EXPERIMENTAL APPROACHES TO PHONOLOGY

EXPERIMENTAL APPROACHES TO PHONOLOGY

Edited by

Maria-Josep Solé,
Patrice Speeter Beddor, and Manjari Ohala

OXFORD

UNIVERSITY PRESS

This book has been printed digitally and produced in a standard specification
in order to ensure its continuing availability

OXFORD

UNIVERSITY PRESS

Great Clarendon Street, Oxford OX2 6DP
United Kingdom

Oxford University Press is a department of the University of Oxford.
It furthers the University's objective of excellence in research, scholarship,
and education by publishing worldwide. Oxford is a registered trade mark of
Oxford University Press in the UK and in certain other countries

British Library Cataloguing in Publication Data
Data available

Library of Congress Cataloguing in Publication Dat
Data available

ISBN 978-0-19-929682-8

CONTENTS

Abbreviations   ix

Preface   xi

PART I. THEORY AND BACKGROUND   1

1. **Methods in Phonology**   3
   John J. Ohala
2. **Elicitation as Experimental Phonology: Thlantlang Lai Tonology**   7
   Larry M. Hyman
3. **Decisions and Mechanisms in Exemplar-based Phonology**   25
   Keith Johnson
4. **Beyond Laboratory Phonology: The Phonetics of**
   Speech Communication   41
   Klaus J. Kohler
5. **Area Functions and Articulatory Modeling as a Tool**
   for Investigating the Articulatory, Acoustic, and Perceptual
   Properties of Sounds across Languages   54
   Jacqueline Vaissière

PART II. PHONOLOGICAL UNIVERSALS   73

6. **Phonological Universals and the Control and**
   Regulation of Speech Production   75
   Didier Demolin
7. **Issues of Phonological Complexity: Statistical Analysis**
   of the Relationship between Syllable Structures, Segment
   Inventories, and Tone Contrasts   93
   Ian Maddieson
8. **Linking Dispersion–Focalization Theory and the Maximum**
   Utilization of the Available Distinctive Features Principle in
   a Perception-for-Action-Control Theory   104
   Jean-Luc Schwartz, Louis-Jean Boë, and Christian Abry

PART III. PHONETIC VARIATION AND PHONOLOGICAL
CHANGE   125

9. Applying Perceptual Methods to the Study of Phonetic
   Variation and Sound Change   127
   Patrice Speeter Beddor, Anthony Brasher, and Chandan Narayan
10. Interpreting Misperception: Beauty is in the Ear of the Beholder   144
    Juliette Blevins
11. Coarticulatory Nasalization and Phonological Developments: Data
    from Italian and English Nasal–Fricative Sequences   155
    M. Grazia Busà
12. A Perceptual Bridge Between Coronal and Dorsal /r/   175
    Olle Engstrand, Johan Frid, and Björn Lindblom
13. Danish Stød: Phonological and Cognitive Issues   192
    Nina Grønnum and Hans Basbøll

PART IV. MAINTAINING, ENHANCING, AND MODELING
PHONOLOGICAL CONTRASTS   207

14. Articulatory Movements and Phrase Boundaries   209
    Patrizia Bonaventura and Osamu Fujimura
15. Physiological and Physical Bases of the Command–Response
    Model for Generating Fundamental Frequency Contours
    in Tone Languages: Implications for the Phonology of Tones   228
    Hiroya Fujisaki, Wentao Gu, and Sumio Ohno
16. Probabilistic "Sliding Template" Models for Indirect Vowel
    Normalization   246
    Terrance M. Nearey and Peter F. Assmann
17. The Variations, Quantification, and Generalizations
    of Standard Thai Tones   270
    Rungpat Roengpitya
18. Controlled and Mechanical Properties in Speech:
    A Review of the Literature   302
    Maria-Josep Solé

PART V. PHONOTACTIC AND PHONOLOGICAL
KNOWLEDGE   323

19. What's in CVC-like Things? Ways and Means to
    Look at Phonological Units Across Languages   325
    Bruce L. Derwing
20. The SLIP Technique as a Window on the Mental
    Preparation of Speech: Some Methodological Considerations   339
    Sieb Nooteboom and Hugo Quené

21. **Experimental Methods in the Study of Hindi Geminate Consonants** 351
Manjari Ohala
22. **Morphophonemics and the Lexicon: A Case Study from Turkish** 369
Anne Pycha, Sharon Inkelas, and Ronald Sprouse
23. **IIow Do Listeners Compensate for Phonology?** 386
Eurie Shin

Notes on Contributors 405
References 411
Index 457

ABBREVIATIONS

AE	American English
AM	autosegmental metrical phonology
ANOVA	analysis of variance
AUSR	Average up-ramp slope ratio
CART	classification and regression tree
CD	Convertor–Distributor model
CP	categorical perception
CT	cricothyroid muscle
DFT	Dispersion–Focalization Theory
DT	Dispersion Theory
EGG	electroglottography
EMG	electromyography
EMA	electro-magnetic articulometer
F	falling tone
FFT	Fast Fourier transform
FR	falling–rising tone
GToBI	German Tone and Break Index
H	high–level tone
HMM	Hidden Markov model
HR	high–rising tone
HSAP	heightened subglottal pressure feature
ID	internal diameter
IPO	Instituut voor Perceptieonderzoek (Institute for perception research)
IRF	impulse response function
KIM	Kiel Intonation Model
L	low–level tone
LF	low–falling tone
LPC	linear predictive coding
LR	low–rising tone
M	mid–level tone
MAP	maximum a posteriori
MFDR	maximal flow-declination ratio
MIA	Middle Indo-Aryan
MRI	magnetic-resonance imaging
MUAF	maximum utilization of the available distinctive features
MVS	maximum vowel space

NC	nasal coupling
PACT	Perception-for-Action-Control Theory
PCA	Guided Principal Component Analysis
PENTA	Parallel Encoding and Target Approximation
PLSD	protected least-significant difference
R	rising tone
RF	rising–falling tone
RS	reading score
SH	sternohyoid muscle
SLIP	Spoonerisms of Laboratory-Induced Predisposition
SPE	Sound Pattern of English
STEM-ML	Soft Template Mark-Up Language
TBU	tone-bearing unit
TELL	Turkish Electronic Living Lexicon
TH	thyrohyoid muscle
TMS	transcranial magnetic stimulation
TTS	text to speech
ToBI	Tone and Break Index
UPSID	UCLA Phonological Segment Inventory Database
VOC	vocalis muscle
VOT	voice-onset time
VP	velopharyngeal
VT	vocal tract
WALS	World Atlas of Language Structures

PREFACE

In May 2004 a conference on "Methods in Phonology" was held in Berkeley, California. Many of the chapters in this volume emerged from that conference, although other invited chapters have been added so as to represent a yet broader range of approaches to the discipline. The conference was held in honor of John J. Ohala, and the contents of this book reflect his influence on the empirical methods that shape phonological inquiry.

The book focuses on two central facets of experimental approaches to phonology. One focus is on the experimental methods which, in our view, are foundational to testing hypotheses concerning speakers' and listeners' knowledge of their native sound systems, the acquisition of those systems, and the laws that govern sound systems. Methods, of course, are not static in any empirical science. In recent years there has been increased use of experimental methods in phonology along with the rise of new experimental techniques, and we see several factors as responsible for this change. First, phonology is addressing increasingly diverse questions about the structure of grammars and the representation of sound patterns in the mind and brain, about the relation between phonetic and phonological constraints, about categorization of sensory data, sound change, socially and geographically indexed variation, and so on; thus, phonology needs to be multifaceted in its methods. Second, technologies relevant to phonological inquiry continue to evolve, as does the availability of large-scale linguistic corpora; new technologies and databases open up new opportunities, new questions, and new grounds on which to test hypotheses. Third, there is growing recognition that phonological inquiry should be embedded within a framework informed by the biological, social, and cognitive sciences; application of standardized experimental techniques from these disciplines allows us to account for phonological structure in ways that are both consistent with established knowledge in these fields and (arguably) better able to provide a unified account of language and speech. Fourth, a clear demonstration that we understand phonetic and phonological principles is the ability to model relevant behaviors and patterns; consequently, the use of articulatory synthesis, stochastic methods, learning algorithms, pattern recognition techniques, and neural networks are of increasing importance to phonological inquiry.

A second focus of the volume is on the phonological findings that emerge from the use of experimental techniques and their theoretical implications. This is not a "how to" volume on methods in phonology, but is rather a volume on the types of answers and insights into phonological structure and phonological knowledge provided by experimental approaches to phonology. The most convincing case for the usefulness of a particular methodology is to demonstrate that it can provide solid evidence bearing on specific issues, and can tease apart alternative hypotheses.

All chapters in the collection represent both of these facets of experimental approaches to phonology. For this reason, and because some chapters demonstrate that applying multiple methods to phonological questions provides particularly compelling answers, the book is organized in terms of major phonological issues: (1) explaining phonological universals; (2) understanding the phonetic factors that may give rise to phonological change; (3) maintaining, enhancing, and modeling phonological contrast; and (4) assessing phonological knowledge (such as knowledge of phonotactic well-formedness).

Specific contributions illustrate how a given technique or set of techniques is being applied to these core issues. Reviewed and illustrated are traditional field methods (Hyman), psycholinguistic methods (Derwing; Grønnum and Basbøll; Nooteboom and Quené; M. Ohala), corpus-based methods (Kohler; Maddieson; Pycha, Inkelas, and Sprouse), aerodynamic and articulatory methods (Bonaventura and Fujimura; Busà; Demolin; Solé), acoustic–perceptual methods (Beddor, Brasher, and Narayan; Blevins; Roengpitya; Shin), and statistical and modeling methods (Engstrand, Frid, and Lindblom; Fujisaki, Gu, and Ohno; Johnson; Nearey and Assmann; Schwartz, Boë, and Abry; Vaissière).

Taken together, the contributions demonstrate that the application of well-established methods from other disciplines to phonology has created new theoretical perspectives that have changed, for many, the window through which we view phonology. In this regard, not only does the maturity of the discipline emerge, but also its thriving, dynamic nature. That is, we see among these authors and more generally within the field a remarkable willingness of researchers to take on new ways of asking what are often long-standing questions, and to recognize the new theoretical territory that has opened up.

The five chapters in Part I delineate various theoretical considerations and provide background concerning the application of methods from other sciences. J. Ohala examines the significance of methods in scientific research and in advancing phonological theories, and explores methods as a means of change within a discipline. Hyman's paper makes a case, using data from Thlantlang Lai tonology, for the continued importance of direct data elicitation from a consultant (along with deductive reasoning) in testing linguistic hypotheses, thus meriting status as a branch of experimental phonology. Johnson explores exemplar-based theories, illustrating how phonological generalizations can emerge from phonetically detailed speech exemplars and investigating in more detail key issues to be addressed when phonology is situated in a cognitive model of human memory. Concentrating on the issues of German word-final devoicing and f0 alignment with articulation, Kohler's chapter illustrates the advantages of a paradigm that studies phonology in its communicative context using large databases of connected natural speech. Vaissière's paper demonstrates how experimentation using articulatory synthesis can inform phonological inquiry by exploring the acoustic–perceptual contribution of language-specific articulatory maneuvers to the realization of phonological contrasts.

The contributions in Part II, "Phonological Universals", are concerned with providing explanations for the similarities that hold across the sound systems of many of the world's languages. Demolin presents aerodynamic evidence in support of the view that changes in fundamental frequency are controlled by the speaker whereas changes in subglottal pressure are due to low-level mechanical effects, and discusses the implications for phonological universals. Maddieson's chapter illustrates the use of a large phonological database to test hypotheses about cross-language patterns; he shows that the hypothesis that phonological systems might tend toward equal complexity finds little support when tested against a database of over 600 languages. Applying modeling techniques to assess the forces constraining phonological systems, Schwartz, Boë, and Abry find evidence reflecting maximum auditory distance, focalization, and maximum use of distinctive features, which they integrate in the perceptuo-motor framework PACT.

The chapters by Beddor, Brasher, and Narayan and by Busà in Part III, "Phonetic variation and phonological change", use experimental methods to illustrate the principle that sound changes due to universal phonetic and cognitive factors have their origins in synchronic variation. Beddor *et al.* examine methods of speech perception as applied to variation and change, focusing on coarticulatory variation and the perceptual factors that underlie loss of the source of coarticulation but retention of its effects. Language-specific variation in coarticulatory effects is explored by Busà in aerodynamic and articulatory terms, with selected sound patterns being attributed to variation in articulatory coordination. Blevins reviews the authority and imprint of experimental methods in phonology, underscoring the insights into sound change (and into the recurring synchronic sound patterns that result from phonetically motivated changes) provided by speech perception experimentation. Engstrand, Frid, and Lindblom also bring to bear perceptual evidence by identifying the perceptual preconditions for historical and ongoing changes involving rhotics, demonstrating that the acoustic signal may be ambiguous as to the articulatory configuration that produced it, possibly leading to articulatory reinterpretation. The final chapter of this section, by Grønnum and Basbøll, investigates the acoustic properties of Danish stød and uses a naturalistic database (radio recordings) to investigate ongoing changes—in this case, simplification of the morphological and phonological contexts in which stød occurs.

The chapters in Part IV, "Modeling, Maintaining, and Enhancing Phonological Contrast", address how phonological contrasts or features can be modeled and how they are manifested in the phonetic domain. Bonaventura and Fujimura's contribution uses articulatory techniques for investigating the influences of prosody on gestural strength, and assesses the results within the Converter/Distributor model of speech production. Fujisaki, Gu, and Ohno consider the role of modeling in relating the physical characteristics of speech to phonological structure, illustrating how f0 contours in tone languages are generated by the Command–Response model and offering a new phonological representation of tonal systems. Focusing on the ability of listeners to categorize the vowels of their language, Nearey and Assmann illustrate and assess several statistical pattern-recognition methods for modeling listeners' responses to vowel stimuli, and overall demonstrate the power of the "sliding template" approach. The chapter by Roengpitya offers a quantified analysis of Thai tones and shows that their canonical shape is altered by processes such as end truncation and phase realignment when the tone-bearing unit is longer or shorter (e.g. due to stress) than the canonical duration. The chapter by Solé teases apart targeted and mechanical properties in the speech signal by varying temporal factors, proposing that phonetic dimensions which adjust to variations in speaking rate/stress/pitch accent (i.e. which show an interaction effect) are under the control of the speaker, whereas properties that do not are mechanical.

The chapters in Part V, "Phonotactic and phonological knowledge", demonstrate the use of psycholinguistic, phonetic, and corpora-based methods to test fundamental claims concerning speakers' and listeners' knowledge of phonological processes and representations. Nooteboom assesses the SLIP technique as a window to speech planning, error detection and self-repairs, proposes improvements in the analysis of spoonerisms elicited with this technique, and draws relevant implications for theories of self-monitoring. A variety of psycholinguistic methods are used by Derwing and M. Ohala to determine the phonological status of selected linguistic units. Derwing, reporting on a series of experiments testing for the psychological reality of the onset-plus-rime theory of the syllable, finds support for this notion for English but not for Korean and Minnan, which seem to have a body-plus-coda structure. M. Ohala tests phonetic and phonological issues regarding Hindi geminates, including their durational status vis-à-vis singletons, clusters, and "apparent geminates" (i.e. assimilated consonant sequences), long-distance effects of geminates, and geminate syllabification. Pycha, Inkelas, and Sprouse assess the statistical and phonological bases for exceptional morphophonemic patterning in Turkish, using large-scale electronic corpora, and conclude that a phonological analysis in which the underlying representation of each root contains the information needed to derive the alternating forms offers the more insightful account. Shin's study of perception of assimilated sequences in Korean examines whether listeners have implicit knowledge of assimilatory processes, and evaluates current theoretical proposals in light of evidence suggestive of compensation for assimilation.

The use of experimental methods in phonology has created a research environment in which rigorous argumentation often depends on integrating data from an array of traditionally distinct disciplines. The work of John Ohala is a fine example of this. His own broad perspective on experimental phonology, which he views as an approach to phonology that might involve any number of methods but is characterized by the experimentalist's chief concern with "taking as much care as possible to refine one's beliefs" (Ohala and Jaeger 1986: 3), has had a defining influence on the study of the relation between phonetics and phonology and has helped set the stage for the present volume. John Ohala has encouraged generations of researchers to be imaginative, to look to other disciplines for methods that enrich the study of phonology, and to test hypotheses against evidence from novel, non-traditional sources. We hope that the present volume will serve as a stimulus to promote further forays into experimental approaches to phonology.

September 2006
Maria-Josep Solé
Patrice Speeter Beddor
Manjari Ohala

ACKNOWLEDGEMENTS

The editors are pleased to acknowledge the contributions of many people in the preparation of this book. We thank the following reviewers of chapters for their valuable comments: Jean Andruski, Thomas Berg, Juliette Blevins, Gösta Bruce, Joan Bybee, Dani Byrd, Abigail Cohn, Gary Dell, Didier Demolin, Bruce Derwing, Jacques Durand, Gunnar Fant, Edward Flemming, Hiroya Fujisaki, Nina Grønnum, Susan Guion, Carlos Gussenhoven, John Hajek, Jeri Jaeger, Keith Johnson, Mark Jones, Kenneth de Jong, Jongho Jun, Shigeto Kawahara, John Kingston, Rena Krakow, the late Peter Ladefoged, Björn Lindblom, Anders Lofqvist, Shinji Maeda, Grant McGuire, Robert McMurray, John Ohala, Doug O'Shaughnessy, Robert Port, Pilar Prieto, Daniel Recasens, Charles Reiss, Jorgen Rischel, Joaquín Romero, Rodney Sampson, Stefanie Shattuck-Hufnagel, Jean-Luc Schwartz, Rebecca Treiman, Jacqueline Vaissière, Gary Weismer, Yi Xu, Alan Yu, Eric Zee, and Jie Zhang. The editors also thank John Davey, Consultant editor in Linguistics, Oxford University Press, for his continued support during the publication of this volume. Anthony Brasher, Andrea Pearman and Sílvia Rustullet also provided much-appreciated assistance with manuscript preparation.

This book is dedicated to John J. Ohala

PART I
Theory and Background

1

Methods in Phonology

John J. Ohala

1.1 INTRODUCTION

With the advent of the new millennium it would be an appropriate time to examine the methodological achievements of phonology. This volume does that. The focus on methodology, rather than exclusively on particular theories or questions is motivated by the all-important role that methodology has in determining the scientific rigor and maturity of a discipline. Furthermore, it may be argued that one of the newest and potentially revolutionary aspects of phonology as it has developed in the past few decades is its new methodology. This work should be a valuable resource for linguists and stimulus to promote further attention to methodological matters in phonology.

1.2 QUESTIONS, ANSWERS, METHOD

Broadly speaking, a scientific discipline can be characterized by:

- the questions it asks;
- the answers given to the questions, that is, hypotheses or theories;
- the methods used to marshal evidence in support of the theories.

1.2.1 Questions

The broad questions that are asked in a discipline remain remarkably constant over time. In phonology (which I take as including phonetics; J. Ohala 1990c), these would include the following.

1. How is language and its parts, including words and morphemes, represented in the mind of the speaker; how is this representation accessed and used? How can we account for the variation in the phonetic shape of these elements as a function of context and speaking style?

2. How, physically and physiologically, does speech work—the phonetic mechanisms of speech production and perception, including the structures and units it is built on?

3. How and why does pronunciation change over time, thus giving rise to different dialects and languages, and different forms of the same word or morpheme in different contexts? How can we account for common patterns in diverse languages, such as segment inventories and phonotactics?

4. How can we ameliorate communication disorders?

5. How can the functions of speech be enhanced and amplified, for example, to give permanency to ephemeral speech, to permit communication over great distances, and to permit communication with machines using speech?

6. How is speech acquired as a first language and as a subsequent language?

7. How is sound associated with meaning?

8. How did language and speech arise or evolve in our species? Why is the vocal apparatus different as a function of the age and sex of the speaker? What is the relation, if any, between human speech and non-human communication?

Some of these questions have good candidate answers. For example, we know a fair amount about how speech production works (Question 2), which has allowed us to give partial answers to Question 5 as to how speech can be a medium of communication between human and machine. Of course, as soon as any question receives an answer at one level, more detailed questions arise and, experience tells us, will forever arise no matter how good an answer is provided at any given level. Some of these questions do not yet have widely accepted answers. An example is Question 8, as to how speech evolved.

1.2.2 Theories

If the questions have some constancy over time, the theories or candidate answers given to the questions vary a great deal. Even within the past 40 years of phonology, there has been an abundance of theories regarding the psychological representation of sound patterns in language and the operations performed on them. Similarly, there have been many theories concerning the mechanisms of sound change. Some of these suggest that sound change represented a continual competition between the goals of making speech easier to produce and making it easier to perceive, both of which involve teleological elements. Other theories emphasize the role played by listeners' misperception or misparsings of the speech signal, eliminating a teleological element (J. Ohala 1989).

1.2.3 Methods

But it is the methods employed by scientific disciplines—especially those that are experimental or fundamentally empirical—that constitute the principal engine for refinement and productive change in a discipline, helping to moderate the pace with which one theory supplants another. Insofar as methodology achieves a gradual refinement of the evidence marshaled in support of theories, hardier, more long-lived theories evolve.

Methods tend to accumulate in a discipline. In chemistry, although ever more accurate means of weighing samples have appeared, by itself the method of weighing as a way of determining the molecular structure of substances has not been abandoned since it was introduced in the late eighteenth century by Lavoisier, Bergman, and Klaproth.

Occasionally the development of new methods can revolutionize a discipline. Astronomy was forever changed by the invention of the telescope and results obtained with it by Galileo. The refinement of the kymograph by E. J. Marey in the late nineteenth century—so that it was capable of recording relatively rapid physiological events—was a landmark in the history of experimental phonetics and experimental phonology. One of the first applications of the kymograph in linguistics was the study by Rosapelly (1876), done in Marey's laboratory, to attempt to understand the physical phonetic basis of coarticulation and assimilation. Although the kymograph is obsolete today one may say that it created a demand for the refined recording methods which supplanted it.

Three key elements of what has been called the "scientific method" are, first, to present data in an objective way, second, in a quantified way—that is, numerically—and, third, to present evidence that overcomes doubt as to its relevance to a particular hypothesis or theory. Data obtained objectively—with minimal or no influence from the act of observing, especially that from the observer—helps to insulate the data from the biases and beliefs of those who espouse the theories. Data presented quantitatively avoids ambiguity; it is more precise, less likely to be misinterpreted. And, for the same reason, it is optimal if the hypothesis or theory or model being tested is also expressed quantitatively. Finally, the way to overcome doubt is to gather the data with controls which permit competing theories a chance to determine the outcome and to give a statistical analysis of the data to evaluate whether or not the patterns observed could have arisen by chance.

Adhering to these principles, what may be called a "methodological revolution" has occurred within phonology over the past few decades. This is manifested by:

- the emergence of linguistic phonetics (Ladefoged 1971) and experimental phonology (J. Ohala and Jaeger 1986);
- the Laboratory Phonology conferences, now seeing its tenth meeting in the series (Kingston and Beckman 1990);
- the greater incidence of papers at professional conferences where phonetic and psycholinguistic evidence is given in support of phonological theories at meetings of the Linguistic Society of America, the Acoustical Society of America, the Acoustical Society of Japan, the International Conference on Spoken Language Processing, Eurospeech (these latter two now unified as Interspeech, a yearly meeting of the International Speech Communication Association), the International Congress of

Phonetic Sciences, and the annual meetings of regional societies such as the Chicago
Linguistic Society, and the Berkeley Linguistic Society, to mention just two of such
with the longest lineage;

- several volumes or series of volumes, including Academic Press's Phonetics and
  Phonology (e.g. Huffman and Krakow 1993), Blackwell's Handbooks (e.g. Hardcastle and Laver 1997), Hume and Johnson (2001*b*);
- an increase in the number of experimental and large corpus-based phonology papers
  in scholarly journals such as *Language, Journal of Phonetics, Speech Communication,
  Journal of the International Phonetic Association, Language and Speech*, and *Phonology*.

This volume gives further evidence of this encouraging trend.

2

Elicitation as Experimental Phonology

Thlantlang Lai Tonology

Larry M. Hyman

2.1 INTRODUCTION

The field of phonology has changed a great deal over the past several decades, not just conceptually, but also in terms of methodology. Throughout the structuralist and generative eras it was not only acceptable but, in fact, standard, for phonologists to acquire their information from two sources: (i) primary data derived from the field or "informant sessions"; (ii) secondary data derived from written sources, most likely based in turn on the same kind of primary data.

Starting in the 1970s, John Ohala argued for a more "experimental phonology", whereby phonological hypotheses would be tested rigorously in a laboratory setting—thereby making phonological research much more like phonetics, psychology, and other experimental sciences. As can be seen by what is going on in current research, the field has transformed dramatically: whether phonetically and/or psycholinguistically grounded, phonologists have recognized that the methods required to solve the kind of questions in which they are interested often require more than deductive reasoning and a face-to-face analysis with an informant.

In fact, the bar has been raised considerably. An old-style tonal analysis, for example, which would have been accepted based on the word of an informant worker, might now instead be met by demands to see pitch tracings—and I myself constantly demand quantitative distributions based on an extensive lexical database. Within the context of optimality theory, with its preoccupation with universality and its orientation towards surface outputs, there has been a distinct move away from doing the kind of thick description and theoretically informed "deep" phonology for which generative grammar gave us the first adequate tools.

I am especially grateful to Bawi Lianmang and Milan Za for their help with Thlantlang Lai and Falam Lai, respectively. Their toleration of and ease of dealing with unusual word combinations requested of them has made this study possible. I would also like to thank Kenneth VanBik, who first got me into Kuki-Chin tonology, and who made the arrangements for me to meet with the above speakers.

It is convenient to view phonology as in (1).

(1)   Phonology = "the intersection of phonetics and grammar"

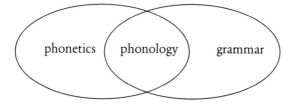

Phonetics accounts for the historical phonologization process, but once something passes into the structured phonology, it can take on a life of its own—which I will call grammatical. Of course not every structured property implies a productive phonological rule or speaker awareness of the pattern. One method to test for the "psychological reality" of phonological relations is through controlled experiments (J. Ohala 1987; J. Ohala and Jaeger 1986). Another method is through direct elicitation, which I will argue to be another form of experimental phonology. Either way there is a shared belief that there is something called phonology which, although often stated in terms of grounded rules or constraints, is distinguishable from phonetics.

This belief contrasts with recent attempts to integrate phonetics further into phonology. This view takes a number of forms. For some, deep phonology still exists, but it has to be described in strictly phonetic terms. For others, deep phonology does not exist at all. Thus, some surface-oriented phonologists have entertained the possibility that there are no underlying forms, just correspondences between surface outputs. From the perspective of the history of the field, this move is particularly subversive: If asked to state what was the principal contribution of generative phonology, I would say that it gave us a way to do morphophonemics—what I am calling "deep phonology". However, a belief has been expressed that there is not much of that either. Consider the view expressed by Hayes (1995: 67–8) in (2).

(2)   Where have all the phonemes gone?
       "... all phonology might ultimately be redistributed between the theory of phonetic rules and the theory of lexical organization.... insofar as rules apply postlexically, they are phonetic and gradient, and insofar as they treat discrete categories, they are part of the lexicon rather than applying to the output of syntax."
       Of the Ilokano rules [I] studied... either they seemed phonetic in character, so that my conventional phonetic transcription represented an over idealized categorization of continuous data, or they struck me as not fully productive, lexicalized rules. At the time I occasionally wondered, "Where is the normal phonology that I was trained to study?"

By "normal phonology" Hayes has in mind the lessons of *The Sound Pattern of English* (*SPE*) (Chomsky and Halle 1968) and post-*SPE* generative phonology that one might have learned, for example, from Kenstowicz and Kisseberth (1979).

Hayes has two concerns. First, word-level phonology largely consists of lexical patterns and irregularities which cannot be captured by fully general rules, for example, the [k] ~ [s] alternation in *cyclic* vs. *cyclicity*. Second, what passes for phonological rules at the phrase level is instead quite phoneticky. Claimed to be (almost) missing are the two classes of phenomenon:

(3) a. word-level phonology that is completely regular;
    b. phrase-level phonology that is not broad phonetics.

The more phonology is not completely regular, but is subject to phonetic variation, the more need there will be for large databases, instrumentation, and controlled experimentation—that is, raising-of-the-bar, as referred to above. But can one assume lesser roles for deductive reasoning and face-to-face elicitations with an informant? It is thus appropriate to raise the question, What is left of the "old" methodology?

In the next section, I will respond to the claimed absence in (3b) and present a systematic source of phrasal phonology that is clearly not "an over-idealized categorization of continuous data". In Section 2.3, I consider the phonology–phonetics working relation. In Section 2.4, I conclude that "normal phonology" does exist and that elicitation, a traditional approach to phonology, is a form of "experimental phonology".

2.2 THLANTLANG LAI TONOLOGY

As will be seen in this section, tone provides an excellent source of material through which to examine the claims in (3). Phrasal tonology in particular has properties that directly contradict Hayes's "impression". The postlexical input–output (I/O) relations I shall discuss are completely regular in the language. Their morphophonemic and opacity-producing properties show that they are not "phonetic and gradient". Since these I/O relations hold across words, they are also quite distinct from the notion of lexical organization which Hayes attributes to word-internal phonology.

The data to be discussed here come from the Thlantlang dialect of Lai, spoken in Chin State, Burma, which I was able to elicit with a speaker over a six-hour period, given my previous experience with other Kuki-Chin languages. The exposition to follow will thus demonstrate both productive phrasal morphophonemics, as well as the "old" methods of working with an informant.

As seen in (4), Thlantlang is a monosyllabic language whose words have the unusual property of being limited to either falling or rising tone in isolation (*Ch* = aspiration; *ng* = [ŋ]):

(4) Thlantlang Lai words in isolation (F = falling, R = rising)

    a. F lûng rock   hnâa ear   tlâang mountain
       [ˆ] lâm road   zôong monkey   râal   enemy
           mêy fire, tail zûu   beer   rûul   snake

b. F   mân   price   vôk   pig   kôoy   friend
[ˆ]   kêe   leg   kût   hand   tsâan   time
      kûm   year   mît   eye   thlâan   grave

c. R   sǎa   animal   zǔu   mouse   bǒoy   chief
[ˇ]   mǐi   person   kǎl   kidney   tsěep   beetle
      bǔu   nest   sěy   basket   hnǎak   rib

The reason for distinguishing two falling tones in (4a,b) can be seen in (5).

(5)   Isolation tones compared to those found after *ká* "my"

    a. F   lûng   rock   F   ká lûng   my rock
          lâm   road   ká lâm   my road
          mêy   fire, tail   ká mêy   my fire, tail

    b. F   mân   price   R   ká <u>mǎn</u>   my price
          kêe   leg   ká <u>kěe</u>   my leg
          kûm   year   ká <u>kǔm</u>   my year

    c. R   sǎa   animal   R   ká sǎa   my animal
          mǐi   person   ká mǐi   my person
          bǔu   nest   ká bǔu   my nest

The falling tone nouns in (5a) remain falling when they follow (high tone) pronominal proclitics such as *ká* "my", while those in (5b) change to rising tone. This was the first alternation I discovered, and it was quite puzzling. Let's call these F/R words, as indicated in (6).

(6)   Four F/R nouns

    a. F   vôk   pig   R   ká vǒk   my pig
    b. F   kôoy   friend   R   ká kǒoy   my friend
    c. F   thlâan grave   R   ká thlǎan my grave
    d. F   mân   price   R   ká mǎn   my price

In order to see how the above alternation might be accounted for, we must first determine how the tone of F/R nouns should be represented underlyingly. In (7) we observe what happens when we take strings of two, three, and four F/R words in sequence:

(7)   Sequences of F/R nouns

    a. H–HL   vók kôoy   pig's friend
    b. H–H–HL   vók kóoy thlâan   pig's friend's grave
    c. H–H–H–HL   vók kóoy thláan mân   pig's friend's grave's price

In (7) I have represented the output tones in terms of H (high) vs. L (low) tonal features, where ['] = H tone. The generalization is clear: the F/R tone words all have H tone except for the last which has a H to L falling tone. Since the nouns in (5a) have a HL falling tone both in isolation and after *ká*, we can assume that they are underlyingly /HL/. The underlying representation of F/R nouns therefore cannot be /HL/.

The data in (7) are straightforwardly accounted for if we adopt the hypotheses in (8).

(8) a. F/R words are underlyingly /H/;
    b. H → HL / __ pause.

Now let us take a look at so-called rising tone nouns such as those in (9).

(9) Four R nouns

    a. R bǒoy chief   R ká bǒoy my chief
    b. R tsěep beetle   R ká tsěep my beetle
    c. R kǎl   kidney   R ká kǎl   my kidney
    d. R sěy   basket   R ká sěy   my basket

When we put these four nouns in sequence in (10), we find exactly the inverted situation of the previous set: R-tone words all have L tone [`] except for the last, which has a L to H rising tone:

(10) Sequences of R nouns

    a. L–LH   bòoy tsěep   chief's beetle
    b. L–L–LH   bòoy tsèep kǎl   chief's beetle's kidney
    c. L–L–L–LH bòoy tsèep kàl sěy chief's beetle's kidney basket

I therefore adopt the second set of hypotheses in (11).

(11) a. R words are underlyingly /L/;
    b. L → LH / __ pause.

Although not as common in the world's languages, (11b) is at least parallel to (8b): both underlying level tones become contour tones before pause.

Consider now F tone words like those in (12).

(12) Four F nouns

    a. F zôong monkey   F ká zôong my monkey
    b. F râal   enemy   F ká râal   my enemy
    c. F rûul   snake   F ká rûul   my snake
    d. F hnâa ear   F ká hnâa   my ear

When F nouns are sequenced, we get the outputs in (13).

(13) Sequences of F nouns

    a. H–LH   zóong rǎal   monkey's enemy
    b. H–L–LH   zóong ràal rǔul   monkey's enemy's snake
    c. H–L–L–LH zóong ràal rùul hnǎa monkey's enemy's snake's ear

In this case, the surface generalizations are those in (14).

(14) a. the first word is realized H;
    b. the last word is realized LH;
    c. intervening words are realized L i.e. H–L*–LH.

Given the presentation in (14), one might ask whether the previous two hypotheses in (8) and (11) might instead be reformulated as the parallel surface generalizations in (15) and (16).

(15)   /H/ nouns in sequence (cf. "F/R" forms in (7))
    a. the first word is realized H;
    b. the last word is realized HL;
    c. intervening words are realized H i.e. H–H*–HL.

(16)   /L/ nouns in sequence (cf. "R" forms in (10))
    a. the first word is realized L;
    b. the last word is realized LH;
    c. intervening words are realized L i.e. L–L*–LH.

Whereas the surface generalizations in (15) and (16) can be straightforwardly derived from the underlying forms, /H/ and /L/, respectively, plus a pre-pausal contouring rule, the outputs of sequences of F nouns in (13) require more. Two competing hypotheses are stated in (17).

(17)   a. There is some kind of mapping algorithm (cf. Yip's 1988 edge-in association).
     b. The outputs are derived by local tone rules.

How do we decide? I suggest that we have to call up the "old methods" and look at more data, specifically, at sequences of unlike tones. We have to do this rigorously and systematically, considering all of the logically contrasting inputs, as in (18):

(18)   a. two words: $3 \times 3 = 9$;
     b. three words: $3 \times 3 \times 3 = 27$;
     c. four words: $3 \times 3 \times 3 \times 3 = 81$, etc.

These combinations should be studied and presented in a grid-like fashion, making sure that nothing is overlooked. The forms in (19) thus illustrate the nine possible combinations of noun + noun (N1 + N2) sequences:

(19) 3×3 grid of tone patterns plotted in noun + adjectival verb combinations

	HL		**H**		**L**	
a. **HL**	ráal	zŏong	ráal	vŏk	ráal	răng
b. **H**	kóoy	zôong	kóoy	vôk	kóoy	răng
c. **L**	bòoy	zŏong	bòoy	vŏk	bòoy	răng
	enemy's monkey		enemy's pig		enemy's horse	
	friend's monkey		friend's pig		friend's horse	
	chief's monkey		chief's pig		chief's horse	

The output tones are summarized in (20), where we clearly see that there are only three output sequences: H–LH, H–HL and L–LH:

(20) Summary of N1 + N2 tonal alternations

	HL		**H**		**L**	
a. **HL**	H	LH	H	LH	H	LH
b. **H**	H	HL	H	HL	H	LH
c. **L**	L	LH	L	LH	L	LH

As a second illustration, all 27 combinations of three-word phrases are given in (21), their tonal summary in (22).

(21) Combinations of N1 + N2 + N3

a. râal + zôong + hmâa → ráal zòong hmǎa enemy's monkey's wound
râal + zôong + kée → ráal zòong kěe enemy's monkey's leg
râal + zôong + bùu → ráal zòong bǔu enemy's monkey's nest

b. râal + vók + hmâa → ráal vòk hmâa enemy's pig's wound
râal + vók + kée → ráal vòk kêe enemy's pig's leg
râal + vók + bùu → ráal vòk bǔu enemy's pig's nest

c. râal + ràng + hmâa → ráal ràng hmǎa enemy's horse's wound
râal + ràng + kée → ráal ràng kěe enemy's horse's leg
râal + ràng + bùu → ráal ràng bǔu enemy's horse's nest

d. kóoy + zôong + hmâa → kóoy zóong hmǎa friend's monkey's wound
kóoy + zôong + kée → kóoy zóong kěe friend's monkey's leg
kóoy + zôong + bùu → kóoy zóong bǔu friend's monkey's nest

e. kóoy + vók + hmâa → kóoy vók hmâa friend's pig's wound
kóoy + vók + kée → kóoy vók kêe friend's pig's leg
kóoy + vók + bùu → kóoy vók bǔu friend's pig's nest

f. kóoy + ràng + hmâa → kóoy ràng hmǎa friend's horse's wound
kóoy + ràng + kée → kóoy ràng kěe friend's horse's leg
kóoy + ràng + bùu → kóoy ràng bǔu friend's horse's nest

g. bòoy + zôong + hmâa → bòoy zòong hmǎa chief's monkey's wound
bòoy + zôong + kée → bòoy zòong kěe chief's monkey's leg
bòoy + zôong + bùu → bòoy zòong bǔu chief's monkey's nest

h. bòoy + vók + hmâa → bòoy vòk hmâa chief's pig's wound
bòoy + vók + kée → bòoy vòk kêe chief's pig's leg
bòoy + vók + bùu → bòoy vòk bǔu chief's pig's nest

i. bòoy + ràng + hmâa → bòoy ràng hmǎa chief's horse's wound
bòoy + ràng + kée → bòoy ràng kěe chief's horse's leg
bòoy + ràng + bùu → bòoy ràng bǔu chief's horse's nest

(22) Summary of tones of N1 + N2 + N3 sequences

a. HL + HL + HL → H–L–LH   f. H + L + HL → H–L–LH
   HL + HL + H → H–L–LH   H + L + H → H–L–LH
   HL + HL + L → H–L–LH   H + L + L → H–L–LH

b. HL + H + HL → H–L–HL   g. L + HL + HL → L–L–LH
   HL + H + H → H–L–HL   L + HL + H → L–L–LH
   HL + H + L → H–L–LH   L + HL + L → L–L–LH

c. HL + L + HL → H–L–LH   h. L + H + HL → L–L–HL
   HL + L + H → H–L–LH   L + H + H → L–L–HL
   HL + L + L → H–L–LH   L + H + L → L–L–LH

d. H + HL + HL → H–H–LH   i. L + L + HL → L–L–LH
   H + HL + H → H–H–LH   L + L + H → L–L–LH
   H + HL + L → H–H–LH   L + L + L → L–L–LH

e. H + H + HL → H–H–HL
   H + H + H → H–H–HL
   H + H + L → H–H–LH

As seen, there are only six output sequences: H–L–LH, H–L–HL, H–H–LH, H–H–HL, L–L–LH, L–L–HL.

There are two striking facts about the outputs in the above tables. First, all non-final tones must be either H or L. This accords with the fact that contour tones are often restricted to final position (Clark 1983; Zhang 2002). Second, and less commonly attested, all final tones must be either falling or rising. In Thlantlang we thus have a complete complementarity: prefinal syllable tones must be level (H, L), while final syllable tones must be contours (HL, LH). Any prefinal contour tone must therefore be simplified to a level tone, and any final level tone must acquire a following [-αT] "polar boundary tone": H% after final /L/, L% after final /H/, where % = pause boundary. When /HL/ is realized as a falling contour, it does not acquire a boundary tone.

The above tables also reveal that a H feature is lost whenever it immediately follows a L feature. Example (23) demonstrates that both /H/ and /HL/ are potentially affected.

(23)   A H feature is lost following a L feature
       a. L + H̲   → L–LH bòoy vǒk   chief's pig
       b. L + H̲L̲ → L–LH bòoy zhǒong chief's monkey

As shown in (24), a reasonable analysis involves left-to-right L tone spreading.

(24)   a.   L-H → L-LH   b.   L-HL → L-LH

             σ   σ   σ   σ
             |---'| |---'|⧸
             L   H   L   H L

Whether L tone spreading applies to a following /H/ or /HL/ syllable, a LH rising tone is observed before pause. We might try to motivate L tone spreading in one of two ways. First, by a constraint Lag-IO(L) (cf. Bickmore's 2000 Extend):

(25)   Lag-IO (L): An input L tone should extend onto the following syllable.

A second way to motivate L tone spreading is by a static output constraint such as (29), which prohibits a jump up from L to H across syllables (cf. Hyman and VanBik's 2004 constraint NoJump proposed for closely related Hakha Lai):

(26)   *Jump(up)

$$\begin{array}{cc} {}^{*}\sigma & \sigma \\ | & | \\ L & H \end{array}$$

This constraint rules out *L–H and *L–HL, as well as *HL–H and *HL–HL, although these latter two sequences are also ruled out by a constraint that prohibits contours on prefinal syllables.

While the I/O relation in (25) is exceptionless, the output constraint in (26) is readily violated, for example, when /L–H–H/ is realized [L–L–H] (~ [L–L–HL] before pause):

(27)   A L to H "jump up" is observed when "intermediate" LH–H is simplified to L–H

bòoy + vók + kée   →   bòoy vŏk kée   →   bòoy vòk kêe   'chief's pig's leg'

$$\begin{array}{ccc} | & | & | \\ L & H & H \end{array} \quad \begin{array}{ccc} | & | & | \\ L & H & H \end{array} \quad \begin{array}{ccc} | & | & | \\ L & H & H \ (L\%) \end{array}$$

In a derivational approach, one might propose that L-tone spreading first produces an LH rising tone, which then must be simplified to L because contour tones are only allowed in final position. This first way of interpreting L tone spreading or Lag (L) is schematized in (28a).

(28)   Two of the ways of interpreting Lag-IO(L)

   a.   Lag creates L–LH, which is simplified to L–L medially
       Rule 1:   L–H   →   L–LH   also L–HL   →   L–LH
       Rule 2:   L–LH   →   L–L   / __ X

   b.   Lag creates L–L, which is contoured to L–LH finally
       Rule 1:   L–H   →   L–L   also L–HL   →   L–L
       Rule 2:   L–L   →   L–LH   / __ %

A second interpretation in (28b), however, is that Lag produces an L–L sequence everywhere, that is to say that when the L spreads into a following /H/ or /HL/ syllable, the H automatically delinks. By rule 2, L tone will contour to an LH rising tone phrase-finally (%). I know of no way to choose between the two interpretations which make the same empirical predictions.

With the above understanding of Thlantlang tonology, we are now in a position to address the following non-resolved question, Why is /H/ realized LH after ka= "my"? We saw in (6) that /H/ (= "F/R") nouns are realized HL in isolation, but as LH after proclitics: vôk "pig"; ká vŏk "my pig". For this reason such nouns were originally designated as F/R. In fact, depending on the context, /H/ nouns are pronounced with any of the four surface tones in Thlantlang:

(29) a. HL: vǫ̀k   pig   /H/
          H: vók kêe   pig's leg   /H + H/
      b. LH: bòoy vǫ̌k   chief's pig   /L + H/
          L: bòoy vòk kêe   chief's pig's leg /L + H + H/

Turning to *ká vǒk* "my pig", it can be verified in the table in (20) that there are exactly four input sequences which surface as H–LH before pause: /HL + HL/, /HL + L/, /H + L/, /HL + H/. We can eliminate the first three inputs for *ká vòk*, since we know that /vók/ is underlyingly /H/. The underlying /H/ is further verified in phrases such as *ká vòk kêe* "my pig's leg", where the derived L of [vòk] has not conditioned L tone spreading on /kée/ "leg" (cf. (27)). But why is this /H/ realized as [LH] (nonfinally, [L]) when preceded by *ká=* "first person" (or the other pronominal proclitics *ná=* "second person" and *á=* "third person")? While the ultimate explanation is undoubtedly a historical one, the synchronic analysis requires one or another form of allomorphy. It is undesirable to say that /H/ nouns have a /LH/ allomorph after pronominal proclitics, since underlying /LH/ does not otherwise exist in the language. This leaves us with the alternative of attributing the tonal allomorphy to the proclitics, as in (30).

(30) a. /ká/ : before /HL/ or /L/
          /ká + râal/   → ká râal   my enemy
          /ká + bòoy/   → ká bǒoy   my chief
      b. /kâ/ : before /H/
          /kâ + kóoy/   → ká kǒoy   my friend

Whereas proclitic /H/ has no effect, the L of proclitic /HL/ causes the following /H/ to undergo L tone spreading. With this accomplished we now consider how the Thlantlang analysis contributes to our understanding of phonology and experimental approaches to it.

2.3 PHONOLOGY AND PHONETICS

In Section 2.2, a descriptive analysis was proposed to account for the observed tonal observations. This analysis required us to recognize a process of L tone spreading, as well as constraints on the distribution of contour tones: a prefinal syllable may not carry an HL or LH contour, whereas a final syllable must. This latter observation was accounted for by means of a polar boundary tone (L% ∼ H%). Finally, it was necessary to recognize tonal allomorphs in the case of proclitics. The system that emerges from the approach in Section 2 is an interesting one from which important lessons can be drawn (cf. Sect. 4). In this section I discuss how the Thlantlang system contributes to the working relation between phonetics and phonology.

We are all accustomed to the notion that phonetics informs phonology. What is "natural" in phonology is "deeply grounded in the universal phonetic properties of speech" (Hyman 1975a: 171). In fact, the relation is bidirectional: by pinpointing and defining the problem, phonology informs phonetics. The LAG(L) process in Thlantlang is clearly an example of Hyman and Schuh's (1974: 88) tone spreading: "Spreading is an assimilatory process of the progressive or perseverative type, rather than of the regressive or anticipatory type. That is, the earlier tone appears to last too long, rather than the later tone starting too early." Hyman and Schuh speculated that the perseverative bias of tone-spreading probably has an articulatory basis (cf. Xu 2004b), whereas Javkin (1979) and Silverman (1997) have instead sought perceptual accounts. Either way, it was on the basis of phonological patterning that Hyman and Schuh (1974: 104) extrapolated a phonetic basis: "the rightward principle was conceived as a purely phonetic one, i.e. as motivated by nothing more than the juxtaposition of nonidentical tones." Subsequent instrumental studies of both tone and intonation have confirmed that "the f0 target for a single static tone tends to occur at the (temporal) end of the associated phonetic region." (Akinlabi and Liberman 2000: 5).

The Hyman and Schuh perseverative generalization represents the first step of "structure-first research" in (31).

(31) a. Discover linguistically significant generalizations based on the structural properties of sound systems.
    b. Hypothesize possible motivations for these generalizations.
    c. Seek evidence to support these hypotheses—i.e. do experimental phonology and phonetics!
        i. Measure "intrinsic" variation that may feed into the "phonologization" process;
        ii. conduct perceptual experiments, etc. (see J. Ohala 1987, 1989, 1993b)

Traditionally, phonologists have stopped short, doing just (31a), or perhaps (31a,b). This correlates with what I have referred to as the "old" methods. But how far can we get by doing this?

Let us return to Thlantlang Lai. Up to now non-final contour simplification has been indicated with an "X", as in (32).

(32) a. LH simplification: LH   →   L   / ___ X
    b. HL simplification: HL   →   H   / ___ X

But what is this X, about which I have been deliberately vague? As shown in (33), one can distinguish two different interpretations of non-final contour simplification:

(33) a. Contour tones are simplified when followed by another syllable (σ)

b. Contour tones are simplified when followed by another tone (T)

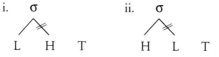

   i.   σ   ii.   σ

        L   H   T   H   L   T

As Clark (1983) originally pointed out, many languages are like Thlantlang in restricting contour tones to the final syllable. The usual assumption in (33a) is that non-final contour simplification is conditioned by the presence of a following syllable. However, as indicated in (33b), another possible interpretation is that contour simplification is conditioned by a following tone.

In most cases the two interpretations will be empirically equivalent. The difference comes from cases where a contour is followed by a toneless syllable, as in Luganda. The prediction of (33a) is that contour simplification will occur, while the prediction of (33b) is that it will not. Rather than citing the evidence that (33b) is needed for Luganda, let us work backwards from Thlantlang in (34) to see if we cannot reach the same conclusion.

(34)   Structure-first research: the example of contour simplification

       a. Discover the linguistically significant generalization that many languages restrict
           contour tones to the final syllable (Clark 1983; Gordon 2001; Zhang 2002).
       b. Hypothesize possible motivations for these generalizations.
       c. Seek evidence to support these hypotheses:
            i. phonetic approach: test against articulatory and perceptual generalizations;
           ii. phonological approach: test against structural generalizations.

What are the phonetic properties which might be at play in non-final contour simplification? One approach, cited in (35), correlates the cross-linguistic distribution of contour tones with the phonetic properties of syllables or syllable rimes:

(35)   a. Gordon (2001), based on a survey of 105 languages

           "[there is] an implicational hierarchy of tone bearing ability, whereby long vowels
           are most likely to carry contour tones, followed by syllables containing a short
           vowel plus a sonorant coda, followed by syllables containing a short vowel plus
           an obstruent coda, followed by open syllables containing a short vowel" (p. 405).

       b. Zhang (2002), based on a survey of 187 languages

           "the distribution of contour tones is found to correlate closely with the duration
           and sonority of the rime. Syllables with longer rime duration, e.g. those that are
           long-vowelled, sonorant-closed, stressed, prosodic-final, or in a shorter word,
           are more likely to carry contour tones" (pp. xiv–xv).

Especially important is the role of duration, which may be sensitive to position; compare the phenomena of "final lengthening" (Lehiste 1970; Beckman and Edwards 1990) and "anticipatory shortening" (Lehiste 1970; Nooteboom 1995).

The alternative in (36) is that contours are harder to implement when followed by another tone. I refer to this as "the principle of ups and downs" (Hyman 1978: 261):

(36) Tonally induced changes tend to minimize the number of ups and downs over a given stretch. In the case of contour simplification, the "stretch" may be as short as a syllable.... The principle of ups and downs not only accounts for most instances of vertical assimilations and contour levelings, but also predicts that change will occur first where the ups and downs are the most complex. Thus, a H–LH or HL–H sequence is much more likely to undergo change than a L–LH or HL–L sequence.

As discussed in Hyman (2004), the situation is more complex than this; some languages permit LH–L, but not *LH–H; other languages permit LH–H, but not *LH–L. The proposal is that LH–L is preferred to LH–H in terms of the perceptibility of the contour, but dispreferred in terms of the articulatory complexity imposed by the drop to L that follows it—cf. (39).

The first hypothesis has to do with rime duration: Thlantlang must simplify non-final contours because their rimes are shorter in that position than finally. That this is not likely is seen in (37).

(37) Presentation of the tones by syllable structure (R = sonorant; T = stop; glosses in (4))

| | Smooth syllables | | | Stopped Syllables | |
	CVV	**CVR**	**CVVR**	**CVT**	**CVVT**
/HL/	zûu	lûng	tlâang		
	tîi	mêy	râal		
/H/	kée	mán	tsáan	vók	
	tháa good	kúm	kóoy	kút	
/L/	sàa	kàl	bòoy		tsèep
	bùu	sèy	pòol gray		hnàak

As indicated, Thlantlang has an underlying vowel-length contrast only in closed syllables. All three tones contrast on so-called smooth syllables which are either open or end in a sonorant consonant. On the other hand, short stopped syllables are underlyingly /H/ tone while long stopped syllables are underlyingly /L/. While syllable structure affects tone in this way, there is no glottalization or breathiness associated with the underlying or surface tones.

Despite the lack of tonal contrast on /CVT/, and despite the restricted duration of the vowel in short stopped syllables, we saw in (29) that words such as /vók/ "pig" can bear all four phonetic tones. On the other hand, as seen in (38), quite long, sonorous rimes fail to carry contour tones when they are not in final position:

(38) a. HL: râal   enemy   /HL/
          H : r<u>áal</u> kǎl   enemy's kidney   /HL + L/
     b. LH: bòoy kǒoy   chief's friend   /L + H/
          L : bòoy k<u>òoy</u> kǎl chief's friend's kidney /L + H + L/

The two underlined forms in (38) show that a falling or rising tone will be simplified even though the rime is both long and sonorous—clearly longer than [vôk] and [vǒk] in (29).

The data in (38) show that we cannot predict the distribution of contour tones based solely on duration. Note that Gordon and Zhang attribute the restriction of contour tones to final syllables to the phenomenon of final lengthening. However, there is no way that the vowels in final [vôk] and [vǒk] can be lengthened to surpass the long underlined vowels in (38a, b). While we know that final lengthening and anticipatory shortening are widespread phenomena, they do not predict the facts in Thlantlang.

I therefore conclude that the alternative view in (33b) is correct; tonal contours are not allowed to be followed by another tone in Thlantlang. In fact, when we look at contours in terms of the tonal contexts in which they occur, we find the typology in (39).

(39)   Typology of contour distribution by following tone

	[LH–H]	**[LH–L]**	**Language**	
Type I	*	✓	Falam Lai	contour disallowed before like tone
Type II	✓	*	Hakha Lai	contour disallowed before unlike tone
Type III	*	*	Thlantlang Lai	contour disallowed before any tone

Type I is illustrated from Falam Lai in (40).

(40)   Falam Lai: only LH tones change (Osburne 1975; examples from my informant
        work)

    a. LH   →   L / ___   {H, HL}   (tone absorption)
       e.g.   tlǎang + lám   →   tlàang lám   mountain road
              LH   H   L   H

    b. LH + L   → no change if L occurs on a smooth syllable
       e.g.   tlǎang + sèer ′ →   tlǎang sèer   mountain lemon
              LH   L   LH   H

In (40a) the H of a rising is absorbed into the following H or HL tone. There is no change in (40b), when the rising tone is followed by a L on a smooth syllable. However, as seen in (41), the H of the rising tone will shift to the right if followed by a L on a CV or CVT syllable:

(41)   Falam Lai: LH + Ľ → L–H

    a. tlǎang + sàriʔ   →   tlàang sáriʔ   seven mountains
    b. tlǎang + vòk   →   tlàang vók   mountain pig
        tlǎang + khàt   →   tlàang khát   one mountain

This appears to indicate that a LH requires greater duration on *a following L* tone rime! This follows from the principle of ups and downs, but not from Zhang's local requirement that contour syllables require longer rimes. In fact, anticipatory shortening might also make the wrong prediction, if the longer sonorous rimes of smooth syllables cause greater anticipatory shortening than CV or CVT syllables. I contend that it is the shortness of the L tone CV or CVT syllable which makes the LH–L sequence problematic.

This is not to say that duration is not a or the determining factor in accounting for surface contour tone distribution in other cases. Both Gordon (2001) and Zhang (2002) have documented scores of languages in which contour tones are prohibited on rimes of restricted sonority or duration. The present study attempts to show that both (33a) and (33b) are needed. While Zhang (2005) appears to allow that more may be involved (see below), he defends the durational account by citing the realization of Tone 3 in Standard Beijing Mandarin, which has the following realizations (Chao 1968):

(42) Realizations of Standard Beijing Mandarin Third Tone (1=lowest, 5=highest pitch)

    a. 214: before pause (also characterized as 213 or 315)
    b. 21 : before Tone 1 (55), Tone 2 (35), Tone 4 (51)
    c. 35 : before another Tone 3 (i.e. $214 + 214 \rightarrow 35 + 214$)
    d. 21 : before neutral (Ø) tone (i.e. $214 + 0 \rightarrow 21\text{–}4$)

Assuming that the starting point is some featural representation of /214/, that is a falling–rising tone, two changes are needed; in (42b) the endpoint of the rise [4] is "absorbed" into a phonetically similar [3] or [5] pitch. In (42c), the same [4] level, which is wedged between relatively low pitches, fuses with the preceding [21] to create a [35] rising tone (similar or identical to Tone 2). In my review of Cheng's (1973) characterization of these processes, I noted that "the result is that the number of ups and downs is decreased," but cautioned that "while contour simplification provides the primary motivation for the tone sandhi rule, the role of duration should not be overlooked" (Hyman 1975b: 94). A full [214] contour before pause is quite long, especially when emphatic and when the vowel is rearticulated, as in [ma.a] "horse". Only Tone 3 can have this "superheavy" property—and only before pause. On the other hand, it is markedly shorter (normal) in non-final position, where the /214/ is obligatorily simplified.

As seen from the above, there is a clear relationship between rime duration and the realization of contour tones, which has been recognized for decades. It is, however, harder to see this relationship in the Thlantlang Lai tone system where contrasting long CVVR syllables lose their contour tones in pre-final position, but contrastively short CVT syllables keep their contour in final position. Zhang (2005: 59) responds to this situation by introducing the constraint REALIZE-HL, which expresses "the intuition ... that a non-final HL can be manifested by other means, such as downstepping the following H, or realizing the L tone on the following syllable, but a final HL does not have such options." Among others, he cites the examples in (43a, b).

(43) Tone spreading and tone preservation

    a. râal + vók $\rightarrow$ ráal vǒk   enemy's pig
        HL   H   H LH

    b. râal + ràng $\rightarrow$ ráal rǎng   enemy's horse
        HL_1 L_2 H $L_{1,2}H\%$

c. /bòoy + vók + bùu/   →   bòoy vòk bǔu   chief's pig's nest
    L   H   L   L   L   L H%

As seen, the HL of /râal/ "enemy" is simplified as a H tone, but the L of the HL fall spreads onto /vók/ "pig" to create a rising tone in (43a). As indicated by the subscripts, the L of the HL fall fuses with the L of /ràŋ/ "horse" in (43b). All of the input tones are thus preserved, thereby satisfying Zhang's constraint REALIZE-HL ("realize the HL contour in some fashion"). Because a final short HL does not have the option to realize its L on the following syllable, it will surface even on a short and less sonorous rime, as in vòk "pig", from /H + L%/.

While Zhang's main illustration comes from Kɔnni, he adds, "I suspect that the Thlantlang Lai data can [be] similarly interpreted. The disyllabic sandhi pattern documents in [the current paper] supports this suspicion." (p. 61). In Thlantlang Lai we have seen that both prefinal HL and LH contours have to be simplified (to H and L, respectively), hence, I assume Zhang would introduce the analogous constraint REALIZE-LH. However, trisyllabic sandhi patterns, to which Zhang also had access, show that this approach cannot work. The output of the phrase in (43c) reveals that the /H/ of /vók/ is not realized. Although L tone spreading has applied, we do not get a rising tone on *[vǒk]. The H is knocked off, and we obtain [vòk]. Rather than REALIZE-CONTOUR constraints (which may be needed elsewhere), Thlantlang Lai (and related tone systems) are effectively analyzed by having the REALIZE (or MAX) constraints refer directly to the individual tone features. Given that a L tone feature is never lost in Thlantlang Lai, we can assume that MAX(L) is inviolable, while MAX(H) is low-ranked. The relevant ranking therefore is MAX(L) >> SPREAD(L) >> MAX(H).

Further support for this approach is observed in Kuki-Thaadow, another Kuki-Chin language which does not allow prefinal contours:

(44)   Properties of L tone spreading in Kuki-Thaadow

    a. hùon + zóong   →   hùon zǒong   garden monkeys
        L   H   L   LH

    b. hùon + zóong + gùup → hùon zòong gùup six garden monkeys
        L   H   L   L   L   HL

    c. hùon + zóong + gîet   → hùon zóong gîet   eight garden monkeys
        L   H   HL   L   H   HL

    d. hùon + zóong + thúm → hùon zóong thúm three garden monkeys
        L   H   H   L   H   H

In (44a) we see that Kuki-Thaadow also has L tone spreading. Example (44b) shows the combined operation of L tone and H tone spreading: The L of /hùon/ "garden" spreads onto the H of /zóoŋ/ "monkey", which in turn spreads onto the L of /gùup/ "six". As also seen, "monkey" is realized L because a LH contour is not tolerated on a prefinal syllable.

What is particularly striking are the facts in (44c, d). Here, L tone spreading does not apply, and /zóoŋ/ is realized H on the surface. To understand why, consider how these phrases would have to be realized if L tone spreading did apply. If the /L–H/ sequence of /hùon zóoŋ/ became L–LH, the H would have to be delinked because the LH contour is not in final position in (44c, d). In (44b) this was no problem, because the H can combine with the L on the final syllable of /gùup/ "six". In (44c,d) the final syllable begins H. Because (44c, d) cannot surface as L–L–HL and L–L–H, respectively, we can conclude that the fusion option, $H_{1,2}$, is not available to satisfy MAX (H). L tone spreading is effectively blocked by the ranking MAX(H) >> SPREAD(L) >> MAX(L), in other words, the opposite ranking of Thlantlang Lai.

It is not my purpose here to develop a full constraint-based account of Thlantlang Lai (or the related Kuki-Chin tone systems cited earlier), but, rather, to show that more is involved than the durational generalizations. Zhang seems to agree when he writes that "the Luganda example indicates that there might be other non-durationally-based conditions that must be taken into consideration for a full account of contour tone licensing." (p. 58). As I have shown, his REALIZE-CONTOUR "intuition" fails to account for the Thlantlang Lai facts. Given his commitment to phonetically grounded constraints, it is hard to understand Zhang's resistance to (33b) and the principle of ups and downs. As I have demonstrated elsewhere (Hyman 2004), expanding on Hyman and Schuh (1974), some contour simplifications are sensitive to the preceding and/or following tone. The summary in (39) shows that Thlantlang Lai falls into a natural typology if we assume that the prohibition against prefinal contours in Kuki-Chin tone systems is not motivated by durational considerations but by the tendency to simplify contours when followed by either an identical tone, a non-identical tone, or both.

2.4 CONCLUSIONS

The above treatments of Thlantlang and Falam tonology reveal that a structure-first approach is successful as a means of identifying important issues in the phonetics–phonology relation. More specifically, the phonological patterning on which the approach relies can provide important clues concerning phonetic mechanisms which feed into phonologization. There are two other conclusions that can be drawn from this study:

(i) *Regular phonology exists*

The tonal properties examined in Section 2 are completely regular. All of the tonal alternations illustrated with combinations of nouns are exactly duplicated elsewhere in the noun phrase, within the verb phrase, and in simple and complex clauses. As in the other Kuki-Chin languages I have investigated (Hakha Lai, Falam Lai, Kuki-Thaadow), the relevant prosodic domain is the intonational phrase within which the tonal alternations occur without exception. Recall Hayes's view in (2) that "*all phonology might ultimately be redistributed between the theory of phonetic rules and the theory of lexical organization.*" It should be clear, however, that the L tone spreading rule of Thlantlang fails both tests. Being regular and applying across words, L tone spreading has nothing to do with lexical organization. Also, L tone spreading is not a phonetic rule. We can see this from the fact that it is not surface true; examples such as *bòoy vòk kêe* "chief's pig's leg" in (27) show that the *Jump prohibition against transsyllabic L + H as was at first hypothesized in (26) is not surface-true. Rather, L tone spreading must be approached either as a derivational rule or as the consequence of a two-level constraint, Lag-IO (L), as envisioned in (25).

(ii) Elicitation is experimental phonology

I've tried to make the case that there is still a lot to learn from the old methods. In a 1970s course description prepared for Linguistics 210 "Methods of Phonological Analysis", John Ohala wrote, "This course will provide the student with practice in the methods of gathering and analyzing phonological data: field methods, laboratory methods, and paper-and-pencil methods. Those enrolled will be required to "try their hand" at all three methodologies." While one might accept or modify the above characterization, the distinctions have become fused over recent decades—for instance, some colleagues have taught courses in field phonetics or field laboratory methods. Similarly, I suggest that one might refer to informant work as experimental elicitation. All of the data presented in the preceding sections were obtained by direct elicitation with a single speaker of Thlantlang (or Falam). The "methodology" to a large extent consisted of asking, "How do you say X?" Clearly the speaker had never heard or conceptualized noun phrases such as those in (45).

(45)   a. pig's friend's grave's price   (cf. (7c))
       b. chief's beetle's kidney basket   (cf. (10c))
       c. monkey's enemy's snake's ear   (cf. (13c))

It would not impress any psychologist, and it would definitely horrify an anthropologist, but who else but an experimental linguist could present such stimuli? As an informant worker I do not prefer semantically odd collocations such as those in (45). However, when I need to get $3 \times 3 \times 3 \times 3 = 81$ tonal combinations to test my rules, the available data may be limited, or the language may make it difficult to find certain tone combinations. I am personally thankful that speakers of Kuki-Chin languages are willing to entertain such imaginary notions. It is most significant that the novel utterances are produced with the appropriate application of tone rules. If the goal is to test the linguistic knowledge of speakers, our finding is that the proposed tone rules have what phonologists used to call "psychological reality". The experimental nature of elicitation should therefore not be underestimated.

3

Decisions and Mechanisms in Exemplar-based Phonology

Keith Johnson

3.1 INTRODUCTION

In the leaf in Figure 3.1 you can see a branching structure—an almost crystalline organization that could be described with a clean mathematical generative formalism. Now, if we raise our gaze only a little we see a forest—diversity formed from interlaced systems of water and light, plant and insect.

We can approach language, too, from these two perspectives. Looking at the geometric regularities in the structure of the leaf is analogous to adopting a structuralist linguistic framework inspired by mathematical/physical theories of mathematics and physics. Generative phonology (Chomsky and Halle 1968) is the most prominent instance of this approach to language in the domain of phonology, adopting such familiar research strategies as idealization of the speaker/hearer and the use of formal symbolic representation of generalizations observed in linguistic data.[1]

Seeking to understand the leaf's structure in the interacting systems of a forest is analogous to approaching language from an ecological or systemic framework inspired by theories in biology and history. Phoneticians have approached language in this way for many years (Lindblom *et al.* 1984; Blevins 2004; see also Baudouin de Courtenay 1972a) "explaining" language sound patterns in terms of phonetic tendencies in speaking and listening that operate in the history of language (Hume and

This paper benefited from comments and discussions at the 3rd Seoul International Conference on Phonology, where it was presented in June, 2005. Parts of this research were supported by NIH Grant #R01 DC04330.

[1] Chomsky and Halle (1968) used the term "grammar" to refer both to "the system of rules represented in the mind of the speaker/hearer" and to "the theory that the linguist constructs" while analyzing forms produced by speakers. Although many of the patterns discovered by linguists are no doubt psychologically real (Halle *et al.* 1981) and thus are part of the cognitive ecology of language, it is nonetheless accurate to identify Chomsky and Halle's linguistic research strategy as a continuation of American structuralism—an insular approach to linguistics that is fundamentally incapable of accommodating a broader, contextualized, view of language.

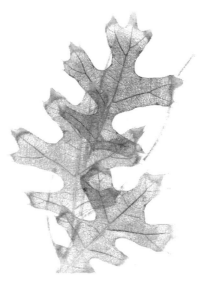

FIGURE 3.1. A leaf

Johnson 2001*a*). John Ohala, in particular, emphasized the historical part of the equation (1974, 1981*b*).

It is important to keep in mind that the structural and ecological perspectives feed each other. For example, many of the observations about English sound patterns given by Chomsky and Halle (1968) were derived from the history of English, so that much of the explanatory power of their analysis of English was gained because the authors explicitly referred to the historical development of rules like vowel shift and velar softening. Ohala objected to their method of packing the history of the language into the head of the speaker—incorporating this explanatory power into a synchronic grammar—but at the same time Ohala was pursuing a very similar project, finding the explanation of the current linguistic state (described in formally expressed generalizations) in the historical path that the language took through an ecology made up of the physiological and perceptual contexts of speech transmission. My point here is simply that the strictest formal description of language sound patterns benefits from historical explanation, and the most ardent biological description benefits from formalized generalizations.

The topic of this chapter is exemplar-based theories of phonological knowledge. From my point of view, exemplar-based theories may be used to increase our understanding of language from an ecological perspective by providing a framework within which we can account for generalizations in language sound systems while incorporating phenomena such as historical drift and contextual variation in phonetic detail. Whereas in phonetic research we have been primarily interested in effects on language sound systems that arise from speech perception and production, the exemplar-based approach is concerned more particularly with the cognitive grounding of phonological knowledge.

The sections to follow will outline what exemplar-based phonology is (Section 3.2), discuss two decisions that must be made in exemplar-based phonology (Section 3.3), and, finally, discuss two mechanisms used in constructing an exemplar-based phonology (Section 3.4).

3.2 WHAT IS EXEMPLAR-BASED PHONOLOGY?

3.2.1 Background

The exemplar-based orientation to sensory memory has a long history in cognitive psychology, and from the work in general cognition we get some ideas about how exemplar-based phonology might look.

Richard Semon (1923) in his *Mnemic Psychology* distinguished *sensation* and *image*. For him the term "image" refers to memories of sensory experience that persist in neural structure and of these he says, "Every moment of individual life adds something to the already existing sum of simultaneous engram-complexes" (p. 171), which is to say that each instant of life adds exemplars to memory. In Semon's view then, these images of sensory experience are used in recognition, which he describes as "partial return of the inner energetic situation which was present at the formation of the engram-complex" (p. 180). Two points in Semon's approach are important. First, his view that each moment of life adds to the sum of images illustrates that exemplars on this view are tokens of experience not types. That is, exemplar-based models envision the storage of instances as they occur, without any abstraction at all. Second, Semon envisions that new experiences are recognized as being similar to old experiences by a partial re-experiencing of images/instances in memory. This is an early conception of an activation model of perception.

These characteristics of exemplar-based models of memory have been carried forward into modern cognitive psychology by a number of researchers. For example, Hintzman's (1986) "multiple-trace" memory model MINERVA (which has been applied to speech perception by Goldinger 1992) implemented a simple version of Semon's images and developed an explicit account of "re-experiencing" during recognition that we will come back to in a subsequent section. Here, the main point that I want to make is that exemplar-based memory models are current in cognitive psychology research and that they are considered one of the mainstream approaches to modeling memory (Baddeley 1997; Tulving and Craik 2000; Neath and Surprenant 2003).

This point is further illustrated by a series of influential papers by Nosofsky (1986, 1988, 1991; Cohen *et al.* 2001). In his models of recognition and categorization processes Nosofsky assumes that people store in memory each instance of the members of a perceptual category and that various effects in categorization performance (frequency effects, "prototype" effects, recency effects) all emerge from this memory storage system. This work has been very influential, and provocative.

In the study of language as well, the idea of representing linguistic categories in terms of experienced instances of linguistic objects has been a focus of study for some years now. For example, Skousen (1989) used an exemplar-based memory system to account for processes of analogy in phonology and historical linguistics. Goldinger (1992) found evidence for exemplar-based storage of auditory words in listeners' word recognition performance. Jusczyk (1993) and Morgan *et al.* (2001 and Anderson *et al.* 2003) have proposed exemplar-based models of child phonology acquisition. Johnson (1997b) proposed that an exemplar-based model can account for the process of talker normalization in speech perception. Coleman (2002) proposes exemplar-based phonetic representations. Pierrehumbert (2001a, 2003a) models pronunciation variation and phonological learning using an exemplar-based phonetic storage system. Bybee (1985) modeled paradigm leveling and other patterns of change in historical morphology using prototype theory, and has more recently (2001) explored instance-based models to account for both prototype effects and the role of frequency of occurrence in these processes. All of these exemplar-based approaches to phonology assume that language sound systems are represented in the set of phonetically detailed exemplars of speech that the speaker/hearer has experienced, and that phonological generalizations—the stuff of phonological rules—emerge from the detailed exemplars. The models thus implicitly entail the radical claims that phonology is represented in phonetic detail rather than in featural abstraction, and that the phonetic definition of phonological contrast is language specific.

It should be noted, however, that there is no one "exemplar theory". Skousen has an explicit model, Goldinger uses MINERVA, Jusczyk called his model WRAPSA, Morgan's model is called DRIBBLER, and I called my simulations XMOD (which may or may not be the best model, but it is definitely the best name). In addition, there are relatively few studies that test the basic assumption of exemplar-based modeling—that people remember exemplars of speech (but see Lightfoot 1989; Schacter and Church 1992; Palmeri *et al.* 1993; Goldinger 1992, 1996, 1997; Nygaard and Pisoni 1998; Goldinger and Azuma 2004). My take on this last point is that the memory literature pretty convincingly demonstrates that an exemplar-based memory does exist for sensory experience, and there is a tendency on the part of people who have read that literature to accept the assumption and start modeling. However, additional work on this topic would be welcome.

The main point of this section is that exemplar-based models of human memory have been considered for at least 100 years. Exemplar theory is not an invention of linguists—there is a large body of work out there for us to draw on and benefit from—and even among linguists a variety of exemplar-based approaches are being tested.

3.2.2 An exemplar-based approach to phonology

So we have these two general approaches to language sound systems. One, the approach used in constructing grammars and dictionaries, is to find generalizations among pronunciations and use phonetic details noted during close inspection of people's pronunciations to formulate rules that describe generalizations among pronunciations. The second, more tentative, exemplar-based approach situates language in a cognitive model of human memory by assuming that people use an exemplar-based memory system to store phonetic details. Generalizations then are computed by the talker flexibly on-demand over this large store of phonetic exemplars.

To illustrate the exemplar-based approach and how it relates to our more familiar grammar and dictionary approach we will consider a couple of analogies. First, consider the field linguist's note cards and their use in formulating phonological observations. At the outset of the linguist's exposure to a language he or she writes words, noting as many phonetic details as possible. Eventually, though, after some time spent hearing and speaking words, and some analysis of the distinctive sounds of the language, we begin to use a more abstract alphabet—a phonemic representation. As it turns out, though, sometimes this move from detailed to abstract representation is taken too early and the linguist must go back and re-elicit forms because a missing or neglected phonetic detail turns out to be important. Now, in the exemplar-based approach, the linguist's note cards are exemplars. One interesting research question is: do learners form abstract representations such that they must essentially re-elicit forms when a generalization proves to be wrong, or do these data exist for learners in detailed phonetic exemplars available for wholesale reanalysis?

Second, consider the difference between definition by extension and definition by rule. For example, among the important numbers in my life I would include my birthday, telephone number, address, and various identification and code numbers. This set of numbers must be defined by extension—simply listed on scraps of paper in my wallet or memorized. This is a very different mode of generation than the sets of numbers that can be generated by rules such as the set of all numbers less than eleven, or the Padovan sequence $[P(n)=P(n-2)+P(n-3)$ with $P(0)=P(1)=P(2)=1]$ 1, 1, 2, 2, 3, 4, 5, 7, 9, 12, ... In the generative view, pronunciation variation is defined by rules of assimilation, deletion, and the like, so we assume that the speaker/hearer does not need to memorize every variant encountered or produced, but instead is able to derive variants by rule the way we can derive 4410 as the thirty-first number in the Padovan sequence.

The exemplar-based approach views pronunciation more like a problem in definition by extension. We note that many aspects of pronunciation variation don't seem to fit the rule-governed approach. For example, individual talker-specific variation and dialect variation may not be rule governed. Stollenwerk (1986) illustrates this with a report of idiolectal variation in the American English [ɑ]/[ɔ] contrast. For this speaker, high-frequency words that should have [ɔ] do, while low-frequency /ɔ/-words are pronounced with [ɑ]. Stollenwerk's explanation for this idiosyncratic distribution is that the speaker picked up high frequency words in a speech community where the distinction is maintained early in life and then moved to a community where the distinction is not made and acquired the low-frequency words with [ɑ].

Obviously the speaker memorized particular variants according to the norms of her speech community at the time of acquisition, but also her interlocutors have to also be able to tolerate such variation within the individual. That is, a listener who has a dialect-mapping rule so that if speakers are from the upper Midwest we expect the [ɑ]–[ɔ] contrast to be maintained, will be confused by them. The outstanding feature of an account of variation like Stollenwerk's is that the personal history of particular words has explanatory value.

We see this also in studies of word-specific pronunciation variation. Lavoie (2002) found that *four* and *for* have different reduction patterns in connected speech (see also Pierrehumbert 2002). I explored this further by taking counts from the *Variation in Conversation* corpus of conversational speech (Pitt *et al.* 2005) as shown in Table 3.1. This table illustrates that in normal conversational speech homophones do not have identical variant frequencies, and sometimes they do not even have the same leading pronunciation. This is true whether we compare content word and function word, as Lavoie did with *four* and *for*; two function words, as in the pairs *your–you're* and *there–they're*; or two content words, as in *one–won, right–write, hole–whole*. Here we see that words may have their own phonetic history (W. Wang 1969) so that it would not be a surprise at all to find that in some future version of American English, *right* is pronounced with a phonemic glottal stop while *write* retains the older final /t/. It may be that we can describe pronunciation variation in terms of simple rules, like the one that palatalizes and devoices the /j/ of *your* and *you're* after [t, s, ʃ, tʃ], so that we can argue that the observed variation does not emerge from word-specific variation, but only that the most typical contexts of the homophones differ and therefore their most typical contextual variants do too. In an exemplar-based view, though, the frequency distribution of variants is part of the representation of the word; thus the representation needs to change very little to support a sound change from /raɪt/ to /raɪʔ/ because the prevalence of [raɪʔ] variants is a part of the representation of *right*.

Coming back to the main point of this section, talker-specific patterns of pronunciation as studied by Stollenwerk (1986) and word-specific patterns of variation as studied by Lavoie (2002) illustrate the type of phenomenon that exemplar-based models handle by defining language sound patterns by extension rather than by rule.

3.2.3 Recognition memory and declarative memory

Before turning to the decisions and mechanisms of the title of this chapter, I would like to mention briefly a relevant distinction that has been made in research on memory. This distinction is justified in part by the tragic case of an epilepsy patient known as Patient HM (see Gluck and Meyers 2000 for a lucid discussion). HM underwent surgery to remove the portion of his brain that was the initiating focal point for his severe epileptic seizures. The part of his brain that was removed was the hippocampus. This was done in the days before the crucial role of the hippocampus in

TABLE 3.1. Relative frequency of occurrence of the leading variants of homophones in a 100,000-word phonetically transcribed corpus of conversational English. The number of tokens of words that occur less than 10 times in the corpus is indicated

four	for		won	one
[fɔr] 53%	[fɚ] 58%		[wən] 94%	[wən] 73%
[foʊr] 34%	[tɔr] 16%		[wə̃n] 6%	[wəɾ] 12%
	[fə] 8%			[wə̃] 5%

two	to		past (n=5)	passed
[tu] 84%	[tə] 21%		[pæs] 80%	[pæst] 80%
[tə] 11%	[tɪ] 11%		[pæst] 20%	[pæs] 17%
	[tu] 10%			[pæʃ] 6%
	[ə] 10%		write	right
eye (n=4)	I		[raɪt] 39%	[raɪʔ] 38%
[aɪ] 100%	[aɪ] 58%		[raɪr] 39%	[raɪt] 28%
	[ə] 16%		[raɪʔ] 10%	[raɪ] 14%
	[ɑ] 16%			[raɪr] 7%

buy	by	bye (n=5)	they're	there
[baɪ] 96%	[baɪ] 86%	[baɪ] 80%	[ðɛr] 53%	[ðɛr] 54%
[bæ] 4%	[bɑ] 5%	[bɑ] 20%	[ðɚ] 15%	[ɛr] 12%
knew	new		[ɛr] 6%	[nɛr] 8%
[nu] 96%	[nu] 77%		[nɛr] 5%	[ðɛ] 5%
[nɪ] 4%	[nə] 11%		threw (n=6)	through
	[ni] 6%		[θru] 67%	[θru] 55%
hire (n=5)	higher		[θu] 33%	[θu] 12%
[haɪɚ] 60%	[haɪɚ] 92%			[θrə] 5%
[hɑr] 40%	[hɑr] 8%		wear	where
hear	here		[wɛr] 69%	[wɚ] 36%
[hir] 62%	[hɪr] 49%		[wər] 13%	[wɛr] 28%
[hɪr] 31%	[hir] 36%		[wɚ] 13%	[wər] 7%
hole (n=7)	whole			[ʌɚ] 6%
[hoʊl] 71%	[hoʊl] 81%		wore (n=5)	war
[hoʊ] 14%	[hoʊ] 16%		[wɔr] 100%	[wɔr] 67%
[hoʊl] 14%				[wər] 22%
hour	our			[woʊr] 11%
[aʊɚ] 50%	[ɑr] 72%		your	you're
[aʊr] 29%	[ər] 13%		[jɚ] 70%	[jɚ] 72%
know	no		[ʃɚ] 6%	[jɪ] 7%
[noʊ] 80%	[noʊ] 81%		[jɪ] 3%	[ʃɚ] 4%
[nə] 9%	[nə] 13%			

memory was known. As a result of the surgery, HM was unable to store any new memories. His doctor had to reintroduce himself each time he entered HM's room because HM did not remember him from one visit to the next. Readers who have seen the movie *Memento* will recognize the memory deficit.

However, more careful testing of HM's memory revealed that he did have the ability to remember *some* things from day to day. In particular, researchers taught him a game that he had never played before and found that even though they had to explain the rules of the game again each day that they visited (after introducing themselves) HM got better and better at the game. He was learning how to play it, using a memory system not available in his conscious life.

This type of priming without conscious memory, and research with normal subjects that reveals a difference between implicit and explicit memory, have led researchers to distinguish recognition memory from declarative memory. Declarative memory, on this view, is made up of one's knowledge of expressible facts, the sort of knowledge you could gain by reading books. Contrasting with this is the type of memory that HM seemed to be acquiring (but without the ability to transfer it to a declarative memory store) as he played the game. This implicit recognition memory is comprised of knowledge acquired through direct experience of an event or object. It is detailed in nature but often hard to describe in words. For instance, you can recognize close friends quickly and often from very limited sensory stimulus (in a quick glance, for example), but if you are asked to describe them to someone who will pick them up at the airport you may find yourself struggling for words. Recognition memory is thus the type of knowledge you get from direct experience while declarative memory is a kind of encoded representation of knowledge that can be passed from person to person in language.

It seems inevitable that the richness and directness of recognition memory is the language-user's knowledge that underlies linguistic performance, while our description of this knowledge in grammars and dictionaries is an impoverished representation in the same way that my description of my friend to the person who will pick him up at the airport is an impoverished representation of my true mental representation of him. While grammars and dictionaries are indeed powerful representations of language, exemplar-based modeling of phonology seeks to explore a representation of phonological knowledge that may be a little closer to the richness of language as it is experienced and stored by native speakers.

In what follows, then, I will recommend answers to two key decisions that must be made in exemplar-based phonology, and then discuss two mechanisms (one old and one new) that I think are required to model successfully language sound patterns in an exemplar-based phonology.

3.3 TWO DECISIONS

The first decision that we make in implementing an exemplar-based model of phonology is that of choosing a unit of representation. Some researchers have proposed to represent exemplars of speech sounds (Skousen 1989; Pierrehumbert 2001a) while others suggest that exemplars in memory are exemplars of words (Wedel 2003; Johnson 2005b).

I assume that exemplars are "of" experiences, that the waves of sensation that we are subject to are segmented into conscious experiences.[2] Searle (1998) argues that nonconscious brain states or events like neurotransmitter release, and my belief while sleeping that airplanes can fly, are not experiences. I accept his suggestion that experiences are the product of the conscious mind. Related to this, Edelman (1987) suggests that conscious experience is generated by the interaction between neuronal maps in the brain. So, in considering what a linguistic experience is, and, thus, the level of representation in an exemplar-based model of phonology, I would suggest that in language people generally experience words and not sounds. One line of support for this decision is in noticing how speakers and listeners talk to each other about language. Nonlinguists ask about words—word meanings and word pronunciations—without noticing or commenting on sub-word regularities. For example, in southeastern Ohio, *fish* is pronounced [fiʃ] and *push* is pronounced [puʃ] (instead of Standard American English [fɪʃ] and [pʊʃ]). Of course, this is a pretty general phenomenon—high lax vowels followed by [ʃ] in Standard American English are pronounced tense in the southern midlands dialect. But this is not how speakers seem to experience this phenomenon at least in conscious experience—we talk about words not sounds. I think this makes sense from Edelman's perspective on the neural formation of consciousness because words are where form and meaning, which are represented in different neuronal structures, interact with each other. So if, as Edelman suggests, the interaction of neuronal structures is the locus of the generation of conscious experience, it would make sense that words would be the fundamental building blocks in the conscious experience of language, while sounds are much less accessible to consciousness. In light of this perspective on the speaker's experience of language, then, exemplar-based phonology should start with word-sized exemplars.

The second decision has to do with how to represent the dimensions of exemplars. Nosofsky (1986) used multi-dimensional scaling to select perceptual dimensions, and in many ways this makes great sense because the representation is compact and based on data. The alternative is for the modeler to make assumptions about how to represent speech (as e.g. Pierrehumbert 2001a; Wedel 2004a) using perceptual dimensions that may or may not be important to listeners. Nosofsky had very simple stimuli (circles of various sizes with one radial line at various angles in the circle) and his two perceptual dimensions were very highly correlated with the two stimulus dimensions. In order to make a perceptual map of speech stimuli, on the other hand, we need *many* more dimensions than this—including auditory, visual, proprioceptive, and motor-control representations. Just considering the auditory representation of speech

---

[2] One reviewer asks how HM, who could not consciously remember experiences after hippocampus removal, could have conscious awareness without the ability consciously to remember those experiences. As I understand it, the hippocampus is involved in recoding experience to declarative memory and that hippocampus injury does not change experience. Thus, HM still had conscious experience after surgery and his experiences could still be treated as exemplars in recognition memory, though he lost the ability to access exemplars consciously.

we could code in terms of F1, F2, F3, f0, duration, spectral shape parameters, plus dynamic representations of each of these. The first two formant values have been shown to be important dimensions in vowel perception but multidimensional scaling spaces for larger sets of phonetic segments (Winters, p. c., Heeringa, p. c.) have not proven to be so coherent. In Johnson (1997*b*) I used formant values as the dimensions of a vowel exemplar space, but in Johnson (1997*a*) I stored exemplars as auditory spectrograms of words. This rich auditory representation is realistic because it is based on psychoacoustic data, and it also avoids making assumptions about which of the many potential acoustic features should be measured and kept in an exemplar of heard speech. I think that currently this is the best approach, not because it gives the cleanest and easiest modeling results—because this is definitely not the case—but because there is not enough data-driven evidence for a more compact representation. Detailed auditory spectrograms are problematic partly because they are so detailed and one would like to be able to reduce the information stored for each exemplar to a small number of significant parameters. However, though parameterizing, the per-ceptual space may make our models easier to work with, the data that could guide us to a particular parameterization do not exist. So, my decision has been to stick close to the signal in the model representation of exemplars—attempting in essence to have the same memory representation support modeling of low-level speech perception phenomena like talker normalization, while also aiming to account for higher-level language sound patterns.

The ideal model of exemplar-based phonology (and perhaps the only way to make this enterprise work) is to include visual and articulatory information in (some) exemplars. I speculated (Johnson 1997*b*) that inclusion of "seen" and "self" exemplars would provide a measure of phonetic coherence in perception that is lacking in current models. This remains an important research task.

3.4 TWO MECHANISMS

This section is a discussion of two key mechanisms used in exemplar-based phon-ology. These two mechanisms are methods for calculating activation of exemplars in response to input and the spread of that activation in a network of exemplars. In a model of speech perception the input is a detailed stimulus token and the pattern of activation is used to determine the category membership of the exemplar. In a model of speech production the input is a desired category output and the pattern of activation is used to determine the phonetic details of the speech to be produced. In either case, we must specify a mechanism of exemplar similarity matching, and we must specify a mechanism of activation spreading.

The first mechanism in exemplar-based phonology (similarity matching) has been used in exemplar-based memory models for many years. It is reviewed here for the sake of making an aspect of exemplar-based modeling explicit. Some authors have emphasized that exemplar-based models produce "on-line" generalizations. Hintzman (1986) was perhaps most explicit about this, even in the title of his article mentioning "abstraction". There is sometimes the misapprehension that because there are no abstract category prototypes in exemplar-based models, it must follow that exemplar-based models may not exhibit prototype effects such as generalization or abstraction. This is not the case because the aggregate response of category exemplars displays exactly these generalization characteristics. The question is not whether people behave as if they have stored abstract category prototypes, but, rather, whether this behavior arises from exemplar storage or prototype storage—because exemplar-based systems do exhibit abstraction behavior. The argument in favor of the exemplar-based generalization mechanism is that people also exhibit exemplar-tuned behavior, so if some sort of exemplar storage system is needed anyway, and if such a system can exhibit generalization behavior (via a similarity matching process) then why would one posit a parallel, totally redundant, prototype system?

The similarity matching process, then, is a key feature of exemplar-based memory systems. Several similarity matching algorithms have been proposed. I will discuss the model given by Nosofsky (1986) because it is the similarity-matching model that I have used in my own work, but many people find Hintzman's MINERVA a more intuitively approachable model.

The first step in similarity matching is to calculate the euclidian distance between the input auditory spectrogram (j) to all exemplars (i). One trick here is in temporally aligning the auditory spectrograms with each other. The strategy taken in XMOD is to slide x_i by x_j (permitting all possible alignments) and let d_{ij} be the smallest observed distance between them.

$$d_{ij} = \sqrt{\sum (x_i - x_j)^2} \quad \text{Auditory distance}$$

Now each exemplar's activation is calculated from auditory distance. The amount of activation of exemplar i caused by input token j is an exponential function of the auditory distance between the exemplar and the input token. One model parameter c scales the activation and is constant for all of the exemplars.

$$a_{ij} = e^{-cd_{ij}} \quad \text{Exemplar activation}$$

Finally, the evidence that input token j is an example of category k is then a sum of the activations of all of the exemplars of category k. In this formula w_{ki} is a weight set to 1 if exemplar i is a member of category k and 0 otherwise.

$$E_{kj} = \sum a_{ij} w_{ki} \quad \text{Category activation/evidence}$$

This simple similarity-matching algorithm produces prototype behavior from a set of detailed exemplars. As we will discuss shortly, a second mechanism may tune the output of the matching algorithm causing the "prototype" of the category to shift in response to various sorts of contextual factors.

The second mechanism that is important for exemplar-based phonology is an exemplar resonance mechanism that permits activation to spread through the set of exemplars via non-phonetic properties. In this approach, each exemplar of language has phonetic properties and nonphonetic properties and similarity between exemplars on their non-phonetic aspects changes the phonetic response of the system. Thus, for example, when you hear a token of a particular word some word properties (e.g. meaning, spelling, usage) may become active and then in a resonance loop feed that activation back to the exemplar memory so that the similarity-matching process becomes weighted toward the word. Hintzman (1986) envisioned a loop of this kind that sharpens the response of the system so that even on relatively equivocal evidence the exemplar-based system will come to a definite recognition decision. In cognition research generally, resonance is one of the key building-blocks in neural modeling. Semon (1923) described a resonance loop in the generation of "mnemic" excitations. Grossberg (Carpenter and Grossberg 1987) calls his influential neural modeling approach the "Adaptive Resonance Theory", with resonance as one of the key explanatory mechanisms. And Edelman (1987) emphasizes the power and importance of re-entrant mapping between neural subsystems in the generation of consciousness.

Coming back to Hintzman's (1986) MINERVA model as an illustration of resonance with exemplars that contain phonetic and nonphonetic information, we can extend Hintzman's ideas to phonology by modeling exemplars (Fig. 3.2) as a set of phonetic and nonphonetic properties. If the input to the system is purely phonetic (though often it is not, as we will see), the aggregate similarity response (the "echo") from a set of exemplars that do have specification for both phonetic and nonphonetic properties will contain an *altered* specification for the phonetic properties and a *new* specification for nonphonetic properties. For example, if one group of the nonphonetic properties of the stored exemplars codes the identity of the word, and another group codes the identity of the talker, then after a number of resonance echos the system will settle into stable categorization responses for both the talker and the linguistic item.

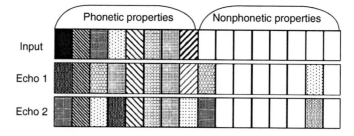

FIGURE 3.2. An input exemplar composed of phonetic property values (shaded cells) and with no nonphonetic properties specified. The first echo from a set of exemplars has a few nonphonetic properties activated and some of the phonetic property values altered. The second echo increases this trend

Given this, it is easy to see also how "topdown" activation could alter perception. Pickett and Pollack (1963) reported that context improves the perception of words produced in conversational speech, and Lieberman (1963) found that speakers produce clearer variants of words when the words appear in nonpredictive environments. In Hintzman's approach we suppose that some nonphonetic semantic properties are provided in the input with the phonetic properties, so that now the phonetic properties do not have to be so distinct in order for the correct word to be recognized because additional topdown information is involved in the similarity matching. In a Nosofsky-style exemplar model (Fig. 3.3) we would allow nonphonetic contextual information to alter the resting activation level of exemplars according to how well the exemplar matches the context, so that if the topic of conversation includes the notion <fish>, all exemplars that match this notion in their nonphonetic properties will get a boost of activation, and an incoming stimulus that sounds (taken out of context) more like *cot* than *cod* will nonetheless be recognized as *cod* because the overall activation of *cod* exemplars is higher in the combination of top–down and bottom–up evidence. In either Nosofsky's approach or Hintzman's we have interacting activation between phonetic and nonphonetic information that alters the perception of phonetic material allowing topdown information to change the perceptual process.

Another illustration of this comes from sociophonetics. It has been observed that listener expectations can alter perception (Johnson *et al.* 1999). One particularly striking illustration of this was shown by Strand (2000). She found that listeners were slower in naming words produced by nonstereotypical-sounding male and female voices than they were in naming words produced by speakers who sounded

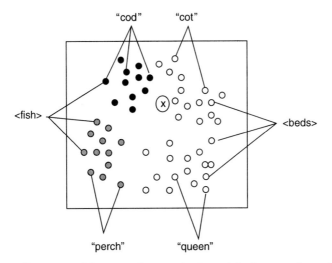

FIGURE 3.3. An illustration of how top–down activation might increase the activation of all exemplars related to <fish> so that a phonetically ambiguous token that sounds more like *cot* than *cod* will be recognized as *cod*

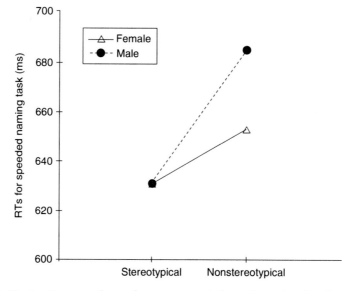

FIGURE 3.4. Naming times were longer for nonstereotypical-sounding voices than for stereotypical-sounding voices (after Strand 2000)

stereotypical (Fig. 3.4). The suggestion here is that voice "stereotypicality" arises in the interaction between phonetic and nonphonetic properties coded in exemplars. The resonance process is quick and decisive with stereotypical-sounding voices producing an easily classified coherent response, while nonstereotypicality results in at least momentary ambiguity in a resonance process that is thus slower to match phonetic detail to categorical representation.

As with the effect of top–down semantic information, we can envision the effect of talker information (via the acoustic signal, a visual signal, a listener bias) as producing an effect on perception by altering the resting activation levels of exemplars associated with the talker. This is illustrated in Figure 3.5. If the gender of the talker can be clearly identified, then the evidence for word identity is sharpened by reducing the amount of competition, thus supporting faster word-identification response.

Finally, the resonance mechanism in exemplar-based phonology permits phonological generalization as well. Some aspects of phonological patterning "emerge" from resonance between semantic and phonetic information. A sketch of this idea is given in Figure 3.6. The allophonic relationship between [d] and [ɾ] emerges from semantic/phonetic resonance. Forms associated with both the word "odd" and the word "odder" are activated in response to presentation of a token of "odd" because there is a semantic relationship between "odd" and "odder". At first only exemplars of "odd" will be activated because the input token with [d] is somewhat different from the exemplars of "odder". However, the resonance loop linking exemplars on the basis of semantic similarity results in the pattern of activation illustrated in Figure 3.6.

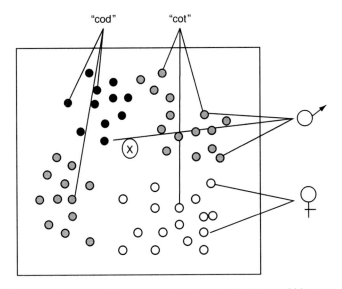

FIGURE 3.5. Illustration that an ambiguous word, indicated with "x", could be interpreted as *cod* more quickly when the speaker is clearly male than when the identity of the speaker is not clear. Each dot stands for an exemplar and the shading of the dot corresponds to the exemplar's activation upon presentation of the "x" token after some resonance. In this case, two categories, "cod" and "male", reinforce each other to categorize the ambiguous token

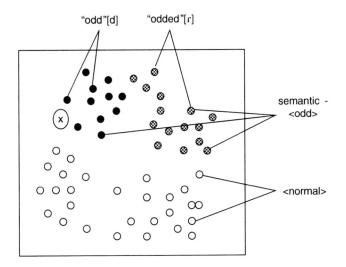

FIGURE 3.6. Illustration of allophonic resonance in the interaction between semantic and phonetic information in exemplar-based phonology. After a new token "x" has been encountered, phonetically similar tokens of "odd" are activated (indicated by darker shading). As a result of semantically guided resonance, the allophonic relationship between [d] and [ɾ] is represented in the pattern of exemplar activation

In this resonance-driven exemplar activation response, the phonological relationship between [d] and [ɾ] is represented as a pattern of exemplar activation in which exemplars of "odd" and "odder" are co-active despite their phonetic differences.

3.5 CONCLUSION

In this chapter I have suggested that exemplar-based models of phonological knowledge may increase our understanding of the ecology of language—particularly of the cognitive basis of phonological knowledge. I see this project as a continuation of the research aims illustrated so well by John Ohala's work on the phonetic and historical basis of language sound patterns.

One of the main goals of the chapter was to point out that exemplar-based phonology is based on a long tradition of research and theorizing in cognitive psychology and that this general approach to phonological modeling is being pursued by many linguists. There is no one exemplar-based phonology theory, but, rather, a number of nascent models seeking to use this class of memory models to help us better understand, among other things, phonological generalizations and the coexistence of gradience and categoriality in phonological knowledge.

In addition to these general considerations, the chapter outlined my answers to a few important decisions that must be made in exemplar-based modeling of phonological knowledge, suggesting (1) that exemplars in linguistic memory are examples of words from which smaller phonetic/phonological units emerge, and (2) that the representation of exemplars in model simulations should be rich with phonetic detail. The paper also described two important mechanisms in exemplar-based phonology, noting that similarity-matching results in generalization behavior without explicit storage of prototypes and that resonance interactions between phonetic and non-phonetic information in exemplars produces top–down processing influences as well as a representation of linguistically significant sound patterns.

4

Beyond Laboratory Phonology

The Phonetics of Speech Communication

Klaus J. Kohler

4.1 INTRODUCTION: PARADIGMS IN SPEECH RESEARCH

Every science develops paradigms—sets of theoretical and methodological principles—which are only partly determined by scientific phenomena, far more so by
the sociology of science. They are passed on through teaching and an influential, often
missionary discipleship, and are finally codified in textbooks and degree curricula.
Changing them is the equivalent of a scientific revolution (Kuhn 1970).

Looking at the history of linguistics of the last 125 years, we can distinguish three
such scientific revolutions in the study of language:

- the positivist codification of "historical linguistics" by the Neogrammarians at the
  end of the nineteenth century (Paul 1880);
- the behaviorist codification of "structural linguistics" in the first half of the
  twentieth century (Bloomfield 1933);
- the mentalist codification of "generative linguistics" in the second half of the
  twentieth century (Chomsky 1957).

They are reflected in the analysis of the spoken medium. Within the framework of
historical linguistics, phonetics developed two strands—descriptive and experimental.
Sievers's introduction to descriptive phonetics (Sievers 1876) was the first volume in the
series *Bibliothek Indogermanischer Grammatiken* under the editorship of a Neogrammarian
team, which included Delbrück and Leskien. It carried the subtitle *for the introduction to
the study of the phonetics of Indo-European languages*, and it was to lay the foundations for
the evaluation of sound change in the historical development of languages.

On the other hand, Rousselot (1897–1901) approached the study of the sounds of
languages through instrumental and experimental analysis of the physics of speech

production, but again with the aim of elucidating sound change, since he also applied his techniques to the modifications of pronunciation in the dialect of a family in order to deduce general sound laws (Rousselot 1892). It was the positivist conviction that the detailed study of sound curves and the numbers derived from them could provide the objective basis of speech sounds, which cannot be captured by subjective auditory impressions and their description. Instrumental measurement, then, was assumed to unfold the truth. Thus, from its inception in the work of Rousselot, and later of Scripture (1902) and Panconcelli-Calzia (1948), experimental, signal-oriented phonetics was conceptualized as a discipline dissociated from, and in opposition to, the symbol-oriented, descriptive framework represented at the turn of the nineteenth century by, among others, Jespersen, Passy, Sievers, Sweet, and Viëtor.

Following on from Saussure (1915), the rise of phonology in the Prague Circle (Trubetzkoy 1962) and in American structuralism (e.g. Bloch 1948) was the systemic answer of the humanities to the focus on atomistic measurement, which had finally dissolved all linguistic categories. Phonology grew into a new discipline within linguistics, establishing a science–humanities dualism in the study of speech: phonetics provides detailed measurements of physical speech parameters; phonology works out the distinctive features of the sound systems of languages. Basically, this dichotomy has stayed with us ever since.

Research groups in psychology and engineering environments—Haskins Laboratories, for instance—imported linguistic concepts such as the phoneme and filled them with phonetic substance in production and perception experiments. The adequacy of the linguistic concepts for these investigations outside linguistics was not questioned but taken as factual. This led to "categorical speech perception", "the speech code", and "the motor theory of speech perception", all anchored on the given linguistic category of the phoneme. The analysis of an array of phonetic parameters, for example to differentiate voiced and voiceless plosive phonemes, gained momentum in production and perception studies within word phonology, which means that phonologically contrastive words (or word-like logatomes) were investigated in isolation or in metalinguistic frames. It soon became obvious that the results were of limited value as regards the explanation of speech communication. In listening experiments, for example, subjects were able to learn to pay attention to fine detail without establishing communicative speech-sound categories.

Within the framework of generative linguistics (Chomsky and Halle 1968), phonology lost its independent status as a level of linguistic analysis and was incorporated into the grammar. This entailed a change of view on the phonologization of morphophonemic alternations, such as the neutralization of voicing of obstruents in morpheme-final position (e.g. German *Kind* [t] "child" ~ *Kinder* [d] "children"). Loss of contrast was recognized as a surface-level phenomenon in final position, but, being accompanied by the maintenance of a phonetic difference in the non-final form of the morpheme, the latter was generally taken to be the *phonological* representation.

So, when researchers started taking these new phonological solutions into the laboratory, it was natural to raise the question whether the postulated non-neutralization in phonology was supported by a phonetic contrast which had not been detected previously due to missing measurements. Attention to phonetic detail of obstruent voicing in a number of languages that had been reported as having morpho-phonologically conditioned neutralization resulted in the rejection of the well-established neutralization phenomena; German was a case in point. In the main part of this chapter, these analyses will be evaluated with regard to the methodology of subject selection, word material, and experiment design.

The essence of this research strategy is that the linguistic form of phonological solutions, arrived at outside the laboratory, is theoretically primary, its phonetic substantiation secondary. It may therefore be called the paradigm of "phonology-going-into-the-lab", which became the methodological core for the Laboratory Phonology conference series and the theoretical pivot of the ensuing conceptualization of laboratory phonology as a natural science (Pierrehumbert *et al.* 2000). Filling phonological categories with phonetic substance is intended to alleviate the modularization into phonetics and phonology.

The blending of phonology (with its discrete categories) and of phonetics (with its scalar variability) into the laboratory phonology paradigm has led to a new dilemma: phonological categories may now turn out to be gradient. To ascertain their category status, inferential statistics comes into play. Statistical significance of sets of measurements is the decisive factor. In perception experiments, attribution to categories is made dependent on categorical perception, which, in its strongest form à la Haskins, requires a sharp change in the identification function coinciding with a sharp increase in the discrimination function.

But this type of phonetic research still does not tell us very much about speech communication. Measurements of signal parameters are related to phonological categories which are established by techniques that result from phonological theories. But neither phonological categories nor phonetic measurements and their statistical evaluation need necessarily represent language structures that are relevant for communicating individuals, and they may even represent incongruous metalinguistic domains. So, extrapolation of such experimental results to categories for real speakers and listeners is problematic, although standard practice in laboratory phonology. In summary, we can say that this type of classic laboratory phonology, has not overcome the philosophy-of-science approach of twentieth-century speech analysis in spite of its sophisticated theorizing and analysis techniques, and although it has contributed a great deal towards a bridging of the phonetics–phonology schism. A new paradigm is needed which has the elucidation of speech communication as its goal and therefore subordinates all phonological categories and phonetic measurements to the relevance for communicative functions. In this approach, phonological form is not primary but results from experimentally relating phonetic substance to independently motivated communicative functions, which include traditional linguistic ones. This is the paradigm of "phonology-coming-out-of-the-lab" or of experimental phonology (J. Ohala and Jaeger 1986; Kohler 2005a).

To illustrate some moot points in the basic tenet of laboratory phonology, two issues will be discussed—one from segmentals, the other from prosody—which have received extensive analysis in the laboratory: (1) the neutralization of voicing in word-final position, with special reference to German, and (2) f0 alignment in intonational phonology. I am well aware that the proponents of laboratory phonology maintain that "laboratory phonology is not a framework . . . it is a coalition amongst groups of people, with some working in one or another of the various current frameworks, and others working in no phonological framework at all." (Pierrehumbert *et al.* 2000: 279). But the "hallmark of a successful community is maintenance of a common vocabulary—which can be used by opposing parties in an argument—even at the expense of a gradual drift in both the meanings of technical terms and the empirical domain under discussion." (ibid.: 276). This stance clearly refers to what I have called "the sociology of science". Although there are researchers working in this community of laboratory phonology who have moved towards the paradigm of experimental phonology referred to above, there is no denying the fact that "phonology-going-into-the-lab" has remained the prevalent core of research.

The discussion of the two areas of laboratory-phonology investigations is followed by some thoughts on categories and methods that will have to be central in a new paradigm for the phonetics of speech communication.

4.2 THE ISSUE OF NEUTRALIZATION OF VOICING IN FINAL OBSTRUENTS

It has been an established statement of fact in German philology for at least a century that there is neutralization of word-final lenis with fortis obstruents (*Auslautverhärtung*) in German. Trubetzkoy (1962: 213) refers to Standard German (besides "Russian, Polish, Czech, etc.") in his discussion of the cancellation of a phonological opposition at the boundaries of words and morphemes, more particularly with regard to final devoicing. Furthermore, it is well-known from foreign-language teaching that native German speakers have great problems in acquiring a word-final voiced–voiceless opposition in languages, such as English or French, where the distinction is made.

This firm stance on complete neutralization of the word-final voicing contrast in German was called into question in the wake of generative phonology, when morphologically related word-forms were given the same underlying phonological representation with the same distinctive phonetic features, and when Dinnsen (1983) maintained that careful phonetic studies would reveal that all declared neutralization rules in the phonologies of languages were in effect not neutralizing at all. An early example of such a phonological reassessment of neutralization is the statement by

Malmberg (1943) that lenis voiced and fortis voiceless plosives in French stay different in the force features even when they lose their voice distinction in regressive assimilation. Partial differences in properties such as duration and intra-oral pressure were subsequently analyzed in read laboratory speech by Thorsen (1966) and Fischer-Jørgensen (1968*a*, *b*).

The first to take the German neutralization issue into the laboratory were Mitleb (1981), Port *et al.* (1981), and O'Dell and Port (1983), followed by more extensive accounts and discussions in Port and O'Dell (1985). In these studies, consistent differences were found, especially in the duration of the vowel preceding the final obstruent, in citation form pronunciations of word lists, containing pairs such as *Rad* "wheel" ~ *Rat* "advice", *Bad* "bath" ~ *bat* "requested", *Alb* "elf" ~ *Alp* "mountain pasture", *weg* "away" ~ *Weck* "breakfast roll" (southern dialect word), *schrag* (imperative form of obsolete *schragen*) "join wooden poles cross-wise or slanting" ~ *schrak* (past tense of intransitive *schrecken*, which only occurs in *erschrecken*) "had a fright". The differences were small (15ms of vowel and burst durations, 5ms of closure voicing on average), but in the same direction as in the non-neutralizing word-medial context, in other words, longer vowel, shorter burst, and more closure voicing in the underlying voiced plosive, some of them reaching statistical significance. The production data were supplemented by listener judgments, which identified the produced member of a pair poorly, but significantly better than chance (59% overall). The authors concluded from these results, supported by inferential statistics, that German had incomplete neutralization of the underlying word-final voicing opposition in obstruents, and that these phonetic differences would have to be taken into account in the phonology of German by the introduction of implementation rules of the generally maintained phonological contrast.

Fourakis and Iverson (1984) argued convincingly, on the basis of data from orthographic vs. free elicitation of relevant words, that the phonetic differences were caused by hypercorrection of isolated words in a reading task, and that there were no grounds for postulating incomplete neutralization in the phonology of German. They also pointed out that *weg* (although etymologically related to the noun paradigm *Weg: Wege*) was not part of a morphological alternation at all, now being an adverb with a short vowel. The orthography argument was further supported by Port and Crawford (1989) in an investigation of the influence of speech style. They found that discriminant analysis to classify productions by underlying final voicing was least successful (about 55%) when target words were embedded in sentences that did not draw attention to minimal pairs, but most successful (78%) when speakers dictated the words. The conclusion from these results was, however, that many small acoustic differences are involved in maintaining the underlying distinction, which surfaces in different degrees depending on speech style.

There is another crucial point that has to be considered in the evaluation of these data and in the inferences for phonological theory and for the phonological explanation of voicing oppositions in German. The authors found it necessary to explain the meanings of some of their words to their subjects before the actual tests. This was certainly necessary for *Alb*, *Alp*, *schrag*, *schrak*, and *Weck*. In view of the complete lack of context for words, which in addition are not all part of common vocabulary of the subjects or are unusual morphological forms, the test items assumed the status of logatomes. It also needs to be taken into account that the data were collected in the US from German speakers who had spent considerable lengths of time in an English-speaking environment and had no doubt been made aware of the need to differentiate final orthographic <b>, <d>, <g> from <p>, <t>, <k>. In view of these experimental design constraints, there is no avoiding the conclusion that the data resulting from this "phonology-into-the-lab" paradigm have neither contributed to the elucidation of the phonetics of speech communication in German, nor have they been able to substantiate the claim of incomplete neutralization; they have thus not advanced our understanding of the phonetics–phonology interface.

The amount of time and effort that went into the attempt to substantiate pre-established phonological categories would have been better spent on assessing the variability of German plosives across different communicative functions, paying attention to situational, syntactic, lexical, and phonetic contexts. In pursuit of this line of research, insights can be gained especially from the following topics of investigation:

- glottalization (Kohler 1994, 1999*a*, *b*, 2001*a*);
- gestural reduction (Kohler 2001*b*);
- lenition, place and manner assimilations (Kohler 2001*c*).

In these studies, the question is not how phonetic data can be fitted into currently proposed linguistic solutions of linear segmental word phonology. Existing phonemic representations of words are not taken as ontologies of cognitive representations, but simply as heuristic devices for accessing labeled acoustic databases to investigate the structured variability of the phonetic dynamics of connected speech in various communicative settings. The aim is to derive general principles of the organization of production units beyond the phoneme under the whole array of contextual constraints from situation to phonetics. The timing and economy of more global gestural units, such as opening–closing and closing–opening movements, become the focus of attention. This allows us to analyze time courses of articulatory and acoustic phonetic parameters in their relation to the production and perception of words and phrasal structures. This also enables the comparison across languages, dialects, and diachronic stages, and opens new perspectives on historical sound change, more akin to the commonly pooh-poohed atomistic approach of the Neogrammarians than to the systemic conceptualization of historical phonology.

One such phonetic property of production and perception beyond the phoneme is glottalization The manifestation of plosives as glottal stops or irregular glottal pulsing in nasal environments is very common in German, for example, *könnten* "could" vs. *können* "can". It is no longer seen as a simple segmental replacement but as the most elementary glottal air stream regulation, allowing continued velic lowering, at the same time conveying to a listener the percept of a break which can be linked to a stop. Glottalization, instead of plosive articulation, thus constitutes a more economical gesture to achieve a constant purpose for a listener. Moreover, the positioning of irregular glottal vibration within the nasal stretch can be highly variable in production, and for a listener its occurrence somewhere in this consonantal configuration, or even towards the end of the preceding vowel, is sufficient to decode a stop.

Similarly, the assimilation of German unreleased coronal plosives to labial or dorsal ones across word boundaries cuts out a gesture without hampering intelligibility because the auditory effect of a coronal closing gesture intertwined with a following labial/dorsal one is only minimally different from that of a labial/dorsal closing + long hold + opening. Again, gestural economy achieves a constant purpose for the listener.

Finally, in German, the realization of voiced approximants instead of intervocalic lenis plosives, and of lenis plosives instead of intervocalic fortis ones, are economical reductions of closing–opening gestures, maintaining the difference in dynamic energy between the two sets of lenis and fortis gestures at lower values, which is sufficient differentiation for the listener.

In all these cases, phonetic-data analysis of connected speech in the laboratory contributes to the linguistic modeling of speech production and perception, no longer filling phonological entities with phonetic measurement, but creating phonological structures from phonetic measurement. Regarding plosive categories from their phonetic manifestations rather than from their positions in phonemic systems also provides a common *tertium comparationis* across languages. So we can assert that German and English show the same phenomenon of glottalization, related to plosives in a nasal environment, as in German *könnten* and English *mountain*, at least in American English (Pierrehumbert and Frisch 1997) and non-RP varieties of British English.

Likewise, a force feature differentiating the two plosive classes /b/, /d/, /g/ and /p/, /t/, /k/ in German, even when lenition reduces them to a distinction between approximants and lenis plosives, can be extrapolated to other languages, for example to English, as a dynamic phonetic property. But at first sight such a cross-linguistic generalization seems to be falsified by data from American English, where /t/ may be deleted in such words as *winter*, coalescing with *winner*, whilst /d/ stays as a plosive in *cinders*, etc. This speaks against referring /t/ and /d/ to a difference in force of articulation, because one would expect the weaker member of the opposition to reduce in a common context.

However, if instead of focusing on an individual consonantal segment, the whole closing–opening gesture is taken into account, all the superficially disparate observations fall into place. Intersyllabic /t/ ~ /d/ is characterized in English generally by /t/ inducing a fast closing movement as against a slow closing movement for /d/. This is an extension of what is found word-finally in for example *bite* ~ *bide*. It takes care of the difference in vowel duration of *writer* ~ *rider*. If the dyad of vowel + stop closure is kept at the same magnitude in both cases the occlusion phases will show complementary duration differences, and this may be supplemented by VOT differences, again stronger for /t/ than for /d/. On the other hand, the faster closing movement for /t/, intervocalically, may change the mechanics of the movement and result in a flap, as against a stop for /d/. This relatively subtle difference can then be easily leveled out, and the difference in vowel duration remains the only distinguishing feature. Even this may be overridden, resulting in complete coalescence.

In the vowel + nasal + /t/ or /d/ context we can expect the same basic dynamics. Here, the nasal is also shorter before /t/ than before /d/; thus, the faster tongue movement is coupled with a faster velic raising to reach the dynamic goal, the establishment of a complete supra-glottal enclosure, more quickly. But the tongue-tip mechanics are already initiated for the nasal, which may become flapped for intervocalic /nt/. In a further step, *winter* could coalesce with *winner*, but /nd/, having the slower closing movement, would stay different.

So, what looks like a reversal of the hypothesized strength relationship in the contextual reduction of /t/ ~ /d/ could be related to the same prototypical category manifestations under changes of the whole syllable dynamics. All these English data would then fit into the lenition patterns one finds in German and in many other languages. With this line of argument, a force-feature difference in stop productions /p/, /t/, /k/ ~ /b/, /d/, /g/ gains further credibility rather than being undermined. This does of course not mean that the force difference is always maintained in a synchronic or diachronic perspective; there is always the possibility of coalescence across dialects, speaking styles, and historical stages of a language, as shown by German *Auslautverhärtung*.

4.3 THE ISSUE OF F0 ALIGNMENT WITH ARTICULATION

The framework of autosegmental metrical (AM) phonology (see Ladd 1996) and its labeling tool ToBI (Beckman *et al.* 2005) postulate the reduction of phonetic f0 patterns to phonological points in the form of pitch accents, phrase accents, and boundary tones, and also to binary oppositions L vs H in each case. For pitch accents, this basic theoretical framework allows four bitonal units L* + H, L + H*, H* + L, and H + L*, besides the two single tones L* and H*. No external grounds have ever been provided to justify the combinatorial restrictions.

If empirical data related to pitch accents in a language under investigation cannot be represented by any of these categories and require further differentiation, there are two ways the theory can deal with the problem: (a) the type of tonal categorization in AM phonology is not adequate and the theory needs fundamental revision, or (b) the theory is kept in its existing detail and new ad hoc categories are added that can cope with the new empirical data. The second solution was adopted by Grice (1995) for English, by allowing three tones in pitch accents in order to account for distinctive pitch phenomena in connection with downstep and with the analysis of "high plus mid accented syllable" as $(H + L) + H^*$ vs. "high plus low accented syllable" as $H + L^*$ (pp. 219 ff.; see also Ladd 1996: 109ff). The argument is circular, in that the empirical data force Grice to expand the categorical repertoire, after which phonology explains the empirical data.

Pitch accents are associated with certain stressed syllables, and in the case of bitonal categories their components either have primary (strong) status, or they are leading or trailing the primary component. This led to the star concept. These primary associations of bitonal components (conceptualized outside the time scale) were subsequently subjected to instrumental measurement, within the laboratory-phonology framework, to analyze their f0 maximum/minimum alignment with the stressed syllable and thus to put the phonetic manifestation of the phonological categories on the time scale post hoc. It turned out that H^* and L^* did not always show the relation in the physics of speech as one would expect from tone association to syllables. Thus the concept of phonetic alignment was born. The question then became, How is *phonological association* mapped onto *phonetic alignment*?

As a way out of this dilemma, Atterer and Ladd (2004) proposed to negate starred accents altogether in collecting phonetic measurements of LH and HL trajectories across different languages. They assume identical cross-linguistic pitch categories without justification, and maintain that "serious investigation of differences between languages and dialects must be based on instrumental data. Notational distinctions such as $L^* + H$ vs. $L + H^*$... are incapable of representing the range of fine phonetic differences that can be discovered instrumentally" (p. 194). This is the reinstatement of the philosophy of science of experimental phonetics at the turn of the twentieth century. It is a step back to the early days of instrumental speech analysis and to Scripture's statement "The 'nature of speech' is a summary of these numbers... The investigator might be—and preferably should be—congenitally deaf and totally ignorant of any notions concerning sound and speech. The entire statement of the results is confined to the measurement-numbers and their harmonies" (Scripture 1936: 135). This is obviously no solution, and should not be considered further.

Alternatively, the incommensurability of theory and data is again resolved by the addition of a new concept, namely, secondary association, set apart from primary tone association by secondary alignment of edge tones to stressed syllables, to moras and to word edges (Pierrehumbert and Beckman 1988). This new phonological concept allows us to "explain" phonetic alignment that deviates from what would be expected from primary association. It becomes a deus ex machina, which always fits and therefore has no explanatory power.

In applying the concept of secondary association to Catalan, Neapolitan, and Pisa Italian, Prieto, d'Imperio, and Gili Fivela (2005) expand it so that not only phrase edges can seek edges of metrical units as anchor points, but also tones in pitch accents. For Catalan, they describe a three-way phonological contrast in rising prenuclear accents and a binary contrast in nuclear position. In commands and in narrow-focus statements, the peak of a prenuclear rise is aligned with the right edge of the accented syllable; in a wide-focus statement, a prenuclear rise has a delayed peak, and in a polar question or a request, the prenuclear rise only starts on the post-tonic syllable. As in prenuclear position, the nuclear accent rise in commands has its peak aligned with the end of the accented syllable, whereas in requests it only starts at that point. The threefold alignment contrast in the prenuclear accent rise cannot be captured by the $L + H^* \sim L^* + H$ dichotomy which the AM framework provides for such rises. This clash between phonological association of pitch accents to syllables and phonetic alignment in and across syllables is again resolved by secondary association. There are two pitch accents, $L + H^*$ and $L^* + H$, which are in primary association with the accented syllable. Their primary associations are sufficient to distinguish the rise with delayed peak and the posttonic rise, respectively. The peak alignment with the edge of the syllable is captured by the addition of a secondary association with the metrical anchor of the accented-syllable edge.

In Neapolitan, narrow focus vs question, there are two contrastively aligned LH rising accents ($L + H^*$ and $L^* + H$) which are nevertheless realized within the stressed syllable boundaries. This means that there is a clash between contrastive earlier vs. later alignment and primary association with the same syllable. The introduction of a secondary association should resolve this clash. It associates the starred tone, H^* or L^*, secondarily to the first mora of the accented syllable, and thus re-establishes a phonological difference of association, as represented by the different star categorizations, in spite of their association with the same syllable.

The postulate of secondary association to account for the manifestation of broad and narrow focus in Pisa Italian is more complex. Again there are two contrastive LH patterns associated with the stressed syllable (and followed by a low intermediate phrase-boundary tone). Both have a phonetic leading tone $[L +]$, narrow focus has a trailing low tone as well. Both pitch accents have H^* associated with the stressed syllable, but this H^* is differently aligned within the syllable. So both have a primary association of H^* with the stressed syllable, but differ in secondary association to the right edge of the syllable for wide focus, but with the right edge of the first mora in narrow focus.

There is no theoretical necessity to deal with the data from these Romance languages in this way; the terms "mora" and "secondary association" are not defined within prosodic theory, but are ad hoc constructs to deal with the empirical data in a clash with the initial phonological representation. For one thing, it can be argued that the introduction of the mora or the syllable edge or the word edge as an anchor for the pitch pattern would make both primary and secondary association superfluous, if it were not for the initial postulate that pitch accents are associated with the stressed syllable. Secondly, although the authors base their analyses on functional contrasts, they nevertheless take pre-established formal phonological categorizations within the AM framework into the laboratory and fill them with measurements, in other words, they adhere to the principal tenet of laboratory phonology. However, this methodological approach forces them to introduce new abstract categories to save the initial postulate and at the same time reconcile it with empirical data.

The much simpler theoretical alternative is to introduce time into the phonological pitch categories in their initial definitions; earlier and later *synchronizations* of pitch contours with syllable articulation can then be differentiated as contrastive categories in the prosodic phonology of Catalan and the two Italian varieties, as well as other languages. The inclusion of time in intonational phonology is comparable to its introduction in articulatory phonology (Browman and Goldstein 1992). But to do this we should aim at the first solution mentioned above, namely, that AM theory needs to be changed.

This was first proposed for the intonational phonology of German in Kohler (1987), long before the application of AM to German and before the codification of the labeling tool GToBI (Grice and Baumann 2002). "Time" became established as a central prosodic category in the development of *KIM* (the *Kiel Intonation Model*; Kohler 1990, 1991*a*, *c*, 1995*b*, 1997, 2003, 2004*a*, *c*, 2005*b*, 2006; Niebuhr 2003; Niebuhr and Kohler 2004). KIM conceptualizes intonation as consisting of sequences of peak or valley or combined peak–valley patterns, each linked to one accented word. They are global pitch units (rising–falling, falling–rising, rising–falling–rising), not series of target pitch points. The distinctive units are established by function-oriented experimental phonetics, that is, the phonological categories are not worked out at the linguist's desk and then carried into the laboratory to be filled with substance. Rather, experimental procedures in functional (contextual) settings lead to the categories.

The peak and valley units have different contrastive phonological "synchronizations" with articulation: early–medial–late peaks, and early–late valleys. These categorizations resulted from perceptual experiments with peak and valley shift paradigms testing discrimination, as well as identification through contextualization (Kohler 1987, 1990, 1991*a*; *c*, Niebuhr 2003; Niebuhr and Kohler 2004). They contain the time dimension, it need not be added post hoc to timeless abstract tonal entities associated with syllables. So the problem of mapping phonological association onto phonetic alignment does not arise.

These peak and valley categories are related to linguistic and paralinguistic functions. In German (Kohler 2004*b*, 2005*b*, 2006, Niebuhr and Kohler 2004), peaks code

- "finality" when "early": *knowing, summarizing, coming to the end of an argument*;
- "openness" when "medial": *observing, realising, starting a new argument*;
- "unexpectedness" when "late": *observing, realising in contrast to one's expectation, surprise, disbelief.*

Valleys differ from peaks by the pragmatic meaning of addressee-orientation, expressing

- "casualness" when "early";
- "friendly concern" when "late".

In addition to these external synchronizations, internal timing of pitch patterns, as in fast rise–slow fall and slow rise–fast fall in peak contours, contributes to their distinctive functions (Niebuhr 2003). The prototypical "early peak" may be defined as slow rising before the accented syllable, followed by fast falling into the accented vowel, as against the prototypical "medial peak" with a fast rise into the accented syllable and a slow fall in the accented vowel. This produces an opposition of a high–low and a low–high pitch contrast in the f0 trajectory into the accented vowel, perceptually accentuating low vs high pitch in the vowel. In the case of the "late peak", the syntagmatic fast rise–slow fall contrast is shifted towards the end of the accented syllable.

The same threefold peak synchronizations have been found in Southern British English (Kleber 2005). The Neapolitan question–narrow focus dichotomy also fits into this frame: a late peak with a slow fall intensifies high pitch late in relation to the accented syllable of a question. Similarly, the Pisa data for wide and narrow (contrastive) focus exhibit a basic contrast in phonological synchronization, combined with internal timing differences to accentuate high pitch in broad focus (see Kohler 2003). The same considerations apply to Catalan question vs. statement, request vs. command, and wide vs. narrow focus.

Within the differently synchronized categories there is phonetic variability. This is what most alignment studies analysed (Atterer and Ladd 2004; Arvaniti *et al.* 1998; Ladd *et al.* 1999, 2000). It is, however, essential to differentiate phonological external and internal timing from phonetic alignment of pitch. In language comparisons, functional timing has to be established before phonetic alignment differences can be evaluated. Placing languages on an alignment scale from early to late, such as English–Dutch–North German–South German–Greek (Atterer and Ladd 2004), presupposes reference to the same functional synchronization across the intonational systems. Then it becomes insightful to say that medial peaks are aligned later in X vs. Y, for example.

4.4 THE NEW PARADIGM OF EXPERIMENTAL PHONOLOGY

A new paradigm is needed for the analysis of segmental and prosodic aspects of languages. Its goal is the elucidation of speech communication, based on function, time, and the listener. Communicative functions, beyond linguistic form, must be at the center of phonetic investigations into speech and language. The analysis is to be based on situational, pragmatic, semantic, syntactic, and phonetic contextualization. Time is central to the paradigm, not just with reference to duration measurements but also as the structuring of the timing of phonation and articulation and their synchronizations; time enters the definitions of segmental and prosodic units. At the prosodic level, different synchronizations of f0 contours for different communicative categories are differentiated from phonetic alignment variation within these categories. The listener also assumes a central role, even in production studies, because communication presupposes that speech is produced for a listener and must therefore be decodable by a listener.

We need to give systematic analyses of large corpora of speech interaction in individual languages a more prominent place in speech research. In a first step these data are annotated, in computer-readable form, with language-specific inventories of segmental and prosodic labels, based on provisional phonemic and prosodic representations; not as linguistic truths about languages, but as heuristic devices to access large corpus data systematically. Segmental transcription starts from canonical word-forms in phonemic representation, and relates signal portions to them with symbolic marking of assimilations, elisions, and insertions. The *Kiel Corpus of Spontaneous Speech* (Institute of Phonetics and Digital Speech Processing (IPDS) 1995, 1996, 1997) is such a database.

Context-sensitive search operations then excerpt, via the symbolic labels, all instances of specific sound classes (and their labeled modifications) in specific segmental and prosodic contexts, or of specific pitch patterns, together with the speech-signal portions the labels have been allocated to. Measurements are performed on the excerpted sound classes and pitch patterns, and descriptive and inferential statistics are applied to the symbol and signal data (e.g. Kohler 2001*b*, 2004*b*).

Based on the results of the corpus analysis, speech data are collected following systematic experimental designs, in production as well as in perception, carefully considering the methods of selection of subjects and speech material, and replacing the metalinguistic levels of isolated word and sentence by contextual and communicative frames. With regard to the application of statistical procedures to the data, inferential significance needs more sophisticated interpretation; in particular, it is necessary to distinguish between categorical perception and category interpretation, as communicative categories may be available to speaker and listener without being supported by categorical perception (Niebuhr and Kohler 2004). A methodology will thus be developed to refine experimental techniques by integrating experimental with corpus data analysis (e.g. Kohler 2004*b*, 2005*b*).

Context-sensitive search operations, measurements on corpus data, and systematic experimental analysis then lead to a revision of the initial heuristic categories. The result is the paradigm of "phonology-coming-out-of-the-lab" or experimental phonology. In parallel, this paradigm needs to be strengthened by function-oriented experimental phonetics, dealing with such concepts as the "frequency code" (J. Ohala 1983*a*, 1984), "minimization of effort", "self-organization in sound systems", "hypo-hyper variation" (Lindblom 1990*a*), "auditory enhancement" (Diehl 1991). There are clear signs of movement among the laboratory-phonology community in the direction of such a refocussed experimental approach, with research beginning to center more on communicative function and large databases of connected natural speech, especially in the analysis of intonation and rhythm. These individual activities deserve wider recognition and should be developed into a coherent model: the "phonetics of speech communication".

5

Area Functions and Articulatory Modeling as a Tool for Investigating the Articulatory, Acoustic, and Perceptual Properties of Sounds Across Languages

Jacqueline Vaissière

5.1 INTRODUCTION

The goal of this chapter is to illustrate the usefulness of articulatory modeling (AM) as a tool for exploring the realization of phonological contrasts. The potential of the method as a tool in phonology is illustrated by addressing some key aspects of French sounds. Because it is based on French, this paper gives a *French* point of view on the vocal tract (VT) as a contrast generator. This is by no means a *fresh* point of view, in the sense that it is based on the strict application of the well-established acoustic theory of speech production (Chiba and Kajiyama 1958; Fant 1960; Stevens 1998).

Different languages contrast their phonemes by exploiting different acoustic possibilities of the VT; from infancy the ear is attuned to the native language's system of contrasts, suggesting a language-specific warping of the perceptual space.[1] For example, the analysis of French reveals the role of the third formant (F3) and of the relative amplitude of the formants, which are often considered negligible in speech perception. In two-formant vowel models, the approximation of the upper formants by a single formant (F2′) has shown the importance of F3 in the /y:/ ∼ /i:/ contrast in Swedish (Carlson *et al.* 1975; Fant 2004b). F3 is also crucial, in French, to the contrast between unrounded and rounded front vowels (/i/, y/; /e/, /ø/; /ɛ/, /œ/), and the

Many thanks to Shinji Maeda for his careful reading and for fruitful discussions, to Gunnar Fant and an anonymous reviewer for very helpful suggestions, and to Kiyoshi Honda and Alexis Michaud for their great help in fixing the final form of the chapter.

[1] Perceptual studies show that 6-month-old infants' magnet regions for vowels are related to adult prototypes in the child's native language (Kuhl *et al.* 1992); for consonants, language-specific reorganization appears later, around 10–12 months (Werker and Tees 1984; see also Strange 1995).

perception of French [u] requires a low amplitude of F3 (Bonneau and Laprie 1998). F2's amplitude relative to F1's plays a role in the contrast between nasal and oral vowels (Delattre 1954).

A reductionist view is necessary to bridge the broad gap from VT deformation to acoustic patterns and then to percepts. VT representation by a straight tube or with two to four uniform tubes connected side by side allows us to predict some essentials of the observed acoustic characteristics of vowels and consonants (see Fant 1960 for Russian vowels and consonants). Modeling by more complex systems of tubes interconnecting smooth adapters (as in Fant's 1960 three-parameter model) is still lacking in anatomical adequacy, and AM is preferable to tubes for approximating the acoustic/auditory range of variations that is articulatorily possible for humans. Both methods are strictly complementary to understand the possibilities of the VT to generate acoustic contrasts.

The structure of the chapter is as follows. First, the notion of F-pattern (Fant 1960), on which this description is based, is summarized briefly. I then focus on the articulatory model used here, namely, Maeda's articulatory model (Maeda 1979; see also Mermelstein 1973). As the detailed realization of each phoneme is partly dependent on the language-specific system of contrasts, some points on French phonemics are presented, followed by an illustration of the method on a few selected points.

5.2 BACKGROUND

5.2.1 The F-pattern

The present line of thought is based on the traditional notion of F-pattern (Fant 1960). The filter function of the VT without branching cavities contains only resonances (i.e. no zeroes), labeled F1, F2, F3, F4, and so on. The term *F-pattern* (Fant 1960: 209) refers to these frequencies. The F-pattern can be calculated for any known VT shape. The F-pattern up to the first two, three, four, and sometimes five, formants is clearly visible on a spectrogram during *oral vowels* (with roughly one formant per kHz). The F-pattern for a consonant is determined by the place, degree, and shape of the main oral constriction, and by the tongue and lip configuration required by the following vowel. For consonants, fewer clues to the formants are visible on spectrograms.

The basic gestures to manipulate formant frequencies (for an adult VT) are indicated in Table 5.1 (see also Fant 1973: 28). As a rule of thumb, there is basically one global gesture for manipulating F1 frequency, two local gestures for F2, and three precise gestures for F3. Fine movements are required to manipulate the upper formants; F4 is very sensitive to the laryngeal region. Lip protrusion and rounding lowers all the formants, especially those affiliated to the front cavity (such as F3 in /i/). Larynx lowering has the same global effect as lip rounding and protrusion, but has a

TABLE 5.1. Main gestures to raise or lower each of the first three formants: location of the constriction

Lowest possible formant	Highest possible formant
⇓F1 Anterior part of the VT	⇑F1 Posterior part of the VT
⇓F2 Velar region Lip rounding	⇑F2 Mid-palatal region Glottal region
⇓F3 Pharyngeal region Bunching of the tongue Retroflexion Lip rounding and/or Lip protrusion	⇑F3 Apical and prepalatal regions Glottal region (*larynx lowering*)

stronger lowering effect on the formants affiliated to the back cavity. The global VT shape influences all the formants. Only in very restricted cases (and with much caution) can a specific formant be interpreted as the resonance of a specific vocal-tract cavity (Fant 1960): the articulatory interpretation of F-patterns depends in part on age and sex; for a girl with a small head producing [i], F2 may have the same perceptual role as the F3 of a male (Fant 1975a).

The F-pattern is invisible during the closure of *stops*. The release of the stop comprises several parts: release, friction, aspiration, and transition into the vowel. The formants due to the front cavity become visible during the release-and-friction part of the consonant. All the formants that correspond to the stop manifest themselves in the aspiration noise (except F1, which is damped and very slightly raised in frequency due to glottal opening, Flanagan 1972: 41–9) and in the transitions into neighboring vowels (where F1 becomes visible). The F-pattern as a whole is visible when the stop closure is not complete, as often happens in continuous speech. The tight and short narrowing for the realization of a fricative divides the VT into a front and a back cavity. During *voiceless fricatives*, the front cavity's resonances are mainly excited by noise created around the constriction. Secondary excitations may play a role in enhancing the contrast among fricatives (Stevens 1998): (i) when the palatal constriction is especially long and narrow, a so-called *palatal noise* may be added to the front cavity resonances; (ii) when the constriction is short, the highest resonances affiliated with the back cavity—which nonetheless remain lower than those of the front cavity—are also excited (though they are often weakened by the accompanying anti-formants due to the back cavity); and again (iii) when the area of the constriction within the VT increases gradually. During *voiced fricatives*, there are two sources of sound, and the resonances due to the back cavities are also excited by the glottal voice source; tracheal coupling reflects in a raising and damping of F1 (this is very similar to the acoustic effect of nasal coupling, and may indeed lead to the perception of nasality). The F-pattern evolves *continuously* across vowels and consonants, reflecting the continuous movements of the articulators, although only those formants that are excited are actually seen on spectrograms. The exact shape of the tongue during the consonant constriction and the lip configuration manifest themselves acoustically in the transition into the vowel. The tongue and lip configurations during the consonant are affected, independently of the place of constriction for the consonant, by those required for the following vowel (illustrations will be provided below), so that the F-pattern of the consonant depends both on the consonant and on the vowel. Due to strong coarticulatory phenomena, the lip and tongue shapes associated with the vowel play a key role in shaping the F-pattern of the preceding consonant (among the most striking instances are pharyngealization, as in Arabic, and palatalization, as in Russian).

Acoustic discontinuities arise from an abrupt change in amplitude of one or more formants, or from the appearance (or disappearance) of energy in certain frequency ranges (Fant 1973: 22; this is reflected in Stevens's 2002 notion of *acoustic landmarks*). Such discontinuities are mainly created by the addition of a side-branch (the nasal, sublingual, lateral, or tracheal cavity) and/or changes in the source location (at the glottis and/or at a supraglottal constriction). The F-patterns at CV boundaries for Swedish and English are analyzed by Fant (1975*b*: 121–5).

5.2.2 Maeda's articulatory model

Like most current models, Maeda's articulatory model has been elaborated by means of a Guided Principal Component Analysis (PCA) of midsagittal X-ray tracings (Maeda 1979). The corpus consisted of ten short French sentences. Using a semi-polar grid, the midsagittal X-ray tracings are transformed into vectors of midsagittal distances that describe the inner vocal-tract contours corresponding to the front laryngeal wall, the tongue and lower lip, as well as the outer contours corresponding to the back laryngeal/pharyngeal wall, soft and hard palates, and upper lip. The Guided PCA of these vector data results in a linear component model in which each component can be interpreted in articulatory terms. A model with seven factors explains more than 90 percent of the observed variance. These factors are interpreted to account for the effect of, respectively, jaw position (1), tongue dorsum position (2) and shape (3), tongue apex position (4), lip aperture—*lipht*—(5) and protrusion—*lippr*—(6), and larynx height (7). In synthesis, the values in standard deviation as units of each of these seven factors (or parameters) are specified, determining the tract shape.

Since the entire profile of the VT, from the glottis to lips, is specified by the seven parameters, its spectral characteristics can be calculated (for details see Maeda 1982). A modified version of the alpha–beta model (Heinz and Stevens 1964) converts the model-derived midsagittal distances into the vocal-tract area function. The alpha–beta model describes cross-sectional areas (A in cm^2) along the midline of the VT from the glottis to the lips as a power function of the corresponding sagittal distances (d in cm) as $A = \alpha d^\beta$, where α and β are empirical constants that depend both on the position along the length of the VT and on characteristics of individual subjects. Since A is determined by the power function of d, the area function is uniquely determined

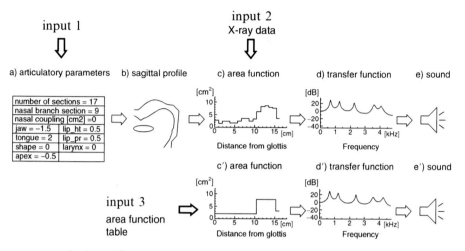

FIGURE 5.1. The three different types of input used in the model (see text).

from the midsagittal profile of the VT, which is specified by the seven articulatory-model parameters.

Figure 5.1 illustrates the three types of input pattern used in the present paper. It corresponds to the vowel [a] and illustrates essential points. To synthesize a vowel, the seven articulatory parameters (a) are given as the input (Input 1) to generate a midsagittal profile (b), from which a cross-sectional area function is derived (c); the transfer function (d) is calculated, and the resulting sound is generated. The area function can also be directly derived from X-ray or Magnetic Resonance Imaging (MRI) data (Input 2); again, it can correspond to simple tubes (Input 3). Each section of the area functions can be manipulated arbitrarily to include details that are observable on X-ray profiles but not reproducible by AM; such manipulation also allows for an estimation of the sensitivity of each formant to a change in area function in a particular region. The sounds created by the different inputs can be then compared with the original sound (if available) and analyzed or used as stimuli for perception tests.

For synthesizing CVC syllables, a series of three or four target-area functions are fed into the program and converted into sounds: one for a fricative, two for a stop (closure and release configurations), and one for each flanking vowel (the description of VCV synthesis with C = fricatives and unvoiced stops is found in Maeda 1996). Noise can be injected at the glottis and at the narrowest section within the VT. A turbulent noise is automatically created 1 cm downstream from the constriction. Its magnitude is controlled in a continuous fashion without using a noise-or-no-noise decision; it is determined by multiplying a weight (or a gain) which varies as a function of the cross-sectional area of the constriction (i.e. the glottal area and the supra-glottal constriction area) and the airflow level (Flanagan 1972: 53–9; for details of the implementation, see Maeda 1996). Numerical analysis related to the constriction area and the magnitude of generated noise is not given by Maeda. In the case of [asa], for example, the oral constriction size is 0.1 cm². A side branch may also be connected to the area function. By default it corresponds to the nasal cavity (with or without sinuses), and it can be manipulated to simulate another side cavity, such as the sublingual cavity (as was done in Espy-Wilson *et al.* 2000 for synthesizing English /ɹ/). In order to synthesize speech sounds, the glottal area and fundamental frequency, too, are specified. Acoustic losses due to yielding walls and radiation effects at the lip opening are added by default.

5.2.3 Some key notions of French phonemics

In Standard French, all vowels are heard as monophthongs. Spectral changes and duration play no role in the identification of oral French vowels (Gottfried 1984; Gottfried and Beddor 1988; Hillenbrand and Nearey 1999). Each oral vowel can be fully specified by a single spectrum, unlike in English.

French /i/, /e/, /ɛ/, /a/, /u/, /o/, /ɔ/, /ɑ/ are often referred to as "good" examples of cardinal primary vowels. Some of Daniel Jones's vowels are represented in Figure 5.2, together with some of the primary and secondary vowels produced by Peter Ladefoged (all these sounds are available at http://phonetics.ucla.edu/course/chapter9/cardinal/cardinal.html).

The IPA symbol set is inadequate for representing cross-language differences in the realization of the same IPA symbol, such as the American and British English /i/ as seen in Figure 5.2; that is, diacritics do not suffice. The new notation set out briefly in the present chapter, originally used in our multilingual spectrogram reading courses, may be useful to supplement the IPA symbols with a short-hand label for the main spectral prominence in vowels and consonants: the brackets indicate a grouping of two

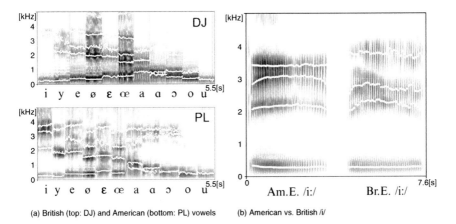

(a) British (top: DJ) and American (bottom: PL) vowels   (b) American vs. British /i/

FIGURE 5.2. Left: spectrograms of Daniel Jones's cardinal vowels (top) and of Peter Ladefoged's cardinal vowels (bottom). Right: prototypical American English /i/, similar to French {palatal (⇑$\underline{F3}$F4)$^{3200\text{Hz}}$} /i/ (left), and British English /i/, with maximal F2 {palatal (⇑$\underline{F2}$)} (right). All sounds are available on the UCLA web site.

consecutive formants, which then form a spectral prominence. Prototypical /i/ in French is represented as a {palatal ($\Uparrow$<u>F3</u>F4)^{3200Hz}} in this notation, where (F3F4) indicates the grouping of F3 and F4. A line drawn underneath a formant (here *F3*) indicates that the formant mainly depends on the front cavity. This information is important since in unvoiced stops and fricatives, only the formants depending on the cavity in front of the constriction are excited during friction and therefore exhibit continuity from consonant to vowel; formants depending on the front cavity are also more sensitive to lip configuration than back cavity formants. "Palatal" means that there is a fronted tongue body position (the other two configurations being *velar*, /u/-like shape, and *pharyngeal*, back, /ɑ/-like shape). $\Uparrow$ corresponds to the highest possible frequency value for the formant, given the tongue position (palatal, velar, or pharyngeal).

It appears that {palatal ($\Uparrow$<u>F3</u>F4)^{3200Hz}} (/i/) is the most acute voiced, noise-free sound among those a VT can generate (for some speakers, F4 and F5 are grouped, rather than F3 and F4, or sometimes more than two formants seem to be grouped around F4; this has to be further investigated). It is almost unanimously accepted (Fant 1960; Stevens 1998) that F2 and F3 can be considered as half-wavelength resonances of the back and the front cavity, respectively, and half-wavelength resonances are the highest first resonances that a uniform tube can produce (a quarter wavelength resonance of the same frequency corresponding to a front tube that is twice as short). A maximally high F3 (noted as ($\Uparrow$F3)) is obtained by a prepalatal position of the constriction along the hard palate (where F4 also tends to be maximal; F3 and F4 are the most correlated formants[2]), whereas a mid-palatal constriction leads to the highest possible F2 (noted as ($\Uparrow$F2)). Mid-sagittal sections suggest that [i] as described by Fant for Swedish (1973: 11 and 2004a: 29) is prepalatal and similar to French [i]. The constriction has actually been observed to be particularly fronted in French, as opposed to English, the acoustic target in the former being most likely *highest F3* and not *highest F2*: see Delattre's comparative X-ray study of French and English in Figure 5.3. Jones's and Ladefoged's /i/s (Fig. 5.2) are equivalent to a prototypical French /i/, where F1 and F2 amplitude is minimal (again enhancing the acuteness of the vowel). As expected, native speakers of Swedish, English, and Spanish choose different /i/ prototypes (Willerman and Kuhl 1996); phonetic transcriptions should reflect the fact that there exist a number of /i/s which are acoustically, articulatorily, and perceptually different. AM simulation allows for an in-depth understanding of these various prototypes. Languages contrasting /i/ and /y/ seem to prefer a prepalatal position for both (Wood 1986), but this is not true of German (Heffner 1950: 99–101) or Swedish (as described by Fant 1973: 94–9); there is a clear lip protrusion for /y/ in French and German, but not in the Scandinavian languages (Malmberg 1974: 139–9). Jones's /y/ does not have the acoustic characteristics of

---

[2] The correlation coefficients are, in decreasing order: 0.656 for F3–F4; 0.525 for F2–F3; − 0.334 for F1–F2; 0.329 for F2–F4; 0.112 for F1–F3 and 0.055 for F1–F4. Calculations are done on 291,011 vowels extracted from the Ester corpus (French broadcast news: http://www.recherche.gouv.fr/technolangue/). Cédric Gendrot, pers. comm.

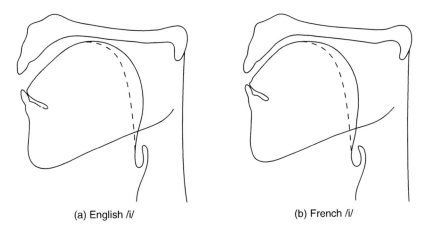

(a) English /i/   (b) French /i/

FIGURE 5.3. English (left) and French (right) configurations for the vowel /i/ (Delattre 1965: 46).

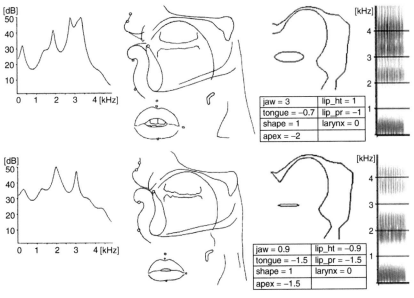

(a) X -ray data for /i/ (top) and /y/ (bottom)   (b) AM simulation for the left data

FIGURE 5.4. Top: vowel /i/ extracted from the word *habit* [abi]. Bottom: vowel /y/ extracted from the word *ambiguë* [ɑ̃bigy]. Left: vowel spectra (note the abnormally high emphasis for masking the noise from the camera). Mid: sagittal profile and associated lip shape (from Bothorel *et al.* 1986: 15–16 and 48). Right: simulation with the AM and associated spectrograms. The values of the seven parameters are indicated.

French /y/, nor does it sound like it, whereas Peter Ladefoged's /y/ qualifies spectrographically and perceptually as a French vowel (Fig. 5.2). Again, this points to an embarrassing shortcoming of the IPA system, if used for phonetic transcription, since such dissimilar sounds are both offered as *reference* for the same unit, /y/.

Prototypical /u/ ({labio-velar ⇓ (F1F2)} in our notation) is the most *grave* vowel: F1 and F2 are grouped and correspond to two Helmholtz resonances. ⇓ ($F^n F^{n+1}$) corresponds to the lowest possible frequency value of the grouped formants. /u/'s F3 and F4 have the lowest possible amplitude, enhancing the gravity of the vowel. English does not have a ⇓ (F1F2) vowel. Jones's and Ladefoged's cardinal /u/ are of the French type. X-ray data for French /u/ offers evidence of two strong constrictions, one at the lips and one at the velar region (witness the X-ray data in Bothorel *et al.* 1986: 46–53). Only the lip configuration seems to have to be tightly controlled (Gay *et al.* 1992); to a large extent, there may be compensation between degree of lip constriction and place of tongue constriction (see examples in Fant and Bävegärd 1997; Boë *et al.* 1992; and also Ouni and Laprie 2001, who use inversion based on Maeda's model). The formants of /u/ depend on the degree of the (labial and velar) constrictions rather than on the place of the constrictions (Lee 1993; on trading relations between tongue-body raising and lip rounding in the production of English /u/, see Perkell *et al.* 1993; see also Savariaux *et al.* 1999 for French).

French seems to favor vowels that have a strong concentration of energy in a specified region in the frequency range. The intra-vowel spectral salience related to the proximity of formants is one of the two perceptual components considered in the Dispersion–Focalization Theory (Schwartz *et al.* 1997b) to predict vowel systems (the other component being global dispersion, which is based on inter-vowel distances; Lindblom 1986). When two formants are close to each other, they are grouped into a single broad peak and their mutual amplitude is strongly enhanced; they are perceptually integrated into a single peak if their separation does not exceed approximately 3.5 Bark (less than 3–4 critical bands; Chistovich and Lublinskaja 1979). The coalescence of F3 and F4 for /i/, of F2 and F3 for /y/, and of F1 and F2 for /u/ and /ɑ/, and all back nasal and oral vowels, creates distinct acoustic patterns, from the high frequencies for /i/ (around 3200 Hz for males, higher for female and children) to the highest possible amplitude in the mid range (around 1000 Hz) for /ɑ/, and finally to the lowest frequency range for /u/. In the case of /i/, palatal friction noise may be created due to the narrow front passage (a *F3*-type noise, of the same type as the alveolo-palatal fricative [ɕ]): French *oui* /wi/ is often pronounced [yiɕ] (see J. Ohala 1997a on the tendency for high vowels to be devoiced because of aerodynamic conditions). The consonant-like constriction in French /i/ and /u/ (as well as /y/) may result in much higher subglottal pressure (P_s) in French as compared to English, as recently discovered by Demolin *et al.* (forthcoming).

Nasal vowels raise additional issues. As is well established for oral vowels, formant amplitude and the overall spectral shape are predictable from the formant frequency and bandwidth values when there is no side-branch cavity, and therefore formant amplitude constitutes redundant information (Fant 1960). In French nasal vowels, the amplitude of the spectral peaks cannot be predicted from formant frequencies; I suspect the relatively higher amplitude of high formants to be the main (and sometimes the only) cue to their identification, at least spectrographically. Further experiments involving French subjects are needed to confirm that French listeners are sensitive to relative formant amplitudes, in contrast to English listeners, who seem to be insensitive (or at least little sensitive) to this parameter (Klatt 1982). Furthermore, the shape of the tongue and lips for back nasal vowels does not correspond to any oral vowel (prototypical /õ/ is more back than /ɔ/ and it is more rounded than the most rounded French oral vowel, /u/; and /ã/ is more back and more protruded than /a/: Bothorel *et al.* 1986, Zerling 1990). Again, I suspect that the speakers adjust lip and tongue configuration to create a *sharp* vowel, even in the case of the two back nasals, /ã/ and /õ/, by grouping the two lowest formants.

In French, there seems to be an especially strong anticipation, during the consonant, of the configuration required for the following vowel (Delattre 1953; Delattre 1965: 101–7 for comparative X-ray data on French and English). To a certain extent, any consonant in French is, as it were, phonetically palatalized, velarized, pharyngealized, or labialized, depending on whether it is followed by a palatal, velar, pharyngeal, or labial vowel (see X-ray illustrations in Bothorel *et al.* 1986). The tongue shape in phonologic-ally palatalized Russian consonants (see X-ray data in Fant 1960: 219) is the main determinant of the value of F2 frequency at vowel onset (around 1900–2000 Hz, Fant 1960: 221) and vowel transitions: the contrast among palatalized consonants (such as [pʲ, tʲ, kʲ] and [fʲ, sʲ, ʃʲ] in Russian) is mainly based on which formants are excited by the friction noise. French has no phonologically palatalized consonants; however, it tends to have a more fronted articulatory setting (the so-called *mode antérieur* as an *habitude articulatoire*, Delattre 1953) than English. French /t/, /d/, /s/, or /z/ (and /n/) are therefore best simulated as half palatalized (leading to a F2 locus around 1800 Hz), regardless of the actual location of the constriction, dental or alveolar, laminal or apical (see Dart 1998 for palatographic comparison of French and English coronals): simula-tion with AM shows that the shape of the tongue is more important for differentiating French and English than the exact place of contact, or the region of the tongue (dental or laminal) involved. Again, this points to another shortcoming of the IPA system concerning the description of the tongue shape for consonants.

5.3 ILLUSTRATIONS OF THE METHOD

The method will be first illustrated by studying the perceptual contribution of anatomical details in the shaping of French /i/.

5.3.1 Testing the perceptual effect of anatomy

In certain cases, AM allows us to test the contribution of anatomical "detail" to the perceptual shaping of the sounds. The laryngeal tube is a cylindrically shaped tube just above the glottis. Its length and shape depend on the speaker (from 2 to 4 cm for an adult, with a diameter of 1 to 2 cm, Stevens 1998:13). The VT may be modeled without a laryngeal tube (as in Stevens 1998: 277; Fant 1960: 66) or with one (Fant

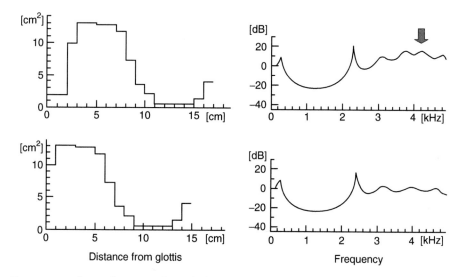

FIGURE 5.5. Left: Area function and transfer function corresponding to /i/, generated by the AM, with a laryngeal tube (top) and after artificial suppression of the effects of the laryngeal tube (bottom).

1960: 108). Direct modification of the area function allows the suppression or change of any part of the VT to test its contribution. The arrow in Figure 5.5 indicates the effect of conserving the laryngeal cavity in the modeling: it raises the spectral amplitude of formants 3 and above by adding an extra formant in that region (Fant 1960: 109); the supplementary formant contributes to a spectral dominance of the high-frequency region, a characteristic sign of French and Swedish /i/ (Fant and Pauli 1974 for Swedish; Schwartz *et al.* 1993 for French). The change is strikingly audible (the sounds are available on our website), pointing to the high sensitivity of the ear to the relative amplitude of the formants in that configuration. In general, the laryngeal tube and the height of the larynx have a considerable effect on the acoustic output (a lower larynx lowers the resonances frequencies, particularly the ones due to the back cavity); these effects are often neglected in the literature (see also Honda *et al.* 2004).

5.3.2 On modeling the lips in the /i/-/y/ contrast in French

In the production of /i/, the lips are spread and F2 (located in the back cavity) is hardly sensitive to perturbations in the area anterior to the prepalatal constriction; sensitivity functions calculated uniformly along the VT would lead to the erroneous generalization that F3 is also insensitive to small perturbations in the lip tube (see e.g. Wood 1986) and that, in the /i/ configuration, both F2 and F3 are insensitive to lip movements. F2 actually becomes very sensitive to these movements when the lips are protruded, because in that case, the front cavity is longer than the back cavity. Fant's nomograms (Fant 1960: 63, 77) indicate that with a constriction at 6 cm (palatal constriction), F3 decreases from 3200 Hz to 2000 Hz if the constriction within the additional 1-cm lip

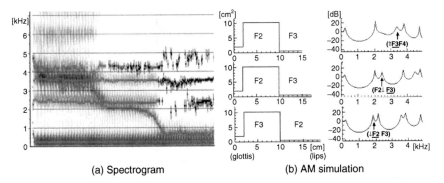

(a) Spectrogram   (b) AM simulation

FIGURE 5.6. Left: spectrograms of the prototypical vowels $(\Uparrow\underline{F3}F4)^{3200Hz}$ /i/, $(\Downarrow\underline{F2}F3)^{1900Hz}$ /y/ and velar /u/$\Downarrow$(F1F2) (uttered by a female speaker). Right: area functions and transfer functions for increasing length of the front cavity for $(\Uparrow\underline{F3}F4)$ /i/ (top), $(F2\uparrow\underline{F3})^{2100Hz}$ /y/ (mid), and $(\Downarrow\underline{F2}F3)^{1900Hz}$ /y/ (bottom) (the three area functions remain the same, except for the lengthening of the front tube). The arrow indicates a resonance associated with the front cavity. The underlined formant, due to the front cavity, is most sensitive to lip configuration.

section decreases from 4 cm² to 0.16 cm² (simulating lip rounding). Indeed, the high sensitivity of F3 to lip configuration is exploited by languages such as French, Swedish or German, which contrast rounded and unrounded palatal vowels. Figure 5.6 illustrates the transition, for one French speaker, from /i/ to /y/ (F3 lowering is mainly due to lip rounding) and from /y/ to /u/ (F2 lowering is due to tongue backing).

The vowel /i/ is currently modeled either with a "lip tube" (Stevens 1998: 277) or without one (Fant 1960: 66). When there is no distinct lip tube, lip rounding or lip protrusion—which have a roughly similar effect—can be simulated by a lengthening of the (narrow) front cavity of /i/.

As the effective length of the front cavity increases in the passage from French /i/ to /y/, F3, a front-cavity resonance, lowers and a change of cavity affiliation takes place, as illustrated in Figure 5.6 (left). The lips are not as protruded for /y/ as for /u/, most likely to keep F2 and F3 close together, and to avoid an extreme lowering of F2. From the frequencies published in Fant (1973: 93–9), it may be proposed that Swedish /y/ is a {palatal rounded $(F2\downarrow\underline{F3})^{2100Hz}$} vowel, F3 remaining a resonance of the front cavity, not exhibiting the typical change of cavity affiliation of the third formant observed in French. Swedish /y/ and Jones's cardinal /y/ (mentioned above, Section 2.3) do not sound like French /y/, whereas Ladefoged's does (see Fig. 5.2).

A close observation of the nomograms (Wood 1986; Stevens 1998, Fig. 6.11) and simulation by AM indicate that there could be several /i/ vowels, as the effective length of the front cavity changes (see Table 5.2). The /i/-/y/ contrast illustrates the leading role of the lips and of F3 in the shaping of close palatal vowels in French: /i/ (F3 and F4 bunched together), /y/ (F2 and F3 bunched together), and /e/ (F3 equidistant between F2 and F4). The three sounds are clearly apart in their F3 values.[3]

---

[3] F1 for /e/ is generally higher than for /i/ so that F1 value helps to distinguish between /i/ and /e/. F2 for /e/ may be as high as for /i/, as observed in Swedish by Fant (1973), and such an observation can also be made for French.

TABLE 5.2. Notation of some typical vowels. (F_nF_{n+1}) indicates a spectral prominence

Palatal	$(\Uparrow\underline{F3}F4)$	$[\text{i}]^{F3=3200\text{Hz}}$	French-type /i/	/i/
	$(\Uparrow\underline{F2})$	$[\text{i}]^{F2=2500\text{Hz}}$	British-type /i/	
	$(F2\downarrow\underline{F3})$	$[\text{y}]^{F2=2100\text{Hz}}$	Swedish-type /y/	/y/
	$(\downarrow\underline{F2}F3)$	$[\text{y}]^{F2=1900\text{Hz}}$		
Pharyngeal	$\Uparrow(\underline{F1}F2)$ or $\Uparrow(F1\underline{F2})$	$[\text{ɑ}]^{F2=1000\text{Hz}}$	French-type	/ɑ/
Labio-velar	$\downarrow(F1F2)$	$[\text{ɔ}]^{F2=900\text{Hz}}$		/ɔ/
	$\downarrow(F1F2)$	$[\text{o}]^{F2=800\text{Hz}}$		/o/
	$\Downarrow(\underline{F1}F2)$ or $\Downarrow(F1\underline{F2})$	$[\text{u}]^{F2=700\text{Hz}}$		/u/

5.3.3 AM as a tool to study compensatory phenomena

An identical F-pattern can be the outcome of more than one articulatory state allowing for compensatory effects and reinforcing gestures across articulators (Gay et al. 1981). Maeda's model has served in a number of laboratories to generate "codebooks" which represent the mapping between articulatory and acoustic formants. Figure 5.7 illustrates four configurations generating a sharp concentration of energy in a specified region in the frequency range.

Jaw lowering and tongue dorsum position compensate for each other in palatal unrounded vowels, as do lip aperture and jaw position in the back rounded series (Maeda 1990). Jaw lowering is sufficient (but not necessary) to create the front unrounded series /i/, /e/, /ɛ/. Furthermore, the tongue constriction has to move back in synchrony with the delabialization gesture for the velar and pharyngeal series, /u/, /o/, /ɔ/, /ɑ/, to keep the first two formants close together (/u/, /o/, /ɔ/, /ɑ/ are (F1F2) vowels). In conclusion, AM and derived codebooks allow us to predict all possible VT configurations producing approximately the same acoustic output and therefore complement X-ray films (one might note in passing that X-ray data are scarce, due to their invasive nature, whereas AM-based experiments can be multiplied and are easy to replicate).

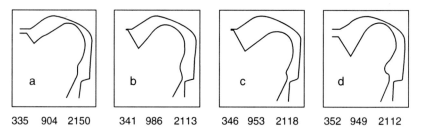

| 335 904 2150 | 341 986 2113 | 346 953 2118 | 352 949 2112 |

FIGURE 5.7. VT configurations giving rise to similar F1, F2, and F3 values, as indicated, using a codebook based on Maeda's model (*Source*: Ouni and Laprie 2001).

5.3.4 The importance of the relative amplitude of the formants

The contextual realizations of two phonemes may seem to have similar poles whilst the relative amplitude of the formants keep them apart. As noted by Fant, "contoids must be described in terms of their envelope contours" (Fant 1960); the numbering of the formants is not important so long as there is an appropriate distribution of energy along the frequency scale. The branching of a side cavity, tracheal or nasal, introduces changes in the relative amplitude of the formants (Stevens 1998). Two examples follow.

(i) As a consequence of the strong anticipatory phenomena in French, /l/ and /ʁ/ in the /i/ context are "palatalized" and show a concentration of energy in the (F3F4) region, similar to that for /i/ and /j/, which are also (F3F4) sounds (the spectral prominence (F3F4) being even higher and more pronounced for /j/, F1 lower, and F2 of weaker amplitude than for /i/). The relative amplitude of the poles contributes to contrasting the four phonemes. F1 amplitude is the strongest for /l/, and very weak for the three others. F2 amplitude for /ʁ/ dominates the whole spectrum (F1 is highly damped), whereas F2 amplitude of /j/ is the weakest (the region (F3F4) dominates). In the same vein, /ʁ/ is pharyngealized in the /a/ context, and /ʁ/ and /a/ have a very similar $\Uparrow(F1F2)^{1000Hz}$ F-pattern: the amplitude of F1 relative to F2 is very weak for /ʁ/ ($\Uparrow(F1F2)^{1000Hz}$), but F1 and F2 have a high amplitude for /a/ ($\Uparrow(F1F2)^{1000Hz}$). Yeou's (1996) simulation of the uvular sounds with Maeda's model (see also Alwan 1989), followed by an EGG study, shows that /ʁ/ is most likely to be uttered with an open glottis (or, when voiced, with a long open-glottis phase), explaining the damping of the amplitude of the first pole relative to F2 (weak for /ʁ/ under 1 kHz, Chafcouloff 1983; see also Calliope 1989), ensuring the realization of the phonemic contrast in all cases.

(ii) When the nasal tract is coupled to the oral cavity, the formant density per kHz (usually one formant per kHz) increases and nasal poles and zeros introduce changes in the relative amplitude of the formants and in formant bandwidth.

As shown in Figure 5.8, with a progressive increase in nasal coupling of the vowel /i/ in AM, the acoustic output successively takes a somewhat [y]-like shape when NC (degree of nasal coupling) = 3cm^2 and a [u] shape when NC = 5cm^2 (for an interpretation of the resonances in terms of oral or nasal cavities, see Maeda 1993; for cross-languages studies, see Beddor and Strange 1982). The difference in acoustic effect depending on the degree of velar lowering (which is difficult to control) probably favors the reduction of the number of nasal vowels in systems where the number of oral vowels is high. In contrast, perceptual data for nasalized high vowels indicate that they tend to be heard as being more open than their oral counterparts (see e.g. Beddor *et al.* 1986) due to the raised spectral prominence of F1 as a result of the perceptual integration of the nasal formant. This sheds light on diachronic change in the French vowel system: nasalized /i/ > nasal /ɛ̃/; nasalized /y/ > nasal /œ̃/ (which has merged with nasal /ɛ̃/ in the present state of the language).

In sum, AM allows us to investigate how far the relative amplitude of the formants can be manipulated while maintaining perceptual integrity. Preliminary results

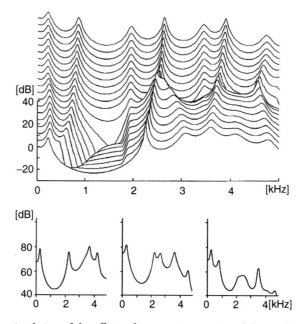

FIGURE 5.8. Top: simulation of the effects of progressive opening of the nasal branch in Maeda's mode on the vowel [i], in 14 steps. Bottom: selected spectra corresponding to different degrees of NC (nasal coupling) indicated in cm² (Maeda 1993).

suggest that the relative amplitude of the formants plays an important role and perceptual experiments are needed to test to what extent the listener's native language influences his/her sensitivity to the relative amplitude and bandwidth of the formants.

5.3.5 Investigating the effects of states of the glottis and of supraglottic constriction

Modeling shows that a very slight change in constriction size and/or in the relative size of the glottis may lead to dramatic changes in source characteristics and hence in the acoustic characteristics of consonants, while preserving their F-pattern. For example, prototypical French /ʁ/ is a {pharyngeal ⇑(F1 **F2**)F3 F4}; the notation can be read as follows: the first two formants (F1F2) are grouped, and the grouped formants are as high as possible (⇑); the underlining of F2 and F4 indicates that these formants are resonances of the cavity in front of the constriction; the bold type of **F2** indicates that the spectrum is dominated by **F2**, its amplitude being enhanced by its grouping with F1; and the dots below F mean that F1 is damped, most likely due to tracheal coupling in the present case. The sound is close to Arabic uvular fricatives, which have been successfully synthesized using the same model (Yeou 1996, see Fig. 5.9). In French, in the case of /ʁ/, voicing is not contrastive, whereas it is contrastive in Arabic. Depending on speaker, phonetic context and prosodic position, French /ʁ/ can be realized as a voiced approximant (the constriction at the glottis is

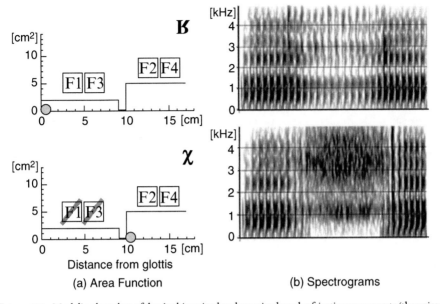

(a) Area Function (b) Spectrograms

Figure 5.9. Modeling by tubes of the Arabic voiced and unvoiced uvular fricative consonants (the voiced fricative looks like a sonorant, Yeou and Maeda 1995). The F-pattern is the same for both consonants, but the formants are excited differently. Top: the glottal area is set to zero in the model, and the oral constriction to 0.2 cm^2 in the present simulation: all formants are excited, F1 and F2 are grouped together, the consonant looks like a (voiced) sonorant; bottom: the glottal area is set to 0.25 cm^2 to simulate glottal opening in the model, and the oral constriction to 0.2 cm^2.

relatively small compared to the upper constriction) or as a voiceless fricative, or sometimes as a mixture of the two. Both variants can be represented by the same F-pattern {pharyngeal ⇑(F1 **F2**) F3 **F4**}, with only the underlined formants (due to the front cavity) being excited in the absence of voicing.

As is well known (see Durand's 1930 palatographic data), the supraglottal constriction for a consonant is less tight in the middle of a word than at the beginning of a word, and the glottal abduction for the unvoiced consonants tends to diminish intervocalically (for Japanese, Sawashima *et al.* 1975), both phenomena leading to lenition (Passy 1890; Martinet 1955). The change from a voiceless fricative to a voiced fricative (through a diminished glottal abduction), to an approximant, to a homorganic vowel (through less and less supraglottal constriction) can be simulated simply by a progressive decrease in glottal abduction and an increase in the area of the tongue constriction. The acoustic and perceptual effects of an increase in the area of the supraglottal constriction and a decrease in glottal opening to simulate lenition can be tested. In the near future, AM should be able to help model the gradual transition from read speech to spontaneous speech and from hyper to hypo-articulated speech, as well as the variety of speaker-dependent strategies (e.g. the speaker-dependent but consistent time-course of the velum, documented by Vaissière 1988).

5.4 OTHER USES OF THE MODEL

AM is extensively used in our lab as a tool for teaching detailed aspects of the acoustic theory of speech production (Vaissière 1995) and as a tool for modeling in phonetic research (for interpreting MRI data concerning the singer's formant, see Pillot 2004; for clinical phonetics, see Crevier *et al.* 2001).

The same AM model has been used in a number of other laboratories in France and abroad for a number of applications. For example, to demonstrate that Neanderthals were not morphologically handicapped for speech (Boë *et al.* 2001); to investigate which sounds and sound contrasts could be produced by humans from birth to adulthood (Ménard *et al.* 2002); and to create codebooks for inversion programs (as in Ouni and Laprie 2001). The model has shown its potential to be adapted to new speakers (Mathieu and Laprie 1997). Using his own model, Maeda showed that the different realizations of /k/ followed by different vowels (from velar to palatal) are not due to the search for ease of articulation, but to perceptual requirements (Maeda 1996). Concatenative (cut-and-paste) synthesis is currently the most widely used approach but, in the long run, biologically motivated articulatory synthesis has more potential (Shadle and Damper 2002).

5.5 CONCLUSION

In this chapter, some principles of speech production and perception that can be explored with articulatory modeling (Maeda's model was presented in Section 5.2.2) have been applied to characterize French sounds. First, the evidence (illustrated in Section 5.2.3 for the nasal and the back vowels, and in Section 5.3.2 on the /i/ ~ /y/ contrast) suggested that the principle which drives auditory spectra towards patterns with close neighboring formants seems to be particularly active in French. In about half of the French prototypical vowels, two formants form a spectral prominence (see Section 5.2.3). It does not come as a surprise that the Dispersion–Focalization theory for explaining vocalic systems in general had been developed by researchers whose native language was French (Schwartz and Escudier 1989). Focalization could benefit speech perception: evidence for increased stability of focal vowels in short-term memory was provided in a discrimination experiment with adult French subjects (Schwartz *et al.* 1989). It may also be one of the reasons why French vowels are often proposed as references for the primary and secondary cardinal vowels (the other reason being that they show no tendency toward diphthongization).

Second, French listeners may have developed a special sensitivity to cues which are not operative at the phonological level in all languages: *labial articulation* (which essentially allows for the manipulation of F3 for the front vowels and F2 for the back vowels) is indispensable in shaping French sounds, to contrast unrounded and rounded front vowels, and to keep F1 and F2 close together in back vowels (see Section 5.3.2); velum lowering (which modifies the relative amplitude of the formants) is used to contrast oral and nasal vowels (see Section 5.3.4).

Third, it is suggested that a new notation may be used to reflect the articulatory, acoustic and perceptual *similarity* between phonemes sharing similar tongue shape and lip configuration but different degrees of glottal and supraglottal constriction (as exemplified on consonants in Section 5.3.5), on the one hand, and the *dissimilarity* among the realizations of the same phonetic symbol, on the other hand (Section 5.3.2 and Table 5.2). This applies to vowels and consonants alike, allowing for a representation of the progressive lenition phenomena observed in spontaneous speech, and for their simulation using an AM model (Section 5.3.5).

Nonetheless, AM has limitations. First, the articulatory parameters, which are based on French data, are not able to reproduce all the observed sagittal profiles for other languages (and sometimes even for French); some tongue deformations have to be introduced by hand, directly on the area function. Second, the approximate relationship assumed between midsagittal distances and the corresponding cross-sectional areas makes a motivated simulation of lateral consonants impossible (3D-MRI data may improve the passage from sagittal profiles to area functions). Third, in the case of important constrictions offering high resistance to outgoing flow, more knowledge on the laws of aerodynamics is needed in the model (J. Ohala 1983b; Badin 1991; Shadle 1997). Fourth, the present model cannot simulate the effect of the state of the vocal folds (which affects the spectral tilt); this is a limitation because, as mentioned by J. Ohala (1996), the phonological end actually seems to exploit any means, and the participation of the entire vocal apparatus, from the lung to lips and to nostrils, may contribute to the realization of a phonemic contrast, especially in the case of hyper-articulated speech. It is a safe guess that some parts of the model will be modified and improved as new physiological data provide new insights into the workings of the speech-production apparatus.

To sum up, AM is a valuable tool for investigating the choice of articulatory manoeuvres made by a specific language to enhance a distinctive feature and to test the role of the perceptual contribution of anatomical details (see Section 5.3.1). These features make it an extraordinary tool to make further progress in the field of phonetics and phonology. AM makes the best use of available X-ray data and it may be used as a complement to EMA data (Electro-Magnetic Articulometer), a non-invasive method. However, no matter how sophisticated models are, they are not the real thing; data remain the basis of sciences. No model should blind us to the complexity of the data which calls for extensive physiological coverage to gain in-depth insight into sound systems. On a personal note, I believe that this is in fact J. Ohala's central message (in the spirit of l'Abbé Rousselot): "Keep experimenting".

PART II
Phonological Universals

6

Phonological Universals and the Control and Regulation of Speech Production

Didier Demolin

6.1 INTRODUCTION

This chapter examines the role of some speech production mechanisms to explain the basis of phonetic and phonological universals. Although there are obviously many automatic processes due to the bio-physical constraints of the vocal tract that explain how speech production is regulated, it is probable that there are more controlled phenomena than is generally assumed. This assumption can and must be demonstrated through various methods of experimentation. One example of how these claims about speech production and phonological universals can be tested is examining the relation between fundamental frequency (f0) and subglottal pressure (Ps). This issue has been addressed in numerous publications, but there is still some debate concerning the contribution of Ps to phonological phenomena, such as whether f0 declination—that is, the global downtrend of f0—is caused by laryngeal or by respiratory activity (J. Ohala 1990b). This is a fundamental issue that has important consequences for the understanding of universals related to intonation and various aspects of prosody as well as to segments.

In the following sections I present new results on the relationship between Ps and f0 in vowels (Section 6.4.3.1), consonants (Section 6.4.3.2), sentences (Section 6.4.3.3) and the effects of changes in Ps and intensity on f0.

I would like to thank Sergio Hassid for his assistance and his invaluable help in collecting the aerodynamic data. Véronique Lecuit, Moges Yigezu, and Alain Soquet contributed to various aspects in the acquisition of the data. Finally, I want to thank Albert Di Cristo, who suggested the set of sentences to be used in the experiments, and Luciana Storto, John Ohala, and Maria-Josep Solé for many helpful suggestions on the manuscript.

The research reported in this chapter has been supported by an ARC convention 98-02 no. 226 of the Belgian ministry of scientific research and by a FNRS grant no.1.5.223.06.

6.2 PHONOLOGICAL UNIVERSALS

Phonological universals are understood here as resulting from production and perceptual constraints shaping spoken language. Besides being universal, these forces influence language in a probabilistic way (J. Ohala 1999). Broadly speaking, production constraints stem from neurological, anatomical, physiological, and aerodynamic conditions, as well from the mapping between vocal tract shape and the resulting acoustic signal, while perceptual constraints derive from the peripheral and central auditory transforms of speech, lateral inhibition, masking, critical bands, short-term memory, and the way in which sounds are stored and retrieved (J. Ohala 1999).

Before we proceed, it is necessary briefly to discuss the concepts of regulation and control used in this chapter. Regulations are defined as the constraints that adjust the rate of production of the elements in a system to the state of the system and its relevant environmental variables. In speech this accounts, for example, for the way respiration is regulated during the production of sentences to sustain a more or less constant pressure. The main operators of these adjustments are feedback loops. In speech production, feedback occurs when the periphery triggers compensatory activity such as when the larynx is lowered to maintain voicing during the production of voiced stops (J. Ohala 1981a). Two types of process can be distinguished in regulatory networks: homeostatic and epigenetic. Homeostatic regulations account for the largest part of the functioning of phonological systems, that is, for their stability, whereas differentiative or epigenetic regulations account for changes in the state of phonological systems, such as sound change (Demolin and Soquet 1999). Therefore, phonological systems and their transformations can be understood by such regulations.

The term "control" used in this chapter is rather different from what is generally understood as motor control (e.g. Perkell *et al.* 1997; Perrier 2005). The chapter follow Kingston and Diehl's (1994) view of articulatory control and phonetic knowledge (see also Solé, in this volume). They suggest that many phenomena are auditorily driven and that speakers control far more articulations than usually assumed. Thus in order to attain a distinctive acoustic result, some specific motor commands or gestures may be targeted or controlled by the speaker.

6.3 EXPERIMENTAL METHODOLOGY
IN PHONOLOGY

The necessity of using experimental methods in phonology has been advocated by J. Ohala (e.g. J. Ohala 1974, 1987, 1995; J. Ohala and Jaeger 1986), who has shown that the multidisciplinary nature of speech requires using and combining various experimental paradigms to explain phonological phenomena. These explanations must be based on a set of limited primitives coming from aerodynamics, production, and perceptual constraints, from principles explaining how the auditory system works, and from an understanding of the statistical variation that is intrinsic to the nature of language (J. Ohala 1990a; Pierrehumbert 1994; Demolin 2002).

A good example of the value of experiments for phonology is shown in M. Ohala and J. Ohala (1972), who demonstrated that the distinctive character of aspirated consonants (including /h/), as observed in the time-course of subglottal pressure, is not the heightened subglottal pressure feature (HSAP) as proposed by Chomsky and Halle (1968). M. Ohala and J. Ohala note that the reduced glottal resistance during a period when there is no oral constriction causes a decrease rather than an increase in subglottal pressure. This was also demonstrated by M. Ohala (1979), who showed that a consistent feature of aspirates in Hindi is reduced Ps immediately after their release. This fact can once be observed more clearly in the Amharic sentence given in Figure 6.1, [kulumc'-wafiino], which shows that Ps diminishes during the production of [ɦ] (Demolin 2004). The Amharic data reinforce M. Ohala and J. Ohala's (1972) claim because a drop of Ps is present not only for voiceless /h/, but also for the voiced glottal fricative [ɦ]. Indeed, such a drop in Ps suggests that there must be either a glottal opening at the posterior end or a wide glottis. The latter, however, would not result in the clear voicing that can be observed in Figure 6.1. The hypothesis of a posterior opening is hence the most likely since it allows simultaneous voicing. Therefore any opening at the level of the glottis, including when there is some voicing as for voiced /ɦ/, lowers Ps. The experimental method shows that the feature HSAP, proposed by Chomsky and Halle, has no empirical support. However, Ladefoged and Maddieson (1996: 67) nuance this claim. Indeed,

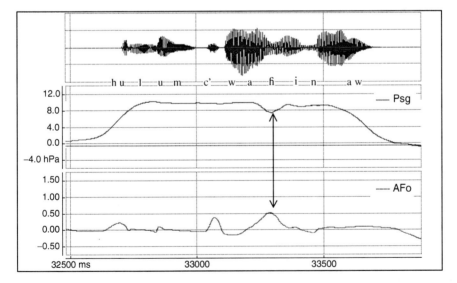

FIGURE 6.1. Audio waveform, subglottal pressure (Ps) [given as Psg in the graph] and oral Airflow (AFo) for the Amharic sentence [kulumc'wafiino] "Everybody is noisy." The arrows indicate the drop in Ps for the voiced [ɦ] and the corresponding increase in oral airflow. Ps is given in hPa (1 cmH$_2$O = 1.2 hPa) and oral airflow in dm^3/s.

the study made by Ladefoged *et al.* (1976) shows that, at least for some Owerri Igbo speakers, Ps is significantly higher during aspirated sounds, lending some support to the suggestion that aspirated sounds are consistently produced with HSAP in some languages. However, as mentioned by Ladefoged and Maddieson (1996: 68), this is a secondary mechanism that can be conjured to enhance the high level of transglottal airflow which a wide open glottal aperture already ensures (Stevens and Keyser 1989). Later, Halle and Stevens (1971) proposed, again without empirical evidence, that the feature HSAP should be replaced by the feature composition [+ spread vocal cords, − constricted vocal cords] in order to characterize aspirates. For example, voiced and voiceless aspirates (e.g. [pʰ] and [bʰ] in Hindi) would be differentiated by the additional feature [stiff vocal cords] versus [slack vocal cords]. As mentioned by M. Ohala and J. Ohala (1972: 45), even if this feature correctly describes the difference between voiced [bʰ] and voiceless [pʰ] aspirates, there is no evidence to support the claim that voiceless aspirates must have stiff vocal folds, nor that voiced aspirates should have spread vocal folds. Later M. Ohala (1979) suggested that only a single binary feature (distinctive release) is needed to differentiate the voiced aspirates from the other stops (see M. Ohala 1979 for more details). These last claims were established by experimental observations, as it should be the case for every primitive of phonology.

6.4 CONTROL AND REGULATION OF PS AND FO IN PHONOLOGICAL PHENOMENA

6.4.1 Overview

The control and regulation of some of the main parameters involved in speech production, such as Ps, f0, and intensity, have been addressed in the literature, but the relation between these parameters and phonological phenomena such as stress, intonation, and tone deserves further investigation.

Several electromyographic studies, such as Hirano and Ohala (1969), Netsell (1969, 1973), J. Ohala (1970), Lieberman *et al.* (1970), Atkinson (1973), Collier (1975), Maeda (1975), Erickson *et al.* (1983), demonstrated that f0 is largely controlled by adjustments of the intrinsic and extrinsic laryngeal musculature rather than by Ps. However, a number of studies claim either that Ps has an important effect on f0 for stress and utterance final fall (Lieberman 1967; Lieberman and Blumstein 1988) or that there is covariation between Ps and f0 during declination (Collier 1974, 1975). Titze (1994: 196) claimed that Ps and f0 are positively correlated when intrinsic laryngeal muscle contraction remains constant. More recently, Herman *et al.* (1996) showed that, in English, utterances with declarative intonation (or with any other contour sharing the phonological specification of a low tone at the end of the tail) consistently display a decline in Ps, whereas utterances with yes–no question intonation (or any other contour sharing the phonological specification of a final high tone) display lesser declines or even increases.

The relation between Ps and intensity has been addressed in several studies (Ladefoged and McKinney 1963; Isshiki 1964; Holmberg *et al.* 1988; Strik and Boves 1992; Lecuit and Demolin 1998; Baken and Orlikoff 2000; Plant and Younger 2000) which show that Ps and intensity are positively correlated. More specifically, Ladefoged (1958), Draper *et al.* (1959), and Benguerel (1970) showed that Ps is raised when a word is focused or emphasized. This suggests that respiratory muscles are involved for higher degrees of prominence.

Since these issues and their relation with linguistic phenomena are still unresolved, it is crucial that we increase our understanding of how these basic speech parameters are controlled and how they are related to phonological phenomena. In this paper I report on recent work done with several French subjects, in which every relevant aerodynamic parameter was measured (Ps by direct tracheal puncture, intraoral pressure, as well as oral and nasal airflow) in synchronization with acoustic data. The purpose of the study was to obtain additional information on how Ps is regulated and controlled by speakers. The study was designed to revisit some issues concerning: the relation between Ps, f0, and intensity; changes in Ps related to the production of segments, particularly trills; and the effect of changes in Ps and intensity on f0.

6.4.2 Experimental procedure

We obtained simultaneous recordings of intraoral (Po) and subglottal (Ps) pressure,[1] as well as oral airflow and the acoustic signal. Recordings were made at the O.R.L. unit of the Hospital Erasme of the Université Libre de Bruxelles. These were made following to the rules of the ethical committee of the Hospital Erasme concerning the participation of human subjects. Intraoral pressure was measured by a small plastic tube (Internal diameter (ID) 2mm) that was inserted through the nasal cavity into the oropharynx. Ps was measured with a needle (ID 2mm) inserted in the trachea. The needle was placed after local anaesthesia with 2 percent Xylocaine was administered. The tip of the needle was inserted just under the cricoid cartilage. A plastic tube (ID 2mm) linked to a pressure transducer was connected to the needle. The tubes were connected to a Physiologia workstation consisting of a computer and an acquisition system equipped with various transducers and the signal editing and processing software Phonedit (Teston and Galindo 1990, 1995). Oral airflow was collected with a rubber mask placed over the subjects' mouth connected to the acquisition device of the computer.

The acoustic signal was recorded with a directional microphone connected to the Physiologia workstation, which was at a constant distance of 4cm from the rubber mask. The signal was sampled at 16,000 kHz and processed with the software Signal Explorer. Intensity was computed by applying the mean root square method to the

---

[1] The values of subglottal (Ps) and intraoral (Po) pressure are given in hPa, 1 $cmH_2O = 1.2$ *hPa*. Oral airflow values are given in dm^3/s.

speech signal. Pitch was computed by the COMB method. In order to obtain a smooth line, the signal was low-pass filtered at 70 Hz.

For the studies described in Sections 6.4.3.1, 6.4.3.2, and 6.4.3.4, two subjects, DD (male) and VL (female), both native speakers of French with a normal larynx and no voice problems, took part in the experiments. For the experiment described in Section 6.4.3.3, the subjects were two male subjects, PW and MC, both native speakers of French with a normal larynx and no voice problems.

6.4.3 Experiments on Ps, intensity, and the control of f0

6.4.3.1 Sustained vowels

Two subjects were asked to pronounce sustained vowels [a, e, i, o, u] while hearing a tone through earphones connected to a synthesizer. Each vowel had to be pronounced at three tones (A–C–E for the male subject and C–F–A for the female subject), at three intensity levels (low–mid–high) each time.

Results show that speakers were able to control f0 independently of Ps and intensity during the production of sustained vowels (see also Lecuit and Demolin 1998). This is illustrated in Figure 6.2 where f0, Ps, and the audio waveform are displayed for the vowel [a] produced by speakers DD and VL. We can observe that f0 is kept constant while Ps drops, which suggests that f0 is independently controlled. This is true for all the vowels investigated for both speakers, [a, e, i o, u].

The results also show that for a certain pitch level, the relationship between Ps and intensity varies across vowels, suggesting that there might be a relative intrinsic intensity corresponding to each vowel and that there is a clear correlation between Ps and intensity. This is shown in Table 6.1, which shows that the correlation coefficient of the linear curve fits between the intensity and the Log of Ps given for each vowel, at each pitch level for each subject. In this table, the row labelled "All" corresponds to the grouping of all the data points for the three levels of intensity and the three pitch levels for each vowel. The value of these coefficients is high enough to prove the linear relationship between intensity and the logarithm of Ps.

6.4.3.2 Consonants: Ps and trills

The next experiment was devised in order to understand the possible relation between segment types, such as trills, and Ps. Specifically, I provide evidence that the variations in Ps during trill production are due to aerodynamic conditions for trills, which are universal, and not to the control of Ps on specific segments.

Two subjects were asked to read words containing the uvular trill [ʀ] followed by the vowels [a, i, u] in a short carrier phrase: for example, *Rara, dis rara encore* [ʀaʀadiʀaʀaɑ̃kɔχ] "Rara, say rara again." Each sentence was repeated five times at a rate and loudness selected by the speaker. The male subject, too, was asked to pronounce the sentences containing the uvular trill [ʀ]; the resulst are presented in Table 6.2. The male subject worked under the same conditions. The results show

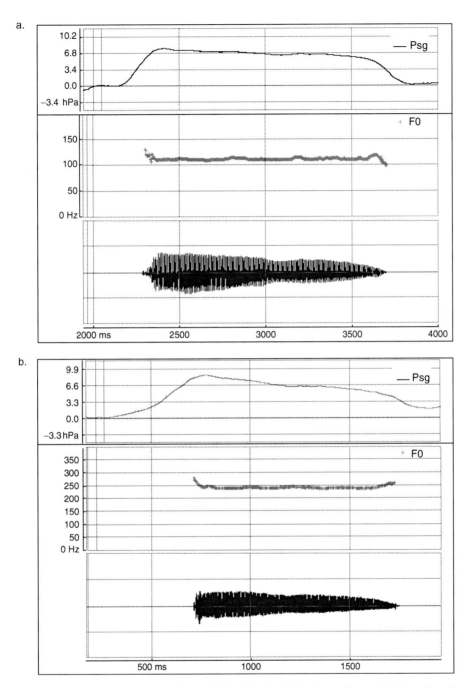

FIGURE 6.2.a. Ps [given as Psg in the graph] in hPa, f0 in Hz (mean f0 = 111 Hz) and audio waveform during the production of the vowel [a] by speaker DD. Note the gradual fall in Ps while f0 remains constant. b. Ps, f0 (mean f0 = 249 Hz) and the audio waveform during the production of the vowel [a] by speaker VL. Note the gradual fall in Ps while f0 remains constant.

TABLE 6.1. Correlation coefficient of the linear curve fit between the intensity and the Log of Ps for each vowel and pitch level (high, mid and low tones correspond to tones A–C–E for the male subject and C–F–A for the female subject)

Speaker VL (female)	[a]	[e]	[i]	[o]	[u]
High pitch level	0.97	0.96	0.90	0.97	0.92
Mid pitch level	0.97	0.78	0.97	0.96	0.87
Low pitch level	0.97	0.97	0.70	0.91	0.94
ALL	0.93	0.92	0.93	0.94	0.94
Speaker DD (male)	[a]	[e]	[i]	[o]	[u]
High pitch level	0.88	0.91	0.95	0.89	0.94
Mid pitch level	0.90	0.94	0.80	0.95	0.98
Low pitch level	0.90	0.83	0.90	0.92	0.91
ALL	0.84	0.85	0.74	0.90	0.87

a clear difference in the pronunciation of the uvular trills between the two subjects. The male subject DD used the voiced uvular trill [ʀ] frequently and the voiced uvular fricative [ʁ] as the main variant. The female subject VL tended to use the voiceless fricative [χ] as the main variant with some voiced fricative [ʁ] realizations. A devoiced trill [ʀ̥] and its voiced counterpart were observed in a few cases for this speaker. The results in Table 6.3 show that Ps tends to be higher for trills than for fricative variants.

Measurements made during the utterances display a consistent elevation of Ps during the production of trills. This can be seen in Figure 6.3 that shows Ps, Po, oral airflow, and the audio waveform of the French sentence *Mon ami Mario Rossi m'a traité de bredin* [mõnamimaʁjoʀosimatχɛtedœbʀœdɛ̃] "My friend Mario Rossi said that I was a fool." The higher Ps around the voiced trills is clearly distinct from the lower Ps around the two fricatives and the rest of the sentence.

6.4.3.3 Sentences

The complexity of the relation between f0 and Ps can also be observed in the intonation contours of various types of sentences. Two male subjects were asked to pronounce a set of sentences with no instructions regarding the speed and the

TABLE 6.2. Test sentences used to study uvular trills

Henri Troyat roule ses [R] comme un Russe.	"Henry Troyat rolls his [R]s like a Russian".
Mon ami Mario Rossi m'a traité de bredin.	"My friend Mario Rossi said that I was a fool".
Remi m'a mis devant la pie qui picore.	"Remy put me in front of the pecking magpie".
Le bébé a réclamé une pomme rapée.	"The baby asked for a sliced apple".
Le bateau n'est pas amarré à la balise.	"The boat is not properly docked".
Le troupeau se repose dans les beaux ormeaux.	"The herd is resting among the nice young elm trees".

TABLE 6.3. Mean value and SD of Ps (in hPa) for uvular trills and uvular fricatives

Subject VL (female)	[ʀ] (n=5)	[ʁ] (n=6)	[R̥] (n=15)	[χ] (n=34)
Mean Ps in hPa	6.9	7	6.5	5.7
SD	1.2	1	1.1	0.8
Subject DD (male)	[ʀ] (n=37)	[ʁ] (n=25)	–	–
Mean Ps in hPa	9.1	8.3	–	–
SD	1.3	1.2	–	–

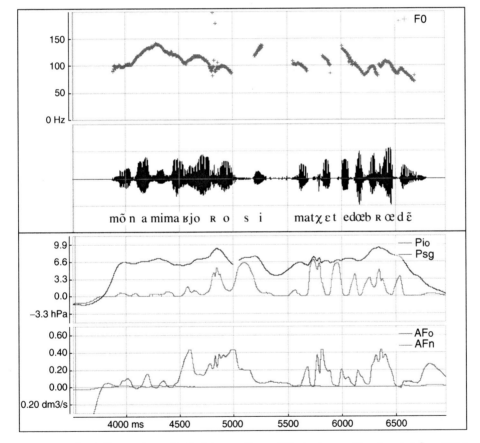

FIGURE 6.3. f0, Audio waveform, Ps, Po [given as Psg and Pio in the graph] and oral airflow (AFo) during the production of the declarative French sentence *Mon ami Mario Rossi m'a traité de bredin* [mõnamimaʁjoʀosimatχɛtedœbʀœdɛ̃] showing a rise in Ps during the production of the voiced uvular trill [R]. Note also the lack of correspondence between f0 declination and Ps.

TABLE 6.4. Test sentences used in the experiment

Tu vois cette maison? C'est la maison que j'aimerais visiter.	"Do you see this house? This is the house that I would like to visit".
Ce n'est pas le château, c'est la maison que j'aimerais visiter.	"It is not the castle, but the house that I wish to visit".
Mais non! Tu n'as rien compris! C'est la maison que j'aimerais visiter, pas le château.	"No! You don't understand! It is the house that I wish to visit, not the castle".
Elle est complètement débile cette histoire de passeport volé.	Literally: "It is completely stupid this story of the stolen passport".
Cette histoire de passeport volé, elle est complètement débile.	"This story of the stolen passport is completely stupid".
Je n'aime pas les films violents qu'on passe à la télé le samedi soir, et toi?	"I don't like the violent films that are broadcast on Saturday nights, do you?"
Anne-Marie dis-lui de venir tout de suite.	"Anne-Marie, tell him to come right away".
Dis-lui de venir tout de suite Anne-Marie.	"Tell him to come right away, Anne-Marie".
Elle n'est pas venue Anne-Marie.	Literally: "She did not come, Anne-Marie".
Selon moi, elle prendra le premier train ou elle ne viendra pas.	"In my opinion, she will take the first train or she won't come".
Elle viendra? Ou elle ne viendra pas?	"Will she come? Or won't she come?"
C'est une maison grise.	"This is a gray house".
C'est une maison qui me grise.	"This is a house that confuses me".
La démonstration du président de l'Assemblée nationale, m'a convaincu de la gravité de la situation.	"The argument of the President of the National Assembly convinced me of the gravity of the situation".
La démonstration du président m'a semblé convaincante.	"The president's argument seemed convincing to me".
Cette nouvelle théorie linguistique provoque, si j'ai bien compris, une nouvelle polémique.	"This new linguistic theory provokes, if I understand correctly, a new controversy".
Tu aurais tout intérêt, si tu tiens à conserver son amitié, à lui téléphoner plus souvent.	"It would be in your best interest, if you hope to keep his friendship, to call him more often".

loudness of their pronunciation. The sentences analyzed in this study are presented in Table 6.4. Sentences involving different f0 contours were selected, including declarative sentences, statements, yes–no questions and sentences with complete vs. incomplete information.

The results show the clear independence of f0 and Ps at the end of yes–no questions, with rising f0. This is shown in Figure 6.4, where there is a clear lowering of Ps at the end of the first interrogative sentence while f0 goes up. The relation between Ps and f0, however, seems to be quite close in the second sentence.

Figure 6.4 also shows a clear drop of Ps between the two sentences. This is quite frequent in the data and is probably due to a reset in the programming of the second sentence (Di Cristo 1998). The large, local modulations of Ps are probably due to changes in the impedance at the glottis and in the vocal tract. They can also reflect the adaptation to a change in the aerodynamic conditions such as those present around voiced fricatives and trills. Note also that although every stressed syllable can be identified on the waveform by a greater duration or amplitude, they have no effect on Ps. In the data examined, it was never possible to establish a clear correlation between Ps and f0, regardless of whether the sentence was interrogative or declarative. Even when Ps and f0 displayed simultaneous declination, there was no clear correspondence between them. This is illustrated in Figure 6.5, which shows the declarative French sentence *C'est une maison grise* [sɛtynœmɛzõɡʀizœ] "This is a grey house." Figures 6.1, 6.3, 6.4, and 6.5 in turn show that Ps is kept rather constant throughout the sentence.

6.4.3.4 The effects of changes in Ps and intensity on f0

This experiment was designed to investigate the effect of changes in intensity and Ps on the f0 of sentences. Two subjects were asked to produce the fourteen sentences in Table 6.5 at three levels of intensity (low, normal, and loud), with no instructions regarding the speech rate at which the sentence should be produced.

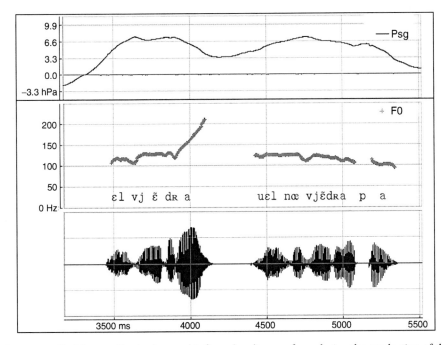

FIGURE 6.4. Ps [given as Psg in the graph], f0, and audio waveform during the production of the interrogative French sentence *Elle viendra? Ou elle ne viendra pas?* [ɛlvjẽdʀauɛlnɲvjẽdʀapa] showing that f0 and Ps are not correlated.

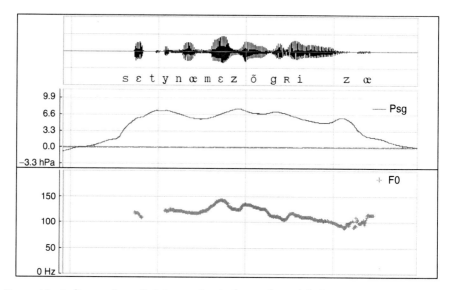

FIGURE 6.5. Audio waveform, Ps [given as Psg in the graph], and f0 during the production of the declarative French sentence *C'est une maison grise* [sɛtynœmɛzõɡʀizœ] showing that f0 declination does not entirely correspond to declining Ps.

The results displayed in Figure 6.6 for the female subject VL show that when there is an increase in intensity, there is also an increase in Ps—as expected—although the values for f0 also increase at high intensity. A closer look shows that for every level of intensity,

TABLE 6.5. Test sentences read at low, normal and high intensity

Le bateau n'est pas amarré à la balise.	"The boat is not properly docked".
Le troupeau se repose dans les beaux ormeaux.	"The herd is resting among the nice young elm trees".
Le borgne empoche un morceau de pomme.	"The one-eyed man is taking a piece of apple".
Le public est ému par Debussy.	"The public is moved by Debussy".
La boue a bouché le poulallier du moulin.	"The mud blocked the mill's henhouse".
Remi m'a mis devant la pie qui picore.	"Remi put me in front of the pecking magpie".
Le bébé a réclamé une pomme rapée.	"The baby asked for a sliced apple".
Le berger mène paître ses maigres bêtes.	"The shepherd leads his thin animals to the feeding trough".
La Meuse devient peu à peu bourbeuse.	"The Meuse is turning muddy bit by bit".
Il a peur que le bœuf meurre de son labeur.	"He is afraid that the bull will die from being overworked".
En attendant le banquet, il se penche sur le commandant.	"Waiting for the banquet, he turns towards the Commander".
Il met une pincée de jasmin dans le bain.	"He puts a pinch of jasmine in the bath".
Mon poupon montre ses bonbons et ses ponpon.	"My baby is showing his sweets and his baubles".

TABLE 6.6. Mean values and SD of f0, Ps, and duration of the thirteen sentences read at low, normal, and high intensity

		f0 Init (Hz)	f0Min (Hz)	Δf0 Init-min	f0Max (Hz)	Ps Max (hPa)	Ps Min (hPa)	ΔPs Max-min	Duration ms
Subject VL									
Low intensity	Mean	208.1	182	26.1	257	5.1	3.6	1.5	2956.4
	SD	5	5.7		13.6	0.5	0.6		307
Normal intensity	Mean	206.5	178.1	28.4	275	6.9	4.6	2.3	2961.6
	SD	8.6	5.2		21.8	1	0.4		341.3
High intensity	Mean	236	197.4	38.6	330.4	9.6	6.6	3	3152.7
	SD	13	11.7		18.7	1.1	0.9		337.4
Subject DD									
Low intensity	Mean	105.1	83	22.1	137.5	7.1	4.3	2.8	2578.9
	SD	4.3	1		11.9	1.2	0.6		459.3
Normal intensity	Mean	104.2	86.2	18	146	8.3	4.9	3.4	2742.6
	SD	2.5	4.5		6.2	0.7	1		278.8
High intensity	Mean	115.5	91.2	24.3	156.2	19.6	6.4	13.2	2629
	SD	10	1.4		12.1	0.6	1.2		330

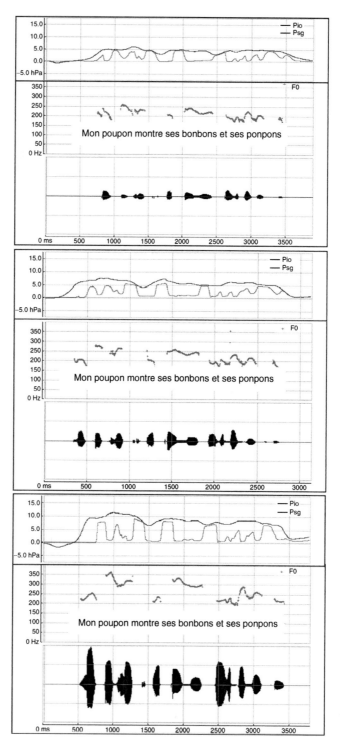

FIGURE 6.6. Ps, Po [given as Psg and Pio in the graph], f0 and audio waveform of the sentence *Mon poupon montre ses bonbons et ses ponpons*, pronounced at low, normal, and high intensity (top to bottom) by subject VL.

the shape of the f0 modulations tend to remain the same and that only the amplitude of f0 movement increases. The same tendencies are observed for the male subject DD. The baseline (see Maeda 1976 and Vaissière and Michaud 2006 for a definition of baseline) is shifted upwards for the high-intensity sentences, even though it is not shifted downwards for low-intensity ones, as it stays almost at the same level as the normal sentences; in fact, it is slightly higher. The results given in Table 6.6, for both subjects, show that there is a clear increase in Ps when the difference between the maximum and the minimum values of Ps is compared across the three intensity levels. Moreover one can observe that there is an overall increase of Ps. Comparison between the Ps line (Max Ps–Min Ps) with the baseline (Initial f0–Min f0) in Table 6.6 shows that the latter does not change in three steps as Ps does: instead, there are only two distinct levels.

When the duration of the sentences are compared, the results in Table 6.6 show that, for one of the subjects, low-and normal-intensity sentences are very similar and that high-intensity sentences have greater duration. For the other subject, in contrast, normal-intensity sentences have a greater duration than either of the other two. The results of this experiment reveal that Ps and Intensity seem to be correlated, whereas Ps and f0 are not, as shown by the differences in Ps across the three intensity levels without corresponding differences in f0.

6.5 DISCUSSION

The experiments on Ps, intensity, and the control of f0 (Section 6.4.3) show that a stable laryngeal configuration, which explains the steady and controlled f0, is always accompanied by a considerable decrease of Ps. Therefore there is no positive correlation between Ps and f0. The experiments on vowels (Section 6.4.3.1) show that a steady f0 can be maintained with a stable laryngeal configuration, even though Ps decreases substantially, suggesting that f0 is controlled independently of Ps. This observation was already made by Holmberg *et al.* (1989) and by Baken and Orlikoff (2000), who stated that under controlled situations there seems to be no clear effect of Ps on f0. When intensity is considered, two main observations can be made. First, there is a positive correlation between Ps and intensity; second, for a given level of pitch and a given level of intensity, there is some variation of intensity across vowels. Open vowels seem to be more stable and less variable than close vowels (Lecuit and Demolin 1998). This is probably due to the fact that the more tensed configuration of the glottis for close vowels, resulting from the contraction of the cricothyroid muscle, is more difficult to control and is more sensitive to changes in Ps. The characteristic setting of the glottis for each vowel combined with a different impedance in the vocal tract might account for differences in the intrinsic intensity of vowels. This was noted by Rossi (1971) and will not be discussed here. Maddieson (1984) shows that in the world's languages, [a] generally has the widest distribution. We could attribute this to the more stable character of open vowels, as shown by Lecuit and Demolin (1998), although this hypothesis remains to be proven by perceptual experiments and descriptive data.

Trills are an interesting case for discussion concerning the relation between Ps and segments (Section 6.4.3.2). Regarding the respiratory component, it seems unlikely that the massive respiratory system with its high inertia would show active modulations to segments in running speech (J. Ohala 1979; J. Ohala 1990b). However, fine modulations of Ps resulting from changes in the impedance at the glottis and in the vocal tract suggest that Ps adapts automatically to those variations. This is clearly illustrated by noticeable increases in Ps during the production of voiced trills. This type of phenomenon is the basis of phonological universals, for example, those explaining the conditions required to produce trills, that is, the maintenance of sufficient pressure differences at the place where the trill is made. Even though this last phenomenon is automatic, it raises questions about the nature of the control speakers exert on phonological processes and units. Solé (2002) relates the phonological patterning of alveolar trills to their aerodynamic characteristics, thus accounting for the absence of nasal trills, the preference for voiced trills, the alternation and co-occurrence of trilling, frication and trill devoicing. As Solé (2002: 682) notes, trills seem to have very similar but more constrained aerodynamic and articulatory requirements than fricatives. She also notes that trills with associated frication are most commonly uvular, and that devoiced trills tend to involve frication. In French, the voiced uvular trill [ʀ], still frequent in Belgian French but realized mostly as a devoiced trill or as a fricative (Demolin 2001), has been replaced by a voiced uvular fricative [ʁ] in other varieties (Fougeron and Smith 1999). Solé's claims seem to be confirmed by the fact that when voiced uvular trills are realized, they are almost invariably produced with a slight increase of Ps in the data presented here. Devoiced trills, although realized with a high Po, do not systematically show an increase in Ps. The constraints at play on voiced uvular trills can then be understood in a quite similar way to those required to produce voiced fricatives. Very precise aerodynamic conditions are required to maintain uvular trilling and voicing: the ΔPs-Po must be maximum for voicing at the same time that the ΔPo-Pa (atmospheric pressure) is also maximum. These two conditions account for the voicing and for the trill. The elevation of Ps for a voiced trill would then be an adaptation[2] to the aerodynamic conditions required to produce a voiced uvular trill.

The relation between segments and Ps is also illustrated in the data from Amharic, presented in Figure 6.1, that replicates the experiment of M. Ohala and J. Ohala (1972) for the glottal fricative [h]. The only difference is that the Amharic consonant is a voiced glottal fricative [ɦ], the allophonic variant of [h] between vowels (K. Hayward and R. Hayward 1999: 48). The significant drop in Ps obtained and the high airflow are probably due to an opening in the inter-arytenoid space. That is, Ps is lowered because

---

[2] Adaptation is taken here as physiological. This is a homeostatic response of the system to a temporary change in the environment. This type of adaptation only implies short-term physiological effects that are considered as adjustments that have no effects on the system (Susanne and Pollet 2005).

of the posterior glottal opening. The important drop in Ps for voiced [ɦ] suggests that there is an opening at the level of the glottis that is part of the phonetic character of this consonant, as is the case for breathy voiced consonants. M. Ohala (1979) made similar observations in a study of Hindi stops that also shows that there is no active participation of the pulmonic system in the production of aspirated stops.

The data presented in Section 6.4.3.3 show that f0 can be controlled independently of Ps in order to realize specific phonological tasks at the prosodic level such as the combination of two interrogative sentences or the production of a declarative sentence. Indeed, Figures 6.4 and 6.5 show that when f0 rises, Ps lowers at the end of yes–no interrogative sentences, therefore some control of the laryngeal muscles is needed to raise f0, whereas Ps is regulated differently. More specifically, Ps falls because the final vowel of the first sentence is prolonged and because of the greater opening of the vocal tract required for vowels as compared to consonants. Movements of f0 depend on a kind of control that can be attributed to phonology while Ps movements depend on regulatory mechanisms. Note, however, that Ps is controlled in the case of focused/emphasized sentences in French as well, as shown by Benguerel (1970). Draper *et al.* (1959) provide EMG data which show that there is a burst of activity for stressed syllables in English.

The data presented regarding the relationship between f0 and Ps (Section 6.4.3.3) show that contrary to the claims that their values tend to decline slightly during the course of a sentence (Lieberman 1967; Maeda 1976), this relation is not so straightforward and needs to be better understood. The present data coincide with the observations made by Plant and Younger (2000), who claimed that the relation between f0, intensity and Ps is much more complex than generally assumed. Although the observation that Ps and f0 are not well correlated is not new, it is significant for those who wish to understand some of the constraints acting on the prosody of languages. The definition of a prosodic unit such as the prosodic or phonological phrase (Vaissière and Michaud 2006) gives central status to the notion of "baseline" that makes reference to the fact that f0 and Ps decline during a sentence. The baseline seems to be perceptually important as a reference for listeners (Pierrehumbert 1979; Vaissière and Michaud 2006), so it is important that we know whether it is related to a specific interaction between Ps and f0.

The results obtained regarding changes of intensity in sentences (Section 6.4.3.4) show that if intensity is increased then Ps and the amplitude of f0 modulations increase too. Sentence duration and f0 baseline are similar for low and normal voice. The experimental results showing that the baseline is modified only when Ps and intensity are high when compared to normal and low intensities are difficult to interpret. The fact that the lines between maximum and minimum Ps are clearly distinct at the three levels of intensity suggests that Ps can change while the f0 baseline remains quite stable. This stability might be acting under a threshold, but this is yet to be proven. The variation between individuals and within different frequency–intensity ranges has been noted by Plant and Younger (2000: 177). The reason why both subjects of the study have a comparable f0 baseline for low and normal intensity may be that it is within the frequency range at which their vocal efficiency is optimized to produce a louder (low to normal) signal without increasing subglottal pressure. Note also that a high intensity level does not involve an increase in Ps larger than for other intensity levels, in other words, there is approximately the same difference between Ps min and Ps max across the three intensity levels for the two speakers (Table 6.6). The reasons why the duration of low-and normal-intensity sentences are similar compared to high intensity sentences are also unknown. One possibility might be the greater effort made to produce high intensity sentences.

Note also that the maximum level of f0 is clearly distinguished for each level of intensity, suggesting that some control is exerted on the level of f0. The data presented here are not conclusive and cannot be explained in full; however, they do suggest that fine details of the relation between Ps and f0 might account for some of the constraints acting on prosodic systems.

6.6 CONCLUSION

This chapter has evaluated the relation between Ps and f0 and its possible effects on phonological universals. Experimental data has been provided indicating that Ps and f0 are not well correlated. Ps variations are mostly regulated by changes in the impedance of the glottis and of the vocal tract. A good part of the f0 control is made by the laryngeal musculature, but in specific cases there is a contribution of Ps. When the global level of Ps rises to a high level, the baseline of f0 is also elevated and the amplitude of f0 modulations increases. Finally, it was shown that the requirements to produce trills depend on the aerodynamic conditions and that there are probably no active modulations of Ps for segments in running speech.

An important conclusion from this chapter points, once more, to the necessity of building physiological models for consonants and for intonation. This has been done in a number of studies, such as Lieberman (1967), Ladefoged (1967b), Collier (1975), Maeda (1976), and Strik and Boves (1994), but as the data presented here show, this enterprise is far from over. Our understanding of phonological universals will certainly benefit from such models.

7

Issues of Phonological Complexity

Statistical Analysis of the Relationship between Syllable Structures, Segment Inventories, and Tone Contrasts

Ian Maddieson

7.1 INTRODUCTION

The value of casting your net wide in order to catch patterns that are widespread across languages is often demonstrated in the work of John Ohala. For example, in his paper "Southern Bantu vs the world: The case of palatalization of labials" (J. Ohala 1978), instances of palatalized bilabials becoming coronals are assembled from Slavic, Daic, Tibetan, Romance, Greek, Germanic, Nupoid, and Bantu language groups to show that this change is not an isolated oddity. Other examples could have been added from Austronesian (Maddieson 1989) and elsewhere. With the data assembled, it is then possible to interrogate the results to look for generalizations concerning the factors that favor the process and hence to gain insights into its cause. Such data-gathering and interpretation can be regarded as an "experiment" in the natural world.

One strand of my work has also involved casting a wide net, in particular through large-scale sampling of salient phonological data from the languages of the world. In this chapter a large database of phonological information is examined in order to investigate an apparently widely held belief among linguists that complexity in one sub-part of the grammar of a language is likely to be compensated for by simplification in another. Such a view seems to be based on the humanistic principle that all languages are to be held in equal esteem and are equally capable of serving the communicative demands placed on them. In rejecting the notion of "primitive"

This work was supported by the National Science Foundation through grant BCS-034578.

languages, linguists seem to infer that a principle of *equal* complexity must apply. For example, in a widely used basic linguistics textbook, Akmajian *et al.* (1979: 4) assert that "all known languages are at a similar level of complexity and detail—there is no such thing as a primitive human language". From this assertion it might seem a logical further step to hypothesize that languages will undergo adjustments to equalize their overall complexity across different subsystems. Thus, as far as phonology is concerned, it seems to be widely believed in the linguistic community (although such beliefs are rarely expressed in print) that, for example, a language with a large number of distinct consonants is likely to have a small number of vowels, or that a language with an elaborated tone inventory will have a tendency to compensate by having simple syllable structure.

Apart from a rather doctrinaire assertion of equal complexity, there are at least two other bases for arguing that complexity will be balanced across subsystems. Some linguists may argue that complexity in individual languages is maintained at a roughly constant overall level because that is the way historical processes work. For example, tone-splitting or tonogenesis is commonly seen as a process in which elaboration of tonal contrast is exchanged for simplification of the consonant inventory (e.g. Matisoff 1973). If it is a typical, or even relatively frequent, characteristic of diachronic phonological processes that they involve exchanging complexity in different subsystems, then apparent compensatory relationships should be detectable across any reasonably inclusive sample of languages.

Others may propose that complexity is held in check because of processing considerations. Overly complex packaging of information may over-stretch our brain's ability to deal with the input in one way or another. For example, Pellegrino *et al.* (2005) have recently suggested that the more complex syllable structure and larger inventory of English allows it to convey more information (in the sense of Shannon 1948) per syllable than does Japanese, which has a simpler syllable canon and fewer distinct segments. However, English compensates for the richer information-per-syllable flow by habitual use of a slower speech rate in terms of syllables per second. Hence the two languages are seen as seeking to optimize the rate at which information is encoded and has to be decoded on-line. Again, if compensatory relationships of this general type are a required characteristic of language design, their impact should be detectable in a survey of phonological properties of languages.

Five relatively simple variables that can be taken to represent certain aspects of the complexity of phonological systems will be compared pairwise to see whether they tend to correlate positively (greater complexity going together on both measures) or negatively (greater complexity on one measure going with lower complexity on the other), or are simply uncorrelated. The variables describe the degree of elaboration of the syllable canon, the size of inventories of consonants, basic vowel qualities, and all vowels, and the complexity of tone systems. The sample of languages examined will first be described, together with how these phonological characteristics are represented in the data.

7.2 LANGUAGE SAMPLE AND DATA

The language sample is essentially an expanded version of the UPSID sample described in Maddieson (1984). This was earlier enlarged from 317 to 451 languages for a version distributed as an interactive database (Maddieson and Precoda 1990). At both these stages, selection of languages for inclusion was governed by a quota principle seeking maximum genetic diversity among extant languages (and those spoken until recently). More recently, the UPSID sample was merged with the 200-language list chosen as the core sample for the *World Atlas of Language Structures* (WALS) (Haspelmath *et al.* 2005). Although representation of genetic diversity was a major goal of this sample, a number of other factors also played a role, including the political importance of a language, the availability of a full-length grammar, the presence of the language in other typological samples, and a desire for wide geographical coverage. Due to overlapping membership of the samples this resulted in a merged list of about 520 languages. The languages previously included in a study of syllable structure (Maddieson 1992) or figuring in a long-term project to investigate the phonetic characteristics of endangered languages have also been added. As part of a plan more fully to examine geographical distribution of phonological characteristics of languages, this database is continuing to be enlarged, with the intention of reaching a total of 1000 or so languages. It should be noted that the addition of more languages, and in particular the relaxation of the requirement that no pair of closely related languages be included, changes the representative nature of the sample from that aimed for in the original UPSID sample.

At the time of writing the database includes 625 languages, with the data for different languages at varying levels of completeness. As shown in Table 7.1, there are about one hundred languages in each of the six major areal/genetic groupings used for subsetting the data for purposes of statistical validation. The composition of these groupings, which are broadly similar to those used by Dryer (1992, 2003), is described in detail in Maddieson (2006). In forming these groupings, genetic factors override purely areal ones in the following way. In order to keep related languages together all languages in a family are included in the area of its major concentration. For example, Semitic languages spoken in Asia Minor are grouped with other Afro-Asiatic languages under the African area, and all Austronesian languages are grouped together in the East and South-East Asian area, including even Malagasy and Maori. The table is included here primarily to confirm the global distribution of the languages in the sample, but occasional reference to differences between the language groups will be made.

The first property to be examined is the complexity of the maximal syllable structure the language permits. In order to reduce a considerable variety of patterns to a manageable number of categories, the languages are divided into Simple, Moderate, and Complex categories based on what is permitted in syllable onset and

TABLE 7.1. Distribution of languages by areal/genetic grouping

Area	No. of languages in sample
Europe, West and South Asia	94
East and South-East Asia	119
Africa	139
North America	91
South and Central America	87
Australia and New Guinea	95

coda positions. Those with Simple structure allow no more than one onset consonant and do not permit codas. In other words, they permit only (C)V syllables. Among languages in this category are Yoruba, Ju|'hoan, Maori, and Guaraní. Languages with a Moderate level of syllabic complexity are those in which the coda may contain not more than one consonant, and the onsets are limited to a single consonant or a restricted set of two-consonant clusters having the most common structural patterns, typically an obstruent followed by a glide or liquid (the 30-language sample used in Maddieson 1992 had shown that simple codas and minimally elaborated onsets tend to co-occur in languages). Among languages in this class are Nahuatl, Tigré, Yanyuwa, and Mandarin (the "medials" of the traditional analysis of Chinese syllables are treated as glides in an onset cluster). Languages which permit a wide range of onset clusters, or which permit clusters in the coda position are classified as belonging to the Complex syllable category. This class includes Georgian, Quileute, Soqotri, and French. No account is taken of the relative frequency of the different syllable patterns in the lexicon, and patterns restricted to relatively recent loanwords are ignored. Values for the syllable complexity category have been entered so far for 564 of the 625 languages, with a large majority belonging to the Moderate category (320 or 56.7%), and Complex languages outweighing Simple ones among the remainder by 180 to 64 (31.9% to 11.3%).

The complexity of the tone system is also reduced to a three-way categorical variable. Languages with no tonal contrasts form the first group, those with a tone system that can be reduced to a basic two-way contrast (usually of level high and low tones) form the second group, and those with a more complex tone system containing three or more levels or contours form the third. A number of languages which do not have canonical tone systems but where pitch patterns make basic lexical distinctions, such as Japanese and Norwegian, have been grouped with the Simple tone languages, as have a few languages with recognized but under-analyzed tone systems. Tone category has been entered for 572 of the 625 languages, with a majority (338 or 59.1%) having no tones, 140 (24.5%) having Simple tone systems (including 14 languages where the tone system has the marginal status mentioned above), and 94 (16.4%) have Complex tone systems. Complex tone systems occur far more frequently in the East and South-East Asian and African groups than elsewhere, but Simple tone systems and languages with no tone system are distributed fairly uniformly across the areal/genetic groupings outside Africa. In the African group a majority of languages have a Simple tone system and languages without tone are few in number.

The remaining three properties compared are numerical rather than categorical. The consonant inventory size is the total number of distinctive consonants recognized for the language in a phonemic-style analysis. The vowel-quality inventory size is the number of distinct vowel types contrasting on the major parameters of height, rounding, and backness, in other words, independent of length, nasalization, voice quality, or other "series-generating" components. Distinctions that are known or hypothesized to be based on tongue-root position are equated with height distinctions, in part because for many languages the role played by tongue root is not known. The total vowel-inventory size is the number of distinct vowel nuclei including distinctions of nasality, phonation type, and length as well as any nuclear diphthongs (that is, those which do not consist of a vowel and a consonantal glide or a sequence of two separate vowels). An attempt has been made to reach interpretations of the consonant and vowel inventories based on uniform principles, so in many cases they depart from the analysis found in published descriptions of the individual languages. Undoubtedly there are errors of judgment or fact affecting the interpretations made, but in a large sample errors in different directions can be expected to cancel each other out, and any robust general patterns can be expected still to emerge.

Consonant inventory and vowel quality inventory values are currently entered for 617 of the 625 languages. Consonant inventory ranges from 6 to 128 with a mean of 22.6, and vowel quality inventory from 2 to 16 with a mean of 6.0. Total vowel inventory is entered for only 535 languages (questions about the status of vowel length and potential diphthongs often being as yet unresolved), and ranges from 2 to 46 with a mean of 10.2. Because a small number of very salient outliers contribute a serious distortion to numerical analyses, languages with more than 30 total vowels or 70 or more consonants are discarded when these variables are considered. Each of these thresholds is exceeded by three languages, one of which, Juǀ'hoan, exceeds both.

7.3 RELATIONSHIPS BETWEEN VARIABLES

In this section, each of the five variables described in the previous section will be compared pairwise with the others, except for the vowel quality and total vowel inventories (which are evidently correlated). When a categorical and a numerical variable are compared, the means of the numerical variable in each category form the basis of the comparison. When two numerical categories are compared, a simple regression is used. The comparison of syllable and tone categories is made using an index. The number of languages in each comparison varies according to the number with values specified for both variables. In each case, the purpose is to see if greater complexity on the two variables tends to co-occur, or if a compensatory relationship exists, or there is no overall trend of either kind.

In the first three comparisons syllable structure is compared with the segment inventory variables. As Figure 7.1 shows, syllable structure complexity and the size of the consonant inventory are positively correlated. The mean number of consonants in the inventory is greater for each increase in complexity of the maximal syllable. Analysis of variance shows a highly significant effect of syllable category on consonant inventory size [$F_{(2, 556)} = 23.26$, $p < .0001$] and all pairwise comparisons are highly significant in a post-hoc comparison (using Fisher's PLSD adjusted for unequal cell sizes). In Figure 7.1 and subsequent figures the error bars show the 95 percent confidence interval.

Neither of the two measures of vowel inventory shows a systematic relationship with syllable complexity. In each case the mean value within each syllable category is essentially the same as the grand mean. These comparisons are shown in Figures 7.2 and 7.3. Neither displays a significant effect for syllable category [$F_{(2, 566)} = .216$, $p = .8054$ for vowel quality and $F_{(2, 488)} = 0.278$, $p = .757$ for total vowel inventory].

The size of the consonant inventory correlates positively (though rather weakly) with increasing complexity of tone system, as shown in Figure 7.4. Analysis of variance shows a significant effect of tone category at better than $p < .05$ [$F_{(2, 566)} = 3.336$, $p < .0363$]. Posthoc comparisons show that only the comparison between "None" and "Complex" reaches significance.

The size of the vowel quality inventory and the complexity of tone system also positively correlate with each other; as tone complexity increases, so does the mean number of distinct vowel qualities. This result is shown in Figure 7.5. In the analysis of variance there is a highly significant effect of tone category [$F_{(2, 566)} = 20.591$, $p < .0001$] and all posthoc pairwise comparisons are significant at better than

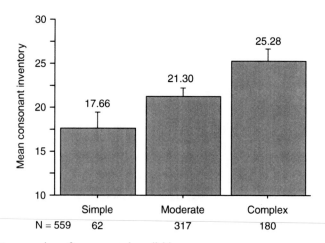

FIGURE 7.1. Mean number of consonants by syllable category.

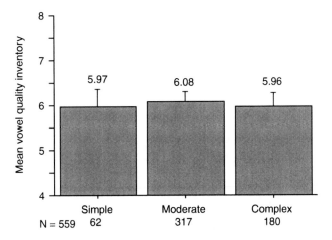

FIGURE 7.2. Mean number of vowel qualities by syllable category.

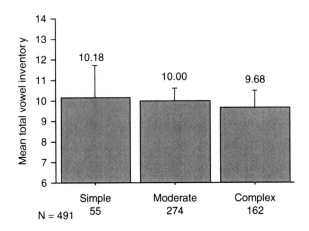

FIGURE 7.3. Mean number of total vowels by syllable category.

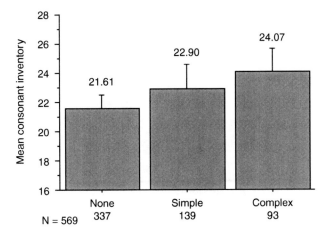

FIGURE 7.4. Mean number of consonants by tone category.

$p < .05$, with the difference between "None" and either category of tonal languages better than $p < .001$.

There is also a correlation between an increase in total vowel inventory size and the presence of a tone system, as shown in Figure 7.6. There is a highly significant overall effect of tone category in the analysis of variance [F $(2, 499) = 16.554$, $p < .0001$], which the posthoc comparisons indicate is due to a highly significant difference between "None" and either tonal category, with no significant difference being found between the two categories of tonal languages.

There is no systematic relationship between the number of vowel qualities and the number of consonants in the inventories of the languages ($N = 612$), nor between the total number of vowels and the number of consonants ($N = 530$). Regression plots are shown in Figures 7.7 and 7.8 for these two comparisons. For the regression in Figure 7.7 the R^2 value is .0002, for that in Figure 7.8 it is .002.

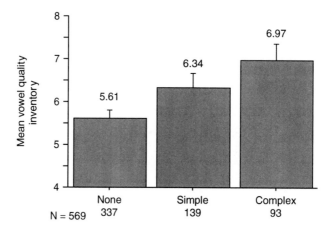

FIGURE 7.5. Mean vowel quality inventory by tone category.

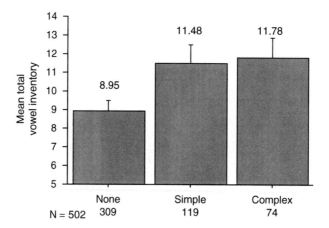

FIGURE 7.6. Mean total vowel inventory by tone category.

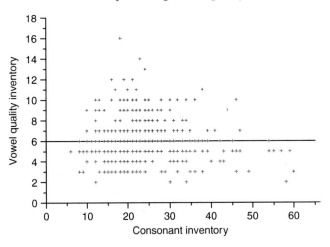

FIGURE 7.7. Regression plot of consonant inventory and vowel quality inventory.

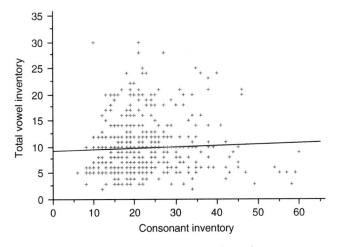

FIGURE 7.8. Regression plot of consonant inventory and total vowel inventory.

The final comparison is between the two categorical variables reflecting complexity of syllable structure and tone system. Tone system complexity does not associate with the complexity of syllable structure; rather, the occurrence of complex syllable structure and lower tonal complexity are associated. In the total sample of 543 languages examined for this relationship, 88 (16.2%) have complex tone systems, but among the 172 languages with complex syllable structure only 11 (6.4%) have a complex tone system. Another way to illustrate this pattern is with a tonal complexity index. Languages with no tones are coded with 1, languages with a simple tonal system as 2, and those with a complex tonal system as 3. The mean value of this index is then computed for each syllable complexity class. Results are shown in Figure 7.9.

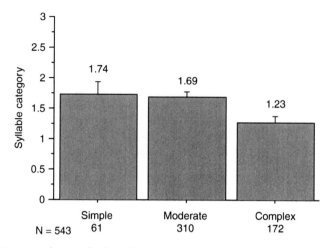

FIGURE 7.9. Tone complexity index by syllable category.

There is a significant overall effect [F (2, 540) = 19.15, $p < .0001$], with the index being significantly lower for the complex syllable structure class than for the other two categories, which are not significantly different in posthoc comparisons.

7.4 SUMMARY AND DISCUSSION OF RESULTS

The nine comparisons made in the preceding section show almost no evidence of any tendency for languages to "compensate" for increased complexity in one of the phonological subsystems surveyed by greater simplicity in another. In fact four of the comparisons show positive correlations of increases in complexity between different subsystems. Increasing syllabic complexity is positively associated with increasing size of consonant inventory, and increasing complexity of tone system is positively associated with increasing size of both consonant and vowel inventories. The mean number of both vowel qualities and total vowels increases with tone complexity. Although these two quantities are generally associated with each other, the two relationships should be considered separately. It would be quite possible for the "series-generating" components that are mainly responsible for the differences between the two numbers to be distributed across the tone categories in a way that created a compensatory relationship between total vowel inventory and tonal complexity.

A further four of the comparisons show no systematic relationship at all between the variables examined. These are the two relationships between syllable complexity and the vowel measures, and the two relationships between consonant inventory size and the vowel measures. Despite anecdotally based belief to the contrary, increasing elaboration of consonant inventory is unrelated to size of vowel quantity inventory (as earlier noted by Stephens and Justeson 1984).

Only one of the relationships shows a tendency to show compensation—that between syllable complexity and tone. Languages with complex syllable structures are most frequent in two language groups, the one uniting the languages of Europe, West, and South Asia, and the one containing the languages of North American and these are two of the four areas (along with South and Central America and Australia and New Guinea) in which relatively few of the languages are tonal.

Although there is no space here for a full discussion of the issues raised it may be useful to point out that the relationships found cannot be obviously accounted for by "natural" or "functional" considerations. For example, the tendency for larger consonant inventory and more complex syllable structure to go together cannot be "explained" by considerations of which types of consonants are more likely, from a cross-linguistic point of view, to occur in clusters. In general, the larger consonant inventories are more likely to contain a higher proportion of consonants that cross-linguistically tend to have their distribution restricted both in clusters and in coda position.

Although individual languages may historically "trade" elaboration in one subsystem for simplification elsewhere, such "compensation" does not seem to be a design feature of language. Nor do we find here evidence that languages are shaped in a compensatory fashion to avoid testing the limits of processing ability. It simply seems to be the case that languages vary quite considerably in their phonological complexity, as measured by the indices used here. Similar variability and absence of compensatory patterning were also found by Shosted (2006b) in comparing phonological and morphosyntactic elaboration.

It should be noted that the results in this chapter are presented as descriptive statistical summaries of the data that is entered into the database. The design and use of language surveys in typological studies and universals research and the nature of the inferences that can fairly be drawn from their analysis have been topics of considerable interest (e.g. Dryer 1989; Perkins 1989, 2001; Cysouw 2005). Much concern centers on the question of whether the languages included in a sample can be considered independent. The concern is particularly acute for those who hope to be able to extrapolate from a sample of documented languages to the universe of *possible* languages. I do not think this step can ever be justified. Moreover, when the hypothesis for which a sample is being used concerns compensatory adjustments, it is not clear that closeness in genetic or areal terms to an included language should disqualify the inclusion of another. After all, in the kind of historical scenario that forms one foundation for the expectation of compensatory adjustments, comparison of dialects of the same language can provide the model. For example, Northern Khmuʔ has tone but has neutralized obstruent voicing, Southern Khmuʔ has no tone and an obstruent voicing distinction (Svantesson 1983). The issue is whether changes that create such patterns occur often enough to leave an overall imprint on language structures. The best way to search for the answer may well be to examine the largest and most inclusive sample possible.

8

Linking Dispersion–Focalization Theory and the Maximum Utilization of the Available Distinctive Features Principle in a Perception-for-Action-Control Theory

Jean-Luc Schwartz, Louis-Jean Boë, and Christian Abry

8.1 INTRODUCTION

The "substance-based" approach to phonology was born some 35 years ago with two seminal contributions, one by Liljencrants and Lindblom (1972)—the first of Lindblom's many variations on dispersion and perceptual contrast (*Dispersion Theories*: Lindblom 1986, 1990b)—the other, Stevens's *Quantal Theory* (1972, 1989). These contributions constituted the starting point for a rich tradition of descriptive and theoretical phonetics, in which the aim is not to refute the existence of a formal phonological level with its intrinsic formal principles and rules, but, instead, to determine and, possibly, model how the emergence of such formal systems could be shaped by the perceptuo-motor substance of speech communication.

The link between substance and form, however, is still not completely clear. In 1979, John Ohala questioned the role of maximization of perceptual dispersion, suggesting that with this principle "we should undoubtedly reach the patently false prediction that a seven-consonant system should include something like the following set: ɗ, kʲ, ts, ɬ, m, r, l" (Ohala 1979: 185), that is, a mixed combination of seven manner and three place contrasts, supposed to enhance perceptual distinctiveness.

This work owes a great deal to Ian Maddieson, whose UPSID database offers researchers a fundamental and invaluable tool. We thank the editor and the two anonymous reviewers for their helpful criticisms on the first versions of this text. We are grateful to Pauline Welby for her helpful comments and for her help with the English translation

He suggested that systems instead tend to limit their use of phonetic features, and that if a new feature is introduced in a system, it tends to combine systematically with the existing features in the system. This is what he called the *Maximum Utilization of the Available Features* (MUAF) principle (see also Clements 2003a, b).

In this chapter, we first review some of the major facts about vowel and consonant systems in human languages and show that both dispersion and MUAF principles seem to be at work in the shaping of these systems. We then present the Dispersion–Focalization Theory (DFT) that we proposed several years ago for predicting vowel systems, adding a new concept, focalization, to the classical dispersion concept inspired by Lindblom (Schwartz *et al.* 1997b). We propose that the integration of dispersion and MUAF forces us to consider speech units as resulting from a perceptuo-motor process. We present the Perception for Action Control Theory (PACT, Schwartz *et al.* 2002), which provides an integrated perceptuo-motor framework in which perception is conceived of as a set of mechanisms that allow the listener to recover speech gestures shaped by multisensory processing. Finally, we discuss how dispersion, focalization, and MUAF can be integrated in PACT in order to predict some of the main components of vowel and consonant systems in human languages.

8.2 DISPERSION AND MUAF IN VOWEL AND CONSONANT INVENTORIES

8.2.1 Systems

Based on databases of phoneme inventories, we estimate that there are about a thousand phonemes in the world's languages. The UPSID Database (Maddieson 1984; Maddieson and Precoda 1990), which groups 451 languages (hereafter $UPSID_{451}$) drawn from the families and sub-families of languages defined in the Stanford classification and selected with a criterion of genetic distance, includes 920 phonemes with 179 vowels, 89 diphthongs, and 652 consonants. (The most recent UPSID version with 566 languages (Maddieson 2001) does not modify this picture.)

As early as 1928, the first typologies of phonological systems of the world's languages proposed by Trubetzkoy (1939) revealed that languages make use of relatively limited choices among all the phoneme possibilities determined by a simple combinatory rule. Thus, there is a strong bias in favor of systems with five vowels and 22 consonants. Within vowel systems, considering the 28 IPA vowel qualities, the theoretical number of five-vowel systems is about 10^5. There are, however, no more than 25 different five-vowel systems attested in the world's languages (Vallée 1994). Moreover, it is important to note that major typological and structural trends bear no clear relationship to linguistic families, either considering typologies proposed long ago by historical linguists (Meillet and Cohen 1924), or the framework of multilateral comparisons proposed by Greenberg (1963). For example, the Indo-European family includes vowel systems ranging from five to 28 vowels considering the sample used by Maddieson in the UPSID$_{451}$ database comprising Greek, Irish, Breton, German, Norwegian, Lithuanian, Russian, Bulgarian, French, Spanish, Farsi, Pashto, Kurdish, Hindi-Urdu, Bengali, Kashmiri, Shinalese, Albanian, Armenian, Nepali, Konkani, and Ormuri. The fact that certain features (e.g. nasality, length, rounding, missing /p/ or missing /g/, three-vowel systems) are associated with certain geographical areas can only confirm that typological classifications of sound structures and genetic classifications according to linguistic families are far from identical, and that languages exhibit geographical (*Sprachbund*) tendencies rather than genetic ones.

8.2.2 Vowels

The 179 vowels in UPSID$_{451}$ are based on 38 plain vowel qualities, combined with secondary features such as nasalization, length, and pharyngealization. The number of units in the vowel systems varies from three for certain North American (e.g. Alabama), South American (e.g. Amuesha) and Australian languages (e.g. Arrente), to 24 (!Xu, Khoisan family) and even 28 (Kasmmiri, Indo-European). However, there is a strong preference for five vowels (comprising 20% of the UPSID$_{451}$ languages), or five vowel qualities (28% of the UPSID$_{451}$ languages, considering /a/, /ã/ and /aː/, for example, as having the same vowel quality).

In general terms, vowel systems seem to combine dispersion and MUAF principles. In fact, if a language has only three vowels, these are the three extreme plain vowels /i a u/, rather than /ə θ ɜ/, which are perceptually too close to each other, or a combination of quality and secondary articulation contrasts (e.g. nasality, length, pharyngealisation) as in /i ã uː/, as argued by Ohala for consonants (1979: 185). In a similar vein, if a language has five vowels, they are mainly the well-formed plain series /i e a o u/, (Crothers 1978; Maddieson 1984; Vallée 1994; Boë 1997; Schwartz *et al.* 1997a), accounting for 20 percent of languages in UPSID$_{451}$, rather than / ə θ ϴ ɜ ɐ/, with no clear perceptual distinctiveness, or /i/ /e/ /a/ /o/ /u/ combined with nasal, breathy, laryngeal, or pharyngeal secondary features. If a language has nine vowels, the preponderant system is /i ɪ e ɛ a ɔ o ʊ u/ (e.g. Tampulma, Niger Congo). Two-thirds of UPSID$_{451}$ languages have only plain vowels, with no secondary features. In systems with more than nine vowels, there generally appears a secondary series, one plain (e.g. /i e a o u/) and the other typically nasal (e.g. /ĩ ẽ ã õ ũ/ in Beembe or Kpan, Niger Congo), or long (e.g. /iː eː aː oː uː/ in Tonkawa, Amerindian). With 24 vowels, as in !Xu, the basic /i e a o u/ series is combined with subsets of secondary articulations combining nasality, length, and pharyngealization. This value of nine provides a kind of threshold above which a sub-space of plain vowels, obeying dispersion criteria, is combined with other features with some trend for MUAF (corroborating different observations; e.g. Crothers 1978: 113; Maddieson 1984: 128, 131; Lindblom and Engstrand 1989: 113; Engstrand and Krull 1991: 13–15; Vallée 1994: 95–6).

Previous analyses allowed us to show that the schwa vowel /ə/ seems to play a specific role in this pattern (Schwartz *et al.* 1997a), escaping in some sense from the traditional vowel space. Our assumption was that schwa, when it does exist in a given system, might be produced by a kind of systematic relaxation procedure based on vowel reduction (see van Bergem 1994), making it a sort of parallel system. To test this idea, we introduced a "transparency rule" which specifies whether or not a vowel interferes with the overall structure of the vowel system. The principle is that if a unit in a given system is "transparent", its presence or absence in the system should not modify the structure of the system. Other units, on the other hand, should do so because of relational interactions patterning the sound systems. For example, /i/ is never a transparent vowel since removing it from preferred systems like /i a u/ or /i e a o u/ leads to /a u/ or /e a o u/, which are unattested in human languages. We showed that schwa is the only vowel which respects this transparency rule since the relative distribution of systems with or without /ə/ is exactly the same. This reinforces the assumption that schwa is a parallel vowel, which exists because of intrinsic principles (probably based on vowel reduction) different from those of other vowels.

The vowels /i/, /a/, and /u/ are systematically used in vowel inventories. Potential counter-examples of systems without these three vowels have been proposed, such as short vowels in Arabic (Kennedy 1960; Mitchell 1962; Tomiche 1964), some Australian languages, or Indo-European reconstructions */e a o/ (about 4000 BC) proposed by Saussure (1879). Note the following points, however.

1. The acoustical analysis of dialectal Arabic vowels (e.g. Allatif and Abry 2004, for Syrian) shows that utterances of short vowels actually have [e] and [o] as their most frequent realizations, but also display clear cases of [iː] and [uː] for their longer counterparts.

2. Though a reduced system typically appears in the 3-vowel Australian indigenous languages (Butcher 1994), extreme [i] configurations are displayed, e.g. for accented phrase final vowels in female speech (Fletcher and Butcher 2003).

3. The oldest attested Anatolian Indo-European languages do not display the abnormal */e a o/ system (no matter how algebraic a speculation it might be, cf. the ± ATR proposals in Greenberg's Eurasiatic), since we regularly find /i a u/ in Luvian, and /i e a u/ in Hittite, Palaic, and Lycian (Melchert 1994).

Therefore it seems that predictions should not only exploit perceptual differentiation, but also incorporate perceptual representation spaces based on a hierarchy of features: first plain (100%) and then, after saturation of this space (generally after nine vowels), various combinations of features such as nasality (22%), length (11%), nasality and length (2%), reproducing to a certain extent the basic /i e a o u/ schema. Perceptual distances should be computed separately in each of these spaces, though not independently, as shown by the MUAF principle.

8.2.3 Consonants

Consonants constitute about three quarters of the available phonemes in the world's languages. Therefore, most languages (97% of the UPSID$_{451}$ languages) have more consonants than vowels. Consonant systems have mainly between 18 and 25 units (minimum 6 for Rotokas and maximum 95 for !Xufi, with a large series of clicks), with a peak at 22. The most frequent consonant systems contain at least six plosives /p t k b d g/, two to four nasals (/m n/, or /m n ŋ/ or / m n ɳ ŋ/), four fricatives including /f s h/, two approximants /j l/ and two affricates /ts tʃ/. It is only with a very large number of consonants that ejectives or clicks appear. UPSID$_{451}$ displays 12 places of articulation (see Fig. 8.1). The distribution of consonant place and manner of articulation is now quite well-known (Laver 1994; Boë 1997) (Table 8.1). In the following sections we focus on plosive systems, to provide some elements for modeling that will be incorporated in Section 8.4.

Like vowel systems, consonant systems seem to combine dispersion and MUAF principles. Indeed, considering plosives, if a language has three plosives (as in 3% of UPSID$_{451}$ languages; Ainu, Maasai, Nicobarese, and Yagua are examples), it has /p t k/, rather than other combinations of place (e.g. a coronal, a palatal, and a velar) or a combination of place and secondary articulation contrasts (e.g. /p tʰ kʷ/). If a language has six plosives, which is the most frequent number (found in 24% of the languages of UPSID$_{451}$), it has /p t k b d g/, rather than /p t c k q ʔ/, /b d g G ʔ/, or /p ⁿt cʰ kˤ qʷ ʔ/. With nine plosives, the basic /p t k b d g/ series combines with

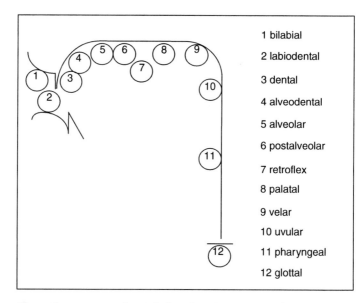

FIGURE 8.1. The twelve consonantal articulation places in UPSID. In the analyses in Section 8.2.3, the "coronal" articulation groups positions 3, 4, 5, and 6 (dental, alveodental, alveolar, and postalveolar)

TABLE 8.1. Percentage of place-of-articulation occurrences (in columns) for the five consonant categories (in rows) in UPSID$_{451}$. The most frequent places for each category are shown in bold type (from Boë 1997)

	Bilabial	Alveodental	Postalveolar	Palatal	Velar	Uvular	Pharyngeal	Glottal
Plosives	**99**	**100**	6	16	**99**	13	1	48
Nasals	**95**	**96**	10	31	**53**	0	0	0
Fricatives	58	**85**	43	8	29	11	4	**62**
Affricates	0	**85**	49	4	1	1	0	0
Approximants	79	78	3	**85**	**75**	0	0	0

secondary feature sets such as aspiration, prenasalization, palatalization, or laryngealization (see Maddieson 1986: 116–20 for details). Altogether, in the UPSID extension to 556 languages (Maddieson 2001), 45 percent of the systems include the six plosives /p t k b d g/. Therefore, it seems that there is both a best-place set including a labial, a coronal, and a velar (possibly for dispersion reasons, as we shall show in Section 8.4) and a combination à la MUAF of this place set with other features, first voicing and then secondary features.

As with schwa in vowel systems, it may be suggested that the glottal articulation could play the role of a "transparent" unit, considering that it often emerges from a "complete reduction" of the consonantal supraglottal gesture, just as schwa emerges from a reduction of the vocalic supraglottal articulation. Actually, it appears that the "transparency" criterion works quite well with /ʔ/. In fact, systems with the three places of articulation /labial, coronal, velar/ constitute 33 percent of the languages in UPSID$_{451}$, while systems with the four places of articulation [labial, coronal, palatal, velar] constitute 7.5 percent of the UPSID$_{451}$ systems. Strikingly, the values for systems with the same distribution plus the glottal articulation are almost the same: 31 percent for [labial, coronal, velar, glottal] and 5 percent for [labial, coronal, palatal, velar, glottal]. Thus the glottal articulation does not seem to intervene in the structural relationship among plosive places. Basically, a given place system (not considering the glottal articulation) has about a 50 percent chance of containing a glottal articulation in addition to its basic structure; this leads to similar frequencies of systems with and without this consonant.

Consonant systems contain many fewer nasals than plosives. Indeed, about 3.5 percent of UPSID$_{451}$ languages have no nasals at all, 6 percent have only one (/m/ or /n/), 28 percent have two (mainly /m n/), 27 percent have three (generally /m n ŋ/), and 27 percent have four, adding /ɲ/. The nasality feature can be combined with other features, as shown by UPSID$_{451}$ languages containing nasals that are retroflex (Khanty, Ural-Altaic), long (Wolof, Niger-Kordofanian), voiceless (Sui, Austro-Tai), laryngealized (Nez Percé, Amerindian), or breathy (Hindi-Urdu, Indic). As with vowels and oral stops, these secondary features appear only if the system contains over a certain number of units, four for nasals.

The overall picture for plosives does not seem so different from that for vowels, with a preferred set of places /p t k/ (corresponding to the preferred /i a u/ or /i e a o u/ sets for vowels), an addition of supplementary features (such as voicing, nasality, and secondary features) more or less in line with the MUAF principle, and the existence of a transparent unit escaping from the structure by the *transparency rule*. An important point to be addressed in the case of nasals is the potential role of the *visual* modality in language system patterns. Of the languages in UPSID$_{451}$, 94 percent contain a contrast between a bilabial /m/ and a coronal /n/. The contrast between these two phonemes is quite easy to lipread, but is acoustically quite weak, as shown by the fact that blind children have some difficulty in learning to distinguish the two (Mills 1987). Hence it is not unreasonable to assume that the high visibility of this contrast plays a part in the fact that it is almost universal. Of course, visual perception is likely to play a role for all other sounds, but it is particularly noticeable in the case of the /m/–/n/ pair.

8.3 THE DISPERSION–FOCALIZATION THEORY OF SOUND SYSTEMS

The first quantitative simulations of vowel inventories are, of course, due to Liljencrants and Lindblom's (1972) Dispersion Theory (DT), based on maximization of perceptual distances in the (F1, F2) or (F1, F'2) plane (F'2 being the so-called "perceptual second formant" integrating F2, F3, and F4 if the higher formants are in the vicinity of F2: see Carlson *et al.* 1970). The basic principle underlying *Dispersion–Focalization Theory* (DFT, Schwartz *et al.* 1997b) is to associate a structural dispersion cost based on inter-vowel perceptual distances (dispersion) and a local cost based on intra-vowel perceptual salience (focalization). The DFT assumes that for a given number of vowels, the preferred system (i.e. the most frequently observed in the world's languages) is obtained by minimizing the sum of these two components, applied to acoustic parameters (formants expressed in Barks) characterizing each vowel located in the Maximal Vowel Space (MVS). This space (Boë *et al.* 1989) groups all possible productions of the human vocal tract, and it is determined from simulations on simplified (e.g. Fant's 4-tube model, 1960) or anthropomorphic (Maeda 1990; Beautemps *et al.* 2001) vocal tract models. The three cardinal vowels [i], [a], and [u] are the three corners of the maximum vowel space in the (F1, F2) plane, [y] being the fourth corner in the (F2, F3) space, allowing a better representation of the rounding dimension (Fig. 8.2).

The energy function of a given system with n vowels is given by: $E_{DF} = E_D + \alpha E_F$ where E_D is the dispersion cost (related to vowel structure) and E_F the focalization cost (related to the nature of each vowel) weighted by a factor α. E_D is defined, as in DT, by the sum of the squared inverse of the perceptual distances (using the

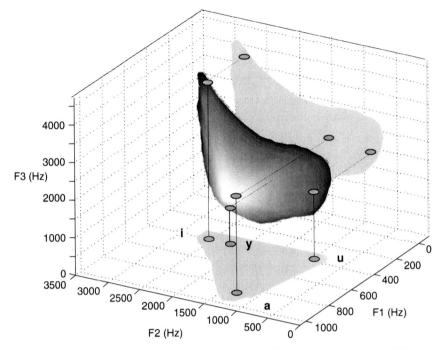

FIGURE 8.2. The F1–F2–F3 Maximal Vowel Space defined with an anthropological model (see text). The four corner-point vowels in this space are [i y a u].

perceptual second formant F2′) between each pair of vowels. In order to deal with the excessive number of high non-peripheral vowels in the DT predictions, we introduce a stretching of the acoustic space along the F1 dimension, assuming that higher formants play a minor role in the phonetic quality of the vowels. The λ parameter sets the weight between F2′ and F1. Simulations suggest that a λ value around 0.3 is necessary to adequately reproduce vowel systems. This raises the question of the possible explanation for a lesser role of higher formants in perceptual dispersion. We suggested three possible reasons for this. The first is due to Lindblom (1986), who showed that if a formant-based distance is replaced by an auditory spectral distance, this results in decreasing the ratio between the [i]–[u] and the [i]–[a] distance by a factor of around 2, which means applying a horizontal shrinking factor λ of 0.5. The same line of reasoning has recently been exploited and refined by Diehl *et al.* (2003) using more realistic auditory representations incorporating temporal neural coding. Secondly, various types of perceptual data suggest that lower-frequency formants are better perceived than higher-frequency ones (e.g. Delattre *et al.* 1952). This may be related to psycho-acoustic facts about the auditory representation of vowels and complex sounds, in which the representation of F1 is shown to be systematically enhanced relative to the representation of higher formants, because of remote suppression of higher-frequency by low-frequency components (see e.g. Stelmachowicz *et al.* 1982, Tyler and Lindblom 1982, and Moore and Glasberg

1983). The third possible cause of F1 stretching relative to F2 and higher formants is based on a non-auditory argument from proprioception. Indeed, it has been proposed that the close–open dimension, mainly related to F1, could be better represented in proprioception than the front–back dimension, mainly related to F2 (Lindblom and Lubker 1985).

The additional focalization term, specific to DFT (and controlled by the second parameter α), diminishes the energy of configurations with vowels with F1 close to F2, F2 close to F3, or F3 close to F4. The focal vowels are produced by articulatory maneuvers changing the formant-to-cavity affiliations (Badin *et al.* 1990), hence making such configurations more stable (see Abry *et al.* 1989 for the relation between focalization and Quantal Theory). This is a very specific way of producing a spectral concentration of energy, which favors integration by the auditory system. Recent production (Ménard *et al.* 2007) and perception (Polka and Bohn 2003; Schwartz *et al.* 2005) data suggest that focalization plays a role in vowel perception just as focal colors play a role in color perception (Brown and Lenneberg 1954; Rosch-Heider 1972).

We thus obtain an energy function combining two terms depending on the λ and α parameters, respectively. DFT allows us to predict not only preferred systems, but also a number of possible variants in the so-called (λ, α) "phase space" (Schwartz *et al.* 1997b), which allows us to simulate about 85 percent of systems with three to seven plain vowel qualities, which is about 65 percent of the UPSID$_{451}$ systems (Boë *et al.* 2002). We illustrate such a "phase space" in Figure 8.3, showing that for an

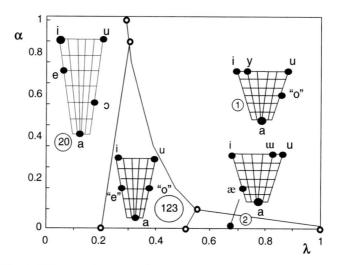

FIGURE 8.3. The DFT five-vowel-systems phase space. The λ-parameter controls the F′2 vs. F1 stretching. Notice how increasing λ leads to adding one vowel between [i] and [u]. The α parameter controls focalization. Notice how increasing α enables incorporation of [y] into the system. The phase space is divided into (α, λ) regions for which a specific system is preferred (i.e. has a lower energy in the DFT framework). All the predicted systems do occur in UPSID$_{451}$ (their number of occurrences is inserted near each system, inside a circle). The preferred system in UPSID$_{451}$ is /i e a o u/ (123 occurrences in UPSID$_{451}$), which is predicted for a λ value around 0.3.

appropriate value of λ around 0.3, the best /i e a o u/ system, present in 123 of the 451 languages of the UPSID$_{451}$ database, is in fact selected. Other simulations allowed us to determine that α should be set to around 0.3 to account for the existence of /y/ in about 8 percent of vowel systems. Unfortunately, though the existence of focalization now seems well established by various experiments, there is no precise evaluation of the α value, apart from the present estimation derived from data fitting. This will be a challenge for future experiments.

8.4 LINKING DFT AND MUAF IN THE PERCEPTION-FOR-ACTION-CONTROL THEORY

8.4.1 Percepts and controls

The description of universals in vowel and consonant systems clearly points to a theoretical difficulty. Sound systems in language inventories seem to exploit both structural and local costs in the perceptual domain (i.e. dispersion and focalization) and a combination principle, which in some sense escapes dispersion and replaces it by some kind of phonological feature economy (Clements 2003*a*, *b*). How can we account for this?

It is tempting to assume that MUAF is based on maximal use of available controls rather than on features, in the sense that once a new articulatory control of the vocal tract has been discovered (e.g. control of the velum for nasals vs. oral stops, or control of the glottis for voiced vs. unvoiced consonants), systems are driven systematically to combine it with other available controls. This is in fact what Lindblom (1998) proposed in his "lexical recalibration" model, according to which speech units are considered both as sounds that should be easy to distinguish (i.e. dispersion) and as gestures that should be easy to learn in the course of development. Learnability would induce a maximum use of available controls, since a system with fewer controls would be preferred over a system with more controls, which should be more difficult to learn. This would lead to a preference for /i a u/ rather than, /e œ o/, for instance (because of dispersion) or /i aː ũ/ (because of learnability). The key question here is to understand better how to combine the concepts of dispersion and available control.

8.4.2 The Perception-for-Action-Control Theory

The Perception-for-Action-Control Theory (PACT) goes one step further in the sensori-motor route. There is a long history of debate between auditory theories (e.g. Massaro 1987; Nearey 1997) and motor theories (A. M. Liberman and Mattingly 1985; Fowler and Rosenblum 1991) of speech perception. Simplifying somewhat, auditory theories consider that speech perception works without action, that is, without incorporating any knowledge about the way sounds are produced by the articulatory system. On the other hand, motor theories consider that the objects of speech perception are gestures and not sounds. Hence in some sense motor theories consider speech perception without audition (this is most clearly expressed in the "speech is special" view, according to which audition does not intervene *per se* in the processing of speech gestures: see Whalen and Liberman 1987; Whalen *et al.* 2006).

Our view is that speech perception is shaped both by auditory processing and motor knowledge (Schwartz *et al.* 2002). PACT assumes that speech perception not only allows listeners to follow the vocalizations of their conversation partner in order to understand then, but also to imitate and learn. In other words, perception allows listeners to specify the control of their future actions as a speaker. There is in this view an integrated process, combining perceptual shaping together with an inversion mechanism, allowing the listener to recover articulatory control in relation to his or her understanding of the perceptual goal. This process is different from both a pure "auditory" and a pure "motor" theory of speech perception. It integrates perceptual processing and articulatory knowledge (possibly in a computational "speech robotics" framework; see Abry and Badin 1996; Serkhane *et al.* 2005). To illustrate this better, let us examine two examples from the patterning of vowel systems.

First, assuming that the Motor Theory of Speech Perception is correct, what would be the possible predictions in terms of oral vowel systems in human languages? There are basically three degrees of freedom for producing oral vowels: height, front-back position, and rounding. This results in a 3-D articulatory space, illustrated in Fig. 8.4a (with a shrinking of the space for open configurations, for which the front–back and rounding dimensions play a less important role). What would be the best three-vowel system in this space? The system /i a u/ is a very good choice, in terms of articulatory dispersion, and it is compatible with the UPSID$_{451}$ data. However, [y a ɯ] should be as

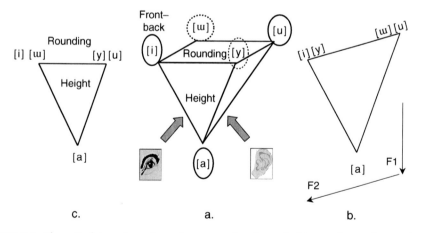

c.   a.   b.

FIGURE 8.4. The articulatory three-dimension space of oral vowels (a), together with its auditory (b) and visual (c) projections.

good a choice. It combines articulatory features differently, but the difference cannot be assessed in articulatory terms. However, this second system never appears in human languages. The reason for this is clearly auditory. Auditory perception is a kind of lateral projection of this 3-D space, in a 2-D (F1, F2) space (Fig. 8.4b) in which [i u] is of course much better (in terms of dispersion) than [y ɯ]. Note that vision (lipreading) can also be incorporated in this schema (Fig. 8.4c). It provides a view from the front, where only height and rounding emerge while the front–back dimension is lost (Robert-Ribes *et al.* 1998), hence [i u] and [y ɯ] are equivalent in this projection. Altogether, the prevalence of /i a u/ and the absence of /y a ɯ/ clearly shows that gestures are shaped by perception.

On the other hand, there are many examples showing that articulatory knowledge seems to intervene in speech perception (e.g. Fowler 1986; A. M. Liberman and Whalen 2000). Let us take the example of vowel reduction. It has long been claimed that listeners are able to recover targets from coarticulated speech and particularly from reduced speech (e.g. Lindblom 1963). Some work from our lab has shown that a stable articulatory target [a] can be recovered by acoustic-to-articulatory inversion, in spite of acoustic variability due to reduction in an [iai] sequence (Lœvenbruck and Perrier 1997). In this vein, there is a very clear case, provided by the coarticulated /u/ in a fronting context, for example, in French *doute* "doubt" /dut/, which becomes acoustically close to a front [y] because of coarticulation. However, it is striking that though most languages contain sequences such as /C_1uC_2/ where C_1 and C_2 are two coronal consonants, /y/ exists in fewer than 10 percent of the languages (see Section 8.2). This shows that listeners are able to recover speaker's intentions, hence the need for introducing "procedural knowledge" (Viviani and Stucchi 1992) about speech production in the course of speech perception.

To summarize, the objects of speech perception for PACT are multi-sensory percepts regularized by knowledge of speech gestures, or speech gestures shaped by perceptual processes. This view has gained some support from recent transcranial magnetic stimulation (TMS) data showing that listening to coronals specifically modulates the excitability of neurons driving the tongue (Fadiga *et al.* 2002), while listening to or looking at labials specifically modulates the excitability of neurons driving the lips (Watkins *et al.* 2003). More generally, the recent literature on mirror neurons and on a "perceptual action understanding system" (e.g. Rizzolati and Arbib 1998) adds a strong neuro-anatomical background to PACT. A plausible cortical circuit for PACT is provided by the "dorsal route" (Hickok and Poeppel 2000), connecting perceptual processes in the temporal region (Superior Temporal Sulcus) with action understanding in the frontal lobe (including Broca's area and motor and premotor areas) passing by parietal regions matching sensory and motor representations (see e.g. Sato *et al.* 2004). In the framework of the current paper, the advantage of PACT is that it intrinsically combines perceptual distinctiveness (modeled in the DFT) with theories of the control of speech gestures, including a number of cognitive aspects about their development and neuro-anatomy.

8.4.3 Vowel and consonant systems resulting from unfolding actions quantally shaped by perception

Since sound systems in language inventories are conceived by PACT as speech gestures shaped by perceptual processing (auditory and visual), we need to know how speech gestures are produced, step-by-step, in a phylogenetically and developmentally plausible scenario.

A central piece here is provided by the Frame/Content theory (hereafter FC theory) developed by MacNeilage and Davis (MacNeilage and Davis 1990a, b, 1993; MacNeilage 1998), which includes ontogenetic, phylogenetic, and neuroanatomical components. FC theory claims that speech production begins with babbling with phonation associated with jaw cycles and no other articulator being controlled online apart from vocal tract pre-settings, which are kept stable throughout the jaw cycles. Besides their alimentary function, jaw cycles would induce alternation of closing and opening patterns (*closants* and *vocants*) and constitute the *frame* of speech. The segmental speech *content* (independent control of consonants and vowels inside the frame) would then progressively emerge from the development of the central and peripheral motor control of the other articulators. Hence, the FC theory provides a natural unfolding sequence of speech gestures. Furthermore, the perceptual shaping of jaw movements is strongly nonlinear. Indeed, jaw closing results in switching from a laminar to a turbulent airflow, and finally to a complete obstruction with no sound. This is a typical case to which Quantal Theory can be applied extremely efficiently (Fig. 8.5a).

Considering that the division between vowels and consonants continues to be generally accepted in phonetics and phonology (Boë and Durand 2001), the FC theory thus provides a natural developmental and evolutionary pathway towards the birth of consonants and vowels, with the emergence of a consonantal /obstruent/ closed pole provided by syllable onset (and maximal jaw closing) and a vocalic /sonorant/ open pole provided by syllable rhyme (and maximal jaw opening). Consonants and vowels do in fact emerge in the FC theory as different objects which occupy different "slots" in the jaw cycle and hence also in the mental representations of language, as displayed in a number of psycholinguistic behaviors (MacNeilage 1998; Levelt 1989). Perceptually, they also correspond to different representation spaces, for instance, formant onset values or burst spectral characteristics after the vocal tract closure for plosives; friction noise for fricatives; harmonic spectrum or formants for vowels (Fig. 8.5). In addition, experimental data suggest that they are indeed processed as separate perceptual streams (Fowler 1986; Fowler and Smith 1986).

8.4.4 [b]–[d]–[g] as a universal triangle as acoustically optimal as [i]–[a]–[u]

From the basic action generator provided by jaw cycles producing frames in the FC theory, the next step is the progressive mastery of vocal-tract shaping. This mastery is

a.

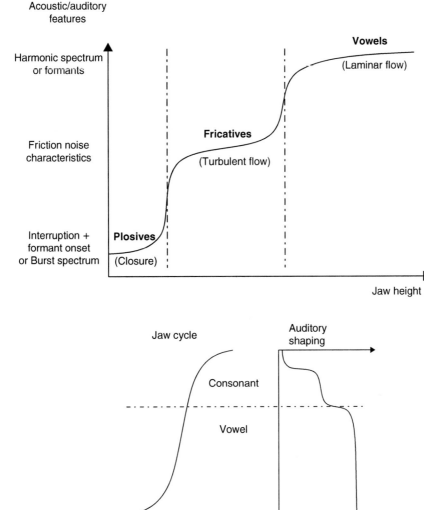

FIGURE 8.5. The articulatory-to-acoustic/auditory quantal transformation along jaw height (a) When jaw position varies from low to high, the acoustic/auditory features change suddenly around two boundary values, separating plosives from fricatives and fricatives from vowels. This is a typically quantal relationship in the sense of Stevens (1972, 1989) (see text). (b) The consequence is that inside jaw cycles, there is a natural division between a consonantal pole for high jaw positions and a vocalic pole for low jaw positions.

developed independently for the control of contacts in plosives and the control of the global tract shape for vowels (discarding fricatives in the discussion to follow). This is the probable sequence of the acquisition of control in speech development (Abry *et al.* forthcoming), and where perceptual shaping comes into play; it should allow us to understand how languages select and combine individual articulators for controlling the vocal tract shape in a perceptually efficient way. In mastering the vocal-tract shaping, the DFT is applied separately to vowels and consonants. For vowels, we showed in Section 8.3 how the height, front–back, and lip rounding dimensions were structured by dispersion and focalization. For plosives, it is also possible to propose the same kind of analysis (Abry 2003).

Indeed, it is noticeable that available Haskins's patterns for the Playback synthesizer allowed one to represent—long before locus equations—a triangle of CV transitions (Cooper *et al.* 1952). In a syllable such as /ga/, when moving towards [a]—in an F2–F3 plane—we can take as a starting point the "hub" locus (velar pinch) at about the [g] release, where F2 equals F3 (Fig. 8.6a). From that point on F3 rises and F2 falls. The pattern for [b] shows F2–F3 rising together towards [a], while they are both falling for [d]. Plotting these starting points (plosive release values) on the F2–F3 plane in Figure 8.6b, we obtain a plosive acoustic triangle [b d g] mirroring the famous acoustic F1–F2 vowel triangle [i a u]. In this right triangle of consonantal formant movements, [g] is at the 90 degrees angle, moving to [a], close to the hypotenuse, while [d] and [b] are also converging to [a] along this hypotenuse. Voiced consonants have their F1 motion in common, which is basically of no use in parsing their place, but only their consonantal nature—their rising formant movement—from wall vibrations (180 Hz) to F1 vowel target value.

Of course, the diagrams in Figure 8.6 are schematic plots rather than articulatory simulations, though they can be interpreted clearly in articulatory terms according to

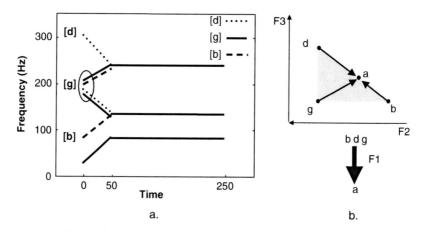

a.   b.

FIGURE 8.6. (a) Schema of VCV transitions for [aba], [aga], and [ada]. All the F1 transitions are the same, and they characterize the transition from vowel to plosive, back to vowel, rather than the plosive's place of articulation. From the consonantal release to the [a] vowel, F2 and F3 change together with similar slopes: both rising for [b], both falling for [d]. [g] is characterized by a convergence of F2–F3 ("hub" locus, circled in the figure) from which F2 decreases and F3 increases towards [a]. (b) This provides a possible "plosive triangle" in the F2–F3 space, while the F1 trajectory is independent of plosive articulation place.

the developmental sequence described earlier. Indeed, plosives are generated in the FC theory by a progressive mastering of contacts inside the vocal tract, produced by upward jaw movements progressively upgraded by the carried articulators (lips and tongue), applied to a basically neutral vocal tract shape. It has long been known that [b], [d], and [g] appear as extrema of F2–F3 configurations in nomograms varying the place of a constriction applied to a neutral tube (see e.g. Fant 1960; Stevens 1998). We provide in Figure 8.7 simplified possible two- and three-tube configurations that correspond rather well to the [b], [d], and [g] configurations that could be generated in the FC theory. Simply closing a neutral tube for labials (Fig. 8.7a); raising and hence flattening the tongue, carried by the jaw, all along the front of the vocal tract towards an [i]-like configuration for [d], typically producing a [djə] as commonly observed in infant babbling (Fig. 8.7b); or for [g] making a constriction connecting a back closed–closed 8 cm long cavity with a half-wavelength resonance at 2180 Hz, and a front closed–open cavity with a fourth-wavelength resonance at the same value, thus

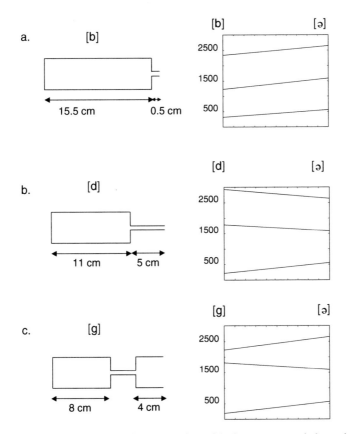

FIGURE 8.7. Simplified geometric configurations for a labial (a), a coronal (b) and a velar (c) constriction applied to a neutral tube (see text). For each configuration, the corresponding formant trajectory towards a 16-cm-long neutral tube is provided on the right.

producing a perfect hub locus with the convergence of F2 and F3 (Fig. 8.7c). Simulations with an articulatory model give more realistic CV patterns (Berrah *et al.* 1995). Therefore, [b], [d], and [g] appear as a possible solution to the perceptual dispersion maximization problem, provided that this problem is raised in a plausible developmental framework in which these three places emerge; they should provide a strong perceptual contrast (in terms of maximal formant transitions towards a neutral or [a] configuration) from basic upward movements of the jaw to which movements of the lips and tongue have been added.

In speech development, F1 is the acoustic/audible movement corresponding to the carrier of speech, the lower jaw, with typical labial [bababa] or coronal [dadada] "frames" (less often velars [gVgV]), following MacNeilage and Davis's (1993) proposal. When carried articulators (lip and tongue) progressively become independent from the jaw, as early as the beginning of the second year, the F2–F3 stream carries information on contact place. Thus the F2–F3 plane is developmentally orthogonal to F1. When coarticulation emerges—typically, after the first year—the [a] vowel in a CV syllable can be produced during the closure phase of the consonant (as evidenced by a case study; see Sussman *et al.* 1999). This means that the vocalic F1 value is coproduced with the intrinsic consonantal F1 closing–opening trajectory. Until four years of age, the mastering of the control of the whole vocal tract for [i] and [u] will be in progress, if they are present in the mother tongue, as is the case for most languages (for the development of timing control for the rounding contrast in high front vowels [i] vs. [y] in French, see Noiray *et al.* 2004). The differentiation process is thus comparable for consonants, in the F2–F3 plane, and for vowels, basically in the F1–F2 plane, and the Dispersion Theory proves efficient for structuring both acoustic planes. Of course, these two orthogonal triangles in the F1–F2–F3 space adjoin each other since they are generated by the acoustic theory of the vocal-tract tube with one or two constrictions (Fig. 8.8). An additional dimension may be used, such as F3 for vowels (e.g. to contrast [i] vs. [y], as in French), or F1 for consonants (contrasting pharyngealized vs. plain segments, as in Arabic).

8.4.5 MUAF emerging from PACT: a computational proposal

In PACT, actions provide the degrees of freedom to combine, and perceptual dispersion and focalization provide the mechanisms driving combination. How could this result in MUAF? The answer is related to the fact that some articulatory degrees of freedom might operate on acoustic dimensions different from those related to another subgroup of articulatory commands. For example, in the case of vowels, lip rounding, and tongue front–back placing basically operate on the same parameters (F2, and to a lesser extent F1 and F3). Adding height, these three articulatory controls interact in the acoustic/auditory (F1–F2–F3 or F1–F'2) space, hence dispersion structures their combination. However, control of the glottis operates on dimensions (e.g. vowel duration or voice quality) other than formant frequencies (though not

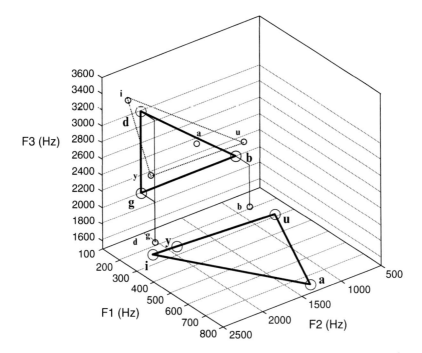

FIGURE 8.8. The three-dimensional vowel/plosive place-space. In bold type, the F1–F2 vowel triangle and the F2–F3 plosive triangle are shown. Circles display focal vowels and maximally distant plosives.

completely unrelated), therefore the combination of place and voice controls may escape dispersion. How then can MUAF (or "feature economy") appear?

A tentative computational answer was proposed a few years ago by Berrah and Laboissière (1997) and Berrah (1998) using a series of simulations of the emergence of a common phonetic code in a society of robots using evolutionary techniques. Robots in this study were simple agents able to produce sustained vowels represented in a perceptual space (including formants, and, possibly, an additional dimension intended to be separable from formants). Each robot had a lexicon composed of a fixed number of randomly initialized items. Pairs of robots, randomly selected, communicated through transactions in which one robot, the speaker, emitted one of its items. The other robot, the listener, related the perceived item to its own repertoire by selecting the nearest item in terms of perceptual distance, moving this item slightly towards the perceived item, and moving all the other items away, in order to avoid further confusions and to maximize perceptual distinction (dispersion). A first series of simulations in a formant space allowed Berrah and Laboissière to reproduce some of the major trends of vowel systems (see also de Boer 2000). In a second series of simulations, Berrah and Laboissière added a "secondary" acoustic dimension (for example, vowel duration). They explored a modified version of their model in which repulsion was not applied simultaneously to all acoustic/auditory parameters, but only to the subset (either formants or secondary dimensions) for which repulsion was the most efficient, that is, most increased the distance between the target item and the competitor items. This means that items were considered as sounds generated by sub-components of an action system selected as perceptually efficient. Typical results are illustrated in Figure 8.9. The right-hand panels represent positions of the items for the whole set of robots on the 3D acoustic space (F1–F2 plus the additional dimension), for a five-vowel (top row), an eight-vowel (middle row) and a ten-vowel system. The left-hand panels display the item projections in the F1–F2 space. It appears that when the number of vowels in the lexicon is small enough (top row), dispersion applies in the F1–F2 space, but the secondary dimension stays unexploited. However, when the number of vowels increases (middle and bottom row), there is an expansion towards the secondary dimension, with a progressive trend for MUAF (partial in the eight-vowel case, and complete in the ten-vowel case). This rather adequately replicates the trends presented in Section 8.2.2, gathered from UPSID vowel inventories. Though

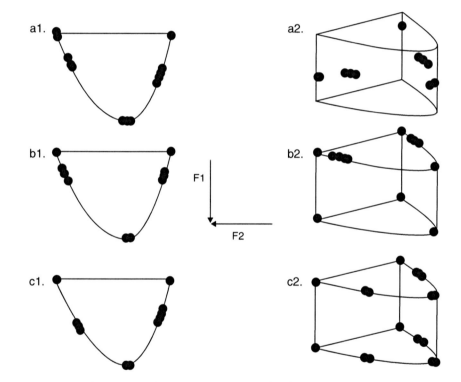

FIGURE 8.9. Vowel-system simulations in a computational evolutionary approach involving a "society of robots" (from Berrah and Laboissière 1997). Robots exchange sounds and adapt their repertoire to their partners, by increasing perceptual distances between items in a 3-D space made of F1–F2 plus an additional secondary parameter (e.g. vowel duration). On the left: projection of the items after convergence in the F1–F2 space. On the right: position of the items after convergence in the 3-D space. From top to bottom: five-, eight-, and ten-vowel systems. Notice how F1–F2 projections are similar in the three rows (due to dispersion), while the use of the third dimension appears only in the second and third row, that is, for a sufficient number of vowels in the system (this simulates MUAF).

preliminary, these simulations show that if a given set of articulatory degrees of freedom is provided, with the possibility of dissociating their acoustic consequences into different sub-spaces leading us to define sub-groups in the set of articulatory controls, PACT may result in both dispersion principles in the specific sub-groups and feature economy. This can lead to either discarding the "secondary" articulatory dimension as in Figure 8.9a or to a partial or systematic combination of the secondary dimension with the primary group as in Figures 8.9b and c.

8.5 "NO INTERFACE BETWEEN PHONOLOGY AND PHONETICS" (J. OHALA 1990C): CONCLUDING REMARKS ABOUT AN INTEGRATED VIEW

Substance-based linguistics is an old dream for phoneticians, and more generally for speech scientists. This was nicely expressed by Lindblom (1984: 78) with his formula "derive language from non-language." We have tried to show that it is now possible to use a theory relying on perceptuo-motor (non-linguistic or pre-linguistic) interactions, a computational framework, and a quantitative methodology inspired by proposals originally formulated by Lindblom and Liljencrants, Stevens, and enriched by J. Ohala, MacNeilage, and Davis for ontogenetical aspects. This provides a number of proposals for predictions of vowel and consonant systems in the PACT framework. This approach has led to further successful predictions concerning, for example, fricative systems (Boë *et al.* 2000) or consonant sequences and the "labial–coronal" effect (Rochet-Capellan and Schwartz 2005a, b). Of course, we do not claim that phonological tendencies in the world's languages can be reduced to explanations formulated solely in terms of linguistic substance. Moreover, a large number of questions remain unsolved or insufficiently developed, and many new simulations will be necessary to provide a completely implemented version of PACT (for example, for extensively simulating vowel and consonant systems). Probably, however, much can be done to anchor a number of seemingly formal regularities, such as MUAF, within perceptuo-motor substance.

Speech is by nature an interdisciplinary area of research, lying at the crossroads of several sensori-motor systems involved in the production and perception of biological communication signals, and of a major human competence, language. The expanding interests and capabilities of phonetics have triggered a reorganization of the scientific connections between phonetic sciences and adjacent disciplines. New interactions are clearly underway between linguistics, cognitive science, and certain sectors of the physical and engineering sciences (Boë 1997). Particularly interesting in this respect is the trend towards "laboratory phonology" which combines experimental phonetics, experimental psychology, and phonological theory (J. Ohala and Jaeger 1986). This approach aims at subjecting hypotheses of phonological organization to the kinds of validation used in the experimental sciences, which has been lacking to date in generative phonology. Phonetic knowledge can thus explore and specify the natural constraints that all phonological theories must respect in order to satisfy concerns of (neuro)physiological plausibility. The integration of phonology into the natural order of things no longer needs to involve a subordinate relationship between the two disciplines.

PART III
Phonetic Variation and Phonological Change

9

Applying Perceptual Methods to the Study of Phonetic Variation and Sound Change

Patrice Speeter Beddor, Anthony Brasher, and Chandan Narayan

Linguists have long recognized phonetic variation as a key factor in sound change (e.g. Paul 1880; Baudouin de Courtenay 1972a), and researchers' ability to study phonetic variation continues to evolve with methodological advances. For example, the use of conversational corpora to study variation in connected speech has opened the door to large-scale investigation of the ways in which variation in speech production mirrors patterns of sound change. At the same time, a comparable large-scale database is not available, nor possible, for speech perception. For natural communicative settings, even if researchers had access to real-time processing information, we could not determine—short of miscommunications—how listeners categorized naturally occur-ring variants independent of their meaningful, real-world, context nor would we know how these variants are discriminated or confused. Indeed, the closest that researchers come to a large-scale naturalistic perceptual database are sound changes themselves—that is, the very patterns we seek to explain. Consequently, systematic investigation of the ways in which perception of phonetic variation mirrors patterns of sound change remains largely within controlled laboratory settings, often using refinements of methods originally designed to answer core questions in speech perception.

It is not surprising that experimental methods developed to address theoretical issues in speech perception can be directly applied to questions about sound change. A main challenge to perceptual theorists over the past 40 or 50 years has been to understand how seemingly highly variable acoustic properties, sometimes spread across long portions of the signal, give rise to relatively constant percepts. Such

The research reported here was supported in part by NSF Grant No. BCS-0118684 to the first author. We thank Kathy Welch for assistance in statistical analysis and Sam Epstein, Sally Thomason, members of the University of Michigan phonetics–phonology research group, and participants in the graduate seminar on phonetic paths to sound change for helpful discussions. We also gratefully acknowledge the helpful comments of John Ohala, Manjari Ohala, Maria-Josep Solé, and an anonymous reviewer on an earlier draft of this paper.

investigations closely parallel the goals of the phonologist or phonetician who seeks to understand the conditions under which listeners are more or less sensitive to phonetic variants that have the potential to lead to sound change.

In this chapter, the phonetic variation under investigation is the structured variability introduced by phonetic context. In laboratory and natural communicative settings, listeners use contextual variation to determine what speakers are saying. Such variation, however lawful, means that not all speaker–listeners in a given speech community arrive at the same phonological grammar for their speech variety, and we are especially interested in the perceptual mechanisms by which such differences might arise. The chapter begins with a highly selective overview of certain basic patterns of experimental findings from speech perception, and their relation to patterns of sound change. The major focus of the paper is to apply a well-established perceptual paradigm to new questions about the role of perception in contextually conditioned sound changes, and to interpret findings emerging from this method in terms of a theoretical account of the phonetic motivation for these changes.

9.1 PERCEPTION OF CONTEXTUAL VARIATION

An issue of central interest to speech perception researchers is to understand how listeners achieve perceptual constancy—for example, how they perceive the same phonological category—across the variations introduced by overlapping articulations for adjacent or nearby sounds. The basic perceptual paradigm for investigating coarticulatory variation is to embed target speech sounds, usually varying along a single acoustic dimension, in different phonetic contexts to determine the effect, if any, of context on target identification or discriminability. Across the wide variety of contexts that have been investigated, listeners' responses under these test conditions are consistent with the interpretation that listeners perceptually reduce or factor out the acoustic effects of a coarticulatory context on the target sound, apparently attributing these effects to their contextual source (e.g. Mann and Repp 1980; Martin and Bunnell 1981; Whalen 1989; Fowler *et al.* 1990; Manuel 1995).

J. Ohala (1981*b*, 1993*a*, 2003) recognized the implications for sound change of perceptual compensation for contextual variation. He argued that, while listeners normally adjust for systematic variation, not adjusting could lead listeners to perceive variation as intrinsic to the target. In that situation, listeners might correctly perceive "how" the target was produced (i.e. the phonetic details), but their linguistic interpretation of the relevant sequence of sounds could differ from what the speaker intended. Consider, for example, what happens when English-speaking listeners judge nasalized vowels (which, predictably, although not exclusively, occur in nasal consonant contexts in English), but the expected flanking nasal consonant is either attenuated or entirely absent. Kawasaki (1986) found that nasal vowels in a nasal consonant context ([NṼN]) sounded quite oral to listeners but, as she lowered the intensity—and hence detectability—of the nasal consonants, listeners were increasingly likely to identify the vowel as nasal. Along similar lines, Beddor and Krakow (1999) found that listeners were accurate in rating acoustically identical nasal vowels as "equally nasal" when both were in non-nasal contexts (e.g. [CṼC]–[Ṽ]), but were much less accurate in rating the same vowels when one, but not the other, was in a nasal context ([NṼN]–[Ṽ]).

Yet the experimental picture is not simply that listeners attribute a phonetic property to its coarticulatory source when the source is detected, and otherwise perceive that property as intrinsic to the target. The more complex outcome that has emerged in recent years is that listeners' perceptual adjustments for contextual variation are partial rather than complete. Here again results for vowel nasalization are illustrative. For example, a second experiment by Beddor and Krakow (1999) tested listeners' judgments of nasal and oral vowels using a discrimination task designed to be a more sensitive perceptual measure than the metalinguistic rating task described above. Listeners' responses were again context-dependent in that judgments were least accurate when one vowel was in a nasal and the other in a non-nasal context; at the same time, discrimination of vowels in such pairings as [NṼN]–[V] was consistently above chance, suggesting that listeners attributed some but not all of the context-dependent variation to a (clearly audible) coarticulatory source. Fowler and Brown (2000) investigated similar types of pairings (e.g. [CṼNə]–[CVCə]) and likewise found that listeners' accuracy and reaction times in a vowel discrimination task indicated that compensation for coarticulatory influences was partial.

The imperfect adjustment of listeners for the acoustic variation introduced by overlapping articulations is not surprising and can be viewed as the normal result of perceptual processing of phonetic properties, whose realization depends on many factors. Yet such contextual "residue"—that is, the acoustic effects of coarticulation not attributed to context—has implications for sound change. On the one hand, having contextual residue on the target sound means that change might take place even when the coarticulatory source is detected. Indeed, this is as expected, since not all assimilatory changes involve loss of the conditioning environment. For example, hearing nasal vowels as nasal even when flanked by a detected nasal consonant could create, for the learner, ambiguity in terms of the primary site of nasalization, Ṽ or N. In this regard, we note that, in some languages with contrastive nasal vowels, these vowels are followed by short epenthetic nasal consonants in certain contexts (e.g. M. Ohala and J. Ohala 1991; Shosted 2006a); thus phonetic [ṼN] sequences may correspond with phonological /Ṽ/ in some languages and /VN/ in others. On the other hand, perceived contextual residue also means that, when the coarticulatory source is *not* detected, the intended utterance might still be correctly perceived because listeners are presumably accustomed to associating the context-dependent properties (in this case, vowel nasalization) with the sporadically undetected source (the nasal consonant).

In the remainder of this chapter we present an experimental approach to contextual variation that recognizes that listeners retain sensitivity to at least some of the fine-grained phonetic effects of a coarticulatory source on the target sound. That listeners have access to phonetic details is a view shared by exemplar-based models of phonology (e.g. Pierrehumbert 2001a; Johnson, in this volume). The view is shared as well by Lindblom *et al.* (1995), although these researchers propose that listeners are only occasionally aware of the unprocessed acoustic form of the input signal, such as when demands on intelligibility are low or when intelligibility is less important than, say, the sociolinguistic information conveyed by phonetic details. In contrast, we see sensitivity to phonetic detail as being systematic, at least for some types of phonetic variation. Our assumption of systematic awareness is based in part on experimental findings such as those just described, and in part on the considerable variation present in the input signal—variation that can render the information contained in such details important to perception. That is, although coarticulatory variation is often viewed as redundant information about segments that are further up or down the speech stream, segments are often deleted in conversational speech. (In one large-scale word corpus of conversational American English, for example, over 20 percent of the words had one or more segments deleted; Johnson 2005a.) Residual phonetic cues from these segments thus might be essential, rather than redundant, information in casual speech.

9.2 INVESTIGATING CONTEXTUAL CO-VARIATION

In our current investigations of the ways that phonetic variation may lead to different phonological grammars and to new lexical forms in a speech variety, we are studying variation in segmental durations, especially context-dependent variation that results in extreme segmental shortening and, at times, deletion of the target segment. It is well known that different stress, phrasal, and phonetic contexts trigger different segmental durations (e.g. Klatt 1976). As discussed below, there is evidence from production that shorter durations of a given segment co-occur with particularly extensive coarticulatory overlap of that segment with surrounding sounds. Our first step has been to further investigate this relation in production (Section 3.1). Our next step has been to explore whether such co-variation in production leads to a comparable trade-off in perception, such that the target segment and the coarticulatory influences of that segment are, to some extent, perceptually equivalent (Section 3.2). We hypothesize that articulatory co-variation and perceptual equivalence between segmental duration and coarticulatory details are important phonetic factors in sound changes in which the segment that conditioned a coarticulated variant is lost while that segment's coarticulatory (now distinctive) effects are retained.

To date, we have studied co-variation between nasal consonant duration and the extent of coarticulatory vowel nasalization, that is, variation possibly relevant to the relatively common sound change VN > Ṽ. However, we expect that the general properties under investigation will hold for conditioned sound changes involving other types of coarticulation. In otherwords, there is no reason to expect that either the coarticulatory or the perceptual mechanisms under investigation here are specific to a given articulator or set of acoustic properties.

9.2.1 Co-variation in production

For some articulatory movements, segmental shortening in certain phonetic contexts is offset in part or in entirety by increased temporal overlap of that movement with one or more flanking segments. Velum lowering for a nasal consonant in English provides clear evidence of this phenomenon. Nasal consonants are shorter before voiceless than before voiced consonants in English, especially when the NC sequence is tautosyllabic, and vowels are correspondingly more nasalized when followed by $NC_{voiceless}$ than by NC_{voiced}. The scatterplots in Figure 9.1 illustrate this relation between segmental duration and extent of coarticulation for the productions of two speakers of American English.[1] The speakers were recorded producing a randomized list of words containing /ɛnC/ sequences, where C was either a voiced or voiceless obstruent (e.g. *spend, spent, bend, bent, dens, dense*). The acoustic measures included duration of the nasal consonant and the temporal extent—that is, the acoustic duration—of vowel nasalization. Acoustic duration of vowel nasalization was assessed by inspecting FFT spectra in 10 ms increments throughout the course of the vowel; nasalization onset was identified as the first spectrum with an identifiable low-frequency nasal formant (which increased in amplitude in subsequent spectra) and/or a broadening of F1 bandwidth accompanied by lowering of F1 amplitude (e.g. Maeda 1993, Stevens 1998). These changes in the FFT spectra were verified against the corresponding wideband spectrogram and the waveform display, with the latter typically showing a decrease in overall vowel amplitude at the onset of vowel nasalization.[2]

As shown in Figure 9.1, Speaker 2's vowels are overall more nasalized than are those of Speaker 1, but both speakers' productions exhibit an inverse relation between the acoustic duration of vowel nasalization and the duration of a following nasal consonant. This inverse relation holds not only across the voiced and voiceless contexts, but also (albeit to a lesser extent) within the voiceless context, where $R^2 \approx 0.2$ for each speaker's $VNC_{voiceless}$ tokens (indicated by squares in Fig. 9.1). Similar patterns of temporal co-variation between a nasal consonant and anticipatory vowel nasalization in English also hold for Malécot's (1960) acoustic measures and Cohn's (1990) aerodynamic data.

Importantly, this pattern of co-variation is not unique to English. In some Italian dialects, for example, nasal consonants are shorter and nasalization extends through

---

[1] The production and perception data reported here belong to a larger set of experiments conducted across languages. See Beddor (forthcoming) for full-scale presentation of the methods and results.

[2] The vowel nasalization measure identifies the point at which acoustically detectable nasalization appears after the initial oral consonant. Comparison of acoustic measures and airflow data (for another group of speakers) is under way.

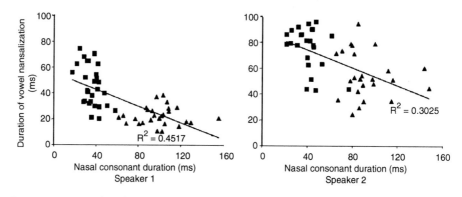

FIGURE 9.1. Scatterplots showing the inverse relation (indicated by the regression line in each plot) between nasal consonant duration and the temporal extent of vowel nasalization for /C(C)εNC/ productions of two American-English speakers in which the coda C was either voiceless (squares) or voiced (triangles). (See text for an explanation of the measure of acoustic vowel nasalization.)

more of the preceding vowel in fricative (e.g. /Vns/) than in stop (/Vnt/, /Vnd/) contexts (Busà 2003 and in this volume); Japanese sequences exhibit a similar relation (Hattori *et al.* 1958). In Thai, which has contrastive vowel length, nasal codas are relatively short after long vowels, but these long vowels are produced with relatively extensive nasalization (i.e. vowel nasalization extends through more of the vowel in V:N than in VN: sequences; Onsuwan 2005). Thus an inverse temporal relation between a nasal coda and its coarticulatory effects holds across various types of coda shortening (or, conversely, lengthening) processes in various languages.

9.2.2 Testing perception of co-variation

Consider, then, the task of a listener conversing with Speakers 1 and 2 (Fig. 9.1), that is, with speakers whose nasal consonants range from quite short (even under laboratory recording conditions) to long and for whom extent of vowel nasalization is likewise highly variable. Presumably the listener–learner must make decisions concerning whether, for these sequences, the speaker intended /εnC/, /εC/, or /ε̃C/; the listener must decide as well if the coda C is voiced or voiceless. English-speaking adult listeners hearing Speaker 1's and 2's productions of these same sequences might be expected to be making decisions between /εnC/ and /εC/ (again, voiced or voiceless), although the extent of vowel nasalization also influences the choices of these more mature listeners, quite possibly in speaker-specific ways.

We are interested in how listeners go about making these decisions. We hypothesize that, in arriving at phonological representations that encompass the wide range of phonetic variants under investigation here, listeners formulate equivalence categories in which the two sites of a lowered velum, N and Ṽ, are perceptually equivalent. In this case, although English-speaking listeners are expected to hear vowel nasalization even in the presence of a nasal consonant, and to use this information in making decisions

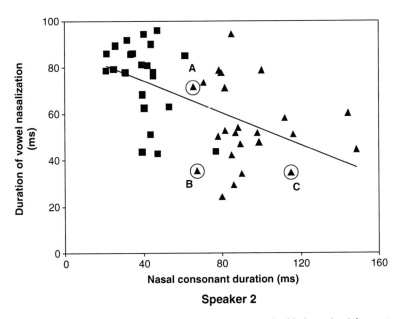

FIGURE 9.2. Scatterplot of productions of Speaker 2 from Fig. 9.1 highlighting *bend* data points with roughly comparable durations of vowel nasalization (B, C), nasal consonant (A, B), and total nasalization across the syllable rhyme (A, C).

about /VNC/, /VC/, and, at least for learners, /ṼC/, they should be relatively insensitive to whether the nasality is primarily on the consonant or on the flanking vowel, possibly formulating the category "nasal" rather than Ṽ or N. Consider, for example, the three data points from Speaker 2 that are circled in Figure 9.2. Under laboratory listening conditions, listeners might be expected to discriminate *bend* tokens B and C, whose nasal consonants differ by 45 ms, as different; the same is expected for *bend* tokens A and B, which differ in more than 35 ms of vowel nasalization. However, if nasalization on the vowel and consonant are heard as perceptually equivalent, then tokens A and C might be heard as similar; despite their relatively large acoustic differences, the total nasalization across the syllable is roughly comparable in these tokens. We hypothesize as well, based on the production data, that the range of variants of Ṽ and N that listeners treat as perceptually equivalent will differ depending on the voicing of the coda consonant. As argued below, such perceptual equivalence might be an important step in the historical loss of a conditioning environment in sound changes such as VN > Ṽ.

9.2.2.1 Methodological approach

We tested for perceptual equivalence between Ṽ and N using a variant of the well-established trading relations paradigm. In this paradigm, two acoustic properties that co-vary for a given phonetic distinction are independently manipulated to determine whether a change in the value for one property can be offset by an opposing change in the other, so that the phonetic percept—measured by identification and / or discrimination tests—remains the same (e.g. Pisoni and Luce 1987). That co-varying acoustic properties perceptually trade with each other is taken as evidence of the coherence among parts of the acoustic signal that "belong" together. In the current work, the duration of /n/ was co-varied with the temporal extent of nasalization on the preceding vowel /ɛ/. To test the hypothesis that post-nasal voicing might influence the expected perceptual trade-off, /ɛ(n)/ sequences were embedded in /b_d/ and /b_t/ contexts.

Waveform-editing techniques were applied to naturally produced utterances to create a nasal consonant continuum and an oral-to-nasalized vowel continuum. The original stimuli, produced by a female American English speaker, were tokens of *bet*, *bed*, and *mend*. The nasal consonant continuum, created from [n] of *mend*, ranged from 0 to 85 ms of [n] murmur and consisted of eight 12–13 ms increments (two glottal pulses each), excised from /n/ onset to offset. To create the vowel nasalization continuum, portions of oral [ɛ] from *bed* were replaced with same-sized portions of nasal [ɛ̃] from *mend* (beginning at vowel offset), yielding a three-step vowel series from oral [ɛ] to 33 percent nasalized (first two-thirds of the vowel from *bed* and final third from *mend*) to 66 percent nasalized (first third from *bed* and final two-thirds from *mend*).[3] Vowel and nasal murmur portions were orthogonally varied and spliced into [b_d] and [b_t] carriers, where the initial [b] (in both carriers) was from *bed*, and the final [d] and [t] were from *bed* and *bet*, respectively. Consistent with coda [t] and [d] in natural speech, whose closures are longer in CVC than in CVNC syllables, we incrementally shortened the oral closure as longer [n] durations were spliced in (such that each 12–13 ms increment of [n] replaced 6–7 ms of [t] or [d] closure).

Thus there were 48 stimuli (eight /n/ durations × three degrees of vowel nasalization × two voicing contexts), with endpoints *bed*, *bend*, *bet*, and *bent*. Stimuli were paired for perceptual testing using a variant of the same-different discrimination task first used by Fitch *et al.* (1980; see also Best *et al.* 1981). For the same pairings, each stimulus was paired with itself. The different pairings were of three types. In all three types, pair members differed in /n/ duration by a constant 37 ms (i.e. three steps along the /n/ continuum). In N-only pairs, /n/ duration was the only difference between pair members; vowel nasalization was held constant (similar to tokens B and C in Fig. 9.2). In the other two types of pairing, the /n/-duration difference was accompanied by a difference in vowel nasalization. For cooperating pairs, the stimulus with the shorter /n/ had *less* vowel nasalization than did the stimulus with the longer /n/ (i.e. pairs were of the type $\tilde{V}_S N_S – \tilde{V}_L N_L$, where $_S$ = slight V nasalization or

---

[3] Because vowels in pre-voiceless contexts are shorter than those in pre-voiced, the original [ɛ] from *bed* was shortened to an intermediate value so that vowel duration would be equally appropriate for [t]-final and [d]-final stimuli; this duration held for all vowels. We note also that, in creating the partially nasalized vowels, the vowel from *mend* rather than *bend* was chosen to ensure that nasalization extended throughout the excised portion. The nasal murmur was extracted from the same stimulus to preserve naturalness.

shorter N duration and $_L$ = longer V nasalization or longer N duration). For conflict-ing pairs, the stimulus with the shorter /n/ had *more* vowel nasalization than did the one with the longer /n/ (i.e. $\tilde{V}_L N_S$–$\tilde{V}_S N_L$; similar to tokens A and C in Fig. 9.2). Table 9.1 summarizes the details of the pairings whose results are reported here.[4] Figure 9.3 gives a spectrographic illustration of one cooperating pair (top panel) and one conflicting pair (bottom) from the series. (Comparable stimuli for the *bent* series are identical except for a (longer) voiceless coda closure and a [t] burst.)

For each of the two voicing contexts (final /t/ and /d/), listeners heard eight randomized repetitions of each different pair, with the order of pair members counterbalanced, and four repetitions of each same pair. Trial presentation was blocked according to final voicing; listeners' task was to determine whether pair members were the same or different.

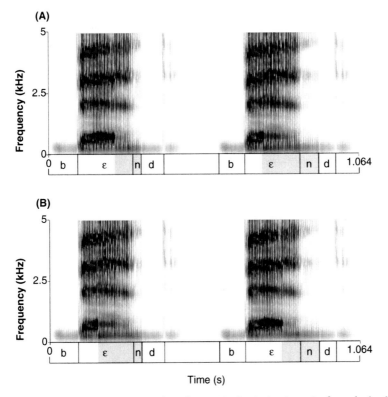

FIGURE 9.3. Illustrative cooperating (A) and conflicting (B) discrimination pairs from the *bend* series. The shaded portion of the transcription grid indicates the nasal (Ṽ and N) portion of each pair member.

---

[4] In the results reported here, all discrimination pairings involved some vowel nasalization (33% or 66%) although the full experimental design included tokens with no vowel nasalization (0%); see Beddor (forthcoming).

TABLE 9.1. Non-identical stimulus pairs for the same-different discrimination task

	N-only $\tilde{V}_S N_S - \tilde{V}_S N_L$	Cooperating $\tilde{V}_S N_S - \tilde{V}_L N_L$	Conflicting $\tilde{V}_L N_S - \tilde{V}_S N_L$
Pair 1	$\tilde{V}_{33\%}N_{0ms} - \tilde{V}_{33\%}N_{37m}$	$\tilde{V}_{33\%}N_{0ms} - \tilde{V}_{66\%}N_{37ms}$	$\tilde{V}_{66\%}N_{0ms} - \tilde{V}_{33\%}N_{37ms}$
Pair 2	$\tilde{V}_{33\%}N_{12ms} - \tilde{V}_{33\%}N_{50m}$	$\tilde{V}_{33\%}N_{12ms} - \tilde{V}_{66\%}N_{50ms}$	$\tilde{V}_{66\%}N_{12ms} - \tilde{V}_{33\%}N_{50ms}$
Pair 3	$\tilde{V}_{33\%}N_{25ms} - \tilde{V}_{33\%}N_{63ms}$	$\tilde{V}_{33\%}N_{25ms} - \tilde{V}_{66\%}N_{63ms}$	$\tilde{V}_{66\%}N_{25ms} - \tilde{V}_{33\%}N_{63ms}$
Pair 4	$\tilde{V}_{33\%}N_{37ms} - \tilde{V}_{33\%}N_{75ms}$	$\tilde{V}_{33\%}N_{37ms} - \tilde{V}_{66\%}N_{75ms}$	$\tilde{V}_{66\%}N_{37ms} - \tilde{V}_{33\%}N_{75ms}$
Pair 5	$\tilde{V}_{33\%}N_{50ms} - \tilde{V}_{33\%}N_{88ms}$	$\tilde{V}_{33\%}N_{50ms} - \tilde{V}_{66\%}N_{88ms}$	$\tilde{V}_{66\%}N_{50ms} - \tilde{V}_{33\%}N_{88ms}$

9.2.2.2 Predictions

As can be determined from Table 9.1, N-only trials have the smallest acoustic difference between pair members of the three trial types, while cooperating and conflicting trials have equally large acoustic differences (33% difference in vowel nasalization and 37–38 ms difference in /n/ duration between pair members). If listeners treat nasalization on the vowel and /n/ as perceptually equivalent, such equivalence should lead to a relatively high proportion of incorrect "same" judgments of pairs whose members are roughly similar in terms of total nasalization across the ṼN sequence. That is, conflicting pairs (illustrated in the bottom panel of Fig. 9.3), despite large acoustic differences between pair members, should be difficult to discriminate—possibly more difficult than the acoustically less distinct N-only pairs. In contrast, cooperating pairs (as in the top panel of Fig. 9.3), whose members have large acoustic differences and large differences in total nasalization, should be correctly judged as different.

The expected influence of coda voicing is that the perceptual judgments of listeners will broadly reflect the distribution of ṼN measures found for the production of VNC_{voiced} and $VNC_{voiceless}$ words, such that vowel nasalization will have a greater influence on judgments in the voiceless (*bent*) than in the voiced (*bend*) context. Specifically, the extreme shortness of N, especially before a voiceless alveolar (shown by our own data, but see also, for example, Kahn 1980), suggests that listeners should be highly sensitive to vowel nasalization in judging *bent*-like stimuli. In this case, it may be that vowel nasalization will override the nasal consonant information, such that discrimination of voiceless conflicting pairs will be similar to that of voiceless cooperating pairs. (In both voiced and voiceless contexts, cooperating pair members should remain relatively easy to judge as different.)

9.2.2.3 Results

Twenty-four native English-speaking listeners participated. The pooled results for each discrimination trial type in which pair members differed, averaged across stimulus pairings (i.e. across the five entries in each column of Table 9.1), are given in Figure 9.4 for final-[d] and final-[t] contexts. Both contexts had a significant main

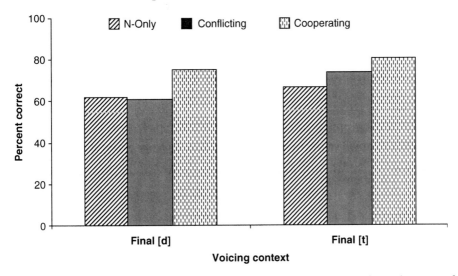

FIGURE 9.4. Pooled responses of 24 listeners to three types of discrimination trial: N-only (extent of vowel nasalization remained constant), conflicting ($\tilde{V}_L N_S - \tilde{V}_S N_L$), and cooperating ($\tilde{V}_S N_S - \tilde{V}_L N_L$).

effect of trial type, as shown by two multivariate repeated measures ANOVAs, one for each voicing context [F(2, 22) = 12.83 for [d] (*bend*) and 13.76 for [t] (*bent*) contexts, $p < .0001$].[5] As expected, for both contexts, discrimination was most accurate for cooperating pairs, whose members differed substantially in total nasalization across the $\tilde{V}N$ sequence ($\tilde{V}_S N_S - \tilde{V}_L N_L$). (It is not surprising that no trial type was highly discriminable across stimulus pairings, which included many within-category judgments for English listeners.) Listeners also showed the expected greater sensitivity to vowel nasalization in the [t] than in the [d] context. That is, as shown by pairwise comparisons, responses for the [d] context to the two trial types in which vowel nasalization varied (conflicting and cooperating) were significantly different ($p < .003$), but this same comparison was not significant for the [t] context ($p > .15$), indicating that listeners were more willing to trade nasalization on the vowel with nasalization on the consonant for the conflicting pairs in the [d] context.

An unexpected outcome was that, in the [d] context, discrimination was not less accurate for the conflicting trials than for the N-only trials. If listeners truly treat nasality on $\tilde{V}$ and N as perceptually equivalent in the conflicting trials, poor discrimination is expected since pair members should sound highly similar, leading to incorrect same responses, but this outcome does not strongly emerge in Figure 9.4. However, closer inspection of the data shows that the pooled results in Figure 9.4 are not representative of the responses of individual listeners, many of whom discriminated the conflicting trials at

---

[5] To control for listener bias, the same analysis was performed with the raw data transformed into d' scores using the independent-observation model from Macmillan and Creelman (1991: 147). The d' scores take into account listeners' performance on identical trials, while the percent correct analysis does not. However, due to listeners' high performance on identical trials, both analyses yielded precisely the same results.

chance level. As shown in Figure 9.5 for the [d] context, two distinct listener groups emerged from this inspection (excluding two respondents who performed at chance level on all trial types): listeners who consistently discriminated the conflicting trials more poorly than the acoustically less distinct N-only trials (left panel), and listeners whose overall accuracy on conflicting trials was similar (within 10%) to that on cooperating trials (right panel). Responses to each stimulus pair are given in order to show that the differences between groups hold across the stimulus set. Moreover, of the ten respondents to the final-[d] stimuli whose responses showed clear evidence of perceptual equivalence between Ṽ and N, only six of these showed the same pattern for the final-[t] stimuli; Figure 9.6 gives these results.

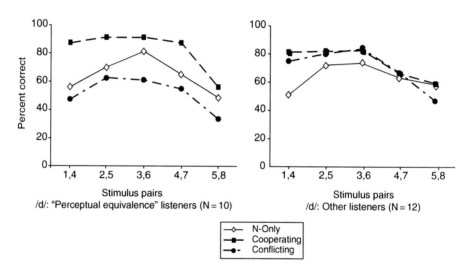

FIGURE 9.5. Responses of two listener groups (see text for explanation) to the /beɛd/–/bɛ̃nd/ stimuli.

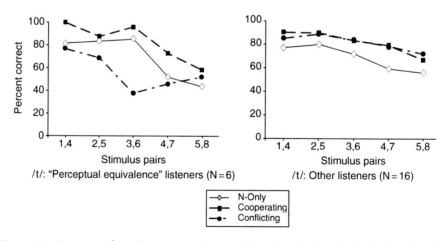

FIGURE 9.6. Responses of two listener groups (see text for explanation) to the /bɛt/–/bɛ̃nt/ stimuli.

Thus the perceptual picture is that, when listeners discriminate stimuli that differ in the acoustic duration of vowel nasalization and the duration of the nasal consonant, they are more likely to treat these two sites of nasality as equivalent when ṼN is followed by a voiced than by a voiceless stop; in the voiceless context, vowel nasalization is the predominant perceptual cue for most listeners. However, hearing Ṽ as the predominant cue when Ṽ and N co-varied in ṼNC$_{voiceless}$ does not mean that listeners are insensitive to N duration for [bɛ̃nt]. For N-only stimuli, listeners were overall as accurate in their judgments in the voiceless as in the voiced context, an outcome that may seem surprising given the shortness of pre-voiceless /n/ in production. However, we attribute this outcome to the fact that nasal murmurs are more likely to be detected when followed by silence (the voiceless closure) than when followed by glottal pulsing (the voiced closure).[6]

At the same time, individual listeners clearly differed in their weightings of these properties. As seen in the results given in Figures 9.5 and 9.6, some listeners heard these properties as perceptually equivalent in both voicing contexts, others did so in the voiced but not the voiceless context; yet others weighed vowel nasalization heavily in both contexts. As would be expected, corresponding across-listener differences emerged in the identification tests conducted with these same listeners on the same (in this case, unpaired) stimuli. In the interest of space, full details of the identification results are not presented here. Instead, Figure 9.7 illustrates the range of identification patterns via the responses of three individual listeners, one from each of the three discrimination categories just described.[7] Listener 1 (top panels), who discriminated conflicting pairs poorly in both voicing contexts (i.e. one of the four listeners who heard nasalization on the vowel and consonant as equivalent; see left panels of Figs. 9.5 and 9.6), in identification systematically traded vowel nasalization and nasal consonant duration for both *bed–bend* and *bet–bent*. For this listener, as vowel nasalization (shown by line types) increased, so did *bent/bend* responses; similarly, as [n] duration (abscissa) increased, so did *bent/bend* responses. Listener 2 (middle panels)—one of the four listeners who poorly discriminated conflicting pairs in the voiced but not voiceless context—traded nasality on the vowel and consonant in identifying *bed–bend*, but in the voiceless condition identified any stimulus that had vowel nasalization as *bent*. Listener 3 (bottom) identified nearly all stimuli—voiced or voiceless—as having /n/ if the vowel was nasalized, and was highly sensitive to vowel nasalization in discrimination pairings (right panel of Figs. 9.5 and 9.6).

---

[6] Malécot (1960) also found evidence of the perceptual importance of vowel nasalization in voiceless contexts but, contrary to our findings, reported that the nasal murmur contributed little to listeners' identifications of words such as *camp* and *can't*. We attribute this difference in the perceptual weight given to pre-voiceless murmurs to stimulus differences in these studies: Malécot's tape-splicing technique included only extremely short "vestigial" murmurs whereas our study included a wider range of N durations (consistent with our production data).

[7] Figure 9.7 shows that ten /n/ murmur durations (stimuli 1–10) were used in the identification experiment, compared to only eight in the same–different discrimination experiment. Identification stimuli 2 and 4, which differed from flanking stimuli by only a single pitch pulse, were omitted from discrimination testing.

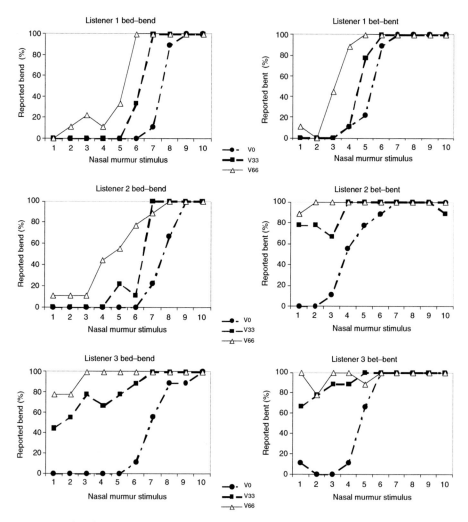

FIGURE 9.7. Identification responses of three listeners to the /bɛd/–/bɛ̃nd/ (left) and /bɛt/–/bɛ̃nt/ (right) stimuli for three degrees of vowel nasalization (oral, 33% nasalized, and 66% nasalized).

9.3 CO-VARIATION IN PRODUCTION AND PERCEPTION: IMPLICATIONS FOR THEORIES OF SOUND CHANGE

The production data (reported here and elsewhere) show that, in VNC sequences, the timing of velum lowering relative to oral closure is systematically variable: less overlap of the lowered velum with the oral closure results in concomitantly greater overlap with the preceding vowel (in other words, the shorter the N, the longer the nasalized portion of the V), and this timing pattern is more likely to occur in VNC$_{voiceless}$ than in VNC$_{voiced}$ sequences.[8] Perception parallels these timing differences. Treiman *et al.* (1995) reported that young children's spellings of English and their responses to phoneme counting tasks indicate that 6–7 year olds sometimes interpret VNC sequences as /ṼC/, and that such interpretations are more common for VNC$_{voiceless}$ than VNC$_{voiced}$ sequences. Our behavioral data show that, in differentiating CVC and CVNC words, some mature listeners are insensitive to the precise timing of velum lowering when differentiating such words, but are highly sensitive to differences in total nasalization across the syllable rhyme (left panels of Figs. 9.5 and 9.6); other listeners are particularly sensitive to differences in vowel nasalization (right panels of Figs. 9.5 and 9.6), especially in pre-voiceless contexts.

We speculate that the production–perception scenario that has emerged here is a factor in the historical change VN > Ṽ. Generally speaking, when coarticulation is phonologized in the transmission from a speaker to a listener or possibly, over time, within a listener, a predictable property of the signal becomes a distinctive one. We propose that, for coarticulatory nasalization, phonologization is facilitated by co-variation in production and equivalence in perception between Ṽ and N. Although the speaker may intend /CVNC/, under equivalence listeners attend less to the segmental source of nasalization and abstract away the feature "nasal" rather than /CVNC/—or /CṼC/. Of course, as we have seen, some listeners do attend to Ṽ as the primary source of nasalization. Clearly we cannot determine whether, at an earlier point in time within the relevant linguistic community, perceptual equivalence of Ṽ and N was an even more prevalent pattern among listeners; phonologized [bɛ̃t] and, to a lesser extent, [bɛ̃d] are arguably already well established for some dialects of American English. Of importance here is that listeners arrive at categorizations of [CṼ(N)C] that do not appear to clearly include Ṽ or N, and a given listener may arrive at context-dependent categorizations of [CṼ(N)C] (e.g. abstracting Ṽ in voiceless but not in voiced contexts).

We have argued that listeners are led to formulate equivalence categories in the face of articulatory co-variation; listeners are sensitive to phonetic detail and arrive at representations that encompass the relevant variation. Of course, sensitivity to phonetic detail depends on the psychoacoustic salience of the details. Perceptual studies that we are currently conducting show that, as duration of vowel nasalization increases in ṼN stimuli, listeners are increasingly unable to detect differences in nasal consonant duration. Specifically, when members of stimulus pairs differed only in N duration (N-only), increasing vowel nasalization in pair members from 25 percent to 75 percent of total vowel duration resulted in a 26 percent decrease (to chance performance) in listeners' discrimination accuracy. Psychoacoustic factors account

---

[8] The timing differences as related to voicing can be understood in terms of a combination of vocal tract aerodynamics and possibly auditory factors. See, for example, J. Ohala and M. Ohala (1993) and Hayes and Stivers (2000) for relevant discussion.

for, or at least contribute to, this outcome, but of interest here is that, even when total nasalization in the syllable rhyme differs, listeners are insensitive to N duration if the preceding vowel is heavily nasalized.

That the production and perception patterns that emerged in this study shed light on the historical change $VN > \tilde{V}$ is supported by the ways in which the phonetic patterns mirror the historical situation in many languages of the world. Our approach predicts that contexts that give rise to the concomitant processes of nasal coda shortening and heavier vowel nasalization should also be those contexts in which phonological nasal vowels are particularly likely to develop historically. At the risk of oversimplifying complex sound changes, broadly speaking, our prediction holds up. Most relevant to the data presented here is that $VN > \tilde{V}$ is more likely to develop when N is followed by a voiceless, as opposed to a voiced, obstruent. For example, Hajek's (1997: 141–2) study of nasalization patterns in Northern Italian dialects showed that six dialects had extensive vowel nasalization and systematic N deletion in $VNC_{voiceless\ stop}$ contexts, but only two of these dialects had the same pattern in $VNC_{voiced\ stop}$ contexts. More generally, Hajek noted that his extensive cross-language study of nasalization showed "no counter-evidence to the claim that the development of distinctive nasalization is predictably affected by the voicing contrast in post-nasal consonants" (1997: 53; see also M. Ohala and J. Ohala 1991; Tuttle 1991; Sampson 1999: 256). Additionally, other phonetic contexts that show a clear inverse relation between the extent of vowel nasalization and nasal consonant duration are also paralleled by the historical data. As discussed in Section 9.2.1, fricative contexts trigger short N durations and temporally extensive vowel nasalization, as shown by phonetic data from Italian and Japanese, and historically $VN > \tilde{V}$ is especially likely to occur in pre-fricative contexts (Foley 1975; Rubach 1977; Tuttle 1991; J. Ohala and Busà 1995; Hajek 1997: 144, Sampson 1999: 182, 253). Similarly, paralleling the phonetic finding from Thai that long vowels are more nasalized than short ones and are followed by short nasal consonants is the historical tendency for long vowels to become distinctively nasalized (Whalen and Beddor 1989; Hombert 1986; Sampson 1999: 340).

To summarize and conclude, our approach to phonetically motivated sound changes takes as its starting point that (a) the coarticulatory variation introduced by phonetic context is lawful and (b) listeners have knowledge of these coarticulatory timing patterns, but their often imperfect adjustments for the consequent acoustic variation mean that listeners remain sensitive to phonetic details. We focused our account on sound changes in which a coarticulatory source is lost over time, but its effects remain on flanking sounds. In such cases, the target gesture is retained, but its coordination relative to other gestures has changed. We hypothesized that we would find evidence of this shifting coordination in production, in terms of increased coarticulatory effects as the duration of the source shortens, and in perception, in terms of overall sensitivity to the acoustic effects of the gesture rather than its precise site. Both hypotheses were upheld, although the responses of some listeners indicated that the predominant cue was the coarticulatory effect rather than the original source.

The convergence of these phonetic patterns with the phonological data leads us to propose that such co-variation in production and perception between coarticulatory source and effect serves as a phonetic path to certain categories of sound changes. We expect that, at a later stage in the evolution of such changes, listener insensitivity to changes in source duration leads to a point at which the original source—which is only variably present in the input—is no longer informative.

10

Interpreting Misperception

Beauty is in the Ear of the Beholder

Juliette Blevins

10.1 INNOCENT MISPERCEPTION

In 1910, forty years after receiving his doctorate in Leipzig, Baudouin de Courtenay (1845–1929) published *O prawach grosowych* ("Phonetic Laws"). In this work Baudouin summarizes much of his life's work in modeling sound patterns and sound change, dissecting phonetic laws into psychological laws (linguistic representations), and laws of the manifestation of linguistic representations by means of organic physical media (implementation of linguistic representations as linguistic forms). It is in this work that Baudouin outlines one of his most significant contributions to the theory and method of phonological analysis: he characterizes misperception as a significant source of sound change, and suggests investigations of the nature of such misperceptions by experimental methods.

I must emphasize the importance of errors in hearing (lapsus auris), when one word is mistaken for another, as a factor of change at any given moment of linguistic intercourse and in the history of language as a social phenomenon. Experimental methods can help to define the types and directions of these errors which depend on the physical conditions, on the sense of hearing of individuals, and on the degree of morphologization and semasiologization of the mobilized articulatory and auditory representations.   (Baudouin 1972b: 267–8)

In the modern era, there is perhaps no single person who has given more substance to Baudouin's insight than John J. Ohala. Ohala has identified recurrent common sound changes with sources in misperception, and has used experimental methods to simulate misperception in the laboratory (e.g. J. Ohala 1981b, 1990a; see also Jonasson 1971). The influence of Ohala's work in this area has been dramatic. In addition to his own numerous publications, there is now a growing literature on sound patterns whose origins are primarily perceptual (e.g. Janson 1983; Beddor *et al.* 1986; Foulkes 1997; Blevins and Garrett 1998, 2004; Guion 1998; Majors 1998; Hume and Johnson

2001b; Plauché 2001). And this work has, in turn, had a dramatic influence on modern phonological theory: within the last decade there has been widespread recognition that certain recurrent sound patterns have phonetic explanations grounded in aspects of speech perception and production. These range from Optimality-Theoretic models (e.g. Steriade 1999, 2001) and generative rule-based accounts (e.g. Hale and Reiss 2000), to functional adaptive approaches (e.g. Lindblom *et al.* 1995), and Evolutionary Phonology (Blevins 2004, 2006), where markedness constraints are eliminated from synchronic grammars.

Nevertheless, there has been some resistance among phonologists to accept two fundamental implications of Ohala's research: (i) that innocent misperception can lead directly to attested recurrent sound patterns; and (ii) that sound change is non-teleological. In this chapter I look at sources of this resistance. In some cases, experimental results are simply ignored. In others, interpretations of perception experiments are not empirically motivated, and fail to recognize lexical effects. A final source of resistance to non-teleological models of sound change involves simplification of the model: "innocent misperception" is argued to be incapable of accounting for a particular phenomenon alone, motivating the implication of markedness effects. This simplification is a serious misinterpretation of Ohala's position and that of many others, where speech perception, speech production, and language use all play important roles in the evolution of sound patterns.

This chapter, then, concerns itself generally with scientific method. More specifically, I review the interpretation of experimental results in the domain of speech perception and their relevance for phonological theory. In phonology, as in many other fields, interpretation of results is often biased by theoretical orientation. Continued constructive dialogue between those carrying out experiments and others who might interpret them can help to identify biases and idealizations within the phonological literature, and can contribute to the common goal of developing plausible and accurate grammatical models.

10.2 VELAR PALATALIZATION: NOT HEARING RESULTS

While coarticulation is the source of many local assimilations, perceptual factors have also been shown to play an important role in sound changes sometimes viewed as assimilatory. One of the most influential papers in this area is J. Ohala (1990*a*), "The phonetics and phonology of aspects of assimilation". In this article, Ohala presents experimental results supporting recurrent asymmetries in the phonology of major place assimilation. In VC_1C_2V sequences, where the medial sequence is heterorganic, listeners misinterpret the sequence as having the place features of C_2 with greater-than-chance frequency when the cluster closure duration is relatively short. This is attributed to the more reliable and robust place cues of the C_2 burst than formant transitions into C_1. Ohala's results are important because they account for two features of sound patterns involving VC_1C_2V sequences: (i) there is a tendency for the consonant sequence to become homorganic; (ii) where major place features are concerned, there is a tendency for assimilation to be regressive. As Ohala (1990*a*) points out, the standard generative account makes neither prediction. There is no explanation for why place, as opposed to, say, manner features assimilate. And there is no account of the directional asymmetry found for major place features.[1]

Another sound pattern often attributed to coarticulation is velar palatalization. Many languages show sound changes or synchronic alternations involving velar palatalization before palatal segments. The most common change of this kind is $^*k > \widehat{tʃ} /$ _{i,j}. Palatalizations of voiced velar stops are less frequent than voiceless ones, and velar palatalization is more common before front high vowels/glides than non-high front vowels. Within the Indo-European family, Old English palatalization of /k, g/ before front vowels and Slavic palatalization of /k, g/ when preceded by front non-low vowels are well documented. Other similar cases are found in the history of Indo-Iranian, Bantu, Chinese, Salish, and Mam (Guion 1998: 20, and references therein). What is remarkable about these velar palatalizations is not only their frequency in the world's languages, but also that the output of the rule is not velar, but coronal. This shift in articulation is problematic for a purely coarticulatory account. Coarticulation predicts fronting of the tongue body, producing $[k^j]$ a palatalized velar, or [c], a pure palatal. But articulatory factors are unable to explain the shift from velar to coronal, which involves a change of articulator: from the tongue body for [k], to the tongue blade for $[\widehat{tʃ}]$.

However, in this case, too, there is evidence that speakers misperceive palatalized velars as coronals with greater-than-chance frequency (Guion 1998). A number of experiments carried out by Guion demonstrate that velar stops before front high vowels are acoustically similar to palatoalveolar affricates and that velar stops in the same contexts are easily confused by listeners with palatoalveolar affricates. An additional finding is that the acoustic and perceptual similarity of voiceless velar stops to palatoalveolars is greater than that for voiced velar stops. In sum, by making reference to perceptual properties of palatalized velars, Guion (1998) is able to explain the high frequency of velar palatalization in the world's languages (in contrast, for example, to labial palatalization), the higher frequency of this change with [k] than [g], the higher frequency of this change with high front vowels than with other vowels, and the shift of articulator from the tongue dorsum to the tongue blade.

In this context, the content of Morris Halle's plenary address "Moving On", given in honor of the 80th anniversary of the founding of the Linguistic Society of America in January 2004, is somewhat surprising. In this lecture, Halle, a founder of modern generative phonology, suggests that synchronic velar palatalizations in a range of

---

[1] Subsequent to this study, Ohala's insights were integrated into phonetically-based Optimality accounts—for example, Steriade (2001).

languages are best accounted for in terms of feature geometry (Halle *et al.* 2000). Front vowels, the triggers of velar palatalization, have both a primary designated articulator, the tongue body (dorsal), and a secondary designated articulator, the tongue blade (coronal). Assimilation expressed as feature spreading accounts for velar palatalization by spreading of the coronal node from a high segment to an adjacent velar.

The question which arises is why Guion's (1998) work is not noted by Halle. Given acoustic similarities between velar stops before front high vowels and palatoalveolar affricates and the confusability of these two consonant types by listeners, should one not rethink a purely articulatory and representational account of the same facts? In this case, as with the regressive major place assimilation, there are fine details which the articulator-feature account does not predict: velar palatalization occurs adjacent to other front vowels, though it is most common with high front vowels; and velar palatalization occurs more often with [k] than [g]. The perceptual account finds further support in context-free shifts from pure palatals to palatoalveolar affricates, like that which occurred in the history of Athabaskan (Krauss 1982). So why are these results ignored?

Interested in the answer to this question, I asked Morris Halle myself, after his plenary address, whether he was aware of Guion's work. He said he had looked at it, but that really, this was all about the results of the articulatory model: sound patterns are the way they are because articulation informs phonological universal feature representations. In general, it seems that results of this sort encroach on territory which generativists are accustomed to viewing as part of the synchronic system. When this happens, there is resistance to the idea of incorporating experimental results. One consequence of this policy is an unrealistic conception of synchronic systems which, in many cases, duplicate explanations in other domains.

10.3 REGRESSIVE PLACE ASSIMILATION IN VNCV: MISHEARING RESULTS

In contrast to Halle's seeming disinterest in the misperception literature, there are recent phonological studies which look in detail at similar experimental results. A case in point is the experimental literature on place assimilation in VCCV sequences referred to earlier. Place assimilation of a nasal stop to a following oral stop is a common sound change, and also reflected by alternations in many of the world's languages. Perception studies, including Fujimura *et al.* (1978) and J. Ohala (1990*a*) show a match between misapprehension and sound change. The CV transition dominates the percept, giving rise to a single homorganic interpretation of place for a medial heterorganic sequence. In Fujimura *et al.*'s experiment, homorganicity correlated with duration of consonantal interlude, while in Ohala's Experiment 1, non-homorganic sequences like [VŋpV], [VnpV] were judged as homorganic 93 percent of the time. Nevertheless, Steriade (2001: 232–3) and Hayes and Steriade

(2004: 26–7) doubt that innocent misapprehension alone is capable of driving system-atic phonological change in nasal place assimilation. What is the source of this doubt?

Steriade (2001) cites the results of Hura *et al.* (1992). In this experiment, where heterorganic VNCV sequences were presented to English speakers (N = [m, n, ŋ] and C = [p, t, k]), nasals showed an error rate of 6.9 percent, significantly higher than the 3 percent error rate for fricatives in the same position. The result of interest to Steriade, however, was that most errors were non-assimilatory. For example, 76.1 percent of all incorrect nasal responses were /n/. If listeners had been responding based on the place of articulation of the following stop, responses would be balanced among the three distinct places of articulation. Steriade takes these results as rejection of the general hypothesis that misperception explains regressive nasal-place assimila-tion. She argues instead that misperception of nasal place in VNCV may be common, but that assimilation (or neutralization to [n]) in this context is the consequence of optimization which characterizes synchronic grammars. She attributes to the speaker the knowledge that the nasal in VNCV is likely to be misperceived. Given this, an "unmarked" nasal is produced instead.

Steriade's interpretation of this particular experiment is surprising, since the authors themselves advise against this conclusion:

it would be a mistake to reject Ohala's hypothesis [of perceptually based assimilation; JB] on the basis of our results, because the VC_1C_2V intervals used in our experiment appear to have been longer than the duration at which perceptual assimilation errors typically occur (Repp 1978; J. Ohala 1990*a*). In other words, our experiment was not designed to provide a clear test of Ohala's hypothesis.   (Hura *et al.* 1992: 69)

Not only were intervocalic consonantal intervals long in this study, but the stimulae were made from a set of nonsense names, with N##C sequences spanning the end of the first name, and the beginning of the last name. In the case of final nasals, the first names were *Shanim*, *Shanin*, and *Shaning*, while the last names were *Perry, Terry,* and *Kerry.* The fact that 76.1 percent of errors in perception of nasals involved hearing *Shanim* or *Shaning* as *Shanin* [ʃanɪn] may be due, not to the default status of /n/ generally, but to very specific facts about the English lexicon, such as the existence of names like *Shannon* and *Sharon*, in the same general phonological neighborhood as the ambiguous tokens, and the fact that disyllabic names with initial stress ending in lax-vowel + nasal sequences are much more likely to end in /n/ than in a non-coronal nasal. Compare *Aaron, Alan, Brian, Brendon, Dustin, Dylan, Evan, Ivan, Jasmine, Karen, Kevin, Kristen, Lauren, Logan, Martin, Megan, Morgan, Stephen,* etc. vs. much less frequent /m/- and /ŋ/-final names like *Adam* or *Henning.*[2]

---

[2] In 1992, the year the Hura *et al.* study was published, the top 100 baby names in the USA. included 31 distinct non-homophonous disyllabic names ending in unstressed /Vn/ (boys: Brandon, Ryan, Justin, Kevin, Steven/Stephen, Dylan, Aaron, Brian/Bryan, Jordan, Christian, Austin, Nathan, Jason, Cameron, Dustin, Evan, Dillon, Devin, Ethan, Logan. Girls': Megan, Lauren, Jasmine, Morgan, Kaitlyn/Caitlin, Erin, Kristen, Kathryn, Jordan, Shannon, Meghan, Kristin), and only two (William, Adam), ending in unstressed vowel + non-coronal nasal (from www.popular-baby-names.org). The bigger the English

In this particular case, reference to synchronic markedness constraints reflects failure to identify and isolate different sources of phonological knowledge: the knowledge of general English phonotactics, and the knowledge of purely contingent patterns involving proper names in the English lexicon.

10.4 VOWEL REDUCTION: AN IMAGINARY PARADOX?

Steriade (2001) is not alone in attributing recurrent sound patterns to teleological constraints invoking enhancement of contrast or minimization of effort. Crosswhite (2001, 2004) looks at vowel reduction in a wide range of languages and argues that there are two distinct types of vowel reduction, with distinct phonetic teleologies. Contrast-enhancing reduction is vowel reduction where non-peripheral vowels within the psycho-acoustic vowel space are avoided in unstressed positions. Since unstressed vowels are more likely to be misperceived than stressed vowels, Crosswhite argues, this type of reduction serves to minimize perceptual confusion by enhancing contrast. A second type of vowel reduction is classified as "prominence reduction". Under this type of reduction, long or otherwise salient vowel qualities are avoided in unstressed syllables.

Crosswhite (2004: 191) claims that this bipartite typology is key to explaining the empirical facts of "reduction paradoxes"—her term for the phenomenon that, cross-linguistically, a particular vowel quality is frequently subject to reduction while at the same time the same vowel quality is frequently the output of reduction.[3] A pair of examples will serve to illustrate the paradox. In Belarusian, unstressed /e, o/ reduce to [a], while unstressed /i, u, a/ undergo no phonemic shifts. In Standard Bulgarian, however, with underlying vowels /i, u, e, o, ə, a/, unstressed /e, o/ raise to [i,u], while unstressed /a/ raises to [ə]. The paradox, Crosswhite suggests, is that [a] is the output of reduction in one language, but the target of reduction in another.

However, nowhere in her work does Crosswhite ask what to many might be an obvious question, namely, Is there a paradox here? Beckman *et al.* (1992) sketch what appears to be a reasonable and well-supported phonetic explanation for prosodically conditioned vowel reduction. On their account:

given-name database, the more skewed ratios are. For example, the top 500 baby names of 2002 show 150 disyllabic names ending in unstressed /Vn/, with only five ending in unstressed V + non-coronal (William, Adam, Liam, Tatum, Malcolm).

Pam Beddor (p.c., 2006) suggests another factor which should be taken into account in comparing Ohala's (1990a) results with those of Hura *et al.* (1992): range of listener choice. Ohala's study offered three choices, two homorganic and one "other", which could have encouraged homorganic responses. This contrasts with the Hura *et al.* study, where listeners were simply asked to identify the first name in each two word sequence. For a different experimental design with assimilation rates intermediate between these two studies, see Beddor and Evans-Romaine (1995).

[3] Of course, it could be that the same phonetic vowel quality is not involved, which would also render the paradox non-existent.

any prosodic effect that increases the gestural overlap, or that decreases the acoustic salience of an overlapped gesture, would increase the likelihood of a listener reinterpreting the coarticulation as an intentional feature of the affected phoneme segment. For example, an unstressed vowel might be very short, so that a greater proportion of its dorsovelar gesture overlaps with the preceding consonant. A listener might misinterpret this resulting coarticulation as an intentional vagueness about the vowel's quality—that is, an underlying full vowel might be replaced with /ə/ (Beckman *et al.* 1992: 48)

Experimental support for this account is found in a study of jaw kinematics, and more general studies of undershoot. As noted by Beckman *et al.* (1992), study of jaw movements in accented vs. unaccented vowels in closed syllables is consistent with an interpretation of "truncation" effects, where a consonantal gesture cuts off the oral gesture for the vowel before the jaw reaches its target. A study of /pɑp/ sequences by Edwards *et al.* (1991) shows that the jaw moves a shorter distance when lowering for shorter unaccented vowels than for longer accented ones, but that the joint kinematic movements are not those associated with a higher target for the unaccented vowels. Beckman *et al.* (1992: 48) also note that Lindblom's (1963) early model of target undershoot as the source of short vowel reduction had good empirical coverage, despite its basis in temporally invariant movements. Taking other facts about gestural organization and timing into account, truncation of closely phased gestures "seems to account for a great deal of vowel reduction synchronically".

Further support for non-teleological models of vowel reduction can be found in the effect of linguistic experience on perceptual similarity and notions of prominence. The paradox suggested by Crosswhite is non-existent if it can be shown that reduced mid vowels /e, o/ can be heard as [a] in one language, while reduced /a/ can be heard as [ə] in another. While I know of no study testing precisely this combination of perception facts, a growing number of studies show that perceptual similarity judgments can reflect language-specific phonetics of one's native language (Bladon and Lindblom 1981; Flege *et al.* 1991; Mielke 2003). More importantly, perhaps, there are significant differences across languages and dialects in the extent to which temporal information is used to distinguish vowel quality. Studies demonstrating that changes in vowel duration give rise to percepts of different qualities include Ainsworth (1972), Mermelstein (1978), Strange (1989), Whalen (1989), and Miller and Grosjean (1997). Finally, there is evidence of cross-speaker differences in the categorization of reduced vowels highlighting difficulties for speakers in distinguishing between acoustic and lexical reduction (van Bergem 1993).

10.5 CONSTRAINTS ON STRONG POSITIONS: MISCONCEPTIONS OF THE MODEL

Another area where diachronic non-teleological explanations have been claimed to be inadequate is in the phonology of prosodic prominence. J. Smith (2004*a*, *b*) argues that the synchronic phonology of prosodically prominent positions is generally incompatible with diachronic phonetic explanations. The two arguments presented in J. Smith (2004*b*) are that (i) the addition of perceptual salience to a strong position is not the kind of sound change that is expected to result from misperception, and (ii) that the relationship between strong positions and salient properties found in augmentation is too abstract to have reliable origins in the acoustic signal.

However, this work simplifies models like Evolutionary Phonology (Blevins 2004), in which phonologization of misperception is just one of multiple mechanisms leading to regular sound change and regular sound patterns. Within Evolutionary Phonology, as in traditional Neogrammarian models, variability along the hyper-to-hypoarticulation continuum provides the exemplar space from which new phonological representations can emerge. The rigid associations in some languages between, for example, a main stress and a heavy syllable (Aguacatec, Yurok) or between a main stress and high tone (Serbo-Croatian, Slave) are expected, given the range of variability in the realization of stress before such patterns are phonologized. For example, variation in syllable duration, pitch contour and amplitude have been observed under emphatic stress (e.g. Dahan and Bernard 1996), and can lead to phonological associations between word stress and distinct types of prominence. As Gordon (2002) demonstrates, a general phonetic feature characterizing most types of "heavy syllable" is greater acoustic energy. Smith's argument, then, is essentially a straw man. No one has claimed that misperception characterizes fortition, or more specifically, that properties associated with phonologically prominent syllables must or typically originate in innocent misperception. Fortition and lenition are processes that occur at opposite ends of the hyper-hypo-articulation continuum, associated with durational expansion and contraction of the utterance as well as more and less forceful articulations respectively.

J. Smith's (2004*b*) second argument for synchronic markedness constraints over historical phonetic modeling of sound patterns involves languages in which roots are stressed. The claim is that since roots have no intrinsic relation to stress, this relationship cannot have evolved through misperception. Again, it is unclear whose claims Smith is contesting. No one, to my knowledge, has ever claimed that root stress is a direct consequence of misperception. Historical studies of the evolution and movement of stress are not numerous, and there seems to be just as many cases of languages where stress shifts between roots and suffixes (e.g. Lithuanian, Japanese), as those mentioned by J. Smith (2004*a*), in which roots are always stressed (e.g. Mbabaram, Tahltan). With respect to this last class, it seems significant that proto-Pama-Nyungan, the ancestral language of Mbabaram, is reconstructed with root-stress. If this is a directly inherited trait, then it is unclear why a synchronic account is necessary for this particular case. Finally, consider the simplest models of grammaticization. A free morpheme becomes a clitic which subsequently becomes an affix: if affixes are fossil clitics, and stress is originally a property of lexemes, then, all else being equal, a pattern of root/stem stress will emerge.

The reductionism found in Smith's arguments is typical of modern generative and post-generative traditions. These approaches show a strong bias to treat recurrent sound patterns as reflections of synchronic markedness or naturalness constraints. But there is continued recognition in the history of phonology, from the Neogrammarians to the school of experimental phonology practised by J. Ohala and others, that there are multiple sources of recurrent sound patterns. Recurrent sound patterns can be the result of direct inheritance among genetically related languages; they can be a consequence of recurrent phonetically motivated sound change, or they can be the result of contact-induced change. Since explanations for the majority of recurrent sound patterns in the world's languages do not require reference to synchronic markedness constraints (Blevins 2004, 2006), the burden of proof lies squarely with those invoking such constraints.[4]

10.6 PHONETIC KNOWLEDGE, PHONOLOGICAL KNOWLEDGE, AND REALISTIC GRAMMARS

Having come to some understanding of sources of resistance in the literature to innocent misperception as the source of regular sound patterns, and to its implication that sound change is non-teleological, we can turn to more constructive questions. Once diachronic phonetic explanation is excised from synchronic phonology, what will grammars look like? What architecture characterizes the description of sounds and sound patterns, and what types of experimental evidence and methods are most likely to shed light on the content of phonological knowledge? Before answering these questions, it will be useful to dispel three common misconceptions of grammatical models in which phonetic explanation is confined primarily to the diachronic component.

One common misconception is that the existence of explanation in the diachronic dimension is only illusory, since language change itself reflects constraints on synchronic grammars. This view is most succinctly stated by Joseph and Janda (1988) and taken by others (e.g. Hume and Johnson 2001b) as a cogent argument for importing phonetic explanations into synchronic grammars. However, when we look closely at the structure of the argument, we can see where it goes wrong:

Diachrony is best viewed as the set of transitions between successive synchronic states, so that language change is necessarily something that always takes place in the present and is therefore governed in every instance by constraints on synchronic grammars.   (Joseph and Janda 1988: 194)

The set of transitions between successive synchronic states is discontinuous, involving an initial state, where the newborn does not have an identifiable grammar of a language, and a final state where the young child or adult does. The claim of models like Evolutionary Phonology is that the majority of regular sound changes have seeds

---

[4] One recent study attempting to provide positive proof of synchronic markedness constraints is Wilson (forthcoming).

in misperception, resolution of ambiguity, and frequency-based choice of "best exemplar" and that these transforms take place in the course of language acquisition (Blevins 2004: 32–44; Blevins 2006).[5] The fact that this acquisition takes place in the present does not mean that change must be governed by constraints on synchronic grammars. On the contrary, if the content of synchronic grammar is what is being discovered in the course of acquisition, then it cannot play a primary role in acquisition. This is the view taken by Lindblom (2000) and Wedel (2004*a*, *b*), for instance, where formal properties of sound patterns are modeled as emergent structures formed in self-organizing ways through the feedback of the perception–production loop in the course of language acquisition.

Two other misconceptions are common regarding localization of phonetic explanation in the diachronic dimension. One is that synchronic systems no longer characterize or incorporate phonetic knowledge.[6] Another is that, with phonetic explanations excised from synchronic grammars, there is nothing left for synchronic systems to characterize. These two misconceptions may stem from the failure to properly distinguish between phonetic and phonological knowledge, explanation and description, or between innate versus learned knowledge of language. Once phonetic explanations are excised from synchronic phonological systems, these systems can describe purely and systematically all and only the phonological knowledge for which speakers show positive evidence, via natural linguistic behavior or experimental data. This phonological knowledge may have a very different character from structuralist, generativist, and optimality conceptions, and explanations for the structure of this knowledge may require deeper understanding of association and categorization strategies of humans more generally (Johnson, this volume). For example, Ernestus and Baayen (2003) show that Dutch speakers interpret neutralized final devoiced segments in Dutch as voiced or voiceless by making use of phonological/phonetic similarity patterns in the lexicon, with new words interpreted in such a way as to conform to these learned patterns. A synchronic grammar of Dutch should be able to characterize knowledge of phonological/phonetic similarity in the sense that it is used by speakers in this particular experiment. In this case, the resulting grammar will be highly descriptive, since word-forms are the basis of analogical generalizations. At the same time, a model of this sort highlights the extent to which knowledge of phonetics and phonology is learned knowledge of language, since the basis of emergent analogical generalizations are learned sound patterns of individual words.

What models of synchronic phonology have this degree of descriptive detail, adopt learning as a primary mechanism, and treat phonetic explanations as primarily

[5] This model accepts that "mature" phonologies change over time, as shown by among others Labov (1994, 2001) and Harrington *et al.* (2000). Indeed, exemplar models (e.g. Pierrehumbert 2001*a*; Johnson, this volume) predict continued change, though at slower rates than initial acquisition transforms, as entrenched system-internal phonological categories have stronger and stronger feedback effects.

[6] I refer here to language-specific phonetic knowledge in the sense of Kingston and Diehl (1994), as well as universal aspects of phonetics, for example, the more sonorous percept of [a] in contrast to [i] implicated in universal sonority scales (cf. Blevins 1995).

historical? One which immediately comes to mind is Stochastic Phonology or Prob-abilistic Phonology (Pierrehumbert 2001b, 2003b; Johnson, this volume). In Stochastic Phonology, phonetic knowledge is represented in detail. Frequencies of sound pat-terns play a crucial role in the acquisition of phonological and phonetic competence, and it is precisely this competence which one attempts to model. At the phonetic level, exemplar theory provides one model of how probability distributions over cognitive maps may be used in speech perception and production (Johnson 1997b, this volume; Pierrehumbert 2001a, 2003b). Modeling of the lexicon is most accurately viewed in terms of stronger and weaker connections between words with more and less shared properties. Finally, in Stochastic Phonology, the actual grammar provides a very concrete tracking of generalizations over the lexicon. The form and content of these generalizations are addressed in work on analogical modeling, from the formal work of Skousen (1989, 1992), and the experimental studies like Ernestus and Baayen (2003), to the computational modeling of Wedel (2004a), for instance. Since, as summarized by Pierrehumbert (2001b), the lexical network and the cognitive map each explain "a large and diverse battery of findings about implicit knowledge of speech, and no viable alternative has been proposed for either concept", it is surpris-ing that more theories of grammar do not take lexical networks and cognitive maps as architectural starting points for the characterization of phonetic and phonological knowledge.

The growing experimental evidence, then, suggests that synchronic phonological grammars are not the domain of phonetic explanation. This is not surprising. Large synchronic systems were proposed as part of an explanation for regular patterns for which no other explanation appeared to be available. But expansive synchronic grammars were a means to an end, not an end in themselves. As compelling phonetic historical explanations for sound patterns have become available, the need to invoke synchronic phonological explanations has receded.

In this chapter I have focused on two of the most important implications of Ohala's research for phonological modeling: that innocent misperception can lead directly to attested recurrent sound patterns; and that sound change is non-teleological. How-ever, the greatest achievement of experimental phonology is not simply being able to account for patterns of sound change, but to provide accounts that make real predictions outside the domain of direct investigation. Validating these predictions reinforces the value of the experimental method, and confirms the discovery of genuine explanations rather than *post facto* descriptions.

11

Coarticulatory Nasalization and Phonological Developments

Data from Italian and English Nasal–Fricative Sequences

M. Grazia Busà

11.1 INTRODUCTION

The relative timing of contiguous oral and nasal articulations in nasal consonant contexts has been shown to vary across languages, with many studies reporting differences in the extent of contextual vowel nasalization and in the coordination of movements at the nasal–oral consonant transition (reviewed by Bell-Berti 1993, Krakow 1993). A particularly challenging pattern of relative timing is called upon in sequences in which a nasal consonant is immediately followed by a fricative. In these sequences, the velum has to move from the extreme low position required for the nasal consonant (an open velopharyngeal port) to the extreme high position required for the fricative (a port that is sealed in order to allow turbulent airflow in the oral tract) (J. Ohala 1975; Bell-Berti 1980; Henderson 1984; Teixeira and Vaz 2001; Rossato 2004). Thus, this change in configuration requires synchronizing the elevation of the soft palate with the release of the oral constriction for the nasal consonant, and the rapid subsequent formation of the constriction for the fricative (J. Ohala 1997b).

Diachronically, sequences in which a nasal consonant is followed by a fricative have been linked to several sound changes, including (1) nasal consonant loss with concomitant nasalization and lengthening of the preceding vowel, and (2) stop epenthesis between the nasal and the fricative. These sound changes may arise due to the phonetic requirements for the production of vowel–nasal–fricative sequences (J. Ohala 1983b, 1993a, b), and may have a perceptual component as well. For example, nasals may be harder to detect before voiceless fricatives than before other consonants because voiceless fricatives are produced with a wider-than-normal glottal opening which, by

I thank Andrea Casotto for writing the .Tcl script and assisting me with the mathematical calculations. I am grateful to Pam Beddor, Maria-Josep Solé, Rena Karkow, and an anonymous reviewer for helpful comments on a previous draft of this chapter.

spreading via coarticulation to the margins of adjacent vowels and causing a lower amplitude and an increased bandwidth of F1, creates an acoustic effect that mimics nasalization. A sound change may occur when listeners factor out nasals actually occurring in this context (J. Ohala and M. Ohala 1993; J. Ohala and Busà 1995).

If both vowel nasalization and stop epenthesis are possible phonological outcomes in vowel–nasal–fricative sequences, are there specific coarticulatory patterns that may have an effect in shaping one or the other outcome? In this study, acoustic and aerodynamic data test the hypothesis that there are specific kinds of coarticulatory patterns in nasal–fricative sequences that may lend themselves to vowel nasalization and/or stop epenthesis. Whether such patterns differ across and within languages is investigated by studying speakers of two varieties of Italian (Northern and Central) as well as speakers of (West Coast) American English. Based on previous studies, reviewed in Section 11.2, the following processes are expected: extensive vowel nasalization in Northern Italian, widespread affrication (stop epenthesis) in Central Italian, and extensive vowel nasalization and not infrequent stop epenthesis in American English.

To test for the generality of the findings, these patterns are investigated across different vowel types in light of the well-known direct relation between velic position and vowel height (e.g. Moll 1962; J. Ohala 1971a; Bell-Berti 1973, 1993; Clumeck 1975; Henderson 1984). Low vowels may provide a better context for vowel nasalization than high vowels because they require a low velic position for their production. However, because high vowels are produced with a narrow tract configuration, small changes in the extent of velic lowering may have large acoustic effects on the spectral envelopes of high vowels, leading to perceptual nasalization (Rochet and Rochet 1991; Bell-Berti 1993; Maeda 1993; Hajek 1997). This study differs from previous cross-linguistic investigations of vowel nasalization and stop epenthesis (e.g. Clumeck 1975; Henderson 1984; Solé 1992; Warner and Weber 2001, 2002) in its focus on linking synchronic nasal coarticulation processes to diachronic change.

11.2 PREVIOUS INVESTIGATIONS OF NASAL-OBSTRUENT SEQUENCES IN ITALIAN AND ENGLISH

Anticipatory vowel nasalization is the result of coarticulatory lowering of the velum for a nasal consonant during a preceding vowel. Anticipatory nasalization occurred extensively in the development of Northern Italian (NI) from Latin, and is still widely attested in NI dialects (Tuttle 1991; Hajek 1997; Sampson 1999). In synchronic standard NI, its frequency of occurrence depends on consonant context, style, and geographical distribution (Mioni and Trumper 1977). Examples are: Latin *rancidu(s)* > Val d'Antrona dialect [rã:^{n}ʃ] ~ [rã:ʃ] "rancid" (from Tuttle 1991); Italian *tanfo* ['taɲfo ~ ['tã:fo] "stink" (from Mioni 2001).

Vowel nasalization in NI seems to be favored by long vowel duration (Hajek 1997, 2003) and by voiceless post-nasal consonants which cause pre-nasal vowels to be as long as those in open syllables (Tuttle 1991). The effect may be greater when the post-nasal consonant is a voiceless fricative (Sampson 1999). Palatographic evidence from NI (Farnetani and Busà 1994) shows that in clusters of a nasal followed by /t/ or /s/, the nasal is assimilated to the following consonant, and is produced with greater contact than an intervocalic nasal. However, before a (voiceless) fricative, the nasal has a fricative-like configuration, which is subject to complete deletion. Busà (2003) also found occurrences of complete nasal consonant loss and longer vowel nasalization before fricatives than stops in NI.

In Central Italian (CI), vowel nasalization has not been thoroughly investigated instrumentally, but reportedly it is not extensive and does not lead to complete nasal consonant loss (Mioni and Trumper 1977). This may be due to different coarticulatory strategies for VNC sequences. Although, phonologically, Italian consonant clusters and geminates are preceded by shorter vowels than singletons are (Bertinetto 1981; Gili Fivela and Zmarich 2005), in NI (unlike CI) the distinction between geminates and singletons is not maintained in casual speech, and vowels tend to be long before phonological geminates and clusters (Renzi 1985; Canepari 1992).

In American English (AE), anticipatory vowel nasalization affects between 80 and 100 percent of the vowel, especially if the vowel occurs before a tautosyllabic nasal (Clumeck 1976; Flege 1988; Solé 1992) and before a voiceless stop (Malécot 1960; J. Ohala 1975; Fujimura 1977; Henderson 1984; Hajek 1997; Beddor *et al.*, this volume). At least for some speakers, this proportion of vowel nasalization is not affected by changes in vowel duration due to post-nasal consonant voicing (Tanowitz and Beddor 1997), or by varying speech rates, showing that in AE vowel nasalization is an intrinsic property of the vowel rather than strictly an effect of coarticulation (Solé 1992).

Stop epenthesis occurs when, in the transition from the nasal to the obstruent, anticipation of velic closure results in denasalization of the final portion of the nasal consonant; when the oral constriction is released it causes a burst at the same place of articulation as the nasal consonant. A sound change occurs when this transitional stop is re-interpreted as a full consonant by the listener (J. Ohala 1997*b*). Examples from Latin and English are, respectively, Latin *sum-p-tus, sum-p-si* < *sumo* "take, spend"; English *glimpse* < O.E. **glimsian*.

In Italian, stop epenthesis occurs in Central (-Southern) Italy, and is part of an affrication process affecting /s/ following /n, r, l/, by which words like *penso* "I think" may be pronounced ['pɛntso] (but ['penso] in the North). This process varies depending on style, age, and geographical location (Tekavčić 1963; Canepari 1992; Giannelli 1997). The existing experimental studies on /s/ affrication in CI (e.g. Endo and Bertinetto 1999; Celata and Kaeppeli 2003; Turchi and Gili Fivela 2004) have focused on the characteristics of the post-nasal consonant rather than on the nasal coarticulation patterns.

In English, epenthetic stops may be produced when the velum is raised before the beginning of the oral constriction for the fricative, as proposed by J. Ohala (e.g. 1997*b*).

They also occur when the velum is raised after the oral release for the fricative, as found by Ali *et al.* (1979). In the latter case, the delayed velum raising causes a delay in the onset of the oral frication, and the nasal occlusion, when released, produces a transient burst at the place of articulation of the nasal.

Stop epenthesis in AE may be the result of language- or dialect-specific rules, as suggested by Fourakis and Port (1986), who found no evidence of epenthesis in South African English. In AE, this process is favored in word-final position and following a stressed vowel, and shows speaker- as well as style-dependent variability (Blankenship 1992; WonHo Yoo and Blankenship 2003).

Because of the reported differences in patterns of vowel nasalization and stop epenthesis in NI, CI, and AE, the three language varieties appear to be good candidates for investigating how nasal coarticulation in vowel-nasal-fricative sequences can condition sound change.

11.3 METHOD

The temporal and dynamic characteristics of the velopharyngeal (VP) opening and closing phases can be appropriately studied by analyzing airflow patterns in speech. Previous findings have shown that there is a positive correlation between oral air emission for the production of oral sounds and the extent of closure of the VP opening, and vice-versa for nasal sounds (Lubker and Moll 1965; Warren *et al.* 1994). Previous research has also successfully used aerodynamic techniques for studying language differences in VP activity in speech (e.g. Cohn 1990; Huffman 1990).

11.3.1 Speech material

The experiment was designed to examine the temporal characteristics of VNF, VNTS, V(F)F, and VTS sequences (where V = vowel, N = nasal, F = voiceless fricative, T = /t/, and S = /s/) in NI, CI, and AE. These sequences were chosen based on the hypothesis that between-group differences in interarticulatory timing factors in VNF sequences would promote either vowel nasalization or stop epenthesis, whereas in VNTS sequences all groups would have a phonological/planned stop.

The words used are listed in Table 11.1. Orthographic "e" and "o" were produced as [e, o] in NI, and as [ɛ, ɔ] in CI. Vowel and consonant durations were measured acoustically. Airflow data were used to study the timing of velopharyngeal opening and closing phases in the sequences, with a focus on airflow patterns at the transitions from V into N and from N into the following consonant. Different pre-nasal vowels were chosen to test the effects of vowel quality.

The words were placed in a carrier sentence (for Italian: *Dico X di nuovo*; for English: *I said X again*) and read five times by each subject. The subjects were three speakers of NI, two of CI (the recordings of a third subject had to be discarded for technical reasons) and three speakers of (West Coast) AE.

TABLE 11.1. Words used in the experiment

Italian				English			
VNF words		VNTS words		VNF words		VNTS words	
Test	Controls	Test	Controls	Test	Controls	Test	Controls
[nf] d'infimo	piffero			[nf] infant	tiffany		
d'enfasi	deficit						
banfi	baffi			Banff	calf		
[ns]		[nts] pinza	pizza	[ns] insect	tea set	[nts]	
penso	spesso			pence	Tess	cents	sets
d'ansa	cassa	danza	tazza	answer	password	pants	pats
[nʃ]				[nʃ] kinship			
consce	cosce			conscious	cautious		

11.3.2 Procedure

Oral and nasal flows were transduced using a two-chamber Glottal Enterprise Rothenberg mask. Simultaneous audio signals were recorded using a high-quality microphone attached to the exterior of the mask. Audio signals were sampled at 11 kHz and airflows at 1375 Hz using the multi-channel data recording and analysis system PCquirer by SciconR&D, Inc. (version 8.9). For each subject, the recording session, including other words not reported in this analysis, lasted about an hour. The participants were allowed short breaks during the recording.

11.3.3 Analysis

The data were first analyzed with PCquirer using simultaneous displays of acoustic waveform, spectrogram, and oral and nasal flow. Four configurations served as criteria to define the onset of vowel nasalization and of the nasal consonant. (1) When the vowel is oral and the nasal is fully articulated, typically the oral flow goes to zero after the vowel, the nasal flow starts rising at the point where the oral flow decreases, and the audio signal shows a reduction in amplitude. On the spectrogram, nasal consonant onset is clearly identifiable at the point where the discontinuities in the signals occur. This is shown in Figure 11.1, right panel. (2) When the vowel is nasalized before a fully articulated nasal consonant, the nasal flow starts during the vowel and rises gradually, the oral flow decreases at the point where the nasal flow begins, and the acoustic signal shows reduced amplitude at the point of onset of nasal flow. The nasal consonant onset is marked by a discontinuity in at least two of the signals (a "bump" in the nasal flow, decrease to zero in the oral flow, and/or low amplitude of the acoustic waveform); the nasal consonant is usually identifiable in the spectrogram. (3) When the vowel is nasalized before a weakly articulated nasal consonant—which typically occurs before a fricative in NI—the vowel's airflow patterns and acoustic waveform are similar to those in (2). However, nasal consonant onset is marked by a sudden increase in nasal flow towards the end of the periodic signal, oral flow that decreases but does not go to zero, and/or lowered amplitude of the acoustic waveform. Spectrographically, this weakly articulated nasal consonant is characterized by voicing in the lower frequencies and frication in the higher frequencies. This configuration is shown in Figure 11.1, left panel. Finally, (4) a fully nasalized vowel shows co-occurrence of nasal flow and reduced oral flow during the periodic signal for the vowel, with the nasal peak occurring at the boundary of the following consonant or during the vowel itself. No nasal consonant is detectable in the acoustic waveform or spectrogram (Fig. 11.1, center).

To perform a quantitative analysis of the airflow patterns, the following steps were taken. The PCquirer data were exported to multiple ASCII files, each containing a VNF/VNTS sequence and relevant time points derived from the acoustic analysis (e.g. beginning of V, beginning of N). Each file was processed using a customized script. Oral and nasal flow signals were low-pass filtered using a fifth-order Butterworth filter with a 40 Hz frequency cutoff. The oral flow was filtered in order to eliminate the high frequency component of the glottal pulse. Because the filter introduces a phase shift, the nasal flow was also filtered to maintain synchronization with respect to the oral flow. The time points derived from the acoustic analysis were then shifted by 13.3 ms, the average phase shift measured by comparing the position of the nasal peaks before and after filtering all the signals.

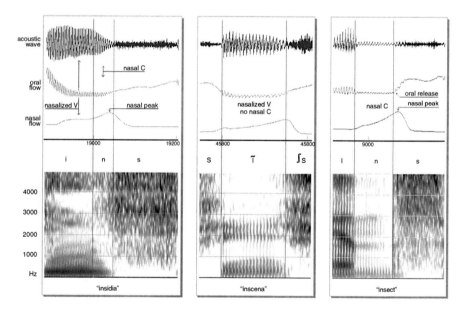

FIGURE 11.1. Acoustic waveform, oral and nasal flow, and spectrogram of the utterances /ins/ (left), /inʃ/ (center), and /ɪns/ (right), showing different production strategies for VNF sequences.

11.3.4 Measures

11.3.4.1 Acoustic analysis

Duration measures were taken of test and control Vs, nasalized portions of pre-nasal Vs, Ns, Fs (both post-nasal and control Fs in VNF and V(F)F sequences respectively), and TSs (both post-nasal and control TS in VNTS and VTS sequences, respectively). Silent periods and bursts of epenthetic or phonological stops were measured with the following consonant.

11.3.4.2 Nasal airflow

The nasal-airflow curve often has an asymptotic shape and there is a slight difference in value at the nasal onset and offset. For this reason, low and high thresholds ($V_{20\%}$ and $V_{80\%}$, respectively) of the nasal flow swing were used to compute the end points of the nasal flow ramps, as shown in Figure 11.2 (bottom). The intersections of the nasal flow with the thresholds were labeled t_{N1}, t_{N2}, t_{N3}, t_{N4}. The "nasal movement" was defined as the interval between t_{N1} and t_{N4}. The peak time of nasal flow was labeled t_{Npeak}. The nasal up-ramp duration was defined as the time from nasal onset to nasal peak ($t_{Npeak} - t_{N1}$), and the nasal down-ramp duration as the time from nasal peak to nasal offset ($t_{N4} - t_{Npeak}$). Following Dotevall *et al.* (2001), across-speaker patterns of decrease of nasal flow were compared using the Maximal Flow Declination Ratio (MFDR), which is defined as the ratio of maximum slope in the down-ramp and the nasal peak value. For the up-ramp, the average rather than the maximum slope was used. The Average Up-ramp Slope was defined as $AUS = (V_{80\%} - V_{20\%})/(t_{N2} - t_{N1})$. To compare across-speaker patterns of increase of nasal flow, in analogy with MFDR, the AUS measure was normalized by dividing it by the nasal peak value, yielding the calculation $AUSR = AUS/V_{Npeak}$. The modeling of the upward nasal movement with just two quantities, namely, up-ramp duration and AUSR, is clearly a first-order approximation and it hides many observable features of the shapes of some up-ramp realizations, like the presence of multiple local maxima. This may be the focus of further studies.

11.3.4.3 Oral airflow

The oral airflow is a more complex curve than the nasal flow. Typically, in a VNF sequence the oral flow is high for V, approaches the baseline for the duration of N, and then increases for F (when the oral cavity opens and the velum closes).

The "oral movement" was approximated with a piecewise linear envelope. The envelope corners were labelled t_{C1} (left corner) and t_{C2} (right corner), as shown in Figure 11.2 (top). The times t_{C1} and t_{C2} approximate, respectively, the time in which the oral constriction comes to its maximum closure and the time in which the oral port starts opening for F.

The envelope was used to compute the time lag from the maximum oral closure to the nasal peak ($t_{Npeak} - t_{C1}$) and the time lag from the nasal peak to the beginning of the oral release for F ($t_{C2} - t_{Npeak}$).

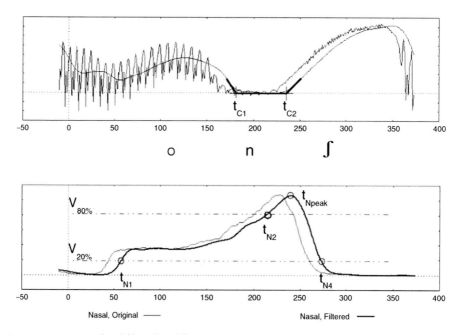

o n ʃ

FIGURE 11.2. Original and filtered oral flow (top) and original and filtered nasal flow (bottom). The filtered flows appear shifted compared to the original. In the top panel, the points t_{C_1} and t_{C_2} are the corners of the envelope used to characterize the times of closure and release of the oral constriction. In the bottom figure, t_{Npeak} is the nasal peak time and t_{N_1}, t_{N_2}, t_{N_4} are the times used in the analysis at which the nasal flow crosses the 20% and 80% thresholds.

11.3.5 Statistical analysis

One-way ANOVAs, having Vowel-Type as a factor, were conducted on the acoustic data for each group of speakers. Moreover, two-way within- and between-group ANOVAs were conducted averaging, by group, all vowels in VNF and in VNTS sequences (factors = Subject/Language and Consonant_Type) to test for the effect of post-nasal consonant context. The dependent variables were: V duration, duration of V nasalization, percentage of V nasalization, N duration, F or TS duration, Control V duration, and Control C. Post-hoc Tukey tests were used to assess which contrasts were significant. Bravais-Pearson measures were used to calculate correlations between variables.

The same statistical tests were used for the aerodynamic data, averaging values across VNF and VNTS contexts. The dependent variables were duration of nasal up-ramp ($t_{Npeak} - t_{N_1}$), Average Up-ramp Slope Ratio of the nasal flow (AUSR), duration of nasal down-ramp ($t_{N_4} - t_{Npeak}$), and Maximal Flow Declination Ratio of nasal flow (MFDR).

One expectation was that longer vowel duration would be associated with longer vowel nasalization and slower nasal flow increase time. Additionally, because NI has been reported to treat VNC sequences as open syllables, NI is expected to show the greatest extent of V nasalization and the fewest occurrences of stop epenthesis. Stop epenthesis should be more frequent where syllabic codas are more strongly coarticulated with the preceding nasal, in other words, in CI and AE.

11.4 RESULTS

11.4.1 Acoustic analysis

Figure 11.1 (left panel) illustrates a typical case in the NI data in which the vowel is heavily nasalized and the nasal consonant is weakly articulated before the following voiceless fricative. In this example, the vowel appears nasalized for most of its duration, as is shown by the co-occurrence of oral and nasal flow during the voiced portion in the acoustic waveform. The "bump" (nasal peak) at the end of the voiced portion is suggestive of a nasal consonant but the fact that the oral flow does not go to zero shows that this sound is characterized by a reduced and incomplete stricture rather than a complete oral closure. In the proximity of the nasal peak, at the point where the stricture is maximal, there are a few milliseconds of low-amplitude voicing. The incomplete closure of the oral cavity causes the anticipation of the frication noise for the post-nasal fricative. Thus, this transitional phase is characterized by simultaneous frication and nasality. This phase is also characterized by considerable intra- and inter-subject variability in terms of the extent and duration of the stricture. As part of this process, cases occur in which the vowel is fully nasalized and there is no nasal murmur, as exemplified in Figure 11.1, center panel, which represents a clear link between coarticulation and sound changes involving nasal consonant loss.

The example in Figure 11.1, right panel, is from AE, but this pattern also occurs in CI. In this example, the release of the oral occlusion for the nasal consonant occurs before the velic closure (nasal peak). Other instances, where the release of the oral closure occurs after the velic closure, acoustically resemble nasal-stop sequences. As the figure shows, at the vowel ending, the oral flow goes to the baseline while the nasal flow starts rising. The vocal cords vibrate throughout the nasal consonant. With the increase in nasal flow, the last portion of the nasal consonant has little acoustic effect, and may appear as a short silent gap, as reported by Ali *et al.* (1979). At the same time, the increase in oral pressure reflects an abrupt change of state in the oral constriction for the following fricative, as shown by the sharp upward movement of the oral flow, which has an acoustic effect similar to a burst. At this point, the oral cavity is not sealed and some frication noise gets into the last portion of the nasal consonant. The waveform shows a short transition between the nasal and the fricative where frication is disrupting the nasal consonant (which explains why this process engenders shorter nasal consonants). During this transition, the VP is still open and turbulence is probably generated at the nostrils. The velum starts raising and is closed after the onset of the fricative. The post-nasal stop may then be cued by the abrupt release of the oral constriction and the preceding acoustic gap, so that listeners may perceive a nasal-stop-fricative sequence.

The results of the acoustic analysis are shown by vowel type, for each group, in Tables 11.2–4. In Table 11.5 the data are averaged by type of post-nasal consonant context. In the tables, p and F values refer to the one-way ANOVAs. The results of the two-way ANOVAs are given in the text. r values indicate the Bravais-Pearson correlation coefficient for the indicated comparison.

The most interesting results can be summarized as follows. Tables 11.2–4 show that, as expected, for all speaker groups there is an effect of vowel quality on vowel duration and duration of vowel nasalization. In NI and AE, lower vowels are significantly longer and more nasalized in both VNF and VNTS contexts. In CI, this effect is significant in VNTS contexts. For all groups, there is a correlation between vowel duration and vowel nasalization in both VNF and VNTS contexts (particularly strong in VNTS contexts for AE), such that the longer the vowel the longer the nasalized portion, as shown in the columns relating to percentage of nasalization.

In addition, in NI and CI, vowels are significantly longer and have a longer nasalized portion in VNF than in VNTS sequences (for NI, $F(1, 108) = 25.0$ and 20.9, respectively, $p < .001$; for CI, $F(1, 73) = 9.0$, $p < .001$ and 6.3, $p < .01$, respectively). Also for both varieties of Italian, N duration is significantly shorter in VNF than in VNTS sequences (for NI, $F(1, 108) = 36.5$, $p < .001$ and for CI, $F(1, 73) = 19.0$, $p < .001$). As shown by the r correlation coefficients for N duration and V nasalization in Tables 11.2–3, in NI, N duration is inversely, though non-significantly, related to V nasalization, whereas in CI, there is a tendency for N duration to be directly related to V nasalization. In NI, post-nasal consonants are significantly longer in VNF sequences than in VNTS sequences ($F(1, 108) = 11.7$, $p < .001$). In contrast to the Italian patterns, AE vowels are significantly longer ($F(1, 128) = 6.3$, $p < .01$) and have a longer nasalized portion ($F(1, 128) = 22.7$, $p < .001$) in VNTS than in VNF sequences. N duration is significantly shorter in VNTS than in VNF sequences ($F(1, 128) = 22.6$, $p < .001$), and is inversely related to vowel duration and duration of vowel nasalization, as shown by the r coefficients values in Table 11.4. AE post-nasal consonants are longer in VNTS than in VNF sequences ($F(1, 128) = 11.2$, $p < .001$).

The duration of vowel nasalization ranges from 59 to 82 percent in VNF sequences and from 43 to 64 percent in VNTS sequences in NI, from 51 to 64 percent in VNF sequences and 43 to 64 percent in VNTS sequences in CI, and from 54 to 71 percent in VNF sequences and from 69 to 92 percent in VNTS sequences in AE.

The data in Table 11.5 show that NI has the longest vowels and shortest oral consonants (F, TS) in both VNF and VNTS sequences. As compared to NI, CI has significantly shorter and less nasalized vowels in VNF sequences but longer oral consonants. This confirms the prediction that in these two varieties of Italian the duration of vowel nasalization is related to differences in segmental durations in VNC sequences. Compared to NI and CI, AE nasal consonants are significantly longer in the VNF context, and significantly shorter in the VNTS context. Finally, while vowel

TABLE 11.2. Northern Italians. Effects by Vowel type in _NF (top) and in _NTS (bottom) sequences

VNF

V	n	Duration of V		Duration of nasalization		Percent. of nasalization		Duration of N		Duration of C		Duration of control V		Duration of control C	
		M	SD	M	SD	M	SD	M	SD	M	SD	M	SD	M	SD
[i]	9	139	21	90	33	63	20	42	25	116	38	94	13	139	21
[e]	30	153	23	91	32	59	16	54	20	98	20	129	28	127	33
[o]	15	171	32	119	44	69	22	50	16	114	20	163	26	129	19
[a]	30	178	27	145	31	82	15	62	25	106	19	155	30	164	25
Prob. $F_{(3, 80)}$		$p < .001$ $F = 7.62$		$p < .001$ $F = 13.85$		$p < .001$ $F = 9.17$		n.s.		n.s.		$p < .001$ $F = 16.65$		$p < .001$ $F = 10.44$	
Dur.V				$r = .70$				$r = .04$		$r = .34$				$r = .36$	
Dur.NasV								$r = -.20$		$r = .17$					
Dur.N										$r = .28$					

VNTS

V	n	Duration of V		Duration of nasalization		Percent. of nasalization		Duration of N		Duration of C		Duration of control V		Duration of control C	
		M	SD	M	SD	M	SD	M	SD	M	SD	M	SD	M	SD
[i]	15	103	20	44	16	43	16	79	15	99	22	80	10	164	23
[a]	15	165	40	106	50	64	24	76	10	90	11	133	32	155	15
Prob. $F_{(1, 28)}$		$p < .001$ $F = 28.83$		$p < .001$ $F = 20.94$		$p < .01$ $F = 7.95$		n.s.		n.s.		$p < .001$ $F = 38.99$		n.s.	
Dur.V				$r = .69$				$r = .02$		$r = .04$				$r = -.16$	
Dur.NasV								$r = -.16$		$r = .02$					
Dur.N										$r = .12$					

Note: Durations in ms. n = number of tokens.

TABLE 11.3. Central Italians. Effects by Vowel type in _NF (top) and in _NTS (bottom) sequences

VNF

V	n	Duration of V		Duration of nasalization		Percent. of nasalization		Duration of N		Duration of C		Duration of control V		Duration of control C	
		M	SD	M	SD	M	SD	M	SD	M	SD	M	SD	M	SD
[i]	10	112	22	59	23	51	13	50	22	139	10	80	9	162	23
[ε]	20	113	29	60	29	51	16	66	19	122	20	97	22	132	53
[ɔ]	10	111	19	61	32	55	24	63	33	152	20	107	17	184	45
[a]	20	129	31	84	29	64	15	61	20	142	19	113	26	186	29
Prob. F(3, 56)		n.s.		$p < .04$ F = 2.90		n.s.		n.s.		$p < .001$ F = 7.49		$p < .001$ F = 5.88		$p < .001$ F = 6.93	
Dur.V				r = .74				r = .54		r = .18				r = .29	
Dur.NasV								r = .32		r = .27					
Dur.N										r = .27					

VNTS

V	n	Duration of V		Duration of nasalization		Percent. of nasalization		Duration of N		Duration of C		Duration of control V		Duration of control C	
		M	SD	M	SD	M	SD	M	SD	M	SD	M	SD	M	SD
[i]	10	82	25	27	21	31	16	77	24	139	23	63	14	188	36
[a]	7	142	32	88	22	63	11	80	20	118	18	110	18	201	30
Prob. F(1, 15)		$p < .001$ F = 18.80		$p < .001$ F = 34.26		$p < .001$ F = 21.71		n.s.		n.s.		$p < .001$ F = 37.58		n.s.	
Dur.V				r = .89				r = .63		r = −.01				r = .19	
Dur.NasV								r = .40		r = .03					
Dur.N										r = .44					

Note: Durations in ms. *n* = number of tokens.

TABLE 11.4. American English. Effects by Vowel type in _NF (top) and in _NTS (bottom) sequences

VNF

V	n	Duration of V		Duration of nasalization		Percent. of nasalization		Duration of N		Duration of C		Duration of control V		Duration of control C	
		M	SD	M	SD	M	SD	M	SD	M	SD	M	SD	M	SD
[ɪ]	45	66	20	36	25	54	35	88	13	108	15	28	28	115	21
[ɛ]	15	77	14	36	32	54	41	64	10	142	33	99	19	130	28
[ɒ]	15	104	21	77	54	67	45	51	8	106	8	138	17	106	8
[æ]	29	157	20	110	24	71	17	51	15	122	21	155	24	116	22
Prob. $F_{(3, 100)}$		$p < .001$ $F = 134.36$		$p < .001$ $F = 35.36$		n.s.		$p < .001$ $F = 62.21$		$p < .001$ $F = 12.83$		$p < .001$ $F = 157.78$		$p < .02$ $F = 3.12$	
Dur.V				$r = .79$				$r = -.59$		$r = .13$				$r = .08$	
Dur.NasV								$r = -.52$		$r = .08$					
Dur.N										$r = -.23$					

VNTS

V	n	Duration of V		Duration of nasalization		Percent. of nasalization		Duration of N		Duration of C		Duration of control V		Duration of control C	
		M	SD	M	SD	M	SD	M	SD	M	SD	M	SD	M	SD
[ɛ]	15	98	11	68	22	69	21	59	15	138	36	99	18	178	12
[æ]	15	139	12	138	12	92		38	19	134	52	119	34	157	57
Prob. $F_{(1, 28)}$		$p < .001$ $F = 102.03$		$p < .001$ $F = 114.56$		$p < .01$ $F = 7.8$		$p < .003$ $F = 10.99$		n.s.		n.s.		n.s.	
Dur.V				$r = .92$				$r = -.53$		$r = .15$				$r = .07$	
Dur.NasV								$r = -.55$		$r = .13$					
Dur.N										$r = -.24$					

Note: Durations in ms. n = number of tokens.

TABLE 11.5. Averaged values, by language group, in _NF (top) and in _NTS (bottom) sequences

VNF

L	n	Duration of V		Duration of nasalization		Percent. of nasalization		Duration of N		Duration of C		Duration of control V		Duration of control C	
		M	SD	M	SD	M	SD	M	SD	M	SD	M	SD	M	SD
NI	84	164*	29	115*	42	69*	20	55	23	106*	23	141*	23	142*	21
CI	60	118*	28	68	30	56	17	61	23	136*	23	101	19	163*	28
AE	104	98*	43	63	45	61	34	69*	21	117*	21	101	17	116*	8
Prob. F(2, 245)		$p < .001$ F = 80.16		$p < .001$ F = 41.89		$p < .01$ F = 4.69		$p < .001$ F = 9.06		$p < .001$ F = 33.1		$p < .001$ F** = 21.89		$p < .001$ F = 42.65	

Note: Durations in ms. n = number of tokens.
*The contrast is significant (Tukey post-hoc).
**$F_{(2, 229)}$.

VNTS

L	n	Duration of V		Duration of nasalization		Percent. of nasalization		Duration of N		Duration of C		Duration of control V		Duration of control C	
		M	SD	M	SD	M	SD	M	SD	M	SD	M	SD	M	SD
NI	30	134*	44	75	48	54	23	77	12	94*	18	107	36	159	20
CI	17	107	41	52	37	44	22	79	22	130	23	83*	28	194*	33
AE	30	119	24	103*	40	81*	26	49*	20	136	44	109	28	168	42
Prob. F(2, 74)		$p < .04$ F = 3.33		$p < .001$ F = 8.04		$p < .001$ F = 15.77		$p < .001$ F = 24.75		$p < .001$ F = 14.53		$p < .01$ F = 4.95		$p < .003$ F = 6.15	

Note: Durations in ms. n = number of tokens.
*The contrast is significant (Tukey post-hoc).

nasalization is significantly longer in NI (the same tendency is observed in CI) in the VNF context, AE has significantly longer durations of vowel nasalization in VNTS sequences. For all three groups, the consonantal context (i.e. NF or NTS) that has the shortest N durations also has the greatest V nasalization.

11.4.2 Temporal airflow measures

To assess any difference in the three groups' VP opening and closing movements, duration and velocity of the upward and downward patterns of airflow were measured and compared across groups. Table 10.6 shows the results of the aerodynamic study, by vowel type, for the three speakers groups. The results of a between-group comparison of the data averaged by group across vowel contexts (with post-hoc Tukey tests) are given in the text.

Nasal up-ramp durations are inversely related to vowel height and directly related to vowel duration (Tables 11.2–4). Speakers group differences in averaged nasal up-ramp durations are significant overall (NI: 153 ms, CI: 114 ms, AE: 124 ms; $F(2, 316) = 27.47$, $p < .001$), with NI durations being significantly longer than AE and CI durations (Tukey). The Average Up-ramp Slope Ratio (AUSR) data show that the nasal flow velocity is significantly influenced by vowel type in NI and CI, although the effect is not consistent across these language groups (and the only significant contrast in CI is between [ɔ] and [a]; Tukey). The between-group comparison for AUSR values was significant ($F(2, 317) = 12.33$, $p < .001$), with NI having a significantly lower value (.0054) than CI (.0086) and AE (.0087).

Overall these data indicate that the nasal flow rising pattern is longer and more gradual in NI than in CI and AE.

Nasal down-ramps have similar durations across vowels and speakers groups. In AE, vowel quality has an overall effect on nasal down-ramp duration, but the contrast is significant only for [ɛ] and [ɒ] (Tukey). Between-group differences (NI: 32 ms, CI: 34 ms; AE: 31 ms) are also non-significant. The nasal down-ramp maximum velocity (MFDR) is significantly influenced by vowel type in AE, but only [ɛ] and [ɒ] contrast (Tukey). MFDR is also similar across speaker groups. Although the main group effect is significant ($F(2, 317) = 3.27$, $p < .03$) only the difference between NI ($-.626$) and CI ($-.699$) is significant (Tukey). Thus, unlike the nasal up-ramp movements, which are characterized by a high intra- and inter-language variability, the observed down-ramp nasal flow patterns can be characterized, for all groups, as a rapid downward movement from the nasal peak.

11.4.3 Oral release in relation to nasal peak time

The difference $t_{C2} - t_{Npeak}$ is the delay between the maximum opening of the velum, represented by the nasal peak t_{Npeak}, and the beginning of the oral release for the following obstruent, approximated by t_{C2}. A positive value indicates that the oral

TABLE 11.6. Temporal airflow measures in Nortern Italian (top), Central Italian (middle), and American English (bottom). (Durations in ms. n = number of tokens)

Vowel type	n	Duration nasal up ramp ($t_{Npeak} - t_{N1}$)		Average Up-Ramp Slope Ratio (AUSR)		Duration nasal down ramp ($t_{N4} - t_{Npeak}$)		Maximal Flow Declination Ratio (MFDR)	
NI		Mean	SD	Mean	SD	Mean	SD	Mean	SD
i	24	112	22	.0074	.0066	32	10	−.651	.205
e	30	130	26	.0062	.0026	32	8	−.609	.198
o	15	163	39	.0046	.0017	33	6	−.629	.120
a	45	186	37	.0041	.0012	32	7	−.624	.172
Prob.		$p < .001$		$p < .001$		n.s.		n.s.	
F(3, 109)		F = 34.05		F = 5.56					
CI									
i	20	97	32	.0092	.0033	33	11	−.629	.124
ɛ	20	108	38	.0097	.0047	31	9	−.759	.237
ɔ	10	111	41	.0109	.0059	34	11	−.798	.481
a	26	133	35	.0066	.0021	36	12	−.668	.237
Prob.		$p < .01$		$p < .01$		n.s.		n.s.	
F(3, 72)		F = 4.20		F = 4.19					
AE									
I	44	105	22	.0089	.0028	34	11	−.662	.188
ɛ	29	109	30	.0093	.0068	30	16	−.730	.159
ɒ	14	127	38	.0102	.0113	38	16	−.552	.152
æ	43	152	31	.0076	.0096	27	9	−.690	.173
Prob.		$p < .001$		n.s.		$p < .02$		$p < .02$	
F(3, 126)		F = 22.33				F = 3.46		F = 3.50	

release occurs after the nasal peak, suggestive of an epenthetic stop, and a negative value indicates that the oral release occurs before the nasal peak, leading to concurrent oral and nasal flow. Based on findings reported in the literature, it was expected that CI and sometimes AE, but not NI, would show evidence of stop epenthesis.

The mean $t_{C2} - t_{Npeak}$ values for the three groups are −19.10 ms (Std.Dev. = 33.05) for NI, 0.78ms (Std.Dev. = 14.98) for CI, and −0.76ms (Std.Dev. = 20.4) for AE. The values close to 0 for CI and AE reflect that, on average, the release of the oral constriction for the nasal and onset of velum raising (i.e., nasal peak) are synchronous (and small variations may result in epenthetic stops), whereas the value of −19.10 ms for NI indicates that onset of velum raising tends to follow the oral release of the nasal, thus precluding epenthetic stops.

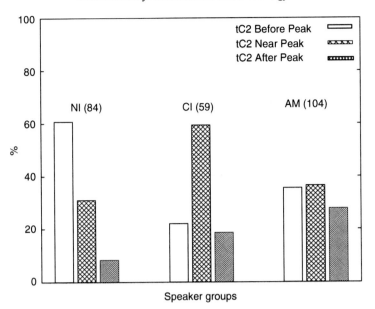

FIGURE 11.3. Time delay between the beginning of the oral release for F (t_{C2}) and the nasal peak (t_{Npeak}). The bar "t_{C2} near peak" shows the percent releases occurring from −10 ms to +10 ms around the nasal peak. The other two bars indicate, respectively, the percentage of all releases occurring more than 10 ms before and after the peak.

A more informative way of viewing the relation between t_{C2} and t_{Npeak} is given in Figure 11.3, which illustrates the tendencies of the three groups for synchronizing the oral–nasal articulators. In this figure, an oral release is considered near the peak if it occurs within an interval centered −10 to +10 ms around t_{Npeak}; before if it occurs more than 10 ms before nasal peak; after, if it occurs 10 ms or more after the peak. The data are in agreement with the hypothesis that in NI, oral releases are anticipated with respect to nasal closures, leading to extensive vowel nasalization but no epenthetic stop. In CI, oral releases occur most often around the time of nasal closure, and in AE, they may occur before, around or, less often, after nasal closures, possibly engendering stop epenthesis.

11.5 SUMMARY AND DISCUSSION

As expected, vowel nasalization correlates with vowel quality and vowel duration for all three groups, with lower, longer, vowels being more nasalized. Also as expected, the extent of vowel nasalization is related to post-nasal consonant context, although the detailed nature of this effect differs across speaker groups. For both Italian groups, anticipatory nasalization is less extensive in VNTS than in VNF sequences, while the reverse order holds for the American English speakers. In addition, pre-nasal vowels are shorter, nasals are longer, and oral consonants are shorter in VNTS than in VNF sequences in Northern and Central Italian, whereas the reverse holds for English, in which pre-nasal vowels are longer, nasals are shorter, and oral consonants are longer in VNTS than in VNF sequences. Finally, nasal consonant duration is inversely related to vowel nasalization in American English and, non-significantly, in Northern Italian.

The English data on VNTS sequences agree with previous findings (reviewed in Section 11.2) that English vowels are extensively nasalized before voiceless stops, with percentages of nasalization ranging between 80 and 100 percent. Nasal consonants are expected to be shortened before tautosyllabic voiceless obstruents, due to an effect of anticipation of devoicing for the following stop (J. Ohala 1971b). The reasons for shorter vowel nasalization and longer nasal duration in VNF than in VNTS sequences require further investigation. However, one may speculate that, in English VNF and VNTS sequences, coarticulation enhances the perceptual distinctiveness of words that, in casual speech, may be pronounced similarly, as in *sense* and *cents*.

In Northern Italian, the greater extent of vowel nasalization in VNF than in VNTS context was expected. In Northern Italian nasal–fricative clusters, nasals are articulatorily weak (Farnetani and Busà 1994). Moreover, being characterized by simultaneous nasality and frication, these nasal consonants are perceptually indistinct (Fujimura 1977; J. Ohala 1993b), and thus more likely to be missed by the listener, rather than developing into some new phonological sound (Solé 1999).

For the two varieties of Italian, the across-group differences in vowel nasalization reflect differences in coarticulation of post-nasal consonants, as well as effects of syllabic boundaries (Krakow 1993). As reviewed in Section 11.2, in Northern Italian, but not in Central Italian, vowels preceding nasal+voiceless consonants are as long as vowels in open syllables. The greater extent of vowel nasalization in Northern Italian vowels as compared to Central Italian may, then, be attributed to pre-nasal vowels being longer in Northern Italian. As pointed out by Hajek (1997), long vowel duration promoted the development of vowel nasalization from Latin to Northern Italian, and vowel length differences may affect the development of distinctive nasalization (Hombert 1986). On the other hand, the greater coarticulatory strength of nasals before post-nasal consonants in Central Italian than in Northern Italian may explain why stop epenthesis is more likely to occur in the former than in the latter dialect (J. Ohala 1981c).

For all speakers groups, nasal up-ramp durations are inversely related to vowel height, and directly related to vowel duration and nasalization. Northern Italian vowels have the longest nasal up-ramp durations, and these durations contrast significantly with those of Central Italian and American English in average rate of increase of airflow during the velum opening phase. This suggests that the nasal flow rises more gradually in Northern Italian vowels than in those of Central Italian or American English, and could be an indication of a slower velic movement. On the other hand, nasal down-ramp durations are similar across groups, and so is the down-ramp maximum velocity (MFDR). Additional data are needed to explore whether the measurements of airflow patterns used in this analysis accurately represent oral–nasal articulations (for a discussion, see Dotevall *et al.* 2001). However, the rather unvaried down-ramp pattern across contexts and groups may suggest that the velum closing movement is rapid and relatively constant. This is unlike nasal up-ramps, reflecting patterns of velic opening movements, which are extremely varied across contexts and groups, depending on where nasalization starts and on how the nasal consonant is articulated. Further investigations of velic movement patterns at different speech rates would help determine whether the observed variability is due to phonetic vs. language-specific factors (Kent *et al.* 1974).

Finally, given the challenging pattern of articulatory timing required for the production of vowel–nasal–obstruent sequences (reviewed in Section 11.1), all speaker groups examined may anticipate or delay the velic closure with respect to the oral closure. However, language-specific coarticulatory patterns cause some patterns to be more frequent than others. In Northern Italian, oral releases are often anticipated before the velic closure; in Central Italian, oral releases occur most often around the time of velic closure, whereas in American English oral releases may occur equally often before or near the time of velic closure, and less often after. Ali *et al.* (1979) also found that the cessation of the nasal consonant, possibly engendering an epenthetic stop, could occur both before and after the nasal peak in English.

11.5.1 Coarticulation strategies and phonological patterns in VNF sequences

How can we relate the observed cross-linguistic differences in coarticulatory patterns to the development of vowel nasalization and stop epenthesis? The results from this study provide insights into the relation between patterns of coarticulation in nasal-fricative sequences and the development of these processes. English and Italian differ in the way in which segmental durations are interrelated, and in the way in which these differences affect the extent of anticipatory vowel nasalization. More importantly, there appear to be language-specific tendencies for synchronizing the opening and closing movements of the oral and nasal ports that parallel the phonological outcomes in the three language groups. In Northern Italian, for example, the anticipation of the oral release with respect to the velic closure causes an anticipation, during the nasal consonant, of the frication noise for the post-nasal fricative. This has a disrupting effect on the nasal consonant. Perceptually, the turbulence associated with frication combined with the voicing of the flanking vowel may have an effect of perceived nasalization on the vowel and lead to vowel nasalization. In Central Italian or English, on the other hand, different patterns of synchronization of the velic closure with respect to the oral closure cause an acoustic effect, between the nasal consonant and the fricative, which is similar to a short silence followed by a burst, which may cue stop epenthesis. For each language, it is the pattern that has higher frequency that determines the direction of the sound change. As expected, the data are characterized by a large inter- and intra-subject variability due to coarticulation. Coarticulatory vowel nasalization can be characterized as a continuum, in which the duration of both vowel nasalization and the nasal consonant span from full to zero. Likewise for stop epenthesis, the silent period preceding the burst before the fricative consonant shows differences in duration.

At the present stage of analysis, it is hard to determine whether, or to what extent, the observed variability is an unintentional by-product of the articulation of vowel–nasal–fricative sequences or is rather the result of the application of some phonological rule, in other words, due to coarticulation that has been phonologized. While in the former case there is a mechanical link between the observed variation and the conditioning environment, in the latter case variation is expected to be disproportionate, either in magnitude or temporal extent, with respect to the contextual environment (J. Ohala 1993b). As shown in previous studies (e.g. Kent et al. 1974; Solé 1992), a possible way to differentiate the nature of variability in speech is through investigations of timing in speech at different rates, which may be the focus of future research.

Though the results of this study give insights on how language-specific differences in coarticulatory patterns parallel vowel nasalization and stop epenthesis, a true account of sound change requires investigations of the listener's perceptual patterns. It is well known that listeners are exposed to the synchronic variability created by the language-specific coarticulation and are generally able to reconstruct the speaker's intended sequence, factoring out the acoustic effects of coarticulation. It has been proposed that sound change occurs when listeners fail to normalize the speech signal, in other words, when they do not recognize the source of contextual variation (J. Ohala 1981b). However, there are indications that listeners may, in fact, take the context into consideration when judging coarticulated speech, and that the perception of coarticulated speech is influenced by the language-specific coarticulatory patterns (Beddor and Krakow 1999; Beddor et al. 2001; Beddor et al. 2002). Thus, it is expected that the language-specific coarticulatory patterns observed in this study could be related to differences in perception of the same sequences. This, too, may be the focus of future research.

11.6 CONCLUSIONS

Though the basic physical production and perception mechanisms giving rise to universal sound patterns are fairly well understood, more insight can be gained by looking at data from individual languages. This study was aimed at investigating how language-specific coarticulatory patterns may condition the development of vowel nasalization and stop epenthesis. The findings call for further investigations of the detailed mechanisms by which the synchronic variability created by language-specific coarticulatory patterns provides the input to the perceptual system and conditions sound change.

12

A Perceptual Bridge Between Coronal and Dorsal /r/

Olle Engstrand, Johan Frid, and Björn Lindblom

12.1 INTRODUCTION

The rhotics (r sounds) are known for having a particularly wide range of phonetic variation (Lindau 1985; Ladefoged and Maddieson 1996; Demolin 2001). Even a small sample of Swedish dialects was shown to contain several /r/ types: "front" (coronal) and "back" (dorsal) approximants, fricatives, trills, taps and flaps, and vocoids (Muminović and Engstrand 2001; but note that front versus back is an over-simplified dichotomy in view of the existence of complex types such as "bunched" /r/s; Delattre and Freeman 1968). These /r/s lack an invariant acoustic basis such as a lowered F3 (Lindau 1985). To be sure, they may be related in terms of a Wittgensteinian family resemblance (Lindau 1985), but this metaphor fails to delimit the category as such. However, all /r/s occupy a liquid slot adjacent to the syllable nucleus (Jespersen 1904).

A geographically large "back" /r/ region includes many of the languages of Western Europe (e.g. French, German, Dutch, Danish, Southern Swedish, and Southern Norwegian). Back /r/s also occur in languages such as English ("Northumbrian burr", Påhlsson 1972), Portuguese (Rogers 1948), Italian (e.g. Calabria and Sicily; Haden 1955; Haller 1987), Czech (Z. Palková, p.c.), Estonian (D. Krull, p.c.), in working-class varieties of Spanish spoken in Central and Eastern Cuba (Penny 2001), and in Northern Swedish rural communities (C.-C. Elert, p.c.). In some southern Swedish transitional dialects, [r] and [ʀ] appear in complementary distribution: /r/ is back only in initial position and after a short stressed vowel (Sjöstedt 1936). Outside this region, southern dialects use [ʀ] and northern dialects use [r]. (Here, we take the liberty to use the symbols [r] and [ʀ] for front and back /r/ regardless of manner of articulation.) Similar allophonic patterns occur in Portuguese (Rogers 1948), in Puerto Rican Spanish (Navarro Tomás 1966; Hammond 2000), and in coastal varieties of Colombian Spanish (Malmberg 1966). Front and back /r/s have until recently provided a basis for lexical contrast in Occitan (Coustenoble 1945).

It has long been debated whether back /r/s in Western Europe have a common historical origin (monogenesis), or whether they developed independently in different languages (polygenesis). One version of the monogenesis theory is that back /r/ originated as a prestige variant in France, later spreading to Germany, Scandinavia, and other areas (Trautmann 1880). The polygenesis view, on the other hand, assumes independent developments in German (Penzl 1961; Howell 1987), Dutch (Howell 1986), English (Grandgent 1920), and Scandinavian (Teleman 2005). An influence from the European [ʀ] region seems likely in adjacent areas (as in Czech), but less likely in southern Italy, Cuba or arctic regions in Sweden.

Why would [r] change into [ʀ] (or vice versa)? If it could be shown that the phonetic preconditions for such changes are inherent in the universal mechanisms for speech production and perception, such changes might be expected to occur from time to time. In particular, the polygenetic scenario for the origins of [ʀ] in Europe would appear phonetically reasonable.

How does sound change begin? Consider a sound that is ambiguous in the sense of having more than one articulatory interpretation (cf. Jonasson 1971). For the rhotics, an example is provided by the retroflex vs. bunched /r/s of American English, all with a characteristically low F3 (Delattre and Freeman 1968; Zawadski and Kuehn 1980; Westbury *et al.* 1998). In spite of the articulatory difference, both are used by American-English speakers. Also, it has been suggested that the change from front to back /r/ in French might be due to the fact that both are trillable and, thus, sound similar enough to trigger change in either direction (Lindau 1985; Demolin 2001).

These observations suggest that perception affects place of articulation in rhotics. The purpose of this chapter is to look for such evidence in yet another corner of the /r/ space—the borderland between coronals and dorsals. For example, observations of Swedish dialects suggest that coronal and dorsal approximant rhotics may be acoustically similar. Figure 12.1 depicts F2 and F3 (Bark) for the two categories as realized by a number of male speakers of dialects in or near the transitional [ʀ]/[r] region. The encircled area contains both dorsals and coronals. Evidently, the two types come close in the F2 / F3 plane and may occasionally be confused in perception (given sufficient similarity in other parameters). Thus, intended coronals could be interpreted as dorsals, or vice versa. Such reinterpretations could remain uncorrected, spread to other speakers and ultimately give rise to a new pronunciation norm (J. Ohala 1993b).

Our purpose was to examine the perceptual preconditions for reinterpretation of place of articulation at the intersection of dorsal and coronal rhotics. An attempt was made to (1) establish an articulatory–acoustic reference system for a number of /r/ types; (2) to evaluate the articulatory–acoustic relationships using articulatory modeling; and (3) to synthesize an /r/ continuum situated in the F2–F3 area in question. The synthetic /r/ sounds were to be used to evaluate the hypothesis that an articulatory discontinuity (coronal–dorsal) corresponds to a perceptual continuum in that area.

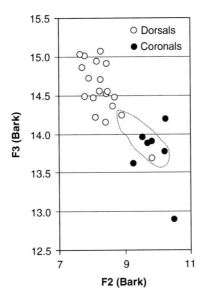

FIGURE 12.1. F2 and F3 (Bark) for approximant rhotics in the word *fara* "to travel" as realized by a number of male dialect speakers. Empty circles: dorsal; filled: coronal. Data points represent individual /r/ productions

12.2 FORMANT FREQUENCIES FOR PLACES OF /ɽ/ ARTICULATION

12.2.1 Data

We recorded reference material to obtain formant frequencies for various approximant rhotics. One male speaker (author OE) produced a number of approximant /r/ variants with five repetitions per variant. The /r/s appeared in the same word as referred to in Figure 12.1, *fara* "to travel". The speaker practiced until all variants could be produced consistently; see Table 12.1.

The distribution in the F2–F3 Bark plane is illustrated in Figure 12.2. These rhotics form a boomerang with pharyngeals, uvulars, and back velars in the top-left corner (low F2, high F3), followed by front velars with lower F3 and higher F2. Adjacent to the front velars, alveolars are found at a higher F2 and slightly lower F3; the front velars and the alveolars are encircled and separated by a dashed line. The changes from alveolar to postalveolar, and from postalveolar to retroflex, involve F3 lowering. This is further emphasized in the strong (sublaminal) retroflexes and the bunched /r/s, the latter also having lower F2. The range ends with labialized retroflexes with even lower F3 and F2.

TABLE 12.1. Mean F1–F4 values (Hz) for five repetitions of the given rhotics. Speaker: Olle Engstrand

Broad types	Places of articulation	Formant frequencies (Hz)			
		F1	F2	F3	F4
Coronals	Alveolars	406	1284	2109	2596
	Postalveolars	405	1265	1798	2513
	Retroflexes	397	1261	1588	2525
	Strong (sublaminal) retroflexes	400	1102	1463	2604
	Labialized retroflexes	328	995	1366	2599
Dorsals	Front velars	471	1055	2217	2943
	Back velars	544	851	2540	3189
	Uvulars	530	926	2425	3150
	Pharyngeals	556	818	2426	3169
Mixed	"Bunched"	459	1097	1542	2937

12.2.2 Comments

The pharyngeals, uvulars, and back velars form separate but adjacent clusters. All three have relatively high F1 and F4 (Table 12.1). This agrees with the auditory impression that the difference between them is rather subtle. The strongly retroflexed and the bunched /r/s overlap to a great extent (see Delattre and Freeman 1968). In the front velar–alveolar region, the F2 difference between categories is slightly greater than 1 Bark, and the F3 difference is smaller than 1 Bark. The F1 and F4 differences are approximately 0.7 and 0.8 Bark, respectively. This is compatible with the auditory similarity between front velars and alveolars—a similarity that seems to provide a

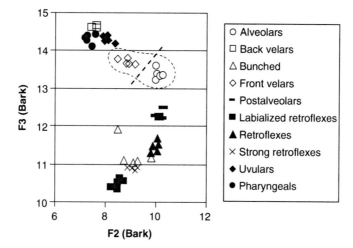

FIGURE 12.2. Various /r/ types in the F2–F3 Bark plane. Data points represent individual productions. The dashed line indicates the division between dorsals and coronals. Speaker: Olle Engstrand

perceptual bridge between coronal and dorsal /r/s. In the next section, these articulatory–acoustic relationships are examined using articulatory modeling.

12.3 APEX SIMULATIONS

12.3.1 The APEX model

The APEX model is an implementation of a framework previously developed for vowels (Lindblom and Sundberg 1971) and subsequently augmented with tongue tip and blade parameters. APEX is a tool for going from articulatory positions to sound in four steps (Stark *et al.* 1999). From specifications for lips, tongue tip, tongue body, jaw opening, and larynx height, APEX constructs an articulatory profile. A coordinate system (defined with respect to fixed vocal tract landmarks) is then applied to this profile to measure the cross-distances along the vocal tract midline at a number of points from the glottis to the lips. The distances are then converted into cross-sectional areas using anatomically motivated and speaker-dependent rules. This area function forms the basis of formant frequency calculations ("formf.c" written by J. Liljencrants) and the generation of a waveform to provide an audible illustration of the configuration under analysis.

The geometry of the APEX vocal tract is based on X-ray data. The generation of an articulatory profile uses contours sampled as x, y points for (i) the shape of the mandible, the hard palate, the posterior pharyngeal wall, and the larynx, and for (ii) the shape of articulators (tongue body, tongue blade, lips). The general philosophy is to have the model represent certain observed key configurations as faithfully as possible and then derive intermediate articulations through physiologically motivated interpolation rules. One of the key features of the model is the mandible-based specification of lip and tongue configurations. To produce a given tongue contour, the APEX user first manipulates the tongue in a mandible-based coordinate system. In other words, its orientation relative to the maxilla is temporarily ignored. This means that the user chooses (i) where the main tongue hump is (position parameter); (ii) how far the tongue is displaced from its neutral configuration (displacement parameter); and (iii), as the third step, the user introduces the mandible and the tongue contour as a whole in a maxilla-based coordinate system so that its location matches the specified jaw opening.

12.3.2 Simulations

In order to supplement the acoustic measurements of /r/ tokens produced by our single speaker (Fig. 12.2) with some articulatory observations, APEX was used to help answer two questions. First, what are the acoustic consequences of varying the place of articulation in /r/-like *coronal* articulations? Second, what are the acoustic consequences of varying the place of articulation in /r/-like *dorsal* articulations?

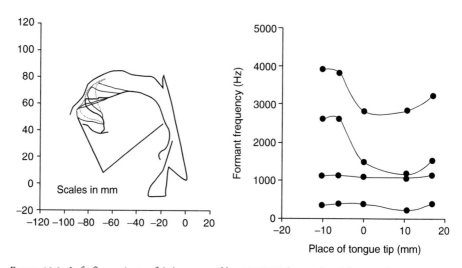

FIGURE 12.3. Left: five variants of /r/ generated by APEX. Right: predicted formant frequencies as a function of position of the tongue tip. The bold contour is based on a tongue shape observed in an X-ray film of a Swedish speaker producing an /r/. Further explanation in text

To address the first question, five variants of /r/ were generated by APEX. These are illustrated in the left panel in Figure 12.3. The bold tongue contour was selected as a reference. It represents the APEX match to a shape observed in an X-ray film of a male Swedish speaker (Branderud et al. 1998). The sample occurs at the onset of the fricative realization of final /r/ in the nonsense utterance [ɑːˈbɑːpʰɑːʐ̩], a sound traditionally classified as a retroflex. The tongue-body shape is specified numerically by parameters derived from a Principal Components analysis of about 400 tongue shapes drawn from the above-mentioned X-ray film (Lindblom 2003). The tongue blade points are obtained by fitting a second-order polynomial to three data points: the tip and the anteriormost two "flesh points" on the dorsal contour. The other four contours differ only in terms of the location of the tongue tip. The anteriormost flesh point on the dorsal contour refers to a given point from which all the tongue blade contours originate. The second-anteriormost flesh point is located a short distance behind the first. The tip and those two points uniquely determine the parabola.

These articulations can be described as dental, prealveolar, postalveolar, retroflex, and strongly retroflex. Running parallel to the hard palate at a constant distance of 4 mm, a curved line can be seen. It indicates the continuum along which the position of the tongue tip was varied. The underside of the blade is anchored at a fixed point on the floor of the mouth. For any given tongue tip location, its shape is derived by scaling the reference underside using the new x, y coordinates of the tip. The tongue-body shape is the same in all four cases.

For an arbitrary articulation, APEX calculates the formant pattern by first measuring cross distances perpendicular to the vocal tract midline, then deriving the cross-sectional areas from distance-to-area rules (Heinz and Stevens 1964, 1965). The speaker in the X-ray film also participated in an MRI study of Swedish vowels (Ericsdotter 2005). Accordingly, these MR images were analyzed to obtain distance-to-area rules specific to the speaker producing the reference sample.

The /r/ variants presented in the left panel of Figure 12.3 differ greatly with respect to the shape of the front sublingual cavity, a crucial feature in retroflex sounds. As the tongue blade moves from a dental/alveolar position to an increasingly retroflex configuration, an acoustically relevant cavity is formed under the blade. Stevens (1998) has shown that this cavity is essential for the lowering of the third formant typically seen in retroflex sounds. At a critical point during the elevation of the blade, the sublingual volume begins to play a significant acoustic role. Small increases in size have a large effect on the frequency of F3.

As seen in Figure 12.3 (right-hand panel), this effect is clearly reflected in the APEX simulations. The x-axis plots the position of the tongue tip relative to its location in the reference articulation (the bold tongue contour) at x=0. For the reference articulation, a formant pattern of F1 = 380, F2 = 1078 and F3 = 1483 is predicted. This is in good agreement with the observed F-pattern, which is F1 = 422, F2 = 1072, and F3 = 1575. There is a rapid "quantal" change in F3 (and F4) separating more anterior from retroflex places. For dental articulations, F3 and F4 remain fairly high, whereas for retroflex variants, they show drastically lowered values. It should be noted that the quantal change observed here is not evident in the corresponding values in Table 12.1. However, we are not aiming at a quantitative modeling of those specific productions; we can claim to be presenting only a set of parallel data which qualitatively show some crude agreement with that speaker's utterances.

To shed some light on the second question ("What are the acoustic consequences of varying the place of articulation in /r/-like *dorsal* articulations?"), we ran a second set of simulations in which APEX was instructed to maintain a constant minimum cross-sectional area of $0.25\,\text{cm}^2$ (a degree of opening deemed appropriate for an approximant) and to vary the place of constriction continuously from a palatal to a pharyngeal position. The resulting formant variations are presented in Figure 12.4.

As expected, F1 rises as the tongue is moved back. F2 and F3 show a region of proximity for the palatal configuration. F2 and F1 approach each other in more posterior articulations. The range of F3 is more limited. These results are in agreement with previous results obtained when the vocal tract is represented by tubes as well as by more physiologically based modeling (Fant 1960, Stevens 1989).

In Figure 12.5, the information in Figures 12.3 and 12.4 is combined and compared with the measurements in Figure 12.2. F3 is plotted against F2 for both measured and simulated variants of /r/. The top ellipse encloses the mean values for the dorsal variants produced by O. Engstrand (solid squares). From left to right, these points represent pharyngeal, back velar, uvular, and front velar. The unfilled squares show the dorsal APEX patterns. From left to right, the points pertain to pharyngeal, uvular, back velar, velar, and front velar. There is, thus, a fair bit of agreement between the sets, although fronting tends to produce somewhat diverging results for F3.

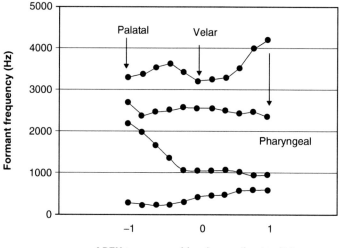

FIGURE 12.4. Acoustic consequences of varying the place of articulation in dorsal articulations. For the front-back dimension a normalized scale is used: palatal $= -1$, velar $= 0$ and pharyngeal $= 1$. The formant patterns corresponding to these locations are indicated by arrows

The retroflex cluster of solid circles refers to the speaker's data and contains (again from left to right) the measurements for rounded retroflex, bunched, strong retroflex, and retroflex. The open circles correspond to the rightmost two points plotted in Figure 12.3. From top to bottom, they represent retroflex and strongly retroflex. Again an acceptable match is obtained.

The circle labeled "alveolar" encloses (from top to bottom) postalveolar and alveolar. For comparison, the F2 and F3 data of Figure 12.3 are replotted as a dashed line connecting the four degrees of tongue-blade elevation. We note that the values fall in the range where the place-dependent formant variations show maximum sensitivity in Figure 12.3. Moreover, it is worth observing that the dashed line falls rather close to the group of dorsal points. No further attempt was made to model the coronal cases.[1]

12.3.3 Conclusions

By and large, it can be seen that APEX corroborates the articulatory properties exhibited by speaker O. Engstrand in producing the test items. It would therefore seem justified to assume that they are descriptively valid not only for him, but, at least qualitatively, also more generally.

---

[1] The reader may note that the F2 and F3 values for the dental articulation in Fig. 12.3 when replotted in Fig. 12.5 fall near the dorsal area. The expected F3 vs F2 location of dentals would be somewhere in between the dorsal and the alveolar articulations. This is because F3 will be slightly higher in dentals than in alveolars. In that respect the predicted dental values appear in approximately the right place. Since the APEX modeling is based on a speaker different from the speaker of the present study, high quantitative accuracy is not possible.

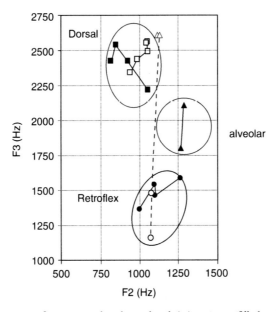

FIGURE 12.5. F3 against F2 for measured and simulated /r/ variants (filled and unfilled symbols, respectively). Further explanation in text

12.4 PERCEPTUAL EVALUATION

12.4.1 Purpose

It needs to be shown that perceived /r/ variants in the dorsal–coronal region may be articulatorily ambiguous. This implies a relatively smooth perceptual transition from dorsal to coronal corresponding to a discontinuous articulatory transition—a reversed quantal relationship as it were (Stevens 1989); see Figure 12.6. Another implication is that the identification function from dorsal to coronal will not display categorical perception (CP) effects such as an abrupt jump between dorsal and coronal perceptions. Categorical perception is also associated with more accurate discrimination near category boundaries, which tends to produce a peak in the discrimination curve at the boundary. If the perception is not categorical, perceived differences between stimuli should be independent of the location of the stimuli along the continuum.

Dorsal and coronal rhotics do not contrast phonologically in any known living language and should not be subject to strong perceptual categorization. If, however, we find evidence of CP of back vs. front /r/ articulations along an acoustic continuum, this would weaken our prediction that perception of place of articulation is ambiguous in that region. Thus, articulatory reinterpretation of ambiguous stimuli would not stand out as a convincing starting point for changes between dorsal and coronal /r/s. The following listening test was designed to address this issue.

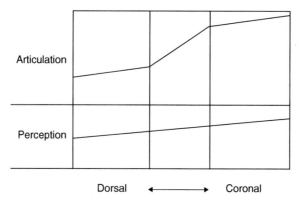

FIGURE 12.6. Hypothetical relationship between articulatory and perceptual representations of dorsal and coronal rhotics

12.4.2 Methods

12.4.2.1 Stimuli

The test was based on the word *fara* "to travel", in which the rhotic gradually changed from dorsal (front velar) to coronal (alveolar) values. Eight stimuli were constructed along a continuum coinciding with the encircled area in Figure 12.2.

Calculation of formant frequencies. F2 and F3 values in Hz given in Table 12.1 for Front velar and Alveolar were used as points of departure. All values were converted into Bark using to the formula

$$z = [26.81/(1 + 1960/f)] - 0.53, \tag{1}$$

where z is Bark and f, Hz (Traunmüller 2005).

The F-values for each stimulus were determined with reference to the mean front-velar value (as measured in Section 12.2.1) and the corresponding Alveolar value. The Bark difference between these is denoted by the symbol Δ in Table 12.2. Stimuli were produced at equal Bark distances ($\Delta/5$) for both F2 and F3, from 8.607 to 10.329 Bark in F2, and from 13.766 to 13.302 Bark in F3. Thus, the series begins at $\Delta/5$ Bark beyond the front velar at one end of the continuum; this location is referred to as "Extreme front velar" in Table 12.2 (observed: F2 = 8.853 Bark, F3 = 13.7 Bark). The series ends at $\Delta/5$ Bark beyond the alveolar at the other end of the continuum, referred to as "Extreme alveolar" (observed: F2 = 10.083 Bark, F3 = 13.368 Bark).

Construction of waveforms. In order to keep the phonetic context of the manipulated /r/ sounds as constant as possible, all stimuli were based on one single recording, henceforth referred to as "the base sound", of a production of the word *fara*. The non-rhotic parts were copied from this recording, whereas the rhotic part was synthesized

TABLE 12.2. Calculation of formant values

	F2 (Hz)	F3 (Hz)	F2 (Bark)	F3 (Bark)
Front velar	1055	2217	8.853	13.7
Alveolar	1284	2109	10.083	13.368
Δ			1.23	3.32
$\Delta/5$			0.246	0.066
Extreme front velar			8.607	13.766
Extreme alveolar			10.329	13.302

using the following method (implemented in the Praat program, Boersma and Wee-nink 2005). The F0 contour of the base sound is re-interpreted as a sequence of points in time, where each point corresponds to a closure phase in the vocal fold vibration; a pulse is generated at each point and converted into a voice-like source by feeding the pulse into the sinc function given in (2).

$$\text{sinc } (0) = 1; \text{ sinc } (x) = \sin x/x \text{ for } x \neq 0. \tag{2}$$

The signal is illustrated in Figure 12.7. Finally, the resulting signal is multiplied by the intensity of the base sound. The result is similar to the base sound in F0 and intensity, but each period is a sinc function instead of the original glottal pulse information. This sound is suitable for spectral manipulation and may be filtered using a spectral shape described by formant frequencies and bandwidths without introducing unnatural qualities or artifacts.

In producing the word *fara*, the synthesized /r/s were integrated into the /faː_a/ context from the original recording using an overlap-and-add paradigm in which windowed frames are cut out of waveforms and added together. The temporal center position of the window is updated for each frame, so that no two frames are copied to the same location in the new sound. However, by using a window that is wider than the update rate, we introduce an overlap from frame to frame. The overlap smoothes

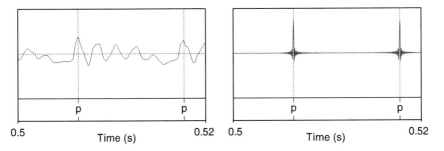

FIGURE 12.7. Left: the original waveform. Right: the signal produced by converting the point sequence into a pulse train using the sinc function. Points designated "p" denote the onset of a new pulse.

the concatenation, thereby avoiding jumps and discontinuities in the resulting wave-form. Each frame consisted of a 32 ms Gaussian window, and the time step for updating the center position of the window was 15.34 ms.

12.4.2.2 Participants and procedures

Twenty-two Swedish speakers, thirteen female and nine male, were tested in one identification and one discrimination test, both using a forced-choice design with one single presentation of each stimulus. With two exceptions, the participants had a linguistic background. Five of the listeners had a back /r/ regional variety. Three listeners had a first language other than Swedish (Estonian, Finnish, and American English, respectively) but had a native-like command of Swedish. Average listener age was 45 (s.d. = 15 years). One hearing-impaired listener was excluded from the present analysis.

Each listener was tested separately. Stimuli were presented through headphones in front of the computer screen. The participants were first exposed to the full range of stimuli a few times, but there was no training session specifically aiming at learning the categorization. Half of the participants completed the identification test first; the other half were tested in the reverse order. Counterbalancing did not result in significant differences. In both tests, the order of presentation of the stimuli was re-randomized for each listener. The participants could not replay a stimulus once heard.

In the identification test, one stimulus (one exemplar of *fara*) was presented at a time. There were eight different stimuli and each stimulus occurred six times. For each of the 48 presentations, listeners were to indicate whether they heard the /r/ in *fara* as back or front. This was done by clicking a "back" or a "front" box that appeared on the screen when the sound stimulus was presented. This response triggered the next stimulus. The identification test took 5 to 10 minutes, depending on individual response rates.

In the discrimination test, listeners were presented with pairs of the same or different exemplars of *fara*. Stimuli were 0, 2, 4, or 6 steps apart (0 steps apart meaning identity). All 32 possible combinations of these step changes in both orders (e.g. stimuli 1–3 and 3–1) were included. Each stimulus combination was presented four times. For each pair, listeners were asked to indicate whether they heard the two members of the pair as being the same or different by clicking on boxes labeled "Same" and "Diff", respectively. This test took 10 to 15 minutes.

12.4.3 Results

Results of the identification test are summarized in Figure 12.8. The horizontal axis shows stimuli (the word *fara* with approximant /r/s separated by equal Bark distances on the F2–F3 plane). The vertical axis shows listener responses as proportions of front judgments and their 95-percent confidence intervals. (The maximum front score was 6 since there were six repetitions of each stimulus in this test.) Stimuli 1–4 (with

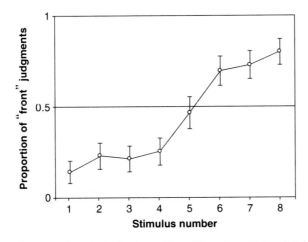

FIGURE 12.8. Identification of synthetic rhotics as "front" based on 21 Swedish listeners. Stimuli change from left to right from more dorsal to more coronal F2–F3 values. The error bars mark 95-percent confidence intervals.

F2 and F3 close to dorsal-/r/ values) evoked more back than front judgments. The opposite was the case for stimuli 6–8 (with F2 and F3 more in accordance with coronal values). Responses to stimulus 5 were random. Thus, the proportion of front judgments tends to increase as the F2–F3 combination approaches front (coronal) values. However, the identification function is non-linear showing a tendency to accelerate at the middle of the range. Both the left and right response series differ significantly from chance in the sense that their 95-percent confidence intervals do not include the horizontal line representing chance. In sum, there is a tendency toward categorical perception of these /r/s, but the curve is less clear-cut than is usually the case in CP. Also note that none of the stimuli is identified with either category at a level near 100 percent.

The data contain considerable between-listener differences. Figure 12.9 illustrates identification curves pertaining to four listeners. Two of the listeners display a "categorical" response type, that is, a steep change from 0 to 100 percent front identifications. The other two listeners represent a more gradual, "non-categorical" response type. Even though we do not have a metric for classifying listeners as categorical or non-categorical, qualitative judgments suggest that eight listeners were predominantly categorical, that two listeners were ambiguous, and that eleven listeners were non-categorical. Thus, the majority of listeners showed non-categorical perception; however, when the identification functions for the different listeners are averaged in Figure 12.8, the more extreme values for categorical listeners make the curve look rather categorical.

Figure 12.10 shows the extent to which members of stimulus pairs were heard as "same" as a function of the magnitude of the difference between the members. The x-axis represents stimuli that were identical (Diff 0) or different to various degrees (Diff 2–Diff 6). For example, Diff 2 means that the distance between pair members

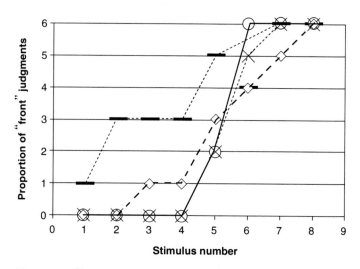

FIGURE 12.9. Two types of listener response: Categorical (circles, solid lines; crosses, dotted lines) and non-categorical (bars, dotted lines; diamonds, dashed lines).

corresponded to two steps in the continuum on the F2–F3 plane (i.e. 2* Δ/5; see. Table 12.2). Evidently, there is a tendency for more similar stimuli to be less well discriminated, but also a striking uncertainty: identical or very similar stimuli are frequently judged as "different", and the most widely differing stimuli (Diff 6) are still heard as "same" to a relatively great extent.

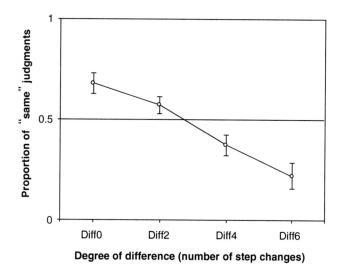

FIGURE 12.10. Discrimination of synthetic rhotics as a function of F2–F3 distance in Barks. Twenty-one Swedish listeners.

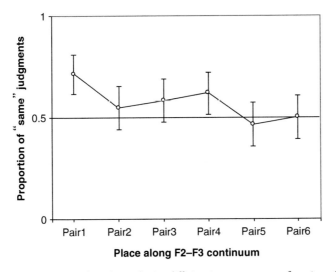

FIGURE 12.11. Discrimination of synthetic rhotics differing in two steps as a function of place along the continuum on the F2–F3 plane. The error bars mark 95-percent confidence intervals. Twenty-one Swedish listeners.

Figure 12.11 illustrates the discrimination results for stimulus pairs in which the individual stimuli differed in two steps on the synthetic continuum (i.e. $2^* \Delta/5$ as defined in Table 12.2; Pair 1 contains stimuli 1 and 3, Pair 2 contains stimuli 2 and 4, etc.). Each data point represents 84 observations (21 listeners and four presentations per stimulus combination). The y-axis shows the extent to which members of the respective pairs were judged to be identical. Except for Pairs 1 and 4, the 95-percent confidence intervals overlap the 50-percent line representing chance. In this sense, Pairs 1 and 4 display significant peaks. However, a categorical discrimination pattern would have shown a significant *downward* peak somewhere along the range suggesting sharper discrimination at a category boundary (this is because the graph displays "same" rather than "different" responses). The absence of such an effect suggests that these listener responses did not meet the basic requirements of CP.

In addition, certain differences were noted between participants whose own productions have back as opposed to front /r/. In particular, listeners who produce back /r/ tended to exhibit less front identification responses to stimuli 6, 7, and 8 (stimuli designed to approximate the front /r/ category). Thus, listeners were inclined to perceive rhotic place of articulation in terms of their own articulatory norm. In the discrimination test, back /r/ producers returned more "different" responses for pairs pertaining to the back region, indicating that these listeners were more sensitive to differences in that area. Finally, the three non-native listeners seemed to display somewhat less categorical identification functions as well as a tendency to more "same" responses. However, in view of the limited data, these observations are quite preliminary.

12.4.4 Conclusions

The identification test showed that front judgments tended to vary as a function of the gradual change in F2–F3 and that many listeners were not able to determine unambiguously whether an /r/ sounded dorsal or coronal. In the discrimination test, greater acoustic differences resulted in more reliable discriminations, but discriminations were not consistent even for stimuli separated by several steps. In this sense, the stimuli were articulatorily ambiguous. Discrimination curves did not show CP effects such as higher rates of discrimination at category boundaries. In sum, these observations corroborate the hypothesis that the observed F2–F3 region is characterized by articulatory ambiguity suggesting a perceptual basis for dorsal/coronal /r/ alternation.

12.5 SUMMARY AND DISCUSSION

It has been argued that articulatory reinterpretation of ambiguous rhotics may constitute a starting point for historical sound change. A listening experiment was conducted based on a synthesized approximant /r/ continuum with stimuli at equal distances in a F2–F3 Bark plane. At one end of the continuum, F2 and F3 were set to values observed in front velars; at the other end, F2 and F3 were set to values observed in alveolars. Formant specifications were guided by a recording of approximant /r/s produced at different places of articulation; acoustic–articulatory relationships in these productions were verified using an articulatory model (APEX).

In essence, listener responses suggested a considerable uncertainty, both in identifying stimuli as back or front and in discriminating members of stimulus pairs. This indicates that, in the region under observation, place of articulation may be ambiguous enough to be mapped to an articulatory configuration different from that intended by the speaker and thus misreconstructed. Potentially, this may lead to a change in phonetic norms. It should be pointed out, however, that this conclusion is limited to approximants—other types will contain additional cues to place of articulation: for example, fricative rhotics will contain prominent noise cues. Also, we have kept F1 and F4 constant in this experiment—the effect of assigning more realistic values to these formants should be tested. On the other hand, the test was carried out in noise-free conditions with a narrowly defined task presented to focused listeners. A more realistic setting could have a negative effect on both identification and discrimination and, thus, lead to even greater articulatory ambiguity.

We have nothing to say here about the typological front /r/ bias in the world's languages. Of the 451 UPSID languages (Maddieson 1984; Maddieson and Precoda 1989), only four (two of which are French and German) have uvular rhotic trills, and two others have uvular rhotic approximants. We do not know whether this bias is due to a perceptual asymmetry or some other factor. It should be noted, however, that [ʀ] may well exist in dialects whose standard varieties have [r]. For example, Norwegian belongs to the UPSID majority of /r/ languages, but /ʀ/ is almost as common (Foldvik 1988).

We began by asking, "Why would front rhotics change into back rhotics?" Whereas many other factors are likely to be involved in this type of change, the experiment described here has offered some evidence for the existence of a perceptual motivation. This suggests that changes in place of articulation for rhotics may be phonetically motivated and, thus, likely to take place from time to time in the world's languages. In particular, the polygenetic scenario regarding the origin of back rhotics in Europe would stand out as reasonable. It should be noted, however, that the front-to-back or back-to-front process is not as straightforward perceptually as, say, the cases Jakobson uses in arguing for the feature "flat", with labialization, retroflexion, and pharyngealization all causing lowering of upper formants (Jakobson *et al.* 1952).

It should be noted, finally, that there is probably considerable place variation between the dorsal rhotics in the world's languages. For example, informal observations suggest that degrees of [ʀ] backing may serve to separate Swedish dialects. Whereas this hypothesis remains to be examined, it is clear that additional developments are necessary for front velars (the "first dorsals" in the sense of this study) to turn into other dorsal categories such as uvulars.

13

Danish Stød

Phonological and Cognitive Issues

Nina Grønnum and Hans Basbøll

13.1 INTRODUCTION

We believe that phonological descriptions gain in acceptability and viability if they can be shown to be reflected in the articulatory, acoustic, and perceptual reality of speakers and listeners. We also believe that phonological theory must ideally always couch its propositions in terms which lay them open to empirical scrutiny. Accordingly, we are compelled to attempt to verify or falsify any phonological statement that lends itself to empirical investigation (confining ourselves to Danish in this case).

Trubetzkoy (1935) and Martinet (1937) suggested an association between mora and the Danish stød, an association explored in a comprehensive comparative context by A. S. Liberman (1982). Basbøll (1988) interpreted stød as a function of specific syllabic-moraic structures in the manner of Hyman (1985). Over the years his ideas about phonology in general, and his theory about Danish stød in particular, developed further. Our investigations took off some time in the late 1990s, and as they developed so did Basbøll's ideas about stød and mora (see Basbøll 2005, particularly chs. 10 and 13–16). That is, his position is no longer exactly identical to the claim which we first set out to test empirically: he started with the strongest hypothesis available about the phonetic reality of morae in Danish (Basbøll 1998), but no longer insists on a strict articulatory or acoustic alignment of stød with the second half of long vowels or the sonorant consonant after short vowels, that is, the second mora.

Danish stød has been the object of previous comprehensive physiological and acoustic analyses (e.g. Riber-Petersen 1973; Fischer-Jørgensen 1987, 1989a, 1989b; and a preliminary perceptual study by Grønnum [Thorsen] 1974). The present study differs from previous ones in that it analyzes natural utterances, albeit read in a laboratory, whereas work by Fischer-Jørgensen and Riber Petersen analyzed citation or quasi-citation forms. The choice of test material itself has also been refined and expanded. Furthermore, we have carried out some perceptual tests to look more closely at the cognitive reality of some of Basbøll's proposals.

Danish stød is highly variable diachronically and geographically (cf. Ejskjær 1990; A. S. Liberman 1982), but the relevance of a moraic analysis for language history and typology is beyond the scope of this chapter. Our aim is to summarize the results of our acoustic and perceptual experiments on stød and to show how highly variable it is in strength and temporal domain, as well as to present some new facts about the distribution of stød. In Section 13.2 we address the phonetic properties of stød which challenge a moraic analysis. In Section 13.3 we give a brief account of how properties of the word stem and the nature of the suffix together govern stød assignment, and we present examples of stød in new and unexpected segmental and morphological contexts and discuss their implication for stød theory. Section 13.4 contains some concluding remarks.

13.1.1 What is stød?

Stød is a kind of creaky voice. It is therefore found only in voiced sounds. It requires more than zero stress. And—most noteworthy—it requires a certain minimum amount of voiced material in the syllable rhyme in order to be present:

- either a long vowel, as in [pʰɛːˀn] *pæn* "nice"[1]
- or a short vowel + a sonorant consonant, as in [pʰɛnˀ] *pen* "pen".

Syllables that fulfill these segmental and prosodic requirements are heavy in Danish phonology. That is how they were characterized in Basbøll (1988), where the notion "weight unit" in Hyman's (1985) sense was used. In later works they are called bi-moraic, and it is claimed that stød characterizes the second mora in bi-moraic syllables (Basbøll 1998, 2003, 2005: 267–72). The idea of stød as a mora-counting device can also be found in the work of some Prague phonologists (Trubetzkoy 1935: sec. 34 and Martinet 1937: 100–2), cf. A. S. Liberman (1982). Fischer-Jørgensen's (1987, 1989a, 1989b) phonetic description of vowels with stød as having two distinct phases, a preparatory non-stød phase succeeded by a stød phase proper is in accordance with such a moraic analysis.

However, Basbøll's (1988, 1998) analysis raised a number of questions about the acoustic manifestation and the cognitive reality of stød which we have addressed in a series of experiments (Grønnum and Basbøll 2001a, b, 2002a, b, 2003a, b). The results of these experiments will be summarized in Section 13.2.

13.1.2 Light and heavy syllables

Onset consonants are commonly considered irrelevant for the assessment of syllable weight; only the segmental structure of the rhyme matters (see e.g. Hyman 1985). But

---

[1] Stød is conventionally marked after the long vowel symbol and after the first post-vocalic sonorant following short vowels. For lack of a more appropriate notation we use a superscript [ˀ].

how a rhyme scores in the balance is language-specific. Here are illustrations of the distinction between light and heavy syllables in Danish according to Basbøll (1988, 1998):

[seːˀ] *se* "see": the long vowel, /eː/, makes the syllable heavy; it potentially carries stød, which would be located in the second half of the long vowel.

[lḁɡ̊s] *laks* "salmon" has a short vowel, /a/, followed by two unvoiced consonants, /ks/. This is not a heavy syllable in Danish. There is not enough voiced material in the syllable rhyme to support a stød.

[sd̥ʁɑmˀd̥] *stramt* "tight" also has a short vowel, /a/, but a sonorant consonant, /m/, follows. The syllable is therefore heavy and it has stød, which would be located in the moraic nasal.

[luːˀn] *lun* "lukewarm" has a long vowel, /uː/, which immediately makes the syllable heavy and qualifies the syllable for stød. The fact that there is a sonorant consonant, /n/, in the coda changes nothing.

13.1.3 The function of stød

Stød is indisputably distinctive on the surface:

['lɛːˀsɐ] *læser* "reads" vs.	['lɛːsɐ] *læser* "reader"[2]
['væːˀln̩] *hvalen* "the whale" vs.	['væːln̩] *valen* "numb"
['huːˀsð̩] *huset* "the house" vs.	['huːsð̩] *huset* "housed"
['tˢœmˀɐ] *tømmer* "timber" vs.	['tˢœmɐ] *tømmer* "empties"
['hɛnˀɐ] *hænder* "hands" vs.	['hɛnɐ] *hænder* "happens"
['sdɛŋˀɐ] *stænger* "rods" vs.	['sdɛŋɐ] *stænger* "locks up"
['ɡ̊ɛlˀɐ] *gælder* "is valid" vs.	['ɡ̊ɛlɐ] *gæller* "gills"

However, as we shall see below, stød is to a very large extent predictable from syllabic and morphological structure.

The stød–non-stød distinction roughly parallels the Accent I–Accent II distinction in standard Swedish and Norwegian. Words with stød in Danish generally correspond to words with Accent I in Swedish and Norwegian, and words without stød correspond to words with Accent II. There are some notable differences, however. (1) The stød–non-stød distinction is a difference in creaky versus modal voice quality; the word-accent distinction is purely tonal. (2) There are segmental restrictions on stød occurrence, see Section 13.1.1; no such restrictions apply to the word accents. (3) Stød is associated with syllables, not words; the opposite is true of word accents. (4) Danish monosyllables may have stød or not; monosyllables in Swedish and Norwegian always carry Accent I. (5) Swedish and Norwegian stressed syllables are always heavy, either because the vowel is long or because a short vowel is followed by a long postvocalic consonant, whereas the

---

² /ər/, and normally also /rə/ and /rər/, are realised as [ɐ], as in ['lɛːsɐ] *læser* "reader" ['hɛnˀɐ] *hænder* "hands", and /ə/ assimilates to a neighboring vowel or sonorant consonant, as in ['b̥ʁuːu] *bruge* "use" and ['væːˀln̩] *hvalen* "the whale".

heavy versus light distinction in Danish depends on the nature of the coda consonant. Together, these differences make any direct comparison of tonal word accent in Swedish and Norwegian with our results for Danish stød in Section 13.2 and the principles in Section 13.3.1 void. In addition, to our knowledge, no trends have been reported for Swedish or Norwegian to match our observations and speculation in Section 13.3.2.

13.2 THE PHONETIC PROPERTIES IN MORE DETAIL

Figure 13.1 presents spectrograms and waveforms of two words which are extracted from connected read speech, as are the words in the figures to follow. ['b̥ɛldð̰] *bæltet* "the belt", on the right, is without stød; ['b̥ɛl'̩dð̰] *Bæltet* (proper name), on the left, has stød in the consonant. In the lower part of the figure the waveform of each [l] is expanded. From Basbøll's original point of view they appear ideal: the stødless [l] on

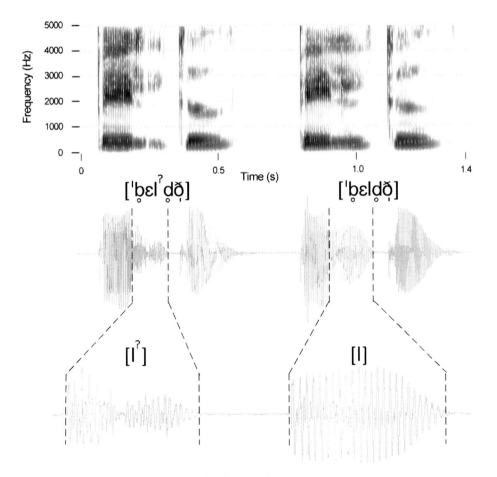

FIGURE 13.1. A word with stød (left) and without stød (right). See text.

the right is regular in terms of periodicity and amplitude. The [lˀ] on the left is irregular both in terms of periodicity and amplitude. This is an archetypical—albeit rare—case, where the stød is confined to the sonorant consonant after the short vowel, or—in Basbøll's terms—it is located in the second mora.

However, stød is much more variable than this, both in acoustic terms and in its temporal domain. At times it is even quite elusive. In Figure 13.2, on the left we see the verb ['sg̊æːˀb̥ɐ] *skaber* "creates"—with stød—and on the right the noun ['sg̊æːb̥ɐ] *skaber* "creator", without stød. In the lower part of the figure the waveforms of the vowels are expanded. The stød vowel on the left has higher pitch (for reasons nothing to do with the stød), but does not appear to be irregular in either periodicity or amplitude.

Cases like this, and they are numerous, are troublesome for a moraic analysis which maintains that the creaky voice is located in the second mora, in this case in the second half of the long vowel in ['sg̊æːˀb̥ɐ] on the left of the figure. Other evidence that is difficult to account for by a strict bi-moraic approach comes from informal perceptual studies. To get a first rough idea about the perceived location of stød, we excised the word ['lɛːˀsɐ] (Fig. 13.3, right) from a read utterance and spliced out the [l] and the first half of the vowel. On three separate occasions the first author (Grønnum)

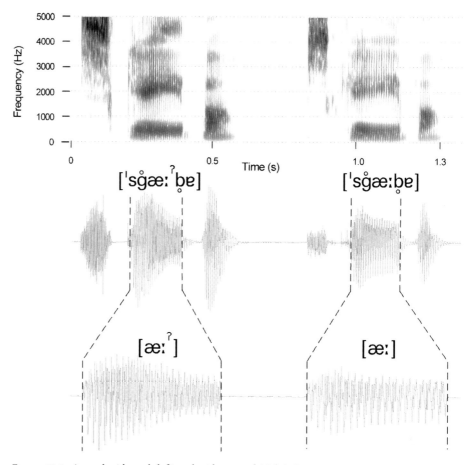

FIGURE 13.2. A word with stød (left) and without stød (right). See text.

presented the resulting truncated item (Fig. 13.3, left) to audiences of about 15, 20, and 70 people, respectively, in a lecture room. She told the audience that they would hear a word spliced out from a larger context; it might therefore sound somewhat abrupt. She then played the truncated word back five times and asked the audience simply: "What do you hear? Could this be a Danish word?" The audience readily responded with *esser* "aces" ['ɛsɐ]. (A trained phonetician would add a glottal stop in the phonetic transcription, to capture the abrupt onset due to the truncation, ['ʔɛsɐ].) Theoretically, three different processing scenarios are possible. (1) Whatever triggers stød identification cannot have been located in the latter part of the vowel, because without the onset consonant and the first half of the vowel the stød was no longer audible. (2a) Perceptible creaky voice was indeed present in the remaining part of the stressed vowel in the truncated item, but the segmental structure—with its acoustically short vowel and following unvoiced obstruent consonant—is not one which normally carries stød. If this fact is part of the implicit knowledge of Danish speakers and hearers about Danish sound structure, as we strongly believe to be the case, then no word with stød in the lexicon was available for identification and the truncated item would have to be rejected as a proper examplar of a Danish word. (2b) Presence of perceptible creaky voice in the truncated vowel initiated a lexical search for an item with the appropriate long vowel (in spite of its indisputable acoustic shortness). However, that road was closed because there is no *['ɛːˀsɐ] in the lexicon, it is a

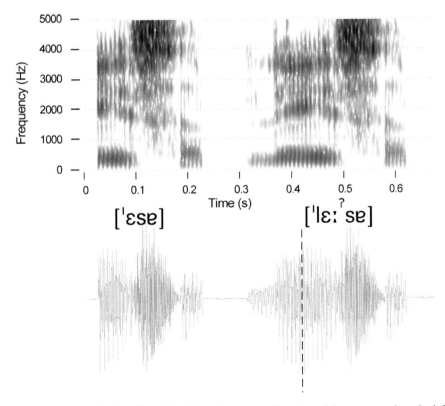

FIGURE 13.3. A word with stød on the right and a truncated version of the same word on the left. The vertical stroke in the righthand waveform indicates the point of incision. See text.

non-word, an accidental gap. Under either (2a) or (2b), listeners would have been free to respond that "this is not a Danish word", "it sounds strange", etc., but they did not. We take this to mean that the simple solution in (1) is the most likely interpretation and that there was indeed no perceptible stød in the latter part of the vowel in this particular instance, at least nothing which prevented identification of the truncated item as a short stød-less vowel in a non-stød syllable.

Similarly, the [l] and the first half of the vowel were removed from the word ['lɛːˀnɐ] *læner* "leans" (Fig. 13.4, right). The truncated item (Fig. 13.4, left) was identified as *ænder* "ducks" ['ɛnˀɐ] (['ʔɛnˀɐ]). And indeed, the stød is seen in the waveform to have spilled way over into the following consonant; no doubt it was perceptible. This item has a perfect match in the lexicon, *ænder* /ɛnˀər/ ['ɛnˀɐ] "ducks". If the stød had actually been confined acoustically to the vocalic portion of the truncated item, in accordance with a strict moraic analysis (Basbøll 1998), or if the audience had perceived it to be thus confined, there are three possibilities to consider, given the clash between an acoustic and/or perceptual reality and the structural impossibility for a short vowel to have stød. (1) The item would still be perceived as *ænder* ['ɛnˀɐ] "ducks" in the absence of a better lexical option. (2) The creaky voice would be

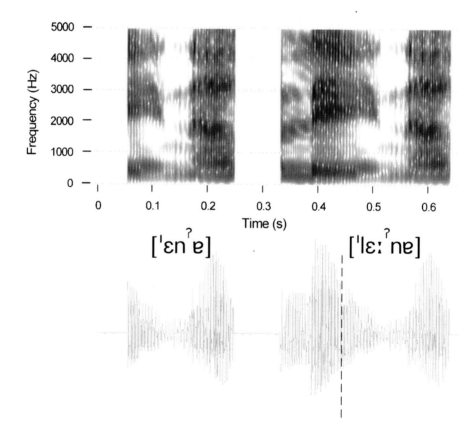

FIGURE 13.4. A word with stød on the right and a truncated version of the same word on the left. The vertical stroke in the righthand waveform indicates the point of incision. See text.

disregarded and a lexical match to the token would be found in the stød-less word with a short vowel, *ender* (n., pl.) /ɛnər/ ['ɛnɐ] "ends." (3) The perceived presence of stød in the vowel would have triggered a lexical search for a word with the appropriate vowel length, but */ɛːˀnər/ [ɛːˀnɐ] happens to be a non-word. Under this assumption, the item should have been rejected as a proper Danish word. Again we opt for the simplest interpretation: the stød was perceived in accordance with its physical presence in the postvocalic nasal.

13.2.1 Empirical issues

Basbøll's (1998) mora-analysis, and Fischer-Jørgensen's previous (1987, 1989*a*, *b*) analyses, posed a number of questions about consonant and vowel duration and about the perception of stød. Over the past three or four years we have addressed some of them:

- Vowels with stød are as long acoustically and perceptually as long vowels without stød. Accordingly, stød vowels could be bi-moraic (Grønnum and Basbøll 2002*a*, *b*).
- Consonants with stød are not generally longer acoustically than consonants without stød across all positions. If consonants without stød are not moraic (as in Basbøll 1998, but cf. Basbøll 2005: 305–10), and if morae in Danish are to have durational correlates in the consonants, as they do in typical mora-counting languages, this is an obstacle for the analysis (Grønnum and Basbøll 2001*a*, *b*).
- Listeners generally perceive the stød onset in long vowels coinciding with vowel onset. In other words, there is no perceptual bipartition, with stød confined to the second part of long vowels (Grønnum and Basbøll 2003*a*, *b*). These results contradict Basbøll's (1988, 1998) and Fischer-Jørgensen's (1987, 1989*a*, *b*) claims.

Our studies led us to conclude that:

- the exact acoustic properties, the timing, and the segmental domain of the stød are highly variable;
- there is no evidence to indicate that vowels with stød have two perceptually distinct phases.

Basbøll's (1988) proposal, "stød as a signal for the second mora of syllables" is therefore not an acoustic nor an immediate cognitive reality. His mora analysis then underwent significant changes in the following years: extra-prosodicity became a central concept, and with it he was able to make a number of important predictions about stød and lexical patterning (Basbøll 2003, 2005: 400–14).

13.2.2 Stød as a ballistic gesture

Fischer-Jørgensen (1987, 1989*a*, *b*) presents an account of various phonation types, particularly creaky voice. She concludes that many features are identical for creaky voice and stød, but that stød is not just creaky voice. We agree entirely. On the basis of our acoustic and perceptual observations, here is how we propose to characterize the stød phonetically:

- the laryngeal activity is a ballistic gesture which, minimally, makes for a slightly compressed voice quality, at one end of a continuum, and, maximally, creates a distinctly creaky voice at the other. Under emphasis it may become a complete glottal closure;
- it is a property of the syllable rhyme as a whole;
- it is aligned with the onset of the rhyme;
- it is variable with respect to strength and to temporal extension.

The proposed ballistic gesture is to be understood as the low-pass filtered muscular response to a transient neural command. The neural command is presumably timed to coincide with the onset of the rhyme. The impulse may be stronger or weaker, resulting in more or less irregular vocal fold vibration of shorter or longer duration, but once the command is executed, the speaker can no longer control the way the vocal folds respond to the excitation, just as one can no longer control the trajectory of a cannon ball once the cannon is fired. This proposal is consistent with the fact that speakers cannot freely choose to increase the duration of the stød the way one may choose to lengthen creaky voice at the end of an utterance. It is also consistent with the way we have seen the stød to behave acoustically: the more or less explicit non-modal vocal fold vibration, the variable timing of the occurrence of creaky voice in the waveform and the spectrogram, and the variable total duration which often makes it continue well into the following syllable. Furthermore, our proposal is consistent with EMG-data: the higher vocalis muscle activity in stød relative to modal voice increases and decreases gradually (Fischer-Jørgensen 1987, 1989*a*, *b*). It would be curious indeed if the actual mechanical change in vocal fold vibration mode were not also gradual. At present we have no indication that the variability in strength and timing is not random. However, investigations of stød in a corpus of non-scripted speech (Grønnum 2006, forthcoming) may reveal individual differences among speakers and variation as a function of speech rate, or, more likely, degree of prominence on the syllable.

Parts of our present proposal could be tested in the future with the high-speed laser light fiberscopic video recording technique (about 1,000 to 2,000 frames per second) developed by Larsen and Goller (2002) at the Institute of Biology at the University of Southern Denmark at Odense, to look at the syringes of small singing birds.

13.3 PHONOLOGICAL AND MORPHOLOGICAL FACTORS IN THE DISTRIBUTION OF STØD

Before focusing on the phonological and morphological factors that are relevant to the distribution of stød, we should note that stød appears where it did not belong originally. This is reflected, inter alia, in the way most Danes pronounce some of the German and Austrian composers:

['beːtˢowʔn̥] *Beethoven*, not ['beːtʰofən]
['hɛnʔd̥l̥] *Händel*, not ['hɛndəl]
['moːsaːʔd̥] *Mozart*, not ['moːtˢsaʁt]
['cuːʔb̥ɐd̥] *Schubert*, not ['ʃuːb̥ɐt]
[b̥ʁaːʔms] *Brahms*, not [b̥ʁaːms]

In other words, stød is productive.

13.3.1 Stød and word structure

This section presents some instantiations of general principles stated in Basbøll (2003, 2005). A general, operative principle of stød is stated in (1)

(1)   Lexically specified properties remain constant throughout.

That is, if a lexical item is marked with stød, the stød will appear in every inflected and derived form and it is not subject to deletion under any circumstances (except as a consequence of stress reduction). Conversely, if a lexical item is marked for non-stød, stød does not turn up in any context. Such well-established lexicalized forms are not considered any further here because they are not the result of productive processes and they are immaterial to our presentation of stød in unexpected contexts and to our suggestion of phonological experiments which may reveal more about the nature of these recent developments.

13.3.1.1 Stød in non-inflected, non-derived words (lexical items)

As noted earlier, stød only occurs in segmentally heavy syllables with more than zero stress.

[muːʔs] *mus* "mouse"   ['muːsə] *muse* "muse (n)"
[pʰanʔd̥] *pant* "lien"   ['tˢaned̥ə] *tante* "aunt"
[vamʔs] *vams* "doublet"   ['b̥amsə] *bamse* "teddy-bear"

If the material above were all the material available to us we would conclude that monosyllabic lexical items have stød (provided the syllable is heavy), di-syllabic lexical items do not. However,

[g̊aˈlanʔd̥] *galant* "chivalrous" is di-syllabic but has stød
[baˈlaŋsə] *balance* "equilibrium" is tri-syllabic without stød
[eləˈfanʔd̥] *elefant* "elephant" is tri-syllabic with stød

The proper general principle at this stage is stated in (2).

(2)   The penultimate syllable of lexical items has no stød.

There are exceptions to this principle, however, in some lexical items ending in /əl, ən, ər/, for example, ['ɛŋʔg̊l̥, 'vɔːʔb̥n̩, 'ilʔd̥ɐ] *enkel, våben, ilter* "simple, weapon, short-tempered", but not all: [ˈɛŋl̩, ˈɔːbn̩, ˈildɐ] *engel, åben, ilter* "angel, open, oxidizes". Most of the lexicalized forms with stød derive historically from monosyllables. According to (1), such lexical items with lexicalized stød properties do not undergo morphological stød-alternations.

13.3.1.2 Inflection and derivation

Matters get more complex in inflected and derived words due to the different behavior of suffixes, depending on their productivity (as described by Basbøll 2003, 2005: 351–63). Danish suffixes, irrespective of their status as inflectional or derivational, come in three degrees of productivity (three degrees of integration with the stem):

(3)   Suffixes are fully productive, semi-productive, or non-productive.

Matters are considerably simplified now, however, compared to previous descriptions, because the pertinent question no longer is which syllables have stød, but rather:

(4)   When does a heavy syllable in a polymorphemic word not have stød?

The answer is given in two stages:

(4)   a. It depends on the productivity of the suffix.
      b. Before semi-productive suffixes it also depends on the stem: monosyllabic versus polysyllabic.

We will look at one suffix only from each of the three productivity groups for illustration, which will suffice to give the reader an idea of the principles regulating stød in inflected and derived forms.

Productive suffixes

An example of a productive suffix is the plural morpheme /ər/, cf.:
[væːˀl] *hval* "whale (sg.)"   [ˈvæːˀlɐ] (pl.)
[eləˈfanˀd] *elefant* "elephant (sg.)"   [eləˈfanˀdɐ] (pl.)
[ˈtˢandə] *tante* "aunt (sg.)"   [ˈtˢandɐ] (pl.)[3]
[faˈjaŋsə] *fajance* "faience (sg.)"   [faˈjaŋsɐ] (pl.).

The lexical items with stød retain it in the plural, and the stød-less lexical items remain without stød, because:

(5)   productive suffixes have no effect on stød as such.[4]

There are many ways to conceptualize this fact; one might be that the productive suffix is so loosely connected with the stem that stem and suffix do not interact.

---

[3]   /ə/+/ə/ contract to /ə/, thus /tantə/+/ər/ > /tantər/.

[4]   However, an added suffix may modify the moraic structure of the stem to the effect that the word receives stød. Thus, *han* "he" is pluralized as /han/+/ər/. The stem-final /n/ cannot be extra-prosodic since it is not word-final (Basbøll 2005: 388–93), and accordingly we get [ˈhanˀɐ] *hanner* "males".

Non-productive suffixes

An example of a non-productive suffix is the plural morpheme /ə/:

[hun?] *hund* "dog (sg.)"   ['hunə] (pl.)
[so:?l] *sol* "sun (sg.)"   ['so:lə] (pl.)
[hu:?s] *hus* "house (sg.)"   ['hu:sə] (pl.)

and myriad other examples. We can then state the principle in (6).

(6)   A non-productive suffix is integrated in the stem.

Since the ensemble behaves like a lexical item, principle (2) is operative: the penultimate syllable of lexical items has no stød. This integration of stem and suffix may be conceived as the effect of a weak boundary between them. It stands to reason that a productive suffix has a more autonomous status cognitively, and is more easily separable from the stem, than a non-productive one.

Semi-productive suffixes

An example of a semi-productive suffix is infinitive /ə/:

['b̥ʁu:u] *bruge* "use"   ['g̊ɛnb̥ʁu:?u] *genbruge* "recycle"
['falə] *falde* "fall"   ['ɒwɛfal?ə] *overfalde* "attack"

(7)   Before semi-productive suffixes monosyllabic stems have no stød

But a stød appears when the stem is expanded to the left. The net result is that phonology and morphology together, by and large, predict the presence and absence of stød. Conversely, stød and its absence will act as a cue to morphological structure. Note especially that the principles governing the presence and absence of stød are not sensitive to word class but exclusively to word structure (syllabic structure) and degree of productivity of the (inflectional or derivational) suffix.

13.3.2 Stød in new and unexpected contexts

The principles for stød assignment seem to be in the process of change, in the direction of simplification and generality, as indicated by data from the Danish radio (channel 1), collected by the first author (Grønnum) during the past decade. Many of the examples given below are unexpected and in disagreement with Basbøll's (2005) model and with all the previous literature. They would generally surprise most speakers of standard Danish.

Simple nouns in the plural

['fɔ:mu:?ɐ] *formuer* "fortunes" but ['fɔ:mu:u] *formue* is always without stød in the
   singular;
['ʌmʁɔ:?ð̞ɐ] *områder* "areas" but ['ʌmʁɔ:ð̞ə] *område* is always without stød in the
   singular.

This is surprising in light of principle 5: productive suffixes have no effect on the stød, and plural /ər/ ([ɐ]) is productive. If we would argue that perhaps the boundary between lexical item and suffix has weakened, then we would be dealing with a penultimate syllable in a (pseudo-) lexical item, and it would have no stød anyway.

Compound nouns in the plural

['viːnnɑwˀnə] *vinnavne* "wine names" but ['nɑwnə] *navne* is always without stød in
    isolation;
['syːyhuːˀsə] *sygehuse* "sickhouses (i.e. hospitals)" but ['huːsə] *huse* is always without
stød in isolation.

Verbal adjectives

['ɛŋˀlsg̊tˢæːˀlnə] *engelsktalende* "English-speaking" but ['tˢæːlnə] *talende* is always
without stød in isolation;
['valb̥əliːˀn̩nə] *hvalpelignende* "puppy-resembling" but isolated ['liːn̩nə] *lignende* is
always without stød.

There is an abundance of similar examples. If the presence of stød is to be accounted for in a principled manner in such examples, we shall have to isolate the compound stem thus:

*engelsktal+e "English-speak"
*hvalpelign+e "puppy-resemble."

Thus, principle (7) would be operative: only monosyllabic stems before semi-productive suffixes, in this case infinitive schwa, are without stød. But such a parse is in stark contrast with our semantic intuitions about the elements in these forms. There is no *engelsktale and no *hvalpeligne in the lexicon. However, although the reasoning about the verbal adjectives here is counter to our semantic intuitions, at least we could rationalize them. But how do we characterize the plurals above (['fɔːmuːˀɐ 'ʌmʁɔːˀðɐ 'viːnnɑwˀnə 'syːyhuːˀsə] *formuer, områder, vinnavne, sygehuse*)?

   We could attempt the following. The stems, whether compound or simple, with unexpected stød have two things in common—they have endings and they are polysyllabic. We could therefore say that perhaps principle (7) is in the process of being generalized to

(7′)   Before any syllabic suffix only monosyllabic stems have no stød.

However, matters get worse—or better—according to temperament:

Non-inflected lexical items

['ɛmb̥eːˀðə] *embede* "office (a post)"
['tˢœɐ̯kʰlɛːˀðə] *tørklæde* "kerchief."

These syllables with stød are penultimate in the lexical item and they do not carry primary word stress. They should be stødless. However, the words end in a vowel which is phonetically identical to a semi-productive suffix (infinitive /ə/) which we have already seen to trigger stød in a preceding polysyllabic stem. So perhaps principle (7) is sneaking in where it does not really belong, namely, within a lexical item. Or perhaps it is the generalization we proposed in (7′) which penetrates the lexical item: before any syllabic suffix only monosyllabic stems have no stød.

Non-inflected compound noun stems

['viːŋɔmˀi] *vingummi* "wine gum" but ['g̊ɔmi] *gummi* in isolation is always without stød;

['uvilˀjə] *uvilje* "ill-will" but isolated ['viljə] *vilje* is always without stød.

However, *vingummi* ends in a vowel, [i], which is phonetically identical to a semi-productive derivative suffix (-*ig* /i/) which, in accordance with (7), induces stød in polysyllabic stems, as in

['moːði] *modig* "courageous" without stød always, but ['ɒwɛmoːˀði] *overmodig* "foolhardy" with stød;

['løːði] *lødig* "valuable" without stød always, but ['ɔnɐløːˀði] *underlødig* "substandard" with stød.

Uvilje ends in schwa, phonetically identical to the semi-productive infinitive suffix which, again in accordance with principle [7], induces stød in polysyllabic stems.

What we are witnessing, as suggested above, may be the change from a specific morphological parse, as in (7), to the mere recognition of morphological complexity which is indiscriminate with regard to the nature of the specific suffix, as in (7′). From there we move to a parse which relies on the identification of certain sounds at the end of the word and their separation from a preceding pseudo-stem, so that we arrive at (7″).

(7″)   In any word which phonetically resembles a stem + a syllabic suffix, only monosyllabic stems have no stød.

The net result is that more and more heavy syllables will have stød, and the need to formulate principles for its absence will diminish accordingly.

If this is not a passing phenomenon, but spreads and gains a foothold, it will have far reaching consequences for stød and its functions: only in paroxytonic di-syllables will stød be truly distinctive and have morphological *raison d'être*. In other contexts it will become entirely predictable from syllable structure and word structure alone, and thus independent of the morphological content.

13.4 CONCLUSION

In this Chapter we presented acoustic and perceptual evidence on Danish stød. The creaky voice characteristic of Danish stød is described phonetically as a property of the syllable rhyme, aligned with the onset of the stressed vowel and highly variable in strength and temporal extension. We argued that the phonetic nature of stød makes it a poor candidate as a signal for the second mora of syllables (Basbøll 1988) at a surface phonological level, thus challenging moraic interpretations. The distribution of stød is shown to be sensitive to phonological and morphological structure, and the productivity of suffixes. Evidence is presented that stød is in the process of spreading to new contexts which may lead to a change and simplification of the distributional facts. Thus the principles governing the presence or absence of stød may be changing from expressing morphological and semantic conditions towards expressing purely formal phonological conditions in the word. The productivity of this purported change in the nature of stød-governing principles can be tested in fairly straightforward production experiments. We intend to address this issue in the future.

PART IV
Maintaining, Enhancing, and Modeling Phonological Contrasts

14

Articulatory Movements and Phrase Boundaries

Patrizia Bonaventura and Osamu Fujimura

14.1 INTRODUCTION

The present study investigates the systematic effect of two prosodic parameters, syllable duration reflecting magnitude of the syllable and magnitude of the gap between two syllables, on the strength of consonantal gestures. In general, consonantal gestures show a larger excursion in phrase-final and -initial, than in phrase-medial position (Kelso *et al.* 1985; Ostry and Munhall 1985; Bonaventura 2003; Keating *et al.* 2003; Cho 2005). For example, previous research on articulatory strengthening by Fougeron and Keating (1997) has shown that the magnitude and duration of consonantal gestures depend on syllable boundaries, position in the phrase, and strength of phrase boundaries. Further research has confirmed these results, showing larger displacements and longer relative durations of consonantal movements during constriction formation and release at phrase edges than in phrase-medial positions (Beckman and Edwards 1992; Byrd and Saltzman 1998; Byrd *et al.* 2000). Such effects have been interpreted as due to the presence of a prosodic gesture (π-gesture; Byrd and Saltzman 2003) that is activated at phrase boundaries, with a strength related to the strength of the juncture, and that slows down adjacent onset and coda gestures at phrase edges (Byrd *et al.* 2005). Although specific measurements of syllable-position (onset, coda) and phrase-position (medial, edge) effects have shown inconsistent patterns of gestural lengthening, both within and across subjects and across consonantal locations in the syllable and consonant types, the general pattern of lengthening of onset and coda consonantal gestures at phrase boundaries, more prominent for consonants adjacent to the boundary and more evident in onsets than in codas, is upheld in the literature (Byrd *et al.* 2005).

The authors wish to acknowledge their sincere gratitude for substantive editorial assistance offered by Dr. Patrice Beddor along with very helpful comments by Dr. Gary Weismar, who reviewed this chapter.

Most previous studies that have observed effects of position on gestural displacement have considered the prosodic position of the consonant as a major factor in determining the spatio-temporal pattern of the consonantal gesture. The research reported here analyzed prosodic influences on gestural strength from a different perspective. Following the interpretative framework of the Converter/Distributor model of speech production (Fujimura and Williams 1999; Fujimura 2003), we tested the hypothesis that the duration of the syllable containing the target consonant, the duration of the gap at the boundary of two syllables, and, of course, the duration of the phrase-final gap, might all have a determinant role in influencing the speed of a gesture. Previous studies have found that excursion (intended as the amount of displacement from one end of a movement to the other end i.e. the total traveling distance) can be considered as a predictor of speed of the consonantal movement (Bonaventura 2003), both in onset and in coda positions. This chapter investigates whether prosodic factors such as syllable magnitude and boundary duration can also be considered as predictors of speed of onset and coda consonantal movements.

We begin with a short introduction to the conceptual approach of the C/D model is provided, followed by the presentation and discussion of the methodology and results of the analysis of the effects of syllable and gap duration on articulator velocity in consonantal movements.

14.2 THE CONVERTER/DISTRIBUTOR MODEL

The Converter/Distributor (C/D) Model is a non-traditional, relatively powerful model of phonetic organization that uses syllables instead of phonemes as the concatenative units of speech signals. It represents the rhythmic organization of an utterance by a magnitude-controlled syllable-boundary pulse train, as illustrated in Figure 14.1. Syllable durations are computed based on the magnitude distribution

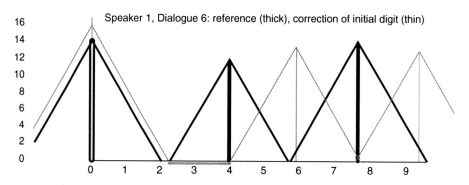

FIGURE 14.1. Effect of contrastive emphasis on the triangle train for reference (thick line) and emphasized (thin line) productions of the digits 959 (with correction of the initial digit in the emphasized form) ("Blue Pine" data; Speaker 1, Dialogue 6, Phrase "No, 959").

of the syllable pulses. Taking temporal gaps between consecutive syllables as representing the boundary pulse magnitudes, syllable-boundary triangles are placed in time
as a contiguous series. The physical magnitude of each boundary as well as of each
syllable is continuously variable according to various utterance factors.

   Fujimura (1986*a*), based on X-ray microbeam data, suggested that a certain aspect
of articulatory movement patterns was characteristically constant for a given demisyllable, even across varying stress conditions. One such relatively invariant pattern was
the speed of movement of the articulator crucially responsible for an obstruent
gesture crossing a fixed height threshold relative to the occlusal plane, for a given
speaker. The time function representing the first time derivative (velocity) of a flesh-
point (pellet) position resembled the tip of the floating iceberg.

   Fujimura (2000, see also 1992) subsequently proposed the C/D model as a new
comprehensive theory of phonetic implementation. The theory assumed, as did
Öhman (1967), that a sequence of vowel gestures for syllable nuclei formed a slowly
changing syllabic gesture (phonetic status contour) as an aspect of what is called
base function, on which local quick gestures for consonants (elemental gestures)
are superimposed, according to syllabic feature specifications. Figure 14.2 gives an

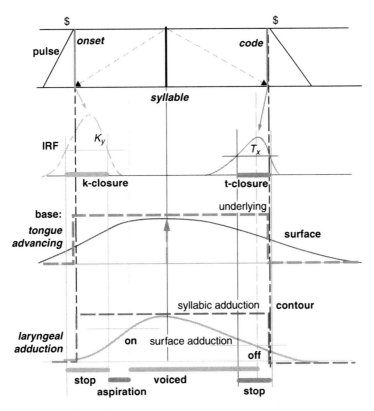

FIGURE 14.2. *kit* (C/D diagram).

example of what is called the C/D model, depicting in this case an utterance of the monosyllabic word *kit* in isolation (the effects of phrase boundaries that always accompany an utterance of a word in isolation are not shown in this illustration). At the top of this figure, the thick vertical bar represents the syllable pulse, the height of which represents the magnitude of the syllable, that is, the degree of stress. On both left and right sides of this pulse, there are slanting lines which form a symmetric triangle (in this case of a light syllable with a simple coda consonant). The angle of the triangle is assumed to be fixed (if all the syllable types involved are the same) throughout the utterance, regardless of stress variation. Therefore, the variation of syllable durations occurs according to the syllable magnitude variation, namely the stress pattern. An example of such magnitude variation is illustrated in Figure 14.1, comparing two prosodically different utterances of the same sentence.

In the second panel of Figure 14.2, the elemental gestures of the onset and coda consonants of this syllable are depicted as abstract control patterns. Each of these gestures is the result of exciting a stored impulse response function (IRF) for the consonant, according to the phonological feature specifications (K for {dorsal}, T for {apical}, tau for {stop}). Both stop gestures, for /k/ in onset and /t/ in coda, are separately defined, the shapes being different according to the choice of design parameters. Generally, the peak amplitude is larger for onset gestures than for coda gestures. The pertinent IRF is selected for the phonologically specified consonant for the intrasyllabic position and it is excited by a pulse, as indicated by the downward arrow for each of the two gestures. The excitation pulse is the same in magnitude as the syllable pulse but shifted in time to the left or right end of the syllable triangle. These local time functions are abstract control functions; when these are implemen- ted as actual speech gestures in the proper articulatory dimensions, the gestures are superimposed onto the pertinent articulatory dimensions of the base function that implement a series of vowel gestures as well as jaw opening gestures. As the consonantal gestures are implemented by the crucial articulator, such as the tongue tip for apical consonants and tongue dorsum for dorsal stops, the movement of the articulator is constrained by physical obstacles according to the anatomical situ- ation and following physical laws. A coarse depiction of the highly nonlinear situation is indicated by the thin horizontal line as a threshold of saturation of the movements of such articulators. The upward and downward crossing of the control function can be conceived as the moments of implosion and explosion of the stop closures in this simple example, as shown by the thick horizontal bars.

The third panel of Figure 14.2 depicts one aspect of the vocalic gesture, one of the (in itself complex) muscular control gestures represented in the C/D model as different dimensions of the base function. The front/back control of the tongue body according to the binary choice of phonological feature {± back} is assumed, and this example uses a high front vowel as the syllable nucleus. A tongue-advancing gesture is prescribed as indicated by the broken line forming a step function, con- necting the resting target and the fronting target. The solid curves represent a coarticulated realization of such an underlying function. The upward arrow suggests that the magnitude of deviation from the neutral position in the pertinent dimension is affected by the syllable magnitude.

The bottom curve portrays the laryngeal abduction–adduction control. Generally, a syllable causes vocal fold approximation around its center, as suggested by the dashed step function in the context of unvoiced boundaries. The base function component of voicing control is a coarticulated version of such a step function, but affected at the syllable edges by obstruent consonantal specifications, which evoke laryngeal abduction at the pertinent edges of the syllable by means of a devoicing IRF (not shown here). The control function governs the temporal change of the glottal aperture by laryngeal muscles. Accordingly, the vocal folds change their position from abducted to adducted and then to abducted again as indicated by the smooth curve. Given the subglottal pressure due to respiratory control, airflow occurs through the glottal aperture and vocal fold vibration occurs at a certain threshold aperture, as depicted by the thin horizontal line (see the mark "on"). As the vocal folds separate toward the end of the syllable, the vibration stops (see the mark "off"). The on and off threshold values are not the same, partly due to hysteresis of the vibrating tissues, and partly due to the change of the respiratory pressure—in other words, due to an interaction between this control variable and another control variable related to pulmonic pressure control, which is not shown in this figure.

With respect to the impulse response function, the C/D model assumes that each elemental consonantal gesture constitutes a fixed ballistic motion pattern, which, as a passive response, is evoked by a time-shifted replica (onset pulse, coda pulse, etc.) of the syllable pulse as the excitation. This conceptual model of the elemental gesture is not necessarily meant to be the exact modeling of the physical process, since the movement process may well include active processes based on localized feedback processes. The point is that, phenomenologically, this picture of the whole course of action for the demisyllable as autonomous and independent from other concomitant gestures helps us to understand and represent quantitatively what occurs in the extremely complex phenomena in terms of phonetically effective control variables. In the case of vocalic gestures, since the temporal change is the effect of basically a syllable-to-syllable slow change, there may well be a significant role of auditory feedback. The C/D model provides a simplified phenomenological description that suffices to capture basic properties of speech production principles and their effective representation. For computation of the phonetic implementation, all elemental gestures for consonants, as demisyllabic constituents (i.e. onsets, codas, or syllable affixes) of the syllable are stored in an impulse-response function (IRF) table, and only its amplitude and triggering time are assumed to be controlled under the government of the syllable pulse, according to the computational algorithm outlined above, in various prosodic situations, except that boundary effects must be computed as discussed below.

Thus, the evoked elemental gesture is amplified, without changing the shape of the local time function, according to the magnitude of the syllable occurring in the utterance, as a linear response to the syllable pulse excitation (shifted in time for the syllable margin). This may sound as though the previous assertions of the iceberg concept were contradicted, since now the consonantal movement should change according to the change of the syllable magnitude for a prosodic condition such as emphasis, contrary to the iceberg concept which says that a fixed part of the movement function should not be affected by any prosodic change. However, it can be shown mathematically that this is not necessarily a contradiction (Fujimura 1996) but an empirical issue. Depending on the time function for the IRF, the speed of crossing a fixed threshold position can be constant when the function is amplified by a multiplication constant. For example, exponential functions have such a property. An amplitude adjustment, by a multiplication of a constant C, of an exponential function of time t, results in a shifting, in time, of the same time function by the logarithm of C, as seen by the mathematical derivation in (1).

(1) $C \times \exp(at + b)$
    $= \exp(ln\ C) \times \exp(at + b)$
    $= \exp(at + b + ln\ C)$

Of course, in reality, the tongue tip cannot move exponentially in time indefinitely, but it is conceivable that the beginning of the rising movement is exponential and later becomes saturated through contact with the hard palate or the upper lip, though the actual process of saturation must be gradual flattening of the function rather than discontinuous change of the time derivative, as the three-dimensional anatomical structure causes many nonlinear interactions among parts of the organ tissues—not only within the midsagittal plane, as we often see in the lateral pictures.

This nearly exponential movement model would imply that the speed is proportional to the distance above the starting (or some reference) point in the initial phase of the movement. If this is the case, then an increase in syllable magnitude by a factor C is observed, not as an increase in the iceberg threshold crossing speed, but as an increase in syllable duration as measured as the time interval between the threshold crossing times for the initial and final demisyllables. Naturally, such a time function representing actual movement may be simply fictitious. Therefore, it remains to be seen whether the relative invariance of the iceberg pattern as suggested by Fujimura (1986b) is actually observed in data when the prosodic condition is systematically controlled *ceteris paribus*.

Bonaventura (2003) has addressed this issue and provided quantitative data using read speech-articulation material. Since "icebergs" were observed on small sets of data in the preliminary analyses (Fujimura 1986b), the first aim of the new study was to extend the observation to a larger corpus of a few selected demisyllables, to test the concept against systematically collected data. Specific issues related to the existence of icebergs that we tested included whether initial and final demisyllables showed similar slope invariance, given the expectation that important prosodic effects such as phrase-final elongation would be more prominent in final than in initial demisyllables.

The effect of the position of the word within a phrase on phrase-final elongation effects was also examined for comparison with the results of Menezes (2003), who analyzed more free-style conversational data of the same street address being corrected repeatedly (Blue Pine data).

14.2.1 Phrase-final elongation

Phrase-final elongation is a phonetic phrase-boundary effect that appears mainly as rhyme elongation in phrase-final position. The elongation could be modeled as an expansion of the time scale, slowing down all gestures in the same way (see the prosodic gesture model of Byrd and Saltzman 2003). Alternatively, the elongation could be a matter of inserting a specific boundary duration, perhaps implemented as an adjustment of the proportionality coefficient in the relation (i.e. the triangle slope) between the magnitude and the duration values of an asymmetric syllable triangle (the right-hand shadow angle adjustment implemented as a function of the magnitude of the immediately following boundary), delaying the occurrences of coda and s-fix (optional affix, placed to the right of the syllable core) gestures, without changing their shapes. Or the elongation could create a pause, whether it is a period of silence or a period filled with spilled over voicing and other articulatory gestures. In the last case, individual control variables may exhibit different deceleration characteristics. It could be a combination of these. Currently available articulatory data are not sufficient to determine which model should be used. Bonaventura (2003), along with Mitchell's (2000) thesis and Menezes's (2003) dissertation, attempted to provide empirical data for developing a quantitative model. The latter two studies, analyzing acoustic syllable duration and magnitude of jaw opening on a corpus of semi-spontaneous speech including repeated digits corrections, found that different speakers used different articulatory implementation strategies in connection with phrase-final lengthening; two of the speakers used reduced jaw opening on the phrase-final digit (as observed articulatorily), in connection with a longer closure phase, with respect to the opening movement (as observed in the acoustic syllable duration). The other two speakers realized the final digit with increased jaw opening, a contrasting strategy possibly linked to syntagmatic alteration of stressed elements (M. Liberman 1975), rather than to phrase-final lengthening. In studies focusing on invariant patterns of articulatory movements of the lower lip and tongue tip as crucial articulators (Bonaventura 2003, from a read speech corpus of corrected digits), results showed evidence of movement patterns in coda in phrase-final position that deviated from patterns of linear dependency of excursion on speed which were more generally found across speakers.

Due to the variability of the speakers' realizations of phrase-final lengthening, and to the difference in the analyzed corpora, it is impossible to propose, on the basis of the current data, an optimal model of representation of phrase-final lengthening effects.

The present study aims at verifying previous results from Bonaventura's (2003) dissertation, Mitchell's (2000) thesis, and Menezes's (2003) dissertation by testing the influence of syllable duration (inferred from articulatory movements, and considered in this paper as a measure of the syllable magnitude) and of gap duration on speed of crucial articulator movement, based on a corpus of read speech.

14.3 METHOD

14.3.1 Data

The articulatory data were acquired at the University of Wisconsin by the X-ray Microbeam system. The data consist of articulatory records, obtained by automatically tracking the movement of gold pellets affixed on selected points of articulatory organs. The positioning of the pellets is illustrated in Figure 14.3. Pellets were affixed on four points of the tongue surface, the lower lip, and on the mandible at the lower incisor and a molar tooth, recording the movement of the articulators with respect to the maxillary occlusal plane (bite plane). Head movements are corrected for, so that articulatory movements relative to the skull were measured.

For the present study, the "New Red Pine 96" corpus was used, collected by Donna Erickson (Erickson 2002). This corpus includes dialogues of the form *Is it 995 Pine Street? No, it's 955 Pine Street. Is it 995 Pine Street? No, it's 595 Pine Street*, etc. Such question–answer exchanges include reference digits (in questions) and corrected and uncorrected digits in correcting utterances, with both the question and answer being spoken by the subject. The corrected digit in the three-digit sequence sounded emphasized, so they will be referred to as "emphasized", whereas the uncorrected digits, in the correcting utterances, will be referred to as "unemphasized". Digits in questions or affirming answers will be referred to as "reference".

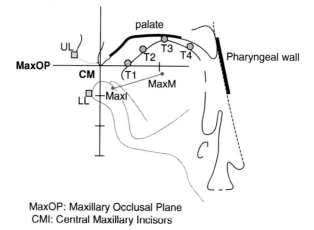

MaxOP: Maxillary Occlusal Plane
CMI: Central Maxillary Incisors

FIGURE 14.3. Pellet configuration (Nadler *et al.* 1987; printed with consent of the author).

14.3.2 Subjects

The subjects were three native speakers of Midwest American English, two males and one female.

14.3.3 Data analysis

14.3.3.1 Analysis of iceberg invariance

Iceberg curves (see Section 14.2) were measured and extracted from the tracings of the crucial articulator for production of the digits 9 and 5 in the dialogs. These monosyllabic words share the same obstruent articulator in initial and final demisyllables (lower lip for *five* and tongue tip for *nine*), and they share the same vocalic nucleus (the diphthong [aj]). The corpus was designed in order to observe variation of prosodic patterns. Iceberg curves were drawn in the original figures, according to the three different emphasis conditions, as illustrated in Figure 14.4 for one speaker's productions of *five*.

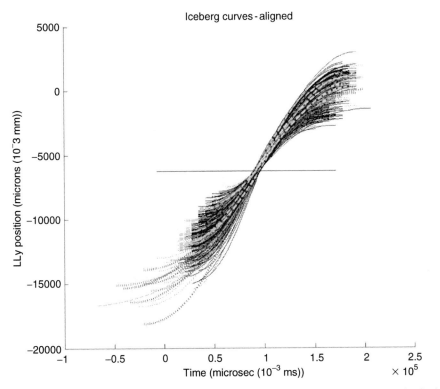

FIGURE 14.4. Speaker DE3, word *five*, 340 iceberg curves of lower-lip vertical displacement for final demisyllables. Solid curves represent reference digits, dashed curves indicate unemphasized digits, and dotted curves emphasized digits.

Invariance of the iceberg slope with respect to excursion distance was tested by obtaining scatterplots of velocity vs. excursion, and by performing linear regression and verifying the strength of the relations. Excursion, defined as the difference of pellet height values between the beginning and ending values of each visually determined demisyllabic movement curve, primarily reflects the vocalic position in the base function, since the consonantal gesture is usually saturated and therefore nearly constant. The C/D model suggests that the speed at each phase of the movement may depend in part on the total excursion, and such dependence may also be observed in the slope in the vicinity of a constant position (height) of the pellet that is selected in the iceberg method as the crossing threshold of the movement of the crucial articulator (Fujimura 1986*a*, 1996). In fact, a linear relation between speed at iceberg crossing and excursion is shown by the scatterplot, again for speaker DE3, in Figure 14.5 (where digits in different emphasis conditions are differentiated by the shape of the markers).

14.3.3.2 Prosodic effects on iceberg invariance

As stated above, there is a clear effect of excursion, or syllable magnitude, on the threshold crossing slope. We now believe this effect is systematic (linear dependence)

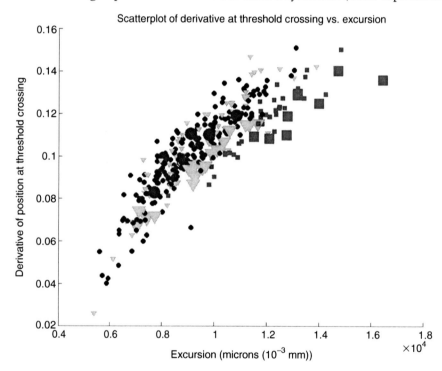

FIGURE 14.5. Speaker DE3, word *five* (340 curves), first derivative at crossing vs. excursion for initial demisyllables. Squares indicate emphasized digits, triangles unemphasized digits, and dots reference digits. Larger symbols indicate digits followed by phrase-final boundary.

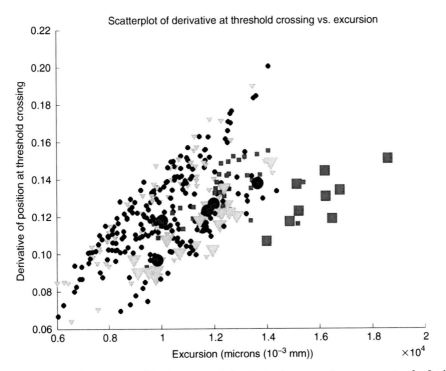

FIGURE 14.6. Speaker DE3, word *five* (340 curves), first derivative at crossing vs. excursion for final demisyllables. Squares indicate emphasized digits, triangles unemphasized digits, and dots reference digits. Larger symbols indicate digits followed by phrase-final boundary.

and therefore can be removed as a predictable component of the variability of the threshold-crossing speed. The non-constant relation between the threshold-crossing speed and excursion contradicts the original assumption by Fujimura about iceberg's invariance of demisyllabic movements (see Section 14.2). In addition, the results show evidence of systematic outliers that deviate from the linear dependence of movement speed on excursion (Fig. 14.6). This deviation may be caused by the phrase-final elongation effect of the immediately following boundary.

A possible approach to this variation may be that target movement of inherent dynamic gestures for each demisyllable might not be observed as an invariant pattern unless at least two effects are removed. One effect is syllable magnitude, which is related to the vocalic target gesture. In order to remove the prosodic effect of syllable magnitude on movement speed, we need to measure the excursion as a reflection of syllable magnitude. The consonantal gesture, as represented by the impulse response function in the C/D model, may or may not affect the iceberg crossing speed, as discussed before. The effect of increased syllable magnitude may be observed mainly by the shift in time of the elemental gesture, away from the syllable center, without affecting the speed. The consonantal gesture is amplified according to the syllable magnitude, but the peak of the position time function is not observed by saturation due to the fixed roof. The factor due to consonantal gesture reflecting syllable magnitude is thus predicted to be more or less insignificant in comparison with the vocalic positions, except that the timing of the movement is removed further out from the center of the syllable when the syllable magnitude is increased by prosodic control.

A second effect that may need to be removed for an invariant pattern of the iceberg threshold crossing speed to emerge is the magnitude of the following boundary, measured as the gap length in the computed series of articulatory syllable triangles. This effect is interpretable in a simple way if the effect of phrase-final lengthening due to the boundary is simply adjustment of the time scale toward the end of the phrase and the excursion magnitude is significantly affected by boundary magnitude only due to coarticulatory undershooting.

The present study aims to investigate and quantify the effect of syllable magnitude and boundary strength on speed of the consonantal movements in the selected syllables.

14.3.3.3 Segmentation for syllable duration and articulatory gap measurement

Segmentation for syllable duration and articulatory gap measurement was performed by the program "ubedit", designed and implemented by Bryan Pardo, who kindly permitted use of the program for the present study; ubedit displays the articulatory trackings from the X-ray microbeam data and aligns them with the corresponding waveform and spectrogram. The program also calculates the pulses corresponding to the center of the syllables by computing local minima, corresponding to max jaw opening, after passing the jaw movement time function through a strong smoothing filter with a time constant comparable to the syllable rate, which is in effect a curve-fitting process for identifying the mandibular minimum timing. No documentation is available for the program.

The example in Figure 14.7 shows segmentation on the Lower Lip vertical movement tracking in the upper window, the corresponding acoustic waveform and syllable pulses with shadows indicating the domain of the extension of the syllable in the lower two windows. The phrase analyzed is "5 9 5 Pine" (from record 32, speaker DE3).

14.4 RESULTS

14.4.1 Relation of speed with articulatory syllable duration

The relation between the speed of the lower-lip vertical movement and the duration of the syllable corresponding to the digit 5, which contains the lower-lip gesture, was investigated by obtaining scatterplots of the speed (as first derivative at the iceberg threshold, see Section 14.2) vs. articulatory syllable duration in initial and final demi-syllables. Syllable duration was measured by manual segmentation of the acoustic signal aligned with the articulatory trackings, and generated automatically by ubedit.

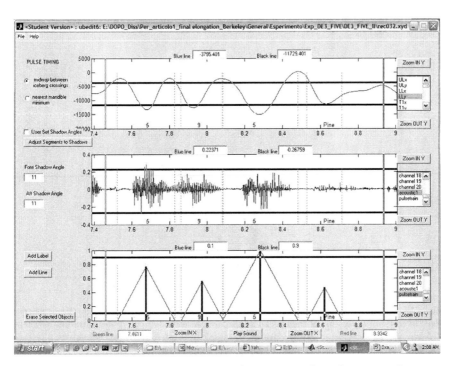

FIGURE 14.7. Program "ubedit": segmentation on the Lower Lip channel (upper window), waveform and syllable triangles. Last phrase "5 9 5 Pine", record 32, speaker DE3.

The speed of the lower lip movement at the iceberg threshold was considered separately for the initial and final demisyllables in the word *five*; the occurrences of the digits were labeled by emphasis (reference, unemphasized, and emphasized utterances) and by position in the phrase (initial, medial, and final). Examples of scatterplots illustrating the relationship of syllable duration with speed at threshold are given in Figures 14.8 and 14.9 for speaker DE3, for both initial and final demisyllables. (Only data from speaker DE3 are reported in this section because more extensive measures were taken for this speaker than for the other two; however, the results from speaker DE3 are not consistent with results from speakers DE1 and DE2, and therefore not representative of a general trend in this study; see Section 14.4.3).

The scatterplots in Figures 14.8 and 14.9 indicate rather weak (but significant) linear correlations of threshold crossing speed and syllable magnitude or duration, and possibly slower speed for emphasized syllables in phrase-final position (represented by asterisks); the latter syllables seem to have a relatively small syllable magnitude (i.e. jaw opening) while being affected by final lengthening. If so, these data support time-scale expansion as phrase-final lengthening (boundary effect) for the lower-lip gesture; the final-lengthening effect must also be tested for other articulatory movements in order to verify whether concurrent articulators besides the crucial one are slowed down by phrase boundary magnitude.

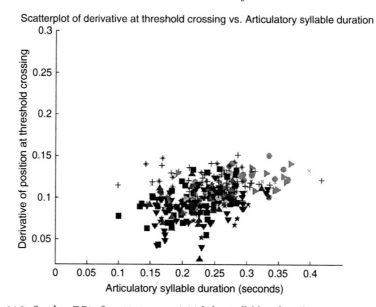

FIGURE 14.8. Speaker DE3, *five*, 334 curves, initial demisyllables, first derivative (i.e. movement speed) at threshold crossing of the crucial articulator vs. articulatory syllable duration, labeled by emphasis and by position. + = reference digit, initial; ■ = reference digit, medial; ▼ = reference digit, final; ● = unemphasized digit, initial; × = unemphasized digit, medial; ▶ = unemphasized digit, final; ✦ = emphasized digit, initial; ▲ = emphasized digit, medial; ★ = emphasized digit, final.

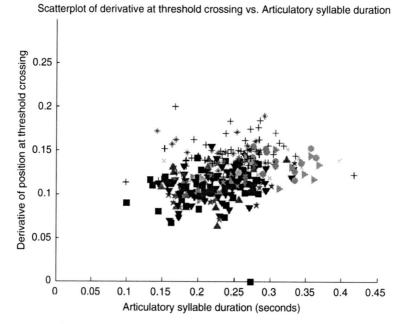

FIGURE 14.9. Speaker DE3, *five*, 334 curves, final demisyllables, first derivative at threshold vs. articulatory syllable duration, labeled by emphasis and by position (symbols as in Fig. 14.8).

14.4.2 Relation of speed with articulatory gap duration

Similarly, the relation between speed of the lower-lip vertical movement and duration of the gap as inferred by the syllable triangle computation following the digit 5 in the utterance, was investigated using scatterplots analogous to the ones described for syllable duration. Examples of the scatterplots showing first derivative at threshold vs. articulatory gap duration, in initial and final demisyllables, are given in Figures 14.10 and 14.11 for speaker DE3. The scatterplots indicate a weak (but significant; see Tables 14.3 and 14.4) negative correlation of threshold crossing speed and gap duration, showing longer gaps (especially in final demisyllables) after all final digits (reference, unemphasized, and emphasized).

These results seem to show that gap duration is affected by final lengthening, regardless of emphasis condition. This effect might be due to the fact that the reading pace of the utterances in the corpus did not induce sensible variations in the pauses following the emphasized vs. non-emphasized productions, pauses which would be more noticeable, instead, in the semi-spontaneous speech corpus of similar material (Menezes 2003).

14.4.3 Correlations of excursion, syllable duration, and boundary strength with speed

A multiple-regression analysis was performed to evaluate how well the prosodic factors of syllable magnitude and gap duration, in combination with excursion,

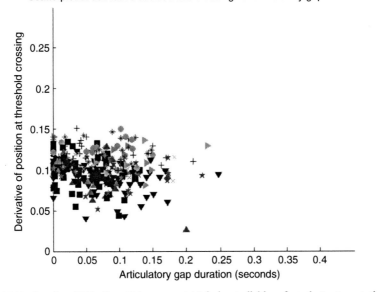

FIGURE 14.10. Speaker DE3, *five*, 334 curves, initial demisyllables, first derivative at threshold vs. articulatory gap duration, labeled by emphasis and by position (symbols as in Fig. 14.8).

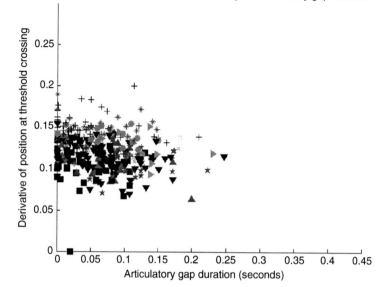

FIGURE 14.11. Speaker DE3, *five*, 334 curves, final demisyllables, first derivative at threshold vs. articulatory gap duration, labeled by emphasis and by position (symbols as in Fig. 14.8).

predicted speed of the movement at an iceberg threshold. Recall that excursion has already proved to be a partial predictor of movement velocity at threshold (Bonaventura 2003).

The linear combination of predictors was significantly related to the speed index. For speaker DE1 (the word *five*), the values are, initial demisyllable (dm), $R^2 = .84$, adjusted $R^2 = .840$ [$F(3, 193) = 343.1$] and final dm, $R^2 = .328$, adjusted $R^2 = .317$ [$F(3, 193) = 31.4$]. For speaker DE2 (*five*) the values are, initial dm, $R^2 = .934$, adjusted $R^2 = .929$ [$F(3, 44) = 207.2$] and final dm, $R^2 = .310$, adjusted $R^2 = .263$ [$F(3, 44) = 6.6$]. For speaker DE3 (*five*), values are, initial dm, $R^2 = .779$, adjusted $R^2 = .777$ [$F(3, 330) = 386.7$] and final dm, $R^2 = .488$, adjusted $R^2 = 484$, $F(3, 330) = 105$. All tests were significant at $p < .001$.

R^2 values of .84, .93, and .78 for speakers DE1, DE2, and DE3, respectively, in initial demisyllables show that high percentages of the criterion variance are accounted for by its linear relationship with the predictor variables in this syllable position. On the other hand, although significant, lower percentages of variance are accounted for by the same linear combination of predictors in final demisyllables, where R^2 of .33, .31, and .5 were found for DE1, DE2, and DE3, respectively.

In Tables 14.1–3, we present indices to indicate the relative strength of the individual predictors. Bivariate and partial correlation coefficients for speakers DE1, DE2, and DE3, for initial and final demisyllables, are reported.

All the bivariate and partial correlations between excursion and the speed index were significant, but the correlations between syllable duration, or magnitude, and gap duration and speed were consistently significant only for speaker DE3. For speakers DE1 and DE2, partial correlations indices for syllable duration and gap duration were not significant except for a mild effect of gap duration on speed in initial demisyllables for speaker DE1.

Bivariate correlations between syllable duration and speed were significant, except for speaker DE2 in initial demisyllables. Bivariate correlations of gap duration and speed were significant for speaker DE3 in initial and final positions and for speaker DE1 in initial demisyllables.

Standardized regression coefficients (Table 14.4) and prediction equations for the standardized variables confirmed the trends shown by the partial correlations: excursion in the present data appears to be the greater contributor to the prediction of speed for all speakers, whereas syllable duration and boundary magnitude show a significant correlation with speed only for speaker DE3 (and low significance for gap in initial demisyllables for speaker DE1).

TABLE 14.1 Speaker DE1, word *five*. The bivariate and partial correlations of the predictors (excursion, syllable duration, and gap duration) with the speed index, initial, and final demisyllables

		Bivariate	Partial
Initial dm	Excursion	$.915^a$	$.910^a$
	Syllable duration	$.219^a$	$.023$
	Gap duration	$.209^b$	$-.165^c$
Final dm	Excursion	$.570^a$	$.562^a$
	Syllable duration	$.129^c$	$-.059$
	Gap duration	$-.042$	$-.036$

$^a p < .001$ $^b p < .01$ $^c p < .05$

TABLE 14.2. Speaker DE2, word *five*. The bivariate and partial correlations of the predictors (excursion, syllable duration, and gap duration) with the speed index, initial and final demisyllables

		Bivariate	Partial
Initial dm	Excursion	$.966^a$	$.962^a$
	Syllable duration	$.153$	$.000$
	Gap duration	$.112$	$.023$
Final dm	Excursion	$.523^b$	$.437^b$
	Syllable duration	$.249^c$	$.141$
	Gap duration	$.033$	$.001$

$^a p < .001$ $^b p < .01$ $^c p < .05$

TABLE 14.3. Speaker DE3, word *five*: The bivariate and partial correlations of the predictors (excursion, syllable duration and gap duration) with the speed index, initial and final demisyllables

		Bivariate	Partial
Initial dm	Excursion	$.870^a$	$.860^b$
	Syllable duration	$.385^a$	$-.181^a$
	Gap duration	$-.189^a$	$-.294^a$
Final dm	Excursion	$.658^a$	$.664^a$
	Syllable duration	$.279^a$	$-.145^b$
	Gap duration	$-.179^a$	$-.313$

$^a p < .001$ $^b p < .01$

TABLE 14.4. Standardized regression coefficients and prediction equations for the standardized variables: excursion, syllable duration, and gap duration

DE1: *five*—initial dm	Z predicted speed $= .934^a$ z exc $+ .009$ z syll dur $- .070^c$ z art gap
DE1: *five*—final dm	Z predicted speed $= .585^a$ z exc $- .051$ z syll dur $- .029$ z art gap
DE2: *five*—initial dm	Z predicted speed $= .965^b$ z exc $+ .000$ z syll dur $+ .009$ z art gap
DE2: *five*—final dm	Z predicted speed $= .501^a$ z exc $+ .194$ z syll dur $+ .002$ z art gap
DE3: *five*—initial dm	Z predicted speed $= .908^a$ z exc $- .107^a$ z syll dur $- .158^a$ z art gap
DE3: *five*—final dm	Z predicted speed $= .725^a$ z exc $- .129^b$ z syll dur $- .263^a$ z art gap

$^a p < .001$ $^b p < .01$ $^c p < .05$

14.5 DISCUSSION

The results show evidence for speaker-specific treatment of the prosodic parameters of syllable duration and boundary strength, in relation to implementation of the velocity patterns of crucial articulator movements, both in initial and final demisyllables. Individual strategies in implementing phrase boundaries and intersyllabic gap durations have also been found by Menezes (2003). Similarly, individual differences were reported by Byrd *et al.* (2005) for effects of syllable and phrase position on consonantal articulatory strength.

The clear relation between speed and excursion, shown by the consistent significant influence of excursion on velocity of the movement at iceberg threshold crossing, substantiates the concept of iceberg in a modified sense, namely, that iceberg patterns are invariant after removing a predictable linear effect of excursion. However, in the present data from a corpus of read speech, the lack of a consistent pattern of syllable magnitude and boundary strength relative to velocity of the crucial articulator movement indicates that these factors do not have a predictable influence on movement speed. Syllable duration appears to relate more consistently to speed than does gap duration. Connections with Fougeron and Keating's (1997) and Byrd *et al.*'s (2005, also Byrd and Saltzman 2003) findings, showing greater lengthening of the consonantal movements at phrase edges, need further investigation.

Although some influence of the boundary duration on the immediately preceding syllable was found only for the productions of one of the three speakers, these results show that overall prosodic rhythmic structure of the utterance has to be taken into account in predicting duration, timing, and excursion of consonantal gestures within the syllable (Fujimura 2000, 2003). In addition, these results appear to be consistent with the hypothesis that durations of syllables and boundaries, and of consonantal and vocalic gestures within the syllables, might be controlled and generated by separate mechanisms (Converter, Distributor, Actuators; Fujimura and Williams 1999) in order to achieve timing coordination during phonetic implementation. The existence of an independent Converter module that encodes relative duration and timing of syllables and boundaries within the utterance, prior to generation of muscle movement patterns, would help explain the dependence of movement speed on the boundary magnitude (duration of articulatory gaps between syllables) that was found phrase medially (albeit to a limited extent). The impact of phrase-medial intersyllabic gap durations on the speed of adjacent movements would, on the other hand, remain unaccounted for by the presence of a "prosodic-boundary gesture" which is hypothesized to occur only at prosodic boundaries (Byrd and Saltzman 2003) and to generate local slowing of surrounding consonantal gestures.

The present results seem to indicate that, at least for these data, only excursion should be considered as a major predictor of speed in designing an approximation model of the movement time functions, due to the unsystematic effects of prosodic parameters as predictors, and that subjective factors in the realization of muscle trajectories in syllable-final position before phrase boundaries have to be taken into account in modeling iceberg patterns. It should be noted that, from the point of view of the C/D model, the excursion as described in this paper is related but somewhat independent from syllable magnitude, which is measurable as syllable duration. Excursion reflects strong nonlinear effects of the speech-signal generating mechanism such as consonantal gesture saturation, while syllable duration is less affected by such peripheral effects.

This study should also be conducted on spontaneous speech (e.g. the X-ray microbeam Blue Pine corpus; Mitchell 2000; Menezes 2003), for which preliminary results seem to indicate similar trends as in read speech (Bonaventura 2006). Another important extension would be the analysis of at least one more crucial articulator (e.g. the tongue tip), both in read speech and in spontaneous speech.

15

Physiological and Physical Bases of the Command–Response Model for Generating Fundamental Frequency Contours in Tone Languages

Implications for the Phonology of Tones

Hiroya Fujisaki, Wentao Gu, and Sumio Ohno

15.1 INTRODUCTION

In many languages of the world, the voice fundamental frequency (F_0) plays an important role in conveying linguistic, paralinguistic, and non-linguistic information. Hence, an accurate representation of the essential characteristics of the contour of the fundamental frequency (F_0 contour) is necessary both for understanding their relationships to the underlying information and for synthesis of high-quality speech.

Although there have been numerous studies on tone and intonation, deriving a fully quantitative representation of continuous F_0 contours of speech is a difficult problem. The existing approaches diverge widely in the density of specified points, in the number of parameters, in the relationship between local accent/tone and global phrase intonation, and in the sophistication of mathematical representation. These approaches fall into two broad categories: model/rule-based approaches and data-driven approaches. The former category can be further divided into two classes: those with explicit representation of only local components of the F_0 contour, usually known as tone-sequence approaches, and those with explicit representation of both

The authors wish to thank Prof. Phil Rose of the Australian National University for helpful discussions and for providing the fundamental frequency data of Lanqi from an unpublished honors thesis at the Australian National University.

global and local components, usually known as hierarchical approaches. Here we give a very brief overview of some well-known examples of these approaches.

The tone-sequence approaches assign sparsely a sequence of local pitch targets based on acoustic characteristics, phonological features, or perceptual attributes, and then apply linear or polynomial interpolations between these target points to give continuous representations of F_0 contours. For example, on the basis of the early work by Pierrehumbert (1980) on English, the intonation module for Mandarin in the Bell Labs TTS system (van Santen *et al.* 1998) represents F_0 contours by specifying a sequence of locally defined high (H) and low (L) tonal targets in each syllable, according to a set of rules for tonal coarticulation. There is no explicit component for global intonation, but the actual F_0 values of tonal targets can be modulated by the downstep and declination effects.

More recently, the Parallel Encoding and Target Approximation (PENTA) model proposed by Xu (2004*a*) also tries to model F_0 contours in terms of local pitch targets. Multiple layers of communicative functions are encoded in parallel into melodic primitives, based on which an F_0 contour is implemented by successively approaching local pitch targets.

In contrast, the IPO model ('t Hart and Cohen 1973) is hierarchical in the sense that it consists of two components—the local rises and falls are imposed between two or three (top, mid, and bottom) global reference lines showing a declining trend. The local movements are classified into a set of stylized "hat" patterns consisting of straight line segments.

As another example of the hierarchical approaches, the Soft Template Mark-Up Language (Stem-ML) proposed recently by Kochanski and Shih (2003) is a tagging system which generates F_0 contours from a set of mathematically defined mark-up tags, including both stress tags for local tone shapes and step and slope tags for global phrase curves. In each syllable, the resulting soft template is a compromise between articulatory effort and communication accuracy, controlled by a strength parameter.

In addition to these model/rule-based approaches, a number of data-driven approaches have also been proposed for modeling F_0 contours using artificial neural networks, classification and regression trees (CART), the hidden Markov model (HMM), and other statistical methods. These data-driven approaches derive the relationships between linguistic features and F_0 values automatically through machine-learning algorithms, requiring little knowledge of linguistics. Although they can produce quite natural F_0 contours on the basis of a specific corpus, they lack the ability to generalize, especially when the training corpus is not large enough or when the speaking styles need to be varied freely to generate expressive and emotional speech.

None of the above mentioned approaches are based on the physiological and physical mechanisms for F_0 control. Although they can approximate F_0 contours with a certain degree of accuracy with the help of various mathematical processes, we believe that an accurate model can only be attained by a sound knowledge of the underlying physiological and physical mechanisms, and by mathematically formulating their characteristics. In this sense, the quantitative models proposed by Öhman (1967) for the F_0 contours of Swedish and by Fujisaki and Nagashima (1969) for the F_0 contours of Japanese are exceptional in that they posit the existence of separate commands of varying amplitude/magnitude for local and global components, and separate mechanisms that produce corresponding components of the F_0 contour from these commands, each with mathematical formulations of their characteristics. This type of model has been called a command–response model (Fujisaki *et al.* 1987). However, these models were not based on an understanding of the actual mechanisms when they were proposed.

The F_0 contour of speech is generated by controlling the frequency of vibration of the vocal folds mainly through various intrinsic and extrinsic laryngeal muscles. As far as the linguistic information is concerned, information on syntactic structure is mainly expressed by relatively slow changes (i.e. global components), while information on word accent / syllabic tone is expressed by relatively rapid changes (i.e. local components) of the F_0 contour. Although the basic mechanism is the same in most languages, certain differences may exist between languages. A previous study by the first author (Fujisaki 1988) clarified the mechanism for F_0 control for languages (e.g. Japanese and English) whose F_0 contours need only positive local components[1] in the model (Fujisaki and Hirose 1984; Fujisaki and Ohno 1995); however, it did not cover tone languages such as Mandarin, which has faster local F_0 changes (Fujisaki *et al.* 1990), nor some non-tone languages such as Swedish, with both acute and grave accents (Fujisaki *et al.* 1993).

In the present chapter, we will first present the physiological and physical properties of the vocal folds and the laryngeal structure (Fujisaki 1988) that underlies a model for the generation process of an F_0 contour with global components and positive local components. We then discuss several tone languages that use both positive and negative local components to express tones, and explain the mechanism involving extrinsic laryngeal muscles for the generation of negative local components (Fujisaki 1995). We also demonstrate that the model with both positive and negative tone commands provides a novel means for the representation and comparison of tone systems of various tone languages, by paying attention to qualitative differences of amplitude and timing of tone commands that are allowed within individual tone languages (Fujisaki and Gu 2006). Thus, unlike most conventional approaches to describing tones, this model-based approach is capable of both qualitative/phonological representations and quantitative/phonetic representations of tones.

---

[1] Positive local components are produced by positive local commands which cause active raising of $\log_e F_0$ above the global components, whereas negative local components are produced by negative local commands which cause active lowering of $\log_e F_0$ below the global components.

15.2 VOCAL FOLD LENGTH AND VOICE FUNDAMENTAL FREQUENCY

15.2.1 Relationship between tension and stiffness of skeletal muscles

The relationship between tension and stiffness of skeletal muscles has been widely studied (Buchthal and Kaiser 1944; Sandow 1958). Figure 15.1 shows the earliest published data on this relationship (Buchthal and Kaiser 1944) which indicate the existence of a very good linear relationship between tension and stiffness over a wide range of tension applied to a skeletal muscle, and can be approximated quite well by the following equation:

$$dT/dl = a + bT, \tag{1}$$

where T indicates the tension, l, the length of the muscle, a, the stiffness at $T = 0$, and b, the slope of the approximated linear function. By solving this differential equation, we obtain the relationship between tension and length of the muscle in (2),

$$T = (T_0 + a/b) \exp\{b(l - l_0)\} - a/b, \tag{2}$$

where T_0 indicates the static tension applied to the muscle, and l_0 its length at $T = T_0$. When $T_0 \gg a/b$, Equation (2) can be approximated by

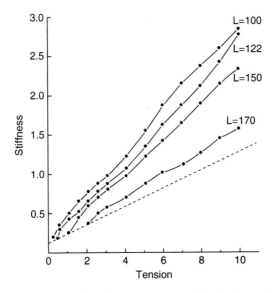

FIGURE 15.1. Stiffness as a function of tension at rest (- - - -) and during isometric tetanic contraction initiated at different original lengths. In the top curve, contraction is initiated at a length below 100 (equilibrium length = 100). Ordinate: stiffness in arbitrary units. Abscissa: tension in arbitrary units (after Buchthal and Kaiser 1944).

$$T = T_0 \exp(bx), \tag{3}$$

where x indicates the change in length of the muscle when T is changed from T_0. This will hold for skeletal muscles in general, including the human vocalis muscles.

On the other hand, the fundamental frequency, F_0, of vibration of an elastic membrane such as the vocal fold is given by[2]

$$F_0 = c_0 \sqrt{T/\sigma}, \tag{4}$$

where σ is the density per unit area of the membrane, and c_0 is a constant inversely proportional to the length of the membrane regardless of its shape (Slater and Frank 1933; Morse 1948). From Equations (3) and (4) we obtain

$$\log_e F_0 = \log_e \{c_0 \sqrt{T_0/\sigma}\} + (b/2)x. \tag{5}$$

Strictly speaking, the first term varies slightly with x, but the overall dependency of $\log_e F_0$ on x is primarily determined by the second term on the right-hand side.[3] This linear relationship was confirmed for sustained phonation by an experiment in which a stereoendoscope was used to measure the length of the vibrating part of the vocal folds (Honda et al. 1980), and will hold also when x varies with time. Thus we can represent $\log_e F_0(t)$ as the sum of an approximately constant term and a time-varying term, such that

$$\log_e F_0(t) = \log_e F_b + (b/2)x(t), \tag{6}$$

where $c_0\sqrt{T_0/\sigma}$ in Equation (5) is rewritten as F_b to indicate the existence of a baseline value of F_0 to which the time-varying term is added when the logarithmic scale is adopted for $F_0(t)$. It is to be noted, however, that the first term ($\log_e F_b$) can be regarded to be approximately constant only as long as the speaker holds T_0 constant by maintaining the same speaking style and emotional state. For example, F_b is found

---

[2] Equation (4) applies both to a string mode and to a membrane mode of vibration. The difference between Flanagan's mass-spring model (Flanagan 1972) and the authors' elastic membrane (string) model is not in the mode of vibration, but in the order of approximation. Namely, the mass-spring model is a zeroth-order approximation of the vocal folds (they are elastic membranes with a finite length, width, and thickness) in terms of lumped-constant mechanical elements. In particular, the idealized lumped stiffness element (spring) in Flanagan's model is a zeroth-order approximation of the stiffness of the vocal fold. Flanagan's model is meant to show the possibility of self-excited oscillation/vibration of the vocal folds in the presence of a certain amount of airflow through the glottis, but does not model the mechanism by which the frequency of vibration is varied. In order to show how the fundamental frequency of vibration (F_0) is controlled, one needs to go to a higher level of approximation, namely, to an elastic string model (the first-order approximation) or an elastic membrane model (the second-order approximation).

[3] As the vocal folds are elongated by the contraction of *pars recta* of the cricothyroid muscle, the following three factors are in operation simultaneously: (i) increase in the tension of vocal folds (through the nonlinear tension-stiffness characteristics of skeletal muscles); (ii) increase in the length of the vibrating part of the vocal folds; (iii) decrease in the density (mass per unit area) of the vocal folds. Of these, (i) and (iii) raise F_0, while (ii) lowers F_0. Although a complete equation describing the dependency of $\log_e F_0$ on the length of the vocal folds is not shown here, its derivation is quite straightforward. From a complete equation it is easy to see that (i) is by far the dominant factor, while the effects of (ii) and (iii) are much smaller.

to be appreciably higher when the speakers are angry than when they are not (Hirose *et al.* 2000). In sum, $\log_e F_0(t)$ rather than $F_0(t)$ varies in proportion to the length of the vocal folds because of the non-linear elastic properties of skeletal muscles.

15.2.2 Role of cricothyroid muscles

Analysis of the laryngeal structure suggests that the movement of the thyroid cartilage relative to the cricoid cartilage has two degrees of freedom (Zemlin 1968: 155–7; Fink and Demarest 1978). One is horizontal translation due, presumably, to the activity of *pars obliqua* of the cricothyroid muscle (henceforth CT); the other is rotation around the cricothyroid joint due to the activity of *pars recta* of the cricothyroid muscle, as illustrated in Figure 15.2. The translation and the rotation of the thyroid can be represented by separate second-order systems as shown in Figure 15.3, and both cause small increments in vocal fold length. An instantaneous activity of *pars obliqua* of the CT, contributing to thyroid translation, causes an incremental change $x_1(t)$ in vocal fold length, while a sudden increase in the activity of *pars recta* of CT, contributing to thyroid rotation, causes

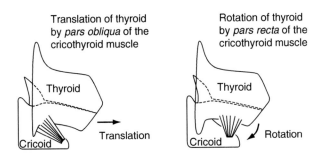

FIGURE 15.2. The role of *pars obliqua* and *pars recta* of the cricothyroid muscle in translating and rotating the thyroid cartilage.

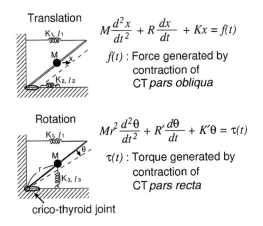

FIGURE 15.3. Equations of translation and rotation of the thyroid cartilage.

an incremental change $x_2(t)$. The resultant change is obviously the sum of these two changes, as long as the two movements are small and can be considered independent from each other. In this case, Equation (6) can be rewritten as

$$\log_e F_0(t) = \log_e F_b + (b/2)\{x_1(t) + x_2(t)\}, \tag{7}$$

which means that the time-varying component of $\log_e F_0(t)$ can be represented by the sum of two time-varying components. According to our preliminary estimate, the translational movement of the thyroid cartilage has a much larger time constant than the rotational movement. Hence the former is used to indicate global phenomena such as phrasing, while the latter is used to indicate local phenomena such as word accent.

15.2.3 Polarity of local components

The foregoing analysis of physiological and physical mechanisms for controlling $F_0(t)$ provides a basis for the command–response model proposed by Fujisaki and his colleagues, for languages with only positive local components (Fujisaki and Nagashima 1969; Fujisaki and Hirose 1984). In this case, a rapid activity of CT *pars recta* for a certain time interval is represented by a positive pedestal function and named "accent command", while a sudden activity of CT *pars obliqua* over a shorter time interval as compared to the time constant of the translational mechanism is represented by an impulse function and named "phrase command". The resulting changes in $\log_e F_0(t)$ caused by these commands are called "accent component" and "phrase component", respectively. For the rest of the chapter, we shall use "F_0 contour" to indicate $\log_e F_0(t)$.

Analysis of F_0 contours of several languages such as Chinese (including various dialects such as Mandarin, Cantonese, Shanghainese, and Lanqi), Thai, Vietnamese, and Swedish, however, indicates that the local components (associated with tones in the case of Chinese, Thai, and Vietnamese) are not always positive but can be both positive and negative. In other words, it is necessary in these languages to posit commands of both positive and negative polarities for the local components, the latter causing active lowering of $\log_e F_0$ below the phrase components.

15.2.4 Role of extrinsic laryngeal muscles

Although several hypotheses have been presented on the possible mechanisms for the active lowering of F_0, none seems to be satisfactory since they do not take into account the activities of muscles that are directly connected to the thyroid cartilage and are antagonistic to CT *pars recta* in rotating the thyroid cartilage in the opposite direction. Several EMG studies have shown that the sternohyoid muscle (henceforth SH) is active when the F_0 is lowered in Mandarin (Sagart et al. 1986; Hallé et al. 1990) and Thai (Erickson 1976) as well as in Swedish (Gårding 1970). The mechanism itself, however, has not been made clear since SH is not directly attached to the thyroid cartilage, whose movement is essential in changing the length and hence the tension of the vocal folds.

On the basis of the above-mentioned study on the production of Thai tones, the first author suggested the active role of the thyrohyoid muscle (henceforth TH) in F_0 lowering in these languages (Fujisaki 1995). Figure 15.4 shows the relationship between the hyoid bone, thyroid, and cricoid cartilages, and TH in their lateral and frontal views; Figure 15.5 shows their relationships with three other muscles: VOC (vocalis muscle), CT, and SH.

The activity of SH stabilizes the position of the hyoid bone,[4] while the activity (hence contraction) of TH causes rotation of the thyroid cartilage around the crico-thyroid joint in a direction that is opposite to the direction of rotation when CT is active, thus reducing the length of the vocal folds, reducing its tension, and eventually

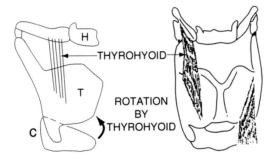

C: cricoid cartilage,   T: thyroid cartilage,   H: hyoid bone.

FIGURE 15.4. Role of the thyrohyoid in laryngeal control.

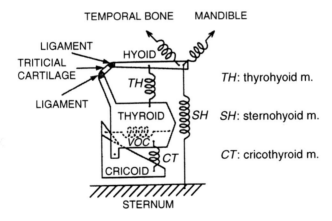

FIGURE 15.5. Mechanism of F_0 lowering by activation of the TH and the SH.

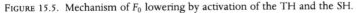

[4] A complete stabilization involves many muscles. Among these are the three major muscles connecting the hyoid bone to different hard structures, namely, the sternohyoid muscle connecting the hyoid bone to the sternum, the geniohyoid muscle connecting the hyoid bone to the mandible, and the stylohyoid and digastric muscles connecting the hyoid bone to the skull. The activity/contraction of the sternohyoid muscle is considered to play a major role in stabilizing the position of the hyoid bone.

lowering F_0. This is made possible by the flexibility of ligamentous connections between the upper ends of the thyroid cartilage and the two small cartilages (triticial cartilages) and also between these triticial cartilages and the two ends of the hyoid bone, as shown in Figure 15.5.

15.3 MATHEMATICAL REPRESENTATION OF F_0 CONTOURS OF TONE LANGUAGES WITH POSITIVE AND NEGATIVE LOCAL COMPONENTS

The foregoing analysis leads to a model for the generation of F_0 contours of tone languages from phrase and tone commands of both positive and negative polarities, as shown in Figure 15.6. In this model, the F_0 contour can be given by the following mathematical formulation:

$$\log_e F_0(t) = \log_e F_b + \sum_{i=1}^{I} A_{pi} G_p(t - T_{0i})$$

$$+ \sum_{j=1}^{J} A_{tj}\{G_t(t - T_{1j}) - G_t(t - T_{2j})\}, \tag{8}$$

where

$$G_p(t) = \begin{cases} \alpha^2 t \exp(-\alpha t), & t \geq 0, \\ 0, & t < 0, \end{cases} \tag{9}$$

$$G_t(t) = \begin{cases} \min[1 - (1 + \beta_1 t)\exp(-\beta_1 t), \gamma_1], & t \geq 0, \\ 0, & t < 0, \end{cases} \tag{10}$$

(for positive tone commands),

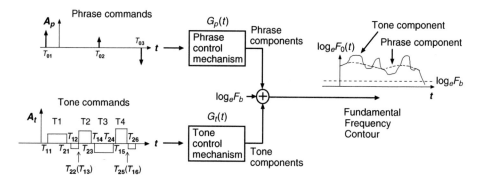

FIGURE 15.6. The command–response model for tone languages (taking Mandarin as an example).

$$G_t(t) = \begin{cases} \min [1 - (1 + \beta_2 t) \exp (-\beta_2 t), \gamma_2], & t \geq 0, \\ 0, & t < 0, \end{cases}$$

(for negative tone commands),

where $G_p(t)$ represents the impulse response function of the phrase control mechanism and $G_t(t)$ represents the step response function of the tone control mechanism. The symbols in these equations indicate:

F_b: baseline value of fundamental frequency;

I: number of phrase commands;

J: number of tone commands;

A_{pi}: magnitude of the ith phrase command;

A_{tj}: amplitude of the jth tone command;

T_{0i}: time of the ith phrase command;

T_{1j}: onset time of the jth tone command;

T_{2j}: end time of the jth tone command;

α: natural angular frequency of the phrase-control mechanism;

β_1: natural angular frequency of the tone-control mechanism for positive tone commands;

β_2: natural angular frequency of the tone-control mechanism for negative tone commands;

γ_1: relative ceiling level of positive tone components;

γ_2: relative ceiling level of negative tone components.

Although both β and γ should take different values depending on the polarity of commands as in Equation (10), the use of a common value for both β and γ irrespective of command polarity was found to be acceptable in almost all cases.

15.4 APPLICATION OF THE MODEL TO THE ANALYSIS OF F_0 CONTOURS OF SEVERAL TONE LANGUAGES

It is possible to use the above-mentioned model to analyze an observed F_0 contour and estimate the underlying commands by the procedure known as analysis-by-synthesis (Bell *et al.* 1961; Fujisaki and Hirose 1984). For a given tone language, a particular tone-command pattern should be specified for each tone type at the initial stage of analysis by direct comparison of all the target tones in a fixed context (Gu *et al.* 2007). We have already applied the model to the analysis of F_0 contours of several tone languages including Mandarin (Fujisaki *et al.* 1987, 1990, 2005), Thai (Fujisaki *et al.* 2003), Cantonese (Gu *et al.* 2004a, 2005, 2007), Shanghainese (Gu *et al.* 2004b), Vietnamese (Mixdorff *et al.* 2003; Gu and Fujisaki n.d.), and Lanqi[5] (Fujisaki and Gu

---

[5] Lanqi is a small subset of Chinese Wu dialects spoken in the area of 兰溪 in the province of Zhejiang, China.

n.d.). Because of space limitations, however, only examples for Mandarin, Thai, and Cantonese are shown here to illustrate the model's ability to generate very close approximations to observed F_0 contours.

Figures 15.7, 15.8, and 15.9 show the results of the analysis on the utterances of Mandarin, Thai, and Cantonese, respectively. The figures show, from top to bottom, the speech waveforms, the measured F_0 values (+ symbols), the model-generated best approximations (solid lines), the baseline frequencies (dotted lines), the phrase commands (impulses), and the tone commands (pedestals). The dashed lines indicate the contributions of phrase components, while the differences between the approximated F_0 contour and the phrase components correspond to the tone components. As seen from the figures, the model generates extremely close approximations to the observed F_0 contours. The patterns of tone commands show a consistent correspondence with each tone type (after taking into account various tone changes such as tone sandhi and tone neutralization in continuous speech), except that the neighboring tone commands of the same polarity can be merged into one. On the other hand, the patterns of phrase commands show the prosodic structure of the utterance, which is closely correlated with but not always identical to the hierarchical structure of the syntax of the utterance.

Figure 15.7 shows the results of the analysis of an utterance of the Mandarin sentence in (11):

(11)   Mu4 ni2 hei1 bo2 lan3 hui4 bu2 kui4 shi4 dian4 zi3 wan4 hua1 tong3.
       "The Munich exposition is really an electronic kaleidoscope."

The results indicate that the patterns of commands for the four tones in Mandarin are positive for Tone 1 (high tone, or H), initially negative and then switched to positive for Tone 2 (rising tone, or R), negative for Tone 3 (low tone, or L), and initially positive and then negative for Tone 4 (falling tone, or F). The occurrences of phrase commands in this utterance are largely consistent with the syntactic structure. Four phrase commands occur at the following points: before the noun *mu4 ni2 hei1* (Munich), before the noun *bo2 lan3 hui4* (exposition) (these two nouns constitute the subject), before the predicate *bu2 kui4 shi4* (is really), and before the noun complement *dian4 zi3 wan4 hua1 tong3* (an electronic kaleidoscope).

Figure 15.8 shows the results of the analysis of an utterance of the Thai sentence in (12).

(12)   Kham0 nii3 phuut2 waa2 naa4 dooj0 khon0 suuan1 jaj1.
       "This word is pronounced /naa4/ by most speakers."

The results indicate that the patterns of commands for the five tones in Thai are negative for Tone 1 (low tone, or L), initially positive and then switched to negative for Tone 2 (falling tone, or F), initially zero and then positive for Tone 3 (high tone, or H), initially negative and then positive for Tone 4 (rising tone, or R), and zero for Tone 0 (mid tone, or M).

Figure 15.9 shows the results of the analysis of an utterance of the following Cantonese sentence:

(13)   Kei4 zung1 jau5 luk9 go3 jan4 kyut8 seoi2, zip8 sau6 zing6 mak9 zyu3 se6.
       "Among them six people were de-hydrated, and received an intravenous injection."

These results as well as those for other utterances of Cantonese indicate that the patterns of commands for the six non-entering tones (tones on syllables not ending with an unreleased stop) in Cantonese are positive for Tone 1 (high level tone, or H), initially negative and then switched to positive for Tone 2 (high–rising tone, or HR), zero for Tone 3 (mid level tone, or M), overly negative for Tone 4 (low–falling tone, or LF), initially negative and then zero for Tone 5 (low–rising tone, or LR), and negative

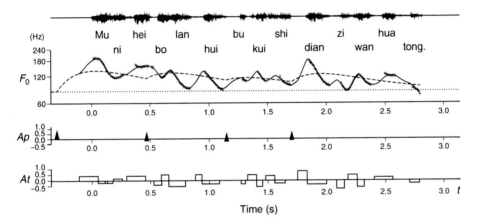

FIGURE 15.7. Analysis of the F₀ contour of an utterance of Mandarin.

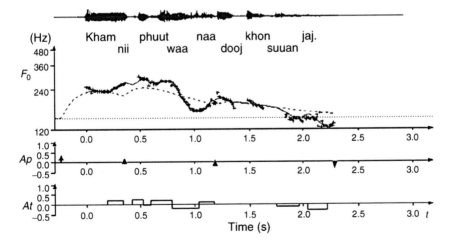

FIGURE 15.8. Analysis of the F₀ contour of an utterance of Thai.

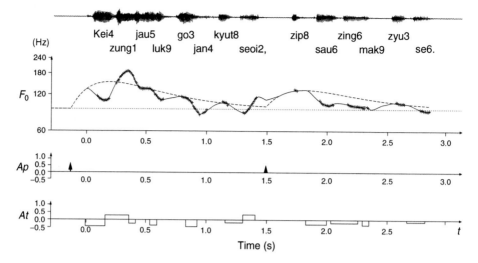

FIGURE 15.9. Analysis of the F_0 contour of an utterance of Cantonese.

for Tone 6 (low level tone, or L). As for the three entering tones (tones on syllables ending with an unreleased stop), the patterns of commands are positive for Tone 7 (high level tone, or H'), zero for Tone 8 (mid level tone, or M'), and negative for Tone 9 (low level tone, or L'). The command duration is always shorter for entering tones than for non-entering tones because in the former voicing is interrupted by the unreleased stop coda. In this utterance, two phrase commands occur before the two clauses separated by a short pause, hence the prosodic structure coincides with the syntactic structure.

The primary advantage of the command–response model over other F_0 models is that it provides a method for representing quantitative aspects of tonal features with a higher degree of accuracy, and thus it is useful in phonetic studies as well as for technological applications such as speech synthesis. In the following sections, however, we will show that it also serves as a novel method for investigating and describing the phonological structures of tone systems of various tone languages.

15.5 CONVENTIONAL DESCRIPTIONS OF TONE SYSTEMS

The description of the tone system of a tone language has always been a challenging problem. Conventional methods of description of tones have not attained the degree of accuracy and generality that have been accomplished for segmental features of speech of various languages, as evidenced by the most recent version of the IPA symbols. This may be due to the fact that the articulatory processes involved in the production of segments are observable, at least partially, by vision, kinesthetic feedback, or proprioception, and thus can be objectively described even without sophisticated instruments, while the phonatory process involved in the production of tones is much more difficult to observe directly, such that scholars in the earlier days had to rely almost exclusively on auditory perception for analyzing and describing tones and their systems. Although recent developments in the technology for observation and measurement are reducing the difference in the difficulty of studying segments and tones, traditional and prevailing approaches in the study of tones still depend heavily on auditory perception and are thus subjective.

Table 15.1 sets out the tone systems of several Chinese dialects that we have studied, and Table 15.2 presents the tone systems of Thai and Vietnamese (the first column for Vietnamese indicates Vietnamese names of the tones). As shown in both tables, there have been at least three major approaches to the description of tones based on perceptual impressions.

The first is the approach that has been adopted by Chinese linguists since as early as the 6th c. AD, representing perceptual impressions of tones in terms of discrete concepts such as the original four tone categories (平 level, 上 elevating, 去 departing, and 入 entering) and the later developed two registers (阴 upper, and 阳 lower, corresponding to voiceless and voiced initials, respectively) for each tone category. Thus, there are eight basic tone types in Late Middle Chinese (9th–10th c. AD). Among them, syllables of entering tones are characterized not by the pitch pattern but by an unreleased stop coda (hence a shorter syllable duration). These traditional tone names are still maintained in contemporary Chinese dialects, but in most dialects they no longer coincide exactly with the actual tonal features which have changed due to diachronic tone mergers and splits (as shown, there are fewer than eight tones in Mandarin, Shanghainese, and Lanqi, whereas Cantonese has nine tones, with an additional 中入 derived from 阴入).

The second is the approach adopted by Western phonologists since the last century, using the discrete categories high (H), mid (M), low (L), rising (R), falling (F), and their combinations, to characterize both height and shape of the pitch patterns of tones.

TABLE 15.1. Tone systems of some contemporary Chinese dialects

Tone name		Mandarin		Shanghainese		Lanqi		Cantonese	
平	阴平	H	55	F	52	M	33	H	55
	阳平	R	35			LF	21	LF	11
上	阴上	L	21(4)			HF	534	HR	35
	阳上							LR	13
去	阴去	F	51	HR	34	HR	45	M	33
	阳去			LR	13	LR	24	L	22
入	阴入			H′	5	HR′	34	H′	5
	中入							M′	3
	阳入			LR′	12	LR′	12	L′	2

TABLE 15.2. Tone systems of Thai and Vietnamese

Thai		Vietnamese			
H	45	ngang	阴平	H	44
M	33	huyền	阳平	LF	31
L	21	hỏi	阴上	D	21(4)
R	14	ngã	阳上	HRG	32 4
F	41	sắc	阴去 or 阴入	HR	<u>35</u>
		nặng	阳去 or 阳入	LG	<u>21</u>

This set of phonological features shares almost the same notions as the traditional Chinese terminology, except that a third register, mid (M), is distinctly introduced. In Table 15.1, a single quotation mark is attached to entering tones to distinguish them from non-entering tones. A uniform description of the tonal features for Vietnamese is still lacking because of great variability across speakers. In our description given in Table 15.2, "D" indicates Dipping (falling with an optional rising), and "G" stands for Glottalized. It should be noted, however, that tones having the same feature specification in different dialects may not share exactly the same pitch pattern. Apparently, these conceptual features are rather vague.

The third is a phonetically oriented approach proposed by Chao (1930) and later adopted by the IPA, using a five-level numerical code or a five-level letter system to describe the subjective pitch pattern for each tone. The five levels, from 1 to 5, corresponding approximately to a musical scale, are used to indicate the relative subjective pitches of low, mid-low, mid, mid-high, and high, respectively. Hence, the subjective pitch pattern of a tone can be described as a string of (at most four but usually no more than three) numbers. Since this system can provide a more accurate description of tones than abstract conceptual features can, it has been widely applied to various tone languages.

For each tone language/dialect in Tables 15.1 and 15.2, the rightmost column shows the five-level tone-code system, though the codes may vary from one author to another. The levels in parentheses are optional, and the underlining indicates a faster rate of change (e.g. <u>34</u> has a duration comparable to that of 3 but is shorter than 34) commonly observed for entering tones or tones involving entering members (e.g. some HR and LG in Vietnamese are entering tones). For Vietnamese, the space inserted in "32 4" indicates a glottal stricture in the middle of the syllable. Based on the five-level tone-code system, more complex phonological systems can be devised to account for finer distinctions. For example, W. Wang (1967) proposed a set of seven distinctive features for tones (i.e. contour, high, central, mid, rising, falling, and convex).

In spite of the above mentioned merits, the tone-code system still has apparent limitations, since it was conceived before any reliable tools for measuring fundamental frequency were available. First, the five levels are usually defined perceptually and are subjective and relative. Hence, there are numerous disputes over the tone codes for a specific language or dialect. The discrepancies in defining the codes reflect quantitative differences between individual speakers as well as between speech samples, or diversity in subjective judgments among researchers, but they may not be phonologically meaningful. As a result, any set of phonological features of tones defined purely on the basis of the five-level tone-code system (e.g. the seven distinctive features proposed by W. Wang 1967) risks being confounded with non-distinctive phonetic variations.

Second, the five-level tone-code system, together with the conventional phonological notations of tones, is valid only for representing tones in citation form. In continuous speech, however, the actual F_0 values differ significantly from those in the canonical forms in isolated syllables since they change with tonal context, word stress, phrase intonation, and various para- and non-linguistic factors.

Third, the five-level codes are discrete and semi-quantitative, and cannot characterize the continuous and dynamic nature of F_0 contours. They cannot therefore be used for quantitative modeling of F_0 contours of continuous speech.

15.6 COMPARISON OF PHONOLOGICAL STRUCTURES OF SEVERAL TONE LANGUAGES ON THE BASIS OF THE COMMAND–RESPONSE MODEL

Since none of the conventional approaches is satisfactory, we introduce here a novel method of describing the phonological structure of the tone system of a tone language, based on the pattern of tone commands in the command–response model. In the following, we use the term "polarity" to indicate, not the binary distinction between positive and negative, but the ternary distinction between positive (+), zero (0), and negative (−). In Figure 15.10 the abscissa indicates the polarity of the tone command occurring in the earlier part of a syllable, and the ordinate indicates the polarity of the tone command occurring in the later part of a syllable. For consistency of representation, we assign two virtual commands respectively to the earlier and the later parts of a syllable, even to tones with null or one tone command.

The phonological structures of the tone systems of Mandarin and Thai can then be represented in panels (a) and (c) of Figure 15.10, respectively. Without considering the complex tone sandhi in polysyllabic words of Shanghainese, the phonological structures of the five lexical tones of Shanghainese (Gu *et al.* 2004b) can be represented in panel (b). Panel (d) indicates the phonological structure of Vietnamese tones based on the results of our recent study (Gu and Fujisaki, n.d.), while panel (e) indicates that of Lanqi tones inferred from the raw fundamental frequency data in Rickard (2005). In the constellation of each panel, the points occupied by the lexical tones in the specific language / dialect are denoted by circles.

In some languages and dialects, two tone types can share the same point in the constellation, for instance, LR and LR′ in Shanghainese, D and LG as well as HR and

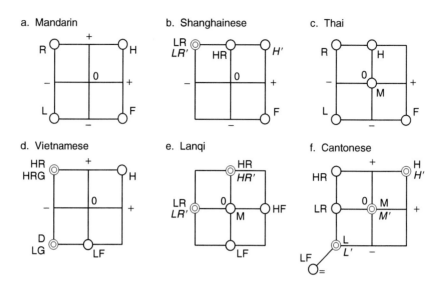

FIGURE 15.10. Phonological structures of the tone systems of six tone languages on the basis of the command–response model.

HRG in Vietnamese, HR and HR′ as well as LR and LR′ in Lanqi, which are indicated by double circles in Figure 15.10. Within each of these pairs, the two tones differ mainly in the duration of tone commands—the non-entering tone is longer than the entering tone or the tone involving entering members (e.g. HR and LG in Vietnamese).

An approximate (but not exact) correspondence can be observed between the proposed way of tone type representation and the traditional five-level tone-code system if we take the mid level 3 as a reference and map the higher and the lower levels to positive and negative commands, respectively. However, the essential difference is that a tone command in our model produces a dynamic F_0 curve (through the tone control mechanism) instead of a static F_0 value. Moreover, the actual amplitudes of the tone commands are not constrained to discrete levels but can assume values along a continuum, and can vary with such para- and non-linguistic factors as emphasis and emotion. Thus, the use of five discrete levels for continuous F_0 contours is misleading. It is an oversimplification in phonetics, and may also result in overdifferentiation in phonology. We consider that the proposed ternary representation for tone commands is sufficient for describing the phonological structure as far as these five tone languages are concerned.

The phonological structure of the tone system of Cantonese can be represented as in panel (f) of Figure 15.10, where + and 0 denote positive and null commands as above, while − and = both denote negative commands but = stands for a more negative one than −. The three entering tones share the same points with their non-entering counterparts. It should be noted that in this dialect we need two phonologically distinct levels for the negative tone command to distinguish between

Tones 4 (LF) and 6 (L). This phonological distinction coincides with the phonetic observations of the command amplitudes of these two tones in our previous studies on citation tones in carrier sentences as well as on tones in arbitrary continuous utterances (Gu *et al.* 2004*a*, 2007).

15.7 CONCLUSIONS

We have explained the physiological and physical mechanisms for controlling the fundamental frequency in speech of languages having both positive and negative local components in the F_0 contour; on the basis of these mechanisms, we also described a model for generating F_0 contours from a set of phrase and tone commands. Analysis-by-synthesis of observed F_0 contours of tone languages including Mandarin, Thai, and Cantonese has shown that the model can generate very close approximations to observed F_0 contours and allows us to estimate the underlying commands that are closely related to the lexical, syntactic, and prosodic information of the utterance. In addition to its validity in quantitative/phonetic representation of continuous F_0 contours, the model also provides a method for qualitative/phonological description of the tone systems of various tone languages. In comparison with the conventional ways of describing tones, the phonological tone features inferred from the model are expected to be less affected by phonetic variations in continuous speech. We do not claim that the current approach is valid for all tone languages. Instead, we are trying to find out what we need to add to cover more tone languages under a common framework.

16

Probabilistic "Sliding Template" Models for Indirect Vowel Normalization

Terrance M. Nearey and Peter F. Assmann

16.1 INTRODUCTION

The relationship between the physical realization of utterances and language-specific categories is a fundamental question in phonology. Although speech perception is often viewed as a branch of experimental phonetics or of psycholinguistics, we believe phonology will not be complete without explicit models of the processes underlying the ability of listeners to label utterances with respect to the phonological categories of their language. For example, an understanding of sound change in progress or of cross-dialect or cross-language comparison of vowels must incorporate knowledge about the perceptual properties of vowels. Much work remains and many perceptual experiments will need to be carried out before a compelling model of vowel perception can be established. Such a model must ultimately provide an detailed account for listeners' response patterns to natural and synthetic stimuli.

The research reported here is in the spirit of our prior work applying explicit statistical pattern-recognition concepts to the perception of phonological categories. Although our focus remains strongly empirical, much of what follows centers on relatively more formal aspects of methodology. The results illustrate how a careful examination of existing empirical data together with an analytic examination of alternate statistical models of production patterns can give insight into perceptual processes.

The results we report show that there are several theoretically interesting models of vowel identification that perform similarly on several moderate to large size

This work was supported in part by SSHRC and by a grant from the National Science Foundation (#0318451). Thanks to the editors, Pam Beddor and Maria-Josep Solé, and to two anonymous reviewers for their many helpful comments on earlier drafts of the chapter.

databases. Some of these allow for the separation of f0 and formant pattern information in ways that we think may be particularly fruitful for modeling the dependence of vowel perception on f0 and formant scaling.

We focus on pattern-recognition models of acoustic measurements of natural vowel productions. The models investigated stem from our initial attempts to account for the results of experiments on the perception of vowels in frequency-scaled speech. The stimuli were produced by processing natural speech samples through a high-quality vocoder (STRAIGHT; Kawahara 1997; Kawahara *et al.* 1999). On resynthesis, the fundamental frequency was scaled by multiplying by a constant, altering the perceived pitch of the stimuli. Simultaneously and independently, using STRAIGHT's built-in capabilities, the spectral envelope frequency axis was scaled (linearly warped by a constant multiplier), resulting in a scaling of formant frequencies. The range of scale factors investigated extended beyond the values observed in human speech. The general pattern of the results showed that vowel intelligibility deteriorated rather quickly unless f0 and envelope scaling were positively correlated in the manner similar to that observed in natural variation across speakers of different sex and age groups. We attempted to model this pattern of results by applying the discriminant analysis methods of Hillenbrand and Nearey (1999) to our perceptual data, using the first three formant frequencies to represent the features of the spectral envelope. Initial results were promising in that the model performed well (high correct identification rates) when f0 and formants shifts were coordinated (e.g. high fundamentals with high formants), but deteriorated when source and filter properties were not coordinated. While this behavior grossly matched that of listeners, it became clear that the Hillenbrand and Nearey model was somewhat too sensitive to the correlation of formants and f0 in the training data. Performance in non-coordinated shifts (e.g. high fundamentals paired with low formants) dropped off considerably faster for the model than it did for listeners.

There are a number of theoretical positions on the role of f0 in the specification of vowel quality (see Nearey 1989, Adank *et al.* 2004, and Johnson 2005c for reviews). Some—for instance, Syrdal and Gopal (1986) and Miller (1989)—incorporate f0 information directly into the initial feature representations of vowels. Others, such as Nearey (1978), are more in accord with the traditional notion of separation of source (f0) and filter (formants, spectrum envelope) properties in perception. The work of Patterson and colleagues (D. Smith *et al.* 2005) can also be viewed as being closer to the latter end of the spectrum. Numerous results with synthetic vowels suggest that the link between f0 and vowel quality perception is not fixed, but may vary considerably in different contexts (Nearey 1989; Johnson 1990, 1997b, 2005c; Nusbaum and Magnuson 1997).

Nearey (1989) suggested the possibility of a graded role for f0 (and possibly other aspects of voice quality), depending on experimental conditions. Fundamental frequency plays its largest role in speaker-randomized conditions, but a lesser one in cases where listeners hear longer stretches of speech from a single individual. This suggests the possibility of an "indirect" role for f0 allowing listeners, in effect, to estimate a likely formant range for a speaker based on f0. Such a hypothesis might be viewed as a version of a "cognitive adjustment" account of normalization as advocated by Nusbaum and Magnuson (1997). This might suggest that when reasonably complete information about a speaker's formant space is available, f0 plays no role at all. However, in our own work there is compelling evidence that substantial f0 effects persist when vowels are presented in sentence contexts (e.g. Assmann and Nearey 2005).

Our current hypothesis is that statistical (rather than deterministic) relations between f0 and formant patterns are at play in perceptual results. We attempt to explore explicit statistical methods that allow for flexible relations between f0 and spectrum envelope characteristics. These models are all based on a formant frequency summary of envelope information. Any problems of formant estimation and interactions of that estimation with the envelope sampling issues associated with high f0 (e.g. Ryalls and Lieberman 1982) are beyond the scope of this study. It is possible, in principle, to apply similar methods to frequency scaling normalization as practiced in modern speech recognition (e.g. Gouvêa and Stern 1997; Welling et al. 1999). Such extensions are also beyond the scope of the present study.

16.1.1 Databases

The methods discussed are evaluated primarily on three databases of measured formant and fundamental frequencies.[1] Since these databases will be referred to frequently, they are assigned three-character abbreviations. H95 refers to the data set presented in Hillenbrand et al. (1995), which is available publicly (http://homepages.wmich.edu/~hillenbr/voweldata.html). This consists of a single replication of 12 vowels, /i, ɪ, eI, ɛ, æ, ʌ, ɑ, ɔ, oU, ʊ, u, ɚ/ in h-V-d syllables spoken by 45 men, 48 women, and 46 children from western Michigan. A00 refers to the data of Assmann and Katz (2000) with the same set of vowels produced by 10 men, 10 women, and 30 children (ages 3, 5, and 7) from the north Texas region. P52 refers to the vowel sample from the classic Peterson and Barney (1952) study (available publicly at http://www-2.cs.cmu.edu/afs/cs.cmu.edu/project/ai-repository/ai/areas/speech/database/).

The measures used are the average fundamental frequency and F1, F2, and F3 for each of the vowels. For the H95 and A00 data, formant measures were taken from two sections at 20 percent and 80 percent of the duration of the vowels. For the P52 data, F1, F2, and F3 measurements are from a single "steady state" section. The P52 data has two replications of each vowel for each speaker, H95 has a single replication

---

[1] Duration is also relevant to vowel categorization in English. However, it not directly germane to the central issue of f0 and formant relations and we do not consider it here, since we want to focus attention on information available from those frequency-based measures.

per vowel per speaker, though a small percentage of measurements of individual formants are missing. A00 has variable numbers of replications per vowel per speaker. Missing values were imputed via a least squares method for some analyses in the H95 and A00 data. See Appendix I for additional details.

16.2 NORMALIZATION ASSUMING UNIFORM SCALING

Many of the models discussed below are variants of the venerable constant-ratio hypothesis, or its logarithmic equivalent, the constant log-interval hypothesis (Nearey 1978, 1989, 1992). It assumes that formant frequencies of the vowels of any speaker, s, of a dialect are related to a reference formant pattern by a single speaker-dependent constant.

Formally, this can be represented as

$$F_{kvs} = F_{kv}^* \cdot \rho_s \tag{1}$$

where F_{kvs} is the k-th formant frequency for vowel v of speaker s; F_{kv}^* is the k-th formant value for the reference pattern of vowel v; and ρ_s is a single speaker-dependent constant. (See Appendix II for a summary of key symbols used in this discussion.)

In the sequel, we rely on the log version of this hypothesis

$$G_{kvs} = G_{kv}^* + \psi_s \tag{2}$$

where each of the terms is the log of the corresponding factors in equation (1); ψ_s is now a speaker-dependent displacement.

Without loss of generality, we can constrain the reference pattern G_{kv}^* such that $\sum_{v=1}^{V} \sum_{k=1}^{3} G_{kv}^* = 0$; this puts the coordinates of the reference pattern at very low values, well below the human range. We could instead place the reference coordinates somewhere in the middle of the observed human range by adding a median value of ψ_s to each coordinate, but the formalization below is somewhat simplified if we define it this way. With these assumptions, we can estimate a particular speaker's displacement consistently as

$$\hat{\psi}_s = \overline{G}_s = \frac{1}{(3 \cdot V \cdot T)} \sum_{k=1}^{3} \sum_{v=1}^{V} \sum_{t=1}^{T} G_{kvst} \tag{3}$$

where G_{kvst} is the measured frequency of formant k of take (repetition) t of vowel v by speaker s, $\overline{G}_s$ is the mean log formant frequency of all vowels of speaker s, V is the number of vowel categories in the dialect, and T is the number of takes. We will assume that G_{kvst} is the sum of two terms: a true speaker average, G_{kvs}, and an additive error term, ε_{kvst}. For this chapter, we make the simplifying assumption that ε_{kvst} is normally distributed with a mean of 0 and with a constant covariance matrix for all subjects and vowels. Under those assumptions, if a complete, balanced set of vowels is available from speaker s, $\overline{G}_s$ is an unbiased estimate of the underlying ψ_s of (2).

16.2.1 Method 1: Normalization when subjects' mean formant values are available

We can define a normalization procedure based on this estimation as

$$\hat{N}_{kvs} = G_{kvs} - \hat{\psi}_s \tag{4}$$

where $\hat{N}_{kvs}$ is the normalized value of formant k for vowel v of subject s. This is an "extrinsic" normalization method since it requires, through $\overline{G}_s$, information about speaker characteristics not available in a single syllable. If the vowels of an arbitrary subject s obey the relations implied by (2) above, then $\hat{N}_{kvs}$ should approximately be equal to G^*_{kv}, the coordinates of the reference pattern.

This model can be visualized in terms of the sliding template model discussed in Nearey (1978: 93 ff.). The original model represents vowels in a two-dimensional G1 by G2 space. It is assumed that the vowels of all speakers of a particular dialect can be represented by a single pattern of holes drilled in a rigid vowel template. One hole is drilled in this template for each vowel category. The holes are centered at the coordinates G^*_{kv} for $k=1$ to 2. It is further assumed (in the most restricted version of the model) that this template is in effect tied to a linear track in this space, allowing translations along the diagonal of the G1 by G2 space. Only one degree of freedom, corresponding to ψ_s, is available to specify the vowels of any given speaker, s. This determines how far along the track the template is moved to produce that speaker's vowel formant frequencies.

In a quantitative implementation, normalized data from a training sample of subjects can be used to tune a conventional pattern-recognition model, and a new subject's vowels can be classified provided ψ_s can be estimated for the new subject. This scheme is quite effective in normalizing vowels for classification when the conditions for its application are met, in other words, where there is a balanced full set of data to estimate the formant pattern of each vowel category for each subject. In the present context, the linear discriminant training procedure consists of calculating the three-dimensional mean vector per vowel and the 3×3 pooled within-groups covariance matrix.

$$\hat{\mu}_{kv} = \frac{1}{S \cdot T} \sum_{s=1}^{S} \sum_{t=1}^{T} N_{kvst} \tag{5}$$

$$\hat{\Sigma}_{jk} = \frac{1}{S \cdot T \cdot (V-1)} \sum_{v=1}^{V} \sum_{s=1}^{S} \sum_{t=1}^{T} (N_{jvs} - \hat{\mu}_{jv})(N_{kvs} - \hat{\mu}_{kv}) \tag{6}$$

When used without the formant number, $\hat{\mu}_v$ will denote the mean vector for vowel v. Similarly, $\hat{\Sigma}$, without subscripts, will denote the estimated pooled within-groups covariance matrix. Given the training data, new vowels from talker s can be classified as follows:

$$P(G_t|v, \hat{\psi}_s) = P(\hat{N}_t|v) = Gau([G_t - \hat{\psi}_s], \hat{\mu}_v, \hat{\Sigma}) \tag{7}$$

where $P(G_t|v, \hat{\psi}_s)$ is the probability density of observing measurement G_t and

$$Gau(x, \eta, \Phi) = \frac{1}{(2\pi)^{3/2}|\Phi|^{1/2}} \exp\left(-\frac{1}{2}(x - \eta)^T\Phi^{-1}(x - \eta)\right) \tag{8}$$

is the probability density of observation column vector x for a multivariate Gaussian with mean (column) vector η and covariance matrix Φ; G_t is the vector of log formant frequencies [G1, G2, G3] for the current trial t, and $\hat{N}_t$ is that vector normalized by subtracting $\hat{\psi}_s$ for the current speaker, s, from each element.

We may then categorize the vowel "crisply" by selecting the vowel for which $P(G_t|v, \hat{\psi}_s)$ is highest;[2] that is, using standard notation, we choose the vowel category c as

$$c = \arg\max_v [P(G_t|v, \hat{\psi}_s)] \tag{9}$$

We can also provide a graded estimate of group membership via *a posteriori* probability estimates over all vowel choices:

$$P(v|G_t, \hat{\psi}_s) = \frac{P(G_t|v, \hat{\psi}_s)}{\sum_{w=1}^{V} P(G_t|w, \hat{\psi}_s)} \tag{10}$$

These *a posteriori* scores have proven useful in our prior work (Nearey and Assmann 1986; Hillenbrand and Nearey 1999) for comparison with listeners' confusion matrices.

There is nothing approaching a consensus about the "best" normalization scheme and we make no claim for universal superiority of any of the methods discussed here.[3] However, the method just described has proven quite successful in a number of applications. For example, it has been used for decades in sociophonetics, where it is referred to as log mean normalization (see Labov 2001: 157–64; Labov *et al.* 2005, ch. 5). It is also included as the standard method in Labov's program Plotnik (http:// www.ling.upenn.edu/~wlabov/Plotnik.html). Furthermore, log mean normalization is closely related to linear scaling or "vocal tract length" normalization widely used in automatic speech recognition applications (Gouvêa and Stern 1997). Finally, it has the advantage of being conceptually compatible with the kind of envelope scaling transformations we have applied in our resynthesis experiments using STRAIGHT. Roughly speaking, sets of vowels whose envelopes are uniformly scaled on the frequency axes will result in formant patterns that are invariant across the scalings.

---

[2] We assume throughout that the prior probabilities of all vowels are equal.
[3] See Adank *et al.* (2004) for a review of a number of methods on Dutch vowels, including a one-degree of freedom log-mean-normalization scheme that includes log (f0). This is contra-indicated by the analyses reviewed in Nearey (1989) and by those discussed below, since log(f0) increases roughly three times more between male and female speakers than do log formant frequencies.

There are two key limitations of this model. First, it appears to require access to more than a single syllable to calculate $\overline{G}_s$. The second is that there is no role for f0 at all. We address these limitations in turn in the next sections.

16.3 NORMALIZATION WITH A LATENT ψ_s

16.3.1 Method 2: Unrestricted (or uniform prior) optimization over ψ_s

Clearly, the normalization method just described cannot apply to listening conditions where speakers are randomized and only one vowel token from one vowel category spoken by one speaker is available at a time. We need tokens from all of a speaker's vowel categories to estimate $\hat{\psi}_s$ from (3).

There are several methods to impute a value of ψ_s in the absence of more complete information. The first is closely related to the maximum likelihood methods of vocal-tract length normalization, spectral scaling or spectral warping in the ASR literature (e.g. Zhan and Westphal 1997; see also Gouvêa 1998 for a lucid review of several approaches). In the present context this involves optimizing the likelihood criterion over all plausible values of ψ_s for a given sample of vowels assumed to be from a single speaker. In the limiting case (corresponding to the one in our experiments) this could be done even on a token-by-token basis as follows. Given the token t with the observation vector G_t, for each vowel category v, we search the range of possible ψ_s and find the value that makes that vowel seem most likely.[4] Formally,

$$\hat{\psi}_{vs}^{(2)} = \arg\max_{\psi_s} [P_v^{(2)}(\psi_s)] = \arg\max_{\psi_s} [P(G_t|v, \psi_s)] \tag{11}$$

where the parenthetical superscript indicates the method of estimation. Note here that we include the subscript v as well as s to emphasize that it is optimized separately for each vowel-category hypothesis being entertained. When the v subscript is absent from an estimator, it implies that the same estimate is used for all vowel hypotheses.

We have included an intermediate expression $P_v^{(2)}(\psi_s)$ as an implicit shorthand for the fuller expression, $\arg\max_{\psi_s} [P(G_t|v, \psi_s)]$. Thus $P_v^{(2)}(\hat{\psi}_{vs}^{(2)})$ is the value of the expression in the square brackets at the maximum for the vowel v. The vowel choice is then based on finding the vowel whose optimum alignment produces the best score of all the vowels, that is, as

$$\arg\max_{v} [P_v^{(2)}(\hat{\psi}_{vs}^{(2)})] \tag{12}$$

Soft classification proceeds analogously, substituting the vowel-dependent $\hat{\psi}_{vs}^{(2)}$ for the global $\hat{\psi}_s$ in (7) and (10).

---

[4] In fact, for the models discussed here, analytic solutions to the optimizations are available and no search is necessary. In more general cases, a grid search can be implemented.

Roughly speaking, (11) and (12) amount to "choose the vowel that looks best when it tries to look its best." This process can be envisioned via a sliding template analog as follows. Imagine a vowel as a point of light under a glass table (see Figure 16.1). The vowel template is constructed on a sheet of mainly opaque material that has clear patches near the vowel centers, with gradually decreasing transparency with distance from each center.

In the analog of (11), for each vowel the template is slid along a track on the table so as to maximize the light coming through its clear patch. In the analog of (12), the vowel patch with the greatest light transmission at its best point is selected. Note again than an optimal value of $\hat{\psi}_{vs}^{(2)}$ is selected independently for each vowel. This means in effect that each vowel choice hypothesis is associated with an implicit choice of speaker-dependent scale factor. In a perceptual modeling context, $\hat{\psi}_{vs}^{(2)}$ and other similar estimators described below might be a source of predictions about listeners' judgments related to speaker size or gender (cf. Smith and Patterson 2005). Furthermore, different vowel choices would in general be associated with different $\hat{\psi}_{vs}^{(2)}$, and some dependency between vowel category and speaker size judgments might be expected for relatively ambiguous vowels.

This scheme imposes no restrictions or preferences on ψ_s, the average formant frequency value, other than that assumed by any global limits on the search range.

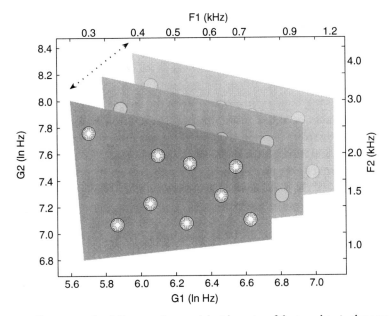

FIGURE 16.1. Illustration of a sliding template model with copies of the template in three positions. These correspond (lower left to upper right) roughly to those of typical adult male, adult female and child speakers, respectively. The double headed arrow represents the direction parallel to the G1 = G2 diagonal along which the template is constrained to slide. (Reference F1 and F2 values are included on the top and right edges).

This would then normalize any formant scaling of each stimulus equally well. In that sense at least, it is compatible with the unrestricted scaling assumptions implicit in the use of Mellin- or scale-transformation based methods (e.g. Umesh *et al.* 1999; Irino and Patterson 2002), which map all scale transformations (subject only to very broad range constraints) of a given spectral envelope to an invariant representation.

16.3.2 Method 3: Optimization of ψ_s with an informative prior

There is evidence from a variety of sources, however, to suggest that there is a preferred range of ψ_s values for human perceivers. Chiba and Kajiyama (1958) report that phonograph recordings of adult male Japanese vowels remain highly intelligible with playback speeds (and hence formant scale factors, relative to adult males) varying from about .8 to 1.5 of normal but that they deteriorate beyond that range. More recently, Fu and Shannon (1999) have summarized the results of several studies of the identification of frequency-shifted vowels and conclude that identification accuracy follows an inverted U-shaped function. Together with our own findings (Assmann and Nearey 2003) these studies provide substantial evidence that there are some range limits on scale factors.

In a statistical modeling of perception, such limits might be accommodated by estimating (or guessing) a prior probability distribution on ψ_s. The rough notion is that values of ψ_s more typical of human populations should be preferred, while those well outside human ranges should be penalized. It is possible to extend the sliding template analogy to incorporate this prior probability. Imagine that the transparency of the glass table varies somehow (perhaps via polarizing filters) with the position of the template along its track. When the template is near the middle of the human range, the table is maximally transparent. When the template is moved away from the midrange, the table becomes more opaque. On a given trial, for a given vowel hypothesis, the template position is adjusted to maximize the light coming through the vowel patch and through the table.

To do this formally, we can augment (11) with an explicit prior (marginal) distribution of ψ_s, $P(\psi_s)$. On a given vowel hypothesis, a listener might be assumed to try to find the best compromise position

$$\hat{\psi}_{vs}^{(3)} = \arg\max_{\psi_s} [P_v^{(3)}(\psi_s)] = \arg\max_{\psi_s} [P(G_t|v, \psi_s) \cdot P(\psi_s)] \tag{13}$$

This optimization corresponds to the estimation of a posterior mode in Bayesian statistics, often referred to as MAP (maximum *a posteriori*) estimation in the speech recognition literature.[5] Crisp vowel identification modifies (12) to $\arg\max_v [P_v^{(3)}(\hat{\psi}_{vs}^{(3)})]$. That is, we pick the vowel that, when optimally adjusted by its own best

---

[5] It would also be possible here (and elsewhere) to use a fuller Bayesian approach by integrating over the values of ψ_s, rather than selecting the maximum. We leave that possibility for future research.

estimate of log-scale factor, produces the largest value of the function in the square brackets of (13) of any of the vowels in the set.

But where does $P(\psi_s)$, the prior distribution, come from? Here we will simply estimate it empirically based on observations of $\overline{G}_s$ (i.e. $\hat{\psi}_s$ as estimated by (7)) in a large sample of the speakers.[6] It is convenient in the analysis below to adopt a single (unimodal) Gaussian distribution $P(\psi_s) = Gau(\mu_{\psi_s}, \sigma^2_{\psi_s})$. Figure 16.2 shows a histogram of $\hat{\psi}_s$ with a fitted Gaussian (scaled to reflect the counts) for the pooled data from the three data sets. The resulting estimate for the log mean, $\mu_{\hat{\psi}_s}$, is 7.2333 with a standard deviation, $\sigma_{\hat{\psi}_s}$, of 0.1284. This corresponds to a geometric mean of 1385 Hz with a coefficient of variation of about 13 percent.[7] We use these values in our models below.

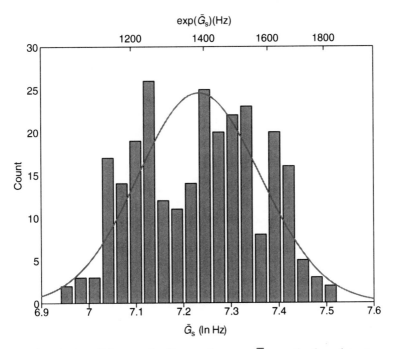

FIGURE 16.2. Distribution of the mean log formant frequency $\overline{G}_s$ over the three datasets.

---

[6] Alternatively, we might impose a "subjective" prior that we regard as a plausible shape for the likelihood distribution of ψ_s values. While not without problems in the philosophy of statistics, such a subjective prior seems plausible in a perceptual application, representing a listener's expectations about the value of ψ_s from experience with many voices, or about the experiment at hand. See the discussion below.

[7] There is some evidence for more than one mode in the histogram. In particular, there appears to be something of a gap near about $\overline{G}_s = 7.18$, or about 1400 Hz. Further graphic analysis shows that the gap in Fig. 16.2 corresponds to a region of limited overlap between adult male and female speakers. It seems likely that at least two distinct modes exist related to the sexual dimorphism between adult males and females. This gap might be filled to some degree by adolescent (and older preadolescent) males. That is, we cannot be certain whether the apparent multimodality is truly representative of the population at large, as samples are taken of rather well-defined subgroups of speakers, but ones that are not scientific stratified samples. Estimates of $\overline{G}_s$ vary somewhat across the three datasets: the corresponding $[\mu_{\hat{\psi}_s}, \sigma_{\hat{\psi}_s}]$

16.4 ESTIMATION OF ψ_s INFORMED BY g0

A number of theories of vowel specification (Syrdal and Gopal 1986; Miller 1989) incorporate f0 information directly as part of the definition of initial vowel features. While we will return to this idea later, here we note that because of the empirical correlation between speakers' g0 ranges and their formant ranges, it is possible to define a reasonable *indirect* g0 normalization scheme that uses a syllable-internal (or intrinsic) property to estimate ψ_s and thence $\hat{N}_{kvs}$ given only the measurements of a single syllable. A conceptually simple way to do this is via simple linear regression of empirical $\overline{G}_s$ from token-wise values of $g0_t$, providing the estimate

$$\hat{\psi}_s^{(4)} = \hat{\overline{G}} = a \cdot g0_t + b \tag{14}$$

where the superscript anticipates its use in Method 4 below. Figure 16.3 shows a scatterplot of this information for the three datasets pooled. Least squares estimates when the three data sets are pooled are $a = 0.3159$, $b = 5.5950$. In the estimation, a single empirical $\overline{G}_s$ value per subject, using (3), is used as a repeated dependent variable for each vowel token (including replicates, when available) from each speaker, s. This seems appropriate as ψ_s is assumed to be invariant, while $g0_t$ varies from trial to trial.[8] (The multiple appearance of each speaker's $\overline{G}_s$ is responsible for the banding apparent on the y-axis.)

16.4.1 Method 4: One-shot plug-in substitution for ψ_s

The most obvious way is to simply plug in $\hat{\psi}_s^{(4)}$ for ψ_s in (7) to estimate the class-conditional probabilities and then to proceed as in Method 1. More precisely, define

$$P_v^{(4)}(\hat{\psi}_s^{(4)}) = Gau(G_t - \hat{\psi}_s^{(4)}, \mu_v, \Sigma) \tag{15}$$

Notice that $\hat{\psi}_s^{(4)}$ is the same for all vowels. This method is closely related to that of Miller (1989). The crisp vowel choice rule is then arg $\max_v [P_v^{(4)}(\hat{\psi}_{vs}^{(4)})]$.

pairs are [7.2389, 0.1017], [7.3382, 0.1303] and [7.1568, 0.1231] for the H95, A00, and P52 datasets, respectively. This corresponds to (geometric) mean values of about 1280 to 1530 Hz with coefficients of variation between 10 and 13 percent. There are several sources of this variation. First, the variation in age of the speakers and exact number of speakers in each group is unequal. The higher geometric means correspond to the subsamples with larger proportion of (and in the case of A00, younger) children. Second, $\overline{G}$ will be affected by the vowel pattern (Disner 1980) of the dialect sampled. Dialect differences in nominally similar vowels and differing vowel inventories could lead to the mean corresponding to a "pattern bias" in $\overline{G}$. This is a difficult problem to solve completely and must remain a topic for future research. [Added in proof. See Morrison and Nearey (2006) for some further development of this issue.]

[8] There is some evidence of a more complex relationship between $\overline{G}_s$ and $g0_t$. Two issues we have explored based on graphics like Fig. 16.3 are that (a) the slope of the relation may be shallower for low values of g0 and (b) the intercepts may differ among the dialects. (The latter may be related to "pattern bias" in $\overline{G}_s$ of n. 6). Although there is statistical support for such differences making reliable improvements in the prediction of $\overline{G}_s$, their use in discriminant analyses provided variable (and at best very modest) improvement in the identification scores. We will continue to study this issue.

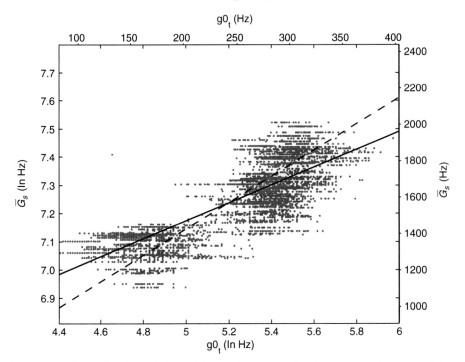

FIGURE 16.3. Scatterplot of $g0_t$, the log of g0 for each token, against the corresponding speaker's log-mean formant frequency. The solid line shows the overall regression line predicting $\overline{G}_s$ from $g0_t$ used in Methods 4 and 5. The dashed line is that predicting $g0_t$ from $\overline{G}_s$ used in Method 6.

16.4.2 Method 5: MAP modulated by conditional probability of ψ_s given g0

Method 4 ignores the error inherent in the estimation of ψ_s from $g0_t$. For the data shown in Figure 16.3, this value $\widehat{\sigma}_{\hat{\psi}_s^{(4)}}$, the standard deviation of the error about the regression line, is 1.284. This corresponds to a reduction of the variance of the prediction of $\overline{G}_s$ by about 2/3 compared to the marginal variance depicted in Figure 16.2. However, the residual variation indicates there could be a range of ψ_s values that might be almost as good, some of which may allow a better matching of the incoming vowel token to a virtual "hole in the template" than the mean predicted value. We can allow for this uncertainty by means of a model for the conditional probability of the value of ψ_s given $g0_t$ based on the regression equation, above.

$$P(\psi_s \mid g0_t) = Gau(\psi_s, \hat{\psi}_s^{(4)}, \hat{\sigma}^2_{\hat{\psi}_s^{(4)}}) \tag{16}$$

We can then incorporate this into a modified g0-guided sliding template optimization by substituting $P(\psi_s|g0_t)$ for the prior $P(\psi_s)$ in (13) as follows.

$$\hat{\psi}_{v,s}^{(5)} = \arg\max_{\psi_s} [P_v^{(5)}(\psi_s)] = \arg\max_{\psi_s} [P(G_t|v, \psi_s) \cdot P(\psi_s|g0_t)] \tag{17}$$

Then crisp vowel identification follows as $\arg\max_v[P_v^{(5)}(\hat{\psi}_{vs}^{(5)})]$. This method tries, in effect, to provide both a reasonable match of ψ_s to the observed g0 while also trying to optimally place the vowel template to maximize the proximity of a vowel mode to the observed vector G_t of formants.

16.4.3 Method 6. Joint maximization of $P(v|G_t, \psi_s)$ and $P(\psi_s, g0_t)$

Method 5 above can be criticized because it represents the conditional probability of ψ_s given $g0_t$ via regression. This does not impose any inherent restrictions on the range of ψ_s. A logically more complete approach incorporating such restrictions considers the joint distribution of ψ_s and $g0_t$. This can be done as follows. From elementary probability theory the joint distribution of ψ_s and $g0_t$ can be expressed as

$$P(\psi_s, g0_t) = P(g0_t|\psi_s) \cdot P(\psi_s) \tag{18}$$

where $P(g0_t|\psi_s)$ is the conditional probability of $g0_t$ given ψ_s and $P(\psi_s)$ is the marginal probability of ψ_s (as illustrated in Fig. 16.2).We again approximate the conditional probability of $P(g0_t|\psi_s)$ by a regression technique that regresses $g0_t$ on $\overline{G}_s$, thus reversing their roles as dependent and independent variables compared to the estimation of (14). The resulting regression equation is

$$\hat{g}0(\overline{G}_s) = 2.14452\overline{G}_s - 10.3233 \tag{19}$$

with an error standard deviation of $\hat{\sigma}_{\hat{g}0} = 0.132703$ (see the broken line of Fig. 16.3). We can then estimate

$$P^{(6)}(\psi_s, g0_t) = Gau\left(g0_t, \hat{g}0(\psi_s), \hat{\sigma}_{\hat{g}0}^{(6)}\right) \cdot \hat{P}(\psi_s) \tag{20}$$

where $\hat{P}(\psi_s)$ is the distribution represented in Figure 16.2. Finally, we can estimate an optimal value of ψ_s for each vowel

$$\hat{\psi}_{v,s}^{(6)} = \arg\max_{\psi_s} [P_v^{(6)}(\psi_s)] = \arg\max_{\psi_s} [P(G_t|v, \psi_s) \cdot P^{(6)}(\psi_s, g0_t)] \tag{21}$$

Crisp vowel classification then selects $\arg\max_v[P_v^{(6)}(\hat{\psi}_{vs}^{(6)})]$ as the winning vowel.

Equation (21) is a complete expression for an estimate of the posterior mode of ψ_{vs} that builds in all the assumptions and empirical relations we have considered so far. Intuitively this model is trying to find, for each vowel, a value of ψ_s that is compatible with three things simultaneously: a good alignment of the template vowel patch with the incoming formant pattern, a reasonable match of template positioning with general human ranges of ψ_s, and a reasonable prediction of observed g0 associated with that position. This may be the only plausible candidate among those discussed here for a model of an ideal observer who knows everything about the statistical distributions we have assumed to be at least approximately valid here.

We note in passing that Methods 5 and 6 provide for very convenient ways to modulate the effects of g0 on vowel identification parametrically. Increasing the variance $\hat{\sigma}^2_{\hat{\psi}_s^{(4)}}$ in Method 5 or $\hat{\sigma}_{\hat{g}0}$ in Method 6 flattens out the likelihood effects with respect to g0 and effectively moves the procedures in the direction of Methods 2 and 3, respectively. Similarly, increasing the variance of the prior distribution of Figure 16.2, $\sigma^2_{\psi_s}$, will move Method 3 toward 2 and Method 6 toward 5, all other things being equal. In a perceptual model, such modulations would probably have to be viewed as *adaptive*, perhaps broadly similar to a kind of "cognitive adjustment" as advocated by Nusbaum and Magnuson (1997).

16.5 METHODS WITH NO EXPLICIT NORMALIZATION

By way of comparison, we include two additional methods that simply avoid explicit normalization or estimation of speaker scale altogether.

16.5.1 Method 7: No explicit normalization, g0 as a free variable

Method 7 treats g0 as an extra feature. This method is equivalent to the approach employed with reasonable success in Nearey and Assmann (1986) and in Hillenbrand and Nearey (1999) to predict listeners' classification of modified natural and resynthesized vowels. (In the latter case, duration was also included as a variable.) More explicitly, define

$$P_v^{(7)} = Gau(X_t, \hat{\mu}_v^{(7)}, \hat{\Sigma}^{(7)}) \tag{22}$$

where X_t is the augmented vector of measurements [g0, G1, G2, G3] for token t, and $\hat{\mu}_v^{(7)}$ and $\hat{\Sigma}^{(7)}$ are the mean vector and covariance matrix estimates from computations analogous to those in (5) and (6), but substituting X_{ksvt} for N_{kvst} in the obvious way. Again, crisp vowel choice comes via arg $\max_v[P_v^{(7)}]$.

Although there is no explicit normalization, aspects of the statistical relationships underlying Figures 16.2 and 16.3 are subsumed in the pooled covariance matrix $\hat{\Sigma}^{(7)}$, as will be discussed further below.

Another potentially important issue is that Method 7 has now, in effect, included g0 as a part of the definition of vowel quality. In principle, this implies there could be specific (register) tones associated with each vowel category. For example, in some hypothetical language, [ɪ] might arbitrarily have a high f0 and [ʊ] a very low f0. In addition, Method 7 could accommodate the small but highly reliable differences among vowel categories associated with vowel height that have long been recognized in phonetics under the rubric of *intrinsic pitch* of vowels (see Whalen and Levitt 1995 for a thorough review). Method 7 would allow even such small pitch differences to play some role in vowel classification. We note, however, that there appears to be no evidence for such effects in speech perception. Katz and Assmann (2001) presented listeners with intrinsic-pitch-neutralized vowels and found no drop in identification accuracy (in both speaker-blocked and speaker-randomized conditions), suggesting that intrinsic f0 has at best limited perceptual importance.

16.5.2 Method 8: No explicit normalization, no g0

Finally, in the comparisons below, it is useful to have as a baseline a model that ignores both explicit normalization and g0 entirely. This is essentially the same as Method 7, but eliminating the g0 variable.

$$P_v^{(8)} = Gau(X_t, \hat{\mu}_v^{(8)}, \hat{\Sigma}^{(8)}) \tag{23}$$

where X_t is the vector of raw measurements [G1, G2, G3] for token t, and $\hat{\mu}_v^{(8)}$ and $\hat{\Sigma}^{(8)}$ are the mean vector and covariance matrix estimates that are the same as those for Method 7, but deleting rows and columns corresponding to g0. Crisp vowel choice comes via arg $\max_v[P_v^{(8)}]$. As in Method 7, although there is no normalization, aspects of the statistical relationship underlying Figure 16.2 (but not that of Fig. 16.3) are subsumed in the pooled covariance matrix $\hat{\Sigma}^{(8)}$.

16.6 APPLICATION TO AUTOMATIC VOWEL CLASSIFICATION

As noted earlier, we have used Method 7 in our earlier work to predict listeners' classification of vowels based on production data. This method works reasonably well in most applications with stimuli in the range of natural speech, but does not appear suited to experiments with vocoded speech where pitch and envelope scaling result in patterns that are not typical of natural speech. Methods 5 and 6 above were originally conceived as ways that might extend better to such cases. Before discussing potential application to such cases, we will evaluate the performance of the models on the classification of natural data.

The general method here was to perform pattern recognition based on each of these methods. In particular, we adopted a leave-out-one-speaker cross-validation technique. Within each dialect dataset, we trained classification models holding out one speaker's data from training, then classifying the held-out speaker's vowels on the models trained on the statistics of the complementary data. In particular, we calcu-lated $\hat{\mu}_v$ and $\hat{\Sigma}$ of (7) used in Methods 1 through 6, and $\hat{\mu}_v^{(7)}, \hat{\Sigma}^{(7)}, \hat{\mu}_v^{(8)}, \hat{\Sigma}^{(8)}$ used in Methods 7 and 8 that way. However, we used pooled-across-dialects datasets (with no holdouts) for the global statistics related to Figures 16.2 and 16.3, namely, those for the prior $P(\psi_s)$, as well as for those of the regression parameters associated with $\hat{\psi}_s^{(4)}$, $\hat{\psi}_s^{(5)}$, or $\hat{\psi}_s^{(6)}$. For the H95 and A00 datasets, we had formant measurements available at two time points and we used them all. Thus, a data vector for Method 7 would include $[g0, G1_a, G2_a, G3_a, G1_b, G2_b, G3_b]$, with the a and b subscripts referring to the 20 percent and 80 percent time points, respectively. For Methods 2 through 6, the estimates of $\hat{\mu}_v$ and $\hat{\Sigma}$ were the same as for Method 1, while method-specific estimates of ψ_s were subtracted from the log formant measurements as appropriate for each method.

16.6.1 Results and discussion

Summary results for the three datasets are shown in Figures 16.4, 16.5, and 16.6. A few general notes are in order. First, the P52 data shows the largest range of variation of the means across the methods, with a spread of more than 10 percentage points. The H95 data shows a spread of only about 3 percentage points, while the A00 data shows an intermediate spread. The relatively higher overall identification rate for H95 data compared to P52 is likely due to the fact that two spectral sections are available in the former, while the somewhat lackluster performance of the A00 data may be due to the presence of relatively variable data from younger children.

There is no firmly established statistical procedure for assessing the statistical significance of differences among models on cross-validated data. Duda *et al.* (2000: 485–6) suggest using *t*-statistics based on a leave-out-one-point (or jackknife) classification. We follow an analogous procedure here for the leave-out-one-speaker

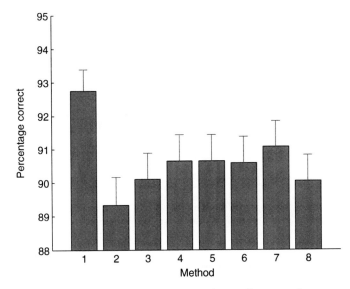

FIGURE 16.4. Results of competing methods for the H95 dataset illustrating the means and standard errors (across 139 subjects) of the cross-validated crisp classification of the vowels.

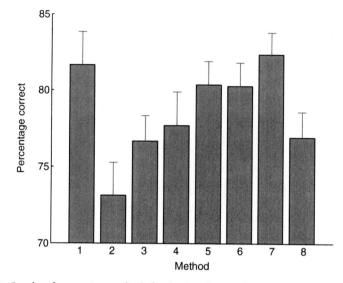

FIGURE 16.5. Results of competing methods for the A00 dataset illustrating the means and standard errors (across 50 subjects) of the cross-validated crisp classification of the vowels.

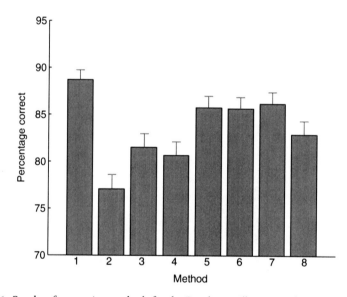

FIGURE 16.6. Results of competing methods for the P52 dataset illustrating the means and standard errors (across 76 subjects) of the cross-validated crisp classification of the vowels.

classification procedure. Nominal significance at the .05 level between any pair of hypotheses corresponds then roughly to separation of about twice the average length of the error bars of the two methods being compared. We use this criterion as a benchmark to guide discussion but do not put great stock in it.

Note first that Method 1 (extrinsic log-mean normalization) and Method 7 (which includes g0 as an extra variable) are on average about tied for the best classification results. Method 1 leads slightly in two of three comparisons, but not significantly so. The t-test criterion shows that Method 1 is superior to Method 2 for all datasets, to Methods 3, 4, and 8 for H95 and P52, and to Methods 5 and 6 for H95. Similarly, Method 7 is superior to Methods 2 and 3 for the A00 and P52 data. It is also superior to Method 8 for A00 data and to Method 4 for the PB52 data.

Methods 5 and 6, using indirect g0-informed estimation of ψ_s, are at most about one standard error inferior to Method 7, which incorporates g0 directly. (The largest t-statistics occur for the A00 data: for Method 7 versus Method 5, $t(98) = 0.9315$, $p > 0.35$; for Method 7 versus Method 6, $t(98)$, $p > 0.32$.) The predictions of the three models are generally quite similar. A comparison of the profile correlations (see Hillenbrand and Nearey 1999) of the *a posteriori* probability of group membership calculated token by token shows that correlations between Methods 5 and 7 are 0.9776, .9879 and .9776 for the H95, A00 and P52 datasets, respectively. The corresponding correlations between Methods 6 and 7 are 0.9954, 0.9875, and 0.9777. For all practical purposes, then, the three models would appear to be equivalent for classifying these datasets.

However, for the sake of argument, let us assume that the slight advantage of Method 7 would hold up in more powerful tests of differences among methods. There is at least one reason[9] why we might expect this to be so; the extra degrees of freedom in Method 7 may be capable of more accurately reflecting the "local" statistics of the sub-samples. In particular, in Methods 4 through 6, the relationship between g0 and $\overline{G}_s$ is modeled over the three datasets combined. For Method 7, however, the covariance between formants and g0 is modeled separately for each dataset. Despite the fact that the classification is based on cross-validation, minor violations (see note 7) of the strong assumptions of the g0 to $\overline{G}_s$ relationship in Methods 3 through 6 might be ameliorated by the local tuning to the data of Method 7.

16.7 IMPLICATIONS FOR PERCEPTUAL MODELING

But why should we bother to go to the trouble of resorting to indirect normalization Methods 5 or 6, when direct incorporation of g0 into the classification of Method 7 seems to be at least as good? Method 7 provides a reasonable solution to vowel recognition as an exercise in statistical classification. We have also argued that similar

---

[9] Additional exploratory modeling makes it seem unlikely that any advantage of Method 7 is due to patterns related to intrinsic pitch. For example, if the g0 components of the mean vectors $\hat{\mu}_v^{(7)}$ of equation (22) for Method 7 are all set to the same value for each vowel (namely, the average of all the vowels), results are essentially identical even though intrinsic pitch information has been eliminated. In fact, average correct identification scores are very slightly higher for the A00 and P52 datasets.

methods provide a reasonable approximation to perceptual behavior in some cases for natural, modified natural and synthetic speech (Nearey and Assmann 1986; Hillenbrand and Nearey 1999). However, differences among the three methods emerge quite clearly when we begin to simulate the effects of independent scaling of f0 and formant frequencies in our vocoding experiments using STRAIGHT. Initial results show that while the behavior of the three methods is similar when f0 to formant relationships match those in natural speech, the behavior is quite different with even moderate departures from that correlation. In particular, Methods 5 and 6 are somewhat less sensitive to such perturbations, while still showing deterioration in performance when the relationship is more severely disturbed. This is also roughly the behavior evinced by human listeners in those conditions.

Figure 16.7 shows the predictions of Methods 5 and 7 for an experiment on the identification of frequency-shifted vowels, using vowels from two male speakers in the A00 database (Assmann and Nearey forthcoming). The STRAIGHT vocoder was used to produce 36 versions of each vowel, with six f0 scale factors (0.25, 0.5, 1.0, 2.0, 4.0, and 8.0) paired with six formant scale factors (0.61, 0.78, 1.00, 1.28, 1.64, and 2.10). Each row in Figure 16.7 shows the results for one f0 shift condition. The left column shows observed and predicted identification accuracy for Method 7; the right column shows Method 6. To generate predictions for the frequency-shifted stimuli, f0 and formant measurements for the baseline (unshifted) condition were scaled up or down, depending on the frequency shifts applied.

Two key aspects of listeners' responses are accurately predicted by both models, namely, the decline in accuracy with more extreme shifts in formant frequency and the fact that the best identified formant scaling values generally increase with increasing f0. Thus, identification accuracy is predicted to be more accurate in conditions where f0 and formant frequencies are both raised (left column, top panel; left side) or both lowered (left column, bottom panel; right side) compared to conditions where shifts are in opposing directions. However, while this general trend is evident in the data from listeners, Method 7 predicts overly narrow peaking along the formant scaling axis, and overly strong linkage with f0. The predictions of Method 6 (right column, unfilled circles) are similar to those of Method 7. Overall, Method 6 does a somewhat better job of predicting the interaction of f0 and formant frequency shifts, with some measure of broadening of the peaks and perhaps somewhat reduced linkage to f0.

Note that the model parameters used to produce the predictions shown with the open circles in Figure 16.7 for Method 6 were tuned only on the unshifted A00 production measurement, and remained "frozen" exactly as they were estimated for the pattern recognition experiments shown in Figure 16.5. We have also included an illustration of "tuning" the parameters of Method 6 by relaxing the relationship between f0 and formant envelope better to account for listeners' data (right column, dashed lines). For these predictions, the parameter $\hat{\sigma}_{\bar{g}0}$ of (20) associated with the regression error of Figure 16.2 has been multiplied by 2.0, thus in effect decreasing the

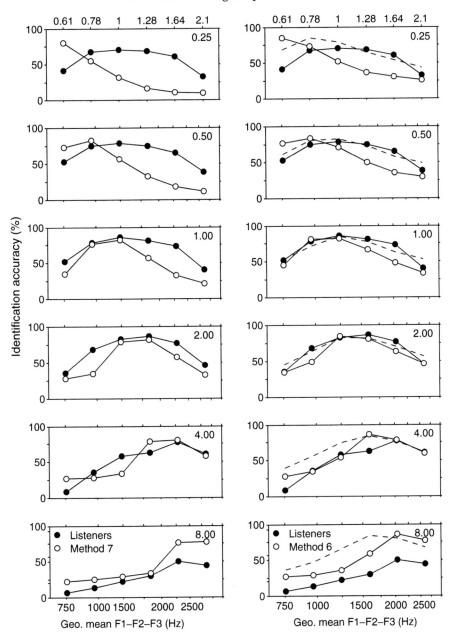

FIGURE 16.7. Vowel identification accuracy for frequency-shifted vowels by listeners (filled circles) and models (unfilled circles). Predictions are based on mean *a posteriori* probabilities from Method 7 (left column) and Method 6 (right column). Spectrum envelope shift factors are shown along the horizontal axis at the top; f0 shift factors are shown in the upper right corner. The dashed lines in the right columns result from modifications to one of the parameters of the model (see text).

degree of correlation between $g0_t$ and $\overline{G}_s$. This improves the fit noticeably. However, thus far even after tuning the parameters to the observed data, there are noticeable discrepancies that remain between predicted and observed means, especially in the condition where f0 is high and formant frequencies are lowered (bottom right panel). In such cases it is often difficult to estimate F1 reliably, and listeners have difficulty identifying these stimuli. In addition, inspection of predicted and observed confusion matrices indicates substantial discrepancies in the pattern of confusion errors in some cases. More work is needed to determine the reasons for these discrepancies.

Whether or not we shall be able to show a compelling advantage for Method 6 in explaining the data of Figure 16.7, the formal separation of f0-dependent effects and expectations about formant averages has potential theoretical advantages in explaining other perceptual effects. There is ample evidence that the effects of f0-to-formant relationships are somewhat malleable (Nearey 1989; Johnson 1990, 1997b, 2005c; Nusbaum and Magnuson 1997). Indirect Methods 5 and 6 can readily allow for this malleability by allowing the variances about the regression lines of Figure 16.3 to vary in different conditions.[10] This effect is similar to what Johnson's (1997b) exemplar model can achieve by changing attentional weights on f0 in different listening conditions.

But what justification might there be for such relaxation? There are many possible answers to this, but we are inclined to favor ones similar in spirit to those of Nusbaum and Magnuson (1997): listeners adapt to the listening conditions at hand. Method 6, in particular, seems to offer the most possibilities for modeling such adaptation. Thus, for example, if over the course of an experiment, f0 variations are extreme because of intonational factors, or if they appear to violate normal expectations of the relationship to formants because of extreme experimental manipulations, then listeners might decrease their reliance on g0 by inflating its expected variance, $\hat{\sigma}_{\hat{g}0}$.

Similarly, if template location (and hence $\overline{G}_s$) appears to be relatively stable within blocks of several trials, listeners might narrow expectations of the distribution of ψ_s to conform more closely to the local average, adjusting (temporarily) the mean,[11] μ_{ψ_s}, toward the recently experienced $\overline{G}_s$ and reducing the current estimate variance, $\sigma^2_{\psi_s}$, of the distribution. It is not difficult to imagine extensions of Model 6 where expectations about μ_{ψ_s} are influenced by other factors, such as visual input (Johnson et al. 1999; Glidden and Assmann 2004), voice quality[12] or even instructions about supposed gender or age of a synthetic voice.

---

[10] It is also possible for this relationship to be relaxed in Method 7 by decreasing the magnitude of the covariance components between g0 and the log formants. While we have experimented with this method, we think the indirect methods proposed here are a clearer way to implement this relaxation.

[11] Such adaptation would likely be similar in effect to the type of trial-to-trial adaptation suggested by Weenink (2003) for simulating improvement in listener performance in speaker-blocked listening conditions.

[12] Suggestions that spectral slope (and perhaps perceived breathiness) of a voice might have an indirect influence on vowel normalization are discussed in passing in Nearey (1989).

Finally, Methods 5 and 6 lead readily to predictions that are not so obviously available in Method 7. The former methods both involve an explicit estimate of ψ_s associated with every act of vowel classification by listeners. This implies that listeners always have a hypothesis about a characteristic that seems likely to be a component of perceived size (Smith *et al.* 2005). It further predicts that, under some circumstances at least, judgments of speaker size should be correlated with judgments of vowel identity. A stimulus that is identified, for example, sometimes as [ʊ] and sometimes as [ʌ] should be associated with a larger value of ψ_s (and hence a smaller apparent speaker size) for the former responses. Experiments that track vowel identification and judgments of speaker size simultaneously would be required to test this prediction.

It is important to note that the adaptations described above do not involve manipulating the basic dialect-specific vowel pattern information illustrated by the template pattern of Figure 16.1 and represented in the statistics associated with equations (6) and (7) of extrinsic log-mean normalization. This is an abstraction. However, normalization does not necessarily involve the stripping away of all indexical information. Rather, methods like 5 and 6 in effect separate out aspects of indexical information from vowel quality in the process of optimizing vowel categorization. The information so extracted could be retained for other purposes, including being coded in episodic memory (in a form distinct from lexical representation) for later use in recognition memory tasks, for example.

In our view, it is far too early to abandon the abstractionist approach in favor of a far less constrained alternative such as the exemplar-based approach of Johnson (1997b).[13] Doing so at this point would seem to rather severely obscure the intuitively appealing notion of a relatively invariant pattern associated with a dialect shared by a number of speakers. Rather, we think that proponents of both approaches should continue to refine their models and compare notes.

---

[13] See Nusbaum and Magnuson (1997: 123–4) for defense of an active normalization process against exemplar-based alternatives.

APPENDIX I. TREATMENT OF MISSING DATA IN THE H95 AND A00 DATA

For H95, a two-stage missing-data imputation scheme was used. First, a three-point running-median smoother was applied to the (maximum of) eight sections available in each of the formant tracks of the original data, ignoring missing values. Then interior gaps were filled in by linear interpolation, while gaps at the beginning and end were copied on from the first or last available estimates. If there were fewer than three non-missing points in a track, then the average of the available one or two points was filled in for the missing values. This procedure "repaired" about 0.4 percent of the data. The remaining (approximately) 0.5 percent of the data were filled in by a least squares procedure described in Hillenbrand and Nearey (1999, n. 5). The data were treated as a complete data set from that point on.

The A00 dataset followed a procedure whereby tokens were rejected unless they had complete records for F1, F2, and F3 at 20 percent and 80 percent time marks. There were, however, a variable number of tokens per subject. Furthermore, about 17 percent of the possible vowel-by-subject combinations did not have even a single accepted token in the database. A large proportion of the dropouts were from 3-year-old children whose voices proved difficult to measure. For the discriminant analyses proper, the unbalanced structure and missing data do not pose a problem, since all measurements are available for every included token. However, the unbalanced design does pose problems for the estimation of $\overline{G}_s$. The strategy adopted was to take a median over all tokens of a given vowel for a given subject. For vowel categories for which there was no acceptable token for a subject, no medians could be taken, so a least-squares data imputation strategy was again adopted. $\overline{G}_s$ was then calculated from the filled-out data.

APPENDIX II. LIST OF KEY SYMBOLS

The number of the formula nearest the first appearance of each symbol is given in ( ).

F_{kvs}	the frequency of k-th formant for vowel v of speaker s (1).
F_{kv}^*	frequency of the k-th formant for the reference pattern of vowel v (1).
ρ_s	speaker-dependent multiplicative constant (scale factor) (1).
G_{kvs}	the log of frequency of k-th formant for vowel v of speaker s (2).
G_{kvst}	an instance of G_{kvs} for take (repetition, trial, or token) t (3).
G_t	vector of log formant frequencies $[G1_t, G2_t, G3_t]$ of observed token t whose vowel identity is unknown (7).
$g0_t$	log of f0 of observed token t whose vowel identity is unknown.
G_{kv}^*	log of frequency of k-th formant for the reference pattern of vowel v (2).
ψ_s	speaker-dependent additive constant (displacement) for log frequency formants (2).
$\hat{\psi}_s = \overline{G}_s$	empirical estimate of ψ_s, average of log formant frequencies (3).
$\hat{N}_{kvs}$	normalized log frequency of formant k for vowel v of subject s (4).
$\hat{\mu}_{kv}$	estimate mean of normalized log frequency of formant k averaged over subjects (5).
$\hat{\mu}_v$	vector of means $[\hat{\mu}_{1v}, \hat{\mu}_{2v}, \hat{\mu}_{3v}]$ for all formants of vowel v (6).
$\hat{\Sigma}_{jk}$	element of covariance between formant k and formant j (or variance when $j = k$) of pooled within vowels covariance matrix estimate, $\hat{\Sigma}$ (6).
$P(G_t\|v, \hat{\psi}_s)$	probability density of observation vector G_t conditional on the assumption that it belongs to vowel v and on an estimate of $\hat{\psi}_s$ (7).
$P(v\|G_t, \hat{\psi}_s)$	a posteriori probability that a given observation vector G_t is a member of category v, when $\hat{\psi}_s$ is also given or assumed (10).
$\hat{\psi}_{vs}^{(m)}$	estimate of ψ_s for a particular vowel v using Method m in a manner defined in the text for each method (11).
$P(\psi_s)$	prior (marginal) distribution of ψ_s over all s, that is, over the population of speakers (13).
$P(\psi_s\|g0_t)$	conditional probability of ψ_s given $g0_t$ (16).
$P(\psi_s, g0_t)$	joint probability of ψ_s and $g0_t$ taking on a specific pair of values (18).
$P(g0_t\|\psi_s)$	conditional probability of $g0_t$ given ψ_s (18).

17

The Variations, Quantification, and Generalizations of Standard Thai Tones

Rungpat Roengpitya

17.1 INTRODUCTION

Standard Thai has five distinctive phonological tones: mid (M), low (L), rising–falling (RF), high (H), and falling–rising (FR) (Abramson 1962; Naksakul 1998; Roengpitya 2001; Yip 2002). The phonetic shapes of these tones in citation form were presented by Abramson (1962, 1997). To illustrate the canonical shapes of the five tones in Thai in citation form, the fundamental frequency (f0) contour of each tone is plotted in real time, in Figure 17.1. The figure shows the five tones in Thai plotted on the same graph. The f0 contours of the five tones show what is regarded as the canonical shape in CVV words in citation form. Tingsabadh and Deeprasert (1997) found, however, that the tones in connected speech had different shapes from the ones in citation form. Gandour (1977) reported that tone shape influenced the duration of the vowel that the tone was superimposed on; vowels on low tones were longer than those on high tones. Saravari and Imai (1983) found that relative initial tone values as well as tonal contours were important for the perceptual differentiation of the tones. They also reported that short and long vowel duration seemed to be not only a cue for differentiating distinctive vowel length but also for identifying the tones.

The focus of this chapter is to determine how the five Thai tones are modified when they appear on tone-bearing units (henceforth TBUs) of different duration (Gussenhoven 2004: 29), not only due to the style of speech or whether we are dealing with citation or connected speech (as noted by Tingsabadh and Deeprasert 1997), but also due to other factors such as vowel length (phonological short vs. long vowels), intrinsic vowel duration (low vowels are longer than high vowels), syllable structure (syllables with final sonorants are longer than ones with final stops; Zhang

The author is grateful to John J. Ohala for guidance, advice, and comments, to reviewers for their comments, to Paul Boersma and David Weenink for the Praat Program, to Ronald Sprouse for the scripts, and to the Phonology Laboratory (University of California at Berkeley). The author also acknowledges and appreciates the support of Dr. Kanita Roengpitya (a former student of John Ohala at UCB), and comments from Ajarn Michael Crabtree (Chulalongkorn University). All errors are my own.

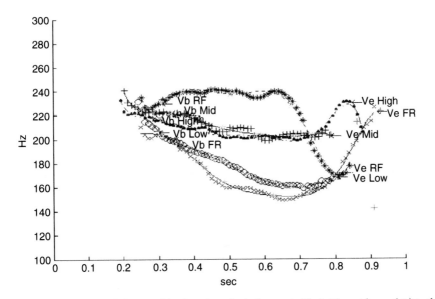

FIGURE 17.1. The canonical shapes of the five phonological tones in Thai: (1) a mid tone (+) in the word /naa/ "field", (2) a low tone (o) in the syllable /nàa/ in the disyllabic word /nɔ́ɔj-nàa/ "custard apples", (3) a rising–falling tone (*) in the word /nâa/ "a face", (4) a high tone (.) in the word /náa/ "an aunt", and (5) a falling–rising tone (x) in the word /nǎa/ "thick". "Vb" indicates the vowel or tone onset, "Ve" shows the end of the vowel or tone offset.

2004: 172), and stress (stressed syllables are longer than unstressed ones: Botinis *et al.* 2002; Gussenhoven 2004: 20). Determining the tonal differences controlled by these factors would pave the way for generalizations about Thai tones.

A direct inspiration for this study came from the work of Alstermark and Erikson on Swedish pitch accent and word length (Alstermark and Erikson 1971; Erikson and Alstermark 1972). These authors found that the realization of acute and grave accents in Swedish depends on word length; there were two ways in which the shorter f0 contours were modified in comparison to the canonical f0 contours. The first process was truncation, where the f0 curves of the canonical and the shortened contours have an identical initial portion, but the end portion of the shortened contour was cut off. This pattern was subsequently also found by Bannert and Bredvad-Jensen (1977) for Gotland Swedish, and by Claßen (2002) for the Swabian dialect of German and the speech of patients afflicted with Parkinson's dysarthria. The second process was f0 rate adjustment, where the f0 curves of the canonical and the shortened contours have the same f0 range (i.e. the same initial and final values), but the f0 curve of the shortened contour has an increased rate of change. These two processes: truncation and rate adjustment, have been found asymmetrically in cross-linguistic studies. Grabe (1998: 138–9) reported that, in the environment of shorter segmental duration with less scope for voicing, both shortened rising and falling accents in English were compressed. On the other hand, in German, shortened falling accents were truncated, but rising accents were compressed. Grabe (1998: 142) added that, within the same language, the behavior of accents may differ across dialects. Later, Grabe *et al.* (2000), on the basis of the results of their experiments, confirmed this claim by showing that four varieties of British English had different f0 realization of the same intonational specification; for example, Southern British English speakers compress H*+L0%, whereas Leeds–English speakers truncate H*+L0% (Grabe *et al.* 2000: 174).

Since Thai tones can occur on longer or shorter TBUs, processes which would alter their canonical shapes may occur in ways similar to the word accents in Swedish. I report my findings on this below. I describe the experimental procedure and analysis criteria used in the study of Thai tones in Section 17.2. In Section 17.3, I examine the factors that induce durational differences in TBUs and how tonal contours adjust to such durational variations. I also introduce some new methods for quantifying the change of tonal shape in Section 17.4, and present generalizations of the behavior of Thai tones in Section 17.5.

17.2 ACOUSTIC ANALYSIS OF THAI TONES

17.2.1 Aim

The aim of this acoustic analysis is to investigate how Thai tones vary when they sit on TBUs of different durations and to find the processes involved in these tonal variations.

17.2.2 Speakers

The speakers were three female native speakers of Standard Thai (RR, JJ, and PS), with the age ranging from 25 to 29 years at the time of recording. They all grew up in Bangkok and did not have any speech or hearing deficiency.

It should be noted here that RR is the author of this chapter. She is a native Thai speaker, who grew up in Bangkok. At the start of the data gathering, she had no preconceptions about the subject of this study and, furthermore, her speech proved similar to that of the others, who were chemists.

17.2.3 Tokens

The test words analyzed for this study were 240 meaningful (45%) and nonsense (55%) Standard Thai words. Each word had a C1V(:)C2T structure, with C1 a nasal /m/, /n/, or /ŋ/; V was a high or low vowel /i/ or /a/ and which could be short or long; C2 was a final nasal /m/, /n/, or /ŋ/ (symbolized "N" below in formulas for word or syllable structure), or a final stop /t/ or /k/ ("O" standing for "obstruent" in formulas); T (the superimposed tone) was mid, low, rising–falling, high, or falling–rising.

Appendix 1 lists all test words, which appeared in six different contexts: (1) in isolation (this was taken as the citation form) (WA for "word alone"); (2) in a sentence (in connected speech) (WS for "word in a sentence"); (3) in an unstressed position in a disyllabic compound spoken in isolation (UA for "unstressed position in a lexeme spoken in isolation"); (4) in an unstressed position in a disyllabic compound in a sentence (US for "unstressed position within a sentence"); (5) in a stressed position in a disyllabic compound (SA for "stressed position in a lexeme spoken in isolation"); and (6) in a stressed position in a disyllabic compound in a sentence (SS for "stressed position in a lexeme spoken in a sentence"). Taken together, these various contexts manifested the main factors giving rise to shorter or longer TBUs: distinctive vowel length, intrinsic vowel duration, stressed vs. unstressed contexts, syllable structure (with a final nasal or a final stop), and citation form vs. connected speech.

17.2.4 Tasks

In Thailand, every student in Grade 1 in primary school is trained to be able to pronounce every combination of both meaningful and nonsense syllables of all five Thai tones, though some nonsense syllables cannot be written in Thai characters, such as the CVO structure with a mid tone. Each student is taught to read a CV(:)(C) syllable in Thai without any tone marker (either mid or low tone), and later s/he learns to pronounce and perceive, natively and naturally, all five tones of each syllable: mid, low, rising–falling, high, and falling–rising. Because of the advantage of this native knowledge of Thai tone pronunciation and perception, the present study was able to cover all possible natively pronounceable combinations of syllables in all five tones.

In this study, first, all speakers were tested for their primary-school knowledge of native pronunciation of all tones in every combination. Then, the CV(:)C test words were introduced to them in Thai script with the tone labels (along with the tone markers, if any). All three speakers (RR, JJ, and PS) read all the test words once with the short and long high vowels /i/ and /ii/, but only Speaker RR read the test words once with the short and long low vowels /a/ and /aa/. All tokens were digitally recorded using the Praat sound-analysis program at a sample rate of 16 kHz. There were a total of 480 tokens in this study ([120 tokens × 3 speakers] +[120 tokens × 1 speaker]).

17.2.5 Processing

Using Praat, each token was marked for the vowel onset (where the formants start) and the vowel offset (where the formants end). Then, each token was measured for its rhyme duration (vowel duration plus, if present, the nasal duration), which constituted the TBU. In this study, each tone's onset was taken to be at the rhyme onset (the vowel onset), and ended at the rhyme offset, that is, at the vowel offset (for CVO or CV:O tokens), or at the final nasal offset (for CVN or CV:N tokens). This is because in connected speech the onset of a targeted token (in this corpus, the syllable-initial nasal) may receive an end portion of the previous tone due to carryover tonal coarticulation (Gandour *et al.* 1994). The reason that all tokens in this study had only nasals as initial consonants was to avoid the effect of pitch perturbation from initial stops, which has been associated with tonogenesis (Matisoff 1973; J. Ohala 1973; Hombert *et al.* 1979; Tumtavitikul 1994). Figure 17.2 presents an example of the landmarks used for the measurement of the rhyme duration of the token /nin/ as in /li-nin/ "linen".

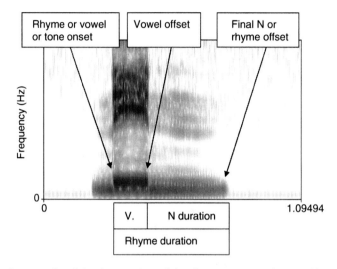

FIGURE 17.2. An example of the demarcation of the rhyme onset (at the vowel/tone onset), the vowel offset, and the rhyme offset of the syllable /nin/ "nonsense" with a mid tone in isolation (WA context), pronounced by PS.

All tokens were measured for their duration, and had their fundamental frequency (f0) extracted as a numerical file using the Praat speech analysis software (http://www.fon.hum.uva.nl/praat/). These numerical files were ported to Matlab (http://www.mathworks.com/) and a seventh-order polynomial was fit to them. The seventh-order polynomial was chosen instead of other orders, because, by trial and error, it seemed to be the order needed for the most complex f0 curves. Such a polynomial was used on all the data for the sake of consistency. The purpose of this quantification of the f0 curves was to permit a more exact characterization of how they changed under different conditions. In the rest of this chapter, reference to a given tone or tonal shape refers to such a fitted polynomial curve. An example of mid-tone f0 curves plotted in Matlab is shown in Figure 17.3.

Two tonal contours are superimposed in Figure 17.3, one from a shorter TBU in "+" (due to a short vowel) and one from a longer TBU in "o" (due to a long vowel) of the same speaker (PS). As these two tokens are in the CV(:)O structure, the contours are aligned at the tone onset, which is taken as the beginning of the vowel (Vb). The tone or rhyme offset is at the vowel offset (Ve). The figure does not show time normalization was used; the tones were plotted in real time.

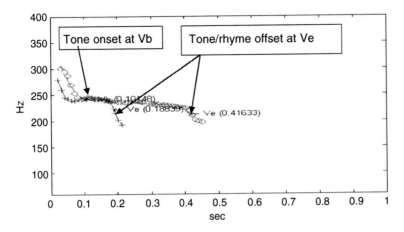

FIGURE 17.3. An example of the f0 contours for a mid tone on a shorter TBU in the word /nit/ "nonsense" (+), and on a longer TBU /niit/ "nonsense" (o) in WA context, pronounced by PS. The symbols "+" and "o" represent the original raw f0 values, and the lines connecting the f0 values together are the seventh-order polynomial lines.

17.3 RESULTS

This section presents the results of this acoustic study (including statistical tests) and examines how the shape of the tones varies with durational variations in the TBUs induced by a variety of factors.

17.3.1 The different TBU durations

As mentioned above, the duration of a TBU can vary due to vowel length, intrinsic vowel duration, syllable structure (final nasals or stops), stress, and context (citation form or connected speech). I first present the results indicating how the TBU durations vary as a function of these factors. T-tests were used to assess the differences.

(i) Vowel length. The phonologically long vowels were on average 1.54 times longer than short vowels.

(ii) Intrinsic vowel duration. Low vowels were longer than high vowels, and this effect was greater in long vowels than in short vowels. The short low vowel /a/ was on average 14 ms longer than the short high vowel /i/ ($p < 0.05$), and the long low vowel /aa/ was about 26 ms longer than the long high vowel /ii/ ($p < 0.05$).

(iii) Syllable structure. Both short and long vowels with final nasals had the same mean duration values (102 ms, and 184 ms, respectively) as the vowels with final stops (104 ms, and 188 ms, respectively). However, as the total rhyme duration of syllables with final sonorants included both vowel and sonorant durations, the average short-vowel rhyme duration with a final nasal (240 ms) was 2.3 times longer than the one with a final stop (104 ms), whereas the average long-vowel rhyme duration with a final nasal (282 ms) was 1.5 times longer than the one with a final stop (188 ms). It can be seen that the effect of different syllable structures on shorter and longer rhyme duration, in this case, was greater for short-vowel rhymes.

(iv) Stressed position. The average short-vowel rhyme duration in the stressed syllable (188 ms) was 1.45 times longer than the one in the unstressed syllable (130 ms), and the average long-vowel rhyme duration in the stressed syllable (257 ms) was 1.51 times longer than the one in the unstressed syllable (170 ms).

(v) Context. The short-vowel rhyme duration in citation form (217 ms) was 1.69 times longer than the one in connected speech (128 ms), and the long-vowel rhyme duration in citation form (306 ms) was 1.86 times longer than the one in connected speech (164 ms).

Figures 17.4a–b summarize the results of different rhyme duration due to the main factors mentioned above and show the TBU duration or rhyme duration in six different contexts: WA (an isolated word), WS (a word in a sentence), UA (an unstressed syllable in a disyllabic compound in isolation), US (an unstressed syllable in a disyllabic compound in a sentence), SA (a stressed syllable in a disyllabic compound in isolation), and SS (a stressed syllable in a disyllabic compound in a sentence), and in two syllable structures (with a final sonorant /N/ or with a final stop /O/).

To illustrate the details of rhyme duration, Tables 17.1–4 below present the mean, n, and SD values of the rhyme duration of tokens, pronounced by the three speakers (RR, JJ, and PS).

In brief, the results show that the TBU or rhyme duration was longer in long vowel rhymes as opposed to short vowel rhymes ($p < 0.05$), in syllables with final sonorants as opposed to final stops ($p < 0.05$), in stressed vs. unstressed syllables ($p < 0.05$), and in citation form vis-à-vis connected speech ($p < 0.05$). Of these factors, the ones which play the most important role are distinctive vowel length and syllable type: final nasal vs. final stop. The results set out in Tables 17.1–4 reveal that different speakers showed similar differences across conditions.

17.3.2 The processes affecting Thai tones

In Swedish, the shapes of the pitch accents were affected by word length, exhibiting two main effects: end truncation, and rate adjustment. For this study of the five Thai tones, I examined the variation in tonal shape due to the factors that have been shown to affect the duration of the TBU. After short and long tones were plotted in the same figure and aligned at the rhyme onset, two processes, truncation and rate adjustment, were found, along with some additional processes: f0 range adjustment, a (so-called)

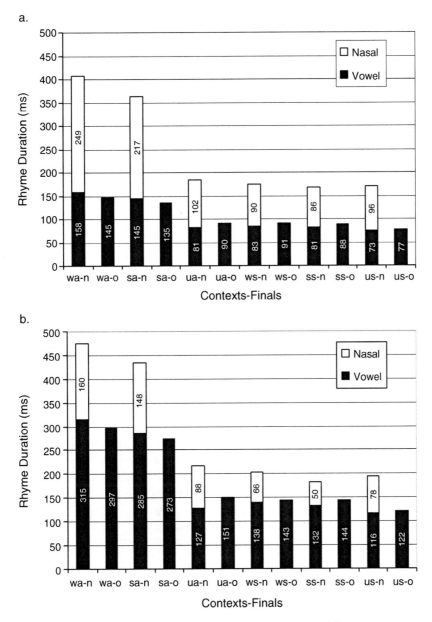

FIGURE 17.4a–b. Average rhyme duration for short and long vowels in six different contexts (wa, ws, ua, us, sa, and ss), and two types of finals (n or o), produced by speakers RR, JJ, and PS.

plateau, and phase realignment (see below). In Figures 17.5–17.9, the symbol "+" represents a shorter tone, and the symbol "o", a longer tone. The frequency distribution of each pattern is reported in Section 17.5.

TABLE 17.1. Mean, n, and SD values of the rhyme duration in Ci(:)N, uttered by RR, JJ, and PS

Context	Speakers	Short-vowel tokens			Long-vowel tokens		
		Mean	n	SD	Mean	n	SD
WA	RR	426.6	5	53	507.0	5	34.08
	JJ	407.0	5	49	408.0	5	40.40
	PS	385.4	5	61	466.8	5	58.84
WS	RR	162.4	5	42	195.4	5	72.10
	JJ	185.2	5	28	222.2	5	29.91
	PS	179.8	5	23	209.4	5	55.36
UA	RR	136.0	5	30	160.0	5	23.25
	JJ	206.2	5	19	257.2	5	34.28
	PS	231.0	5	21	275.6	5	46.00
US	RR	135.0	5	18	151.0	5	9.925
	JJ	183.0	5	30	229.0	5	42.03
	PS	216.6	5	44	242.6	5	27.93
SA	RR	385.6	5	39	439.6	5	28.13
	JJ	340.6	5	77	389.6	5	14.54
	PS	342.6	5	61	424.6	5	55.48
SS	RR	136.6	5	18	162.6	5	19.67
	JJ	194.0	5	12	202.4	5	10.64
	PS	193.4	5	32	204.4	5	50.49

17.3.2.1 Tonal truncation

In this case, tones on short-vowel TBUs have their end portions truncated, when compared to tones on long-vowel TBUs. Examples of tonal end truncation of short tones appear in Figures 17.5a–b. Figure 17.5a illustrates the low tone on a short TBU of the syllable /ŋìt/ "irritated" (+) and the same tone on a long TBU of the syllable /ŋìit/ "nonsense" (o) in word-alone (WA) context, pronounced by JJ. Figure 17.5b presents the low tone on a short TBU of the stressed syllable /ŋìt/ (+) in the compound /ŋùt-ŋìt/ "irritated", and on a long TBU of the stressed syllable /ŋìit/ (o) of the compound /ŋùt-ŋìit/ "nonsense" in stressed-word (SA) context, pronounced by RR.

TABLE 17.2. Mean, n, and SD values of the rhyme duration in Ca(:)N, uttered by RR

Context	Speakers	Short-vowel tokens			Long-vowel tokens		
		Mean	n	SD	Mean	n	SD
WA	RR	410.6	5	27	517.8	5	11.34
WS	RR	170.4	5	32	188.2	5	23.86
UA	RR	161.0	5	13	172.0	5	18.03
US	RR	146.4	5	29	152.4	5	15.71
SA	RR	383.2	5	53	479.2	5	37.37
SS	RR	147.4	5	12	160.0	5	24.09

TABLE 17.3. Mean, n, and SD values of the rhyme duration in Ci(:)O, uttered by RR, JJ, and PS

Context	Speakers	Short-vowel tokens			Long-vowel tokens		
		Mean	n	SD	Mean	n	SD
WA	RR	168.0	5	32.0	287.4	5	30.71
	JJ	142.6	5	40.0	294.2	5	14.06
	PS	100.8	5	13.0	290.0	5	33.55
WS	RR	97.0	5	14.0	122.4	5	19.62
	JJ	86.0	5	16.0	138.6	5	18.24
	PS	77.2	5	10.0	156.4	5	32.91
UA	RR	85.4	5	35.0	119.8	5	28.11
	JJ	102.0	5	22.0	186.2	5	11.69
	PS	76.4	5	15.0	163.8	5	15.27
US	RR	78.2	5	9.7	101.8	5	25.02
	JJ	83.0	5	11.0	142.0	5	14.46
	PS	69.8	5	8.5	137.4	5	14.22
SA	RR	129.2	5	17.0	249.0	5	31.23
	JJ	137.8	5	12.0	257.4	5	16.98
	PS	117.8	5	11.0	292.8	5	25.94
SS	RR	84.0	5	9.4	120.2	5	19.61
	JJ	83.2	5	17.0	144.4	5	13.18
	PS	77.6	5	8.8	157.8	5	24.02

17.3.2.2 Increased rate of change of f0 or f0 rate adjustment

In this case, the rate of change of f0 normally increases when a tone becomes shorter but the f0 range between the f0 maxima and the f0 minima remains approximately the same. Examples of the increased rate of change of short tones when compared to long tones are shown in Figures 17.6a–b. Figure 17.6a illustrates a low tone on a short TBU of the word /ŋìt/ "irritated" (+) and the same tone on a long TBU of the word

TABLE 17.4. Mean, n, and SD values of the rhyme duration in Ca(:)O, uttered by RR

Context	Speakers	Short-vowel tokens			Long-vowel tokens		
		Mean	n	SD	Mean	n	SD
WA	RR	172.4	5	18.0	316.6	5	15.60
WS	RR	106.4	5	6.5	154.2	5	6.38
UA	RR	95.4	5	15.0	135.8	5	20.40
US	RR	77.8	5	22.0	106.8	5	18.70
SA	RR	158.6	5	11.0	293.8	5	23.34
SS	RR	109.6	5	18.0	167.8	5	7.34

/ŋìit/ "nonsense" (o) in word-alone (WA) context, pronounced by RR. Figure 17.6b presents the same tones, words, and context for Speaker PS.

17.3.2.3 f0 range adjustment

In this case, when a tone gets shorter and is compared to a long tone, the f0 range (from the f0 minima to the f0 maxima) is adjusted (compressed or expanded). f0 range adjustment is found mostly for the two contour tones in Thai: rising–falling and falling–rising. Short tones of both RF and FR contours in Thai, when compared to the long counterparts, were found to be adjusted (compressed or expanded). Examples of a compressed f0 range and of an expanded f0 range of short tones are provided in Figures 17.7a–b, respectively. The vertical dashed line indicates the f0 range of a short tone and the solid line the f0 range of a long one.

Figure 17.7a illustrates the compressed range of a falling–rising tone on a short TBU of the syllable /nǐŋ/ in the compound /nǔŋ-nǐŋ/ "a name" (+), vis-à-vis the same FR tone on a long TBU of the syllable /nǐiŋ/ in the compound /nǔŋ-nǐiŋ/ "nonsense" (o) in a stressed-position (SA) context, pronounced by JJ. Figure 17.7b

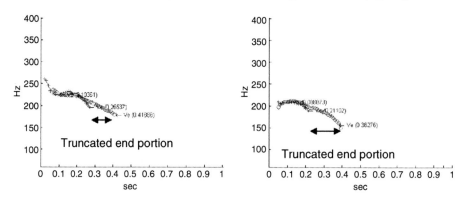

FIGURE 17.5a–b. Examples of end truncation of a low tone in the Thai syllables /ŋìt/ "irritated" (+) (a), and /ŋìit/ "nonsense" (o) (b) (see text).

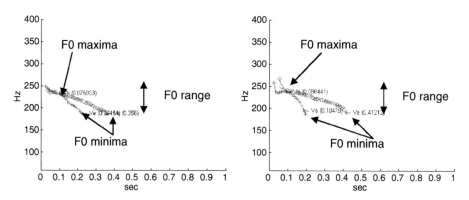

FIGURE 17.6a–b. Examples of f0 rate adjustment (increased rate of change) of a low tone in the Thai syllables /ŋìt/ "irritated" (+) (a), and /ŋìit/ "nonsense" (o) (b) (see text).

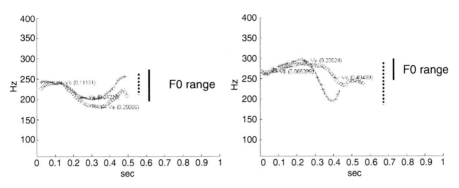

FIGURE 17.7a–b. An example of the compressed f0 range of a falling–rising tone in the syllable /nĭŋ/ "a name" (+) versus /nĭiŋ/ "nonsense" (o) (a); and an example of the expanded f0 range of a rising–falling tone in the syllable /mân/ "strong" versus /mâan/ "blind" (b). The vertical dashed line indicates the f0 range of a shorter tone, and the solid line the f0 range of a longer tone (see text).

presents the expanded f0 range of a rising–falling tone on a short TBU of the word /mân/ "strong" (+) vis-à-vis the same tone on a long TBU of the word /mâan/ "a blind" (o) in a word-alone (WA) context, pronounced by RR.

Further information on the quantitative study of f0 range and the rate of change is provided in Appendix 2, which gives numerical data on the interaction of f0 range (Hz) and the rate of change of f0 or the f0 slope (Hz/sec) of Speaker RR in all contexts. From this information, it can be concluded that short tones have a narrower f0 range, but a more negative f0-slope average.

17.3.2.4 Plateau

In the case of the two contour tones: rising–falling and falling–rising, what may be described as a "plateau"—a relatively flat portion—appears in between the more steeply sloped initial and terminal portions of the tone. This is found only for contour tones on long TBUs such as are found in a word-alone context (WA) or in a stressed-position (SA) context. Examples of short and long plateaus appear in Figures 17.8a–b. Figure 17.8a illustrates the rising–falling tone on a short TBU of the word /nîŋ/ "still" (+, plateau duration in a dashed arrow) and the same tone on a long TBU of the word /nîiŋ/ "nonsense" (o, plateau duration in a solid arrow) in a word-alone (WA) context, pronounced by RR. Figure 17.8b presents the falling–rising tone on a short TBU of the syllable /nĭŋ/ in the compound /nŭŋ-nĭŋ/ "a name" (+, plateau duration in a dashed arrow) and the same tone on a long TBU of the syllable /nĭiŋ/ in the compound /nŭŋ-nĭiŋ/ "nonsense" (o, plateau duration in a solid arrow) in a stressed-position (SA) context, pronounced by PS.

17.3.2.5 Phase realignment

This process occurs only in a rhyme with a final sonorant. Abramson (1962) and Roengpitya (2001) claim that when a vowel in a rhyme is short, the following nasal is longer, and vice versa. Since it is believed that a tone is superimposed on a rhyme, the

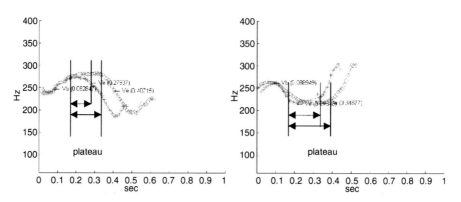

FIGURE 17.8a–b. An example of shorter and longer plateaus of a rising–falling tone (a) and a falling–rising tone (b) (see text).

tone can sit on a short vowel plus a longer nasal or, conversely, on a long vowel followed by a shorter nasal. Thus, this process is called "phase realignment", as shown in the examples in Figures 17.9a–b. Figure 17.9a illustrates the rising–falling tone on a short TBU of the syllable /nîŋ/ "still" in the compound /náam-nîŋ/ "still water" (+) and the same tone on a long TBU of the syllable /nîiŋ/ "nonsense" in the compound /náam-nîiŋ/ "nonsense"(o) in a stressed-position (SA) context, pronounced by PS. Figure 17.9b presents the falling–rising tone on a short TBU of the word /nǐŋ/ "a name" (+) and the same tone on a long TBU of the syllable /nǐiŋ/ "nonsense" (o) in a word-alone (WA) context, pronounced by JJ. In this figure, the relative duration of the vowel and nasal is indicated by boxes, and the values of their duration are given on the right-hand side. In each figure, tones are superimposed on a short vowel followed by a long nasal vis-à-vis on a long vowel followed by a short nasal.

In sum, there are five tonal processes which influence the shape of the five Thai tones on the different TBU durations: truncation, f0 rate adjustment, f0 range adjustment, plateau, and phase realignment.

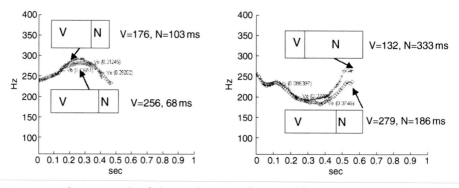

FIGURE 17.9a–b. An example of phase realignment of a rising–falling tone (a) and a falling–rising tone (b) (see text).

17.4 QUANTIFICATION, DERIVATIVES, AND LANDMARKS

The processes affecting Thai tones found in the previous section suggest that end truncation and phase realignment should be examined in more detail to determine which portion of the contours is most prominent and thus preserved, while the less important portions get truncated, and to see whether the two contour tones (rising–falling and falling–rising) would be treated in a similar way.

17.4.1 Methodology

A new method of quantifying the contour tones in Thai was applied to define the landmarks in these two contour tones (see J. Ohala and Roengpitya 2002). These contour tones involve steep f0 slopes towards their beginning and end and a point where there is an inflection (a local maximum or local minimum). The first and second derivatives of the tone slopes were calculated (derived from the seventh-order polynomial fitted to the extracted tonal f0 traces) and used to mark the following three landmarks for each contour.

1. The first landmark was located at the point of the negative rising–falling (RF1) or positive falling–rising (FR1) zero-crossing of the second derivative of f0 (d2). This defines and marks the onset of the deceleration of the f0 contour, preceding the beginning of the plateau of these contour tones.
2. The second landmark was located at the point of the negative rising–falling (RF2) or positive falling–rising (FR2) zero-crossing of the first derivative of f0 (d1). Usually, this defines and marks the location inside a plateau before the plateau offset.
3. The third landmark was located at the point of the positive rising–falling (RF3) or negative falling–rising (FR3) ongoing zero-crossing of the second derivative of f0 (d2). This defines and marks the steepest slope on the second portion of a contour, after the plateau offset.

Figure 17.10 shows these three landmarks for an FR contour: FR1, FR2, and FR3. The top panel shows the raw f0 values of a falling-rising tone in the word /nǐiŋ/ "nonsense" in SA context, uttered by PS, with the seventh-order polynomial fit to connect those f0 values. The d1 and d2 values of this particular token were plotted in the bottom panel, where a zero line is given so as to locate where the d1 or d2 crossings were. The three arrows connecting the two panels indicate the three landmarks both at the d1/ d2 zero crossings and on the raw FR. It can be seen that FR1 is located at the falling portion of an FR tone, FR2 within the plateau, and FR3 at the rising portion of the contour.

After all landmarks were located, the durations between the tone onset, the three landmarks and the tone offset of each contour were measured. The details of

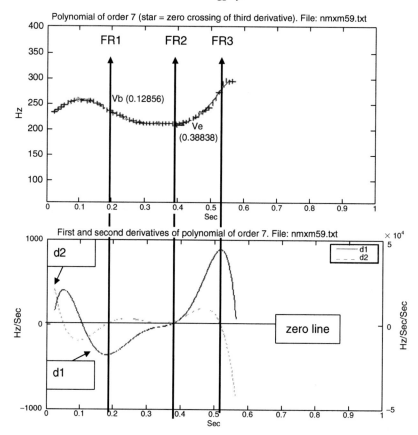

FIGURE 17.10. An example of the demarcation of the three landmarks (FR1, FR2, and FR3) of a falling–rising tone of the word /nîiŋ/ "nonsense" in SA context, uttered by PS (see text for details).

the quantification of the tonal truncation and the phase realignment are described in the following sections.

17.4.2 Quantification of the tonal truncation of Thai contours

The quantification of the tonal truncation for the two contour tones in Thai—rising–falling and falling–rising—was investigated in addition to the acoustic analysis in Section 17.2. Only twelve meaningful and nonsense words in Thai, as listed in Appendix 3, were chosen for this study. Each word had a C1V(:)C2T structure, with C1 a nasal /m/, /n/, or /ŋ/; V(:) a short or long vowel /a/ or /aa/, C2 a voiceless unreleased stop /p/; and T a rising–falling or a falling–rising tone. All words were read in isolation and in the frame sentence /phûut kham _____ naan naan/ "Say the word _____ for a long time" ten times by Speaker RR, and were digitally recorded in the Praat program with a sample rate of 16 kHz. There were a total of 240 tokens (12 words × 10 times × 2 contexts × 1 speaker). The f0 of all tokens was extracted in Praat and transferred to Matlab, a mathematics program. In Matlab, the three landmarks of each contour were located and the durations between landmarks were measured. The results are presented in Figures 17.11a and 17.11b. The figures show four intervals: (1) between the tone onset to the first landmark; (2) between the first and second landmarks; (3) between the second and third landmarks; and (4) between the third landmark and the tone offset, in real-time scale (see also Roengpitya 2003: 1111). Each Figure presents the results for tones with short or long vowels, in citation form (word alone), or in connected speech (in a sentence).

The figure shows that short contour tones (on short vowels or in connected speech) had the end portion truncated when compared to long tones, especially the canonical tones, that is, tones on long vowels in isolation. Furthermore, the falling–rising tone was longer than the rising–falling one (by 9% in isolation and 3–8% in connected speech). However, the RF tone had a longer first tone interval (between the tone onset and the first landmark) than did the FR tone. The results reveal further that, unlike the short RF tone, a short FR tone still preserved its third landmark at the rising portion to make a contrast with the low tone, which shared the same f0 slope and f0 range of the falling portion. It can be summarized that the two contours had different prominent tonal portions.

17.4.3 Quantification of the phase realignment of Thai contours

The quantification of the phase realignment of the two Thai contour tones was computed with another data set (also in J. Ohala and Roengpitya 2002). In this quantification, 24 native Thai meaningful and nonsense words were chosen, as listed in Appendix 4. Each word had a C1V(:)C2T structure, with C1 a nasal /n/, V(:) a short or a long vowel /i/, /ii/, /a/, or /aa/, C2 a nasal /m/, /n/, and /ŋ/, and T a rising–falling or a falling–rising tone. All the words were read in isolation nine times by Speaker RR and were digitally recorded in the Praat program. There were a total of 216 tokens (24 words × 9 times ×1 context × 1 speaker). Processing in the Praat and Matlab programs was conducted in the same way as reported in Section 17.4.2, but, in addition, the duration of vowels and final nasals was measured. The results are presented in Figures 17.12a–d. The figures show the four intervals defined by the three landmarks plotted in the same way as in Figures 17.11a–b, but with a normalized time scale. There is a vertical dotted line in each figure to mark the vowel offset and the nasal onset (the VN juncture).

Figures 17.12a–d also show that tones superimposed on short and long vowels indeed maintained similar phases, even though they had different absolute durations. There were some between-vowel variations in the phase that need to be looked at in

further detail. These temporal "maps" of the duration between the tone onset and
landmarks of each contour tone reveal that the landmark locations of tone tokens
containing both short vowels (with longer final nasals) and long vowels (with shorter
final nasals) were located at similar points (in the same range). This result can be
interpreted as showing that tones on short and long vowels still maintain the same
relative phase relations, although the boundary between the vowel offset and the final
nasal onset may shift depending on whether the vowels and final nasals are short or
long. Furthermore, although the landmarks were chosen for their computability, the
results suggest that they may have some relevance in defining crucial target events in
the execution of these contour tones.

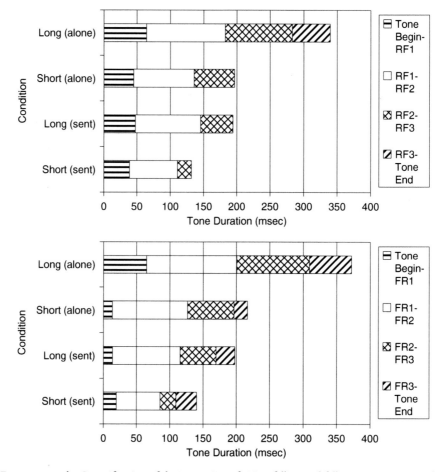

FIGURE 17.11a–b. Quantification of the truncation of rising–falling and falling–rising tones in Thai
(see also in Roengpitya 2003).

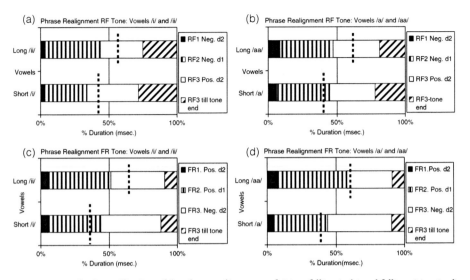

FIGURE 17.12a–d. Quantification of the phase realignment of rising–falling (a, b) and falling-rising (c, d) tones in Thai with long and short high (a, c) and low (b, d) vowels (see also J. Ohala and Roengpitya 2002). The vertical dotted line, as seen in each bar, represents a VN juncture, or the vowel offset and the nasal onset.

17.5 GENERALIZATIONS OF THE BEHAVIOR AND PROCESSES OF THE FIVE THAI TONES

The aim of this chapter was to study the interaction of different durations of tone-bearing units and the effects of short and long TBUs on the shapes of the five Thai tones. The results reveal five basic processes or transformations of the tones; end truncation; f0 rate adjustment; f0 range adjustment; plateau; and phase realignment. From these results it is possible to make several generalizations for these five tones in Thai when they appear on short and long TBUs. The main questions addressed here are whether the five Thai tones behave the same way when the TBU varies in duration, and, if not, which processes favor some tones as opposed to others and, furthermore, the role played by certain factors such as syllable structure (rhymes with final nasals versus rhymes with final stops). To find the answers, each pair of short and long tones was plotted, and the processes which occur in each pair were identified, counted, and computed. The results are shown in Figures 17.13a–b, and described in Sections 17.5.1–4.

17.5.1 Syllable Structures

Figures 17.13a–b show the distribution of the f0 processes by tone type for syllables with final nasals and final obstruents, respectively. The key process that distinguishes the two syllable structures is phase realignment (process 5), which occurs only with

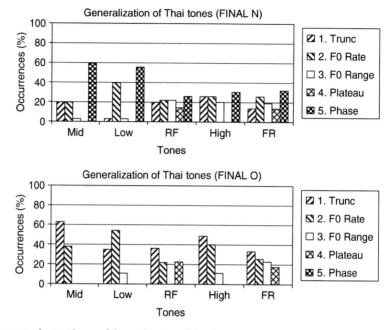

FIGURE 17.13a–b. Incidence of the application of the five processes on the five tones in Thai on two rhyme structures (Fig. 17.13a: final N and Fig. 17.13b: final O).

the tones with final sonorants. Phase realignment was found in as many as 30–60 percent 60 percent of cases of all tones with a final nasal (Fig. 17.13a), while none appeared in the tones involving a final stop (Fig. 17.13b). Besides the absence of the phase realignment process, other processes which can differentiate the two syllable structures (final N versus final O) are end truncation, rate adjustment, and plateau. These three processes show the increased incidence by between 17 and 43 percent in the truncation process, by 10 percent in the rate adjustment process, and by between 5 and 8 percent of longer plateaus, when syllables end with final stops.

17.5.2 Level and contour tones

Of the five tones in Thai, mid and low tones are level tones; rising–falling and falling–rising are contour tones, and the high tone can be interpreted in two ways, namely, as a level or a contour tone. In this section, high tone is classified as a level tone. The main feature that can differentiate level and contour tones is the applicability of the plateau process, which occurs with contours only, as seen in Figures 17.13a–b.

17.5.3 The behavior of each tone

We are now in a position to relate the observed processes to the five tones.

- Mid and low tones: with final nasals and final stops, the truncation process occurs in mid-tone cases more than in low-tone cases, while f0 rate adjustment occurs in low-tone cases more frequently than in mid-tone cases.

- High tone: as with the other level tones, the processes that occur frequently in high-tones are end truncation and f0 rate adjustment. However, high tone with a final nasal shows a high incidence of the occurrence of f0 range adjustment, just as the contours do.
- Rising–falling and falling–rising tones: all five processes can occur with both contours with final nasals, but they lack only the phase realignment process when appearing with final stops. Furthermore, it can be noted that all the processes occur with higher incidence for the RF tone than the FR tone, with final nasals and final stops.

17.5.4 All processes

Generalizing about the incidence of all the five processes, the following can be noted.

- Process 1: tonal truncation. End truncation occurs for all five Thai tones, but this process is found more often in tones with final stops than with final nasals.
- Process 2: increased rate of change of f0 or f0 rate adjustment. This process occurs for all five tones with final nasals and final stops. As noted earlier, a low tone in Thai shows more rate adjustment than end truncation.
- Process 3: f0 range adjustment. This process occurs primarily with contours, and with high tone.
- Process 4: plateau. This process occurs only with contours and with final nasals more than with final stops.
- Process 5: phase realignment. This process occurs with all tones but only with final nasals.

Thus, it can be concluded that the five processes do not occur equally with every tone, but, instead, form a specific pattern for each tone with a particular syllable structure (with final nasal or with final stop). This reflects that each tone has its own tonal behavior. The tonal pattern given in Section 17.5 helps us to differentiate one phonological tone from another.

17.6 CONCLUSION

It can be concluded that the generalizations given in this chapter of the five Thai tones are based on the five different tonal processes when tones appear on short and long TBUs due to vowel length, intrinsic vowel duration, syllable structure, stress position, and citation form versus connected speech. The five tonal processes, discovered by experimental techniques, are truncation (as in Swedish pitch accent), f0 rate adjustment (also as in Swedish pitch accent), f0 range adjustment, plateau, and phase realignment. These five processes reveal the different behavior of each tone, and help to differentiate one phonological tone from another. It is hoped that the results of this research help to shed light on other aspects of the phonological behavior of Thai tones, and on other phonetic and phonological topics in other dialects of Thai or other languages.

APPENDIX 1. TEST WORDS FOR THE ACOUSTIC ANALYSIS OF THAI TONES

In the tables in this appendix and the following appendices, WA stands for "word alone", WS for "a word in a sentence", UA for "a syllable in an unstressed position in a lexeme spoken alone", US for "a syllable in an unstressed position within a sentence", SA for "a syllable in a stressed position in a lexeme spoken alone", and SS for "a syllable in a stressed position in a lexeme spoken in a sentence". The frame sentence was /phûut kham_____nùŋ khráŋ/ "Say the word_____once". It is noted here that some compounds were invented so that all combinations could be covered. They were all tested to ensure that they were naturally and natively pronounceable.

TABLE 17.5. Test words with the Ci(:)N structure in six different contexts

Word/context	WA	WS	UA	US	SA	SS
Mid T.-Short V.	1. /nin/ "nonsense"	2. /nín/ "nonsense"	3. /nin-caa/ "a hero"	4. /nin-caa/ "a hero"	5. /li-niin/ "linen"	6. /li-niin/ "linen"
-Long V.	7. /niin/ "nonsense"	8. /niin/ "nonsense"	9. /niin-caa/ "nonsense"	10. /niin-caa/ "nonsense"	11. /li-niin/ "nonsense"	12. /li-niin/ "nonsense"
Low T.-Short V.	13. /mìn/ "to insult"	14. /mìn/ "to insult"	15. /mìn-mèe/ "imminent"	16. /mìn-mèe/ "imminent"	17. /duu- mìn/ "to insult"	18. /duu- mìn/ "to insult"
-Long V.	19. /mìin/ "nonsense"	20. /mìin/ "nonsense"	21. /mìin-mèe/ "nonsense"	22. /mìin-mèe/ "nonsense"	23. /duu- mìin/ "nonsense"	24. /duu- mìin/ "nonsense"
RF T.-Short V.	25. /nǐn/ "still"	26. /nǐn/ "still"	27. /nǐn-nɔɔn/ "to hesitate"	28. /nǐn-nɔɔn/ "to hesitate"	29. /náam-nǐn/ "still water"	30. /náam-nǐn/ "still water"
-Long V.	31. /nǐin/ "nonsense"	32. /nǐin/ "nonsense"	33. /nǐin-nɔɔn/ "nonsense"	34. /nǐin-nɔɔn/ "nonsense"	35. /náam-nǐin/ "nonsense"	36. /náam-nǐin/ "nonsense"
High T.-Short V.	37. /nín/ "perfect"	38. /nín/ "perfect"	39. /nín-lɤɤj/ "superb"	40. /nín-lɤɤj/ "superb"	41. /kha- nín/ "frozen dew"	42. /kha- nín/ "frozen dew"
-Long V.	43. /níin/ "nonsense"	44. /níin/ "nonsense"	45. /níin-lɤɤj/ "nonsense"	46. /níin-lɤɤj/ "nonsense"	47. /kha- níin/ "nonsense"	48. /kha- níin/ "nonsense"
FR T.-Short V.	49. /nîn/ "a name"	50. /nîn/ "a name"	51. /nîn-nûn/ "nonsense"	52. /nîn-nûn/ "nonsense"	53. /nûn- nîn/ "a name"	54. /nûn- nîn/ "a name"
- Long V.	55. /nîin/ "nonsense"	56. /nîin/ "nonsense"	57. /nîin-nûn/ "nonsense"	58. /nîin-nûn/ "nonsense"	59. /nûn- nîin/ "nonsense"	60. /nûn- nîin/ "nonsense"

Table 17.6. Test words with the Ca(:)N structure in six different contexts

Word/context	WA	WS	UA	US	SA	SS
Mid T.-Short V.	61. /man/ "fat"	62. /man/ "fat"	63. /man-mǔu/ "lard"	64. /man-mǔu/ "lard"	65. /khǎj-man/ "fat"	66. /khǎj-man/ "fat"
-Long V.	67. /maan/ "an evil"	68. /maan/ "an evil"	69. /maan-ráaj/ "a dangerous evil"	70. /maan-ráaj/ "a dangerous evil"	71. /tua-maan/ "an evil"	72. /tua-maan/ "an evil"
Low T.-Short V.	73. /màn/ "to keep on"	74. /màn/ "to keep on"	75. /màn-pʰian/ "to be diligent"	76. /màn-pʰian/ "to be diligent"	77. /mát-sa-màn/ "a curry"	78. /mát-sa-màn/ "a curry"
-Long V.	79. /ŋàaŋ/ "a sound of bells"	80. /ŋàaŋ/ "a sound of bells"	81. /ŋàaŋ-ŋêeŋ/ "a sound of bells"	82. /ŋàaŋ-ŋêeŋ/ "a sound of bells"	83. /ŋêeŋ-ŋàaŋ/ "a sound of bells"	84. /ŋêeŋ-ŋàaŋ/ "a sound of bells"
RF T.-Short V.	85. /mân/ "strong"	86. /mân/ "strong"	87. /mân-caj/ "to be sure"	88. /mân-caj/ "to be sure"	89. /tâŋ-mân/ "to stand on"	90. /tâŋ-mân/ "to stand on"
-Long V.	91. /mâan/ "a blind"	92. /mâan/ "a blind"	93. /mâan-pʰâa/ "a blind made of cloth"	94. /mâan-pʰâa/ "a blind made of cloth"	95. /lǎŋ-mâan/ "behind the curtain"	96. /lǎŋ-mâan/ "behind the curtain"
High T.-Short V.	97. /ŋám/ "to huff"	98. /ŋám/ "to huff"	99. /ŋám-ŋɔɔ/ "to huff"	100. /ŋám-ŋɔɔ/ "to huff"	101. /náa-ŋám/ "a huffy face"	102. /náa-ŋám/ "a huffy face"
-Long V.	103. /náam/ "water"	104. /náam/ "water"	105. /náam-caj/ "kindness"	106. /náam-caj/ "kindness"	107. /tôn-náam/ "water source"	108. /tôn-náam/ "water source"
FR T.-Short V.	109. /năm/ "to be satisfied"	110. /năm/ "to be satisfied"	111. /năm-caj/ "to be satisfied"	112. /năm-caj/ "to be satisfied"	113. /ʔim-năm/ "to be full"	114. /ʔim-năm/ "to be full"
-Long V.	115. /năam/ "a rose thorn"	116. /năam/ "a rose thorn"	117. /năam-tam/ "to be punctured by a thorn"	118. /năam-tam/ "to be punctured by a thorn"	119. /sǐan-năam/ "an enemy"	120. /sǐan-năam/ "an enemy"

TABLE 17.7. Test words with the Ci(:)O structure in six different contexts

Word/context	WA	WS	UA	US	SA	SS
Mid T.-Short V.	121. /nit/ "nonsense"	122. /nit/ "nonsense"	123. /nit-naa/ "nonsense"	124. /nit-naa/ "nonsense"	125. /naa-nit/ "nonsense"	126. /naa-nit/ "nonsense"
-Long V.	127. /niit/ "nonsense"	128. /niit/ "nonsense"	129. /niit-naa/ "nonsense"	130. /niit-naa/ "nonsense"	131. /naa-niit/ "nonsense"	132. /naa-niit/ "nonsense"
Low T.-Short V.	133. /ɲìt/ as in /ɲùt-ɲìt/ "irritated"	134. /ɲìt/ as in /ɲùt-ɲìt/ "irritated"	135. /ɲùt-ɲìt/ "irritated"	136. /ɲùt-ɲìt/ "irritated"	137. /ɲìt-ɲùt/ "nonsense"	138. /ɲìt-ɲùt/ "nonsense"
-Long V.	139. /ɲìit/ "nonsense"	140. /ɲìit/ "nonsense"	141. /ɲùt-ɲìit/ "nonsense"	142. /ɲùt-ɲìit/ "nonsense"	143. /ɲìit-ɲùt/ "nonsense"	144. /ɲìit-ɲùt/ "nonsense"
RF T.-Short V.	145. /nît/ "nonsense"	146. /nît/ "nonsense"	147. /nît-naa/ "nonsense"	148. /nît-naa/ "nonsense"	149. /naa-nît/ "nonsense"	150. /naa-nît/ "nonsense"
-Long V.	151. /nîit/ as in /pra- nîit/ "to be neat"	152. /nîit/ as in /pra- nîit/ "to be neat"	153. /nîit-naa/ "nonsense"	154. /nîit-naa/ "nonsense"	155. /naa-nîit/ "nonsense"	156. /naa-nîit/ "nonsense"
High T.-Short V.	157. /nít/ "little"	158. /nít/ "little"	159. /nít-nɔ́ɔj/ "little+small"	160. /nít-nɔ́ɔj/ "little+small"	161. /nɔ́ɔj-nít/ "a small sum"	162. /nɔ́ɔj-nít/ "a small sum"
-Long V.	163. /nít/ "nonsense"	164. /nít/ "nonsense"	165. /nîit-nɔ́ɔj/ "nonsense"	166. /nîit-nɔ́ɔj/ "nonsense"	167. /nɔ́ɔj-nîit/ "nonsense"	168. /nɔ́ɔj-nîit/ "nonsense"
FR T.-Short V.	169. /ɲǐt/ "nonsense"	170. /ɲǐt/ "nonsense"	171. /ɲǐt-naa/ "nonsense"	172. /ɲǐt-naa/ "nonsense"	173. /naa-ɲǐt/ "nonsense"	174. /naa-ɲǐt/ "nonsense"
-Long V.	175. /ɲǐit/ "nonsense"	176. /ɲǐit/ "nonsense"	177. /ɲǐit-naa/ "nonsense"	178. /ɲǐit-naa/ "nonsense"	179. /naa-ɲǐit/ "nonsense"	180. /naa-ɲǐit/ "nonsense"

TABLE 17.8. Test words with the Ca(:)O structure in six different contexts

Word/context	WA	WS	UA	US	SA	SS
Mid T.-Short V.	181./nat/ "nonsense"	182./nat/ "nonsense"	183./nat-naa/ "nonsense"	184./nat-naa/ "nonsense"	185./naa-nat/ "nonsense"	186./naa-nat/ "nonsense"
-Long V.	187./naat/ "nonsense"	188./naat/ "nonsense"	189./naat-naa/ "nonsense"	190./naat-naa/ "nonsense"	191./naa-naat/ "nonsense"	192./naa-naat/ "nonsense"
Low T.-Short V.	193./nàt/ as in /tha-nàt/ "expertise"	194./nàt/ as in /tha-nàt/ "expertise"	195./nàt-nǎa/ "nonsense"	196./nàt-nǎa/ "nonsense"	197./nǎa-nàt/ "nonsense"	198./nǎa-nàt/ "nonsense"
-Long V.	199./nàat/ as in /kha-nàat/ "size"	200./nàat/ as in /kha-nàat/ "size"	201./nàat-nǎa/ "nonsense"	202./naat-nǎa/ "nonsense"	203./nǎa-nàat/ "nonsense"	204./nǎa-nàat/ "nonsense"
RF T.-Short V.	205./nák/ "nonsense"	206./nák/ "nonsense"	207./nák-naa/ "nonsense"	208./nák-naa/ "nonsense"	209./naa-nák/ "nonsense"	210./naa-nák/ "nonsense"
-Long V.	211./nâak/ "otters"	212./nâak/ "otters"	213./nâak-naa/ "nonsense"	214./nâak-naa/ "nonsense"	215./naa-nâak/ "nonsense"	216./naa-nâak/ "nonsense"
High T.-Short V.	217./nák/ "a person"	218./nák/ "a person"	219./nák-naa/ "nonsense"	220./nák-naa/ "nonsense"	221./naa-nák/ "nonsense"	222./naa-nák/ "nonsense"
-Long V.	223./náak/ "nonsense"	224./náak/ "nonsense"	225./náak-naa/ "nonsense"	226./náak-naa/ "nonsense"	227./naa-náak/ "nonsense"	228./naa-náak/ "nonsense"
FR T.-Short V.	229./nák/ "nonsense"	230./nák/ "nonsense"	231./nák-naa/ "nonsense"	232./nák-naa/ "nonsense"	233./naa-nák/ "nonsense"	234./naa-nák/ "nonsense"
-Long V.	235./nâak/ "nonsense"	236./nâak/ "nonsense"	237./nâak-naa/ "nonsense"	238./nâak-naa/ "nonsense"	239./naa-nâak/ "nonsense"	240./naa-nâak/ "nonsense"

APPENDIX 2. F0 RANGE (Hz) AND AVERAGE F0 RATE OF CHANGE (Hz/sec) OF ALL TOKENS, SPOKEN BY RR

TABLE 17.9. f0 range (Hz) and average rate of change (Hz/ sec) of mid-tone tokens, spoken by RR

Tones	Context	Tones on short vowels		Tones on long vowels	
		f0 range	Average rate of change	f0 range	Average rate of change
Mid	WA	31	−63	32	−23
	WS	17	−29	15.5	−65
Ci(:)N	UA	36	−165	30	−151
	US	10	−118	19.5	−114
	SA	22	−45	31	−52
	SS	11	−49	6.2	−44
Mid	WA	20	−49	29.5	−70
	WS	9	−48	12	−70
Ca(:)N	UA	16	−113	18	−105
	US	4.5	−35	17	−96
	SA	24	−41	34	−44
	SS	31	26	13.5	−85
Mid	WA	15	−79	11.5	−56
	WS	12	−324	44	−224
Ci(:)O	UA	15	−213	17	−152
	US	10	−117	10	−82
	SA	17	−123	7.25	−75
	SS	8	−35	8	−59
Mid	WA	4	−15	8	−41
	WS	10	72	9	−84
Ca(:)O	UA	6	−221	9	−63
	US	9.5	−141	8.5	−80
	SA	6.5	−59	15	−53
	SS	5	−76	9	−93

Note: The negative values of the rate of change indicate that the raw f0 curves of a tone descend.

TABLE 17.10. f0 range (Hz) and average rate of change (Hz/sec) of low-tone tokens, spoken by RR

Tones	Context	Tones on short vowels		Tones on long vowels	
		f0 range	Average rate of change	f0 range	Average rate of change
Low	WA	52	−186	48	−130
	WS	50.5	−314	48	−252
Ci(:)N	UA	25	−172	16	−144
	US	50	−264	35	−309
	SA	64	−259	74	−195
	SS	54	−378	46.5	−293
Low	WA	43	−169	54	−120
	WS	40	−261	43	−205
Ca(:)N	UA	30	−173	25	−160
	US	38	−233	44	−333
	SA	80	−305	37	−83
	SS	60	−440	12	−62
Low	WA	44.5	−320	61	−166
	WS	56	−400	40	−402
Ci(:)O	UA	37	−299	79	−181
	US	48	−426	30	−381
	SA	57.5	−153	17	−193
	SS	9	−364	20	−183
Low	WA	67	−412	62	−200
	WS	49	−480	57	−372
Ca(:)O	UA	38	−481	43	−409
	US	61	−903	49	−391
	SA	65	−473	71	−227
	SS	40.5	−454	77	−838

Note: Negative rate-of-change values indicate that the raw f0 curves of a tone descend.

TABLE 17.11. f0 range (Hz) and average rate of change (Hz/sec) of rising–falling tone tokens, spoken by RR

		Tones on short vowels			Tones on long vowels		
Tones	Context	f0 range (Hz)	Average rate of change (rising)	Average rate of change (falling)	f0 range (Hz)	Average rate of change (rising)	Average rate of change (falling)
Rising–falling	WA	90	183	−405	79	174	−349
	WS	68.5	484	−195	68	403	−289
Ci(:)N	UA	57	267	−158	39	911	−156
	US	65	581	−311	69	232	−106
	SA	65	126	−331	60	192	−366
	SS	59	310	−147	50	236	−10
Rising–falling	WA	102	173	−593	51	89	−274
	WS	48	436	−228	64	375	−358
Ca(:)N	UA	21	195	−474	21	114	−467
	US	38	342	−589	30	272	405
	SA	56	0	−182	56	169	−309
	SS	14	9	−247	66	482	−515
Rising–falling	WA	60	83	−245	26	148	−404
	WS	21	542	−388	63	644	−515
Ci(:)O	UA	52	391	−183	36	256	−597
	US	70	643	−318	64	659	−247
	SA	48	395	−737	56	222	−386
	SS	56	437	−734	75	451	−365
Rising–falling	WA	33	93	−569	58	68	−411
	WS	32	386	−341	48	348	−580
Ca(:)O	UA	12	152	−177	17	136	−679
	US	39	543	−41	35	362	−827
	SA	31	262	−328	29	127	−205
	SS	39	368	−575	42	306	−645

Negative rate-of-change values indicate that the raw f0 curves of a tone descend.

TABLE 17.12. f0 range (Hz) and average rate of change (Hz/sec) of high-tone tokens, spoken by RR

Tones	Context	Tones on short vowels			Tones on long vowels		
		f0 range (Hz)	Average rate of change (level)	Average rate of change (rising)	f0 range (Hz)	Average rate of change (level)	Average rate of change (rising)
High	WA	46	53	239	40	−9	204
	WS	14	361	N/A	39	−35	203
Ci(:)N	UA	15	−46	144	10	−30	180
	US	14	1	232	18	−58	205
	SA	53	−48	194	30	−65	236
	SS	20	−73	274	12	−46	283
High	WA	45	−64	193	43	−47	159
	WS	15	−129	251	37	−161	301
Ca(:)N	UA	16	0	113	16	−156	79
	US	12	−139	277	14	−31	120
	SA	59	−255	181	70	−265	166
	SS	47	−624	182	47	−434	130
High	WA	27	−14	264	26	14	237
	WS	19	260	−505	24	−58	145
Ci(:)O	UA	16	−66	161	11	82	−653
	US	13	280	−128	23	−27	239
	SA	20	−135	9	11	−109	145
	SS	7	70	84	14	−96	45
High	WA	18	−154	145	28	−61	245
	WS	7	−63	137	22	−164	217
Ca(:)O	UA	11	−90	141	15	−126	201
	US	14	−134	204	17	−161	240
	SA	22	−70	197	29	−28	239
	SS	19	−35	207	20	−82	212

Negative rate-of-change values indicate that the raw f0 curves of a tone descend.

TABLE 17.13. f0 range (Hz) and average rate of change (Hz/sec) of falling-rising-tone tokens, spoken by RR

Tones	Context	Tones on short vowels			Tones on long vowels		
		f0 range (Hz)	Average rate of change (falling)	Average rate of change (rising)	f0 range (Hz)	Average rate of change (falling)	Average rate of change (rising)
Falling–rising	WA	67	−176	257	60	−116	275
	WS	54	−396	271	47	−332	240
Ci(:)N	UA	21	−136	264	29	−111	201
	US	43	−269	323	40	−302	281
	SA	65	−228	364	65	−183	405
	SS	24	−185	91	16	−234	191
Falling–rising	WA	27	−166	237	27	−93	183
	WS	26	−268	266	41	−339	382
Ca(:)N	UA	11	−115	81	16	−168	179
	US	26	−319	131	37	−476	206
	SA	23	−144	216	68	−257	302
	SS	12	144	280	84	−769	478
Falling–rising	WA	37	−24	110	27	−23	297
	WS	58	−277	175	37	−420	86
Ci(:)O	UA	21	−46	−10	25	−356	0
	US	40	−280	457	27	−226	−57
	SA	42	−235	−611	26	−230	213
	SS	26	−219	187	21	−135	100
Falling–rising	WA	12	−128	213	27	−168	247
	WS	23	−381	135	37	−489	263
Ca(:)O	UA	12	−291	57	22	−155	0
	US	31	−355	219	21	−394	23
	SA	31	−385	252	41	−391	245
	SS	19	−439	174	24	−464	131

Note: Negative rate-of-change values indicate that the raw f0 curves of a tone descend.

APPENDIX 3. TEST WORDS FOR THE TRUNCATION QUANTIFICATION (SECT. 17.4.2)

TABLE 17.14. Test words for truncation quantification

Rising–falling tone tokens	Falling–rising tone tokens
1. /mâp/ "nonsense"	7. /mǎp/ "nonsense"
2. /mâap/ "a name" as in /mâap-taa-phút/	8. /mǎap/ "nonsense"
3. /nâp/ "nonsense"	9. /nǎp/ "nonsense"
4. /nâap/ "to press on something"	10. /nǎap/ "nonsense"
5. /ŋnâp/ "nonsense"	11. /ŋǎp/ "nonsense"
6. /ŋâap/ "to take something from someone"	12. /ŋǎap/ "nonsense"

APPENDIX 4. TEST WORDS FOR THE PHASE-REALIGNMENT QUANTIFICATION (SECTION 4.3)

TABLE 17.15. Test words for phase-realignment quantification

Rising–falling tone tokens	Falling–rising tone tokens
1. /nîn/ "nonsense"	13. /nǐn/ "nonsense"
2. /nîin/ "nonsense"	14. /nǐin/ "nonsense"
3. /nân/ "that"	15. /nǎn/ "a name"
4. /nâan/ "a name of a Thai province"	16. /nǎan/ "happy" as in /sa- nǎan/
5. /nîm/ "soft"	17. /nǐm/ "a name"
6. /nîim/ "nonsense"	18. /nǐim/ "nonsense"
7. /nâm/ "a type of ice-cream "magnum" loaned from English"	19. /nǎm/ "to be satisfied"
8. /nâam/ "nonsense"	20. /nǎam/ "a thorn"
9. /nîŋ/ "still"	21. /nǐŋ/ "a name"
10. /nîiŋ/ "nonsense"	22. /nǐiŋ/ "nonsense"
11. /nâŋ/ "to sit"	23. /nǎŋ/ "skin"
12. /nâaŋ/ "nonsense"	24. /nǎaŋ/ "nonsense"

18

Controlled and Mechanical Properties in Speech

A Review of the Literature

Maria-Josep Solé

18.1 INTRODUCTION

In the study of speech there is a well-known dichotomy between features that are planned by the speaker (i.e., present in the input to speech production) and mechanical features that emerge due to vocal tract constraints. Those aspects of speech which result from elasto-inertial, biomechanical, or aerodynamic constraints are not targeted by the speaker and can be explained by general phonetic principles. Examples include (a) the few milliseconds' delay in the onset of voicing in vowels and sonorants following unaspirated stops, due to the time needed to release the oral pressure build up for the stop and initiate the transglottal flow needed for voicing (J. Ohala 1983*b*), and (b) coarticulation with adjacent sounds which can be described in terms of the production constraints of the sounds involved (e.g. the "Degree of Articulatory Constraint" model of Recasens *et al.* 1997).

The aspects of speech under the control of the speaker minimally include parameters used to signal segmental and prosodic contrasts, to mark linguistic boundaries and constituency, and language-specific coarticulatory and timing features. Planned effects also include language-specific articulatory maneuvers to inhibit (or facilitate) intrinsic influences on articulation (e.g. active expansion of the oropharyngeal cavity to preserve voicing in obstruents; J. Ohala 1997*a*). In recent years a great deal of evidence has suggested that fine-grained phonetic detail, such as language-specific preferences for certain ranges of voice onset time (VOT) values for prevoiced and

Work on this chapter was supported by grants HUM2005-02746, BFF2003-09453-C02-C01 from the Ministry of Science and Technology, Spain and by the research group SGR 2005-2008 of the Catalan Government. The suggestions of K. de Jong and Peter Ladefoged are gratefully acknowledged.

aspirated stops (Kessinger and Blumstein 1997; Cho and Ladefoged 1999), and detail used to cue social, geographical, and stylistic markers (e.g. Docherty 2003) are also manipulated by speakers. Such language-specific and even dialect-specific features need to be specified in the motor commands, either in the input to speech production or gestures (Browman and Goldstein 1986, 1992), or through language-specific rules of phonetic implementation (Keating 1985; Cho and Ladefoged 1999). Other approaches, such as exemplar models (Johnson 1997b, this volume; Bybee 2000, Pierrehumbert 2001a), choose to include phonetic detail in the stored representations.

There has been long-standing interest in teasing apart mechanical and controlled effects in the speech signal which permeates the literature on a number of different areas. Some of these are: allophonic variation, for example intrinsic vs. extrinsic allophones (W. Wang and Fillmore 1961; Ladefoged 1967a); connected speech processes, for instance, those resulting from vocal tract constraints—increased overlap and decreased magnitude of gestures—or programmed by the speaker (Holst and Nolan 1995; Wood 1996); coarticulatory theories, such as adjusting gestures by coproduction vs. changing targets by feature-spreading (Fowler 1980); speech timing, for instance general vs. language-dependent patterns of motor control (Lubker and Gay 1982), and perceptual reinterpretation and sound change (J. Ohala 1983b). Because the distinction between mechanical and targeted properties of the signal is so central to phonology and to most areas of speech research, it is surprising that we still do not have a clear metric to distinguish between the two.

One of the aims of this chapter is to reinterpret previous work so as to clarify what is language-specific, and hence controlled, and what is the result of inevitable physiological and aerodynamic factors. A second aim is to address how planned properties differ across languages. In order to address these questions I will focus on what aspects of the signal vary consistently from language to language, which would indicate that these variations must be controlled properties, and examine whether these show measurable differences from aspects that can be attributed to vocal tract constraints. I intend to focus on how particular speech features adjust to variations in timing in order to determine their mechanical or purposeful nature.

18.1.1 Distinguishing between language-specific and mechanical properties

Distinguishing between physically measurable effects that are intrinsic to the speech mechanism and language-specific properties under the control of the speaker is not a straightforward task because the actual status of a phonetic feature may not be the same for all speakers at any given time. A physiologically based difference such as intrinsic differences in pitch or duration related to vowel height (with low vowels having a lower pitch and a longer duration than corresponding high vowels) may become part of a perceptual cue distinguishing different vowel heights. Once this association has been established, the concomitant cue may be deliberately used by speakers to enhance the vowel height contrast (Kingston and Diehl 1994). The fact that phonetic features change their status over time implies that what for some speakers may be a purely phonetic effect, for other speakers may have been changed to a phonological or lexical feature. (See Beddor *et al.*, this volume, for an example of phonetic features that appear to be phonological for some speakers of a language but possibly not for other speakers of that language/dialect.) J. Ohala (1981*a*, 1983*b*, 1989, 1993*b*) has provided extensive evidence that mechanical features which follow from constraints of the vocal tract may be reinterpreted by listeners as intended and result in sound change. Similarly, what for one language or dialect may be merely a low-level phonetic effect, may have been phonologized or lexicalized in another language or dialect. Precisely because language-specific (phonetic, allophonic or lexical) features, that is, intended variation, may be the result of phonetically predictable variation, they will look similar and they may not be easy to tease apart.

Previous attempts to provide a metric to differentiate vocal tract constraints from controlled features are available in the literature. J. Ohala (1981*c*) argued that since the duration of segments is influenced by the structure of the syllable, and assuming that timing of the segments in the syllable is phonologically specified, manipulating syllable structure can help us determine if certain phonetic phenomena such as epenthetic stops are planned or not. Planned stops should have consequences on segment duration (specifically, preceding vowel duration), while stops that originate at the vocal tract level should not. Solé (1992, 1995) suggested that acoustic properties targeted by the speaker adjust to durational variations triggered by changes in speaking rate so as to maintain a constant perceptual distance across rates, whereas low-level phonetic effects remain constant across rates or should vary in a way that could be explained by physical and physiological principles of speech motor control. De Jong (1995, 2004) suggested that strong prosodic positions (stressed, accented) enhance features used by speakers to indicate linguistic contrasts but have no effect on features due to vocal tract mechanics. Other recent studies on how prosodic effects affect segmental features have also noted that features distinctive for a contrast are enhanced in stressed and accented positions (e.g. Cho and Jun 2000; Cho and McQueen 2005). What these proposals have in common is that variations in segment duration—prompted by syllable type, speaking rate, and prosodic prominence—trigger the temporal adaptation of features planned by the speaker, but have no consequence (or merely phonetically predictable consequences) on low-level mechanical effects. This is the proposal that will be explored in this chapter.

Although there are numerous intrinsic and extrinsic factors that induce changes in segment duration (see Klatt 1976 for a review), I will focus on three main factors, namely, changes in speaking rate, in prosodic factors, and in syllable structure. These factors have known effects on segment duration: segments are longer at slower than at faster speaking rates (Lehiste 1970; Gay 1981; Magen and Blumstein 1993), though effects may differ for consonants and vowels (Klatt 1976: 1210); in stressed rather than in unstressed position (Houde 1967; Lehiste 1970; Beckman, Edwards, and Fletcher 1992, for English; Straka 1963, for French; Farnetani and Vayra 1991, for Italian; Engstrand 1988, for Swedish); in pitch-accented vs. unaccented syllables (de Jong 1995, for English; Cambier-Langeveld and Turk 1999, for Dutch and English), and in certain syllable types (House and Fairbanks 1953; Klatt 1976, for American English). In addition, the effect of these factors on segment duration is sufficiently large that they produce observable effects on intended properties of the speech signal which can be found in the literature. One caveat is in order. Not all types of durational variation are of the same nature. While syllable type and stress effects are usually local (i.e., they are taken to be a property of a particular syllable; de Jong 2004), speaking-rate effects are global. In spite of this difference, cues that are deliberately controlled by the speaker to convey linguistic information to the listener should be present in the same proportion across durational differences in rate, stress, or syllable types, hence they are expected to scale up or down with changes in these factors.

A number of studies have examined the effect of temporal variation on phonetic properties to assess a variety of issues,[1] but to my knowledge, links between changes in temporal effects induced by these factors on the one hand, and controlled vs. execution features in speech on the other, have not been claimed (apart from the exceptions noted above). The results of these studies, however, offer relevant information in the assessment of the nature of intended and mechanical speech features in different languages and some of their results will be reviewed in this paper.

18.1.2 Experimental approach

Many of the linguistic and indexical properties of speech targeted by the speaker are manifested in the temporal domain or their spectral properties need to be achieved within certain temporal windows. Consequently, changes in the time domain may allow us to ascertain which phonetic features are actively manipulated by speakers. The rationale of the approach is the following. If a particular feature is specified in the input to speech production, and if we assume that the timing characteristics of segments are also specified at that level, then if overall segment duration is varied with changes in speaking rate, stress, or syllable type, the timing of the feature should be reorganized accordingly in order to maintain a constant perceptual distance across conditions. That is, phonetic properties targeted by the speaker should be present in

---

[1] These issues include, for example, stable timing relations in speech production across changes in stress and rate (e.g. Nittrouer *et al.* 1988); the invariant acoustic properties of features across changes in speaking rate (e.g. Port and Dalby 1982; Pickett *et al.* 1999); feature-spreading vs. time-locked theories of coarticulation (e.g. Bell-Berti and Krakow 1991); the role of temporal aspects of speech on speech perception (e.g. Summerfield 1981); segmental alignment of tones and f0 curves under different temporal constraints (e.g. Gandour *et al.* 1999; Grabe *et al.* 2000); and studies on stress, focus, and phrasal boundary effects on the production of segments (e.g. de Jong 1991, 1995, 2004 for stress and focus; Keating *et al.* 2003 for phrasal boundaries).

the same proportion despite differences in the absolute duration of the segment. This is in line with research on speech perception suggesting that listeners rely on constant temporal ratios (e.g. Pickett *et al.* 1999; Boucher 2002); consequently, speakers must control these properties during speech production. It is also in line with the more general claim that speech movements are directed towards perceptual or acoustic goals (Ladefoged *et al.* 1972; Johnson *et al.* 1993; J. Ohala 1995). It is reasonable to assume that this listener-oriented goal constrains the motor strategies used to implement intended features across changes in the temporal dimension.

On the other hand, effects which are not planned by the speaker but are due to physical or physiological constraints are expected not to adjust to rate or stress variations since they do not participate in the higher level reorganization of timing and durational factors and originate at a lower level. Mechanical effects may present slight variations that correlate with temporally induced changes in the causal physical or physiological factors and, thus, they should be predictable from general phonetic principles. In short, linguistically specified features will be scaled up or down depending on rate or stress conditions, whereas physiological effects will not.[2] Note that this proposal differs from that of de Jong (1995, 2004), Cho and Jun (2000), and Cho and McQueen (2005) in that while they claim that stress and focus enhance linguistic specifications, expanding certain specifically phonemic contrasts, I suggest that it is not accentual prominence per se, but rather the need to maintain a constant perceptual distance across durational variations (induced by a number of factors, including accentual prominence) that is responsible for the different behavior of planned vs. biomechanical features.

To review, the assumptions underlying this study are the following: (a) many of the properties encoded in the target pronunciation are manifested in the temporal domain; (b) most of these properties are language-specific and are not phonetic universals resulting from vocal tract constraints; (c) these effects are used by listeners in speech perception and, consequently, should be recoverable from the signal across different rate and prosodic conditions; (d) since perception constrains motor strategies, intended properties will be rescaled in duration across different rate and prosodic variations, whereas low-level effects of phonetic implementation will not. In the following sections I will review evidence to test the predictions of the hypothesis proposed. Specifically, I address the status of vowel nasalization, VOT differences, and vowel duration before voiced and voiceless obstruents in various languages, as well as contrastive vowel length, drawing selectively from the large body

---

[2] One reviewer suggests that the assumption that there are two types of effect—either a property is not sensitive to global timing, or it is proportionally changed—may be a bit of an oversimplification since de Jong's (2001a, b) studies on rate scaling show planned effects which vary with rate but by different amounts. The present chapter makes no claims as to whether all controlled properties show the same rate adjustment. Rather, it claims that controlled properties vary in a proportional way with changes in temporal factors (i.e. the value of the property increases by a constant multiple of the temporal increase), not that they vary by the same amount.

of experimental data accumulated over the past few decades. In my focus on teasing apart properties that are actively controlled as opposed to properties that are a product of execution I do not attempt to distinguish between subphonemic and phonemic effects, both under the control of the speaker.

18.2 VOWEL NASALIZATION

A great deal of allophonic variation can be attributed to coarticulation with adjacent sounds, that is to say, the variation can be described in terms of a numerical model which takes into account the degree and extent of coarticulation and the production constraints of the sounds involved (see e.g. Recasens *et al.* 1997). However, some of the allophonic variation seems to be phonologically encoded, that is, part of the language-specific instructions. Such variants would have different target properties since these differences are made deliberately and are not simply attributable to coarticulation. These have traditionally been called "extrinsic allophones", each with its own set of motor commands.[3]

Solé (1992, 1995) examined evidence that showed that vowels followed by a tauto-syllabic nasal in languages such as Spanish, French, Japanese, Italian, and Swedish show very restricted coarticulatory nasalization due to the necessary time required by the velum to lower for the nasal consonant. She argued that the extensive vowel nasalization found in American English could not be explained in terms of anticipatory nasal coarticulation. To differentiate coarticulatory and deliberate vowel nasalization, she measured the oral and nasalized portions of vowels followed by oral (CVVC) and nasal consonants (CVVN) in the productions of three Spanish and three American English speakers, each at four different speaking rates. A nasograph was used to track the time-varying positions of the velum. Coarticulatorily nasalized vowels should be targeted as oral and onset of velum lowering should be timed relative to the following nasal consonant, thus the nasalized portion of the vowel should be more or less constant in spite of durational differences in the vowel across speaking rates. In contrast, if vowel nasalization were not a coarticulatory effect but an inherent property of vowels preceding nasal consonants (i.e. an allophonic variant), the timing of velum lowering should be independent of the nasal consonant and should be timed relative to the vowel, thus the nasalized portion of the vowel should adjust to differences in vowel duration across rates. Thus, by determining whether speaking rate affected the duration of the oral or the nasalized portion of the vowel, she could establish whether the vowel was articulatorily targeted as oral (with mechanical nasalization)

---

[3] It has been suggested that the origin of such discrete allophones (as for example, taps and alveolar stops in American English; glottal stops and /t/; dark and clear /l/, etc.) may be gradual articulatory variability that, because it is consistent and occurs in a particular context and position, and because it has a distinct perceptual result, has been stored by the listener as discrete allophones; however, they are no longer realizations of the same gesture.

or as nasalized. The results are shown in Figure 18.1, which plots the duration of the oral and nasalized portion of the vowel sequence (including the aspiration period) as a function of varying speech rate for American English and Spanish productions. For the American-English speakers there is a significant positive correlation between rate conditions and duration of the *nasalized* portion of the vowel ($p < 0.0001$, $r^2 = 0.94$). The oral portion of the vowel, in contrast, is very short (corresponding approximately to the aspiration period) and does not vary much with speaking rate as indicated by the low r values. The results indicate that in American English the nasalized portion of the vowel varies with speech rate (the slower the rate, the longer the nasalized portion), as predicted for deliberate nasalization. In other words, in American English, velum lowering is not timed relative to the nasal consonant but to the onset of the vowel, and thus the vowel is nasalized throughout: the vowel has the same percentage of nasalization (100%) across all rates, despite durational differences. Thus, vowel nasalization has been dissociated from the conditioning environment and has become part of the programming instructions for the vowel.[4]

For the vowels of the Spanish speakers, the nasalized portion is very restricted and shows a roughly constant duration across different speaking rates. The slight rate-

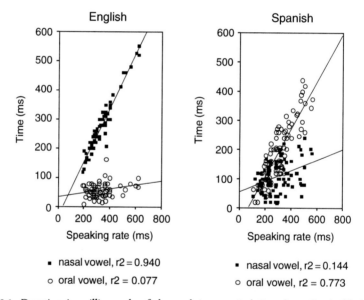

FIGURE 18.1. Duration in milliseconds of the oral (empty circles) and nasalized (filled squares) portions of the vowel sequence (including aspiration) in /tVVN/ for American English and Spanish on the ordinate. Average speech rate in milliseconds appears on the abscissa. Each dot represents an individual measurement. N = 400

---

[4] A similar claim was made by Malécot (1960) for vowels followed by a nasal and a homorganic voiceless stop, such as *camp*.

correlated changes, such that faster rates show a slightly shorter portion of vowel nasalization than slower rates, may be attributed to the higher stiffness in the dynamic characteristics of the velum, and hence higher velocity of movements, at faster rates (Kuehn and Moll 1976; Kelso *et al.* 1985). The relationship between rate conditions and vowel nasalization, however, does not reach significance and the correlation coefficient is low ($r^2 = 0.144$). It is the *oral* portion of the vowel which varies greatly as a function of rate, with a high correlation coefficient ($r^2 = 0.773$). The results suggest that Spanish vowels are targeted as oral (the oral portion adjusts to variations in speech rate) and nasalization is timed relative to the nasal consonant, reflecting the transitional time (which may vary slightly due to stiffness factors) needed to lower the velum for the following nasal consonant. In summary, the results indicate that in Spanish, vowel nasalization is a low-level coarticulatory effect due to the transitional time needed to lower the velum for the upcoming nasal. In American English, vowel nasalization has become part of the language-specific instructions, and the nasalized portion adjusts to changes in the temporal dimension so as to maintain a constant perceptual distance across rates.

In a similar vein, Bell-Berti and Krakow (1991) sought to determine the temporal extent of coarticulatory vowel nasalization in American English by varying the number of vowels in CV_nN and CV_nC sequences, where n was any number of vowels (i.e. V, V:, VV), thus altering the time between the onset of the vocalic segment and the onset of the following consonant. They found that the velum starts to lower at the beginning of the vowel sequence, regardless of the number of vocalic segments, supporting the view that vowel nasalization in American English is an intrinsic property of vowels before coda nasals. Bell-Berti and Krakow, however, attribute early velar lowering to the intrinsic velar position for vowels (oral vowels involve lower velum positions than oral consonants do) since they observe similar velar lowering movements in strictly oral contexts. Solé (1992) reports a difference in magnitude of velar lowering in CVC and CVN sequences, which challenges Bell-Berti and Krakow's interpretation.

Finally, Clumeck's (1976) cross-linguistic study of vowel nasalization in six languages notes restricted vowel nasalization in CVN sequences in Swedish, French, Amoy Chinese, and Hindi, which can be attributed to coarticulatory nasalization, and extensive vowel nasalization in American English and Brazilian Portuguese, which must be attributed to the language-specific organization of speech motor commands. Although Clumeck does not manipulate temporal factors, interestingly, he analyzes Swedish long and short vowels separately (his table 5, p. 341). He finds that velum lowering occurs at a roughly constant time before the onset of the nasal consonant regardless of whether the preceding vowel is long or short, thus resulting in short vowels being more heavily nasalized than long vowels (percentage of vowel nasalization: 0.92 and 0.58, respectively). Since velic lowering begins at roughly the same point in time, it is the oral portion of the vowel which varies with differences in vowel duration; thus Swedish vowels can be said to be targeted as oral, and nasalization is the result of a physiological time constraint. In contrast, Clumeck (his table 11, p. 343) finds that in Brazilian Portuguese, velum lowering for mid vowels begins earlier than for non-mid vowels. He notes that mid vowels are longer in duration than high and low vowels due to their diphthongal realization, thus the earlier velum lowering for the longer mid vowels results in a comparable percentage of vowel nasalization across differences in vowel duration. That is to say, the temporal extent of vowel nasalization varies with differences in vowel duration so as to maintain a constant perceptual distance despite durational differences, as predicted for phonologically encoded effects. Overall, these studies illustrate how temporal factors can be manipulated by varying speaking rate and syllable type, thus providing testable hypotheses about the mechanical or controlled nature of speech features.

18.3 THE STOP VOICING CONTRAST

This experimental approach has also been tested on the well-known phenomenon of the implementation of the voicing contrast in stops in prevocalic (onset) position. Changes in speaking rate affect the duration of aspiration in English (Summerfield 1981; Miller *et al.* 1986; Volaitis and Miller 1992; Kessinger and Blumstein 1997) such that, as speaking rate increases, voice-onset time (VOT) for voiceless stops decreases; as speaking rate decreases, VOT increases. We hypothesize that VOT in English adjusts to variations in speaking rate because the aspiration of syllable initial [p, t, k] is a language-specific property of English used to signal voicing contrasts (Abramson and Lisker 1970). Thus, duration of aspiration should be proportional to the duration of the segments to maintain a constant perceptual contrast across rates. In contrast, in languages such as Catalan, Spanish, and French the voicing contrast is signaled by presence or absence of vocal fold vibration during the consonant constriction (i.e. long voicing lead vs. lack of voicing lead). Clearly, the different perceptual cues to stop voicing arise from different patterns of coordination of oral and glottal gestures in these languages (see Cho and Ladefoged 1999). For voiceless unaspirated stops in the Romance languages, onset of laryngeal vibration is timed with the release of the oral constriction. The short positive VOT values can be attributed to the aerodynamic link between the stop release and voicing onset: the time needed to release the oral pressure behind the constriction for the stop and thus initiate transglottal airflow for voicing. According to our expectations, in the Romance languages aspiration should remain constant in different rate conditions or should present slight variations if changing rate affects the resistance to outgoing airflow and hence the time needed to lower the oral pressure and initiate voicing.

Solé and Estebas (2000) report the results for three Southern British English speakers and three Catalan speakers reading words with all possible combinations of CV, where C = [p, t, k] and V = [i, a], in a carrier phrase at four different speaking rates. The duration of the carrier phrase was used as a measure for speaking rate. The results for the measurements of duration of aspiration (i.e. the time lag between the release burst and the onset of voicing) across different speech rates for English and Catalan speakers are shown in the scatter plots in Figure 18.2. As in previous studies for English, a positive correlation was found between speech rate and duration of aspiration for all stops and vowel contexts ($p < 0.0001$ in all cases). The results indicate that duration of aspiration in English adjusts to durational variations induced by changes in speech rate. Aspiration in English shows a multiplicative effect: VOT in one

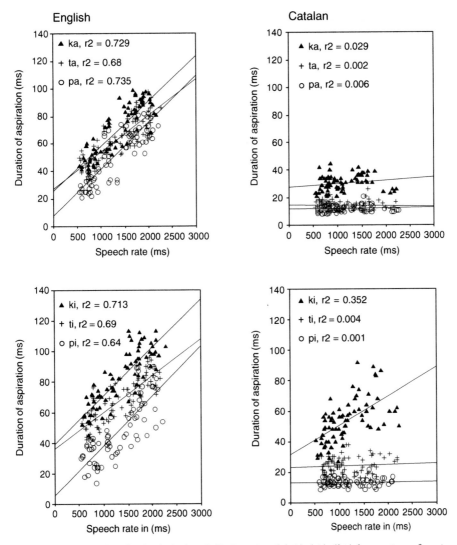

FIGURE 18.2. VOT values for /pa/, /ta/, and /ka/ (top) and /pi/, /ti/, /ki/ (bottom) as a function of speech rate for English (left) and Catalan (right) speakers. Regression lines and r^2 values for each syllable are shown. Each dot represents an individual measurement. N = 900

rate of speech differs from that in another rate by an amount proportional to the duration of the vowel so as to maintain a constant perceptual difference across rates. Thus, it can be deduced that aspiration in English does not occur automatically but that it is part of the programming instructions of the language.

Conversely, for the Catalan speakers (right panels, Fig. 18.2) the relationship between rate conditions and voicing lag is not significant. The short-lag VOT values are consistent across rates (except for [ki] sequences), suggesting that in this language duration of aspiration is independent of changes in speaking rate. The sequence [ki] shows a weak correlation between the two variables, which can be accounted for by physical phonetic principles. The slower articulatory opening for velars vis-à-vis labials and apicals (Stevens 1998: 48, 365), which is exaggerated in slow speech, and the higher tongue position and longer duration for [i] in slow speech (Lindblom 1963) offer a higher resistance to outgoing flow, and hence result in a longer delay in re-establishing the aerodynamic conditions for transglottal airflow and onset of voicing at slow than at faster rates. Thus rate-related variations in VOT values in Catalan [ki] sequences co-vary with aerodynamic effects. In summary, the results indicate that the delay in the onset of voicing in Catalan seems to reflect low-level phonetic effects.[5]

Further data corroborate and complement these results. Acoustic measures of VOT in English (Summerfield 1981; Miller et al. 1986; Kessinger and Blumstein 1997) and Icelandic (Pind 1995) show that whereas there is a significant effect of speaking rate on the VOT values of voiceless long lag stops in these languages, the VOT values of voiced short lag stops are not significantly affected by changes in speaking rate, that is, they exhibit consistent VOT values across rates. This asymmetry in the effects of speaking rate on VOT may be accounted for in terms of the crucial role of aspiration (vs. lack of aspiration), rather than vocal-fold vibration during the constriction, in signaling voicing contrasts in these two languages. Conversely, acoustic measurements of VOT values in French (Kessinger and Blumstein 1997), Spanish (Magloire and Green 1999), and EGG and acoustic measurements in Catalan (Cuartero 2002) reveal that negative VOT values for prevoiced stops vary with changes in speaking rate, which supports the view that in these languages glottal vibration during the constriction (i.e. prevoicing) is the cue that is actively controlled to signal voicing contrasts. The observed asymmetries in Romance and Germanic languages may be described as an interaction between speaking rate and stop voicing on VOT values, such that an increase in segment

---

[5] Note that differences in VOT values induced by the place of articulation of the stop, such that velar stops show a longer period of aspiration than alveolars and labials (Fischer-Jørgensen 1954: 50; Peterson and Lehiste 1960: 701), have been observed cross-linguistically and can be explained from aerodynamic principles (J. Ohala 1983b; Westbury and Keating 1986). Such implementational differences are expected to remain constant across rates and languages. Figure 18.2 shows that, with the exception of Catalan [ki] sequences, the difference in VOT values between any pair of consonants differing in place of articulation is approximately the same in slow and fast speech, that is, the regression lines have roughly the same slope. Thus, the difference in duration of aspiration for various places of articulation has approximately the same magnitude in slow and fast speech, and across the two languages, as predicted for low-level phonetic effects.

duration (at slower rates) increases negative VOT values for voiced stops, but does not affect VOT values for voiceless stops in Romance languages, whereas the opposite is the case for Germanic languages.

Converging evidence for the adaptation of features controlled by the speaker to durational variation comes from studies on acoustic invariance. A number of studies (e.g. Port and Dalby 1982; Miller *et al.* 1986; Boucher 2002) found that in English voiceless stops, the ratios of VOT values to the syllables remained constant across changes in speaking rate. Since the duration of syllables increases substantially at slower rates, a constant ratio implies that the absolute values of VOT increase accordingly in this language, as expected for controlled effects. Crucially, Boucher (2002) also reports VOT measures for English intervocalic voiced stops with voiceless closures. His Figure 3 shows constant short lag VOT values for voiced stops in English, and decreasing ratios at slower speaking rates (due to the substantial increase in syllable duration without a corresponding increase in VOT values), suggesting that voicing during the constriction is not actively targeted by English speakers.

In a similar vein, Port and Rotunno (1979) report that VOT of aspirated stops in American English varies as a function of the duration of the following vowel, such that VOT is longer before long (tense) vowels than before short (lax) vowels, as expected. However, they note that VOT changes by a smaller proportion than the following voiced vowel.

Studies on stable patterns in speech motor control across changes in speaking rate provide further evidence. For example, de Jong (2003) proposes that there are temporal bindings which differ for different syllabic positions and examines the intergestural timing of glottal and subglottal articulators in CV and VC syllables spoken at different rates. De Jong claims stable patterns of oral and glottal gestures in onset consonants across changes in speaking rate (i.e. consistent VOT durations); however, his Figure 14.2, bottom right panel, shows increasing VOT values with decreasing speaking rate for voiceless stops, whereas positive VOT values for voiced stops show constant values (his Fig. 14.2, top right panel), reflecting the language-specific properties of American English observed in other studies rather than general patterns of motor coordination as claimed by de Jong.

Interestingly, in languages with a three-way VOT distinction, such as Thai, both voiced stops and aspirated stops show longer VOT values (negative for prevoiced, and positive for aspirated) at the slow than at the fast rate, whereas VOT for unaspirated stops does not vary with rate (Kessinger and Blumstein 1997).[6] This is compatible

---

[6] Pam Beddor has brought to my attention that conflicting data from Thai has recently appeared. Onsuwan (2005), for example, did not find VOT of Thai aspirated stops to be longer before contrastively long vowels than before short vowels, as my approach would predict (and has been found for English; Port and Rotunno 1979). On the other hand, she did find that the aspiration contrast had an effect on the duration of the voiced portion of the following vowel: voiced vowel duration was shorter after aspirated than after unaspirated stops. (This effect is not due simply to aspiration being a voiceless articulation of the initial portion of the vowel because, although the voiced portion is longer after unaspirated stops, in her data VOT plus voiced vowel duration is longer after aspirated stops.)

It seems that the VOT outcome conflicts with the predictions of the approach presented here (since VOT is clearly under the control of Thai speakers). However, an interpretation that is consistent with this

with the interpretation that vocal fold vibration during the constriction is targeted by Thai speakers for prevoiced stops: since segments are longer in slower speaking rates, negative VOT values are also longer. In a similar way, Thai speakers actively target long-lag VOT for aspirated stops, which adjusts to rate variations. In unaspirated stops, vocal-fold vibration appears to be timed relative to the beginning of the vowel and constant short-lag VOT values result from the time needed to initiate transglottal flow for voicing after the stop constriction.

VOT has also been reported to vary in some languages with changes in stress, focus, and phrasal boundaries, which have known effects on segment duration. Specifically, voiceless stops in English are produced with longer VOT values in lexically stressed vs. unstressed syllables (Lisker and Abramson 1967), in focused vs. non-focused position (Choi 2003), in accented syllables vs. unaccented syllables (Choi 2003; Cole et al. 2003), and in domain-initial syllables vs. within a prosodic constituent (Pierrehumbert and Talkin 1992; Choi 2003, however, did not find a consistent effect of phrasal boundaries on VOT values). Such an increase in VOT at prosodically strong locations has been interpreted as a cue to prosodic structure. If this were the case, one would expect segmental cues to prosodic structure to be present cross-linguistically whenever a certain prosodic location is found. However, increased VOT domain-initially has not been found in French (Fougeron 1999, 2001) or Japanese (Onaka et al. 2002), or in stressed, accented, or domain-initial position in Dutch (Cho and McQueen 2005)—that is, in languages which do not manipulate aspiration to indicate stop voicing.[7] Thus, the different effects of prosodic factors on VOT values seem to reflect language-specific differences in the use of aspiration to signal the voicing contrast rather than prosodic structure.

In summary, the differential effects of durational variation induced by changes in rate, vowel length, and prosodic factors on VOT values across languages can be interpreted as adjusting the motor strategies to the perceptual demands of the language. Thus, aspiration or delayed VOT seems to be the primary cue to indicate the voicing distinction in stops in English, Icelandic, and the aspirated vs. unaspirated/voiced distinction in Thai, and positive VOT values have been found to vary with changes in local and global timing so as to maintain a constant perceptual distance across conditions. In contrast, positive VOT values have not been found to increase

approach is that Thai speakers also control vowel duration, and they instead manipulate this aspect of the signal so that information about aspiration/vowel duration is kept nearly proportional. That is, a stable ratio aspiration-to-voiced vowel can be maintained by changing the aspirated portion, the voiced vowel portion, or both, and Thai speakers may choose to adjust the voiced vowel portion. The difference in the results found by Kessinger and Blumstein (1997) and Onsuwan (2005) is intriguing and the source is hard to pin down. One possibility may be that longer durations due to rate have different effects than longer durations due to phonemic vowel length.

[7] Crucially, Dutch shows longer values for prevoicing in voiced stops in prosodically strong positions (Cho and McQueen 2005), suggesting that the contrast between voiced and voiceless stops in this language is primarily cued by presence or absence of vocal-fold vibration during the consonant constriction.

with changes in rate or prosodic conditions in French, Japanese, Catalan, Spanish, Dutch, or for unaspirated stops in Thai; thus it can be deduced that in these languages onset of glottal vibration is timed relative to the beginning of the vowel and the short VOT values result from known aerodynamic factors. Crucially, these languages use voicing during the consonant constriction for voiced stops as a cue to the voicing contrast. Accordingly, voicing duration (i.e. negative VOT) has been found to adjust to temporal variation.

18.4 VOWEL DURATION BEFORE VOICED AND VOICELESS OBSTRUENTS

Another phenomenon that has been investigated in these terms is the use of vowel duration as a cue to consonant voicing in English (Port and Dalby 1982; Summers 1987; de Jong 1991 1995, 2004). It is known that vowels in English are substantially shorter before tautosyllabic voiceless obstruents than before voiced obstruents (Peterson and Lehiste 1960). The magnitude of the difference in English is much greater than can be explained by purely physiological factors (J. Ohala 1983*b*), thus vowel-duration differences seem to be articulatorily targeted by speakers and used by listeners as a reliable cue to voicing in the obstruent (Chen 1970; Raphael 1972). The cue to postvocalic obstruent voicing has been characterized as a change in the ratio of the vowel-to-consonant duration in the syllable, and a similar difference in vowel/consonant duration ratio has been found for other Germanic languages (Standard German, Bavarian, Swedish, and Icelandic, cited in Port 1996). The shortening of vowels before tautosyllabic voiceless consonants is undoubtedly part of the phonology of these Germanic languages. Other languages do not seem to manipulate vowel duration as a cue to voicing contrasts.

As noted earlier, vowels are known to be longer in stressed than in unstressed position, thus manipulating stress is a natural way to vary segment duration and observe its effects on phonological specifications targeted by speakers vs. mechanical effects. Summers (1987) and de Jong (1991, 1995) investigated the effect of stress on English vowel duration before voiced and voiceless obstruents, and before consonants differing in manner (e.g., vowels are longer before fricatives than stops; House and Fairbanks 1953; Peterson and Lehiste 1960), among other factors. I re-examined de Jong's (1991) results plotting them the same way that I did in Figures 18.1 and 18.2. These are presented in Figure 18.3. Vowel duration is shown on the ordinate, and the stressed and unstressed conditions on the abscissa, for voicing and manner contexts for two speakers.

Figure 18.3 shows that, in general, vowels are longer in stressed than in unstressed position due to the known effects of prosodic prominence on segment duration. The bottom panels show that the difference in the duration of the vowels before stops and

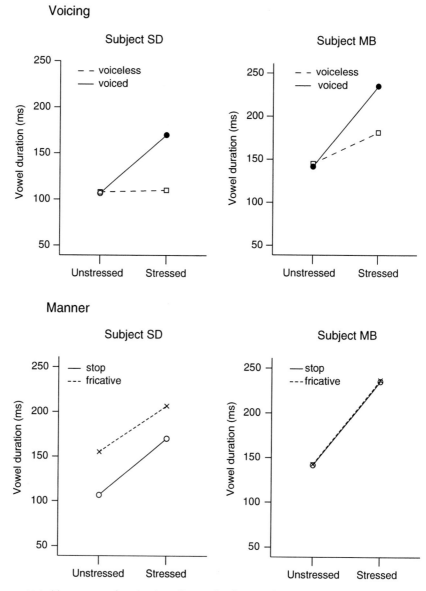

FIGURE 18.3. Top: average duration in milliseconds of vowels followed by voiced (filled circles) and voiceless (empty squares) stops in unstressed and stressed contexts for speakers SD and MB. Bottom: average duration of vowels followed by stops (Xs) and fricatives (empty circles) in unstressed and stressed contexts. (Adapted from de Jong 1991)

fricatives tends to be uniform across prosodic conditions, that is, consonant manner effects on vowel duration remain constant across changes in stress conditions (as shown by the parallel lines). The lack of interaction between stress and consonant manner on vowel duration suggests that manner effects do not participate in the temporal readjustments triggered by changes in stress, but originate at a lower level. The same was not true for vowel duration differences before consonants differing in voicing. The results in the top panels in the figure show a significant interaction between stress and consonant voicing on vowel duration: stress increased the duration of vowels before voiceless consonants by a smaller amount than that before voiced consonants. Similar results were found by de Jong (2004). Such non uniform effects of stress on vowel duration differences cannot be explained from physiological factors, but may be explained for perceptual reasons: if preceding vowel duration is actively controlled by English speakers to cue consonant voicing, then one way to maintain a constant perceptual contrast across stress/rate conditions is to adjust the magnitude of the vowel duration differences before voiced and voiceless consonants to the duration of the vowels (that is, a larger difference for longer, stressed, vowels and a smaller one for shorter, unstressed, vowels). This is what is shown in the top panels in Figure 18.3. The finding that the magnitude of the vowel duration difference is proportional to (i.e. varies with) the duration of the vowels across stress conditions suggests that vowel duration before voiced/voiceless codas is linguistically specified and actively controlled by the speaker.

Summers (1987) found comparable results for his three American English subjects. He interpreted the interaction between stress and consonant voicing on vowel duration as an effect of "incompressibility" of segment durations beyond some minimum value (Klatt 1976). Thus, destressing did not decrease the duration of vowels before voiceless obstruents by a larger amount due to a limit on minimum vowel duration. However, the vowel-duration values before voiceless obstruents found by Summers (mean 162 ms) are over and beyond the minimum vowel durations observed by other investigators (e.g. Peterson and Lehiste 1960). Consequently, the smaller differences in vowel duration before voiceless obstruents found in unstressed vs. stressed position (vis-à-vis those before voiced obstruents) cannot be satisfactorily accounted for in terms of incompressibility. I favor the interpretation that vowel shortening before voiceless codas, used to cue consonant voicing, is a language-specific and conventionalized aspect of English which is adjusted to durational differences induced by stress, while manner influences are a result of speech production processes.

Caisse (1988) examined the effects of post-vocalic consonant voicing and a number of other factors (vowel height, vowel tenseness, post-vocalic consonant manner, and utterance position) on vowel duration in American English. She manipulated the duration of the vowel in a different way. Following Klatt (1976), Caisse considered the vowel in a certain condition to be the inherent duration of the vowel and attempted to model the vowel durations under other conditions as derived from the inherent duration. She found that the duration of vowels before voiced obstruents differed from that before voiceless obstruents by an amount proportional to the duration of the vowel, that is, it showed a multiplicative effect, whereas the duration of vowels in other conditions differed by a constant number of milliseconds, that is, it showed an additive effect. She suggested that multiplicative effects are centrally controlled and occur prior to additive effects, which are peripheral.

Cuartero (forthcoming) examined the effect of varying speaking rate on vowels preceding voiced and voiceless obstruents in Catalan and English. Catalan has a contrast in obstruent voicing (except word-finally) indicated by presence or absence of glottal-fold vibration during the consonant constriction, as stated in Section 18.3. Vowel-duration differences before voiced and voiceless obstruents are presumed to be merely mechanical in this language. Cuartero measured vowel duration before tautosyllabic voiced and voiceless consonants in bisyllabic sequences in English (e.g. *bad day, bat time*) and Catalan (e.g. *pot dur* [dd], *pot tou* [tt]; coda obstruents in Catalan take on the voicing specification of a following voiced or voiceless consonant within the same phrase due to regressive voicing assimilation). The results in Figure 18.4 show that, in English, slower speaking rates increased the size of the intended vowel duration contrast before voiced and voiceless stops, that is to say, vowel-duration differences are proportional to the duration of the vowel, larger for longer vowels at slower rates and smaller for shorter vowels at fast rates. In contrast, Catalan vowels before voiced consonants are slightly longer than before voiceless consonants but the size of the consonant voicing effect remains stable across rates, as predicted for phonetic effects.

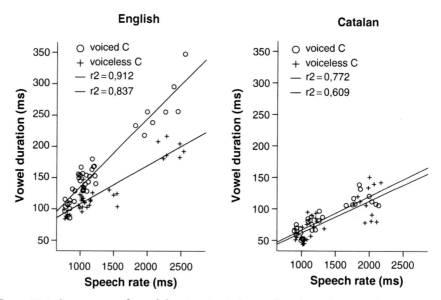

FIGURE 18.4. Scattergrams of vowel duration (vertical axis) plotted as a function of speaking rate (horizontal axis) for English and Catalan vowels followed by tautosyllabic voiceless (crosses) and voiced (empty circles) obstruents. Each dot represents one observation. (Adapted from Cuartero forthcoming).

De Jong and Zawaydeh (2002; see de Jong 2004 for further discussion) studied the effect of stress and focus on vowels followed by voiced and voiceless consonants in Arabic (e.g. *baada* "he extinguished" ~ *baata* "he stayed overnight") and on phonemically contrastive long and short vowels (e.g. *bada* "he started" ~ *baada* "he extinguished"). They found that whereas the voicing effects on vowel duration were the same in stressed and unstressed syllables, the difference between contrastive long and short vowels was larger in stressed than in unstressed position. In other words, stress increased the size of the intended vowel duration contrast, but not the size of the mechanical consonant voicing effect. In fact, de Jong (2004) notes that the most compelling evidence for the claim that English uses vowel duration differences for voicing contrasts in consonants while Arabic does not, is provided by Munro (1993). Munro reports that Arabic speakers, who do not have specified vowel duration cues to consonant voicing (as shown in de Jong and Zawaydeh 2002), exhibit larger durational differences as they become more proficient in English.

Braunschweiler (1997) obtained similar results for German as those found for English, manipulating vowel duration, rather than stress or rate. German has a contrast in obstruent voicing (except word-finally) and in vowel length. Vowels preceding voiced stops are significantly longer than vowels preceding voiceless stops (Kohler 1984), thus vowel duration is a systematic acoustic correlate of consonant voicing. Braunschweiler systematically varied vowel length, /a/ ~ /aː/, before word-medial contrasting stops /p, t, k/ ~ /b, d, g/ in bisyllabic words (e.g. ['bakən], ['laːkən]; ['flagə], ['laːgən]). His study allows us to observe whether consonant voicing effects on preceding vowel duration vary with the length of the vowel. His data (Table 1, p. 363) show a significant interaction between consonant voicing and vowel length on vowel duration, such that phonologically short vowels were lengthened by a smaller amount (i.e. half as much) before voiced stops than long vowels. The difference in absolute durational values, however, results in a constant vowel-duration ratio before voiced and voiceless stops for long (ratio: 1.20) and short vowels (ratio: 1.20), as predicted for effects actively targeted by the speaker. Other temporal correlates of consonant voicing measured by Braunschweiler (e.g. consonant closure) did not result in constant ratios.

18.5 DISTINCTIVE VS. NON-DISTINCTIVE FEATURES

On reviewing the effects of speaking rate, stress, and syllable type on speech features, a confounding factor is that some of the features (e.g. vowel length and aspiration) are phonemic in some languages, whereas they are the result of language-specific phonological processes in others. One would expect that whether features are contrastive or not would have an effect on their phonetic behavior. However, a review of the literature on the effects of durational variation shows very similar effects for "lexically contrastive" and "allophonic" effects. For example, studies on the effects of speaking rate and stress on distinctive vowel length show similar results to those for allophonic vowel duration effects in English and German reviewed in Section 18.4. The contrastive short and long vowel distinction in Arabic (Port *et al.* 1980; de Jong and Zawaydeh 2002), Japanese (Hirata 2004), Icelandic (Pind 1999), and Thai (two speakers[8] in Svastikula 1986) shows a non-uniform effect of stress/speaking rate on vowel duration. A significant interaction is found between rate (stress) and vowel length on vowel-duration, such that a slower speaking rate (stress) lengthens long vowels by a greater amount than it does short vowels, in such a way that the relationship between long and short vowels remains constant across changes in rate/stress. The interaction between speaking rate/stress and vowel length thus reflects centrally controlled vowel-length differences. Conflicting evidence comes from Korean (Magen and Blumstein 1993), where long and short vowels are reported to be equally affected by changes in speaking rate (i.e. rate increases the duration of long and short vowels by an equal amount). Their data (table 4, p. 400), however, show that a slow rate lengthens long vowels by a larger amount that it does short vowels, though the interaction does not reach significance. The small asymmetries found by Magen and Blumstein may reflect the loss of the vowel-length distinction in Seoul Korean, which seems to be an ongoing sound change among younger speakers (Magen and Blumstein 1993; Colhoun and Kim 1976).

Similarly, comparable effects of rate and stress on VOT values in languages where aspiration is contrastive (e.g. Thai) and in languages where it is generally considered to be allophonic (e.g. English, but see Cho and Ladefoged 1999 and Cho and McQueen 2005 for the view that aspiration is the primary contrasting feature in English) were reviewed in Section 18.3. The similar effects of durational variation for contrastive and allophonic effects suggest that features actively targeted by the speaker, whether contrastive, allophonic, or possibly language-and dialect-specific phonetic detail, are present in the input to speech production and participate of the higher level temporal readjustments triggered by changes in durational factors.

18.6 CONCLUSIONS

The conclusion we can draw from the studies reviewed is that not all aspects of speech motor behavior have the same status vis-à-vis the linguistic system. Some are determined by universal physical and physiological factors (or by speaker-specific motor organization, which will vary idiosyncratically from speaker to speaker). Other aspects are under the control of the speaker and reflect some part of the linguistic

---

[8] Two other speakers in Svastikula's (1986) study did not show the expected interaction between rate and vowel length, suggesting idiosyncratic or dialectal variation (e.g. use a phonetic correlate other than vowel duration to cue contrastive vowel length).

code.[9] Manipulating the temporal dimension by changes in speaking rate, stress, and syllable type is a useful tool for determining whether, or the degree to which, a particular phonetic effect is linguistically specified for a given speech community or is merely a product of execution. Thus variations in the timing of segments have no effect, or phonetically predictable effects, on mechanical features, whereas they trigger the temporal readjustment of linguistic specifications in a way that is not predictable from phonetic factors, but which can be explained in terms of the perceptual demands of the language (thus maintaining a constant perceptual distance across changing temporal conditions). I have argued that the effects of durational differences on planned vs. mechanical properties of the speech signal are congruent with what we know about speech production and speech perception.

The results reviewed also show that the effect of temporal variation on phonetic features differs from language to language. The findings suggest language-specific use of phonetic dimensions and corresponding language-specific patterns of motor control in order to achieve the intended acoustic–perceptual goals. Further cross-linguistic studies are needed to identify the phonetic dimensions, and the preferred values of these dimensions, used in different languages that have to be stated in the grammar of the language, and the effects that are governed by phonetic implementation rules. Finally, a word of caution is in order. Studies on general patterns of motor control, prosodic structure, and speech perception too often make general claims based on empirical data from one single language. On occasion such data reflect language-specific patterns that cannot be generalized to other languages before a substantial number of unrelated languages are tested.

---

[9] See also the results of Roengpitya (this volume) on the adjustment of Thai tonal contours to durational variations.

PART V

Phonotactic and Phonological Knowledge

19

What's in CVC-like Things?

Ways and Means to Look at Phonological Units Across Languages

Bruce L. Derwing

19.1 ON DEFINING THE NOTIONS ''LANGUAGE'' AND ''LINGUISTIC STRUCTURE''

Definitions matter. How one defines a problem, in fact, goes a long way in characterizing the nature of that problem, no matter how arbitrary the definition may be. A case in point is the classical dilemma about whether or not "a sound is produced" when a tree falls in the forest if there is no one around to hear it. Clearly, the answer to this question depends crucially on how one defines the term "sound" in the first place. If sound is defined as a physical construct (as "vibrations transmitted through a [physical] . . . medium"; *American Heritage Dictionary*: 172), then, of course, a sound is always produced whenever a tree falls; but if sound is defined as a psychological construct ("the sensation stimulated in the organs of hearing by such vibrations"; *loc. cit.*), then it is critical that a living human (or other hearing creature) be present to appreciate the experience.

In similar terms, the kind of research that is carried out in linguistics, as well as the interpretation of the significance of that research, depends crucially on how such notions as "language" and "linguistic structure" are defined. In the remainder of this section, therefore, I will outline three popular conceptions of the nature of language

Much of the research described here was supported by research grants from the Social Sciences and Humanities Research Council of Canada and by the Chiang Ching Kuo Foundation of Taiwan. Jane Tsay should be especially credited for her assistance in the construction of the Minnan stimuli, as well as for supervising the collection of the list recall data in that language. The author also expresses his thanks to Tracey Derwing, James Myers, Terry Nearey, Sally Rice, and Gary Libben for helpful comments and suggestions, to Ron Thomson for much technical assistance, and to Yeo Bom Yoon and Sam Wang for serving as sounding boards for all things Korean and Chinese, respectively.

and briefly discuss some of their most important ramifications. This is followed in Section 19.2 by an introduction to the kinds of units that this chapter is concerned with, together with some naturalistic evidence in their favor, and in Section 19.3 a variety of kinds of experimental evidence will be adduced, focusing on some key differences between English and Korean. Finally, in Section 19.4, a new study of the syllable structure of the Minnan language will be presented, followed by a few concluding remarks on the rationale for the particular philosophical and methodological positions adopted throughout.

19.1.1 Language as a formal system

One way to view language is as a purely abstract formal system, having no realization in any accessible or even well-defined empirical space. People who adopt this view may talk about language and linguistic structure as "things", implied to have kind of vague existence "out there" somewhere, perhaps, but little is said about either the ontological status of the theoretical constructs involved or what place in our universe these entities may actually occupy. Linguists who regard their field as a fully autonomous discipline would seem to fall into this camp as their practice is consistent with the view of a language as a purely formal object or abstract "set of sentences" (as in Chomsky 1957: 13).[1]

Without debating the full implications of this position here (see Derwing 1980 for further discussion), I see the abstractionist approach as having one serious drawback from the point of view of the aspiring linguistic scientist, in that it provides no real-world empirical entities to test linguistic constructs against. Thus, if a formal linguist proposes—typically on the basis of so-called "primary linguistic data"[2]—that a language has such-and-such a syntactic, morphological, or phonological unit or other structure, they cannot access the "language" itself to check the constructs out, as no hint is provided about where such a thing might be found. (Contrast the case of a geologist who posits a particular internal structure for some new or unusual mineral

---

[1] Chomsky, of course, later changed his philosophy, but not his methodology. What counts in this discussion, naturally, is not so much the philosophical position espoused but rather how language is treated in practice as this is what determines the kind of evidence that actually serves to constrain theory construction. Thus, for example, an approach that disregards psycholinguistic evidence as something "external" to the tasks of theory construction and evaluation in linguistics will certainly be open to a much broader range of theories, but there is a potentially heavy price to be paid in terms of the reduced psychological plausibility—or even testability—of the theoretical constructs and principles that result from such an effort.

[2] This is data about real or potential surface forms (the language product), supplemented by certain native speaker intuitions (often very informally elicited) about those forms and their meanings. It is important to recognize that all grammars—not to mention all linguistic theories—are considerably underspecified by such data, which explains the need to invoke various arbitrary assumptions about seemingly empirical issues. One good example of this is the economy of storage assumption that figured prominently in the theory of classical generative phonology, and which Halle and Clements (1983: 2) characterized as the proposal "that human storage space for memorizing words is at a premium."

or rock formation, who can carry out a microscopic or chemical examination of the physical rock itself.)

As a consequence of this inability to carry out definitive empirical tests, the formal linguist is forced to enlist a variety of subjective evaluation criteria, which typically include some form of simplicity, economy, or universal generality, as if models lacking such properties were of no real theoretical interest.[3]

19.1.2 Language as a physical reality

Suppose, however, that we seek to test some of our fundamental assumptions empirically, transcending the limits of the traditional data in the field; may we in that case follow the geologist's lead and view language as a "physical reality", analogous to a rock, and do our testing in the material domain? Bloomfield seemed to adopt such a tack when he wrote that "[i]n the division of scientific labor, the linguist deals only with the speech-signal" (Bloomfield 1933: 32), implying that linguistic structure was part of the physical stream of speech (acoustic waveform). Halle went even further in this direction when he argued that the status of the phoneme in linguistics was "analogous to that of electrons in physics" and that phonemes were "every bit as real [physically?] as any other theoretical entity in science" (Halle 1964: 325).

However, while physicists have made much progress in accessing their electrons over the years, phoneticians seem no closer today than ever to isolating even the lowly segment as a physical unit—which is to say nothing of all the other kinds of entities (syllables, morphemes, words, lexical categories, phrases, clauses, sentences, etc.) that linguists posit as the raw material of hypothesized linguistic structures. It seems highly unlikely that any of these higher-order theoretical entities are ever going to be found even in the "wetware" of a physical brain, much less as part of the physical "stream of speech".

From the standpoint of accessibility for testing, therefore, linguistic units, structures, categories, etc. all seem to be best viewed neither as purely hypothetical entities, nor as entities that are intrinsic to utterances, but rather as entities that are attributed to utterances by speakers and hearers.

19.1.3 Language as a psychological reality

People who subscribe to the view of language as a "psychological reality"—whether they call themselves linguists, psycholinguists, or psychologists—typically view a language as a "mental code" that speakers know and use to internally convert

---

[3] By way of contrast, research to date on the mental lexicon shows quite convincingly that high redundancy, rather than economy, is the rule for word representations, with a premium placed neither on economy of storage nor even on efficiency of computation/retrieval, but rather on a factor that Libben (2006: 6) calls "maximization of opportunity".

thoughts into words and then into speech articulations, yielding physical sounds, and which hearers also use to convert perceived speech sounds back into meaningful thoughts.

In this conception of language, "language processes" (quite unlike grammatical or generative processes in the description of linguists) involve activities that speakers and hearers actually perform when they use language, whether as speakers or as hearers (or as signers and viewers, in the case of sign language). Theories of the units, structures, categories, and the like that are involved in these real-life, real-time processes can thus be tested (at least in principle) against the linguistic knowledge and abilities that real speakers and hearers have and use. From this perspective, then, "a linguistic unit at any 'level' exists as a unit only because the language user treats it as a unit" and "linguistic structure is not something that is 'built up' out of utterances or 'overlaid' upon [them], but is . . . something which receives its only possible empirical realization as part of the language process of speech production and comprehension" (Derwing 1973: 305). In short, linguistic structure is viewed in this framework as psychological structure, and from this it follows immediately that the appropriate kinds of tests for linguistic constructs ought to be psychological tests.

With this understanding in mind, I will devote the rest of this chapter to an attempt to illustrate how the empirical base of linguistics can be usefully enhanced by interpreting some of its fundamental constructs (such as its basic phonological units) in psychological terms and by exposing them to critical evaluation by various kinds of psycholinguistic experiments.

19.2 NATURALISTIC EVIDENCE FOR SOME POSSIBLE PHONOLOGICAL UNITS

Among the many basic building blocks that linguists employ in theory construction, there are quite a number of phonological units that seem to be excellent candidates for being psychologically real. In particular, the syllable, the rime, the onset, and the segment have all been involved in much theoretical speculation and experimental evaluation, as well as manifesting themselves in a variety of natural language activities that go beyond ordinary everyday language use.

The syllable, for example, plays a role in many English poetic metrical schemes, and the rime is used in rhyming poetry. Likewise, the poetic use of alliteration implies that special status might also be assigned to the onset, the natural complement of the rime, which is the consonant or consonants, if any, that occur before the vowel within the same syllable (such as the *st-* in the first syllable of *storage*).

Natural word blends also support an onset–rime analysis of the English syllable. The word *smog*, for example, created in the early twentieth century by some anonymous natural poet, is a blend of the words *smoke* and *fog*; significantly, the onset *sm-* of the first of these is combined with the rime -*og* of the second, thus slicing both words immediately before the vowel.

It has also been widely observed that the division of the English syllable into onset plus rime constituents is the basis of a once-popular language game called "Pig Latin", in which English-speaking children disguised their speech by pronouncing a word like *street* as *eet-stray*. Notice that this inversion involves removing the onset element *str-* from its original position before the vowel and moving it to a new position after the rime, then appending a new vowel nucleus *ay* (i.e. /e/) at the end. Once again, this kind of manipulation suggests that the natural breaking point within an English syllable is immediately before the vowel, and that the onset and the rime are its two main sub-components.

Finally, while the literature on spontaneous speech errors provides relatively little evidence in support of the rime per se as an intact unit in English (though such slips as *hunk of jeep* for *heap of junk* do, in fact, occur), Laubstein (1987) finds that switches involving the rime's complement, the onset (e.g. *cone fall* for *phone call*) are actually the most common type. Furthermore, an individual segment can be transported both into and out of an onset cluster, as when the accidental form *sprive* is created from *strive for perfection* (Laubstein 1987: 345).

Taken together, such natural, real-life examples usefully supplement the primary data of linguistic analyses, in suggesting that the English syllable may actually have a linguistically (i.e. psychologically) significant representation at three different levels, as shown in the tree diagram in (1) for the English monosyllabic word *dog*.

(1)

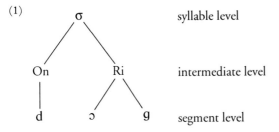

If we view the naturalistic evidence in certain other languages, however, the syllable begins to take on a rather different look. For example, Gim (1987) describes a language game that is played in Korea that involves inserting a phonological string not before the vowel of a monosyllable (i.e. at the boundary between onset and rime) but rather after its vowel, dividing it into components that have come to be known (after Vennemann 1988) as the "body" and the "coda". This kind of manipulation suggests that the onset–rime division may not be universal and that there may be at least two fundamentally different kinds of syllable structure to be found among the world's languages. As shown in (2a), the first of these is the so-called right-branching structure of English, where a CVC syllable is broken into a light onset (C) and a heavy rime, with the vowel joining the heavier, more complex unit on the right (VC); while the second of these, shown in (2b) in the diagram, is the one hypothesized for Korean (see Yoon 1995), where the vowel links with the onset to form a heavy body unit (CV) on the left, with the lighter coda unit (C) on the right. In support of this distinction, it is perhaps also significant that there is no tradition of rhyming poetry in Korean, with poetic meter established instead on the basis of a syllable count (Yoon 1995: 11).

(2) a.   b.

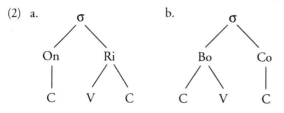

In short, what these scattered, informal observations provide for us is a rather strong indication that units like the syllable and some of its various sub-components, such as the rime, the onset, the body, and the coda, as well as individual V or C segments, may all play a significant role in the mental linguistic codes that different speakers use, and the experimental tests described below were carried out to assess the correctness of these suggestions.

19.3 SOME EXPERIMENTAL PARADIGMS

Consider first the rime, if only because it has attracted the most experimental attention to date. The first studies involved tasks that were quite self-consciously modeled after some of the naturalistic activities already described, but in a controlled, experimental setting.

19.3.1 Experimental word games in English and Korean

Experimental word blending is a case in point. If onset–rime word blends like *smog* occur naturally in English, would we not expect that speakers would split experimental stimuli at the same onset–rime boundary? This possibility was explored first by Treiman (1983), using a production task with nonsense stimuli; she showed that the prevocalic break point was indeed highly preferred by native English speakers.

Was the rime a universal unit, however, as many theorists also suggested (cf. Fudge 1987; Kaye 1989)? The answer to this question required the testing of speakers of other languages, beginning with those, like Korean, where there was already anecdotal evidence that the body and not the rime was the operative sub-syllabic unit. Using a forced-choice version of the word-blending task, Derwing *et al.* (1993) carried out some experimental word blending studies with Korean speakers, comparing their results with those of Wiebe and Derwing (1994), who used the same approach with

English. Examples of stimuli used in those studies, which illustrate the patterns with real-word inputs and nonsense outputs, were as follows:

(3)   a. English: SIEVE   + FUZZ → SUZZ (= onset + rime blend)
                   SIEVE   + FUZZ → SIZZ (= body + coda blend)
      b. Korean: THONG + SEM   → THEM[4] (= onset + rime blend)
                   THONG + SEM   → THOM (= body + coda blend)

As expected, the onset-rime blends were preferred by the English speakers; the Korean speakers, however, preferred the body-coda blends.

A second experimental word game contrasting English and Korean involved an oral unit reduplication exercise, whereby either the rime of a simple CVC syllable was copied at the end of a stimulus (task #1, below) or else the body was copied at the beginning (task #2).

(4)   Task #1: SAN → SAN-AN (= copying rime at end)
      Task #2: SAN → SA-SAN (= copying body at beginning)

Note that both of these tasks involve reduplicating a unit of the same size (two segments), without creating any new consonantal combinations in either case. As reported in Yoon and Derwing (2001), these results, too, showed a difference between the two languages, with the English speakers proving better at the rime-copying task, while the Korean speakers were better at the body-copying task.

19.3.2 Global sound-similarity judgments in English and Korean

A third approach used with these languages involved the elicitation of global sound similarity judgments (SSJs) for selected word pairs. Following up on the earlier work of Vitz and Winkler (1973) and others with English speakers, Derwing *et al.* (1986) found that, for simple CVC pairs, a shared rime element (VC) contributed more to similarity judgment scores than a shared initial CV.

In the much more elaborate Korean study carried out by Yoon (1995), real word CVC-pairs were incorporated that illustrated all possible types of segmental comparisons, ranging from no segments in common to all segments in common, as illustrated in Table 19.1. Fifty-six such test pairs were presented to 30 university students in Korea, who rated each for similarity in sound on a ten-point scale. The mean similarity ratings that emerged from this experiment for the seven non-identical pair-types were partitioned into four Fisher Least Significant Difference groupings, as summarized in (5) (where the numbers in parentheses indicate the number of segments that were matched in each case).

---

[4] The Korean nonsense syllables THONG and THEM are written in a standard transliteration system that affords them a purely superficial visual similarity to real English words.

TABLE 19.1. Types of stimulus pairs used in the Korean SSJ experiment

No. of matched phonemes	Sub-syllabic units matched	Examples
0	None	pan-mət
1	Onset	pan-pət
1	Vowel	pan-mat
1	Coda	pan-mən
2	Body	pan-pat
2	Rime	pan-man
2	Margins	pan-pən
3	All	pan-pan

(5) | Bo(2) | > | Ri(2), Mar(2) | > | On(1), V(1), Co(1) | > | None(0) |

Notice that the three comparisons involving just one matched segment (in the third box from the left) were not differentiated in the similarity judgments of the speakers; however, when two matched segments were involved, the items that shared a common body unit (CV) were judged to be significantly more similar than those that shared either a rime (VC) or the consonantal margins (C . . . C). Thus, for Korean, it was a shared initial CV that enhanced judged sound similarity ratings, while a shared final rime contributed no more to the similarity scores than a shared initial and final consonant, which was just the opposite of the English result.

19.3.3 Concept formation in Korean

Another approach that has been used with Korean is concept formation. Though too complex to describe in any detail here, an experiment using this technique demonstrated that a set of disyllabic words containing the common body sequence KA- as part of either syllable (e.g. *KANG.CO* or *SIM.KAK*, where the period is used to show the syllable break) were significantly easier to identify as a class than a set containing the common rime sequence -AK in either syllable (e.g. *CAK.SIM* or *SIM.KAK*). Although this task has not yet been used with English speakers, the results for Korean were consistent with all of the other findings in showing that the body was a more salient element in this language than the rime (see Yoon and Derwing 2001 for details).

19.3.4 A new list-recall task for non-literate participants

Despite these many congruent findings, there was still a nagging concern that literacy might have been a factor in our results, particularly for Korean. This was because there is a feature in the standard Korean orthography that might of itself have inclined

FIGURE 19.1. Korean orthographic representation for the word SAN 'mountain'

the university students we tested to associate the vowel of a CVC syllable more closely with its preceding consonant than its following consonant. This convention is one that often involves writing the CV ("body") portion of a syllable on a line above the final C ("coda") portion, as in the example at Figure 19.1 above for the Korean word SAN (meaning "mountain"), where the letters representing SA occur over the one representing "N". Since this convention affects roughly half of the Korean syllabic inventory, the only recourse, it seemed, was to design a completely new type of experiment that could be used with non-literate speakers, whose results would not be influenced by knowledge of the writing system at all. For this purpose it was convenient to target non-literate preschoolers, for whom the following "list-recall" experiment proved quite manageable.

Thinking that having a shared rime might enhance the recall of a list of otherwise heterogeneous words in English, I devised a study using nonsense CVC syllables as stimuli (to avoid frequency effects). These syllables were assigned to lists of three or four words each, each of which belonged to one of two sets, designated as either "rime-sharing" or "body-sharing". In the first set, the words in each list rhymed, while all those in the second had a common initial CV element, as shown in the following examples for English:

(6)   a. One list in rime-sharing set: HOKE, MOKE, NOKE, LOKE
       b. One list in body-sharing set: TEM, TEP, TENG, TETCH

Each list (which, of course, involved a different specific rime or body element in each case) was then assigned to a card containing pictures of nonsense creatures, with the words designated as their "names".

In the experiment itself, the picture cards were presented in random order to young English-speaking children who had been categorized either as "readers" or "non-readers" on the basis of a simple but carefully constructed multiple-choice reading test, which is described in Yoon and Derwing (2001). After a fixed number of repetitions, each participant was then asked to recall the names of the creatures described on each card, and tabulations were made of the number of correct responses. As expected, the English-speaking children, both readers and non-readers, were able to remember more names from the rime-sharing lists than from the body-sharing ones, attesting once again to the special status of a rime unit in this language.

A corresponding study was then carried out for Korean, which also involved both rime-sharing and body-sharing sets, as well as a Korean version of the reading test.

When sufficient readers and non-readers were identified to conduct the main experiment, the list recall test was carried out with 20 participants in each reading category, and with 20 items in each rime-sharing or body-sharing set. The results were very clear: just as in the English case, the readers and non-readers performed in much the same way, but this time performance was better for both groups in recalling the body-sharing items than the rime-sharing items.

Even when orthographic knowledge was eliminated from the picture, therefore, the body still emerged as the more salient unit in Korean, as opposed to the rime in English, strongly attesting to a fundamental difference in the structures employed by speakers in the two languages.

19.4 ADAPTING THE LIST RECALL PARADIGM TO MINNAN CHINESE

In a new study reported for the first time here, Jane Tsay and I extended the list recall paradigm to a Chinese language called Minnan, a dialect of which is widely spoken in Taiwan. This language was selected primarily because it manifests a phenomenon of nasal harmony between a voiced onset of a syllable and its vowel, whereas a nasalized vowel is incompatible with a following nasal coda (see H. Wang 1995 for further discussion). Thus the following syllable types either occur or do not occur, as indicated, ignoring tones:

(7)   ba bat ban mã vs. *bã *ma *mãn

In short, when a syllable begins with a voiced consonant, either both the initial C and the V are nasalized, or neither is, and a nasal coda consonant can follow only in the latter situation. Taken together, these constraints conspire to suggest that the syllable in Minnan may have a left-branching structure, much like Korean, in which the body (CV) is separated from the coda as a distinct and cohesive phonological unit.[5] An extension of the list-recall paradigm to this language thus seemed very much in order. Unfortunately, however, Minnan, like Mandarin, uses almost all of its syllabic resources for purposes of real vocabulary, thus manifesting a rather extreme paucity of "nonsense" syllables, certainly far too few to allow for the completion of multiple lists of even three rhyming or body-sharing monosyllables each, all with matching tone. In the Minnan version of this experiment, therefore, we decided to make up sets of novel compound words, combining nine meaningless first elements (for convenience I will

---

[5] Traditionally, Mandarin Chinese has a right-branching syllable structure, like English, and there is speech error evidence (e.g. Shen 1993; Wan 1999) to support this for the modern language, as well. It should not be assumed that Minnan is the same, however, as its phonology differs in many respects from Mandarin.

loosely refer to these as the "prefixes") with 27 real, meaningful second elements (the "roots") that had the requisite rime- or body-sharing properties.

Using the nonsense syllable $*GA^{53}$ as an example of a Minnan "prefix",[6] one three-item rime-sharing list of novel compounds was created using the three real words LAM^{55} "cage", KAM^{55} "orange", and $TSAM^{55}$ "hairpin" as "roots" (i.e. $*GA^{53}$-LAM^{55}, $*GA^{53}$-KAM^{55}, $*GA^{53}$-$TSAM^{55}$), and a parallel body-sharing list was created by combining the same prefix with the real words LAM^{55} "cage", LAN^{55} "callus", and $LANG^{55}$ "sparse" (i.e. $*GA^{53}$-LAM^{55}, $*GA^{53}$-LAN^{55}, $*GA^{53}$-$LANG^{55}$). Eighteen such lists of three items each were thus created for the Minnan list recall study, half with rime-sharing and half with body-sharing elements, and these were randomly ordered and assigned as names to nonsense creatures that were pictured on a separate card for each list.

Although all of the stimuli were now meaningless *in toto* (since their first elements were all meaningless), each did have a meaningful sub-component as their second elements, so the problem of frequency could not be ignored. The approach we took to deal with that is illustrated in the two sample lists provided above, which both contain the root LAM^{55}. By the judicious selection of roots to go with the prefixes, the 27 roots in each set were identical for the two tasks, albeit distributed differently on the lists that were assigned to the picture cards. Thus any frequency effects for the real elements were distributed equally across both sets, giving neither an advantage over the other. And since all of the picture cards were mixed together for presentation to participants and shuffled anew before each presentation, a rough parity was also established between the first and the second exposure to each element for the participants overall, thereby neutralizing any order or recall effects.

Otherwise, the procedures used for the Minnan version of the experiment were the same as in the earlier English and Korean versions, although a few new complications did arise in the scoring. For example, how should a response be scored if participants erred in their recall of the "prefix" element but recalled the "root" perfectly well? Under a completely strict scoring system, of course, any errors at all would be sufficient to label a response as incorrect. Some errors, however—such as errors in the prefix and even some mistakes involving the roots, such as using the wrong tone—did not seem to bear on the crucial research question, which was whether the roots would be easier to recall if they all rhymed or if they shared a common CV-element instead. In the end, therefore, we developed a dual scoring system: a "strict" one in which any mistake in a response was sufficient to score it as an error, and also a "broad" one which ignored those mistakes that seemed to be irrelevant to the main issue at hand.

In order to distinguish readers from non-readers, a simple multiple-choice reading test was constructed along the same general lines as the one used in the earlier English and Korean research. Since Minnan is not a written language, this test was constructed

---

[6] The suprafixed numbers indicate tones.

in Mandarin, which is the medium of instruction in all of the Chinese schools in Taiwan. Like its English and Korean counterparts, this was a 20-item picture test involving simple high frequency words (such as MAO[1] "cat", CHUAN[2] "ship", and MA[3] "horse"), with four systematically varied orthographic representations presented below each picture to choose from. Unlike the English and Korean versions, however, the Mandarin reading test was presented in two forms, one for each of the orthographic systems that are used in Taiwan.

The first of these writing systems involves the traditional Chinese "characters", which we had no reason to suspect would influence the results of the study in any particular way and which were included merely as a standard test of literacy. The main focus of the reading test, therefore, was on the second writing system learned in school, called Zhuyin Fuhao. This alphabet-like system is unique to Taiwan, where it is used for written work in the early grades while children are still struggling with the major task of learning the standard ideographic characters. Its relevance here is highlighted by the fact that it is based on the traditional initial-final interpretation of the Chinese syllable, which is roughly equivalent to an onset–rime scheme. As seen in the following example for the Mandarin words SAN[1] "three" and SHAN[1] "mountain" in Figure 19.2, this system provides a common symbol for the rime element -AN[1] that is shared by these words.

Since this transcription system consistently provides symbols for all of the possible rime elements in Mandarin, it is clear that it might easily inculcate a bias in speakers who know it to regard the syllables of their language as having an onset–rime structure, too, and this awareness might in turn affect their judgments and responses in psycholinguistic experiments intended to explore such issues, even in a different but closely related language.[7] In any event, all readers and non-readers involved in the study now under discussion were assigned to these categories on the basis of their performance on both versions of the Mandarin reading test, using the same reading

SAN[1]   SHAN[1]

Figure 19.2. Zhuyin Fuhao transcriptions for the Mandarin words SAN[1] "three" and SHAN[1] "mountain"

[7] H. Wang (1996) presents a compelling case that skill at manipulating segments in Minnan can indeed be radically affected by familiarity with transcription systems learned for Mandarin.

score (RS) criteria as in the earlier English and Korean studies (see Yoon and Derwing 2001 for a statistical justification of the threshold values used).

All testing was carried out on the campus of the National Chung Cheng University, located near the city of Chiayi, Taiwan. The study involved 40 children, 20 of whom were classified as readers and 20 as non-readers; the list-recall results for all of these are summarized in Table 19.2 below.

Although the readers, who were typically older, performed better overall on both the rime-sharing and body-sharing sets, it can be seen from the table that their response pattern was the same on both, and the same was true whether the "strict" or the "broad" scoring system was used. In brief, the expected results emerged throughout, showing consistently better recall by all participant groups on the 27 names when they appeared on the body-sharing cards than when the same names appeared on the rime-sharing cards. We take this as good evidence that Minnan speakers do indeed treat the syllables of their language as a synthesis of distinct body and coda elements, with the nasal harmony phenomenon confined to the first of these.[8]

TABLE 19.2. Results of Minnan list recall experiments for Readers and Nonreaders ($N = 20$ each), using both "strict" and "broad" scoring systems; RS = score on 20-item Reading Test

Group results using the "strict" scoring system:

Nonreaders (RS < 9)			Readers (RS > 13)		
	Rime	*Body*		*Rime*	*Body*
Total correct	54	103	Total correct	85	121
Mean correct	2.7	5.2	Mean correct	4.3	6.1
Ttests:	$p < .001$			$p < .01$	
	(Body > Rime)			(Body > Rime)	

Group results using the "broad" scoring system:

Nonreaders (RS < 9)			Readers (RS > 13)		
	Rime	*Body*		*Rime*	*Body*
Total correct	140	176	Total correct	193	226
Mean correct	7.0	8.8	Mean correct	9.7	11.3
Ttests:	$p < .01$			$p < .01$	
	(Body > Rime)			(Body > Rime)	

[8] Notwithstanding this congruence of our results with the nasal harmony phenomenon, one reviewer expressed concern that the consistent CV shape of the nonsense "prefixes" might somehow have made it easier to recall the CVC-shaped "roots" from the body-sharing lists than from the rime-sharing lists. While this possibility cannot be dismissed out of hand and ought to be addressed in future research, we found no such effect in a parallel Mandarin study (not reported here) in which the recall stimuli all had a similar *CV-CVC structure.

19.5 CONCLUDING REMARKS

In this chapter I have discussed a variety of ways to look at the structure of language (from a philosophical perspective), as well as several means (from a methodological standpoint) to explore theoretical questions through psycholinguistic experimentation, focusing attention primarily on the problem of phonological units. It was obviously crucial to the exercise to have chosen the psychological domain as the one in which concepts like "language" and "linguistic structure" could be empirically defined, as this opened the door to evidence about how native speakers dealt with the hypothetical units postulated by linguistic theory. Such a step serves, of course, to reduce somewhat the autonomy of linguistics as a discipline, but the potential reward is great, for the more that assumptions can be replaced by psychologically valid constraints in linguistic theorizing, the more likely the resulting theoretical constructs are to be relevant to our understanding of what it means to learn and use a language.

As always, future research may force a reinterpretation of some or even all of the particular conclusions that have been arrived at here about the syllable structures of the three languages investigated, but even if that happens, we have no reason to think that the focus on language as a psychological phenomenon and the utilization of psycholinguistic experimentation to clarify its internal structure will likely be changed in any fundamental way. This is because we now have a sense that real progress is at last being made, largely for reasons predicted by our honoree two decades ago:

Real progress . . . would [likely] follow if an equal amount of imagination and enthusiasm were to be spent in the design and conduct of experiments as is currently spent in formulating the hypotheses that require testing.   (J. Ohala 1986: 12)

In short, after a surprisingly long gestation period, linguistics seems to be reaching the point where theory and experimentation are coming to be widely recognized to be but two sides of the same coin, and that this coin is the currency most readily accepted by the enterprise called "science".

20

The SLIP Technique as a Window on the Mental Preparation of Speech

Some Methodological Considerations

Sieb Nooteboom and Hugo Quené

20.1 INTRODUCTION

This chapter is about the so-called SLIP (Spoonerisms of Laboratory-Induced Predisposition) technique for eliciting spoonerisms. This technique was introduced in 1974 and has since been used by a number of researchers to study aspects of the mental production of speech. Recently the technique has seen a revival. A major question in many of the published studies is, "What is the cause of lexical bias?" Lexical bias is the phenomenon by which phonological speech errors more often lead to real words than to non-words, when a priori probabilities are equal. According to some, lexical bias is caused by feedback of activation between phonemes and words (Stemberger 1985; Dell 1986), whereas others claim that lexical bias is caused by self-monitoring of inner speech rejecting and correcting non-words more often than real words (Levelt 1989; Levelt *et al.* 1999). This issue is important because it reflects two different ways of looking at the architecture of the mental processes involved in human speech production. Researchers in the feedback camp believe that, although one may distinguish between different hierarchically related components of the speech-production system, such as a component for retrieving and ordering lexical items and a component for retrieving and ordering phonemes, the hierarchical relation is only partial because there is interaction in the form of immediate feedback of activation between successive components.

Researchers in the self-monitoring camp, on the contrary, are convinced that there is no immediate feedback between successive components of the production system. For that reason, they have to account for lexical bias with a mechanism other

We are grateful to Huub van den Bergh for his assistance in running the logistic regression analyses.

than feedback. The alternative explanation is found in self-monitoring of inner speech detecting, rejecting, and repairing non-words more often than real words. This long-standing debate has not been settled, mainly because of some problems with the SLIP technique and how it is used. The aim of this chapter is three-fold: (1) to discuss some of these problems and make some suggestions as to how to deal with them in future research; (2) to present a new view of what might happen to elicited spoonerisms in inner speech that potentially leads to a new way of analyzing data obtained in SLIP experiments; and (3) briefly to present a re-analysis of some data obtained in an earlier experiment reported in Nooteboom (2005b) supporting the assumption that the main cause of lexical bias is to be found in self-monitoring. But first we will give some more information on the SLIP technique and the lexical bias effect.

20.2 THE SLIP TECHNIQUE AND THE LEXICAL-BIAS EFFECT

The SLIP technique was introduced by Baars and Motley (1974), and used by Baars *et al.* (1975) to study lexical bias in phonological speech errors, among other things. The technique was inspired by the observation that inappropriate lexical responses may result from anticipatory biasing. For example, a child asks another child to repeat the word *poke* many times, then asks, "what is the white of egg called?" In this way the (wrong) answer "yolk", induced by the rhyming relation with "poke", may be elicited (Baars 1980). The SLIP technique works as follows. Participants are successively presented visually—for example, on a computer screen—with word-pairs such as DOVE BALL, DEER BACK, DARK BONE, BARN DOOR, to be read silently. On a prompt, for example a buzz sound or a series of question marks ("?????"), the last word-pair seen (the test word-pair as opposed to the priming word-pairs), in this example BARN DOOR, has to be spoken aloud. Interstimulus intervals are in the order of 1000 ms, as is the interval between the test word-pair and the prompt to speak. Every now and then a word-pair like BARN DOOR will be mispronounced as DARN BORE as a result of phonological priming by the preceding word pairs.

When the SLIP technique is used to study lexical bias, two types of stimulus are compared, one generating lexical spoonerisms, such as BARN DOOR turning into DARN BORE, and another one generating non-lexical spoonerisms, such as BAD GAME turning into GAD BAME. Although both types of stimulus are equally frequent, responses commonly show that lexical spoonerisms are made more frequently than non-lexical ones. This lexical-bias effect has been found not only in errors elicited in the laboratory with the SLIP technique, but was also clearly demonstrated in spontaneous speech errors (Dell 1986; Nooteboom 2005a), despite some failures to do so (Garrett 1976; del Viso *et al.* 1991). Baars *et al.* (1975) explained lexical bias from "prearticulatory editing" of inner speech, more particularly on the assumption that in inner speech, speech errors forming non-words are more often covertly detected and repaired than speech errors forming real words. However, Stemberger (1985) and Dell (1986) explained lexical bias in phonological speech errors from immediate feedback of activation from phonemes to words for the mental preparation of speech. Such immediate feedback causes reverberation of activation between the planned phoneme string and all word forms containing this phoneme string or part of it. This gives an advantage in activation to phoneme strings corresponding to real words over those corresponding to non-words, because the latter have no lexical representations. This advantage in activation would explain (among other things) the phenomenon of lexical bias.

The idea that there is immediate feedback from phonemes to lexical representations is not generally accepted. Notably, Levelt (1989) and Levelt *et al.* (1999) assume that the mental preparation of speech is strictly serial and feedforward only, allowing no feedback between different levels of processing. These authors essentially support the original assumption by Baars *et al.* (1975) that lexical bias is caused by prearticulatory editing or self-monitoring of inner speech. Levelt assumes that this self-monitoring of inner speech employs the same speech comprehension system that is also used for self-monitoring of overt speech, and for listening to other-produced speech. The self-monitoring system is supposed to employ a general criterion of the form "Is this a word?" Therefore non-words are more often covertly suppressed and repaired before overt production than real words. This would explain lexical bias in phonological speech errors.

To complicate matters, recently, Hartsuiker *et al.* (2005) found experimental evidence that led them to assume that the relative frequencies of real-word and non-word speech errors are affected both by immediate feedback and by self-monitoring of inner speech. Their basic finding is that in a well-controlled experiment eliciting word–word and non-word–non-word spoonerisms with the SLIP technique testing for lexical bias, in which the kind of context is varied from mixed (word–word and non-word–non-word priming and test word pairs) to nonlexical (non-word–non-word pairs only), it is not the case that non-words are suppressed in the mixed context, as claimed by Baars *et al.* (1975), but rather that word–word errors are suppressed in the non-lexical context. This suppression of real words in the non-lexical context is explained by adaptive behavior of the self-monitoring system, but this explanation presupposes that there is an underlying pattern, before operation of the self-monitoring system, that already shows lexical bias. This underlying pattern would be caused by immediate feedback as proposed by Dell (1986). Thus we now have three competing views on the possible origin of lexical bias in phonological speech errors: (1) immediate feedback of activation alone; (2) self-monitoring of inner speech alone; and (3) both immediate feedback of activation and self-monitoring of inner speech. It is important to realize that in principle feedback and self-monitoring are successive processes that do not exclude each other. Before self-monitoring operates, feedback has the effect that more real-word than nonword errors are made (Dell 1986). In the absence of feedback, numbers of real-word and nonword errors are supposed to be equal before self-monitoring. We look for a way to count real-word and nonword errors in inner speech before self-monitoring operates.

20.3 SOME PROBLEMS WITH THE SLIP TECHNIQUE

Obviously, it is still controversial whether or not there is feedback of activation from phonemes to words, and whether lexical bias is caused by such immediate feedback or by self-monitoring of inner speech, or by both. A major problem in putting an end to this long-standing controversy one way or the other is that the SLIP technique is only marginally successful in generating spoonerisms of the primed-for kind. This has led to ways of analyzing the data that may have obscured important strategies used by participants in a SLIP task. Notably, instead of focusing on the predicted spoonerisms (BARN DOOR > DARN BORE), Baars *et al.* (1975)—and, in their wake, most later researchers—in order to assess whether more speech errors are made in the word-word than in the nonword-nonword priming condition, have collapsed "full exchanges" and "partial spoonerisms". "Full exchanges" are exchanges of the two initial consonants without regard for what happens in the remainder of the two words as in BARN DOOR > DARN BORE or DARK BOARD or DARK BO.. where in the latter example one does not know how the second word would end or ended in inner speech. "Partial spoonerisms" are cases like BARN DOOR > DARN DOOR, but also DA.. BARN DOOR where overt speech was initiated too hastily and then interrupted.

Even given the practice of collapsing different error types, the numbers and percentages of spoonerisms obtained are not impressive and vary widely, from c. 8 percent "full exchanges" in one of the experiments described by Baars *et al.* (1975) to only 1 percent in one of the experiments by Dell (1986), 100 percent being the number of test trials. The variation in yield appears to be related to the method of stimulus presentation. More particularly, constant time pressure during the experiment appears to give more errors than more relaxed conditions. Notably, Baars *et al.* gave their participants no time for repairs, thus keeping time pressure on during the whole experiment. Dell, who wanted to make certain that elicited spoonerisms were not reading errors, followed the following procedure. After test-stimulus presentation, a sequence of question marks appeared on the screen as a signal for the participant to speak the last word-pair seen aloud. The onset of the question marks was followed by a buzz signal after 500, 700, or 1,000 ms. Participants were instructed to speak the last word-pair seen before the buzz sound. Then, 500 ms after the buzz, for 2,500 ms, the participant saw the phrase "Did you make an error?", and the participant answered this with "yes" or "no". Then the phrase "repeat words" was presented, also for 2,500 ms, upon which the participant repeated the words that were, according to her or him, the correct words seen. The participant pressed a key on the terminal keyboard when she or he was ready to continue. This procedure made it possible to remove all errors from the data that might have been reading errors, under the assumption that, when participants were not aware of a discrepancy between the target seen and their spoken erroneous response, the error might have been a reading error. The yield of this procedure was very low, certainly for the time limit of 1,000 ms (0.8% of all test stimulus presentations). The same time limit was used in the original experiments by Baars *et al.* (1975), where the yield was an order of magnitude higher in experiment II (8.2%). The low yield in Dell's experiment may be attributed to the leisurely procedure with always more than 5,000 ms between each test stimulus word-pair and the following biasing word-pair. It may also be relevant that it is uncertain how well the time pressure induced by the buzz sound following the test stimulus worked. Dell mentions that he removed responses starting after the onset of the buzz sound. This suggests that there were many cases where the participant certainly did not finish the response before the onset of the buzz sound, as they were instructed to do. As Dell's extensive measures to ensure that possible reading errors were removed from the responses apparently led to an extremely low yield, it seems more attractive to go along with the plausible assumption by Baars *et al.* that reading errors resulting in initial consonant exchanges are unlikely.

Similar to this comparison between two extremes, other differences between published experiments in percentages of elicited spoonerisms can potentially be explained by differences in the method of stimulus presentation and instruction to the participants. So the relatively low yield (4% and 2.29%) in the two experiments by Hartsuiker *et al.* (2005) is possibly related to their attempts to hide the purpose of the experiments from the participants by mixing the priming word pairs that preceded the target word pair with non-priming word pairs. However, even the maximum yield of 8 percent "full exchanges" is low. The problem of the scarcity of data is aggravated when there are good reasons not to collapse speech errors of different types. Of course, one way of dealing with this problem is simply to obtain more measurements. This can be done in two ways: presenting more test stimuli per participant, or using more participants. However, the requirements on the test-stimulus language material usually restrict the range of possible word-pairs to be used. This is so because a number of properties of words and word-pairs affect the propensity of word-pairs to elicit spoonerisms. This propensity has been shown to depend on the transitional probability of initial consonants and vowels in the word pair (Motley and Baars 1975), whether the vowels in the two words are the same (Dell 1986), the frequency of usage of the stimulus words involved (Dell 1990), the phonetic distance between the two initial consonants (Nooteboom 2005b), the semantic relations between the biasing word pairs and the predicted spoonerisms (Motley and Baars 1976), and even the phonological patterns particular to the stimulus word pairs in the experiment in question (Dell and Warker 2004). Although it is impossible to keep word pairs constant on all the properties mentioned, one should at least try to balance differences in these properties over different experimental conditions. This aspect of setting up SLIP experiments generally seems to get less attention than it deserves.

With the possibilities for using many more test stimuli thus limited, more data should be obtained by running more participants per experiment. However, in doing this the number of elicited relevant speech errors per participant remains low. In fact, it is a common finding that in a SLIP experiment, whereas some participants make a satisfactory number of errors, there are others who never make a relevant speech error. Also, it cannot be excluded that participants differ not only in their tendency to spoonerize, but also in the kind of speech errors they make. If this is so, there is a fair chance that in a blocked design, apparent significant differences between experimental conditions or between relative numbers of error types may have their real source in differences between participants. As far as we can see, the only way to deal with this problem is to use as many participants as possible, and test whether large enough non-overlapping subgroups in the same experimental condition show the same behavior. This is bad news for those who want to economize on these experiments.

These quantitative problems with the SLIP task are, of course, closely related to the chosen method of statistical analysis. In publications reporting SLIP experiments the most frequent statistical methods are (a) the Mann-Whitney U test, the Wilcoxon signed ranks test, and the binomial (or sign) test, when only the difference between two conditions is to be assessed; (b) the traditional analysis of variance (ANOVA), when the interaction between independent variables is of interest; and (c) the chi^2 (chi square) test, if one is interested in knowing whether distributions of error types are the same or different across conditions. Of these, the Mann-Whitney U test, the Wilcoxon test, and the binomial test are the most straightforward, although here, too, one should be aware that the scarcity and strong variability of data per participant may in some cases lead to spurious significance (capitalization on chance). Therefore it might be advisable to test whether non-overlapping subgroups give the same results. The use of traditional analysis of variance is not recommended for analyzing SLIP data, because the data is binomial (for which it was not designed) and the design matrix has more than 90 percent of the cells with zeroes. This causes the data to deviate strongly from the normal distribution. It also brings the power of the analysis down, often to below 0.3, making spurious acceptance of the null hypothesis unacceptably probable. Finally, the chi^2 test requires that the observations counted in the contingency table are independent (Devore and Peck 2005). Given that the same participants contribute to each cell, and that participants tend to differ in the kind of errors they make, independence cannot be guaranteed. Here, too, the problem might be alleviated by repeating the test for non-overlapping subgroups of participants or by repeating the experiment with different participants.

Clearly, problems with the various statistical techniques in analyzing data obtained with the SLIP task arise mainly because of the variability of both stimuli and participants in their behavior, combined with the scarcity of data per participant and per stimulus. In our opinion, the most promising technique for analyzing such data is multi-level logistic regression, which we will briefly introduce in Section 20.5. The main point in this section is that, if the SLIP task is to be used in further research on the possible origins of the lexical bias effect, each experiment requires a sufficient number of participants to test whether the relevant patterns in the data occur in independent subgroups of participants.

20.4 A NEW VIEW OF WHAT MAY HAPPEN TO ELICITED SPOONERISMS IN INNER SPEECH

In the self-monitoring account of lexical bias, one would predict that "early interruptions" of elicited spoonerisms, of the type D..BARN DOOR, and G..BAD GAME, are more frequent in the nonword-nonword priming condition than in the word-word priming condition. This is so because, according to Levelt's lexicality criterion, in inner speech, nonwords are more easily detected than real words. Such early interruptions must be reactions to inner speech, not to overt speech, because the brief fragments of the elicited errors are shorter than humanly possible reaction times (see Levelt 1989: 473, 474 for an alternative argument). Not only the interruptions but also the following repairs, often with an offset-to-repair interval of 0 ms, presumably result from self-monitoring of inner speech (Blackmer and Mitton 1991; Nooteboom 2005b). Nooteboom (2005b) found that indeed early interruptions are more frequent in the nonword-nonword than in the word-word priming condition. This finding suggests that early interruptions should not be collapsed with full or partial (but not interrupted) exchanges, as has been done in many published reports.

As mentioned before, it has been standard practice among those employing the SLIP technique for eliciting spoonerisms in pairs of monosyllable words, to define as completed spoonerisms or full exchanges all those speech errors in which the initial consonants of the words are exchanged, irrespective of what happens to the remainder of the words. It has also been common practice to remove all speech errors from the data that can be interpreted as intrusions from earlier parts of the experiment. Now consider that one is studying lexical bias in elicited spoonerisms. A possible test stimulus word pair in the nonword-nonword outcome condition is BAD GAME, provoking the nonword-nonword error GAD BAME, but as it happens potentially also GAD BA..., where one does not know how the second error word would end (or ended in inner speech), or even GAS BAME, where one part of the pair is an intruding lexical item, or GAS BAIT, where both error words are real words. Those errors can hardly be taken for nonword-nonword spoonerisms.

The real question is, "Why would a primed-for nonlexical spoonerism like GAD BAME turn into a lexical or partly lexical spoonerism like GAS BAME or GAS BAIT, or GAS BA..?" It turns out that, under certain conditions, this happens more often in the nonword-nonword than in the word-word priming condition (Nooteboom 2005c).

This seems to be an effect of self-monitoring. In inner speech, non-lexical spoonerisms would be detected and replaced more often than lexical spoonerisms, being replaced by either the correct targets (this would not become observable in the error data), or by other, but now lexical, errors. A possible rich source of these secondary, lexical, errors would be the lexical items that were recently encountered in the same experiment, and thus would be still relatively active. These secondary errors provide valuable information on a possible strategy in self-monitoring, in which nonlexical errors in inner speech are replaced by lexical ones before speech is initiated. It should also be observed that an operation where one error (GAD BAME) is made in inner speech, which is then (partly) replaced by another error like GAS BAME or GAS BAIT, before pronunciation is started, should be time-consuming. Nooteboom (2005c) found that response times for the GAS BAIT cases are some 100 ms longer than those for the GAD BAME cases. This supports the hypothesis that errors like GAS BAIT for BAD GAME are indeed secondary errors, replacing the elicited spoonerisms, and made after the elicited speech error in inner speech has been rejected.

These reflections on error types lead to the following view of what may happen to elicited spoonerisms in inner speech as elicited in a SLIP task. The basic assumption of this view is that all speech errors made in a SLIP task that start with the initial consonant of the second word have their origin in the elicited spoonerisms in inner speech. If the speech errors deviate from the predicted spoonerisms this is caused by some operation of the self-monitoring system. Of course, the elicited spoonerisms may go undetected, and then are articulated. This gives a category of predicted completed spoonerisms of the type BARN DOOR > DARN BORE or BAD GAME > GAD BAME. Secondly, the elicited spoonerisms may be detected in inner speech, but overt speech will be initiated too hastily, and then interrupted early, giving rise to a category of early interruptions of the type BAD GAME > G..BAD GAME. Thirdly, the elicited spoonerisms will be detected in inner speech and then replaced by another speech error, also starting with the initial consonant of the second word, generating a category of so-called replacement errors of the type BAD GAME > GAS BAME or > GAS BAIT. Fourthly, the elicited spoonerisms will be covertly repaired before speech initiation: BAD GAME > GAD BAME > BAD GAME. Unfortunately these covert repairs disappear from the error counts. Errors not beginning with the initial consonant of the second word are discarded.

Let us assume for a moment that there are no covert repairs. We will come back to these later. Under this assumption, the current view of what may happen to elicited spoonerisms in inner speech has an interesting property. The sum of the number of completed spoonerisms (GAD BAME), early interrupted spoonerisms (G..BAD GAME), and replacement errors (GAS BAIT) equals the number of predicted spoonerisms in inner speech before self-monitoring operates. This is important, because the feedback-account predicts that, before self-monitoring operates, there are more word-word than nonword-nonword spoonerisms (Dell 1986), but if there is no effect of feedback on lexical bias, this sum would be the same for the word-word and the nonword-nonword priming condition. Given this new view of self-monitoring inner speech, let us now see what predictions we can derive from each of the three accounts of the origin of lexical bias, keeping in mind that covert self-repairs may cause elicited spoonerisms to become unobservable.

The first possibility is that immediate feedback alone is responsible for lexical bias. This would not mean that there is no self-monitoring, but, rather, that self-monitoring would not employ a lexicality criterion and therefore would not cause a bias towards word-word spoonerisms. This is the position taken by Stemberger (1985) and Dell (1986). From this position, together with our new view of self-monitoring, we derive the following predictions:

1. The sum of 'completed spoonerisms', 'interrupted spoonerisms', and 'replacement errors' is larger for the word-word than for the nonword-nonword priming conditions, corresponding to the lexical bias effect caused by feedback before self-monitoring operates.
2. For each error type separately the number of errors is also larger for the word-word than for the nonword-nonword priming condition. Note that only in this 'feedback only' account the lexical bias effect is equally strong in all error types.

A second possibility is that self-monitoring alone is responsible for lexical bias by employing a lexicality criterion in the detection of speech errors in inner speech. This is the position taken by Levelt (1989) and Levelt *et al.* (1999). We will assume that the lexicality criterion equally affects both error types following detection of a speech error. From this the following predictions can be derived:

3. For the word-word priming conditions, the sum of completed spoonerisms, interrupted spoonerisms, and replacement errors is the same as or only slightly larger than for the nonword-nonword priming conditions. Before self-monitoring operates, the number of elicited spoonerisms would be equal. However, there may or may not be more covert repairs in the nonword-nonword than in the word-word priming condition, but if there are, this effect would be notably smaller than the lexical bias effect in the 'completed spoonerisms'. This is so, because of the next prediction.
4. As a result of the lexicality criterion in self-monitoring inner speech there should be fewer interruptions plus replacement errors—and as a consequence more completed spoonerisms—in the word-word than in the nonword-nonword priming condition. Note that if this were indeed the case, even when the sums of all error types were equal for the two priming conditions, both feedback and covert repairs contribute little or nothing to lexical bias.

Finally, as suggested by Hartsuiker *et al.* (2005), it is possible that lexical bias is caused by both feedback and self-monitoring. This leads to the following predictions, which are basically the same as predictions 1 and 4:

1′. The sum of all errors is larger in the word-word than in the nonword-nonword priming condition.

4'. There are, relative to the sum of all errors, fewer interruptions plus replacement errors and more completed spoonerisms in the word-word than in the nonword-nonword priming condition.

Although a significant difference in the sum of all errors combined with a significant difference in the distribution of interruptions and replacement errors in the predicted direction would be consistent with Hartsuiker's hypothesis, such a finding should be interpreted with care. A difference in the sum of all errors between priming conditions could be attributed either to feedback or to the unobservable covert repairs being more frequent in the nonword-nonword than in the word-word priming condition, as a result of the lexicality criterion employed in self-monitoring.

20.5 A RE-ANALYSIS OF SOME EARLIER DATA

We will apply the above reasoning to data obtained in an experiment reported by Nooteboom (2005b) which gives more details on the experiment. The observed numbers and percentages of completed spoonerisms, early interruptions, and replacement errors are set out in Table 20.1, for the word-word and nonword-nonword priming conditions separately.

The data in Table 20.1 show a strong and significant lexical bias in the completed spoonerisms (binomial test, $p = .012$). The data also show a mirror image of the lexical-bias effect: there are fewer interrupted and replaced spoonerisms in the word-word than in the nonword-nonword priming condition, as predicted by a self-monitoring account of lexical bias. The distributions of error types are significantly different for the two priming conditions ($chi^2(2) = 12.44; p = .002$). Importantly, the sum of error types does not differ significantly between priming conditions (binomial test, $p = .173$), suggesting that there is no contribution of immediate feedback or of the number of covert repairs to lexical bias. These results are not in line with the predictions of the feedback-only account, and lend support to the self-monitoring-only explanation of lexical bias. Lexical bias in this experiment can be completely

TABLE 20.1. Numbers of completed, interrupted, and replaced spoonerisms separately for the word-word and nonword-nonword priming conditions as observed in a SLIP task with $N = 1,800$ test stimuli (Nooteboom 2005b). Regression coefficients from the mixed-effects, multi-nomial logistic regression (in logit units, see text) are given in parentheses

	Word-word	Nonword-nonword	TOTAL
Completed	39 (-3.10)	19 (-3.84)	58
Interrupted	27 (-3.48)	45 (-2.94)	72
Replaced	22 (-3.69)	30 (-3.37)	52
TOTAL	88	94	182

accounted for by a self-monitoring process interrupting and replacing nonword-non-word spoonerisms more frequently than word-word spoonerisms.

The frequency-based chi^2 analysis above, however, assumes that all cell values are independent, which cannot be guaranteed here. Moreover, it is quite likely that individual participants and items vary in their propensity to produce speech errors. These sources of random variation should not be ignored, because they may result in capitalization on chance (Quené and van den Bergh 2004). To remedy these problems, the same data were also analyzed by means of multi-nomial logistic regression[1] (Hosmer and Lemeshow 2000; Pampel 2000). The proportion P of responses within each error category is converted to logit units (i.e. to the logarithm of the odds of P, or logit(P)= log $(P/(1 - P))$). These logit units, in the model functioning as regression coefficients, can here be seen best as estimated cell means with all participants and all items kept apart. Negative values indicate proportions lower than 0.5. Lower values stand for lower cell means. There are three response variables, corresponding to the three error categories in Table 20.1, which are then regressed simultaneously on the lexicality factor. For the resulting logit values see the table. This analysis was chosen because logistic regression is perfectly suitable for regression analysis with one or more dichotomous dependent variables. The multi-nomial logistic regression was done by means of a mixed-effects model with participants and items as additional random factors (Goldstein 1995; Snijders and Bosker 1999; Luke 2004; Quené and van den Bergh 2004). This type of model is similar to a repeated-measures, within-participant, analysis of variance.

This analysis confirms the effects summarized above. First, the lexical bias yields a significant contrast between word-word and nonword-nonword priming conditions in the completed spoonerisms $(F(1, 36) = 6.83, p = .013)$.[2] Second, this bias is reversed in the interrupted and replaced spoonerisms, yielding a significant interaction effect between the two priming conditions and the three error categories $(F(2, 36) = 9.49, p = .004)$. Thus the effects observed in the raw counts aggregated over participants and over items (Table 20.1) hold out under more advanced statistical analysis in which the random variation over response categories, between participants and between items, is taken into account. This multi-level multi-nomial regression overcomes the methodological problems discussed in Section 20.3 (in chi^2 analyses or ANOVA). The analysis suggests that the results cannot be ascribed to random variation between participants or between items, although some uncertainty remains because of the scarcity of observations per participant. In addition, the power of the analysis is not very good because of the limited number of participants.

Although this re-analysis raises hopes for the suitability of this method for SLIP data, and although its results are certainly suggestive, our current interpretation

---

[1] We are aware that many readers may be unfamiliar with this type of analysis, which is unfortunately computationally complex. We refer to Quené and van den Bergh (2004) for an accessible introduction.

[2] In logistic regression analysis it is customary to give diagnostic chi^2 values where in ANOVA F ratios are given. In order to avoid confusion with the earlier chi^2 analysis in this chapter, we have recalculated the chi^2 values of the logistic regression analysis to the more familiar F ratios.

awaits confirmation from further experiments with many more participants. Analyses of further data sets were underway at the time of writing.

20.6 CONCLUSIONS

The SLIP task for eliciting spoonerisms has inherent shortcomings as an experimental technique, stemming from its low yield in terms of spoonerisms per participant, combined with variability of both participants and items in their propensity to spoonerize. This can easily lead to spuriously significant effects. This inefficiency of the technique has also led to a standard practice in coding and analyzing the data that may obscure important strategies of participants in this task. Notably, it has become customary to collapse error types that had better be kept apart. A new view of self-monitoring inner speech is presented, which makes different predictions for completed spoonerisms on the one hand, and for both early interruptions and other errors beginning with the initial consonant of the second word, on the other. This view is briefly tested here on data obtained in an earlier experiment, using two methods of analysis. The results suggest that lexical bias in phonological speech errors is caused by elicited spoonerisms in inner speech being more often interrupted after speech initiation, or replaced by other speech errors before speech initiation, in the nonword-nonword than in the word-word priming condition. The results also suggest that there is no contribution of immediate feedback and no contribution of covert repairs to lexical bias.

21

Experimental Methods in the Study of Hindi Geminate Consonants

Manjari Ohala

21.1 INTRODUCTION

In this chapter I attempt to provide answers to some of the issues raised by phoneticians and phonologists about long consonants or geminates (these two terms are used interchangeably here), using an experimental approach in the analysis of Hindi geminates. A number of different methodologies have been proposed to address issues in phonetics and phonology experimentally (J. Ohala 1995) which can be applied directly to the question being addressed or, with some creativity, modified and adapted. In the first part of the chapter, Sections 21.2–4, I report on experiments using standard experimental phonetic procedures. The second part reports on a phonological experiment for which I modified and developed an available methodology (Section 21.5). In the last part of the chapter I use a recently proposed methodology for gathering phonetic data and apply it to address some phonological questions regarding geminates (Sections 21.6 and 21.7). Although the data and claims being made are from Hindi, the methodological techniques used could be relevant to address similar issues in other languages.

The specific topics addressed in this paper are (a) the duration of geminates and of the vowels preceding them (Section 21.2); (b) long distance durational effects (e.g. do geminates behave as a prosody; Section 21.3); (c) the duration of geminates vis-à-vis clusters and of the vowel preceding these (Section 21.4); (d) the syllabification of geminates and the issue of their integrity (Section 21.5); and (e) the status of "apparent"

For some of the experiments reported on here the data were gathered at the laboratories at the University of Alberta and the University of California, Berkeley, and at Jawaharlal Nehru University. I am grateful to Terry Nearey, John Ohala, and Anvita Abbi for making their facilities available to me. I am grateful to all my subjects for their time. I am especially grateful to John Ohala for his help, inspiration, and guidance in conducting all the experiments and for his help in the statistical analysis and figures in the preparation of this chapter. Thanks also to Heriberto Avelino for help with quantitative analysis. I also thank Patrice Beddor, Maria-Josep Solé, and two anonymous reviewers for their detailed and insightful comments. Parts of this research were supported by the San José State University College of Humanities and the Arts Dean's Small Grant.

geminates (i.e. those that are formed across morpheme boundaries or due to total assimilation) as compared to phonemic geminates (Sections 21.6 and 21.7). Some of the results presented are rather preliminary and should be taken as a first attempt to address these issues empirically using experimental methodology.

21.1.1 Some facts about geminates in Hindi

Geminates involve the consonantal closure held for a longer period than that of non-geminate counterparts. Phonetically, they are not two separate consonants, as the term "geminate" might imply. The Devanagari orthography does, however, represent them as two consonants (using a half symbol for the first consonant) thus overtly indicating a cluster. Almost all of the consonants of Hindi can occur as geminates and they are phonemic (although not all yield minimal pairs with singletons). A detailed list of the consonants and vowels of Hindi can be found in M. Ohala (1983, 1994). However, unlike singletons or consonants clusters, the geminates have severe phono-tactic restrictions: they occur only intervocalically (but see n. 13) and are always preceded by the non-peripheral vowels, the short vowels, [ə ɪ ʊ].

21.1.2 Diachronic data on development of geminates

Diachronically, geminates came about due to cluster simplification in the develop-ment of Middle Indo-Aryan (MIA) from Sanskrit. In the case of heterorganic stop + stop clusters only the second stop's place of articulation was maintained, giving rise to a geminate version of the second stop as exemplified in (1) (data from Masica 1991).

(1) Examples of geminate formation in the history of Indo-Aryan[1]

Sanskrit *bhakta* meal, food > Pali / Prakrit *bhatta*
Sanskrit *sapta* seven > Pali / Prakrit *satta*
Sanskrit *dugdha-* milk > MIA *duddha-*

2 EXPERIMENT I: DURATION OF GEMINATE VS. SINGLETON CONSONANTS AND THE DURATION OF THE VOWEL PRECEDING THEM

I first present the experimental procedures used, then the results in Figures 21.1 and 21.2, and finally the relevant statistics. Although geminate and singleton consonants are usually differentiated by the longer consonantal hold for the geminate (Pickett *et al.* 1999 and references therein), the magnitude of the difference between these classes of

---

[1] The transcription given for words in Sanskrit and other intermediate historical stages between that and Modern Hindi is given not in IPA but in the traditional transliteration.

consonants can vary from one language to another (Lahiri and Hankamer 1988). Thus, it is of interest to provide data from one more language with geminates. Moreover, it is acknowledged that they may differ by other secondary features such as the duration of the preceding vowel or RMS amplitude (Lehiste 1970; Maddieson 1985; Abramson 1987; Lahiri and Hankamer 1988; Esposito and Di Benedetto 1999). Of these, I examined vowel duration.

21.2.1 Experimental procedures

21.2.1.1 Speakers and speech corpus

The speakers were three male native speakers of Standard Hindi with home towns in Uttar Pradesh, Bihar, and Delhi. Recordings of their speech were made in the Language Laboratory of the Jawahar Lal Nehru University, Delhi, using high-quality analog portable equipment. Minimal pairs involving the singleton–geminate contrast given in Table 21.1 were read in two different random orders five times each (i.e. ten renditions per word) in the frame [vo _____ ḍo] "that __ give".[2]

21.2.1.2 Analysis methods

The recorded speech was band-pass filtered at 68 Hz to 7.8 kHz, digitized at 16.7 kHz and analyzed with the aid of waveform and LPC spectral displays produced by the CSRE™ speech analysis software and related programs. Segmentation criteria were those conventionally used in phonetics: boundaries between consonants and vowels were based on the location of abrupt changes, especially in amplitude. Occasionally there was perseveratory voicing from the preceding vowel into the closure of voiceless stops; in these cases the boundary between the vowel and the consonant was determined by the sudden drop in amplitude of the second formant. Voice onset time (VOT) was defined by the time interval between the onset of the stop burst (in cases of multiple bursts, this was the first such burst) to the abrupt increase in the amplitude of the first formant.[3] In the statistical analysis detailed below, I give means based on a maximum of three tokens per word per speaker, in other words, nine tokens per word; 3.5 percent of the target tokens were unusable but usable tokens never fell below five per word.

---

[2] Stress is not relevant here. The existence of word stress in Hindi is disputed (M. Ohala 1991). Researchers giving stress algorithms for Hindi (e.g. Gupta 1988; Pandey 1989) do not provide instrumental data on the phonetic correlates of stress, which means that we cannot verify their claims. For example, Gupta claims that [mʊhəlːɑ] "locality" and [sʊtʃɪʈrɑ] "a good picture, proper name for a girl" are stressed differently, the former on the second syllable and the latter on the first. However, in my experience native speakers of Hindi (and I am one) give the same prosodic contour to both words.

[3] For breathy or aspirated stops, the question can be asked as to how vowel duration was measured. M. Ohala and J. Ohala (1992) suggest that, for Hindi, including half of the aspiration period in the vowel duration would make the duration congruent with the vowel duration after a non-aspirate. That study did not include affricates. In the case of the present chapter, for affricates just the closure duration was measured.

TABLE 21.1. List of minimal pairs with singleton vs. geminate consonants

Singleton	Translation	Geminate	Translation
bət͡ʃa	save	bət͡ʃːa	child
gəd̪a	mace (weapon)	gəd̪ːa	mattress
gəʈʰa	muscular body	gəʈʰːa	bundle
kəʈʰa	narrative	kəʈʰːa	powdered red bark
pəka	cook (v.)	pəkːa	firm
pəla	nurture	pəlːa	edge of sari
pəʈa	address (n.)	pəʈːa	leaf
pəʈa	make someone agree	pəʈːa	type of animal collar
ʈəpa	to cross over	ʈəpːa	type of song
rəsa	juice	rəsːa	rope
t͡ʃʊni	selected (fem.)	t͡ʃʊnːi	scarf
d̪ʱəd͡ʒi	decorated; adorned	d̪ʱəd͡ʒːi	strip of cloth or paper

21.2.2 Results

Figure 21.1 shows the mean durations for singletons and geminates. On average, the geminates were 76 ms longer than the singletons, a ratio of 1.96:1. Although ratios around 2:1 between geminates and singletons are common in languages (Lahiri and Hankamer 1988; Hankamer *et al.* 1989), the ratio is significantly higher in some cases, such as Japanese (Han 1992).

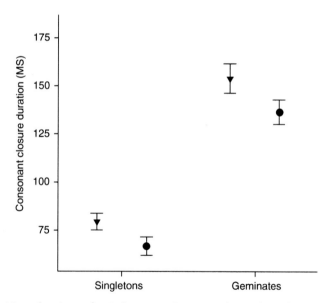

FIGURE 21.1. Mean durations of voiceless (triangle) (▼) and voiced (circle) (●) singleton and geminate consonants, word-medially. (For the various categories from left to right, N = 71, 30, 71, 38.) Here and in all subsequent figures the 95 percent confidence interval is shown by the bars.

As mentioned, prior phonetic literature reports on the occasional presence of shorter vowel duration before geminates than singletons,[4] although the magnitude of the difference is much less than that of the duration of the consonants, in other words, there is no compensation which leads to a relatively constant V + C duration. Figure 21.2 shows that Hindi also has this pattern, the vowels before geminates being on average 10.5 ms shorter than those before singletons. For possible explanations for this pattern see Kluender *et al.* (1988) and the discussion in Section 21.3.3.

A factorial ANOVA (durations of the medial consonant and preceding vowel as the dependent variables, and $\pm$ geminate, $\pm$ voice as factors) yielded a significant effect due to $\pm$ geminate for both the consonant duration ($F(1, 205) = 422, p < .0001$) and the duration of the preceding vowel ($F(1, 205) = 17, p < .0001$). There was also a significant effect due to $\pm$ voice for both consonant duration ($F(1, 205) = 21, p < .0001$) and vowel duration ($F(1, 205) = 101, p < .0001$) paralleling similar findings for singleton $\pm$ voiced segments and the vowels preceding them (Lehiste 1970).[5] These trends were found for all three subjects except that one subject showed no difference in the duration of the preceding vowel due to $\pm$ geminate.

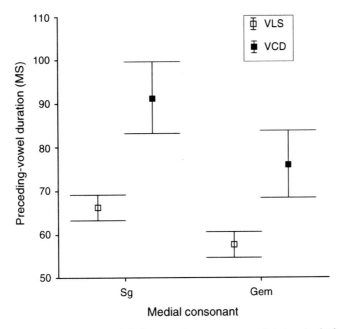

FIGURE 21.2. Mean durations of vowels before voiceless (open squares) (□); voiced (closed squares) (■) singleton and geminate word medial consonants. (For the various categories from left to right, N = 71, 71, 27, 38).

[4] A few languages, including Japanese (Han 1994) and Persian (Hansen 2004), have been reported to have longer vowel duration before a geminate.
[5] A manner difference was not included because there were not enough tokens clearly to define this and other categories.

21.3 EXPERIMENT 2: IS GEMINATION
A PROSODY?

In a study of Malayalam sonorant singletons and geminates, Local and Simpson (1999) found not only the expected durational differences between these segment types but also small duration differences in the preceding, non-contiguous, consonant. For example, in a near-minimal pair like *purli* "tamarind" vs. *purlli* "spot", the initial [p]s were slightly different, the [p] before the geminate being shorter than the [p] before the singleton (this effect was significant before singleton and geminate laterals but not before contrasting nasals). I sought to determine if a similar effect could be found in Hindi, another language containing geminates.

21.3.1 Experimental procedures

The words given in (2) were read by three male and three female native speakers of Standard Hindi. (The male speakers were recorded in India and the female ones in the US due to opportunity.) The words were presented in the Devanagari script and spoken in the frame [vo_____ ɖo] "that___give", which permitted demarcation of the initial consonant onset. The words were spoken 5 times each in two different random orders (i.e., ten renditions per word).

(2)   [pəlɑ] nurture   [pəlːɑ] edge of sari
       [bətʃɑ] save   [bətʃːɑ] child
       [pəʈɑ] address (n.)   [pəʈːɑ] leaf
       [gəɖɑ] mace (weapon)   [gəɖːɑ] mattress

The recordings of the male speakers were from the same corpus as described earlier in Section 21.2.1, so that the recording conditions were the same as those mentioned there. The three female subjects were recorded in a quiet room in the experimenter's home. These recordings were done digitally. The digitization for all six subjects was done at 16kHz, 16-bit sampling. Some tokens were unmeasurable due to misreading by the speakers or due to pauses inserted before the target word. Between all the speakers, however, the number of tokens per word ranged from 12 to 15. The duration of the vowel preceding the geminate/singleton was measured as well as the duration of the initial consonant; for example, both the [p] and the [ə] in [pəlɑ] "nurture", and, for reference, the duration of the medial singleton or geminate consonant. Segmentation criteria were as described in Section 21.2.1.

21.3.2 Results

The results are given in Figure 21.3. The geminates averaged 146 ms and the singletons 70 ms, for a difference of 76 ms. Once again we see that the vowels before

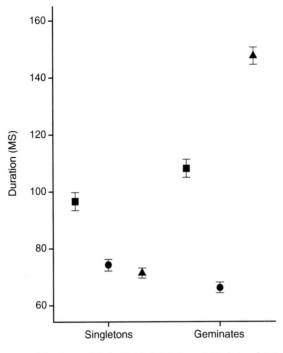

FIGURE 21.3. Durations of C1 (square) (■), V (circle) (●), and C2 (triangle) (▲) in singleton and geminate minimal pairs.

geminates are consistently shorter (this time by about 6.5 ms). (The small difference between the vowel durations in Figs. 21.2 and 21.3 could be due to different software used for analysis as well as different speakers.) Interestingly the *initial* consonant (C1VC:V) is *longer* by about 10 ms before a geminate.

The data were analyzed by one-way ANOVAs where the durations of C1, V, and C2 (which was singleton or geminate) were the dependent variables, and singleton vs. geminate was the factor. There were significant effects due to $\pm$ geminate for all three duration measures, such that C1 duration was significantly longer when C2 was geminate ($F (1,430) = 26.3$, $p < .001$), and V duration was shorter before geminates ($F (1,430) = 29.5$, $p < .001$) and, of course, C2 was significantly longer when it was a geminate ($F (1,429) = 1868$, $p < .001$). Thus, these results are similar to those of Local and Simpson in that the initial consonant shows a duration effect depending on the nature of the medial consonant. However, my results are different in that they found the initial consonant to be *shorter* before geminates, whereas I found it to be *longer*.[6]

---

[6] Local and Simpson also found differences in formant frequencies of the vowels before geminates and singletons. I looked for similar effects in Hindi but concluded that any differences that might be present were small in comparison to the differences that would arise by chance due to slight variation in the placement of the analyzing window in these short vowels having marked spectral dynamics.

21.3.3 Discussion of studies on gemination as a prosody

The results show that not only do geminates show a longer closure duration than singletons, but also that the stop preceding them in the same word is longer. To explain this difference in the C1 duration, the following three hypotheses can be entertained.

- Hypothesis A. It might reflect some sort of measurement artifact. Measurement error could arise through a systematic error in the placement of a between-segments boundary but I think this is unlikely in this case because the apparent conditioning environment, the singleton vs. geminate medial consonant, does not share a segment boundary with C1. Although one might imagine that measurement error could be responsible for the inverse relation between the durations of the C2 (singleton or geminate) and the immediately preceding V,[7] there is no conceivable way such an error would influence the preceding between-segments boundary.
- Hypothesis B. It is possible that a length contrast on segment i (S_i) is enhanced by making an adjacent segment, S_{i-1}, shorter (Kluender et al. 1988). It is true that the vowel immediately preceding a geminate is shorter by about 15 ms, which may enhance the geminate duration. It is unclear what this theory would predict about segment S_{i-2} (e.g. the initial consonant in words like [təpːɑ] "type of song"). One might propose that (a) this segment should also be short in order to enhance the perceived length of S_i (this is what Local and Simpson's findings would support), or the opposite, (b) that it should be longer to enhance the shortness of S_{i-1}, which in turn would enhance the length of S_i. Prediction (b) coincides with the result I obtained but this hypothesis is viable only if it can be shown that these small differences in C1 duration really do contribute to the perception of geminates.
- Hypothesis C. In languages like Hindi there is some sort of "meta command" issued during motor programming of geminate consonants which has the effect of making a consonant closure hold longer than usual. The effects of this meta-command may spread to the initial consonant.

In order to test hypothesis B, I conducted an informal test. The tokens of the dental and retroflex singleton/geminates of one of the subjects were digitally manipulated by a phonetician (not the author) in the following way: the original geminate closure duration was shortened until one listener (the author) judged it to be ambiguous between

---

[7] I do not actually think my measurements were subject to this error, for several reasons; (a) the magnitude of the duration difference between a singleton and geminate consonant is an order of magnitude greater than the difference in the durations of the immediately preceding vowels; and (b) there have been other reports of intrasyllabic effects—in a C1VC2 syllable, where the character of C2 influences some subphonemic aspects of C1 (Port and Rotunno 1979; Weismer 1979; Port et al. 1980; Local and Simpson 1999; Nguyen and Hawkins 1999).

singleton and geminate. Similarly, the closure duration of the original singleton was manipulated (increased) until it was judged ambiguous (the listener was not told what the original token was). In the case of singletons, the closure duration of 111 ms seemed to make a retroflex ambiguous and a closure duration of 113 ms had the same effect on a dental.[8] Then for each of the four ambiguous tokens (two places of articulation × two contrastive durations) the duration was further bracketed by increasing it by 7 ms and decreasing it by 7 ms. Then for each of these tokens (three versions for each given type judged ambiguous) the duration of the initial consonant (C1) was increased or decreased by 10 ms and played to the listener. This latter temporal alteration did not change the percept, in other words, the increase did not lead to more "geminate" responses and the decrease did not lead to more "singleton" responses.

Could the 10 ms increase be too short a difference to be noticeable? To see if this was the case, for a subset of these ambiguous tokens, the incremental increase was changed by 15 ms, then 30 ms, then 70 ms. This still did not change the responses towards geminate. Fujisaki *et al.* (1975) found that to differentiate singleton and geminate consonants, listeners could make use of duration differences that were in the range of 7 to 10 percent of their crossover duration. The manipulations that were made were of this order or more, so the failure of these durational changes in C1 to trigger a perceptual change probably cannot be attributed to insufficient auditory resolution of the temporal magnitudes involved.

I conclude therefore that hypothesis C has the firmest basis. If this hypothesis holds up under further testing it would support the view that at least in speech production geminates are singletons plus an added prosody-like feature of extra length. This would be in line with the position of non-linear phonology which separates the timing of geminates (i.e. the durational aspects) from their melodic structure (Lahiri and Hankamer 1988; Goldsmith 1990; Clements and Hume 1995, among others). It would be a simple extension to consider the feature [+long] for geminates in some languages as a spreading feature similar to what is done for vowel harmony with harmonizing vocalic features.

21.4 EXPERIMENT 3: GEMINATES VS. CLUSTERS: DURATION MEASUREMENTS

This experiment and the one to be reported on in the next section are relevant to the issue of whether geminates are different from clusters in that the process of vowel epenthesis that can apply to clusters cannot be applied to geminates (Kenstowicz and Pyle 1973; Hayes 1986; Goldsmith 1990). It is therefore of interest to examine the phonetic manifestation of clusters and geminates and to attempt to assess their

---

[8] These findings are similar to those reported in Shotriya *et al.* (1995) and to those reported for Marathi by Lisker (1958).

representation in the mental grammar of a native speaker. This section reports on duration measurements of geminates and clusters as well as the vowel preceding them.

21.4.1 Experimental procedures

Four native speakers of Hindi (not the same subjects as those involved in the experiment in the previous sections) read the words given in (3) in the frame [vo___ḍo] "that____give". This time the list also contained the word [bəsṭa] "back-pack" which contains a cluster:

(3) [pəka]   ripe, cooked
     [pəkːa]   firm
     [pəṭa]   address
     [pəṭːa]   leaf
     [bəsṭa]   back-pack

The readings were digitized and analyzed using the Praat program. The duration results given below are based on multiple tokens (three to ten per subject). In order to keep the vowel the same, the word with the cluster had to be [bəsṭa] even though the medial cluster starts with a fricative and not a stop. I could find no existing word with the same syllable structure having a stop + stop cluster after a schwa.[9]

21.4.2 Results

Figure 21.4 and 21.5 present the average duration of clusters, geminates, and singletons, and the duration of the vowels preceding these segments, respectively. A one-way ANOVA on the medial consonantal duration indicated significant differences ($F(2, 157) = 259$, $p < .001$). A post-hoc Tukey HSD showed that there was no significant difference between the geminates and clusters ($p = .57$, n.s.); the other pair of comparisons was highly significant: the duration of singletons was significantly shorter than the durations of clusters or geminates ($p < .001$). A one-way ANOVA on the vowel durations indicated significant differences ($F(2,157) = 68.7$, $p < .001$). A post-hoc Tukey HSD showed that the durations before geminates were significantly shorter than those before singletons ($p < .02$) and the durations before geminates and singletons were significantly shorter than of the vowels before clusters ($p < .001$).

Figure 21.4 shows that geminates and clusters have approximately the same duration.[10] However, as Figure 21.5 shows, the vowel before the cluster is

---

[9] Words such as[pəṭka] "cause something to fall with a jerk" are derived by a schwa-deletion rule (M. Ohala 1983) from the related verb form [pəṭək] "to let fall with a jerk". Thus, at the underlying level there was no medial cluster. It is not clear whether this would have an effect, therefore I did not use it.

[10] Of course, before a definitive statement can be given on this point a more detailed study would have to be done to establish for Hindi the duration for all fricatives versus stops. Lehiste (1970) reports that languages differ on this point.

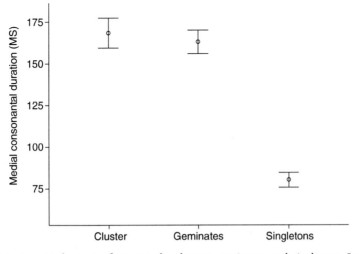

FIGURE 21.4. Average duration of intervocalic clusters, geminates, and singletons. See text for details.

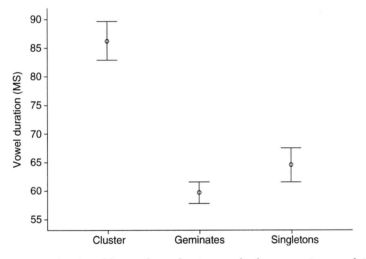

FIGURE 21.5. Average duration of the vowel preceding intervocalic clusters, geminates, and singletons.

longer.[11] But before this increased duration can be attributed to a property of the cluster per se, one would need to eliminate the possibility that the vowel was longer because of the fricative. I do not know of any study on Hindi reporting on vowel duration differences before fricatives. Caisse (1988), studying English segment durations,

---

[11] Although the effect here of geminates and singletons on preceding vowel duration seems to be smaller than that given in Fig. 21.2, it should be noted that the results reported in Fig. 21.5 are based on a smaller sample.

did find a modest effect of consonant manner on the duration of the preceding vowel with the effect of fricative vs. stop being on the order of 20–80 ms. (See also Peterson and Lehiste 1960; Klatt 1976.) It cannot therefore be ruled out that the vowel-duration difference observed was due to the effect of the fricative.

If indeed vowels are shorter before geminates but not before consonant clusters then this could be explained by Kluender *et al.*'s theory (mentioned above): vowels are shorter before geminates in order to enhance their major perceptual cue, namely, duration. They are not shorter before clusters because such enhancement is not needed. The short duration of vowels before geminates but not clusters is also relevant to the claim of Maddieson (1985), who ties the cross-linguistic tendency of vowels to be shorter before geminates to the tendency of vowels being shorter in closed syllables. He assumes that both geminates and clusters are syllabified VC.CV. My results indicate that vowels are not shorter before clusters even though clusters are syllabified VC.CV. Experimental evidence for such syllabification is presented in M. Ohala (1999*a*, 2006).

21.5 EXPERIMENT 4: THE SYLLABIFICATION OF INTERVOCALIC GEMINATES

Although I tentatively conclude, based on the results given above, that geminates and clusters are phonetically the same as far as their closure duration is concerned, could they nevertheless be different phonologically, at least as far as syllabification is concerned? This section addresses the issue of the syllabification of geminates and introduces a new experimental methodology (see also M. Ohala 2006) to answer the question, "Is the syllabification of geminates VC.CV or V.C:V?"

For Hindi, as for many other languages, intervocalic geminates have traditionally been syllabified as VC.CV (Kelkar 1968; Maddieson 1985). Although moraic phonology treats geminates as being the moraic coda of one syllable and the non-moraic onset of the next, it too, in general, syllabifies them between two syllables as given above (Hayes 1989). However, such syllabification proposals have largely been based on descriptive studies.[12] The two most widely used methodologies for addressing issues of syllabification experimentally are those of Fallows (1981) and Derwing (1992).[13] However, as mentioned

---

[12] A list of a number of experimental studies dealing with syllabification can be found in M. Ohala (2006).

[13] Derwing's methodology involves a pause–break technique in which the experimenter presents subjects with different alternatives for syllabifying the word and asks them to choose one. For example, for *melon* the experimenter pronounces *me-lon*, *mel-on* (the hyphen represents where the experimenter paused) and subjects indicate their preference. Fallows's methodology involves subjects repeating twice the first (or last) part of the word given by the experimenter. For example, given *shampoo*, the subject could respond *shamshampoo* for repeating the first part and *shampoopoo* for repeating the second part, evidencing the syllabification *sham.poo*.

in M. Ohala (2003, 2006), both of these methodologies have serious limitations when applied to geminates because of problems with phonotactic/pronunciation constraints since in Hindi, geminates usually are not pronounced in word-initial or word-final position.[14] For example, in an earlier experiment done using Fallows's methodology (reported in M. Ohala 1999a), when syllabifying the geminate in a word such as [gədːɑ] "mattress", subject responses such as [gə-ɖa] or [gəɖ-a] could be considered either (1) as deletion of the first consonant of the geminate (if it is conceived of as two consonants as implied by the orthography) with no import as to how it is syllabified, or (2) as an indication that subjects were treating geminates as single consonants with either V.CCV or VCC.V syllabification (i.e. as intended/psychological /gə-ɖːɑ/ or /gəɖː-ɑ/) with the medial stop modified to a non-geminate to conform to phonotactic/pronunciation constraints. Because of this problem, the results of the study were inconclusive. Therefore I developed another methodology involving a word game, a variation on the concept formation technique (J. Ohala 1986), which attempts to access mental representations by circumventing the problems associated with phonotactic/pronunciation constraints. A summary of the methodology and the results is given in the next section.

21.5.1 A new experimental technique[15]

The subjects were 21 literate native speakers of Standard Hindi, residents of New Delhi, who also spoke English. The instructions to the subjects indicated that a new game for children was being devised in which [ɪ] is inserted in the middle of a word. The experiment was administered to them individually by me. For words involving intervocalic single consonants they were trained to insert the [ɪ] before the C but for intervocalic clusters it was to be inserted between the CC. Thus, for example, [tʃʰupa] "hidden" was to be rendered as [tʃʰuɪpa] but [bəsʈa] "knapsack" as [bəsɪʈa]. In the training session, which involved 45 words, subjects were given feedback as to what the correct response should be. Once subjects reached criterion at 13 correct responses in a row,[16] they turned to the test session in which no feedback was provided. (There was no signal to subjects as to when the training session ended and the test session started.) The results to be presented are based on 15 subjects because three of them did not reach criterion in the training session and three others did not give correct answers to the control words in the test session.

Forty-five words were used in the training session, 22 containing intervocalic single consonants and 23 a variety of intervocalic two-consonant clusters, none involving geminates. The test session consisted of nine words, including four words with intervocalic geminates (those given in Table 21.2), two words with intervocalic single

---

[14] Word-final geminates occur in a few loanwords such as Sanskrit [mʌtː] "intoxicated" and Perso-Arabic [rʌɖː] "destroyed". However, in casual speech even these are usually pronounced with singletons.

[15] This experiment is described in more detail in M. Ohala (2006).

[16] This criterion was used because it is unlikely that a subject could respond correctly this many times by chance (see Jaeger 1986 for similar reasoning and further details).

consonants, and three with intervocalic clusters which were similar to the training session. The latter five words acted as a control to see if the subjects had indeed learned the word game. (If subjects made errors on these it would indicate that they had not learned the word game.)

21.5.2 Results and discussion

Table 21.2 presents the results. Here, -C:- indicates a geminate kept as a unit (i.e. [ɪ] was inserted *before* the geminate). CɪC indicates [ɪ] was inserted to divide the geminate (i.e. the geminate was treated as a cluster). The responses listed under "other" were either of the type in which the vowel of the first syllable was changed, for example, in response to [gəɖːɑ] if the subject responded [gɪɖːɑ], or they were of the type in which [ɪ] was added at the end of the word, as in [gəɖəɪ] for [gəɖːɑ]. The responses in the "other" column have not been included in the statistics.

Ignoring the "other" responses, the majority of the responses kept the geminate intact ($\chi^2 = 7.692$, df $= 1$, $p < .01$). The issue of possible orthographic influence also needs to be addressed. It seems unlikely that this majority response could be due to orthographic influence since, with geminates always being written as clusters in Devanagari, that influence would have favored the -CɪC- response (reflecting a VC.CV syllabification). Thus, the syllabification VC.CV appears not to be justified for Hindi geminates. (It should be noted that such syllabification *is* justified for clusters (M. Ohala 2006)). I should also point out that this experiment does not rule out VC:.V syllabification (since in the training session, subjects were taught to insert the vowel before the single consonant, not after.) These results are relevant to the issue of the integrity of geminates. Phonologists have noted that geminates seem to have integrity in that they are not subject to the process of epenthesis (Kenstowicz and Pyle 1973; Hayes 1986; Clements and Hume 1995; Perlmutter 1995; among others). My results support the notion that in the mental grammar of these native speakers geminates are treated as units, not clusters.

Finally, the following question also needs to be addressed, "Is it possible that although geminates are treated as units with respect to epenthesis (i.e. they show integrity), they are nevertheless syllabified like clusters (i.e. VC.CV)?" In other words, perhaps my experiment does not address syllabification since the task was to

TABLE 21.2. Results for the syllabification of intervocalic geminates

	-C:-	-CɪC-	other
[pəkːɑ] firm	9	5	1
[gəɖːɑ] mattress	9	4	2
[gənːɑ] sugarcane	9	3	3
[gʊsːɑ] anger	9	4	2
TOTALS	36	16	8

epenthesize a vowel. This is of course theoretically possible. However, I know of no experimental evidence for any language demonstrating that such an analysis (that is one where subjects would not epenthesize in the middle of a geminate but nevertheless break up the geminate for syllabification) reflects psychological reality. In the case of Hindi, there are no phonological rules dictating a particular syllabification (syllable weight is not relevant since, as mentioned in n. 2, word stress is controversial).[17] Also, even though Hindi shows the cross-language pattern of vowels being shorter before geminates, Maddieson's hypothesis tying this to closed syllables can still be viable with a VC:.V syllabification for geminates. Moreover, the definitive explanation for such a pattern (from speech production/perception) is still to come. Thus, in the absence of any evidence for a VC.CV syllabification for geminates, I consider the claims justified that Hindi geminates are a unit and syllabify like a unit.

21.6 EXPERIMENT 5: CLUSTERS ACROSS MORPHEME/ WORD BOUNDARIES BECOME GEMINATES[18]

This section reports on results obtained by using data-gathering methodology promoted by Kohler (1991*b*, 1995*a*, and in this volume). Kohler demonstrated the usefulness of acoustic analysis done using connected casual speech (also called "unscripted speech") as opposed to what can be called "laboratory" speech, in which data is collected from a subject using words embedded in a carefully selected frame sentence.

In order to investigate the type of reductions/assimilations that take place in unscripted speech in Hindi, I analyzed a small corpus of unscripted speech gathered from one male and one female speaker of Hindi. The speech was taped using high-quality portable recording equipment. The signal was digitized and select portions were analyzed via waveform, spectrograms and close auditory study, using Kay Elemetrics's Multispeech. In such analyses I found cases of assimilation that involved complete assimilation of abutting segments, thus leading to consonants similar in duration to geminates (187–200 ms or so). (M. Ohala and J. Ohala 1992 presented data which showed that the average duration of geminates in Hindi is 146 ms.)

As shown in Figure 21.6, intended [lʌgt̪i] "feels" is rendered with a very long voiceless stop. Although looking at the formant transitions it might appear that there is some ambiguity as to whether there is a cluster [kt̪] or just [t̪ː], in the close auditory study I did using Multispeech (mentioned above), this sounded like [t̪ː] to me and not [kt̪]. The perception test reported below also shows that this was judged [t̪ː]. Table 21.3 gives additional examples of such assimilation.[19]

---

[17] Although Gupta (1988) claims that there is a rule of vowel shortening before geminates, this is actually a general rule of vowel shortening in compounds, and not due to the geminate. For example, /pɑni + gʰɑt̪/ "water + a special type of area on the shore" is [pʌngʰət̪].

[18] This study is described in more detail in M. Ohala (1999*b*, 2001).

[19] In the first example of Table 21.3, the voicelessness of the whole cluster can be explained by the aerodynamic voicing constraint (J. Ohala 1983*b*).

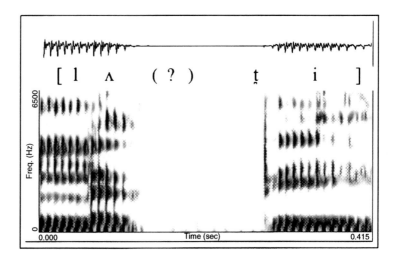

FIGURE 21.6. Intended [lʌgʈi] pronounced with a long voiceless consonant showing voicing and place assimilation. The frequency-scale of the spectrogram is 0 to 6500 Hz, the time scale is 0 to .415 sec.

The data in Figure 21.6 are also relevant to a claim made in Masica (1991: 189). Since the two stops here are across morpheme boundaries [lʌg + ʈi] "feel + present participle marker (FEM)", he considers them pseudo-clusters and claims that basic assimilations such as voicing do not take place in such clusters. However, the data to be presented below show that such assimilations *do* take place. Lahiri and Hankamer (1988) report similar cases of total assimilation for Bengali. However, their examples are based on regular phonological rules, not unscripted speech data. As they point out in their paper, non-linear phonology recognizes geminates as coming from three sources (Goldsmith 1990; Perlmutter 1995; and the references therein): underlying geminates (also called "true geminates"), concatenation of identical consonants across a morpheme boundary, and total assimilation (such as the example in Fig. 21.6). (The latter two types are also referred to as "apparent geminates".) Lahiri and Hankamer address the issue of whether in Bengali, geminates from these three sources differ acoustically. Their results show that they do not. However, they did not conduct a perceptual test.

TABLE 21.3. Examples of the formation of geminates across word boundaries. Canonical forms indicate citation forms

Canonical	Realized as
/saʈ+ disʌmbər/ seven + December	[saʈːisʌmbər]
/ kut͡ʃʰ+t͡ʃoʈ/ some + hurt	[kut͡ʃːoʈ]
/rok+ dija/ stop + did (= stopped)	[rodːija]
/bagʱ + ke/ lion + genitive postposition	[bakːe]

21.7 EXPERIMENT 6: ARE DERIVED GEMINATES PERCEPTUALLY THE SAME AS UNDERLYING GEMINATES?

I combined the unscripted-speech data-gathering technique with a perception test to address this question for underlying geminates and those derived by total assimilation.

21.7.1 Experimental procedures

The VCV portion of such derived geminates was extracted from the speech data of one of the speakers along with some examples from the same speaker of the same consonants in V_V environments where they were either clear singletons or underlying geminates. Samples were short with only a fraction of the surrounding vowels such that the constituent words were not identifiable (in order to avoid subjects being influenced by any existing words). A total of 16 such tokens (nine singletons, six derived geminates, and one underlying geminate)[20] were extracted from unscripted speech and were randomized in a tape and were played over earphones to five native speakers of Standard Hindi (all currently in the USA). Each token was heard three times with an inter-stimulus-interval of two seconds and with six seconds between trials. Subjects were asked to identify "single" and "double" consonants just by hearing a small portion of a word ("double consonant" refers to the orthographic representation of geminates and was a term familiar to the subjects).[21] They were given an answer sheet containing in the Devanagari orthography, singletons in one column and geminates in a second column (just the consonant part was included) and were instructed to circle the appropriate consonant. Table 21.4 lists some examples of the types of token used and their durations.

TABLE 21.4. Examples of tokens used in the listening test plus the durations of the relevant intervocalic consonant

Stop type	Duration in ms	canonical word or phrase yielding token	Translation
Derived geminate	155	/lʌgti/[lʌgti] (in this corpus spoken as [lʌʈːi])	"seems"
Underlying geminate	131	/mɪʈːʌl/[mɪʈːʌl]	"proper name"
Singleton	53	/pəʈa/[pəʈa]	"address"

---

[20] The number of tokens used was dictated by what was obtainable in the data. This was unscripted speech data, not data obtained by methods used in laboratory speech.
[21] Although this was a forced choice, I do not think it distorted the results because, once assimilation takes place, for the listener, derived geminates are identical to underlying geminates.

TABLE 21.5. Proportion of geminate responses to the underlying geminates, singletons, and derived geminates

Underlying geminate (N = 1)	0.8
Singletons (N = 9)	0.29
Derived geminates (N = 6)	0.7

21.7.2 Results

The results given in Table 21.5 show that the derived geminates are generally perceived as underlying geminates:

They support Hayes's (1986) claim that heteromorphemic geminates created by assimilation are similar to underlying geminates; see also Goldsmith (1990: 81). Thus the answer to the question as to whether such geminates are different from underlying geminates seems to be that, at least as far as perception is concerned, no, they seem to be treated as similar. (For a more detailed discussion see M. Ohala 2001.)

21.8 CONCLUSIONS

The results of experiments reported in this paper indicate that in Hindi geminates differ from singletons in their closure duration as well as in the duration of the vowel preceding them. Interestingly, they also differ from singletons in the duration of the initial consonant (i.e. the consonant preceding the vowel) which is longer for geminates. Thus gemination seems to act as a prosody. Tentative results indicate that they also differ from clusters in that the vowel preceding the geminates is shorter than that before a cluster. Results of a psycholinguistic experiment are suggestive of geminates showing what has been called "integrity". Thus the weight of evidence suggests that geminates are not two adjoining singletons, that is to say that they are not clusters, but, rather, a different type of unitary consonant. Experimental results also support the view that apparent geminates are perceived the same as underlying geminates. This chapter, then, has attempted to demonstrate the usefulness of the experimental approach to phonological issues. I do not claim that any of these results are definitive answers to the questions raised. However, they provide some firm ground which other researchers can build on rather than the quicksand characteristic of speculation without empirical evidence.

22

Morphophonemics and the Lexicon

A Case Study from Turkish

Anne Pycha, Sharon Inkelas, and Ronald Sprouse

22.1 INTRODUCTION

A large body of recent work has focused on statistical properties of the lexicon and their possible consequences for the grammar (e.g. Luce 1986; Content *et al.* 1990; Baayen 1993; Plag *et al.* 1999; Hay and Baayen 2002; Ernestus and Baayen 2003). The basic idea of this line of research is that every word can be meaningfully characterized by way of its relationship to other words in the same lexicon. Individual words are therefore not isolated entities; instead, their grammatical behavior can best be understood by considering lexicon variables such as frequency, neighborhood density, and cohort size. For example, Rhodes (1992) claims that flapping in American English tends to occur in frequent words like *winter* but not in infrequent words like *banter*. Frequent words are produced with more gestural overlap and hence greater tendency for reduction, so the lexical-statistics approach offers a plausible explanation for this gradient alternation. It is less clear what the approach offers for semi-regular alternations, where a majority of words undergo a categorical change but others do not. Consider stem-final alternations in Turkish nouns, in which coda /p, t, t͡ʃ, k/ alternate with onset /b, d, d͡ʒ, g/. Most nouns undergo the alternation (1a), but some resist it (1b).

(1) a. kana**t** wing   kana**d**-a wing-DAT
     b. sana**t** art   sana**t**-a art-DAT

Traditional generative phonology partitions words like *kanat* and *sanat* into two categories: those that alternate and those that do not. This partition can be accomplished either with underlying representations or with indexed rules, but it is in any event category-based. The lexical-statistics approach, on the other hand, claims that the difference between *kanat* and *sanat* can be attributed to how and where they are stored relative to other words in the lexicon, and that their alternation patterns should therefore correlate with lexicon variables.

These variables have been shown to impact word recognition and production processes in the laboratory (e.g. Wingfield 1968; Marslen-Wilson and Welsh 1978; Luce and Pisoni 1998; Gaskell and Marslen-Wilson 2002), but few or no studies exist which directly measure them—for Turkish or any other language. Instead, most studies have performed calculations using dictionaries, which are normative and conservative, or text corpora, which are compiled from disparate sources. Both text corpora and dictionaries represent the linguistic community as a whole, but neighborhood density and cohort size are ultimately facts about a single speaker's lexicon. The linguistic literature which speculates on the functional role of lexicon variables in natural language use (e.g. Wedel 2002) is thus getting ahead of itself because the variables themselves have not really been measured.

In this chapter, we employ a single-speaker corpus of Turkish to calculate lexicon variables, and to test correlations with semi-regular alternations. This novel methodology allows us to model lexical storage more directly, without relying on text-based substitutes. Furthermore, it allows us to study the idiolectal, rather than the normative, application of semi-regular alternations. If the lexical statistics approach has teeth for semi-regular alternations as well as gradient ones, for example, we should find that words such as *kanat* and *sanat* reside in clusters of similar words that exhibit similar grammatical behavior, and these clusters should be characterizable by variables like neighborhood density, which have been claimed to correlate with applicability of gradient alternations. Our question is, "Do any of the variables predicting gradient alternation applicability also predict the applicability of semi-regular alternations?"

Section 22.2 describes the Turkish alternations in more detail and reviews a previous proposal—by Wedel (2002)—for applying the lexical-statistics approach to them. Section 22.3 describes the single-speaker corpus and overall methodology. The results of our examination of lexicon variables are presented in Section 22.4 for word frequency, Section 22.5 for cohorts, and Section 22.6 for neighborhood density. Section 22.7 examines etymology. Section 22.8 concludes by reviewing the predictions of the lexical statistics approach and comparing them with those made by a generative account.

22.2 THE PROBLEM

Our test case is the occurrence of stem-final alternations in Turkish nouns. These semi-regular alternations take two forms: velar deletion, in which /k/ and /g/ delete intervocalically when stem-final (2a), and plosive voicing alternations, in which coda /p, t, t͡ʃ, k/ alternate with onset /b, d, d͡ʒ, g/ (2b):[1]

---

[1] Velar deletion is systematically inhibited following a phonemically long vowel, as in words like [meraːk-ɯ] *meraki* "curious-ACC"; see Sezer (1981). On plosive voicing alternations and velar deletion, see Lewis (1967), Zimmer and Abbott (1978), Inkelas (1995), Inkelas and Orgun (1995), Orgun (1995), Inkelas (2000), among others. The data in (2) are presented in IPA. In the dialect we describe, velar deletion is absolute; in other more conservative dialects, velars fricate or glide in the same environment.

(2)   a. *Velar deletion*

bebek   baby   bebe[Ø]-e   baby-DAT
arkeolog   archeologist   arkeolo[Ø]-a   archeologist-DAT

b. *Plosive voicing alternations*

kanat   wing   kanad-a   wing-DAT
peroksɪt   peroxide   peroksid-e   peroxide-DAT
kitap   book   kitab-a   book-DAT
gyvetʃ   clay pot   gyvedʒ-e   clay pot-DAT
kepenk   shutter   kepeng-e   shutter-DAT

These alternations do not apply to verb stems.[2] Both patterns are productive in the sense of being applied to loans (e.g. *bifstek* [bifstek], *bifsteği* [bifstei] "steak(-ACC)"; *ofsayt* [ofsajt], *ofsaydı* [ofsajduɪ] "offside(-ACC)"), but they are nonetheless semi-regular rather than fully regular. As observed by Lewis (1967), most polysyllabic words undergo the alternations, but most monosyllabic words and a substantial subset of polysyllabic words do not:

(3)   a. Some polysyllabic words resist stem-final alternations

metod   method   metod-a   method-DAT
sanat   art   sanat-a   art-DAT
jourt   yogurt   jourt-a   yogurt-DAT
tʃaput   rag, patch   tʃaput-a   rag, patch-DAT
krep   crepe   krep-e   crepe-DAT
almanak   almanac   almanak-a   almanac-DAT
sinagog   synagogue   sinagog-a   synagogue-DAT

b. Most (C)VC words resist stem-final alternations

ad   name   ad-a   name-DAT
kod   code   kod-a   code-DAT
at   horse   at-a   horse-DAT
kep   mortar board   kep-e   mortar board-DAT
hadʒ   pilgrimage   hadʒ-a   pilgrimage-DAT
satʃ   hair   satʃ-a   hair-DAT
ok   arrow   ok-a   arrow-DAT
lig   league   lig-e   league-DAT

c. Some (C)VC words display alternations:

tat   taste   tad-a   taste-DAT
dʒep   pocket   dʒeb-e   pocket-DAT
tʃok   a lot   tʃo[Ø]-a   a lot-DAT

Inkelas and Orgun (1995) have offered a generative analysis of the Turkish facts, in which cyclicity and word minimality account for the special status of (C)VC stems, while lexical prespecification of consonant features accounts for the fact that within size categories, some nouns alternate while others do not. The prespecification

---

[2] Velar deletion does apply, however, to velar-final suffixes, as in the future: *al-adak-sin*, take-FUT-2SG "you will take", *al-adʒa[Ø]-ɯz*, take-FUT-1PL.SUBJ "we will take".

analysis not only covers the relevant empirical ground, but also extends readily to other phonological problems such as geminate inalterability (Inkelas and Cho 1993) and non-derived environment blocking (Inkelas 2000).

Wedel (2002) has offered a lexical-statistics account of the same facts, starting with the experimental finding, from other studies in the literature (e.g. Luce and Pisoni 1998), that high neighborhood density inhibits word recognition. Wedel suggests that if morphophonemic alternation also inhibits recognition, there may be a trading relationship in which the higher the neighborhood density of a word, the lower its probability of alternating and vice versa. According to Wedel, "If complexity within a lexical entry slows processing in any way (for example, if sub-entries compete with one another), alternation may be marked [i.e. less likely] in dense neighborhoods, where lexical access is already inefficient." Presumably the same argument should also hold for other lexicon variables that inhibit word recognition, such as low frequency (e.g. Wingfield 1968) or large cohort size (e.g. Marslen-Wilson and Welsh 1978; Gaskell and Marslen-Wilson 2002). Using lexicon variables calculated from a dictionary of Turkish, Wedel reports an inverse correlation between neighborhood density and alternation rate within (C)VC nouns.

The experimental literature actually presents a rather mixed view of the functional consequences of neighborhood density and surface alternations, casting doubt on the likely correctness of Wedel's hypothesis (on neighborhood density, see Luce and Pisoni 1998; Vitevitch and Sommers 2003; on surface alternations, see Otake *et al.* 1996; McLennan *et al.* 2003). Yet even if we could be sure that both neighborhood density and surface alternation had a consistent inhibitory effect in lexical access, Wedel's hypothesized relationship between lexicon variables and alternations cannot be meaningfully evaluated using statistics from a dictionary. Only a single-speaker corpus provides an accurate model of lexical storage at the level of the individual speaker.

22.3 METHODOLOGY: TELL AND A FREQUENCY CORPUS

The primary source of data for this study comes from the Turkish Electronic Living Lexicon (TELL), compiled at the University of California, Berkeley.[3] In addition, we use data on word frequency from a large text corpus developed by Kemal Oflazer at Sabancı University, Turkey.

22.3.1 The Turkish Electronic Living Lexicon

The Turkish Electronic Living Lexicon (TELL) is a searchable database of some 30,000 words in Turkish whose inflected forms have been elicited from a native

---

[3] TELL is available online at http://linguistics.berkeley.edu/tell

speaker and transcribed phonologically (for a complete description of TELL, see Inkelas *et al.* 2000). The lexemes in TELL include roughly 25,000 headwords from the 2nd and 3rd editions of the Oxford Turkish–English dictionaries, along with 175 place names from an atlas of Istanbul and some 5,000 place names from a telephone area code directory of Turkey. A 63-year-old native-speaker resident of Istanbul, who speaks standard Istanbul Turkish, was presented with the entire list, in random order. For each word in the list that the speaker knew—approximately 17,500—he was asked to pronounce the word in isolation as well as in several other morphological contexts designed to reveal any morphophonemic alternations in the root. For nouns, words were elicited in the nominative case (no suffix), in the accusative case (vowel-initial suffix -*I*), in the first person predicative context (vowel-initial pre-stressing suffix -(*y*)*Im*), in the possessive case (vowel-initial suffix -*Im*) and with the derivational "professional" suffix (consonant-initial suffix -*CI*).[4]

These pronunciations were transcribed and posted online on the TELL website, where users can search the list using regular expressions. In addition to the phonological transcriptions, both morphological and etymological information are provided. The morphological information shows the breakdown of complex stems, which were excluded from the current study and do not concern us here. The etymological information, provided for a large number of lexemes, gives the source language for the word. Thus, a user interested in information about the Turkish word *kitap* "book" could search TELL and turn up the following information:[5]

Simple search of TELL

Citation	kitap
Accusative	kitabı
Predicative	kitabım
Possessive	kitabım
Professional	kitapçı
Etymology	Arabic

For all of the discussion that follows, any "root" in Turkish may be either a stand-alone word (such as when *kitap* appears in the nominative) or the basis for further suffixation. For calculating lexicon statistics such as neighborhood density, we consider only those TELL entries in which the root is also a word (this includes the nominative *kitap*, but excludes the accusative *kitabı* and all other suffixed forms). Suffixed forms are used only to determine alternation rates.

---

[4] Following standard convention, uppercase letters in the representations of affixes refer to segments which alternate, predictably, for a particular feature; in the case of vowels, the harmonic features [back] and [round]; in the case of consonants, [voice].

[5] Transcriptions are presented, in this chapter, in Turkish orthography or in IPA, as appropriate. This example uses orthography. In the TELL database itself, an ASCII transcription is used instead, with a code allowing users to translate to orthography and/or IPA.

TABLE 22.1. Overall noun count from TELL, and alternation rates

	% (C)VC nouns that alternate	% Longer nouns that alternate	COUNT
Voicing	17	52	1,065
Velar deletion	8	93	495

22.3.2 Stem-final alternations: A snapshot from TELL

A search of all words in TELL, carefully hand-edited to eliminate errors as well as morphological compounds, yielded a total of 1,560 monomorphemic nouns that are potential candidates for stem-final alternations. Of these, approximately two-thirds end in plosives and are therefore potential undergoers of the semi-regular voicing alternation. The remaining one-third end in velars and are therefore potential under-goers of the semi-regular velar alternation.

The actual alternation rates for the TELL speaker are shown in Table 22.1. These data confirm that stem-final alternations are in fact semi-regular for this speaker: they apply to most, but certainly not all, nouns in the lexicon. The data also show that alternation rates vary with word size, confirming Lewis's (1967) generalization that monosyllabic roots tend to resist these alternations. Interestingly, the TELL data also reveal a significant effect of alternation type. While voicing alternation is three times as likely for longer roots than for (C)VC roots, velar deletion is over ten times as likely for longer roots.

22.3.3 Frequency corpus

To supplement the data on the single speaker represented in TELL, we used a text corpus compiled and morphologically analyzed by Kemal Oflazer, at Sabancı University in Istanbul, Turkey, for information about word frequency. The corpus consisted of some 12 million words drawn from newspapers, novels and other sources. The top and bottom ends of the word list, sorted by frequency, are illustrated in Table 22.2. The most frequent item is a conjunction, *ve* "and"; the least frequent item, *heyecanlan-dığımda*, is a highly morphologically complex word: *heyecan-lan-dığ-ım-da* "excitement-VERBALIZER-PARTICIPLE-1.SG.POSSESSIVE-LOCATIVE".

22.4 FREQUENCY

The first variable that we considered as a possible correlate of the semi-regular pattern in Turkish is word frequency. Previous work has proposed direct correlations between frequency and grammatical behavior. Studies such as Rhodes (1992) on American English flapping and Bybee (2001) on coronal deletion have found that high-frequency words undergo these alternations at higher rates than low-frequency words do. Of

TABLE 22.2. Sample frequency counts

Turkish word	Gloss	No. of occurrences
ve	"and"	284,663
bir	"one, a"	247,294
bu	"this"	153,903
da	"and, also"	94,994
için	"for"	94,642
de	"and, also"	94,530
çok	"very"	55,210
ile	"with"	51,175
...		...
mutsuzluktan		3
minyatürden		3
çikiverdim		3
korunabilirsiniz		3
heyecanlandığımda		3

course, both flapping and coronal deletion are gradient alternations that occur due to gestural overlap and are sensitive to speech rate. By contrast, the semi-regular Turkish alternations are not gradient but categorical. That is, they apply categorically to a certain subset of Turkish nouns and are not affected by rate of speech. One question we ask in this section, then, is whether frequency has the same correlation with semi-regular, morphophonemic alternations as it does with gradient, phonetic alternations. Frequency is somewhat different from the other variables examined in this study because it can be calculated in absolute terms, without reference to other items in the lexicon. The real explanatory value of frequency, however, can only be gauged in relative terms, by asking whether alternations tend to occur more often with high-frequency words than low-frequency words, or vice versa. If frequency has a role to play in the grammatical status of a given word, therefore, it would require a computation over the whole range of frequency counts in the lexicon.

To test for a frequency effect in Turkish, we took frequency counts from the text corpus described in Section 22.3.3 and examined the correlation between mean frequency and alternation rate for nominal roots with lengths of one, two, and three syllables. The results are mixed. In the case of roots which are candidates for velar deletion, alternators overall had a much higher mean text frequency than non-alternators (Fig. 22.1). For roots which are potential undergoers of voicing alternations, however, the results are the opposite: for one-syllable roots, the only category with roots of sufficiently high frequency to allow for comparisons, the class of alternating roots has a much lower mean frequency than the category of non-alternating roots (Fig. 22.2).

Our findings for the velar alternation are thus in the same direction as that proposed by Rhodes (1992) and Bybee (2001) for gradient alternations in English: more-frequent words are more likely to alternate. Our findings for the voicing

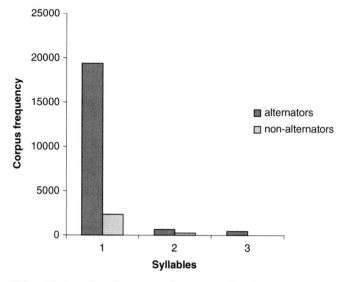

FIGURE 22.1. Velar deletion: Cumulative root frequencies for alternating and non-alternating velar-final roots

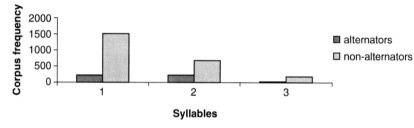

FIGURE 22.2. Voicing alternation: Cumulative root frequencies for alternating and non-alternating nonvelar-final roots

alternation, however, are in the opposite direction: less-frequent words are more likely to alternate. If frequency is to have any explanatory value for Turkish, then, its effects must be teased apart in a way that can account for these divergent results. One natural question to ask is whether the velar alternation has more in common with gradient, phonetic, patterns (such as flapping) than the voicing alternation does, but in fact the opposite would appear to be true.

22.5 NEIGHBORHOOD DENSITY

The next variable that we examined is neighborhood density, using standard measures from the literature (Luce and Pisoni 1998). For any given word, its neighbors are those words which are most phonologically similar to it, and its "neighborhood density" is the number of words that differ from it by the addition, deletion, or featural change of a single segment. For example, the Turkish word *amut* "a perpendicular" has neighbors that differ by the insertion of one segment (*mamut* "mammoth"), the deletion of one segment (*mut* "happiness"), and the change of one segment (*avut* "to soothe").

As discussed in Section 22.2, Wedel (2002) proposed a direct correlation between neighborhood density and Turkish voicing and velar alternations. Using dictionary data, Wedel found that neighborhood density decreases with word length, a fact that presumably holds cross-linguistically. Specific to the Turkish alternation question, however, Wedel also found that within the class of (C)VC nouns, there was an inverse correlation between neighborhood density and alternation rate; the non-alternators had neighborhood densities that were approximately 40 percent higher than those of the alternators.

Wedel used a print dictionary of Turkish (the Redhouse Turkish–English dictionary; Alkım 1968) both as the source of information on individual word alternations and to calculate neighborhood density. The fact that a print dictionary includes many words that an average speaker might not know skews the computation of neighborhood density to a large degree. A print dictionary also acts as a normative, rather than descriptive, source of information about alternations. A single-speaker corpus, however, permits us to study only those words known to that speaker—in effect, idiolect-specific pattern of alternation. We therefore revisit the hypothesized correlation between neighborhood density and alternation rate, using TELL as the source for both neighborhood-density calculations and word alternations.

22.5.1 Neighborhood density with a single-speaker corpus

Using the same definition of neighborhood employed in Wedel's study, we tested whether alternating nouns and non-alternating nouns had different mean neighborhood densities. We first produced a list of neighbors for each monomorphemic noun in TELL; counting these neighbors produced the "neighborhood density" variable. Table 22.3 presents examples of some of the nouns in the database and their neighbors. As discussed in Section 22.2, only nouns can potentially undergo the alternations in question but both nouns and verbs are included as potential neighbors for nouns. Our first finding is that mean neighborhood density is inversely correlated with word length (see Fig. 22.3). This finding is similar to what Wedel found using data from the Redhouse dictionary.

Unlike the dictionary study, however, we found no correlation between mean neighborhood density and alternation rate. As seen in the charts in Figure 22.4 for voicing alternations and Figure 22.5 for velar deletion, while mean neighborhood density varies according to word length, it is virtually identical for alternators and nonalternators within a given word-size category as measured by syllable count (note the almost complete overlap in Fig. 22.4 between the solid and dashed lines). The only size category for which we observed mean neighborhood density to be a factor in

TABLE 22.3. Some near-minimal pairs for neighborhood density

Root	Alternates? (accusative shown)	Neighbors	Neighborhood density
aɯt	Yes; aɯd-ɯ	azɯt, ait, acɯt, ast, ant, kɯt, aɯn, aɯz, at, aɯl, anɯt, zɯt, art, baɯt, aft, alt, aut, arɯt, akɯt, aɯr	20
ait	No; ait-i	vait, bit, ast, ant, git, aɯt, at, d͡ʒit, asit, it, alt, art, aft, fit, eit, aut, akit, sit, zait, ahit, mit	21
amut	Yes; amud-u	mamut, anut, umut, aut, mut, armut, hamut, avut	8
anut	No; anut-u	amut, aut, unut, ant, anot, anɯt, angut, avut	8
armut	Yes; armud-u	amut	1
angut	No; angut-u	anut	1

alternation rates is monosyllabic velar-final roots. Mean neighborhood density for non-alternators is higher than that for alternators (15 vs. 10), but the difference is not significant.

Neighborhood density can be defined in several ways, however. If the speaker/ listener performs computations that refer only to highly similar words in the lexicon, a narrower definition of "neighbor" could yield different results. In particular, since the Turkish alternations affect stem-final segments, we can hypothesize that neighborhood densities calculated according to changes in the final segment (as opposed to

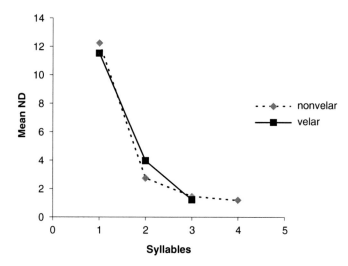

FIGURE 22.3. Mean neighborhood density as a function of root length: mean neighborhood density declines with root length

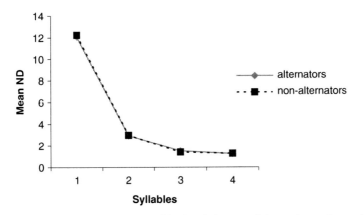

FIGURE 22.4. Voicing alternation: Mean neighborhood density of alternating and non-alternating plosive-final roots

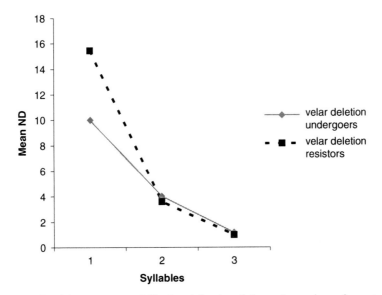

FIGURE 22.5. Velar deletion: Mean neighborhood density of alternating and nonalternating velar-final roots

the addition, deletion, or change of a segment anywhere in the word) are more likely to correlate with alternation rates.

We tested this hypothesis using neighbors that differed only in the final segment. For example, under this definition, the word [aɯt] has just four neighbors (instead of 20): [aɯn], [aɯz], [aɯl], and [aɯr]. We also tested the hypothesis using neighbors that differed only in the voicing of the final segment. For example, the word [at] has the neighbor [ad], but the word [aɯt] has no neighbors (*[aɯd]). Changing the definition of neighbor had no effect on our findings. The results were the same.

In summary, then, there is no evidence that neighborhood density explains the semi-regular pattern of alternation in Turkish; there is only evidence that mean neighborhood density is correlated with word size. We know that alternation rate is also correlated with size, but in a different way. Mean neighborhood density declines abruptly from monosyllabic to polysyllabic words (see Figs. 22.4 and 22.5), but within polysyllabic words, it declines gradually with increasing size. By contrast, as shown in Figure 22.6, alternation rates increase abruptly at the one-syllable mark but hold relatively steady across two-, three- and four-syllable roots (see Fig. 22.6).[6] This categorical difference between one-syllable roots and all others is also recognized by Wedel (2002), who ultimately concludes that the special behavior of one-syllable roots cannot be explained synchronically by mean neighborhood density although it may be—according to Wedel—the result of grammaticalization of what once was a statistical lexical effect of mean neighborhood density on alternation.

22.5.2 Frequency-weighted neighborhood density

Thus far we have found that neither word frequency nor neighborhood density correlates in a consistent way with alternation rate (word frequency makes opposite predictions for velar deletion and voicing alternations, while neighborhood density makes no predictions at all). It is conceivable, however, that the speaker/listener performs a computation over the entire lexicon using multiple variables at once. A composite variable, then, might reveal correlations with alternation rate that single variables do not.

A composite variable can also address one problem with interpreting the frequency results presented earlier: the impact of a single, highly frequent word can be enormous, obscuring what might be a more general pattern. For example, the word *çok*

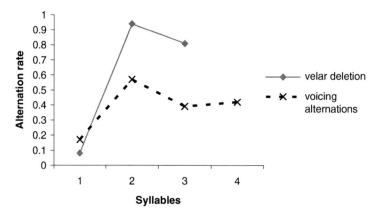

FIGURE 22.6. Alternation rate as a function of number of syllables in the root

---

[6] There were no four-syllable velar-final roots in the database.

TABLE 22.4. A near-minimal pair for neighborhood frequency

Word	Alternates? (accusative shown)	Number of neighbors	Neighborhood frequency
aɯt	Yes; aɯd-ɯ	20	113,091
ait	No; ait-i	21	106,297

[t͡ʃok] "very", a monosyllabic word that undergoes the velar deletion alternation (çoğ- u [t͡ʃo[Ø].u] "very-ACC"), occurs 55,210 times in the corpus, a number which may well be responsible for the spike in the chart in Figure 22.1. We therefore calculated a composite lexicon variable called "neighborhood frequency". This is the sum of the corpus frequencies of the neighbors of each root. Our example minimal pair for neighborhood density ([aɯt], [ait]) is a near-minimal pair for neighborhood frequency, as illustrated in Table 22.4.

Our results indicate that in general, there is no correlation between neighborhood frequency and alternation rates. For the voicing alternation, mean neighborhood frequencies are almost identical for both alternators and nonalternators (see Figs. 22.7 and 22.8). For the velar alternation, two- and three-syllable roots do not show any correlation either. For monosyllabic roots, though, higher neighborhood frequencies are correlated with the non-alternating pattern. Recall that word frequency exhibited very different relationships to voicing and velar deletion. Neighborhood frequency, on the other hand, shows a more consistent pattern across the two alternation types, at least for words that are two or more syllables in length. And for both alternations, neighborhood frequency is highest for one-syllable roots and roughly even for roots of two and three syllables.

In summary, neighborhood frequency does not in general correlate with alternation rate. Instead, what we see is a big difference between monosyllabic and larger roots, with no difference in mean neighborhood frequency between alternators and non-alternators in longer roots.

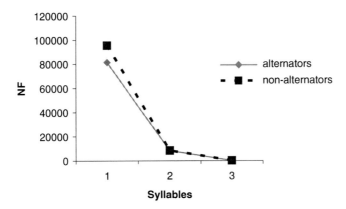

FIGURE 22.7. Voicing alternation: Neighborhood frequency for alternators and non-alternators

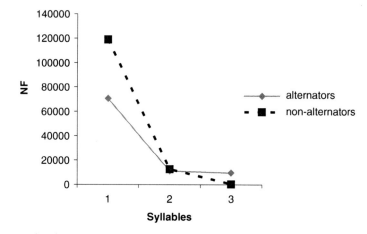

FIGURE 22.8. Velar alternation: Neighborhood frequency for alternators and nonalternators

22.6 COHORTS

The final lexicon variable that we tested is cohort size (and its related variable, uniqueness point) (Marslen-Wilson and Welsh 1978; Luce 1986; Gaskell and Marslen-Wilson 2002). Starting from the initial segment of a word, the uniqueness point is the segment at which the word becomes uniquely distinguishable from all other words in the lexicon. Some words have no uniqueness point at all. In the current study, the cohort of a word is that set of words sharing the initial substring ending one segment before the uniqueness point. Thus, in TELL the root *sokak* "street" has a uniqueness point at the fourth segment, [*a*]. No other word in the lexicon begins with the substring *soka-*, so *sokak* is uniquely identifiable at [*a*]. However, five words (including *sokak* itself) begin with the substring *sok-*; this is the cohort of *sokak*:

(4)   *sokak* street
      Uniqueness point at fourth segment (*soka-*)
      Cohort size = 5 (*sokul, sokus, sokum, sokak, sok*)

Like neighborhood density, cohort size is a way of measuring a word's phonological similarity to the rest of the lexicon. But while neighborhood density is by definition restricted to measuring words of a similar length (neighbors can differ by one segment at most), cohort size is not so restricted. Using cohort size as a lexicon variable, then, allows us to test whether phonologically similar words of any length are relevant for the speaker/listener's hypothesized computations over the lexicon.

Using TELL, we examined cohort sizes as well as uniqueness points for (C)VC roots and longer (>CVC) roots, looking separately at voicing alternations and velar deletion. We compared cohorts of small (two to three words), medium (four to nineteen words), and large (more than twenty) sizes, as well as uniqueness points that are early (before the last segment), late (at the last segment), and non-existent

TABLE 22.5. Voicing alternation in roots longer than CVC

	Cohort size		
	Small (2–3)	Medium (4–19)	Large (>19)
Number of alternators	242	174	49
Number of nonalternators	505	333	81
Alternators	32%	34%	38%

TABLE 22.6. Voicing alternation in roots longer than CVC

	Uniqueness point		
	Early	Late	None
Number of alternators	244	196	25
Number of nonalternators	662	189	68
Alternators	27%	51%	27%

(roots with no uniqueness point). The findings were negative: in no case did we find that cohort size or uniqueness point correlated with alternation rates. Rather, alternation rates were remarkably stable across all cohort and uniqueness point categories, with one exception.

Consider, for example, the figures for voicing alternation in longer roots shown in Table 22.5. The small differences in alternation rates across the cohort size groups is not significant. Figures for velar deletion are similar.

For uniqueness point, we also found essentially no difference, and certainly no statistically significant difference, except in one case: voicing alternations in roots longer than CVC (see Table 22.6). In this case, the difference between roots with a late uniqueness point and all other roots (early or no uniqueness point) is significant. Precisely in roots where the final consonant served uniquely to disambiguate the root, more alternation was found than in all other roots.

22.7 ETYMOLOGY

A simple hypothesis that immediately springs to mind but can be dismissed almost as easily is that whether or not a given noun alternates is predictable from its etymological status. If voicing alternations and velar deletion are frozen morphophonemic alternations, perhaps it is simply the case that native nouns exhibit them and loans do not. Data to test this conjecture are available in TELL, which supplies etymological information for 7,917 lexemes. Of these, the majority (6,014, or 76%) are identified as non-native. This proportion is undoubtedly exaggerated due to the fact that the

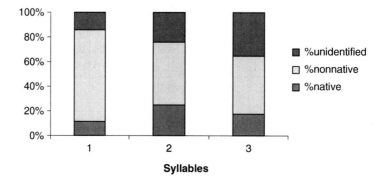

FIGURE 22.9. Etymological sources of nouns by size

etymological information in TELL came in part from dictionaries of loanwords, and is therefore biased in the direction of non-native words. Nonetheless, Turkish is noted for having borrowed heavily from a variety of languages—for example, Arabic, Persian, French, Italian, Greek—and therefore it is not surprising that TELL contains so many loanwords.

The chart in Figure 22.9 illustrates graphically the proportion of one-, two- and three-syllable nouns in TELL which are identified as native, non-native, and not identified either way. The statistical question at issue is whether native nouns differ from non-native nouns in their overall rates of alternation. The figures in Table 22.7 pose this question for roots ending in -*t* or -*d*, that is, coronal-final roots that are potential participants in the voicing alternation. As seen, the alternation rates of native and nonnative words are similar. While the number of nouns identified in the TELL database as native (which is likely to underestimate the actual representation of native roots in the lexicon) is perhaps too small to generalize from (12 only), the number of nonnative nouns is quite large (412), and it is clear that for these nouns, alternation is quite a common pattern. Many of the words in the alternating nonnative category are quite familiar items; the list includes *kilit, kilid-i* "lock(-ACC)", from Greek; *armut, armud-u* "pear(-ACC)", from Farsi; and *orkit, orkid-i* "orchid(-ACC)", probably from French.

In summary, etymological origin appears not to be a factor in overall alternation rates. As has often been remarked on in descriptions of Turkish, a large portion of the lexicon is non-native to begin with, and non-native words, old and new, are readily assimilated into patterns of morphophonological alternation, rather than resisting alternations in numbers large enough to account for the figures in Table 22.1.

TABLE 22.7. No pattern of alternation based on native status

	Polysyllabic coronal-final nouns
Native (N = 12)	50% alternation rate
Nonnative (N = 412)	42% alternation rate

22.8 CONCLUSIONS

Thus far we have found no lexicon variable that predicts or explains why (C)VC roots in Turkish alternate less than longer roots and why voicing alternations are less consistent than velar deletion within words of a given size. When a single-speaker corpus is employed, an appeal to one word's relationship with other words in the lexicon—in the form of neighborhood density, neighborhood frequency, or cohort size—does not predict whether a word is more or less likely to undergo alternation. By contrast, recall from Section 22.4 that we did find a positive correlation between raw word frequency, as calculated from a large text corpus, and velar alternation rate, though there was an inverse correlation in that same corpus between raw frequency and voicing alternation rate. Our single-speaker study thus finds no support for Wedel's (2002) hypothesis that roots with larger neighborhood densities (and presumably, lesser frequencies and larger cohorts) will be less amenable to undergoing phonological alternations.

For existing roots in Turkish, there is simply no way to predict whether a given root will alternate other than to hear the accusative (or other relevant suffixed) form. The more insightful analysis for Turkish velar deletion and voicing alternations thus appears to be the generative one, in which the underlying representation of each root contains the information necessary to predict its grammatical behavior (Inkelas and Orgun 1995). Words undergo, or resist, morphophonemic alternation in a manner unrelated to the noun's relationship to other lexical items.

23

How Do Listeners Compensate for Phonology?

Eurie Shin

23.1 INTRODUCTION

Words produced by speakers in connected speech are not identical with their intended forms; the signal that reaches the listener's ears has undergone phonological and phonetic processes of assimilation, reduction, coarticulation, and so on, leading researchers to ask how listeners map acoustic realizations to linguistic meanings. Assimilatory processes have especially attracted researchers' attention because these processes may result in phonemic change resulting in lexical ambiguity, which can challenge the listener's recognition of the intended utterance. Yet human listeners generally seem to have little or no difficulty recognizing the intended forms from assimilated forms in everyday speech. Surface-form variations resulting from assimilation do not hinder communication (Koster 1987).

Various proposals have been offered to explain how listeners cope with assimilation in order to correctly arrive at the intended forms (McClelland and Elman 1986; Lahiri and Marslen-Wilson 1991; Gaskell *et al.* 1995; Gaskell and Marslen-Wilson 1996, 1998; Coenen *et al.* 2001; Gow 2001, 2002, 2003; Weber 2001; Mitterer and Blomert 2003; Gow and Im 2004). In this chapter, I will focus on two approaches, the phonological-inference account and the feature-parsing account.

Gaskell and Marslen-Wilson (1996, 1998) proposed that speakers gain knowledge of assimilation rules through language learning, and the perceptual system applies this implicit knowledge to infer the underlying form from the assimilated form in a viable context. In a cross-modal repetition priming study, Gaskell and Marslen-Wilson (1996) found that *leam* in an unviable context (*leam gammon*) disrupts activation of the underlying form *lean*, but *leam* in a viable context (*leam bacon*) does not show this

I thank Patrice Speeter Beddor, Ian Maddieson, John J. Ohala, Manjari Ohala, Maria-Josep Solé, and two anonymous reviewers for their valuable comments and encouragement. All errors are of course mine.

inhibition effect. They argued that this viability effect originates from listeners' ability to attribute the non-coronal place of assimilated segments to the following context based on their phonological knowledge. In a subsequent phoneme monitoring experiment, Gaskell and Marslen-Wilson (1998) found that listeners' false detection of [t] was higher in a viable context (e.g. *frayp bearer* and *prayp bearer*) than in an non-viable context (e.g. *frayp carrier* and *prayp carrier*) both in real words and non-words. This result indicates that listeners can reconstruct the lawful underlying forms from assimilated forms even in non-words, and it supports the claim that listeners know the assimilation rules of their language and use them in spoken-language processing.

Gow (2002) questioned Gaskell's assumption and that of his and colleagues that assimilation creates lexical ambiguity. Unlike Gaskell and Marslen-Wilson (1996, 1998), whose stimuli deliberately produced assimilated forms, Gow used naturally occurring assimilated forms in his study. In a form-priming experiment, he found that an underlying non-coronal token *ripe berries* correctly accessed *ripe*, and an assimilated token *right berries* correctly accessed *right*, even when the assimilated form was judged as non-coronal in a perceptual-rating task. He argued that assimilated segments encode both original and assimilated place features, and listeners can map encoded features onto segments primarily by perceptual analysis of the acoustic signal without knowledge of language-specific phonological rules.

Gow's feature-parsing account is based on the assumption that assimilation occurs in a graded fashion; therefore, segments that have lost all the underlying features by complete assimilation are unlikely to have their underlying forms recovered. Although assimilation has been found to be gradient in many previous works (Barry 1985; Kerswill 1985; Nolan 1992), assimilation can also be a categorical process, resulting in phonemic changes (Silverman and Jun 1994; Holst and Nolan 1995; Jun 1996; Ellis and Hardcastle 2002; Gow and Im 2004). For example, Ellis and Hardcastle (2002) found, using electropalatography, that velar-assimilated coronals, $[_n{}^{\eta} \#k]$, were not different from underlying velars, $[\eta\#k]$, in the productions of four out of ten native English speakers, and gradient assimilation was produced by only two out of the ten speakers.[1]

Gow and Im's (2004) results from cross-linguistic form-priming tests appear to support the claim that completely and incompletely assimilated forms differ in the information available for resolving signal ambiguities, as well as the claim that recognition of assimilated forms is not influenced by language-specific assimilation rules. Their tests of incomplete voicing assimilation in Hungarian showed that these partial effects had an influence on target detection. In contrast, their investigation of complete labial-to-velar assimilation in Korean, in which F2 and F3 transitions of velarized labials $[_m{}^{\eta}\#g]$ are significantly different from unmodified [m#g] but not different from unmodified $[\eta\#g]$, failed to show context effects in the same type of

---

[1] Among the remaining four speakers, two never assimilated, and the other two showed either no assimilation or complete assimilation.

task. Moreover, in both sets of experiments, non-native speakers unfamiliar with the targeted phenomenon showed the same pattern of results as did native speakers, leading Gow and Im to conclude that listeners use general perceptual mechanisms rather than a language-specific knowledge-driven mechanism in spoken language processing.

Gow and Im (2004) did not examine whether Korean speakers can reconstruct underlying labial segments from assimilated forms in their study, but the feature-parsing account would seem to predict that they would fail to recover underlying labials from assimilated forms because no labiality remains in the speech signal. However, this is an unlikely possibility because Korean listeners can correctly produce and understand this process in everyday speech.

The goal of this study is to examine whether listeners can cope with complete assimilation. Korean place assimilation was chosen as the focus. This language has anticipatory place assimilation, with the occurrence depending on factors such as speech rate and style (Jun 1996). Coronals always undergo assimilation before non-coronals (i.e. /t.p/ → [p.p], and /t.k/ → [k.k]), labials assimilate to velars but not to coronals (i.e. /p.k/ → [k.k] but /p.t/ → [p.t]), and velars never undergo assimilation (i.e. /k.p/ → [k.p], and /k.t/ → [k.t]). Labial-to-velar assimilation is particularly interesting because it is a categorical process in Korean (Silverman and Jun 1994; Jun 1996; Gow and Im 2004) unlike the gradient coronal-to-non-coronal assimilation that Gaskell and Marslen-Wilson (1996, 1998) investigated in English.[2]

The phonological-inference and feature-parsing accounts make different predictions for how listeners will compensate for complete assimilation in Korean. For underlying heterorganic sequences that are phonetically homorganic, the phonological-inference account predicts that listeners will be able to restore the intended underlying forms using their implicit knowledge, whereas the feature-parsing account predicts that listeners will be unable to reconstruct the underlying forms.

In order to ensure that underlying features of assimilated segments are completely absent in the acoustic signal, I used only underlying homorganic consonant sequences as stimuli in this study. Stimuli of the type used by Gaskell and Marslen-Wilson (1996, 1998), for example, were not appropriate to test the possibility of phonological inference under complete assimilation because they used forms deliberately produced with assimilation. If their stimuli had traces of underlying segment features that were not detected in an off-line perception-judgment test as Gow (2002, 2003) showed, then the regressive effects they found could be also explained by feature parsing. Because the current study used stimuli devoid of residual place information, it cannot directly test the feature-parsing account; however, if the results show that listeners can reconstruct all and only possible underlying forms from the stimuli, they will support

---

[2] Existing results agree in that Korean labial-to-velar assimilation is complete, but a direct comparison between Korean labial-to-velar assimilation and Korean coronal-to-non-coronal assimilation is found in few studies. In Gow and Im (2004), one Korean male speaker's production showed partial assimilation for /n#b/ and complete assimilation for /m#g/.

the interpretation that listeners employ a knowledge-driven mechanism in speech recognition.

In addition, non-words were adopted as stimuli in this study in order to eliminate possible lexical, semantic, and frequency effects. Gow (2003) argued that the application of phonological inference in spoken word recognition is limited to "cases in which lexical or semantic factors mitigate against accepting the surface form of an item" (p. 580). If listeners can restore underlying forms from phonetically completely assimilated non-words with no lexical or semantic factors given, it will corroborate that listeners use phonological inference more extensively than Gow suggested.

The present study consists of three experiments that use an offline task, as opposed to the on-line tasks described above. Although offline measures allow post-perceptual effects to come into play, they provide the opportunity to test listeners' explicit awareness of assimilation processes—in this case, to test their judgments of possible underlying forms for assimilated segments. Experiment 1 used VCCV sequences generated by cross-splicing. The intervocalic consonants were always labial, coronal, or velar homorganic clusters and the flanking vowels were limited to [i], [ɛ], [a], [o], and [u]. In Experiment 2, non-words of the form (C)VCCV(C) were tested. The stimuli in Experiment 2 sounded more like real words than did the stimuli in Experiment 1, because there was more variability in flanking consonants and vowels, and also in syllable structures. In Experiment 3, pseudo-compounds consisting of two non-words of the form (C)(V)(C)(C)VC#CVC were used in an attempt to examine morpheme-boundary effects. If a new word does not have a recognizable morpheme, listeners might be likely to treat it at face value; if listeners could identify a morpheme in a new word, they might be more attentive to possible phonological changes occurring across morpheme boundaries. Comparison of the results of Experiments 2 and 3, of which the stimuli resemble monomorphemic words and compounds respectively, will be able to show any morpheme boundary effects in speech recognition.

23.2 EXPERIMENT I

23.2.1 Methods

A linguistically naive female Korean speaker recorded seven repetitions of the original stimuli, [Vp.pV], [Vt.tV], and [Vk.kV], in five different vowel environments [i], [ɛ], [a], [o], and [u] (where $V_1 = V_2$ and C.C are phonologically lax).[3] Using waveform editing techniques, original VCCVs were segmented into VC and CV portions which were cross-spliced with each other to create all possible homorganic VCCV stimuli, for a total of 450 tokens (five initial vowels × five final vowels × three homorganic clusters × six different tokens of each of the stimulus types = 450).[4]

---

[3] Tensing post-obstruent lax stops, a regular phonological process in Korean, occurred in all recordings.
[4] The cross-splicing technique was adopted to reduce the speaker's fatigue.

Response options were written in Korean orthography. Although Korean has three series of voiceless stops (lax, tense, and aspirated), only lax stops were used in the response options, except that the coronal coda was represented as /s/ instead of /t/ because /s/ is the most common coronal coda in Korean orthography, and also because Korean native speakers tend to reanalyze [t˺] in syllable coda as /s/ regardless of its original form.[5] All possible homorganic and heterorganic clusters were used as response options for homorganic tokens (i.e. /p.p/, /s.p/, and /k.p/ for [p.p] tokens; /p.t/, /s.t/, and /k.t/ for [t.t] tokens; /p.k/, /s.k/, and /k.k/ for [k.k] tokens). Alternative syllable-initial consonants for a given cluster (e.g. /p.t/ and /p.k/ for [p.p]) were not included because place assimilation is exclusively anticipatory in Korean.

The listeners were twelve native Korean speakers whose task was to determine whether the stimulus they heard could be transcribed as indicated in Korean orthography on the answer sheet. They were to choose either YES or NO for their answer. For example, if listeners judged /p.k/ on the answer sheet as a possible underlying form of a token containing [k.k], they chose YES.

Non-parametric tests were used for statistical analyses because of the non-normal distribution of the data. A Friedman test, a non-parametric test for related samples, was performed on YES responses to test for a main effect of coda consonant in each homorganic cluster condition. A subsequent Wilcoxon Signed-Rank test, a non-parametric test for two related samples, was carried out for post hoc comparisons.[6]

23.2.2 Results

The results of only eleven listeners were analyzed because one participant did not complete the experiment. The pooled results for these listeners are given in Table 23.1, which shows that listeners accepted homorganic clusters as possible representations for phonetic homorganic sequences over 95 percent of the time for all three places of articulation. In comparison, participants much more rarely accepted heterorganic clusters, regardless of the legitimacy (indicated by + or −) of the corresponding assimilatory patterns. Significant main effects were found for coda consonant types in all three homorganic conditions ($\chi^2 = 15.125$, $p < 0.001$ for labial, $\chi^2 = 25.485$, $p < 0.001$ for coronal, and $\chi^2 = 29.121$, $p < 0.001$ for velar stimuli). Small differences were observed among the heterorganic options for a given homorganic

---

[5] Obstruents in coda position are always unreleased and obligatorily neutralized in Korean: /p, pʰ, p*/ → [p˺], /t, tʰ, t*, s, s*, c, cʰ, c*, h/ → [t˺], and /k, kʰ, k*/ → [k˺]. Only lax types were used in the response options because Korean orthography dictates that phonetic tense sounds are represented as lax equivalents when tensing is predicted from context. Korean speakers' reanalysis of syllable coda [t] as underlying /s/ is observed in the following example: /patʰ/ "a field" is pronounced as [pat˺] in isolation; when the object particle /il/ is added, some speakers pronounce /tʰ/ as [s], i.e. /patʰ/ + /il/ → [pa.sil] instead of [pa.tʰ il].

[6] In order to monitor for any artifacts from the non-parametric tests, one-way ANOVAs were also performed with Tukey HSD post hoc tests for all three experiments. All parametric test results were found to be consistent with the non-parametric test results.

TABLE 23.1. Results of Experiment 1: YES responses for each coda condition for all stimuli

Stimuli	[p.p]	[p.p]	[p.p]	[t.t]	[t.t]	[t.t]	[k.k]	[k.k]	[k.k]
Transcription	/p.p/	/s.p/	/k.p/	/p.t/	/s.t/	/k.t/	/p.k/	/s.k/	/k.k/
Occurrence	+	+	−	−	+	−	+	+	+
Count	524/550	41/550	34/550	25/550	530/550	33/550	26/550	59/550	526/550
Percent	95.3%	7.5%	6.2%	4.5%	96.4%	6%	4.7%	10.7%	95.6%
SD	1.402	2.136	4.006	1.505	1.585	3.059	1.621	1.71	1.402

cluster, with the main difference being that listeners were more than twice as likely to respond YES when the coda option for [k.k] was coronal (10.7% YES) than when the coda option was labial (4.7% YES), which was found significant ($z = -2.82$, $p < 0.01$). No significant differences were found between coronal and velar coda responses for [p.p], and between labial and velar coda responses for [t.t].

23.2.3 Discussion

The purpose of Experiment 1 was to determine whether listeners can reconstruct the legal underlying forms from the given stimuli, which were phonetic homorganic clusters occurring in VCCV sequences. Under this condition, in which there are no phonetic cues for underlying heterorganic sequences, listeners would not be able to choose lawful heterorganic clusters over unlawful ones unless they inferred the possible underlying forms using their knowledge of phonological rules. The results of Experiment 1 suggest that listeners did not successfully infer the possible underlying forms from what they heard. Their preference for homorganic cluster transcriptions was high in each condition, and acceptance of heterorganic cluster transcriptions was consistently low, notwithstanding their legitimacy in natural speech. The results show no evidence in favor of the phonological-inference account, but the feature-parsing account can handle the results straightforwardly.

Another possibility is that subjects may not have treated the stimuli in the way they process natural speech, and instead responded depending on what they actually heard. In this scenario, that they highly preferred homorganic clusters but not heterorganic clusters is not surprising at all, because homorganic clusters were what they actually heard. This result might be due to the nature of the stimuli used in Experiment 1. These stimuli did not sound like real words because the only difference between tokens was the flanking vowels, chosen from a limited set, namely, [i], [ɛ], [a], [o], and [u]. A post hoc analysis of individual items suggested that listeners' performance was possibly affected by artificial-sounding stimuli. Twenty-seven out of 225 transcriptions tested in Experiment 1 were either real words or possible combinations of real words, such as nouns followed by case markers and verbs followed by suffixes, but these transcription options did not elicit different YES response rates compared with non-word transcriptions. Furthermore, there were five heterorganic transcriptions that are the only lawful underlying forms for the phonetic homorganic stimuli (e.g. /us.ki/ for [uk.ki] and /ip.ku/ for [ik.ku]), and these also did not elicit higher YES responses. Lexical factors are known to influence normal speech recognition (Ganong 1980; Fox 1984), yet the results of Experiment 1 do not appear to reflect such processing.

In either case, the significant difference between coronal and labial coda options for [k.k] clusters (i.e. the preference for /s.k/ over /p.k/ as an underlying form of [k.k]) is puzzling. If YES responses to heterorganic clusters are performance errors, all such clusters are expected to elicit about the same error rate. Given that the YES response rate for /s.p/ was not significantly higher than /k.p/ for [p.p] stimuli, the relatively high YES response rate for /s.k/ cannot be interpreted as listeners' general preference for coronals as assimilatory targets. At the same time, considering that the YES response rates for homorganic clusters were over 95 percent, but that for /s.k/ was only 10.7 percent, the significant difference in the YES responses to /s.k/ and /p.k/ may not be meaningful for the purpose of this experiment; this issue cannot be solved at this point.

In summary, the feature-parsing account correctly predicts the results of Experiment 1 but this interpretation is tentative due to the concern that subjects did not respond in ways consistent with what is known about the processing of natural speech. In order to resolve this issue, non-word stimuli that exhibited greater variation were used as stimuli in Experiment 2.

23.3 EXPERIMENT 2

23.3.1 Methods

In Experiment 2, monomorphemic non-words in (C)VCCV(C) form were used. The target items were 270 disyllabic non-words containing homorganic clusters [p.p], [t.t], and [k.k] (90 per each type) across a syllable boundary. Other consonants and vowels in the target words were uncontrolled to give more variability to the stimuli. Care was taken to exclude any recognizable morphemes in target words and transcription options. The target words and their transcriptions are given in Appendix A. Forty real words about farming and fishing were chosen as fillers so that the target words might sound as if they were real, and the filler items were carefully monitored to ensure that they did not contain place assimilations.

A linguistically naive female native Korean speaker recorded the stimuli. She read the stimuli at a relatively fast rate from a randomized list in which each of the 310 different items (30 tokens × three coda options × three homorganic cluster types = 270 target words, and 40 filler words) occurred twice. Stimuli that were not consistent in intonation were discarded from the stimulus set presented to listeners. For target stimuli, transcriptions of labial, coronal, and velar codas were created in the same way

TABLE 23.2. Results of Experiment 2: YES responses for each coda condition for all stimuli

Stimuli	[p.p]	[p.p]	[p.p]	[t.t]	[t.t]	[t.t]	[k.k]	[k.k]	[k.k]
Transcription	/p.p/	/s.p/	/k.p/	/p.t/	/s.t/	/k.t/	/p.k/	/s.k/	/k.k/
Occurrence	+	+	−	−	+	−	+	+	+
Count	288/300	81/300	40/300	31/300	279/300	24/300	32/300	88/300	286/300
Percent	96%	27%	13.3%	10.3%	93%	8%	10.7%	29.3%	95.3%
SD	0.871	4.11	2.966	2.587	1.513	1.625	1.833	5.192	1.281

as in Experiment 1. For each homorganic condition, transcriptions with 30 labial codas, 30 coronal codas, and 30 velar codas were provided.[7]

Ten Korean native speakers were recruited as listeners. They were told that all the words they heard were real words about farming and fishing, still used in different parts of Korea. Listeners were asked to judge whether what they heard could be transcribed as indicated on the answer sheet.

23.3.2 Results

Listeners showed high rates of correct response (96.8%) to the fillers, which indicates that participants fully understood their task and had competence in spelling. Table 23.2 gives the results, pooled across the ten listeners, for the target items. Response patterns to target items were similar to those in Experiment 1 in that listeners favored homorganic clusters far more than permissible heterorganic clusters as possible underlying forms. There were significant main effects for coda consonant types in all three homorganic conditions ($\chi^2 = 16.8$, $p < 0.001$ for labial, $\chi^2 = 15.8$, $p < 0.001$ for coronal, and $\chi^2 = 17.897$, $p < 0.001$ for velar stimuli). Listeners were more likely in Experiment 2 than in Experiment 1 to accept heterorganic transcriptions for homorganic productions. Gradient effects were observed among heterorganic response options, with labial and velar coda responses being less common—or more resistant to assimilation—than coronals. For labial stimuli, coronal coda responses were significantly more frequent than were velar responses ($z = -2.346$, $p < 0.05$). Of particular interest is that, although labials and coronals assimilate to velars in natural speech, listeners had a significantly higher rate of YES responses to coronal coda options than to labials for [k.k] stimuli ($z = -2.49$, $p < 0.05$). No significant difference was found between labial coda and velar coda responses to [t.t] tokens.

23.3.3 Discussion

The goal of Experiment 2 was to determine whether listeners can infer the lawful underlying forms from phonetic homorganic clusters in non-words, which Experiment

---

[7] Fillers were presented with 20 correct transcriptions, and 20 wrong transcriptions containing errors resulting from a random place feature change (e.g. /pu.ju/ for [ku.ju] "trough").

1 failed to show using a relatively simple form of stimuli. The more variable forms of stimuli used in Experiment 2 yielded different results from those of Experiment 1. Listeners in Experiment 2 generally preferred lawful heterorganic clusters over unlawful ones, indicating at least some compensation for assimilation. For labial stimuli, the YES response rate for the lawful coronal codas was significantly higher than that for the impermissible velar codas. For coronal stimuli, the YES response rates for illicit labial and velar codas were significantly lower than that for the permissible coronal coda option, and no significant difference was found between labial and velar coda options, consistent with phonological assimilatory patterns in Korean.

An interesting result for the velar stimuli is that, although both /s.k/ and /p.k/ assimilate to [k.k] in natural speech, the YES response rate for coronal codas was significantly higher than that for labial codas. Previous findings that labial-to-velar assimilation is categorical whereas coronal-to-noncoronal assimilation is gradient appear to be responsible for this result, but neither the phonological-inference account nor the feature-parsing account can explain why coronal codas were more accepted than labial codas for [k.k] in this experiment. The phonological-inference account predicts that listeners can infer the underlying labials from velar homorganic clusters to the same extent that they can infer the underlying coronals; the feature-parsing account predicts that listeners can retrieve neither coronal nor labial codas from the stimuli used in Experiment 2.

I speculate that the frequency of occurrence of labial-to-velar assimilation and coronal-to-noncoronal assimilation in natural speech might account for the lower YES response rate for labial underlying forms. If coronal-to-noncoronal assimilation occurs far more frequently than labial-to-velar assimilation in natural speech, then the knowledge-driven mechanism might learn from experience that coronal-to-noncoronal assimilation needs to be inferred more often than labial-to-velar assimilation. If this is the case, the phonological-inference account can explain the low YES response rate for the labial underlying forms in velar homorganic clusters. Due to the lack of available frequency data, however, this issue will remain unsolved at this point.[8]

In summary, the results of Experiment 2 revealed that listeners can infer the underlying forms from homorganic clusters in non-words, at least to a limited extent. In Experiment 3, pseudo-compounds consisting of two non-words were used as stimuli in order to see if listeners cope with assimilation across word boundaries differently from the way they deal with assimilation within monomorphemic words. If listeners' recognition of assimilated forms is influenced by morpheme boundaries, Experiment 3 is expected to yield different results from those of Experiment 2.

---

[8] Jun's (1996) production study of labial-to-velar assimilation found that 14 Korean speakers produced 63percent of [p#k] clusters with a reduced [p] gesture in casual speech, which were mostly perceived as [kk] rather than [pk] in a perception study. However, I know of no study on frequency of Korean coronal-to-velar assimilation production.

23.4 EXPERIMENT 3

23.4.1 Methods

In Experiment 3, the stimuli were pseudo-compounds consisting of two non-words. The first non-word element of each compound was a monosyllabic CVC or disyllabic (C)(V)(C)(C)VC form, ending with a labial, coronal, or velar. Ninety forms were created for each final coda for a total of 270 first elements. The second element of each compound was /paŋ/, /taŋ/, or /kaŋ/.[9] Initial-element non-words ending with labials, coronals, and velars were combined with /paŋ/, /taŋ/, and /kaŋ/, respectively, to create homorganic consonant sequences at word boundaries (i.e. [p+paŋ], [t+taŋ], and [k+kaŋ]). Target stimuli for the experiment are given in Appendix B. The filler items were 42 real words ending with vowels, and these were also combined with /paŋ/, /taŋ/, or /kaŋ/. The speaker from Experiment 2 read, in fast speech, a randomized list of the stimuli in which each item occurred twice. Items with inconsistent intonation were discarded and 312 stimuli (270 targets and 42 fillers) were chosen for presentation to listeners.

The listeners were provided with transcription options that were created in the same way as in the previous experiments. For labial coda, stimuli combined with /paŋ/ (i.e. [p+paŋ]), three different transcriptions (i.e. /p.paŋ/, /s.paŋ/, and /k.paŋ/) were created. Transcription options for the coronal and velar stimuli were made in the same fashion. None of the transcriptions contained real words.

Listeners were ten Korean native speakers. Made-up meanings of /paŋ/, /taŋ/, and /kaŋ/, and examples of compounds were presented to subjects as if they were real words. To make the task more realistic, real words that were not used in fillers were used in the demonstrations. Table 23.3 shows the examples.

23.4.2 Results

The rate of YES responses for the filler words was 96.3 percent, which indicates that subjects understood their task well. Table 23.4 sets out the results for the target words, for which, as in the previous experiments, listeners nearly always accepted homorganic cluster transcriptions as underlying forms (96% for all three groups). Significant main effects were found for coda consonant types in all three homorganic conditions ($\chi^2 = 20$, $p < 0.005$ for labial, $\chi^2 = 15.2$, $p < 0.005$ for coronal, and $\chi^2 = 17.59$, $p < 0.005$ for velar stimuli). For heterorganic cluster options, overall YES response rates were higher than in the previous experiments but listeners again showed a preference for coronal targets—in fact, an even stronger preference than in

---

[9] To make them sound more natural, these words were chosen from existing words, and made-up meanings were given to them. Presented with the made-up glosses and made-up examples as in Table 23.3, subjects accepted them as homonyms of the familiar words without difficulty.

TABLE 23.3. Meanings and examples of compounds given in the instruction of Experiment 3

Words with gloss	Example
[homi] "a weeding hoe"	[homipaŋ-in homi-ɾil cal taɾu-nin saram-ita]
[paŋ] "an expert in dealing with a tool"	"Homipaŋ is a person who handles a weeding hoe very well."
[tomi] "a sea bream"	[tomitaŋ-in tomi-ɾil cap-nin pɛ-ta]
[taŋ] "a boat used to catch certain fish"	"Tomitaŋ is a boat used to catch sea breams."
[co] "millet"	[cokaŋ-in co-ɛsʌ hik-il kollanɛ-nin toku-ta]
[kaŋ] "a tool used to filter soil from grains"	"Cokaŋ is a tool that filters soil from millet."

TABLE 23.4. Results of Experiment 3: YES responses for each condition in all three groups

Stimuli	[p.paŋ]	[p.paŋ]	[p.paŋ]	[t.taŋ]	[t.taŋ]	[t.taŋ]	[k.kaŋ]	[k.kaŋ]	[k.kaŋ]
Transcription	/p.paŋ/	/s.paŋ/	/k.paŋ/	/p.taŋ/	/s.taŋ/	/k.taŋ/	/p.kaŋ/	/s.kaŋ/	/k.kaŋ/
Occurrence	+	+	−	−	+	−	+	+	+
Count	287/300	185/300	49/300	58/300	288/300	57/300	57/300	188/300	288/300
Percent	95.7%	61.7%	16.3%	19.3%	96%	19%	19%	62.7%	96%
SD	0.9	7.697	4.504	3.894	0.98	4.92	6.051	7.743	0.872

Experiment 2. The YES response rate for the coronal coda option was significantly higher than for the velar coda option for labial stimuli ($z = -2.807$, $p < 0.01$). As in Experiment 2, coronal codas were more accepted than labial codas for velar stimuli, although both were lawful codas in this context, and the difference was significant ($z = -2.71$, $p < 0.01$). No significant difference was found between the labial coda and the velar coda responses (both unlawful) for coronal stimuli.

23.4.3 Discussion

The purpose of Experiment 3 was to test the expectation that, if listeners identified the initial morpheme in a new compound word, they might show greater assimilation across a word boundary compared with assimilation occurring within monomorphemic words. The finding that listeners compensated for assimilation more successfully in Experiment 3 than in the previous experiments suggests that there were some word-boundary effects, which I will return to in the next section. The rates of YES responses for heterorganic clusters across all homorganic conditions were higher in Experiment 3 than in Experiment 2. However, the larger standard deviations suggest that between-subject variability also increased. Interestingly, more false positives were observed as well: the YES response rates for illegitimate assimilatory patterns were higher in Experiment 3 than in Experiment 2.

Although the overall YES response rates for heterorganic clusters were higher in Experiment 3 than in the previous experiments, the patterns paralleled those found in

Experiment 2 in that homorganic clusters again consistently showed the highest YES response rates, and heterorganic options with coronal codas elicited more YES responses than those with noncoronal codas did. All non-coronal coda options, including legal /p.k/ and illegal /k.t/ and /p.t/, elicited about the same rate of YES responses. The low preference for labials as assimilatory targets (especially the low preference for lawful /p.k/) may indicate a different strategy Korean speakers employ when they deal with labial-to-velar assimilation.

23.5 GENERAL DISCUSSION

Similar response patterns emerged across three experiments. First, subjects always preferred homorganic clusters as underlying forms. Even lawful heterorganic clusters were accepted significantly less often than were homorganic clusters. Second, subjects preferred coronals as targets of assimilation over noncoronals. These two characteristics were found in all conditions across three experiments, except that listeners disallowed coronal and velar codas equally for labial stimuli in Experiment 1.

The response patterns found in both Experiments 2 and 3 support the phonological-inference account. Although the offline task used in this study cannot determine when the phonological inference occurs in the recognition process, the results of Experiment 2 and Experiment 3 suggest that Korean listeners know the Korean place assimilation rules and made use of this knowledge while they were doing the offline task. If listeners retrieved underlying forms purely based on the acoustic signal, they should not choose heterorganic consonant sequences as underlying forms at all since the given stimuli were unmodified homorganic clusters.

That listeners did not completely recover legal heterorganic clusters as underlying forms (i.e. they consistently chose homorganic options over even legal heterorganic ones) may be due to the absence of lexical and semantic factors. In natural speech, much phonetic, lexical, semantic, and sentential information—which helps listeners fully to reconstruct the designated form—is available to listeners (Ganong 1980; Fox 1984; Bard *et al.* 2001), but this information was missing in the experimental stimuli.

Another effect observed across the three experiments was that YES response rates to heterorganic clusters increased from Experiment 1 to Experiment 2 to Experiment 3, with significantly greater increases in the selection of legal heterorganic options than in the selection of illegal ones. The lower acceptance of heterorganic clusters in Experiment 1 seems to be due to the less natural nature of stimuli. For the VCCV stimuli used in Experiment 1, the only difference between the tokens (within a medial cluster type) was in the flanking vowels; the stimuli used in Experiment 2 and 3 had much more variability in the choice of consonants, vowels, and syllable structure. Additionally, the stimuli in Experiment 2 and 3 were presented to listeners as if they were real words.

The fact that listeners more successfully retrieved possible underlying forms in Experiment 3 than in Experiment 2 suggests that they rely more on phonological inference when analyzing assimilation occurring across word boundaries than within words. I speculate that this effect may due to the different degrees of assimilation occurring within words and across word boundaries in Korean. Cho (2001) found greater intergestural overlap across a morpheme boundary than within a morpheme in [t-i] and [n-i] sequences in Korean. Given that gestural overlap can lead to assimilation (Browman and Goldstein 1990), Cho's findings lead to the prediction that assimilation will occur to a greater extent across morpheme boundaries than within morphemes. If this is what actually occurs in natural speech, then listeners will know that homorganic clusters in compounds are more likely to be assimilated forms than are those in monomorphemic words. The phonological-inference account predicts that listeners will more successfully retrieve underlying forms across morpheme boundaries than within monomorphemic words because this morpheme boundary effect can be learned by native speakers through language experience. On the other hand, the feature-parsing account does not posit that listeners use this kind of knowledge in speech recognition; listeners should be able to restore assimilated forms as long as there are residual features of underlying forms, regardless of morpheme boundaries. The results of this study, which showed that listeners performed better across morpheme boundaries than within monomorphemic words, are thus in favor of the phonological-inference account. However, the effect of morphological factors in assimilation needs further investigation because it cannot account for the fact that listeners allowed more illegal heterorganic clusters in Experiment 3 than in Experiment 2.

23.6 CONCLUSION

This study examined whether listeners use their phonological knowledge to infer original forms in speech recognition. The results suggest that phonological inference is a part of the speech recognition process, working as an active device to map the speech signal onto the designated form, at least to some extent. The finding of this study—that listeners generally choose legal underlying forms over illegal ones even when the stimuli are non-words produced with underlying homorganic clusters—suggests that listeners can compensate for assimilation using their implicit knowledge. Due to the nature of the stimuli used in the experiments, in which homorganic stimuli included no residual phonetic information about possible underlying heterorganic clusters, the present study was not intended to examine the feature-parsing account. It is possible and also plausible that listeners make extensive use of the place features in the acoustic signal in natural language processing. Natural speech has rich, often redundant, acoustic, phonological, semantic, and sentential information, and listeners are likely to make use of any available information in processing speech signal. The results of this study should be interpreted as positive evidence for the knowledge-driven mechanisms that are active in speech recognition—not as evidence against other mechanisms.

APPENDIX A

Target Stimuli of Experiment 2

Stimuli	Transcription	Stimuli	Transcription	Stimuli	Transcription
kap.pʌl	kap.pʌl	kʌt.tam	kʌp.tam	kok.kon	kop.kon
kap.pon	kap.pon	kʌt.tun	kʌp.tun	nʌk.kon	nʌp.kon
kjʌp.pu	kjʌp.pu	kʌt.tʌm	kʌp.tʌm	nak.kʌn	nap.kʌn
kop.poŋ	kop.poŋ	nʌt.tan	nʌp.tan	nak.kan	nap.kan
kup.pak	kup.pak	nʌt.tɛ	nʌp.tɛ	nʌk.ku	nʌp.ku
kup.pʌl	kup.pʌl	nʌt.toŋ	nʌp.toŋ	tak.kan	tap.kan
nap.paŋ	nap.paŋ	nut.til	nup.til	tak.kin	tap.kin
nʌp.pun	nʌp.pun	tat.tʌl	tap.tʌl	tʌk.kan	tʌp.kan
nup.pon	nup.pon	tot.tʌl	top.tʌl	pak.kan	pap.kan
tap.pul	tap.pul	tut.toŋ	tup.toŋ	pak.ko	pap.ko
tap.pi	tap.pi	pot.tu	pop.tu	pok.kol	pop.kol
tʌp.puk	tʌp.puk	pot.tal	pop.tal	sak.kaŋ	sap.kaŋ
top.paŋ	top.paŋ	sat.tal	sap.tal	sak.kon	sap.kon
tup.pul	tup.pul	sat.tʌk	sap.tʌk	sʌk.kaŋ	sʌp.kaŋ
pap.pu	pap.pu	sʌt.tum	sʌp.tum	sok.kʌm	sop.kʌm
pʌp.pan	pʌp.pan	sot.tʌk	sop.tʌk	sik.kul	sip.kul
pop.pjʌŋ	pop.pjʌŋ	sit.tom	sip.tom	ak.kaŋ	ap.kaŋ
sap.pak	sap.pak	at.tok	ap.tok	ak.kun	ap.kun
sʌp.po	sʌp.po	at.toŋ	ap.toŋ	ʌk.ku	ʌp.ku
sip.pon	sip.pon	ɛt.ton	ɛp.ton	cak.kan	cap.kan
ap.pun	ap.pun	ʌt.taŋ	ʌp.taŋ	cak.kun	cap.kun
ʌp.pak	ʌp.pak	ʌt.tom	ʌp.tom	cʌk.kon	cʌp.kon
op.pan	op.pan	it.tak	ip.tak	cuk.kan	cup.kan
ip.pʌn	ip.pʌn	cat.tʌk	cap.tʌk	cik.kjʌm	cip.kjʌm
cap.pan	cap.pan	cʌt.toŋ	cʌp.toŋ	cʰak.kon	cʰap.kon
cʌp.pok	cʌp.pok	cut.tak	cup.tak	cʰak.kol	cʰap.kol
cup.pɛ	cup.pɛ	cut.tol	cup.tol	cʰik.ku	cʰip.ku
cip.po	cip.po	cit.tun	cip.tun	hak.kon	hap.kon
cip.pun	cip.pun	cʰit.ton	cʰip.ton	hak.kʌl	hap.kʌl
tʰap.pan	tʰap.pan	cʰut.tan	cʰup.tan	hok.kaŋ	hop.kaŋ
kap.pak	kas.pak	kʌt.tak	kʌs.tak	kok.kɛ	kos.kɛ
kap.pʌn	kas.pʌn	kʌt.tɛ	kʌs.tɛ	nʌk.kam	nʌs.kam

(contd.)

Target Stimuli of Experiment 2 (*Contd.*)

Stimuli	Transcription	Stimuli	Transcription	Stimuli	Transcription
kop.pak	kos.pak	kʌt.tum	kʌs.tum	nak.kam	nas.kam
nap.pok	nas.pok	nʌt.tal	nʌs.tal	nak.kʌl	nas.kʌl
nap.pul	nas.pul	nʌt.tap	nʌs.tap	nʌk.kuŋ	nʌs.kuŋ
nap.pin	nas.pin	nʌt.tok	nʌs.tok	tak.kak	tas.kak
nʌp.pok	nʌs.pok	nut.tʌk	nus.tʌk	tak.kaŋ	tas.kaŋ
nup.pu	nus.pu	tat.tam	tas.tam	tʌk.kol	tʌs.kol
tap.pan	tas.pan	tot.tʌk	tos.tʌk	pak.kon	pas.kon
tap.pɛ	tas.pɛ	tut.tan	tus.tan	pak.kup	pas.kup
top.pal	tos.pal	pot.tɛ	pos.tɛ	pok.kal	pos.kal
top.pʌn	tos.pʌn	pot.tak	pos.tak	sak.kak	sas.kak
tup.pan	tus.pan	sat.tak	sas.tak	sak.kʌl	sas.kʌl
tup.pʌl	tus.pʌl	sat.tʌm	sas.tʌm	sʌk.kam	sʌs.kam
pap.pan	pas.pan	sʌt.tok	sʌs.tok	sok.kʌn	sos.kʌn
pʌp.pak	pʌs.pak	sot.tʌm	sos.tʌm	sik.kaŋ	sis.kaŋ
pop.pu	pos.pu	sit.tal	sis.tal	ak.kan	as.kan
sap.po	sas.po	at.tom	as.tom	ak.kum	as.kum
sʌp.pon	sʌs.pon	at.tɛ	as.tɛ	ʌk.kum	ʌs.kum
sip.pi	sis.pi	ɛt.tam	ɛs.tam	cak.kak	cas.kak
sip.puk	sis.puk	ʌt.tam	ʌs.tam	cak.kop	cas.kop
ap.pi	as.pi	ʌt.toŋ	ʌs.toŋ	cʌk.kop	cʌs.kop
ʌp.pʌm	ʌs.pʌm	it.tɛ	is.tɛ	cuk.kum	cus.kum
ip.pak	is.pak	cat.tʌl	cas.tʌl	cik.kal	cis.kal
cap.pon	cas.pon	cʌt.tu	cʌs.tu	cʰak.ko	cʰas.ko
cʌp.pu	cʌs.pu	cut.tam	cus.tam	cʰak.kom	cʰas.kom
cʌp.pi	cʌs.pi	cut.tʌk	cus.tʌk	cʰik.koŋ	cʰis.koŋ
cup.pun	cus.pun	cit.toŋ	cis.toŋ	hak.kan	has.kan
cip.pak	cis.pak	cit.tol	cis.tol	hak.kuŋ	has.kuŋ
tʰap.pak	tʰas.pak	cʰut.ton	cʰus.ton	hok.kon	hos.kon
kap.puk	kak.puk	kʌt.taŋ	kʌk.taŋ	kok.ka	kok.ka
kʌp.pak	kʌk.pak	kʌt.toŋ	kʌk.toŋ	nʌk.kap	nʌk.kap
kjʌp.pan	kjʌk.pan	kʌt.tap	kʌk.tap	nak.kop	nak.kop
kop.pal	kok.pal	nʌt.to	nʌk.to	nak.kum	nak.kum
kop.pon	kok.pon	nʌt.tol	nʌk.tol	nʌk.kom	nʌk.kom
kup.pʌm	kuk.pʌm	nʌt.tun	nʌk.tun	tak.kʌm	tak.kʌm
nap.pak	nak.pak	nut.tʌn	nuk.tʌn	tak.kʌl	tak.kʌl
nap.pɛ	nak.pɛ	tat.tom	tak.tom	tʌk.kal	tʌk.kal
nap.pʌl	nak.pʌl	tot.tʌm	tok.tʌm	pak.kop	pak.kop
nap.puŋ	nak.puŋ	tut.tap	tuk.tap	pak.kul	pak.kul

nap.pi	nak.pi	pot.tom	pok.tom	pok.kon	pok.kon
nʌp.pal	nʌk.pal	pot.tap	pok.tap	sak.kɛ	sak.kɛ
nup.pan	nuk.pan	sat.ton	sak.ton	sak.kom	sak.kom
nup.pʌn	nuk.pʌn	sat.tʌl	sak.tʌl	sʌk.kon	sʌk.kon
tap.pa	tak.pa	sʌt.toŋ	sʌk.toŋ	sok.kap	sok.kap
tap.pʌl	tak.pʌl	sot.tʌl	sok.tʌl	sik.kop	sik.kop
tʌp.paŋ	tʌk.paŋ	sit.tok	sik.tok	ak.ko	ak.ko
top.pu	tok.pu	at.tu	ak.tu	ak.kop	ak.kop
tup.poŋ	tuk.poŋ	at.tum	ak.tum	ʌk.kan	ʌk.kan
sap.pʌn	sak.pʌn	ɛt.tal	ɛk.tal	cak.kam	cak.kam
sʌp.puk	sʌk.puk	ʌt.tap	ʌk.tap	cak.kol	cak.kol
sip.poŋ	sik.poŋ	ʌt.tum	ʌk.tum	cʌk.ko	cʌk.ko
ap.pɛ	ak.pɛ	it.tum	ik.tum	cuk.kup	cuk.kup
ʌp.pu	ʌk.pu	cat.tʌm	cak.tʌm	cik.kum	cik.kum
op.pʌn	ok.pʌn	cʌt.tam	cʌk.tam	cʰak.kɛ	cʰak.kɛ
ip.pu	ik.pu	cut.tʌm	cuk.tʌm	cʰak.kop	cʰak.kop
ip.pi	ik.pi	cut.tom	cuk.tom	cʰik.kap	cʰik.kap
cʌp.pi	cʌk.pi	cit.taŋ	cik.taŋ	hak.kok	hak.kok
cip.pan	cik.pan	cit.tap	cik.tap	hak.kul	hak.kul
tʰap.pu	tʰak.pu	cʰut.tal	cʰuk.tal	hok.kɛ	hok.kɛ

APPENDIX B

Target Stimuli of Experiment 3

Stimuli	Transcription	Stimuli	Transcription	Stimuli	Transcription
kan.nop.paŋ	kan.nop.paŋ	kan.tut.taŋ	kan.tup.taŋ	kam.cʌk.kaŋ	kam.cʌp.kaŋ
kaŋ.cʰip.paŋ	kaŋ.cʰip.paŋ	kam.hat.taŋ	kam.hap.taŋ	kʌ.pak.kaŋ	kʌ.pap.kaŋ
ku.kʌp.paŋ	ku.kʌp.paŋ	kʌ.hot.taŋ	kʌ.hop.taŋ	kʌ.cʰik.kaŋ	kʌ.cʰip.kaŋ
ki.nop.paŋ	ki.nop.paŋ	kok.sat.taŋ	kok.sap.taŋ	ku.cak.kaŋ	ku.cap.kaŋ
na.ap.paŋ	na.ap.paŋ	ku.hot.taŋ	ku.hop.taŋ	na.kuk.kaŋ	na.kup.kaŋ
nʌn.tap.paŋ	nʌn.tap.paŋ	nan.sʌt.taŋ	nan.sʌp.taŋ	na.cak.kaŋ	na.cap.kaŋ
nʌp.paŋ	nʌp.paŋ	nʌ.hot.taŋ	nʌ.hop.taŋ	nʌ.tʌk.kaŋ	nʌ.tʌp.kaŋ
no.kap.paŋ	no.kap.paŋ	nu.sat.taŋ	nu.sap.taŋ	no.ʌk.kaŋ	no.ʌp.kaŋ
no.sip.paŋ	no.sip.paŋ	ta.ot.taŋ	ta.op.taŋ	ta.cik.kaŋ	ta.cip.kaŋ
ta.hop.paŋ	ta.hop.paŋ	to.kɛt.taŋ	to.kɛp.taŋ	tan.nok.kaŋ	tan.nop.kaŋ
taŋ.nʌp.paŋ	taŋ.nʌp.paŋ	to.ot.taŋ	to.op.taŋ	tʌn.sik.kaŋ	tʌn.sip.kaŋ
tʌn.tap.paŋ	tʌn.tap.paŋ	tun.nʌt.taŋ	tun.nʌp.taŋ	to.ʌk.kaŋ	to.ʌp.kaŋ
toŋ.ap.paŋ	toŋ.ap.paŋ	ma.rat.taŋ	ma.rap.taŋ	tu.sik.kaŋ	tu.sip.kaŋ
ma.kop.paŋ	ma.kop.paŋ	man.sit.taŋ	man.sip.taŋ	mo.nok.kaŋ	mo.nop.kaŋ
man.cip.paŋ	man.cip.paŋ	mun.nat.taŋ	mun.nap.taŋ	mo.sʌk.kaŋ	mo.sʌp.kaŋ
maŋ.ʌp.paŋ	maŋ.ʌp.paŋ	mun.not.taŋ	mun.nop.taŋ	mi.tak.kaŋ	mi.tap.kaŋ
mo.ʌp.paŋ	mo.ʌp.paŋ	mi.rʌt.taŋ	mi.rʌp.taŋ	pam.sʌk.kaŋ	pam.sʌp.kaŋ
mu.hop.paŋ	mu.hop.paŋ	sa.kut.taŋ	sa.kup.taŋ	sam.kɛk.kaŋ	sam.kɛp.kaŋ
mun.cʌp.paŋ	mun.cʌp.paŋ	su.cʌt.taŋ	su.cʌp.taŋ	sʌ.ʌk.kaŋ	sʌ.ʌp.kaŋ
mi.nup.paŋ	mi.nup.paŋ	ʌ.cʌt.taŋ	ʌ.cʌp.taŋ	su.nʌk.kaŋ	su.nʌp.kaŋ
sʌ.tʌp.paŋ	sʌ.tʌp.paŋ	un.tʌt.taŋ	un.tʌp.taŋ	si.nʌk.kaŋ	si.nʌp.kaŋ
ʌ.ip.paŋ	ʌ.ip.paŋ	cam.not.taŋ	cam.nop.taŋ	a.sik.kaŋ	a.sip.kaŋ
ʌn.sip.paŋ	ʌn.sip.paŋ	caŋ.hot.taŋ	caŋ.hop.taŋ	ʌ.cak.kaŋ	ʌ.cap.kaŋ
un.tap.paŋ	un.tap.paŋ	cu.kut.taŋ	cu.kup.taŋ	cʌ.tok.kaŋ	cʌ.top.kaŋ
cʌ.rap.paŋ	cʌ.rap.paŋ	cin.tʌt.taŋ	cin.tʌp.taŋ	cuŋ.tʌk.kaŋ	cuŋ.tʌp.kaŋ
cu.nʌp.paŋ	cu.nʌp.paŋ	cʰu.kɛt.taŋ	cʰu.kɛp.taŋ	cʰʌ.nok.kaŋ	cʰʌ.nop.kaŋ
cʰʌŋ.tap.paŋ	cʰʌŋ.tap.paŋ	ha.kot.taŋ	ha.kop.taŋ	cʰu.tak.kaŋ	cʰu.tap.kaŋ
cʰi.kʌp.paŋ	cʰi.kʌp.paŋ	ho.kʌt.taŋ	ho.kʌp.taŋ	ha.cʌk.kaŋ	ha.cʌp.kaŋ
han.tup.paŋ	han.tup.paŋ	hu.kɛt.taŋ	hu.kɛp.taŋ	hʌm.tak.kaŋ	hʌm.tap.kaŋ
ho.tap.paŋ	ho.tap.paŋ	hu.kot.taŋ	hu.kop.taŋ	ho.nak.kaŋ	ho.nap.kaŋ
ka.hup.paŋ	ka.hus.paŋ	kʌ.kat.taŋ	kʌ.kas.taŋ	kʌ.tʌk.kaŋ	kʌ.tʌs.kaŋ
ko.nɛp.paŋ	ko.nɛs.paŋ	ko.rat.taŋ	ko.ras.taŋ	ko.rʌk.kaŋ	ko.rʌs.kaŋ

ku.nup.paŋ	ku.nus.paŋ	kun.not.taŋ	kun.nos.taŋ	kon.sʌk.kaŋ	kon.sʌs.kaŋ
nan.tup.paŋ	nan.tus.paŋ	na.ɾot.taŋ	na.ɾos.taŋ	kil.lak.kaŋ	kil.las.kaŋ
nʌ.kap.paŋ	nʌ.kas.paŋ	nan.tot.taŋ	nan.tos.taŋ	nam.suk.kaŋ	nam.sus.kaŋ
no.tup.paŋ	no.tus.paŋ	nʌ.kɛt.taŋ	nʌ.kɛs.taŋ	nʌ.sak.kaŋ	nʌ.sas.kaŋ
nu.kop.paŋ	nu.kos.paŋ	no.kot.taŋ	no.kos.taŋ	no.cik.kaŋ	no.cis.kaŋ
ta.ɾop.paŋ	ta.ɾos.paŋ	nu.cut.taŋ	nu.cus.taŋ	nu.tok.kaŋ	nu.tos.kaŋ
tʌ.kʌp.paŋ	tʌ.kʌs.paŋ	ta.nɛt.taŋ	ta.nɛs.taŋ	tʌ.kok.kaŋ	tʌ.kos.kaŋ
tʌ.sop.paŋ	tʌ.sos.paŋ	tam.cit.taŋ	tam.cis.taŋ	tʌ.cak.kaŋ	tʌ.cas.kaŋ
to.kop.paŋ	to.kos.paŋ	tʌ.kat.taŋ	tʌ.kas.taŋ	tʌŋ.ak.kaŋ	tʌŋ.as.kaŋ
tu.nɛp.paŋ	tu.nɛs.paŋ	to.kʌt.taŋ	to.kʌs.taŋ	to.ɾak.kaŋ	to.ɾas.kaŋ
tu.ap.paŋ	tu.as.paŋ	toŋ.cʌt.taŋ	toŋ.cʌs.taŋ	tun.cʌk.kaŋ	tun.cʌs.kaŋ
tun.top.paŋ	tun.tos.paŋ	tu.ɾot.taŋ	tu.ɾos.taŋ	man.tok.kaŋ	man.tos.kaŋ
mo.kop.paŋ	mo.kos.paŋ	mo.kʌt.taŋ	mo.kʌs.taŋ	mo.ak.kaŋ	mo.as.kaŋ
mjo.cʌp.paŋ	mjo.cʌs.paŋ	mu.nɛt.taŋ	mu.nɛs.taŋ	mi.hok.kaŋ	mi.hos.kaŋ
sa.nop.paŋ	sa.nos.paŋ	mi.tot.taŋ	mi.tos.taŋ	pam.cak.kaŋ	pam.cas.kaŋ
sʌ.nɛp.paŋ	sʌ.nɛs.paŋ	min.kot.taŋ	min.kos.taŋ	sa.kʌk.kaŋ	sa.kʌs.kaŋ
su.ɾʌp.paŋ	su.ɾʌs.paŋ	min.cʌt.taŋ	min.cʌs.taŋ	sam.nak.kaŋ	sam.nas.kaŋ
si.kop.paŋ	si.kos.paŋ	pam.sʌt.taŋ	pam.sʌs.taŋ	sʌl.cʌk.kaŋ	sʌl.cʌs.kaŋ
an.cʌp.paŋ	an.cʌs.paŋ	sʌ.cʰut.taŋ	sʌ.cʰus.taŋ	an.sʌk.kaŋ	an.sʌs.kaŋ
ʌ.tʌp.paŋ	ʌ.tʌs.paŋ	sun.nut.taŋ	sun.nus.taŋ	ʌ.rik.kaŋ	ʌ.ris.kaŋ
ul.top.paŋ	ul.tos.paŋ	sin.tʌt.taŋ	sin.tʌs.taŋ	u.tʌk.kaŋ	u.tʌs.kaŋ
co.nop.paŋ	co.nos.paŋ	ʌ.kut.taŋ	ʌ.kus.taŋ	ca.tak.kaŋ	ca.tas.kaŋ
cʰʌ.tap.paŋ	cʰʌ.tas.paŋ	u.cʌt.taŋ	u.cʌs.taŋ	co.tak.kaŋ	co.tas.kaŋ
cʰun.tʌp.paŋ	cʰun.tʌs.paŋ	cu.ɾʌt.taŋ	cu.ɾʌs.taŋ	cu.hok.kaŋ	cu.hos.kaŋ
cʰi.tap.paŋ	cʰi.tas.paŋ	cʰo.sat.taŋ	cʰo.sas.taŋ	cʰo.tʌk.kaŋ	cʰo.tʌs.kaŋ
tʰup.paŋ	tʰus.paŋ	cʰu.not.taŋ	cʰu.nos.taŋ	cʰuk.kaŋ	cʰus.kaŋ
ha.nop.paŋ	ha.nos.paŋ	ho.ɾut.taŋ	ho.ɾus.taŋ	cʰi.sik.kaŋ	cʰi.sis.kaŋ
hon.cip.paŋ	hon.cis.paŋ	hut.taŋ	hus.taŋ	hul.tok.kaŋ	hul.tos.kaŋ
kʌ.nup.paŋ	kʌ.nuk.paŋ	kʌ.rat.taŋ	kʌ.rak.taŋ	kaŋ.uk.kaŋ	kaŋ.uk.kaŋ
koŋ.up.paŋ	koŋ.uk.paŋ	ko.pot.taŋ	ko.pok.taŋ	kʌ.hak.kaŋ	kʌ.hak.kaŋ
kuŋ.cʰop.paŋ	kuŋ.cʰok.paŋ	ki.ot.taŋ	ki.ok.taŋ	ko.ɾak.kaŋ	ko.ɾak.kaŋ
na.ɾap.paŋ	na.ɾʌk.paŋ	na.kat.taŋ	na.kak.taŋ	ki.tak.kaŋ	ki.tak.kaŋ
nan.cʌp.paŋ	nan.cʌk.paŋ	na.sit.taŋ	na.sik.taŋ	na.ok.kaŋ	na.ok.kaŋ
nʌ.ɾap.paŋ	nʌ.ɾak.paŋ	no.cut.taŋ	no.cuk.taŋ	nan.hok.kaŋ	nan.hok.kaŋ
nʌn.cʰip.paŋ	nʌn.cʰik.paŋ	non.cʰot.taŋ	non.cʰok.taŋ	nʌ.ak.kaŋ	nʌ.ak.kaŋ
nu.ap.paŋ	nu.ak.paŋ	nu.ʌt.taŋ	nu.ʌk.taŋ	noŋ.tʌk.kaŋ	noŋ.tʌk.kaŋ
ta.kʌp.paŋ	ta.kʌk.paŋ	nɨt.taŋ	nɨk.taŋ	nu.sik.kaŋ	nu.sik.kaŋ
tʌ.ɾup.paŋ	tʌ.ɾuk.paŋ	taŋ.kɛt.taŋ	taŋ.kɛk.taŋ	nuk.kaŋ	nuk.kaŋ
tʌ.ʌp.paŋ	tʌ.ʌk.paŋ	tʌn.sat.taŋ	tʌn.sak.taŋ	tʌ.nuk.kaŋ	tʌ.nuk.kaŋ
to.sop.paŋ	to.sok.paŋ	to.not.taŋ	to.nok.taŋ	tu.kʌk.kaŋ	tu.kʌk.kaŋ

(contd.)

Target Stimuli of Experiment 3 (*Contd.*)

Stimuli	Transcription	Stimuli	Transcription	Stimuli	Transcription
toŋ.cʰop.paŋ	toŋ.cʰok.paŋ	tu.kut.taŋ	tu.kuk.taŋ	ma.sʌk.kaŋ	ma.sʌk.kaŋ
tu.sap.paŋ	tu.sak.paŋ	tu.it.taŋ	tu.ik.taŋ	mo.ɾak.kaŋ	mo.ɾʌk.kaŋ
mo.kap.paŋ	mo.kak.paŋ	mo.sot.taŋ	mo.sok.taŋ	mo.cak.kaŋ	mo.cʌk.kaŋ
mon.tʌp.paŋ	mon.tʌk.paŋ	mun.cʰut.taŋ	mun.cʰuk.taŋ	mul.tak.kaŋ	mul.tak.kaŋ
mi.kʌp.paŋ	mi.kʌk.paŋ	mi.cut.taŋ	mi.cuk.taŋ	pon.sak.kaŋ	pon.sʌk.kaŋ
min.tup.paŋ	min.tuk.paŋ	min.tat.taŋ	min.tak.taŋ	so.tʌk.kaŋ	so.tʌk.kaŋ
pan.cʌp.paŋ	pan.cʌk.paŋ	pu.kʌt.taŋ	pu.kʌk.taŋ	su.hok.kaŋ	su.hok.kaŋ
so.nʌp.paŋ	so.nʌk.paŋ	san.tut.taŋ	san.tuk.taŋ	ʌ.tak.kaŋ	ʌ.tak.kaŋ
su.nop.paŋ	su.nok.paŋ	so.ɾat.taŋ	so.ɾak.taŋ	o.sʌk.kaŋ	o.sʌk.kaŋ
sin.nap.paŋ	sin.nak.paŋ	ʌ.ɾut.taŋ	ʌ.ɾuk.taŋ	in.tok.kaŋ	in.tok.kaŋ
u.cap.paŋ	u.cak.paŋ	o.sat.taŋ	o.sak.taŋ	cʌ.ɾak.kaŋ	cʌ.ɾʌk.kaŋ
cʌ.tap.paŋ	cʌ.tak.paŋ	can.tʌt.taŋ	can.tʌk.taŋ	cʌn.sak.kaŋ	cʌn.sak.kaŋ
cun.tap.paŋ	cun.tak.paŋ	cʌ.nɛt.taŋ	cʌ.nɛk.taŋ	cʰam.cʌk.kaŋ	cʰam.cʌk.kaŋ
ci.kop.paŋ	ci.kok.paŋ	cu.nat.taŋ	cu.nak.taŋ	cʰʌ.sik.kaŋ	cʰʌ.sik.kaŋ
cʰo.tap.paŋ	cʰo.tak.paŋ	cin.tat.taŋ	cin.tak.taŋ	cʰu.kʌk.kaŋ	cʰu.kʌk.kaŋ
ha.sip.paŋ	ha.sik.paŋ	cʰo.nut.taŋ	cʰo.nuk.taŋ	cʰin.nak.kaŋ	cʰin.nak.kaŋ
han.tap.paŋ	han.tak.paŋ	cʰi.kat.taŋ	cʰi.kak.taŋ	hʌm.sik.kaŋ	hʌm.sik.kaŋ
ho.tɛp.paŋ	ho.tɛk.paŋ	ha.sat.taŋ	ha.sak.taŋ	hun.cʌk.kaŋ	hun.cʌk.kaŋ

NOTES ON CONTRIBUTORS

Christian Abry is Professor of Experimental Phonetics (Stendhal University, Grenoble), founder of the Speech, Multimodality & Development group at ICP (CNRS). His main interests are speech production, control and robotics, perceptuo-motor interactions, speech working memory, bimodal speech, speech development, speech evolution, and narratives. He has published in among others *Journal of Phonetics*, *Journal of the Acoustical Society of America*, *Speech Communication*, *Interaction Studies*, *Behavioral and Brain Sciences*, *NeuroImage*, *Journal of Neurolinguistics*, *Perception & Psychophysics*, and co-authored a chapter in *Phonetics, Phonology, and Cognition* (2002, Oxford University Press).

Peter F. Assmann is Professor in the School of Behavioral and Brain Sciences at the University of Texas at Dallas. His research investigates the perceptual strategies used by listeners to recognize and understand speech, especially under adverse conditions where background noise and interfering sounds are present. His recent work examines the effects of frequency shifts on speech perception. The ability to understand frequency-shifted speech is a fundamental component of everyday speech communication because listeners must adapt to the frequency shifts that result from differences in larynx and vocal tract size across talkers.

Hans Basbøll is Professor of Scandinavian Linguistics at the Institute of Language and Communication, University of Southern Denmark. He has directed projects on Danish language acquisition. Among his recent publications is *The Phonology of Danish* (2005, Oxford University Press). Hans Basbøll is a Fellow of The Royal Danish Academy of Sciences and Letters.

Patrice Speeter Beddor is Professor of Linguistics and currently Chair of the Department of Linguistics at the University of Michigan. Her primary research interests are in the areas of speech perception, coarticulation, and the phonetic factors underlying sound change, and her major recent publications focus on the intersection of these areas of inquiry.

Juliette Blevins is a Senior Scientist in the Department of Linguistics, Max Planck Institute for Evolutionary Anthropology, Leipzig. She received her doctorate in Linguistics from MIT in 1985 and, the same year, joined the Department of Linguistics at the University of Texas at Austin. Her research interests in phonology range from historical, descriptive, and typological studies to theoretical analysis with a synthesis in her recent book *Evolutionary Phonology* (2004, Cambridge University Press). Other interests include Oceanic languages, Australian Aboriginal languages, and Native American languages. She is currently working on a database of regular sound change, and preparing a grammar of Yurok, an endangered language of northwestern California.

Louis-Jean Boë is senior researcher at the Institute of Speech Communication (ICP) at the University of Grenoble. His main interests lie in sound structure in relationship with ontogenesis and phylogenesis, the origin of speech and language, the history of speech sciences, and the deontological problems of forensic application of speech sciences.

Patrizia Bonaventura is Assistant Professor in Speech and Hearing Science at Case Western Reserve University, Cleveland, OH. She has a background in phonetics, speech science, linguistics, and speech processing. She worked in multilingual speech recognition and synthesis for Italian Telecom, Hamburg University, and in the US; she received her Ph.D. from the Ohio State University in 2003. Her present research focuses on motor control mechanisms in normal and disordered speech production, by x-ray microbeam and EMA analyses. Her second field of interest is intonation modeling, based on semio-syntactic analysis, for applications to speech synthesis.

Anthony Brasher is a doctoral student at the University of Michigan, Ann Arbor. His interests include historical linguistics, socio-phonetics, and speech perception and articulation, especially as pertaining to phonology and sound change. Past work has examined the perception of breathy stops in Hindi. He is currently investigating the effects of speech style on (nasal) coarticulation in English.

M. Grazia Busà is Associate Professor of English Linguistics and Phonetics at the University of Padova, Italy. Her research interests include speech perception and production, especially in relation to sound change, second language acquisition, and discourse analysis. She has also worked on acoustic, articulatory, and aerodynamic characteristics of Italian.

Didier Demolin is Professor of Linguistics, Music Acoustics, Ethnomusicology, and Director of the Laboratory of Experimental Phonology at the Université Libre de Bruxelles in Belgium. He is also Visiting Professor at the Universidade de São Paulo and a member of the Académie Royale des Sciences d'Outre Mer in Belgium.

Bruce Derwing is Professor Emeritus in the Department of Linguistics at the University of Alberta (Edmonton, Canada). He was a pioneer in the development of non-chronometric psycholinguistic techniques for the cross-linguistic investigation of phonological units, involving languages as disparate as Arabic, Blackfoot, Korean, Minnan, and Swiss German. His current research focuses on the phonological and morphological aspects of the form, structure, and organization of the mental lexicon, with a special interest in the role of orthographic knowledge on the perceived segmentation of speech.

Olle Engstrand is Professor of Phonetics with an interest in early speech development, speaking styles, phonetic typology including dialectology, and in intersection between these areas. He has coordinated the national research project "Phonetics and phonology of the Swedish dialects around the year 2000".

Johan Frid is a Research Fellow in Phonetics with a specialization in speech technology. His main interests are text-to-speech, speech synthesis, automatic processing of speech, and prosody. He is working with automatic methods of analysis and recognition of speech, as well as on synthesis-related software and tools.

Osamu Fujimura is Professor Emeritus of Speech and Hearing Science at The Ohio State University and Fellow of the International Institute for Advanced Studies in Kyoto, Japan. He was formerly Head of AT&T Bell Laboratories Departments of Linguistics and Artificial Intelligence Research, after having directed the Research Institute of Logopedics and Phoniatrics of the University of Tokyo as Professor of the Faculty of Medicine and of the Department of Linguistics, Faculty of Letters. His major research interests are theoretical and experimental phonetics, integrating speech physiology, physics, and general linguistics.

Hiroya Fujisaki is Professor Emeritus of the University of Tokyo, where he was affiliated with the Faculties of Engineering, Letters, and Medicine, working on various aspects of spoken language. He served as leader on Japanese national projects on spoken-language processing and on human–machine spoken-dialogue systems. He also founded the International Conference on Spoken Language Processing. He is an honorary member of the Acoustical Society of Japan, a fellow of the Acoustical Society of America, a fellow of the Institute of Electronics, Information and Communication Engineers, a Board member of the International Speech Communication Association, and a corresponding member of the Academy of Sciences of Göttingen, Germany.

Nina Grønnum works at the Department of Nordic Studies and Linguistics, University of Copenhagen. She received her M.A. in phonetics in 1972, her Ph.D. in 1981 (*Studies in Danish Intonation*), and her Danish Doctorate in 1992 (*The Groundworks of Danish Intonation*). From 1972 to 1976 she was an Assistant Professor, between 1976 and 1993 she was an Associate Professor, and since 1993 she has been an Associate Professor with Special Qualifications. She is a Fellow of The Royal Danish Academy of Sciences and Letters.

Wentao Gu is a member of the research staff at the Department of Electronic Engineering, Chinese University of Hong Kong. He was a Lecturer at Shanghai Jiatong University (1999–2005), and JSPS Postdoctoral Research Fellow at the University of Tokyo (2004–2006). His interests include prosody modeling, speech synthesis, automatic speech recognition, second-language acquisition, and computational phonology, especially for tone languages. He is a member of the International Speech Communication Association, and the Acoustic Society of Japan.

Larry M. Hyman received his Ph.D. in Linguistics from UCLA in 1972. He taught at the University of Southern California from 1971 to 1988. He came to Berkeley's Department of Linguistics in 1988, which he chaired from 1991 to 2002. He has worked extensively on phonological theory and other aspects of language structure, concentrating on the Niger-Congo languages of Africa, especially Bantu. He has published *Phonology: Theory and Analysis* (1975, Holt, Rineholt and Winston), *A Theory of Phonological Weight* (1985, Foris; 2003, CSLI), and numerous articles in both theoretical and Africanist journals. He is currently writing a book entitled *Tone Systems: Typology and Description* for Cambridge University Press.

Sharon Inkelas received her Ph.D. in 1989 from Stanford University. She is now a Professor in the Department of Linguistics at the University of California, Berkeley, where she has taught since 1992. She has also taught at UCLA, the University of Maryland, and summer linguistics institutes in the United States and the Netherlands. Her specialities are phonology and morphology. Her most recent book, *Reduplication: Doubling in Morphology,* with Cheryl Zoll, appeared in 2005 with Cambridge University Press.

Keith Johnson is a Professor in the Department of Linguistics at the University of California, Berkeley. He received his Ph.D. in 1988 from Ohio State University. He has held postdoctoral fellowships at Indiana University (with David Pisoni) and UCLA (with Pat Keating and the late Peter Ladefoged) and faculty positions at the University of Alabama, Birmingham, and at the Ohio State University. His research interests include the phonetic description of Native American Indian languages, talker normalization in speech perception, cross-linguistic speech perception, and the influence of perception on language sound systems.

Klaus J. Kohler is Professor Emeritus of Phonetics and Digital Speech Processing, Institute of Phonetics and Digital Speech Processing, University of Kiel. His research interests include prosody, phrase-level phonetics and phonology, sound patterns of spontaneous speech, and synchronic articulatory reduction and historical sound change. He has a major research project on Sound Patterns of German Spontaneous Speech. His numerous publications include *Aspects of the History of English Pronunciation in Scotland* (Ph.D., Edinburgh 1964), *Einführung in die Phonetik des Deutschen* (1977, Erich Schmidt Verlag; 2nd edn 1995), and an edited volume *Progress in Experimental Phonology. From Communicative Function to Phonetic Substance and Vice Versa* (*Phonetica* 2005).

Björn Lindblom is Professor Emeritus of Speech Physiology and Speech Perception. His main research interest is the biology of spoken language. In the past he has done experimental research on speaking, listening, and learning to speak. His current work is focused on the modeling of the phonetics and phonology of speech development.

Ian Maddieson was born and educated in the UK but after teaching in Nigeria he moved to the US to complete his doctorate at UCLA in 1977. He remained at the UCLA Phonetics Laboratory for many years until joining UC Berkeley, where he is now Emeritus. His major research interest is in the variety of sound systems in the world's languages. Major publications are *Patterns of Sounds* (1984, Cambridge University Press) and *Sounds of the World's Languages* (with Peter Ladefoged, 1996, Blackwell). He was a major contributor to the recent *World Atlas of Language Structures* (2005, Oxford University Press); this project has renewed his interest in mapping the global distribution of phonological features around the world.

Chandan Narayan is a postdoctoral fellow at the Institute for Research in Cognitive Science at the University of Pennsylvania. He received his Ph.D. in Linguistics from the University of Michigan in 2006. His primary areas of research are acoustic phonetics, the development of speech perception in infancy, and explanations for phonological patterns in speech perception.

Terrance M. Nearey is Professor of Linguistics at the University of Alberta. His area of interest is the relationships among acoustic cues, candidate phonological structures, and human speech perception. This work focuses on the development and statistical evaluation of phonetically explicit pattern-recognition models. These models are designed to account for the fine structure of listeners' categorization of natural and synthetic speech signals in controlled perception experiments.

Sieb Nooteboom received his Ph.D. in 1972 from Utrecht University. He has had positions as Researcher in Philips Research in Eindhoven (1966–1988), part-time Professor of Phonetics in Leyden University (1980–1988), part-time Professor of Experimental Linguistics in Eindhoven Technical University (1986–1988), full-time Professor of Phonetics in Utrecht University (1988–2004), and part-time Professor of Phonetics in Utrecht University (2004–2006).

John J. Ohala is Professor Emeritus in the Department of Linguistics, University of California, Berkeley. He received his Ph.D. from UCLA in 1969 and joined UCB in 1970 after a one-year post-doctoral fellowship at the University of Tokyo. He has held research or teaching positions at Bell Telephone Labs, University of Copenhagen, UCLA, and City University of Hong Kong, among others. His research has centered on speech production and perception, especially as this relates to sound change, and on the ethology of vocal communication as manifested in intonation and sound symbolic vocabulary.

Manjari Ohala received her Ph.D. from UCLA in 1972. She is now Professor, and currently Chair, of the Department of Linguistics and Language Development at San Jose State University, where she has taught since 1974. She has also taught at University of Maryland (Linguistic Society of America Summer Institute), UC Davis, UC Berkeley, and the University of Alberta, Edmonton. Her research interests in phonetics and phonology include experimental phonology and the phonetics and phonology of Indo-Aryan languages. She is the author of numerous articles on Hindi phonetics and phonology, and *Aspects of Hindi Phonology* (1983, Motilal Banarsidass).

Sumio Ohno is Associate Professor at the Tokyo University of Technology. His interests include speech perception, prosody, and automatic speech recognition, with special emphasis on analysis and processing of emotional speech. He is a member of the Institute of Electronics, Information and Communication Engineers, and the Acoustical Society of Japan.

Anne Pycha is completing her doctorate in the Linguistics Department at the University of California, Berkeley.

Hugo Quené received his Ph.D. from Utrecht University in 1989. He has held positions as Research Scientist in Utrecht University (1986–1989), Assistant Professor of Phonetics at Leyden University (1989–1990), Assistant Professor of Phonetics (1989–2004), and Associate Professor of Phonetics at Utrecht University (2004–). He was Fulbright Visiting Scolar at Indiana University, Bloomington, in 2001 and 2002.

Rungpat Roengpitya received her Ph.D. from the University of California at Berkeley in 2001. She is a Lecturer of English and Linguistics at the College of Religious Studies, Mahidol University, Thailand. Her research interests are phonetics, Southeast Asian languages and linguistics, and language learning.

Eurie Shin is a Ph.D. candidate in Linguistics at the University of California, Berkeley. Her dissertation research focuses on the interaction of micro- and macro-prosodic effects on the fundamental frequency in Korean and English. Her primary research interests include the phonetics–phonology interface, phonetic variation, listener-directed speech phenomena, psycholinguistics, and second-language acquisition.

Jean-Luc Schwartz, a member of the French CNRS, has been leading the ICP (Institut de la Communication Parlée) since 2003. His main areas of research involve auditory modeling, audiovisual speech perception, perceptuo-motor interactions, speech robotics, and the emergence of language. He has been involved in national and European projects, and authored or co-authored more than forty publications in international journals and about thirty book chapters.

Maria-Josep Solé is a Professor in English Phonetics and Linguistics at the Autonomous University of Barcelona, Spain. She has been a Fulbright Visiting Scholar at the University of California, Berkeley, on various occasions. She has published on speech production (interarticulatory coordination and aerodynamics of speech sounds), the articulatory and perceptual basis of sound change, cross-linguistic phonological patterns, and the phonetics–phonology interface. She has directed a number of funded research projects in phonetics. Her current work is on variability in the speech signal and categorization.

Ronald Sprouse is a graduate student in Linguistics at the University of California at Berkeley, currently employed as Programmer/Analyst in the UC Berkeley Phonology Lab, where he has worked with John Ohala since 2000 on issues of speech production and perception. Ohala and Sprouse have jointly published several papers, including "Effects on speech of introducing aerodynamic perturbations" in the Proceedings of ICPhS in 2003.

Jacqueline Vaissière is Professor of Phonetics at the Sorbonne Nouvelle University and current Head of the CNRS Phonetics and Phonology Laboratory in Paris. Her fields of research are acoustic phonetics, clinical phonetics, prosody, articulatory synthesis, automatic speech recognition, and language comparison at the segmental and suprasegmental levels. She is a member of the Permanent Council for the International Congress of Phonetic Sciences.

REFERENCES

Abramson, A. (1962). *The Vowels and Tones of Standard Thai: Acoustical Measurements and Experiments*. Bloomington: Indiana University Center in Anthropology, Folklore, and Linguistics, Publication 20.

—— (1987). "Word-Initial Consonant Length in Pattani Malay", *Proceedings from the 11th International Congress of Phonetic Sciences, Tallinn, Estonia*, vi, 68–70.

—— (1997). "The Thai Tonal Space", in A. Abramson (ed.), *Southeast Asian Linguistic Studies in Honour of Vichin Panupong*. Bangkok: Chulalongkorn University Press, 1–10.

—— and Lisker, L. (1970). "Discriminability Along the Voicing Continuum: Cross-language Tests", in B. Hala, M. Romportl and P. Janota (eds.), *Proceedings of the VIth International Congress of Phonetic Sciences*. Prague: Academica, 569–73.

Abry, C. (2003). "[b]-[d]-[g] as a Universal Triangle as Acoustically Optimal as [i]-[a]-[u]", *Proceedings of the 15th International Congress of Phonetic Sciences, Barcelona*, [CD-ROM] 727–30.

—— and Badin, P. (1996). "Speech Mapping as a Framework for an Integrated Approach to the Sensori-Motor Foundations of Language", *Proceedings of the 4th Speech Production Seminar*, 175–8.

—— Boë, L. J., and Schwartz, J. L. (1989). "Plateaus, Catastrophes and the Structuring of Vowel Systems", *Journal of Phonetics*, 17: 47–54.

—— Cathiard, M.-A., Vilain, A., Laboissière, R., and Schwartz, J.-L. (forthcoming). "Some Insights in Bimodal Perception Given for Free by the Natural Time Course of Speech Production", in G. Bailly, P. Perrier and E. Vatikiotis-Bateson (eds.), *Festschrift Christian Benoît*. Cambridge, MA: MIT Press.

Adank P., Smits, R., and van Hout, R. (2004). "A Comparison of Vowel Normalization Procedures for Language Variation Research", *Journal of the Acoustical Society of America*, 116(5): 3099–3107.

Ainsworth, W. A. (1972). "Duration as a Cue in the Recognition of Synthetic Vowels", *Journal of the Acoustical Society of America*, 51: 648–51.

Akinlabi, A., and Liberman, M. (2000). "Tonal Complexes and Tonal Alignment", *Northeastern Linguistic Society*, 31: 1–20.

Akmajian, A., Demers, R. A., and Harnish, R. M. (1979). *Linguistics: An Introduction to Language and Communication*. Cambridge, MA: MIT Press.

Ali, L., Daniloff, R., and Hammarberg, R. (1979). "Intrusive Stops in Nasal-fricative Clusters: An Aerodynamic and Acoustic Investigation", *Phonetica*, 36: 85–97.

Alkım, U. B. (1968). *Redhouse Yeni Türkçe-İngilizce Sözlük [New Redhouse Turkish-English Dictionary]*. Istanbul: Redhouse Yayinevi.

Allatif, O., and Abry, C. (2004). "Adaptabilité des paramètres temporels et spectraux dans l'opposition de quantité vocalique de l'arabe de Mayadin (Syrie)", *JEP-TALN, Fez, Morocco*. (http://www.lpl.univ-aix.fr/jep-taln04/proceed/actes/jep2004/Allatif-Abry.pdf).

Alstermark, M., and Erikson, Y. (1971). "Speech Analysis. A Swedish Word Accent as a Function of Word Length", *Speech Transmission Laboratory Quarterly Progress and Status Report (STL-QPSR)*, 1: 1–13.

Alwan, A. (1989). "Perceptual Cues for Place of Articulation for the Voiced Pharyngeal and Uvular Consonants", *Journal of the Acoustical Society of America*, 86: 549–56.

The American Heritage Dictionary of the English Language (1992). (3rd edn). Boston: Houghton Mifflin.

Anderson, J. L., Morgan, J. L., White, K. S. (2003). "A Statistical Basis for Speech Sound Discrimination", *Language and Speech*, 46/2–3: 155–82.

Arvaniti, A., Ladd, D. R., and Mennen, I. (1998). "Stability of Tonal Alignment: The Case of Greek Prenuclear Accents", *Journal of Phonetics*, 26: 3–25.

Assmann, P. F., and Katz, W. F. (2000). "Time-varying Spectral Change in the Vowels of Children and Adults", *Journal of the Acoustical Society of America*, 108: 1856–66.

—— and Nearey, T. M. (2003). "Frequency Shifts and Vowel Identification", in M. J. Solé, D. Recasens, and J. Romero (eds.) *Proceedings of the 15th International Congress of Phonetic Sciences*. Rundle Mall: Causal Productions, 1397–1400.

—— —— (2005). "Relationship Between Fundamental and Formant Frequencies in Speech Perception", *Journal of the Acoustical Society of America*, 117: 2374(a).

—— —— (forthcoming). "Identification of Frequency-shifted Vowels".

Atkinson, J. (1973). "Aspects of Intonation in Speech: Implications from an Experimental Study of Speech", Ph.D. dissertation (University of Connecticut).

Atterer, M., and Ladd, D. R. (2004). "On the Phonetics and Phonology of 'Segmental Anchoring' of F0: Evidence from German", *Journal of Phonetics*, 32: 177–97.

Baars, B. J. (1980). "Eliciting Predictable Speech Errors in the Laboratory", in V. A. Fromkin (ed.), *Errors in Linguistic Performance*. New York: Academic Press, 307–18.

—— and Motley, M. T. (1974). "Spoonerisms: Experimental Elicitation of Human Speech Errors", *Journal Supplement Abstract Service, Fall 1974. Catalog of Selected Documents in Psychology*, 3: 28–47.

—— —— and MacKay, D. G. (1975). "Output Editing for Lexical Status in Artificially Elicited Slips of the Tongue", *Journal of Verbal Learning and Verbal Behavior*, 14: 382–91.

Baayen, H. (1993). "On Frequency, Transparency and Productivity", *Yearbook of Morphology 1992*: 181–208.

Baddeley, A. (1997). *Human Memory; Theory and Practice* (revised edn). East Sussex: Psychology Press.

Badin, P. (1991). "Fricative Consonants: Acoustic and X-ray Measurements", *Journal of Phonetics*, 19: 397–408.

—— Perrier, P., Boë, L. J., and Abry, C. (1990). "Vocalic Nomograms: Acoustic and Articulatory Considerations Upon Formant Convergences", *Journal of the Acoustical Society of America*, 87: 1290–1300.

Baken, R. J., and Orlikoff, R. F. (2000). *Clinical Measurements of Speech and Voice*. San Diego: Singular.

Bannert, R., and Bredvad-Jensen, A. (1977). "Temporal Organization of Swedish Tonal Accents: The Effect of Vowel Duration in the Gotland Dialect", *Working Papers, Phonetic Laboratory, Lund University* 15: 133–8.

Bard, E. G., Sotillo, C., Kelly, M. L., and Aylett, M. P. (2001). "Taking the Hit: Lexical and Phonological Processes Should Not Resolve Lexical Access", *Language and Cognitive Processes*, 16: 731–7.

Barry, M. C. (1985). "A Palatographic Study of Connected Speech Processes", *Cambridge Papers in Phonetics and Experimental Linguistics*, 4: 1–16.

Basbøll, H. (1988). "The Modern Danish Stød and Phonological Weight", in P. M. Bertinetto and M. Lopocaro (eds.), *Certamen Phonologicum. Proceedings from the Cortona Phonology Meeting*. Torino: Rosenberg and Sellier, 119–52.

—— (1998). "Nyt om stødet i moderne rigsdansk: Om samspillet mellem lydstruktur og ordgrammatik", *Danske Studier 1998*: 33–86.

—— (2003). "Prosody, Productivity and Word Structure: The Stød Pattern of Modern Danish", *Nordic Journal of Linguistics*, 26: 5–44.

—— (2005). *The Phonology of Danish*. Oxford: Oxford University Press.

Baudouin de Courtenay, J. (1972a). "An Attempt at a Theory of Phonetic Alternations", in E. Stankiewicz (ed.), *A Baudouin de Courtenay Anthology: The Beginnings of Structural Linguistics*. Bloomington: Indiana University Press, 144–212 (originally pub. 1895).

—— (1972b). "Phonetic Laws", in E. Stankiewicz (ed.), *Selected Writings of Baudouin de Courtenay*. Bloomington: Indiana University Press, 260–77 (originally pub. 1910).

Beautemps, D., Badin, P., and Bailly, G. (2001). "Linear Degrees of Freedom in Speech Production: Analysis of Cineradio- and Labio-film Data and Articulatory-acoustic Modeling", *Journal of the Acoustical Society of America*, 109: 2165–80.

Beckman, M. E., and Edwards, J. (1990). "Lengthenings and Shortenings and the Nature of Prosodic Constituency", in J. Kingston and M. E. Beckman (eds.), *Papers in Laboratory I: Between the Grammar and Physics of Speech*. Cambridge: Cambridge University Press, 152–78.

—— —— (1992). "Intonational Categories and the Articulatory Control of Duration", in Y. Tohkura, E. Vatikiotis-Bateson, and Y. Sagisaka Ohmasha, (eds.), *Speech Perception, Production, and Linguistic Structure*. Tokyo: OHM Publishing Co., 359–75.

—— —— and Fletcher, J. (1992). "Prosodic Structure and Tempo in a Sonority Model of Articulatory Dynamics", in G. Docherty and D. Ladd (eds.), *Papers in Laboratory Phonology II: Gesture, Segment, Prosody*. Cambridge: Cambridge University Press, 68–86.

—— Hirschberg, J., and Shattuck-Hufnagel, S. (2005). "The Original ToBI System and the Evolution of the Tobi Framework", in Sun-Ah Jun (ed.). *Prosodic Typology. The Phonology of Intonation and Phrasing*. Oxford: Oxford University Press, 9–54.

—— de Jong, K., Jun, S.-A., and Lee, S-H. (1992). "The Interaction of Coarticulation and Prosody in Sound Change", *Language and Speech*, 35: 45–58.

Beddor, P. S. (forthcoming). "A Phonetic Path to Sound Change".

—— and Evans-Romaine, D. (1995). "Acoustic-perceptual Factors in Phonological Assimilations: A Study of Syllable-final Nasals", *Rivista di Linguistica*, 7: 145–74.

—— and Krakow, R. A. (1999). "Perception of Coarticulatory Nasalization by Speakers of English and Thai: Evidence for Partial Compensation", *Journal of the Acoustical Society of America*, 106: 2868–87.

—— —— and Goldstein, L. M. (1986). "Perceptual Constraints and Phonological Change: A Study of Nasal Vowel Height", *Phonology Yearbook*, 3: 197–217.

—— —— and Lindemann, S. (2001). "Patterns of Perceptual Compensation and Their Phonological Consequences", in E. Hume and K. Johnson (eds.), *The Role of Perceptual Phenomena in Phonology*. New York: Academic Press, 55–78.

—— and Strange, W. (1982). "Cross-language Study of Perception of the Oral-nasal Perception", *Journal of the Acoustical Society of America*, 71 (6): 1551–156.

—— Harnsberger, J., and Lindemann, S. (2002). "Language-specific Patterns of Vowel-to-Vowel Coarticulation: Acoustic Structures and Their Perceptual Correlates", *Journal of Phonetics*, 30: 591–627.

Bell, C. G., Fujisaki, H., Heinz, J. M., Stevens, K. N. and House, A. S. (1961). "Reduction of Speech Spectra by Analysis-by-Synthesis Techniques", *Journal of the Acoustical Society of America*, 33: 1725–36.

Bell-Berti, F. (1973). *"The Velopharyngeal Mechanism: An Electromyographic Study*, Ph.D. dissertation. (*Haskins Laboratories Status Report on Speech Research, Supplement*, Sept. 1973).

—— (1980). "Velopharyngeal Function: A Spatial-temporal Model", in N. J. Lass (ed.), *Speech and Language: Advances in Basic Research and Practice.* New York: Academic Press 4: 291–316.

—— (1993). "Understanding Velic Motor Control: Studies of Segmental Context", in M. K. Huffman and R. A. Krakow (eds.), *Nasals, Nasalization, and the Velum.* [*Phonetics and Phonology Series*, v]. San Diego: Academic Press, 63–85.

—— and Krakow, R. A. (1991). "Anticipatory Velar Lowering: A Coproduction Account", *Journal of the Acoustical Society of America*, 90(1): 112–23.

Benguerel, A.-P. (1970). "Some Physiological Aspects of Stress in French", Ph.D. dissertation (University of Michigan).

Berrah, A. R. (1998). *Évolution d'un société artificielle d'agents de parole: un modèle pour l'émergence des structures phonétiques.* Doctorat Sciences Cognitives INPG, Grenoble. http://tel.ccsd.cnrs.fr/documents/archives0/00/00/48/68/index_fr.html.

—— and Laboissière, R. (1997). "Phonetic Code Emergence in a Society of Speech Robots: Explaining Vowels Systems and the MUAF Principle", *Proceedings of EuroSpeech '97*, 5: 2399–2402.

—— Boë, L.-J., and Schwartz, J.-L. (1995). "Emergent Syllable Using Articulatory and Acoustic Principles", *Proceedings of the 13th International Congress of Phonetic Sciences*, 396–9.

Bertinetto, P. M. (1981). *Strutture Prosodiche dell'Italiano.* Firenze: Accademia della Crusca.

Best, C. T., Morrongiello, B., and Robson, R. (1981). "Perceptual Equivalence of Acoustic Cues in Speech and Nonspeech Perception", *Perception and Psychophysics*, 29: 191–211.

Bickmore, L. S. (2000). "Downstep and Fusion in Namwanga". *Phonology*, 17: 297–331.

Blackmer E. R., and Mitton J. L. (1991). "Theories of Monitoring and the Timing of Repairs in Spontaneous Speech", *Cognition*, 39: 173–94.

Bladon, R. A. W., and Lindblom, B. (1981). "Modeling the Judgment of Vowel Quality Differences", *Journal of the Acoustical Society of America*, 69: 1414–22.

Blankenship, B. (1992). "What TIMIT Can Tell Us about Epenthesis", *UCLA Working Papers in Phonetics*, 81: 17–25.

Blevins, J. (1995). "The Syllable in Phonological Theory", in J. Goldsmith (ed.), *Handbook of phonological theory.* London: Basil Blackwell, 206–44.

—— (2004). *Evolutionary Phonology: The Emergence of Sound Patterns.* Cambridge: Cambridge University Press.

—— (2006). "A theoretical synopsis of Evolutionary Phonology", *Theoretical Linguistics*, 32: 117–65.

—— and Garrett, A. (1998). "The Origins of Consonant-vowel Metathesis", *Language*, 74: 508–56.

—— —— (2004). "The Evolution of Metathesis", in B. Hayes, R. Kirchner, and D. Steriade (eds.), *Phonetically Driven Phonology.* Cambridge: Cambridge University Press, 117–56.

Bloch, B. (1948). "A Set of Postulates for Phonemic Analysis", *Language*, 24: 3–46.

Bloomfield, L. (1933). *Language.* New York: Henry Holt and Company.

Boë, L. J. (1997). "Sciences phonétiques et relations forme/substance", *Histoire, Épistémologie et Langage*, 19 I: 5–41, 19 II: 5–25.

—— and Durand, J. (2001). "L'opposition consonne/voyelle: Avatar historique ou dichotomie opératoire", *Orbis Supplementa*, 17, 2, 785–810.

Boë, L. J., Heim, J. L., and Maeda, S. (2001). "Neanderthal Man Was Not Morphologically Handicapped for Speech", *Evolution of Communication*, 3 (1): 49–77.

—— Perrier, P., and Bailly G. (1992). "The Geometric Vocal Tract Variables Controlled for Vowel Production: Proposals for Constraining Acoustic-to-articulatory Inversion", *Journal of Phonetics*, 20: 27–38.

—— —— Guérin, B., and Schwartz, J. L. (1989). "Maximal Vowel Space", *Proceedings of Eurospeech'89* 281–4.

—— Vallée N., Schwartz J. L., and Abry C. (2002). "The Nature of Vowel Structure", *Acoustical Science and Technology*, 23: 221–8.

—— —— Badin P., Schwartz J. L., and Abry, C. (2000). "Tendencies in Phonological Structures: The Influence of Substance on Form", *Bulletin de la Communication Parlée*, 5: 35–55.

de Boer, B. (2000). "Self Organization in Vowel Systems", *Journal of Phonetics*, 28: 441–65.

Boersma, P., and Weenink, D. (2005). "Praat: Doing Phonetics by Computer" (Version 4.3.29) [Computer program]. Retrieved 11 Nov. 2005, from http://www.praat.org/

Bonaventura, P. (2003) *Invariant patterns in articulatory movements*, PhD Dissertation, The Ohio State University.

—— (2006). "Prosodic Effects on Articulatory Movements at Phrase Boundaries in Spontaneous Speech", presented at the 5th International Conference on Speech Motor Control, Nijmegen, The Netherlands, 7–10 June 2006.

Bonneau, A., and Laprie, Y. (1998). "The Effect of Modifying Formant Amplitudes on the Perception of French Vowels Generated by Copy Synthesis", *Proceedings of the 5th International Conference on Spoken Language Processing*. Sydney, 2131–4.

Bothorel, A., Simon, P., Wioland, F., and Zerling, J-P. (1986). *Cinéradiographie des voyelles et consonnes du français*. Strasbourg: Publications de l'Institut de Phonétique de Strasbourg.

Botinis, A., Bannert, R., Fourakis, M., and Pagoni-Tetlow, S. (2002). "Prosodic Effects and Crosslinguistic Segmental Durations", *Speech Transmission Laboratory Quarterly Progress and Status Report (STL-QPSR)*, 44: 77–80.

Boucher, V. (2002). "Timing Relations in Speech and the Identification of Voice-Onset Times. A Stable Perceptual Boundary for Voicing Categories Across Speaking Rates", *Perception and Psychophysics*, 64 (1): 121–30.

Branderud, P., Lundberg, H.-J., Lander, J., Djamshidpey, H., Wäneland, I., Krull, D., and Lindblom, B. (1998). "X-ray Analyses of Speech: Methodological Aspects", *FONETIK 98, Papers Presented at the Annual Swedish Phonetics Conference*. Stockholm: Dept. of Linguistics, Stockholm University, 168–71.

Braunschweiler, N. (1997). "Integrated Cues of Voicing and Vowel Length in German: A Production Study", *Language and Speech*, 40(4): 353–76.

Browman, C., and Goldstein, L. (1986). "Toward an Articulatory Phonology", *Phonology Yearbook*, 3: 219–52.

—— —— (1990). "Articulatory Gestures as Phonological Units", *Phonology*, 6: 201–31.

—— —— (1992). "Articulatory Phonology: An Overview", *Phonetica*, 49: 155–80.

Brown, R., and Lenneberg, E. (1954). "A Study in Language and Cognition", *Journal of Abnormal and Social Psychology*, 49: 454–62.

Buchthal, F., and Kaiser, E. (1944). "Factors Determining Tension Development in Skeletal Muscles", *Acta Physiologica Scandinavica*, 8: 38–74.

Busà, M. G. (2003). "Vowel Nasalization and Nasal Loss in Italian", in M. J. Solé, D. Recasens, and J. Romero (eds.), *Proceedings of the 15th International Congress of Phonetic Sciences*. Barcelona: Universitat Autònoma de Barcelona, 711–14.

Butcher, A. (1994). "On the Phonetics of Small Vowel Systems: Evidence from Australian Languages", *Proceedings of the 5th Australian International Conference on Speech Science and Technology* I: 28–33. http://www.flinders.edu.au/speechpath/Butcher SST1994.pdf

Bybee, J. (1985). *Morphology: a Study of the Relation between Meaning and Form*. Amsterdam: John Benjamins.

—— (2000). "Lexicalization of Sound Change and Alternating Environments", in M. Broe and J. Pierrehumbert (eds.), *Papers in Laboratory Phonology V*. Cambridge: Cambridge University Press, 250–69.

—— (2001). *Phonology and Language Use*. Cambridge: Cambridge University Press.

Byrd, D., and Saltzman, E. (1998). "Intragestural Dynamics of Multiple Prosodic Boundaries", *Journal of Phonetics*, 26: 173–99.

—— —— (2003). "The Elastic Phrase: Modeling the Dynamics of Boundary-adjacent Lengthening", *Journal of Phonetics*, 31: 149–80.

—— Kaun, A., Narayanan, S., and Saltzman, E. (2000). "Phrasal Signatures in Articulation", in M. B. Broe and J. B. Pierrehumbert (eds.), *Papers in Laboratory Phonology*, v. Cambridge University Press, London, 70–87.

—— Lee, S., Riggs, D. and Adams, J. (2005). "Phrase and Syllable Effects on Articulation", *Journal of the Acoustical Society of America*, 118 (6): 3860–3.

Caisse, M. (1988). *Modeling English Vowel Durations*. Ph.D. Dissertation (University of California, Berkeley).

Calliope (1989). *La parole et son traitement*. Collection Technique et Scientifique des Télécommunications. Paris: Masson.

Cambier-Langeveld, T., and Turk, A. (1999). "A Cross-linguistic Study of Accentual Lengthening: Dutch vs. English", *Journal of Phonetics*, 27: 255–80.

Canepari, L. (1992). *Manuale di pronuncia italiana*. Bologna: Zanichelli.

Carlson, R., Granström, B., and Fant, G. (1970). "Some Studies Concerning Perception of Isolated Vowels", *Speech Transmission Laboratory, Quaterly Progress Speech Report*, 2–3: 19–35.

—— Fant, G., and Granström, B. (1975), "Two-formant Models, Pitch and Vowel Perception", in G. Fant and M. A. A. Tatham (eds.), *Auditory Analysis and Perception of Speech*. London: Academic Press Inc, 55–82.

Carpenter, G. A., and Grossberg, S. (1987). "ART 2: Stable Self-Organization of Pattern Recognition Codes for Analog Input Patterns", *Applied Optics*, 26: 4919–30.

Celata, C., and Kaeppeli, B. (2003). "Affricazione e rafforzamento in Italiano: Alcuni Dati sperimentali", *Quaderni del Laboratorio di Linguistica, Pisa: Scuola Normale Superiore*, 4: 243–55.

Chafcouloff, M. (1983). "A propos des indices de distinction /l-R/ en français", *Speech Communication*, 2: 137–9.

Chao, Y. R. (1930). "A System of Tone Letters", *Le Maître Phonétique*, 45: 24–7.

—— (1968). *A Grammar of Spoken Chinese*. Berkeley: University of California Press.

Chen, M. (1970). "Vowel Length Variation as a Function of the Voicing of the Consonant Environment", *Phonetica*, 22: 129–59.

Cheng, C. C. (1973). *A Synchronic Phonology of Mandarin Chinese*. the Hague: Mouton.

Chiba, T., and Kajiyama, M. (1958). *The Vowel: Its Nature and Structure*. Tokyo: Phonetic Society of Japan (first publ. 1941, Tokyo: Kaiseikan).

Chistovich, L. A., and Lublinskaya, V. V. (1979). "The 'Center of Gravity' Effect in Vowel Spectra and Critical Distance between the Formants: Psychoacoustical Study of the Perception of Vowel-like Stimuli", *Hearing Research*, 1: 185–95.

Cho, T. (2001). "Effect of Morpheme Boundaries on Intergestural Timing: Evidence from Korean", *Phonetica*, 58: 129–62.

—— (2005). "Prosodic Strengthening and Featural Enhancement: Evidence from Acoustic and Articulatory Realizations of /a, i/ in English", *Journal of the Acoustical Society of America*, 117 (6): 3867–78.

—— and Jun, S. (2000). "Domain-initial Strengthening as Featural Enhancement: Aerodynamic Evidence from Korean", *Chicago Linguistics Society*, 36: 31–44.

—— and Ladefoged, P. (1999). "Variation and Universals in VOT: Evidence from 18 Languages", *Journal of Phonetics*, 27: 207–29.

—— and McQueen, J. M. (2005). "Prosodic Influences on Consonant Production in Dutch: Effects of Prosodic Boundaries, Phrasal Accent and Lexical Stress", *Journal of Phonetics*, 33: 121–57.

Choi, H. (2003). "Prosody-induced Acoustic Variation in English Stop Consonants", in M. J. Solé, D. Recasens and J. Romero (eds.), *Proceedings of the 15th International Congress of Phonetic Sciences*, iii. Barcelona, 2661–4.

Chomsky, N. (1957). *Syntactic Structures*. The Hague and Paris: Mouton.

—— and Halle, M. (1968). *The Sound Pattern of English*. New York: Harper and Row.

Clark, M. (1983). "On the Distribution of Contour Tones", *West Coast Conference on Formal Linguistics*, 2: 44–55.

Claßen, K. (2002). "Realisations of Nuclear Pitch Accents in Swabian Dialect and Parkinson's Dysarthria: A Preliminary Report", paper presented at Speech Prosody 2002, Aix-en-Provence, France.

Clements, G. N. (2003a). "Feature Economy as a Phonological Universal", *Proceedings of the 15th International Congress of Phonetic Sciences*, Barcelona. [CD ROM] 371–4.

—— (2003b). "Feature Economy in Sound Systems", *Phonology*, 3: 287–333.

—— and Hume, E. V. (1995). "The Internal Organization of Speech Sounds", in J. Goldsmith (ed.), *Handbook of Phonological Theory*. Oxford: Blackwell, 245–306.

Clumeck, H. (1975). "A Cross-Linguistic Investigation of Vowel Nasalization: An Instrumental Study", in C. A. Ferguson, L. M. Hyman, and J. J. Ohala (eds.), *Nasálfest: Papers from a Symposium on Nasals and Nasalization*. Stanford: Language Universals Project, 133–51.

—— (1976). "Patterns of Soft Palate Movements in Six Languages", *Journal of Phonetics*, 4: 337–51.

Coenen, E., Zwisterlood, P., and Bölte, J. (2001). "Variation and Assimilation in German: Consequences for Lexical Access and Representation", *Language and Cognitive Processes*, 16: 535–64.

Cohen, A. L., Nosofsky, R. M., and Zaki, S. R. (2001). "Category Variability, Exemplar Similarity, and Perceptual Classification", *Memory and Cognition*, 29: 1165–75.

Cohn, A. (1990). "Phonetic and Phonological Rules of Nasalization," *UCLA Working Papers in Phonetics*, 76: 1–224.

Cole, J., Choi, H., Kim, H., and Hasegawa-Johnson, M. (2003). "The Effect of Accent on the Acoustic Cues to Stop Voicing in Radio News Speech", in M. J. Solé, D. Recasens and

J. Romero (eds.), *Proceedings of the 15th International Congress of Phonetic Sciences*, iii. Barcelona, 2665–8.

Coleman, J. (2002). "Phonetic Representations in the Mental Lexicon", in J. Durand, and B. Laks, (eds.), *Phonetics, Phonology and Cognition*. Oxford: Oxford University Press, 96–130.

Colhoun, E. R., and Kim, T. W. (1976). "English Loanwords in Korean: Lexical and Phonological Problems", *Applied Linguistics*, 8 (2): 237–50. Seoul: Language Research Institute, Seoul National University.

Collier, R. (1974). "Laryngeal Muscle Activity, Subglottal Pressure, and the Control of Pitch in Speech", *Status Report on Speech Research [Haskins Labs.]* SR-39/40: 137–70.

—— (1975). "Physiological Correlates of Intonation Patterns", *Journal of the Acoustical Society of America*, 58: 249–55.

Content, A., Mousty, P., and Radeau, M. (1990). "BRULEX: Une base de données lexicales informatisées pour le français écrit et parlé", *L'Année Psychologique*, 90: 551–66.

Cooper, F. S., Delattre, P. C., Liberman, A., Borst, J. M., and Gerstman, L. J. (1952). "Some Experiments on the Perception of Synthetic Speech Sounds", *Journal of the Acoustical Society of America*, 24: 597–606.

Coustenoble, H. N. (1945). *La phonetique du provençal moderne en terre d'Arles*. Hertford: Austin.

Crevier-Buchman, L., Maeda, S., Bely, N., Laccourreye, O., Vaissière, J., and Brasnu, D. (2001). "Articulatory Compensation after Supracricoid Partial Laryngectomy with Cricohyoidoepiglottopexy", *Ann Otolaryngol Chir Cervicofac*, 118 (2): 81–8.

Crosswhite, K. (2001). *Vowel Reduction in Optimality Theory*. New York: Routledge.

—— (2004). "Vowel reduction", in B. Hayes, R. Kirchner, and D. Steriade (eds.), *Phonetically Driven Phonology*. Cambridge: Cambridge University Press, 191–231.

Crothers, J. (1978). "Typology and Universals of Vowel Systems", in J. H. Greenberg (ed.), *Universals of Human Language*. Standford: Stanford University Press, 93–152.

Cuartero, N. (2002). "Voicing Assimilation in Catalan and English", Ph.D. dissertation (Universitat Autònoma de Barcelona).

—— (forthcoming). "Phonetic Cues to Voicing Contrasts: A Cross-Linguistic Study".

Cysouw, M. (2005). "Quantitative Methods in Typology", in G. Altmann, R. Köhler, and R. Piotrowski (eds.), *Quantitative Linguistik–Quantitative Linguistics: An International Handbook*. Berlin and New York: Mouton de Gruyter: 554–77.

Dahan, D., and Bernard, J.-M. (1996). "Interspeaker Variability in Emphatic Accent Production in French", *Language and Speech*, 39: 341–74.

Dart, N. (1998). "Comparing French and English Coronal Consonant Articulation." *Journal of Phonetics*, 26: 71–94.

de Jong, K. (1991). "An Articulatory Study of Consonant-induced Vowel Duration Changes in English", *Phonetica*, 48: 1–17.

—— (1995). "The Supraglottal Articulation of Prominence in English", *Journal of the Acoustical Society of America*, 97: 491–504.

—— (2001a). "Rate-induced Resyllabification Revisited", *Language and Speech*, 44: 197–216.

—— (2001b). "Effects of Syllable Affiliation and Consonant Voicing on Temporal Adjustment in a Repetitive Speech Production Task", *Journal of Speech, Language, and Hearing Research*, 44: 826–40.

de Jong, K. (2003). "Temporal Constraints and Characterising Syllable Structuring", in J. Local, R. Ogden and R. Temple (eds.), *Phonetic Interpretation. Papers in Laboratory Phonology VI.* Cambridge: Cambridge University Press, 253–68.

—— (2004). "Stress, Lexical Focus, and Segmental Focus in English: Patterns of Variation in Vowel Duration", *Journal of Phonetics*, 32: 493–516.

—— and Zawaydeh, B. (2002). "Comparing Stress, Lexical Focus, and Segmental Focus: Patterns of Variation in Arabic Vowel Duration", *Journal of Phonetics*, 30: 53–75.

de Saussure, F. (1879). *Mémoire sur le système primitif des voyelles dans les langues indo-européennes.* Leipzig: B. G. Teubner.

—— (1915). *Cours de linguistique générale.* Paris: Payot.

del Viso, S., Igoa, J. M., and Garcia-Albea, J. E. (1991). "On the Autonomy of Phonological Encoding: Evidence from Slips of the Tongue in Spanish", *Journal of Psycholinguistic Research*, 20: 161–85.

Delattre, P. (1953). "Les modes phonétiques du français.", *The French Review*, 27 (1): 59–63. (Repr. in *Studies in French and Comparative Phonetics, Selected Papers in French and English by Pierre Delattre*, The Hague: Mouton, 1966, 9–13).

—— (1954). "Les attributs acoustiques de la nasalité vocalique et consonantique", *Studia Linguistica*, 8 (2): 103–9.

—— (1965). "Comparing the Vocalic Features of English, German, Spanish and French", *International Review of Applied Linguistics*, 2: 71–97.

—— and Freeman, D. C. (1968). "A Dialect Study of American r's by X-ray Motion Picture", *Linguistics*, 44: 29–68.

—— Liberman, A. M., Cooper, F. S., and Gertsman, J. (1952). "An Experimental Study of the Acoustic Determinants of Vowel Color; Observations on One- and Two-Formant Vowels Synthesized from Spectrographic Patterns", *Word*, 8: 195–210.

Dell, G. S. (1986). "A Spreading-Activation Theory of Retrieval in Sentence Production", *Psychological Review*, 93: 283–321.

—— (1990). "Effects of Frequency and Vocabulary Type on Phonological Speech Errors", *Language and Cognitive Processes*, 5: 313–49.

—— and Warker, J. A. (2004). "The Tongue Slips Into (Recently) Learned Patterns", in H. Quené and V. van Heuven (eds.), *On Speech and Language: Studies for Sieb Nooteboom.* Netherlands Graduate School of Linguistics, Occasional Series, 47–56.

Demolin, D. (2001). "Some Phonetic and Phonological Observations Concerning /R/ in Belgian French", in H. van de Velde and R. van Houdt (eds.), Studies on /R/. *Études et Travaux*: 63–73.

—— (2002). "The Search for Primitives in Phonology and the Explanation of Sound Patterns: The Contribution of Fieldwork Studies", in C. Gussenhoven and N. Warner (eds.), *Papers in Laboratory Phonology*, 7. Berlin and New York: Mouton de Gruyter, 455–513.

—— (2004). "Acoustic and Aerodynamic Characteristics of Ejectives in Amharic", *Journal of the Acoustical Society of America*, 115: 2610.

—— and Soquet, A. (1999). "The Role of Self-Organization in the Emergence of Phonological Systems", *Evolution of Communication*, 3: 5–29.

—— Hassid, S., Ladefoged, P., and Soquet A. (forthcoming). "Vowel and Consonant Effects on Subglottal Pressure".

Derwing, B. L. (1973). *Transformational Grammar as a Theory of Language Acquisition: A Study in the Empirical, Conceptual, and Methodological Foundations of Contemporary Linguistics*. Cambridge: Cambridge University Press.

—— (1980). "Against Autonomous Linguistics", in T. Perry (ed.), *Evidence and Argumentation in Linguistics*. Berlin and New York: Mouton de Gruyter, 163–89.

—— (1992). "A 'Pause-break' Task for Eliciting Syllable Boundary Judgments from Literate and Illiterate Speakers: Preliminary Results for Five Diverse Languages", *Language and Speech*, 35: 219–35.

—— Nearey, T. M., Beinert, R. A., and Bendrien, T. A. (1986). "On the Role of the Segment in Speech Processing by Human Listeners: Evidence from Speech Perception and from Global Sound Similarity Judgments", in J. J. Ohala, T. M. Nearey, B. L. Derwing, M. E. Hodge, and G. E. Wiebe (eds.), *Proceedings of the 1992 International Conference on Spoken Language Processing*, i. Edmonton: University of Alberta, 289–92.

—— Yoon, Y. B., and Cho, S. W. (1993). "The Organization of the Korean Syllable: Experimental Evidence", in P. M. Clancy (ed.), *Japanese/Korean Linguistics*, ii. Stanford: Center for the Study of Language and Information, 223–38.

Devore, J., and Peck, R. (2005). *Statistics: The Exploration and Analysis of Data* (5th edn.). Belmont, CA: Brooks/Cole.

Di Cristo, A. (1998). "Intonation in French", in D. Hirst and A. Di Cristo (eds.), *Intonation Systems: A Survey of Twenty Languages*. Cambridge: Cambridge University Press, 193–218.

Diehl, R. (1991). "The Role of Phonetics within the Study of Language", *Phonetica*, 48: 120–34.

—— Lindblom, B., and Creeger, C. P. (2003). "Increasing Realism of Auditory Representations Yields Further Insights Into Vowel Phonetics", *Proceedings of the 15th International Congress of Phonetic Sciences*, Barcelona, [CD ROM] 1381–4.

Dinnsen, D. A. (1983). *On the Characterization of Phonological Neutralization*. Bloomington: Indiana University Linguistics Club.

Disner, S. F. (1980). "Evaluation of Vowel Normalization Procedures", *Journal of the Acoustical Society of America*, 67: 253–61.

Docherty, G. (2003). "Speaker, Community, Identity: Empirical and Theoretical Perspectives on Sociophonetic Variation", in M. J. Solé, D. Recasens and J. Romero (eds.), *Proceedings of the 15th International congress of Phonetic Sciences*, i. Barcelona, 11–16.

Dotevall, H., Ejnell, H., and Bake, B. (2001). "Nasal Airflow Patterns during the Velopharyngeal Closing Phase in Speech in Children with and without Cleft Palate", *Cleft Palate-Craniofacial Journal*, 38 (4): 358–73.

Draper, M., Ladefoged, P., and Whitteridge, D. (1959). "Respiratory Muscles in Speech", *Journal of Speech and Hearing Research*, 2: 16–27.

Dryer, M. (1989). "Large Linguistic Areas and Language Sampling", *Studies in Language*, 13: 257–92.

—— (1992). "The Greenbergian Word Order Correlations", *Language*, 68: 81–138.

—— (2003). "Significant and Non-significant Implicational Universals", *Linguistic Typology*, 7: 108–12.

Duda, R. O., Hart, P. E., and Stork, D. G. (2000). *Pattern Classification* (2nd edn). New York: Wiley-Interscience.

Durand, M. (1930). *Étude sur les phonèmes postérieurs dans une articulation parisienne*. Paris, Petite collection de l'Institut de Phonétique et du Musée de la Parole et du Geste, vii. Paris: H. Didier.

Edelman, G. M. (1987). *Neural Darwinism: The Theory of Neuronal Group Selection*. New York: Basic Books.

Edwards, J., Beckman, M. E., and Fletcher, J. (1991). "The Articulatory Kinematics of Final Lengthening", *Journal of the Acoustical Society of America*, 89: 369–82.

Ejskjær, I. (1990). "Stød and Pitch Accents in the Danish Dialects", *Acta Linguistica Hafniensia*, 22: 49–76.

Ellis, L., and Hardcastle, W. J. (2002). "Categorical and Gradient Properties of Assimilation in Alveolar to Velar Sequences: Evidence from EPG and EMA Data", *Journal of Phonetics*, 30: 373–96.

Endo, R., and Bertinetto, P. M. (1999). "Caratteristiche prosodiche delle così dette 'rafforzate' italiane", in R. Delmonte, and A. Bristot, *Aspetti computazionali in fonetica, linguistica e didattica delle lingue: Modelli e algoritmi. Atti delle IX giornate di studio del gruppo di fonetica sperimentale*. Venice: Università Ca' Foscari, 243–55.

Engstrand, O. (1988). "Articulatory Correlates of Stress and Speaking Rate in Swedish VCV utterances", *Journal of the Acoustical Society of America*, 83: 1863–75.

—— and Krull, D. (1991) "Effects of the Inventory Size on the Distribution of Vowels in the Formant Space: Preliminary Data from Seven Languages", *Phonetics Experimental Research Institute of Linguistics, University of Stockholm*, 13: 15–18.

Erickson, D. (1976). "A Physiological Analysis of the Tones of Thai", Ph.D. dissertation (University of Connecticut).

—— (2002). "Articulation of Extreme Formant Patterns for Emphasized Vowels". *Phonetica*, 59: 134–49.

—— Baer, T., and Harris, K. S. (1983). "The Role of the Strap Muscles in Pitch Lowering", in D. M. Bless and J. M. Abbs (eds.), *Vocal Fold Physiology. Contemporary Research and Clinical Issues*. San Diego: College-Hill Press, 279–85.

Ericsdotter, C. (2005). "Articulatory-Acoustic Relationships in Swedish Vowel Sounds", Ph.D. dissertation (Stockholm University).

Erikson, Y., and Alstermark, M. (1972). "Speech Analysis. A. Fundamental Frequency Correlates of the Grave Word Accent in Swedish: The Effect of Vowel Duration", *Speech Transmission Laboratory Quarterly Progress and Status Report (STL-QPSR)*, 1: 1–13.

Ernestus, M., and Baayen, H. (2003). "Predicting the Unpredictable: Interpreting Neutralized Segments in Dutch", *Language*, 79: 5–38.

Esposito, A., and Di Benedetto, M. G. (1999). "Acoustical and Perceptual Study of Gemination in Italian Stops", *Journal of the Acoustical Society of America*, 106: 2051–64.

Espy-Wilson, C. Y., Boyce, S. E., Jackson, M., Narayanan, S., and Alwan, A. (2000). "Acoustic Modeling of American English /r/", *Journal of the Acoustical Society of America* 108 (1), 343–56.

Fadiga, L., Craighero, L., Buccino, G., and G. Rizzolatti, G. (2002). "Speech Listening Specifically Modulates the Excitability of Tongue Muscles: A TMS Study", *European Journal of Neuroscience* 15: 399–402.

Fallows, D. (1981). "Experimental Evidence for English Syllabification and Syllable Structure", *Linguistics*, 17: 179–392.

Fant, G. (1960). *Acoustic Theory of Speech Production*. The Hague: Mouton.

—— (1973). *Speech Sounds and Features*. Cambridge, MA: MIT Press.

—— (1975a). "Non-Uniform Vowel Normalization, Speech, Music and Hearing", Stockholm, Quarterly Progress and Status Report, STL/QPSR 2–3/1975, 1–19 (http://www.speech.kth.se).

—— (1975b). "Stops in CV Syllables," in G. Fant (ed.), *Speech Sounds and Features*. Cambridge, MA: MIT Press, 10–139.

Fant, G. (2004a). "Swedish Vowels and a New Three-parameter Model", in G. Fant (ed.), *Speech Acoustics and Phonetics*, Dordrecht: Kluwer, 58–67.

—— (2004b). "Vowel Perception and Specification", in G. Fant (ed.), *Speech Acoustics and Phonetics*. Dordrecht: Kluwer, 201–15.

—— and Bävegård, M. (1997). "Parametric Model of Vocal Tract Area Functions: Vowels and Consonants", ESPRIT/BR Speechmaps (6975), Delivery 28, WP2.2, 1–30.

—— and Pauli, S. (1974). "Spatial Characteristics of Vocal Tract Resonance Modes", *Proceedings Speech Communication Seminar*, Stockholm, 121–32.

Farnetani, E., and Busà, M. G. (1994). "Consonant-to-consonant Interactions in Clusters: Categorical or Continuous Processes?", *Quaderni del Centro di Studi per le Ricerche di Fonetica del CNR* XIII: 219–45.

—— and Vayra, M. (1991). "Word- and Phrase-level Aspects of Vowel Reduction in Italian", in *Proceedings of the 12th International Congress of Phonetic Sciences*, ii. Aix-en-Provence, Université de Provence, 14–17.

Fink, B. R., and Demarest, R. J. (1978). *Laryngeal Biomechanics*. Cambridge, MA: Harvard University Press.

Fischer-Jørgensen, E. (1954). "Acoustic Analysis of Stop Consonants", *Miscellanea Phonetica*, 2: 42–59.

—— (1968a). "Voicing, Tenseness and Aspiration in Stop Consonants, with Special Reference to French and Danish", *Annual Report Institute of Phonetics University of Copenhagen (ARIPUC)*, 3: 63–114.

—— (1968b). "Les occlusives françaises et danoises d'un sujet bilingue", *Word* 24: 112–53.

—— (1987). "A Phonetic Study of the Stød in Standard Danish", *Annual Report of the Institute of Phonetics, University of Copenhagen*, 21: 55–265.

—— (1989a). *Phonetic Analysis of the Stød in Danish*. Turku: University of Turku.

—— (1989b). "Phonetic Analysis of the Stød in Standard Danish", *Phonetica*, 46: 1–59.

Fitch, H. L., Halwes, T., Erickson, D. M., and Liberman, A. M. (1980). "Perceptual Equivalence of Two Acoustic Cues for Stop–consonant Manner", *Perception and Psychophysics* 27: 343–50.

Flanagan, J. L. (1972). *Speech Analysis, Synthesis and Perception* (2nd ed.). New York: Springer.

Flege, J. E. (1988). "Anticipatory and Carryover Coarticulation in the Speech of Children and Adults", *Journal of Speech and Hearing Research* 31: 525–36.

—— Munro, M. J., and Fox, R. A. (1991). "The Interlingual Identification of Spanish and English Vowels", *Journal of the Acoustical Society of America* 90 (4): 2252–3.

Fletcher, J., and Butcher, A. R. (2002). "Vowel Dispersion in Two Northern Australian Languages: Dalabon and Bininj Gun-wok", *Proceedings of the 9th Australian International Conference on Speech Science and Technology* 343–8. (http://www.flinders.edu.au/speechpath/ FandB SST2002.pdf).

—— —— (2003). "Local and Global Influences on Vowel Formants in Three Australian Languages" *Proceedings of the 15th International Congress of Phonetic Sciences*, Barcelona, [CD-ROM] 905–8. (http://www.flinders.edu.au/speechpath/FandB Barcelona.pdf).

Foldvik, A. K. (1988). "Spredning av skarrning i Norge i löpet av om lag 70 år", *Norsk lingvistisk tidskrift* 1 (2): 55–62.

Foley, J. (1975). "Nasalization as Universal Phonological Process", in C. A. Ferguson, L. M. Hyman, and J. J. Ohala (eds.), *Nasálfest: Papers from a Symposium on Nasals and Nasalization.* Stanford, CA: Stanford University, 197–212.

Fougeron, C. (1999). "Prosodically Conditioned Articulatory Variations: A Review", *UCLA Working Papers in Phonetics*, 97: 1–74.

—— (2001). "Articulatory Properties of Initial Segments in Several Prosodic Constituents in French", *Journal of Phonetics*, 29: 109–35.

—— and Keating, P. A. (1997). "Articulatory Strengthening at Edges of Prosodic Domains", *Journal of the Acoustical Society of America*, 101: 3728–40.

—— and Smith C. (1999). "Illustrations of the API: French", *Handbook of the International Phonetic Association.* Cambridge: Cambridge University Press, 78–81.

Foulkes, P. (1997). "Historical Laboratory Phonology—Investigating /p/ > /f/ > /h/ Changes", *Language and Speech*, 40: 248–76.

Fourakis, M., and Iverson, G. K. (1984). "On the 'Incomplete Neutralization' of German Final Obstruents", *Phonetica*, 41: 140–9.

—— and Port, R. (1986). "Stop Epenthesis in English", *Journal of Phonetics* 14: 197–221.

Fowler, C. A. (1980). "Coarticulation and Theories of Extrinsic Timing Control", *Journal of Phonetics*, 8: 13–133.

—— (1986). "An Event Approach to the Study of Speech Perception from a Direct-Realist Perspective", *Journal of Phonetics*, 14: 3–28.

—— and Brown, J. M. (2000). "Perceptual Parsing of Acoustic Consequences of Velum Lowering from Information for Vowels", *Perception and Psychophysics* 62: 21–32.

—— and Rosenblum, L. D. (1991). "The Perception of Phonetic Gestures", in I. G. Mattingly and M. Studdert-Kennedy (eds.), *Modularity and the Motor Theory of Speech Perception.* Hillsdale, NJ: Erlbaum, 33–59.

—— and Smith, M. R. (1986). "Speech Perception as 'Vector Analysis': An Approach to the Problems of Invariance and Segmentation", in J. S. Perkell and D. H. Klatts (eds.), *Invariance and Variability in Speech Processes.* Hillsdale, NJ: Erlbaum, 123–39.

—— Best, C. T., and McRoberts, G. W. (1990). "Young Infants' Perception of Liquid Coarticulatory Influences on Following Stop Consonants", *Perception and Psychophysics* 48: 559–70.

Fox, R. A. (1984). "Effect of Lexical Status on Phonetic Categorization", *Journal of Experimental Psychology: Human Perception and Performance* 10: 526–40.

Fu, Q.-J., and Shannon, R. V. (1999). "Recognition of Spectrally Degraded and Frequency-Shifted Vowels in Acoustic and Electric Hearing", *Journal of the Acoustical Society of America* 105: 1889–1900.

Fudge, E. (1987). "Branching Structure within the Syllable", *Journal of Linguistics*, 23: 359–77.

Fujimura, O. (1977). "Recent Findings on Articulatory Processes—Velum and Tongue Movements as Syllable Features", in R. Carré, R. Descout, and M. Wajskop (eds.), *Modelès Articulatoires et Phonétique/Articulatory Modeling and Phonetics.* Grenoble: Groupe de la Communication Parlée, 115–26.

—— (1986a). "A Linear Model of Speech Timing", in R. Channon and L. Shockey (eds.), *In Honor of Ilse Lehiste.* Dordrecht: Foris, 109–23.

Fujimura, O. (1986*b*). "Relative Invariance of Articulatory Movements", in S. Perkell and D. L. Klatt (eds), *Invariance and Variability in Speech Processes*. Hillsdale, NJ: Lawrence Erlbaum.

—— (1992). "Phonology and Phonetics. A Syllable-based Model of Articulatory Organization", *Journal of the Acoustical Society of Japan* (E) 13: 39–48.

—— (1996). "Icebergs Revisited", paper presented at the 133rd meeting of the Acoustical Society of America Meeting, PennState University, 17 June 1997.

—— (2000). "The C/D Model and Prosodic Control of Articulatory Behaviour", *Phonetica*, 57: 128–38.

—— (2003). "Temporal Organization of Speech Utterance: A C/D Model Perspective", *Cadernos de Estudos Lingüísticos*, 43: 9–35.

—— and Williams, J. C. (1999). "Syllable Concatenators in English, Japanese and Spanish", in O. Fujimura and J. B. D. Palek (eds.), *Proceedings of LP '98*, Prague: Charles University Press.

—— Macchi, M. J., and Streeter, L. A. (1978). "Perception of Stop Consonants with Conflicting Transitional Cues: A Cross-Linguistic Study", *Language and Speech*, 21: 337–46.

Fujisaki, H. (1988). "A Note on the Physiological and Physical Basis for the Phrase and Accent Components in the Voice Fundamental Frequency Contour", in O. Fujimura (ed.), *Vocal Physiology, Voice Production, Mechanisms and Functions*. New York: Raven Press, 347–55.

—— (1995). "Physiological and Physical Mechanisms for Tone, Accent and Intonation", *Proceedings of the XXIII World Congress of the International Association of Logopedics and Phoniatrics*. Cairo, 156–9.

—— and Gu, W. (2006). "Phonological Representation of Tone Systems of Some Tone Languages Based on the Command–Response Model for F_0 Contour Generation", *Proceedings of the Second International Symposium on Tonal Aspects of Languages*, La Rochelle, 59–62.

—— —— n.d. Unpublished work on modeling Lanqi tones.

—— and Hirose, K. (1984). "Analysis of Voice Fundamental Frequency Contours for Declarative Sentences of Japanese", *Journal of the Acoustical Society of Japan* (E), 5 (4): 233–42.

—— —— Hallé, P., and Lei, H. T. (1990). "Analysis and Modeling of Tonal Features in Polysyllabic Words and Sentences of the Standard Chinese", *Proceedings of the 1990 International Conference on Spoken Language Processing*, ii. Kobe, 841–4.

—— and Nagashima, S. (1969). "A Model for the Synthesis of Pitch Contours of Connected Speech", *Annual Report of the Engineering Research Institute*, 28. Tokyo: University of Tokyo, 53–60.

—— and Ohno, S. (1995). "Analysis and Modeling Fundamental Frequency Contours of English Utterances", *Proceedings of the 4th European Conference on Speech Communication and Technology*, ii. Madrid, 985–8.

—— Hallé, P., and Lei, H. T. (1987). "Application of F_0 Contour Command–Response Model to Chinese Tones", *Proceedings of 1987 Autumn Meeting of the Acoustical Society of Japan*, i: 197–8.

—— Ljungqvist, M., and Murata, H. (1993). "Analysis and Modeling of Word Accent and Sentence Intonation in Swedish", *Proceedings of the 1993 International Conference on Acoustics, Speech, and Signal Processing*, ii. Minneapolis, 211–14.

—— Nakamura, K., and Imoto, T. (1975). "Auditory Perception of Duration of Speech and Non-speech Stimuli", in G. Fant and M. A. A. Tatham (eds.), *Auditory Analysis and Perception of Speech*. New York: Academic Press, 197–219.

—— Ohno, S., and Luksaneeyanawin, S. (2003). "Analysis and Synthesis of F_0 Contours of Thai Utterances Based on the Command–Response Model", *Proceedings of the 15th International Congress of Phonetic Sciences*, Barcelona, Spain, 2: 1129–32.

Fujisaki, H., Wang, C. F., Ohno, S., and Gu, W. (2005). "Analysis and Synthesis of Fundamental Frequency Contours of Standard Chinese Using the Command–Response Model", *Speech Communication*, 47 (1–2): 59–70.

Gandour, J. (1977). "On the Interaction between Tone and Vowel Length", *Phonetica*, 34: 54–65.

—— Potisuk, S., and Dechongkit, S. (1994). "Tonal Coarticulation in Thai", *Journal of Phonetics*, 22: 477–92.

—— Tumtavitkul, A., and Salthamnuwong, N. (1999). "Effects of Speaking Rate on Thai Tones", *Phonetica*, 5: 123–34.

Ganong, W. F. I. (1980). "Phonetic Categorization in Auditory Word Perception", *Journal of Experimental Psychology: Human Perception and Performance*, 6: 110–25.

Gårding, E. (1970). "Word Tones and Larynx Muscles", *Working Papers*, 3. Lund: *Lund University, Department of Linguistics*, 20–46.

Garrett, M. F. (1976). "Syntactic Process in Sentence Production", in R. J. Walker and E. C. T. Walker (eds.), *New Approaches to Language Mechanisms*. Amsterdam: North-Holland, 231–56.

Gaskell, M. G., and Marslen-Wilson, W. D. (1996). "Phonological Variation and Inference in Lexical Access", *Journal of Experimental Psychology: Human Perception and Performance*, 22: 144–58.

—— —— (1998). "Mechanisms of Phonological Inference in Speech Perception", *Journal of Experimental Psychology: Human Perception and Performance*, 24: 380–96.

—— —— (2002). "Representation and Competition in the Perception of Spoken Words", *Cognitive Psychology*, 45: 220–66.

—— Hare, M., and Marslen-Wilson, W. D. (1995). "A Connectionist Model of Phonological Representation in Speech Perception", *Cognitive Science*, 19: 407–39.

Gay, T. (1981). "Mechanisms in the Control of Speech Rate", *Phonetica*, 38: 148–58.

—— Boë, L.-J., and Perrier, P. (1992). "Acoustic and Perceptual Effects of Changes in Vocal Tract Constrictions for Vowels", *Journal of the Acoustical Society of America*, 92 (3), 1301–9.

—— Lindblom, B., and Lubker, J. (1981). "Production of Bite-block Vowels: Acoustic Equivalence by Selective Compensation", *Journal of the Acoustical Society of America*, 69 (3), 802–10.

Giannelli, L. (1997). "Tuscany", in M. Maiden and M. Parry (eds.), *The Dialects of Italy*. London: Routledge, 297–302.

Gili Fivela B., and Zmarich, C. (2005). "Italian Geminate under Speech Rate and Focalization Changes: Kinematic, Acoustic and Perception Data", *Proceedings of INTERSPEECH 2005—EUROSPEECH*, Lisboa, 2897–2900.

Gim, C. G. (1987). "A Study on Syllable Structure and Some Processes in Its Nucleus in Korean", *Mal [Speech]*, 12: 25–69.

Glidden, C. M., and Assmann, P. F. (2004). "Effects of Visual Gender and Frequency Shifts on Vowel Category Judgements", *Acoustics Research Letters Online*, 5 (4): 132–8.

Gluck, M. A., and Myers, C. E. (2000). *Gateway to Memory: An Introduction to Neural Network Modeling of the Hippocampus and Learning*. Cambridge, MA: MIT Press.

Goldinger, S. D. (1992). "Words and Voices: Implicit and Explicit Memory for Spoken Words", Ph.D. dissertation (Indiana University).

—— (1996). "Words and Voices: Episodic Traces in Spoken Word Identification and Recognition Memory", *Journal of Experimental Psychology: Learning, Memory, and Cognition*, 22: 1166–83.

Goldinger, S. D. (1997). "Words and Voices: Perception and Production in an Episodic Lexicon", in K. Johnson and J. Mullennix (eds.), *Talker Variability in Speech Processing*. New York: Academic Press.

—— and Azuma, T. (2004). "Episodic Memory Reflected in Printed Word Naming", *Psychonomic Bulletin and Review*, 11: 716–22.

Goldsmith, J. A. (1990). *Autosegmental and Metrical Phonology*. Oxford: Basil Blackwell.

Goldstein, H. (1995). *Multi-level Statistical Models*. New York: Halstead Press.

Gordon, M. (2001). "A typology of Contour Tone Restrictions", *Studies in Language*, 25: 405–44.

—— (2002). "A Phonetically Driven Account of Syllable Weight", *Language*, 78: 51–80.

Gottfried, T. L. (1984). "Effects of Consonant Context on the Perception of French Vowels", *Journal of Phonetics*, 12, 91–114.

—— and Beddor, P. S. (1988). "Perception of Temporal and Spectral Information in French Vowels", *Language and Speech*, 31: 57–75.

Gouvêa, E. B. (1998). "Acoustic-feature-based Frequency Warping for Speaker Normalization", Ph.D. dissertation (Carnegie Mellon University).

—— and Stern, R. M. (1997). "Speaker Normalization through Formant-based Warping of the Frequency Scale", *5th European Conference on Speech Communication and Technology*, iii: 1139–42.

Gow, D. W. (2001). "Assimilation and Anticipation in Continuous Spoken Word Recognition", *Journal of Memory and Language*, 45: 133–59.

—— (2002). "Does English Coronal Place Assimilation Create Lexical Ambiguity?", *Journal of Experimental Psychology: Human Perception and Performance*, 28: 163–79.

—— (2003). "Feature Parsing: Feature Cue Mapping in Spoken Word Recognition", *Perception and Psychophysics*, 65: 575–90.

—— and Im, A. M. (2004). "A Cross-Linguistic Examination of Assimilation Context Effect", *Journal of Memory and Language*, 51: 279–96.

Grabe, E. (1998). "Pitch Accent Realization in English and German", *Journal of Phonetics*, 26: 129–43.

—— Post, B., Nolan, F., and Farrar, K. (2000). "Pitch Accent Realization in Four Varieties of British English", *Journal of Phonetics*, 28: 161–85.

Grandgent, C. (1920). *Old and New: Sundry Papers*. Cambridge: Harvard University Press.

Greenberg, J. H. (1963). *The Languages of Africa*. Bloomington: Indiana University Press.

—— (1987). *Language in the Americas*. Cambridge: Cambridge University Press.

Grice, M. (1995). "Leading Tones and Downstep in English", *Phonology*, 12: 183–233.

—— and Baumann, S. (2002). "Deutsche Intonation und GToBI", *Linguistische Berichte*, 191: 267–98.

Grønnum, N. (2006). "DanPASS—A Danish Phonetically Annotated Spontaneous Speech Corpus", in N. Calzolari, K. Choukri, A. Gangemi, B. Maegaard, J. Mariani, J. Odijk, and D. Tapias (eds.), *Proceedings of the 5th International Conference on Language Resources and Evaluation (LREC)*. Genova.

—— (forthcoming). "DanPASS—A Danish Phonetically Annotated Spontaneous Speech Corpus", in D. House, I. Karlsson, K. Elenius and M. Blomberg (eds.), *Research Challenges in Speech Technology. Festschrift to Rolf Carlson and Björn Granström on the Occasion of Their 60th Birthdays*.

Grønnum, N., and Basbøll, H. (2001a). "Consonant Length, Stød and Morae in Standard Danish", *Phonetica*, 58: 230–53.

—— —— (2001b). "Consonant Length, Stød and Morae in Danish", in A. Karlsson and J. van de Weijer (eds.), *Fonetik2001, Working Papers*, 49, Department of Linguistics, Lund University, 46–9.

—— —— (2002a). "Stød and Length: Acoustic and Cognitive Reality?", in B. Bel and I. Martin (eds.), *Proceedings of the Speech Prosody 2002 Conference*. Aix-en-Provence, 355–8.

—— —— (2002b). "Stød and Vowel Length: Acoustic and Cognitive Reality?", *Fonetik 2002*, Tal Musik Hörsel, *Quarterly Progress and Status Report* 44, Royal Institute of Technology, Stockholm, 85–8.

—— —— (2003a). "Two-phased Stød Vowels—A Cognitive Reality?", *Fonetik2003, Lövånger, Phonum*, 9, Reports in Phonetics, Department of Philosophy and Linguistics, Umeå University, 33–6.

—— —— (2003b). "Stød and Length in Standard Danish: Experiments in Laboratory Phonology", in M. J. Solé, D. Recasens and J. Romero (eds.), *Proceedings of the 15th International Congress of Phonetic Sciences*. Barcelona: Universitat Autònoma de Barcelona, 455–8.

Gu, W., and Fujisaki, H. n.d. Unpublished work on modeling Vietnamese tones.

—— Hirose, K., and Fujisaki, H. (2004a). "Analysis of F_0 Contours of Cantonese Utterances Based on the Command–Response Model", *Proceedings of the 2004 International Conference on Spoken Language Processing*, Jeju, 781–4.

—— —— —— (2004b). "Analysis of Shanghainese F_0 Contours Based on the Command–Response Model", *Proceedings of the 2004 International Symposium on Chinese Spoken Language Processing*. Hong Kong, 81–4.

—— —— —— (2005). "Identification and Synthesis of Cantonese Tones Based on the Command–Response Model for F_0 Contour Generation", *Proceedings of the 2005 IEEE International Conference on Acoustics, Speech, and Signal Processing*, Philadelphia, 289–92.

—— —— —— (2007). "Analysis of Tones in Cantonese Speech Based on the Command–Response Model", *Phonetica*, 64: 29–62.

Guion, S. G. (1998). "The Role of Perception in the Sound Change of Velar Palatalization", *Phonetica*, 55: 18–52.

Gupta, A. (1988). *Peculiarities of Geminates in Hindi*. Ms. University of Arizona, Tucson.

Gussenhoven, C. (2004). *The Phonology of Tone and Intonation*. Cambridge: Cambridge University Press.

Haden, E. (1955). "The Uvular r in French", *Language*, 31: 504–10.

Hajek, J. (1997). *Universals of Sound Change in Nasalization*. Oxford: Blackwell.

—— (2003). "Patterns of Vowel Nasalization in Northern Italy: Articulatory versus Perceptual", *Proceedings of the 15th International Congress of the Phonetic Sciences*, Barcelona, 235–8.

Hale, M., and Reiss, C. (2000). " 'Substance Abuse' and 'Dysfunctionalism': Current Trends in Phonology", *Linguistic Inquiry*, 31: 157–69.

Halle, M. (1964). "On the Bases of Phonology", in J. A. Fodor and J. J. Katz (eds.), *The Structure of Language: Readings in the Philosophy of Language*. Englewood Cliffs, NJ: Prentice-Hall, 324–33.

—— (2004). "Moving on". Plenary address given in honor of the 80th anniversary of the founding of the Linguistic Society of America. LSA Winter Meeting, Boston, January, 2004.

Halle, M., and Clements, G. C. (1983). *Problem Book in Phonology: A Workbook for Introductory Courses in Linguistics and Phonology.* Cambridge, MA: MIT Press.

—— and Stevens, K. N. (1971). "A Note on Laryngeal Features", *MIT Quarterly Progress Report,* 11: 198–213.

—— Bresnan, J., and Miller, G. A. (1981). *Linguistic Theory and Psychological Reality.* Cambridge, MA: MIT Press.

—— Vaux, B., and Wolfe, A. (2000). "On Feature Spreading and the Representation of Place of Articulation", *Linguistic Inquiry,* 31: 387–444.

Hallé, P., Niimi, S., Imaizumi, S., and Hirose, H. (1990). "Modern Standard Chinese Four Tones: Electromyographic and Acoustic Patterns Revisited", *Annual Bulletin of the Research Institute of Logopedics and Phoniatrics,* 24. University of Tokyo, 41–58.

Haller, H. (1987). "Italian Speech Varieties in the United States and the Italian-American Lingua Franca", *Italica,* 64: 393–409.

Hammond, R. (2000). "The Phonetic Realizations of /rr/ in Spanish: A Psychoacoustic Analysis", *Papers from the Hispanic Linguistics Symposium 3:* 80–100.

Han, M. S. (1992). "The Timing Control of Geminate and Single Stop Consonants in Japanese: A Challenge to Non-native Speakers", *Phonetica,* 49: 102–127.

—— (1994). "Acoustic Manifestations of Mora Timing in Japanese", *Journal of the Acoustical Society of America,* 96 (1): 73–82.

Hankamer, J., Lahiri, A., and Koreman, J. (1989). "Perception of Consonant Length: Voiceless Stops in Turkish and Bengali", *Journal of Phonetics,* 17: 283–98.

Hansen, B. B. (2004). "Production of Persian Geminate Stops: Effects of Varying Speaking Rate", in A. Agwuele, W. Warren, and S. H. Park (eds.), *Proceedings of the 2003 Texas Linguistics Society Conference.* Somerville, MA: Cascadilla Proceeding Project, 86–95.

Hardcastle, W. J., and Laver, J. (eds.) (1997). *The Handbook of Phonetic Sciences.* Oxford: Blackwell.

Harrington, J., Palethorpe, S. and Watson, C. I. (2000). "Does the Queen Speak the Queen's English?", *Nature,* 408: 927–28.

't Hart, J., and Cohen, A. (1973). "Intonation by Rule: A Perceptual Quest", *Journal of Phonetics,* 1: 309–27.

Hartsuiker, R., Corley, M., and Martensen, H. (2005). "The Lexical Bias Effect Is Modulated by Context, but the Standard Monitoring Account Doesn't Fly: Related Beply to Baars, Motley, and MacKay (1975)", *Journal of Memory and Language,* 52: 58–70.

Haspelmath, M., Dryer, M. S., Gil, D. and Comrie, B. (eds.) (2005). *The World Atlas of Language Structures.* Oxford and New York: Oxford University Press.

Hattori, S., Yamamoto, K., and Fujimura, O. (1958). "Nasalization of Vowels in Relation to Nasals", *Journal of the Acoustical Society of America,* 30: 267–74.

Hay, J., and Baayen, H. (2002). "Parsing and Productivity", *Yearbook of Morphology 2001:* 203–35.

Hayes, B. (1986). "Inalterability in CV Phonology", *Language,* 62: 321–51.

—— (1989). "Compensatory Lengthening in Moraic Phonology", *Linguistic Inquiry,* 20: 253–306.

—— (1995). "On What to Teach the Undergraduates: Some Changing Orthodoxies in Phonological Theory", *Linguistics in the Morning Calm,* 3. Seoul: Hanshin Publishing, 59–77.

—— and Steriade, D. (2004). "Introduction: The Phonetic Basis of Phonological Markedness", in B. Hayes, R. Kirchner, and D. Steriade (eds.), *Phonetically Based Phonology.* Cambridge: Cambridge University Press, 1–33.

—— and Stivers, T. (2000). "Postnasal Voicing". MS.

Hayward, K., and Hayward, R. J. (1999). "Illustrations of the API: Amharic", *Handbook of the International Phonetic Association*. Cambridge: Cambridge University Press, 45–50.

Heffner, R.-M. S. (1950). *General Phonetics*. Madison: University of Wisconsin.

Heinz, J. M., and Stevens, K. N. (1964). "On the Derivation of Area Functions and Acoustic Spectra from Cinéradiographic Films of Speech", *Journal of the Acoustical Society of America*, 36: 1037–8.

—— —— (1965). "On the Relations between Lateral Cinéradiographs, Area Functions and Acoustic Spectra of Speech", *International Congress of Acoustics*, 5(Ia), paper A44.

Henderson, J. B. (1984). "Velopharyngeal Function in Oral and Nasal Vowels: A Cross-language Study", Ph.D. dissertation (MIT).

Herman, R., Beckman, M., and Honda, K. (1996). "Subglottal Pressure and Final Lowering in English", *Proceedings of the Fourth International Conference on Spoken Language Proceedings of the Fourth International Conference on Spoken Language Processing '96*, i. Philadelphia, 145–8.

Hickok, G., and Poeppel, D. (2000). "Towards a Functional Neuroanatomy of Speech Perception", *Trends in Cognitive Science*, 4: 131–8.

Hillenbrand, J. M., and Nearey, T. M. (1999). "Identification of Resynthesized /hvd/ Utterances: Effects of Formant Contour", *Journal of the Acoustical Society of America*, 105: 3509–23.

—— Getty, L. A., Clark, M. J., and Wheeler, K. (1995). "Acoustic Characteristics of American English Vowels", *Journal of the Acoustical Society of America*, 97: 3099–3111.

Hintzman, D. L. (1986). "'Schema Abstraction' in a Multiple-Trace Memory Model", *Psychological Review*, 93: 411–28.

Hirano, M., and Ohala, J. J. (1969). "Use of Hooked-wire Electrodes for Electromyography of the Intrinsic Laryngeal Muscles", *Journal of Speech and Hearing Research*, 12: 362–73.

Hirata, Y. (2004). "Effects of Speaking Rate on the Vowel Length Distinction in Japanese", *Journal of Phonetics*, 32: 565–89.

Hirose, K., Minematsu, N., and Kawanami, H. (2000). "Analytical and Perceptual Study on the Role of Acoustic Features in Realizing Emotional Speech", *Proceedings of the 2000 International Conference on Spoken Language Processing*, ii. Beijing, 369–72.

Holmberg, E. B., Hillman R. E., and Perkell J. S. (1988). "Glottal Airflow and Transglottal Air Pressure Measurements for Male and Female Speakers in Soft, Normal and Loud Voice", *Journal of the Acoustical Society of America*, 84 (2): 511–29.

—— —— —— (1989). "Glottal Airflow and Transglottal Air Pressure Measurements for Male and Female Speakers in Low, Normal and High Pitch", *Journal of Voice*, 3: 294–305.

Holst, T., and Nolan, F. (1995). "The Influence of Syntactic Structure on [s] to [ʃ] Assimilation", in B. Connell, and A. Arvanti (eds.), *Papers in Laboratory Phonology, iv: Phonology and Phonetic Evidence*. Cambridge: Cambridge University Press, 315–33.

Hombert, J. (1986). "The Development of Nasalized Vowels in the Teke Language Group, Bantu", in K. Bogers and H. van der Hulst (eds.), *The Phonological Representation of Suprasegmentals*. Dordrecht: Foris, 359–79.

—— Ohala, J. J., and Ewan, W. (1979). "Phonetic Explanations for the Development of Tones", *Language*, 55: 37–58.

Honda, K., Hibi, S., Kiritani, S., Niimi, S., and Hirose, H. (1980). "Measurement of the Laryngeal Structure during Phonation by Use of a Stereoendoscope", *Annual Bulletin of the Research Institute of Logopedics and Phoniatrics*, 14. Tokyo: University of Tokyo, 73–8.

Honda, K., Takemoto, H., Kitamura, T., Fujita, S., and Takano, S. (2004) "Exploring Human Speech Production Mechanisms by MRI", *IEICE Transactions on Information and Systems*, 87 (5): 1050–8.

Hosmer, D. W., and Lemeshow, S. (2000). *Applied Logistic Regression* (2nd edn). New York: Wiley.

Houde, R. A. (1967). "A Study of Tongue Motion during Selected Speech Sounds", Ph.D. dissertaion (Speech Communication Research Laboratory, Santa Barbara).

House, A. S., and Fairbanks, G. (1953). "The Influence of Consonant Environment upon the Secondary Acoustical Characteristics of Vowels", *Journal of the Acoustical Society of America*, 25: 105–13.

Howell, R. B. (1986). "Notes on the Rise of the Non-apical R in Dutch: Denying the French Connection", *Canadian Journal of Netherlandic Studies*, 7: 24–66.

—— (1987). "Tracing the Origin of Uvular R in the Germanic Languages", *Folia Linguistica Historica*, 7: 317–49.

Huffman, M. K. (1990). "Implementation of Nasal: Timing and Articulatory Landmarks". *UCLA Working Papers on Phonetics*, 75.

—— and Krakow, R. (eds.) (1993). *Phonetics and Phonology 5: Nasals, Nasalization and the Velum*. San Diego: Academic Press.

Hume, E., and Johnson, K. (2001*a*). "A Model of the Interplay of Speech Perception and Phonology", in E. Hume and K. Johnson (eds.) *The Role of Speech Perception in Phonology*. San Diego: Academic Press, 3–26.

—— —— (eds.) (2001*b*). *The Role of Speech Perception in Phonology*. San Diego: Academic Press.

Hura, S. L., Lindblom, B., and Diehl, R. L. (1992). "On the Role of Perception in Shaping Phonological Assimilation Rules", *Language and Speech*, 35: 59–72.

Hyman, L. (1975*a*). *Phonology: Theory and Analysis*. New York: Holt, Rineholt and Winston.

—— (1975*b*). Review of C. C. Cheng, "A Synchronic Phonology of Mandarin Chinese", *Journal of Chinese Linguistics*, 3: 88–99.

—— (1978). "Historical tonology", in V. A. Fromkin (ed.), *Tone: A Linguistic Survey*. New York: Academic Press, 257–69.

—— (1985). *A Theory of Phonological Weight*. Dordrecht: Foris.

—— (2004). "Universals of Tone Rules: 30 Years Later". To appear in C. Gussenhoven and Tomas Riad (eds), *Tones and Tunes: Studies in Word and Sentence Prosody*. Berlin and New York: Mouton de Gruyter.

—— and Schuh, R. G. (1974). "Universals of Tone Rules: Evidence from West Africa", *Linguistic Inquiry*, 5: 81–115.

—— and VanBik, K. (2004). "Directional Rule Application and Output Problems in Hakha Lai Tone", *Phonetics and Phonology, Special Issue, Language and Linguistics* v. Taipei: Academia Sinica, 821–61.

Inkelas, S. (1995). "The Consequences of Optimization for Underspecification", in J. Beckman (ed.), *Proceedings of the Northeastern Linguistics Society 25*. Amherst MA: Graduate Linguistic Student Association, 287–302.

—— (2000). "Phonotactic Blocking through Structural Immunity", in B. Stiebels, and D. Wunderlich (eds.), *Lexicon in Focus*. Berlin: Akademie Verlag, 7–40.

—— and Cho, Y.-M. Y. (1993). "Inalterability as Prespecification", *Language*, 69: 529–74.

—— and Orgun, C. O. (1995). "Level Ordering and Economy in the Lexical Phonology of Turkish", *Language*, 71: 763–93.

Inkelas, S. Küntay, A., Orgun, O., and Sprouse, R. (2000). "Turkish Electronic Living Lexicon (TELL)", *Turkic Languages*, 4: 253–75.

Institute of Phonetics and Digital Speech Processing (1995). *The Kiel Corpus of Spontaneous Speech*, i, CD-ROM#2. Kiel: Institute of Phonetics and Digital Speech Processing.

—— (1996). *The Kiel Corpus of Spontaneous Speech*, ii, CD-ROM#3. Kiel: Institute of Phonetics and Digital Speech Processing.

—— (1997). *The Kiel Corpus of Spontaneous Speech*, iii, CD-ROM#4. Kiel: Institute of Phonetics and Digital Speech Processing.

Irino, T., and Patterson, R. D. (2002). "Segregating Information about the Size and Shape of the Vocal Tract Using a Time-domain Auditory Model: The Stabilised Wavelet-Mellin Transform", *Speech Communication*, 36: 181–203.

Isshiki, N. (1964). "Regulatory Mechanisms of Voice Intensity Variation", *Journal of Speech and Hearing Research*, 7: 17–29.

Jaeger, J. J. (1986). "Concept Formation as a Tool for Linguistic Research", in J. J. Ohala and J. J. Jaeger (eds.), *Experimental Phonology*. Orlando, FL: Academic Press, 211–37.

Jakobson, R., Fant, G., and Halle, M. (1952). *Preliminaries to Speech Analysis: The Distinctive Features and Their Correlates*. Cambridge, MA: MIT Press.

Janson, T. (1983). "Sound Change in Perception and Production", *Language*, 59: 18–34.

Javkin, H. (1979). *Phonetic Universals and Phonological Change. Report of the Phonology Laboratory*, 4. Berkeley: University of California.

Jespersen, O. (1904). *Phonetische Grundfragen*. Leipzig and Berlin: Teubner.

Johnson, K. (1990). "The Role of Perceived Speaker Identity in f0 Normalization of Vowels", *Journal of the Acoustical Society of America*, 88: 642–54.

—— (1997a). "The Auditory/Perceptual Basis for Speech Segmentation", *OSU Working Papers in Linguistics*, 50: 101–13. Columbus, Ohio.

—— (1997b). "Speech Perception without Speaker Normalization: An Exemplar Model", in K. Johnson and J. Mullennix (eds.), *Talker Variability in Speech Processing*. San Diego: Academic Press, 145–66.

—— (2005a). "Massive Reduction in Conversational American English". MS.

—— (2005b). "Resonance in an Exemplar-based Lexicon: The Emergence of Social Identity and Phonology", *UC Berkeley Phonology Lab Annual Report, 2005*, 95–128 (http://linguistics. berkeley.edu/phonlab/annual_report.html) (to appear in *Journal of Phonetics*).

—— (2005c). "Speaker Normalization in Speech Perception", in D. B. Pisoni and R. Remez (eds.), *The Handbook of Speech Perception*. Oxford: Blackwell, 363–89.

—— Ladefoged, P., and Lindau, M. (1993). "Individual Differences in Vowel Production", *Journal of the Acoustical Society of America* 94 (2): 701–14.

—— Strand, E. A., and D'Imperio, M. (1999). "Auditory-Visual Integration of Talker Gender in Vowel Perception", *Journal of Phonetics*, 27: 359–84.

Jonasson, J. (1971). "Perceptual Similarity and Articulatory Re-interpretation as a Source of Phonological Innovation", *Quarterly Progress and Status Report*, 1. Stockholm: Speech Transmission Laboratory, 30–41.

Joseph, B., and Janda, R. (1988). "The How and Why of Diachronic Morphologization and Demorphologization", in M. Hammond and M. Noonan (eds.), *Theoretical Morphology*. New York: Academic Press, 193–210.

Jun, J. (1996). "Place Assimilation Is Not the Result of Gestural Overlap: Evidence from Korean and English", *Phonology*, 13: 377–407.

Jusczyk, P. W. (1993). "From General to Language-specific Capacities—The WRAPSA Model of How Speech-perception Develops", *Journal of Phonetics*, 21 (1–2): 3–28.

Kahn, D. (1980). *Syllable-based Generalizations in English Phonology*. New York: Garland.

Katz, W. F., and Assmann, P. F. (2001). "Identification of Children's and Adults" Vowels: Intrinsic Fundamental Frequency, Fundamental Frequency Dynamics, and Presence of Voicing", *Journal of Phonetics*, 29: 23–51.

Kawahara, H. (1997). "Speech Representation and Transformation Using Adaptive Interpolation of Weighted Spectrum: Vocoder Revisited", *Proceedings of the ICASSP*, 1303–6.

—— Masuda-Katsuse, I., and de Cheveigné, A. (1999). "Restructuring Speech Representations Using a Pitch-Adaptive Time-Frequency Smoothing and an Instantaneous-Frequency-based F0 Extraction", *Speech Communication*, 27: 187–207.

Kawasaki, H. (1986). "Phonetic Explanation for Phonological Universals: The Case of Distinctive Vowel Nasalization", in J. J. Ohala and J. J. Jaeger (eds.), *Experimental Phonology*. Orlando, FL: Academic, 81–103.

Kaye, J. (1989). *Phonology: A Cognitive View*. Hillsdale: Lawrence Erlbaum.

Keating, P. A. (1985). "Universal Phonetics and the Organization of Grammars", in V. A. Fromkin (ed.), *Phonetic Linguistics. Essays in Honor of Peter Ladefoged*. Orlando, FL: Academic Press, 115–32.

—— Cho, T., Fougeron, C., and Hsu, C. (2003). "Domain-Initial Strengthening in Four Languages", in J. Local, R. Ogden, and R. Temple (eds.), *Papers in Laboratory Phonology*, vi. Cambridge: Cambridge University Press, 143–61.

Kelkar, A. R. (1968). *Studies in Hindi-Urdu, i: Introduction and Word Phonology*. (Building Centenary and Silver Jubilee, 35). Poona: Deccan College.

Kelso, J. A. S., Vatikiotis-Bateson, E., Saltzman, E., and Kay, B. (1985). "A Qualitative Dynamic Analysis of Speech Production: Phase Portraits, Kinematics, and Dynamic Modeling", *Journal of the Acoustical Society of America*, 77: 226–80.

Kennedy, N. M. (1960). *Problems of Americans in Mastering the Pronunciation of Egyptian Arabic*. Washington DC: Center for Applied Linguistics.

Kenstowicz, M., and Kisseberth, C. W. (1979). *Generative Phonology: Description and Theory*. New York: Academic Press.

—— and Pyle, C. (1973). "On the Phonological Integrity of Geminate Clusters", in M. J. Kenstowicz and C. W. Kisseberth (eds.), *Issues in Phonological Theory*. The Hague: Mouton, 27–43.

Kent, R. D., Carney, P. J., and Severeid, L. R. (1974). "Velar Movement and Timing: Evaluation of a Model of Binary Control", *Journal of Speech and Hearing Research*, 17: 470–88.

Kerswill, P. E. (1985). "A Sociophonetic Study of Connected Speech Processes in Cambridge English: An Outline and Some Results", *Cambridge Papers in Phonetics and Experimental Linguistics*, 4: 17–39.

Kessinger, R. H., and Blumstein, S. E. (1997). "Effects of Speaking Rate on Voice-onset Time in Thai, French and English", *Journal of Phonetics*, 25: 143–68.

Kingston, J., and Beckman, M. E. (eds.) (1990). *Papers in Laboratory Phonology*, i. Cambridge: Cambridge University Press.

—— and Diehl, R. L. (1994). "Phonetic Knowledge", *Language*, 70: 419–54.

Klatt, D. H. (1976). "Linguistic Uses of Segmental Duration in English: Acoustic and Perceptual Evidence", *Journal of the Acoustical Society of America*, 59: 1208–21.

Klatt, D. H. (1982). "Prediction of Perceived Phonetic Distance from Critical-band Spectra: A First Step", *Proceedings of the International Conference on Acoustics, Speech, and Signal Processing,* ICASSP-82, 1278–81.

Kleber, F. (2005). "Experimentalphonetische Untersuchungen zu Form und Funktion fallender Intonationskonturen im Englischen", MA dissertation (University of Kiel).

Kluender, K. R., Diehl, R. L., and Wright, B. A. (1988). "Vowel-length Differences between Voiced and Voiceless Consonants: An Auditory Explanation", *Journal of Phonetics,* 16: 153–69.

Kochanski, G., and Shih, C. (2003). "Prosody Modeling with Soft Templates", *Speech Communication,* 39 (3–4): 311–52.

Kohler, K. J. (1984). "Phonetic Explanation in Phonology: The Feature Fortis/Lenis", *Phonetica,* 38: 116–25.

—— (1987). "Categorical Pitch Perception", *Proceedings of the 11th International Congress of Phonetic Sciences,* v, Tallinn, 331–3.

—— (1990). "Macro and Micro F0 in the Synthesis of Intonation", in J. Kingston and M. E. Beckman (eds.), *Papers in Laboratory Phonology,* i: *Between the Grammar and Physics of Speech.* Cambridge: Cambridge University Press, 115–38.

—— (1991*a*). "A Model of German Intonation", *Arbeitsberichte des Instituts für Phonetik der Universität Kiel (AIPUK),* 25: 295–360.

—— (1991*b*). "The Organization of Speech Production. Clues from the Study of Reduction Processes", *Proceedings 12th International Congress of Phonetic Sciences,* i. Aix-en-Provence, 102–6.

—— (1991*c*). "Terminal Intonation Patterns in Single-accent Utterances of German: Phonetics, Phonology and Semantics", *Arbeitsberichte des Instituts für Phonetik der Universität Kiel (AIPUK),* 25: 115–85.

—— (1994). "Glottal Stops and Glottalization in German. Data and Theory of Connected Speech Processes", *Phonetica,* 51: 38–51.

—— (1995*a*). "Articulatory Reduction in Different Speaking Styles", in K Elenius and P. Branderud (eds.), *Proceedings 13th International Congress of Phonetic Sciences,* i. Stockholm, 12–19.

—— (1995*b*). "The Kiel Intonation Model (KIM), its Implementation in TTS Synthesis and its Application to the Study of Spontaneous Speech" (http://www.ipds.uni-kiel.de/kjk/forschung/kim.en.html).

—— (1997). "Modelling Prosody in Spontaneous Speech", in Y. Sagisaka, N. Campbell, and N. Higuchi (eds.), *Computing Prosody: Computational Models for Processing Spontaneous Speech.* New York: Springer, 187–210.

—— (1999*a*). "Articulatory Prosodies in German Reduced Speech". *Proceedings of the 14th International Congress of Phonetic Sciences,* San Francisco, 89–92.

—— (1999*b*). "Plosive-Related Glottalization Phenomena in Read and Spontaneous Speech. A Stød in German?" Poster presented at ICPhS 99 Satellite Meeting on Non-modal Vocal-fold Vibration and Voice Quality, San Francisco, 31 July, 1999. (http://www.ipds.uni-kiel.de/kjk/pub_exx/kongrbtr/plosglot.html).

—— (2001*a*). "Plosive-related Glottalization Phenomena in Read and Spontaneous Speech. A Stød in German?", in N. Grønnum and J. Rischel (eds.), *To Honour Eli Fischer-Jørgensen. Travaux du Cercle Linguistique de Copenhague,* 31. Copenhagen: Reitzel, 174–211.

—— (2001*b*). "The Investigation of Connected Speech Processes: Theory, Method, Hypotheses and Empirical Data", *Arbeitsberichte des Instituts für Phonetik der Universität Kiel (AIPUK),* 35: 1–32.

Kohler, K. J. (2001c). "Articulatory Dynamics of Vowels and Consonants in Speech Communication", *Journal of the International Phonetic Association*, 31: 1–16. (http://www.ipds.uni-kiel.de/kjk/publikationen/audiobsp.en.html).

—— (2003). "Neglected Categories in the Modelling of Prosody: Pitch Timing and Non-pitch Accents", *Proceedings of the 15th International Congress of Phonetic Sciences*, Barcelona, 2925–8.

—— (2004a). "Wieviele späte Gipfel braucht die Modellierung der Prosodie im Deutschen? Methodische und theoretische Reflexionen zur prosodischen Phonologie" (http://www.ipds.uni-kiel.de/kjk/forschung/lautmuster.en.html, section 4(b)).

—— (2004b). "Pragmatic and Attitudinal Meanings of Pitch Patterns in German Syntactically Marked Questions", in G. Fant, H. Fujisaki, J. Cao, and Y. Xu (eds.), *From Traditional Phonology to Modern Speech Processing. Festschrift for Professor Wu Zongji's 95th Birthday.* Beijing: Foreign Language Teaching and Research Press, 205–14. (http://www.ipds.uni-kiel.de/kjk/publikationen/audiobsp.en.html).

—— (2004c). "Categorical Speech Perception Revisited", *Proceedings of the Conference "From Sound to Sense: 50+ Years of Discoveries in Speech Communication"*. MIT, 11–13 June 2004. (http://www.ipds.uni-kiel.de/kjk/forschung/lautmuster.en.html, section 4(b)).

—— (ed.) (2005a). *Progress in Experimental Phonology: From Communicative Function to Phonetic Substance and Vice Versa.* (*Phonetica*, 62).

—— (2005b). "Timing and Communicative Functions of Pitch Contours", *Phonetica*, 62: 88–105.

—— (2006). "Paradigms in Experimental Prosodic Analysis: From Measurement to Function", in S. Sudhoff, D. Lenertová, R. Meyer, S. Pappert, P. Augurzky, I. Mleinek, N. Richter, and J. Schließer (eds.), *Methods in Empirical Prosody Research.* (= *Language, Context, and Cognition*, 3) Berlin and New York: Mouton de Gruyter, 123–52. (http://www.ipds.uni-kiel.de/kjk/publikationen/audiobsp.en.html).

Koster, C. J. (1987). *Word Recognition in Foreign and Native Language: Effects of Context and Assimilation.* Dordrecht: Foris.

Krakow, R. A. (1993). "Nonsegmental Influences on Velum Movement Patterns: Syllables, Sentences, Stress, and Speaking Rate", in M. K. Huffman and R. A. Krakow (eds.), *Nasals, Nasalization, and the Velum.* (*Phonetics and Phonology*, v). San Diego: Academic Press, 87–116.

Krauss, M. E. (1982). "Proto-Athapaskan *ḵ in Chipewyan, 1742–1800: Philological Evidence", *International Journal of American Linguistics*, 48: 73–82.

Kuehn, D., and Moll, K. (1976). "A Cineradiographic Study of VC and CV Articulatory Velocities", *Journal of Phonetics*, 4: 303–20.

Kuhl, P. K., Williams, K. A., Lacerda, F., Stevens, K. N., and Lindblom, B. (1992). "Linguistic Experience Alters Perception in Infants by 6 Months of Age", *Science*, 255: 606–8.

Kuhn, T. S. (1970). *The Structure of Scientific Revolutions.* (2nd edn). Chicago: University of Chicago Press.

Labov, W. (1994). *Principles of Linguistic Change*, i: *Internal Factors.* Oxford: Blackwell.

—— (2001). *Principles of Linguistic Change*, ii: *Social Factors.* Oxford: Blackwell.

—— Ash, S., and Boberg, C. (2005). *Atlas of North American English.* Berlin and New York: Mouton de Gruyter.

Ladd, D. R. (1996). *Intonational Phonology.* Cambridge: Cambridge University Press.

—— Mennen, I., and Schepman, A. (2000). "Phonological Conditioning of Peak Alignment in Rising Pitch Accents in Dutch", *Journal of the Acoustical Society of America*, 107: 2685–96.

Ladd, D. R. Faulkner, D., Faulkner, H., and Schepman, A. (1999). "Constant 'Segmental Anchoring' of F0 Movements Under Changes in Speech Rate", *Journal of the Acoustical Society of America*, 106: 1543–54.

Ladefoged, P. (1958). "Syllables and Stress", *Miscellanea Phonetics*, 3: 1–14.

—— (1967a). "Linguistic Phonetics", *UCLA Working Papers in Phonetics*, 6.

—— (1967b). *Three Areas of Experimental Phonetics*. London: Oxford University Press.

—— (1971). *Preliminaries to Linguistic Phonetics*. Chicago: University of Chicago Press.

—— and Maddieson, I. (1996). *The Sounds of the World's Languages*. Oxford: Blackwells.

—— and McKinney, N. P. (1963). "Loudness, Sound Pressure and Subglottal Pressure in Speech", *Journal of the Acoustical Society of America*, 35: 454–60.

—— DeClerk, J., Lindau, M., and Papçun, G. (1972). "An Auditory-motor Theory of Speech Production", *UCLA Working Papers in Phonetics*, 22: 48–75.

—— Williamson, K., Elugbe, B. O., and Uwalaka, A. (1976). "The Stops of Owerri Igbo", *Studies in African Linguistics* Supplement 6: 147–63.

Lahiri, A., and Hankamer, J. (1988). "The Timing of Geminate Consonants", *Journal of Phonetics*, 16: 327–338.

—— and Marslen-Wilson, W. D. (1991). "The Mental Representation of Lexical Form: A Phonological Approach to the Recognition Lexicon", *Cognition*, 38: 245–94.

Larsen, O. N., and F. Goller (2002). "Direct Observation of Syringeal Muscle Function in Songbirds and a Parrot", *Journal of Experimental Biology*, 205 (1): 25–35.

Laubstein, A. S. (1987). "Syllable Structure: The Speech Error Evidence", *Canadian Journal of Linguistics*, 32(4): 339–63.

Laver, J. (1994). *Principles of Phonetics*. Cambridge: Cambridge University Press.

Lavoie, L. (2002). "Some Influences on the Realization of *For* and *Four* in American English", *Journal of the International Phonetic Association*, 32: 175–202.

Lecuit, V., and Demolin, D. (1998). "The Relationship between Intensity and Subglottal Pressure with Controlled Pitch", *Proceedings of the The 5th International Conference on Spoken Language Processing*. Sydney, 3079–82.

Lee, S. (1993). "Formant Sensitivity in the Vocal Tract", *Journal of the Acoustical Society of America*, 94 (3): 1764.

Lehiste, I. (1970). *Suprasegmentals*. Cambridge, MA: MIT Press.

Levelt, W. J. M. (1989). *Speaking: from Intention to Articulation*. Cambridge, MA: MIT Press.

—— Roelofs, A., and Meyer, A. S. (1999). "A Theory of Lexical Access in Speech Production", *Behavioral and Brain Sciences*, 22: 1–75.

Lewis, G. (1967). *Turkish Grammar*. Oxford: Oxford University Press.

Libben, G. (2006). "Why Study Compound Processing? An Overview of the Issues", in G. Libben and G. Jarema (eds.), *The Representation and Processing of Compound Words*. Oxford: Oxford University Press, 1–22.

Liberman, A. M, and Mattingly, I. G. (1985). "The Motor Theory of Speech Perception Revised", *Cognition*, 21: 1–36.

—— and Whalen, D. H. (2000). "On the Relation of Speech to Language", *Trends in Cognitive Science*, 4: 187–96.

Liberman, A. S. (1982). *Germanic Accentology*, i: *The Scandinavian Languages*. Minneapolis: University of Minnesota Press.

Liberman, M. (1975). "The Intonational System of English", Ph.D. dissertation (MIT).

Lieberman, P. (1963). "Some Effects of Semantic and Grammatical Context on the Production and Perception of Speech", *Language and Speech*, 6: 172–87.

—— (1967). *Intonation, Perception and Language*. Cambridge, MA: MIT Press.

—— and Blumstein, S. (1988). *Speech Physiology, Speech Perception, and Acoustic Phonetics*. Cambridge: Cambridge University Press.

—— Sawashima, M., Harris, K. S., and Gay, T. (1970). "The Articulatory Implementation of Breath Group and Prominence: Cricothyroid Muscular Activity in Intonation", *Language*, 46: 312–27.

Lightfoot, N. (1989). "Effects of Talker Familiarity on Serial Recall of Spoken Word Lists", *Research on Speech Perception Progress Report*, 15. Bloomington: Indiana University, Department of Psychology, 419–43.

Liljencrants, J. "Formf.c" (C-program for the calculation of formant frequencies from area functions). *Speech Transmission Laboratory Quarterly Progress and Status Report* 4. Stockholm: Royal Institute of Technology, Department of Speech, Music and Hearing, 15–20.

—— and Lindblom, B. (1972). "Numerical Simulations of Vowel Quality Systems: The Role of Perceptual Contrast", *Language*, 48: 839–62.

Lindau, M. (1985). "The Story of /r/", in V.A. Fromkin (ed.), *Phonetic Linguistics, Essays in Honor of Peter Ladefoged*. Orlando: FL: Academic Press, 157–68.

Lindblom, B. (1963). "A Spectrographic Study of Vowel Reduction", *Journal of the Acoustical Society of America*, 35 (11): 1773–81.

—— (1984). "Can the Models of Evolutionary Biology Be Applied to Phonetic Problems?", *Proceedings of the 10th International Congress of Phonetic Sciences*. Utrecht, 67–81.

—— (1986) "Phonetic Universals in Vowel Systems." in J. Ohala and J. Jaeger (eds.), *Experimental Phonology*. Orlando, FL: Academic Press, 13–44.

—— (1990a). "Explaining Phonetic Variation: A Sketch of the HandH Theory", in W. J. Hardcastle and A. Marchal (eds.), *Speech Production and Speech Modelling*. Dordrecht: Kluwer, 403–39.

—— (1990b). "On the Notion of Possible Speech Sound", *Journal of Phonetics*, 18: 135–52.

—— (1998). "Systematic Constraints and Adaptive Change in the Formation of Sound Structure", in J. R. Hurford, M. Studdert-Kennedy and C. Knight (eds.), *Approaches to the Evolution of Language*. Cambridge: Cambridge University Press, 242–64.

—— (2000). "Developmental Origins of Adult Phonology: The Interplay between Phonetic Emergents and Evolutionary Adaptations", in K. Kohler, R. Diehl, O. Engstrand, and J. Kingston (eds.), *Speech Communication and Language Development: Adaptation and Emergence*. *Phonetica* 57: 297–314 (special issue).

—— (2003). "A Numerical Model of Coarticulation Based on a Principal Components Analysis of Tongue Shapes", *Proceedings of the 15th International Congress of Phonetic Sciences*, Barcelona, 427–30.

—— and Engstrand, O. (1989) "In What Sense Is Speech Quantal?", *Journal of Phonetics*, 17: 107–21.

—— and Lubker, J. (1985). "The Speech Homonculus and a Problem of Phonetic Linguistics", in V. A. Fromkin (ed.), *Phonetic Linguistics*. Orlando, FL: Academic Press, 169–92.

—— and Sundberg, J. (1971). "Acoustical Consequences of Lip, Tongue, Jaw and Larynx Movement", *Journal of the Acoustical Society of America*, 50: 1166–79.

—— MacNeilage, P., and M. Studdert-Kennedy. (1984). "Self-organizing Processes and The Explanation of Language Universals", in B. Butterworth, B. Comrie and Ö. Dahl, (eds.), *Explanations for Language Universals*. Berlin: Walter de Gruyter.

—— Guion, S., Hura, S., Moon, S., and Willerman, R. (1995). "Is Sound Change Adaptive?", *Rivista di Linguistica*, 7: 5–37.

Lisker, L. (1958). "The Tamil Occlusives: Short vs. Long Or Voiced vs. Voiceless?", *Indian Linguistics*, 19: 294–301.

—— and Abramson, A. S. (1967). "Some Effects of Context On Voice Onset Time in English Stops", *Language and Speech*, 10: 1–28.

Local, J., and Simpson, A. (1999). "Phonetic Implementation of Geminates in Malayam Nouns", in J. J. Ohala, Y. Hasegawa, M. Ohala, D. Granville (eds.), *Proceedings of the XIVth International Congress of Phonetic Sciences*, i. Berkeley: University of California, Department of Linguistics, 595–8.

Lœvenbruck, H., and Perrier, P. (1997). "Motor Control Information Recovering from the Dynamics with the EP Hypothesis", *Proceedings of the European Conference on Speech Communication and Technology*, iv. Rhodes, 2035–8.

Lubker, J., and Gay, J. (1982). "Anticipatory Labial Coarticulation: Experimental, Biological, and Linguistic Variables", *Journal of the Acoustical Society of America*, 71 (2): 437–48.

—— and Moll, K. L. (1965). "Simultaneous Oral-Nasal Air Flow Measurements and Cinefluorographic Observations During Speech Production", *Cleft Palate Journal*, 2: 257–72.

Luce, P. A. (1986). "A Computational Analysis of Uniqueness Points in Auditory Word Recognition", *Perception and Psychophysics*, 39: 155–8.

—— and Pisoni, D. B. (1998). "Recognising Spoken Words: The Neighborhood Activation Model", *Ear and Hearing*, 19: 1–36.

Luke, D. A. (2004). *Multi-level Modeling* (Quantitative Applications in the Social Sciences, 143). Thousand Oaks, CA: Sage.

McClelland, J. L., and Elman, J. L. (1986). "The TRACE Model of Speech Perception", *Cognitive Psychology*, 18: 1–86.

McLennan, C. T., Luce, P. A., and Charles-Luce, J. (2003). "Representation of Lexical Form", *Journal of Experimental Psychology: Learning, Memory, and Cognition*, 29: 539–53.

Macmillan, N. A., and Creelman, C. D. (1991). *Detection Theory: A User's Guide*. Cambridge: Cambridge University Press.

MacNeilage, P. F. (1998). "The Frame/Content Theory of Evolution of Speech Production", *Behavioral and Brain Sciences*, 21: 499–546.

—— and Davis, B. L. (1990a). "Acquisition of Speech Production: Frames Then Content", in M. Jeannerod (ed.), *Attention and Performance*, XIII. Hillsdale, NJ: Lawrence Erlbaum, 453–75.

—— —— (1990b). "Acquisition of Speech Production: The Achievement of Segmental Independence", in W. J. Hardcastle and A. Marchal (eds.), *Speech Production and Speech Modelling*. Dordrecht: Kluwer, 55–68.

—— —— (1993). "Motor Explanations of Babbling and Early Speech Patterns", in B. de Boysson–Bardies, S. de Schonen, P. Jusczyk, P. F. MacNeilage and J. Morton (eds.), *Developmental Neurocognition: Speech and Face Processing in the First Year of Life*. Dordrecht: Kluwer, 123–37.

Maddieson, I. (1984). *Patterns of Sounds*. Cambridge: Cambridge University Press.

Maddieson, I. (1985). "Phonetic Cues to Syllabification", in V. Fromkin (ed.), *Phonetic Linguistics*. Orlando, FL: Academic Press, 203–21.

—— (1986). "The Size and Structure of Phonological Inventories: Analysis of UPSID", in J. J. Ohala, and J. J. Jaeger (eds.), *Experimental Phonology*. Orlando, FL: Academic Press, 105–23.

—— (1989). "Linguo-Labials", in R. Harlow and R. Hooper (eds.), *VICAL, Papers from the Fifth International Conference on Austronesian Linguistics*, i: *Oceanic Languages*. Auckland: Linguistic Society of New Zealand, 349–75.

—— (1992). "The Structure of Segment Sequences", in J. J. Ohala *et al.* (eds.) *Proceedings of the Second International Conference on Spoken Language Processing*. Banff, Addendum, 1–4.

—— (2001). "Typological Patterns, Geographical Distribution and Phonetic Explanation", paper presented at the Conference on the Phonetics-Phonology Interface, Zentrum für Allgemeine Sprachwissenchaft, Berlin, 11 Oct. 2001.

—— (2006). "Correlating Phonological Complexity: Data and Validation", *Linguistic Typology*, 10: 108–25.

—— , and Precoda, K. (1989). "Updating UPSID", *Journal of the Acoustical Society of America*, 86 (suppl. 1): S19.

—— —— (1990). "Updating UPSID", *UCLA Working Papers in Phonetics*, 74: 104–14.

Maeda, S. (1975). "Electromyographic Study of Intonational Attributes", *Quaterly Progress Report, Research Laboratory of Electronics*, MIT: 261–9.

—— (1976). "A Characterization of American English Intonation", Ph.D. dissertation (MIT).

—— (1979). "An Articulatory Model of the Tongue Based on a Statistical Analysis", *Journal of the Acoustical Society of America*, 65: S22.

—— (1982), "A Digital Simulation Method of the Vocal-tract System", *Speech Communication*, 1: 99–229.

—— (1990). "Compensatory Articulation During Speech: Evidence from the Analysis and Synthesis of Vocal-tract Shapes Using an Articulatory Model", in W. J. Hardcastle and A. Marchal (eds.), *Speech Production and Speech Modelling*. Dordrecht: Kluwer Academic, 131–49.

—— (1993). "Acoustics of Vowel Nasalization and Articulatory Shifts in French Nasal Vowels", in M. K. Huffman and R. A. Krakow (eds.), *Nasals, Nasalization and the Velum: Phonetics and Phonology*. San Diego: Academic Press, 174–67.

—— (1996). "Phonemes as Concatenable Units: VCV Synthesis Using a Vocal-tract Synthesizer", in A. Simpson (ed.), *Sound Patterns of Connected Speech: Description, Models and Explanation*. Arbeitsberichte des Instituts für Phonetik und digitale Sprachverarbeitung der Universität Kiel, AIPUK 31 (Proceedings of the symposium held at Kiel University on 14–15 June 1996).

Magen, H., and Blumstein, S. (1993). "Effects of Speaking Rate on the Vowel Length Distinction in Korean", *Journal of Phonetics*, 21: 387–409.

Magloire, J., and Green, K. P. (1999). "A Cross-language Comparison of Speaking Rate Effects on the Production of Voice Onset Time in English and Spanish", *Phonetica*, 56: 158–85.

Majors, T. J. (1998). "Stress Dependent Harmony: Phonetic Origins and Phonological Analysis", Ph.D. dissertation (University of Texas, Austin).

Malécot, A. (1960). "Vowel Nasality as a Distinctive Feature in American English", *Language*, 36: 222–9.

Malmberg, B. (1943). *Le système consonantique du français moderne: études de phonétique et phonologie. Etudes Romanes de Lund VII.*

—— (1966). *Spansk fonetik.* Lund: Liber läromedel.

—— (1974). *Manuel de phonétique générale.* Paris: Éditions A. and J. Picard.

Mann, V. A., and Repp, B. H. (1980). "Influence of Vocalic Context on Perception of the [ʃ] - [s] Distinction", *Perception and Psychophysics,* 28: 213–28.

Manuel, S. Y. (1995). "Speakers Nasalize /ð/ after /n/, but Listeners Still Hear /ð/", *Journal of Phonetics,* 23: 453–76.

Marslen-Wilson, W. D., and Welsh, A. (1978). "Processing Interactions and Lexical Access During Word Recognition in Continuous Speech", *Cognitive Psychology,* 10: 29–63.

Martin, J. G., and Bunnell, H. T. (1981). "Perception of Anticipatory Coarticulation Effects", *Journal of the Acoustical Society of America,* 69: 559–67.

Martinet, A. (1937). *La phonologie du mot en danois.* Paris: Libraire C. Klincksieck. Also in *Bulletin de la Société Linguistique de Paris,* 38: 69–266.

—— (1955). *Economie des changements phonétiques: traité de phonologie diachronique.* Berne: Francke.

Masica, C. P. (1991). *The Indo-Aryan Languages.* Cambridge: Cambridge University Press.

Massaro, D. W. (1987). *Speech Perception by Ear and Eye: A Paradigm for Psychological Inquiry.* London: Laurence Erlbaum Associates.

Mathieu, B., and Laprie, Y. (1997). "Adaptation of Maeda's Model for Acoustic to Articulatory Inversion", *Proceedings of the 5th European Conference on Speech Communication and Technology,* 2015–18.

Matisoff, J. (1973). "Tonogenesis in South-East Asia", in L. M. Hyman (ed.), *Consonant Types and Tone.* Los Angeles: University of Southern California, 71–95.

Meillet, A., and Cohen, M. (1924). *Les langues du monde.* Paris: CNRS.

Melchert, H. C. (1994). *Anatolian Historical Phonology.* Amsterdam and Atlanta: Rodopi.

Ménard, L., Schwartz, J. L., and Boë, L. J. (2007). "Production-perception Relationships During Vocal Tract Growth for French Vowels: Analysis of Real Data and Simulations with an Articulatory Model", *Journal of Phonetics,* 35 (1): 1–19.

—— —— —— Kandel, S., and Vallée, N. (2002). "Auditory Normalization of French Vowels Synthesized by an Articulatory Model Simulating Growth from Birth to Adulthood," *Journal of the Acoustical Society of America,* 111 (4): 1892–1905.

Menezes, C. (2003). "Rhythmic Pattern of American English: An Articulatory and Acoustic Study", Ph.D. dissertation (The Ohio State University).

—— Pardo, B., Erikson, D., and Fujimura, O. (2003). "Changes in syllable magnitude and timing due to repeated correction", *Speech Communication,* 40: 71–85.

Mermelstein, P. (1973). "Articulatory Model for the Study of Speech Production", *Journal of the Acoustical Society of America,* 53: 1070–82.

—— (1978). "On the Relationship between Vowel and Consonant Identification When Cued by the Same Acoustic Information", *Perception and Psychophysics,* 23: 331–36.

Mielke, J. (2003). "The Interplay of Speech Perception and Phonology: Experimental Evidence from Turkish", *Phonetica,* 60: 208–29.

Miller, J. D. (1989). "Auditory-Perceptual Interpretation of the Vowel", *Journal of the Acoustical Society of America,* 85 (5): 2114–34.

Miller, J. L., and Grosjean, F. (1997). "Dialect Effects in Vowel Perception: The Role of Temporal Information in French", *Language and Speech,* 40: 277–88.

Miller, J. L., Green, K. P., and Reeves, A. (1986). "Speaking Rate and Segments: A Look at the Relation between Speech Production and Speech Perception for the Voicing Contrast", *Phonetica*, 43: 106–15.

Mills, A. E. (1987). "The Development of Phonology in the Blind Child", in B. Dodd and R. Campbell (eds.), *Hearing by Eye: the Psychology of Lipreading*. London: Lawrence Erlbaum Associates, 145–61.

Mioni, A. (2001). *Elementi di Fonetica*. Padova: Unipress.

—— and Trumper, J. (1977). "Per un'Analisi del 'Continuum' Linguistico Veneto," in R. Simone and G. Ruggiero, *Aspetti Sociolinguistici dell'Italia Contemporanea, Atti dell'VIII Congresso Internazionale di Studi*. Roma: Bulzoni, 329–72.

Mitchell, C. J. (2000). "Analysis of Articulatory Movement Patterns According to the Converter/Distributor Model" MA thesis (The Ohio State University).

Mitchell, T. F. (1962). *Colloquial Arabic: The Living Language of Egypt*. London: Hodder and Stoughton.

Mitleb, F. (1981). Segmental and Non-segmental Structure in Phonetics: Evidence from Foreign Accent", Ph.D. dissertation (Indiana University).

Mitterer, H., and Blomert, L. (2003). "Coping with Phonological Assimilation in Speech Perception: Evidence for Early Compensation", *Perception and Psychophysics*, 65: 956–69.

Mixdorff, H., Bach, N. H., Fujisaki, H., and Luong, M. C. (2003). "Quantitative Analysis and Synthesis of Syllabic Tones in Vietnamese", *Proceedings of the 8th European Conference on Speech Communication and Technology*, i. Geneva: 177–80.

Moll, K. (1962). "Velopharyngeal Closure on Vowels", *Journal of Speech and Hearing Research*, 5: 30–7.

Moore, B. C. J., and Glasberg, B. R. (1983). "Masking Patterns for Synthetic Vowels in Simultaneous and Forward Masking", *Journal of the Acoustical Society of America*, 73: 906–17.

Morgan, J. L., Singh, L., Bortfeld, H., Rathbun, K., and White, K. (2001). "Effects of Speech and Sentence Position on Infant Word Recognition", paper presented at the Boston University Conference on Language Development, Boston, MA.

Morrison, G. S., and Nearey, T. M. (2006). "A cross-language vowel normalisation procedure", *Canadian Acoustics*, 43 (3): 94–5.

Morse, P. M. (1948). *Vibration and Sound*, 2nd edn. New York: McGraw-Hill.

Motley, M. T., and Baars, B. J. (1975). "Encoding Sensitivities to Phonological Markedness and Transitional Probabilities", *Human Communication Research*, 2: 351–61.

—— —— (1976). "Semantic Bias Effects of Verbal Slips", *Cognition*, 4: 177–87.

Muminović, D., and Engstrand, O. (2001). "/r/ i några svenska dialekter" [/r/ in some Swedish dialects], in M. Sundman, and A.-M. Londen (eds.), *Svenskans Beskrivning*, 25. Åbo: Förhandlingar vid Tjugofemte sammankomsten för svenskans beskrivning, 200–7.

Munro, M. J. (1993). "Productions of English Vowels by Native Speakers of Arabic: Acoustic Measurements and Accentedness Ratings", *Language and Speech*, 36: 39–66.

Nadler, R. D., Abbs, J. H., and Fujimura, O. (1987). "Speech Movement Research Using the New X-ray Microbeam System", *Proceedings of the XIth International Congress of Phonetic Sciences*, vi. Tallin: Academy of Sciences of the Estonian SSR, 10–27.

Naksakul, K. (1998). *Ra-bob-siang-phaa-saa-thai*. [The Thai Sound System]. Bangkok: Chulalongkorn University Press.

Navarro Tomás, T. (1966). *El español en Puerto Rico*. Rio Piedras: Universidad de Puerto Rico.

Nearey, T. M. (1978). *Phonetic Feature Systems for Vowels*. Bloomington: Indiana University Linguistics Club.

—— (1989). "Static, Dynamic, and Relational Properties in Vowel Perception", *Journal of the Acoustical Society of America*, 85 (5): 2088–2113.

—— (1992). "Applications of Generalized Linear Modeling to Vowel Data", in *Proceedings Fourth International Conference on Spoken Language Processing 92*, i. Edmonton: University of Alberta, 583–6.

—— (1997). "Speech Perception as Pattern Recognition", *Journal of the Acoustical Society of America*, 101: 3241–54.

—— and Assmann, P. F. (1986). "Modeling the Role of Inherent Spectral Change in Vowel Identification", *Journal of the Acoustical Society of America*, 80: 1297–1308.

Neath, I., and Surprenant, A. (2003). *Human Memory*, (2nd edn). Belmont, CA: Thompson, Wadsworth.

Netsell, R. (1969). "Subglottal and Intraoral Air Pressures During the Intervocalic Contrast of /t/ and /d/", *Phonetica*, 20: 68–73.

—— (1973). "Speech Physiology", in F. D. Minifie, T. J. Hixon and F. Williams (eds.), *Normal Aspects of Speech, Hearing and Language*. Engelwood cliffs, NJ: Prentice Hall, 211–34.

Nguyen, N., and Hawkins, S. (1999). "Implications for Word Recognition of Phonetic Dependencies between Syllable Onsets and Codas", in J. J. Ohala, Y. Hasegawa, M. Ohala, D. Granville (eds.), *Proceedings of the XIVth International Congress of Phonetic Sciences*, i. Berkeley: Department of Linguistics, University of California, 647–50.

Niebuhr, O. (2003). "Perceptual Study of Timing Variables in F0 Peaks", *Proceedings of the 15th International Congress of Phonetic Sciences*, Barcelona, 1225–8.

—— and Kohler, K. J. (2004). "Perception and Cognitive Processing of Tonal Alignment in German", in B. Bel and I. Marlien (eds), *Proceedings of the International Symposium on Tonal Aspects of Languages. Emphasis on Tone Languages*. Beijing: The Institute of Linguistics, Chinese Academy of Social Sciences, 155–8.

Nittrouer, S., Munhall, K., Kelso, J. A. S., Tuller, B., and Harris, K. S. (1988). "Patterns of Interarticulator Phasing and Their Relation to Linguistic Structure", *Journal of the Acoustical Society of America*, 84: 1653–61.

Noiray, A., Ménard, L., Cathiard, M.-A., Abry, C., and Savariaux, C. (2004). "The Development of Anticipatory Labial Coarticulation in French: A Pionneering Study", *Proceedings of the 8th International Conference on Spoken Language Processing (ICSLP '04)*, i: 53–6.

Nolan, F. (1992). "The Descriptive Role of Segments: Evidence from Assimilation", in D. R. Ladd, and G. Docherty (eds.), *Papers in Laboratory Phonology*, ii: *Gesture, Segment, Prosody*. Cambridge: Cambridge University Press, 261–80.

Nooteboom, S. G. (1995). "Limited Lookahead in Speech Production", in F. Bell-Berti and L. R. Raphael (eds), *Producing Speech: Contemporary Issues*. New York: AIP Press, 3–18.

—— (2005a). "Listening to One-self: Monitoring Speech Production", in R. Hartsuiker, Y. Bastiaanse, A. Postma, and F. Wijnen (eds.), *Phonological Encoding and Monitoring in Normal and Pathological Speech*. Hove: Psychology Press, 167–86.

—— (2005b). "Lexical Bias Revisited: Detecting, Rejecting, and Repairing Speech Errors in Inner Speech", *Speech Communication*, 47 (1–2): 43–58.

—— (2005c). "Lexical Bias Re-revisited. Secondary Speech Errors as a Major Source of Lexical Bias", in J. Véronis and E. Campione (eds.), *Disfluency in Spontaneous Speech* (An ISCA Tutorial and Research Workshop). Équipe DELIC, Université de Provence, 139–44.

Nosofsky, R. M. (1986). "Attention, Similarity, and the Identification-Categorization Relationship", *Journal of Experimental Psychology: General*, 115: 39–57.

—— (1988). "Exemplar-based Accounts of Relations between Classification, Recognition, and Typicality", *Journal of Experimental Psychology: Learning, Memory, and Cognition*, 14: 700–8.

—— (1991). "Tests of an Exemplar Model for Relating Perceptual Classification and Recognition Memory", *Journal of Experimental Psychology: Human Perception and Performance*, 17: 3–27.

Nusbaum, H., and Magnuson, J. (1997). "Talker Normalization: Phonetic Constancy as a Cognitive Process", in K. Johnson and J. Mullennix (eds.), *Talker Variability in Speech Processing*. San Diego: Academic Press, 109–32.

Nygaard, L. C., and Pisoni, D. B. (1998). "Talker-Specific Learning in Speech Perception", *Perception and Psychophysics* 60: 355–76.

O'Dell, M., and Port, R. (1983). "Discrimination of Word-Final Voicing in German", *Journal of the Acoustical Society of America* 73: S31, N17.

Ohala, J. J. (1970). "Aspects of the Control and Production of Speech". *Working Papers in Phonetics*, 15. Berkeley: UCLA.

—— (1971a). "Monitoring Soft Palate Movements in Speech", *Project on Linguistic Analysis [POLA] Reports*, 15. Berkeley: University of California at Berkeley, 25–40.

—— (1971b). "How to Represent Nasal Sound Patterns", *Project on Linguistic Analysis, [POLA] Reports*, 16. Berkeley: University of California at Berkeley 40–57.

—— (1973). "The Physiology of Tones", in L. Hyman (ed.), *Consonant Types and Tone. Southern California Occasional Papers, Linguistics*, 1: 1–14. Los Angeles: The Linguistics Program, University of Southern California.

—— (1974). "Experimental Historical Phonology", in J. Anderson and C. Jones (eds.), *Historical Linguistics*, ii. Amsterdam: North-Holland, 353–89.

—— (1975). "Phonetic Explanations for Nasal Sound Patterns", in C. A. Ferguson, L. M. Hyman, and J. J. Ohala (eds.), *Nasálfest: Papers from a Symposium on Nasals and Nasalization*. Stanford, CA: Language Universals Project, 289–316.

—— (1978). "Southern Bantu vs the World: The Case of Palatalization of Labials", *Proceedings of the Berkeley Linguistic Society*, 4: 370–86.

—— (1979). "Moderator's Introduction to Symposium on Phonetic Universals in Phonological Systems and Their Explanation", *Proceedings of the 9th International Congress of Phonetic Sciences*, 3: 181–5.

—— (1981a). "Articulatory Constraints on the Cognitive Representation of Speech", in T. Myers, J. Laver, and J. Anderson (eds.), *The Cognitive Representation of Speech*. Amsterdam: North-Holland, 113–24.

—— (1981b). "The Listener as a Source of Sound Change", in C. S. Masek, R. A. Hendrick, and M. F. Miller (eds.), *Papers from the Parasession on Language and Behavior*. Chicago: Chicago Linguistic Society 178–203.

—— (1981c). "Speech Timing as a Tool in Phonology", *Phonetica*, 38: 204–17.

—— (1983a). "Cross-Language Use of Pitch: An Ethological View", *Phonetica*, 40: 1–18.

—— (1983b). "The Origin of Sound Patterns in Vocal Tract Constraints", in P. F. MacNeilage (ed.), *The Production of Speech*. New York: Springer, 189–216.

—— (1984). "An Ethological Perspective on Common Cross-Language Utilization of F0 of Voice", *Phonetica*, 41: 1–16.

—— (1986). "Consumer's Guide to Evidence in Phonology", *Phonology Yearbook*, 3: 3–26.

Ohala, J. J. (1987). "Experimental Phonology", *Proceedings Berkeley Linguistics Society*, 13: 207–22.

—— (1989). "Sound Change Is Drawn from a Pool of Synchronic Variation", in L. E. Breivik and E. H. Jahr (eds.), *Language Change: Contributions to the Study of Its Causes*. Berlin: and New York: Mouton de Gruyter, 173–98.

—— (1990a). "The Phonetics and Phonology of Aspects of Assimilation", in J. Kingston and M. Beckman (eds.), *Papers in Laboratory Phonology, i: Between the Grammar and the Physics of Speech*. Cambridge: Cambridge University Press, 258–75.

—— (1990b). "Respiratory Activity in Speech", in W. J. Hardcastle and A. Marchal (eds.), *Speech Production and Speech Modelling*. Dordrecht: Kluwer, 23–53.

—— (1990c). "There is No Interface between Phonetics and Phonology. A Personal View", *Journal of Phonetics* 18: 153–71.

—— (1993a). "Coarticulation and Phonology", *Language and Speech*, 36 (2–3): 155–70.

—— (1993b). "The Phonetics of Sound Change", in C. Jones (ed.), *Historical Linguistics: Problems and Perspectives*. London and New York: Longman, 237–78.

—— (1995). "Experimental Phonology", in J. A. Goldsmith (ed), *The Handbook of Phonological Theory*. Oxford: Blackwell, 713–22.

—— (1996). "Speech Perception Is Hearing Sounds, Not Tongues", *Journal of the Acoustical Society of America* 99: 1718–25.

—— (1997a). "Aerodynamics of Phonology", *Proceedings 4th Seoul International Conference on Linguistics [SICOL]*. Seoul, 92–7.

—— (1997b). "Emergent Stops", *Proceedings of the 4th Seoul International Conference on Linguistics [SICOL]*. Seoul, 84–91.

—— (1999). "Phonetic and Phonological Universals", Seminar given on 25 Jan. 1999 at the Laboratoire Dynamique du Langage, Université de Lyon 2.

—— (2003). "Phonetics and Historical Phonology", in B. D. Joseph and R. D. Janda (eds.), *The Handbook of Historical Linguistics*. Malden, MA: Blackwell, 669–86.

—— and Busà, M. G. (1995). "Nasal Loss Before Voiceless Fricatives: A Perceptually-based Sound Change", *Rivista di Linguistica*, 7: 125–44.

—— and Jaeger, J. J. (eds) (1986). *Experimental Phonology*. Orlando, FL: Academic Press.

—— and Ohala, M. (1993). "The Phonetics of Nasal Phonology: Theorems and Data", in M. K. Huffman, and R. A. Krakow (eds.), *Nasals, Nasalization, and the Velum. [Phonetics and Phonology Series, 5]*. San Diego: Academic Press, 225–49.

—— and Roengpitya, R. (2002). "Duration Related Phase Realignment of Thai Tones", in J. H. L. Hansen and B. Pellom (eds.), *Proceedings of the 7th International Conference on Spoken Language Processing*. Denver. 2285–8.

Ohala, M. (1979). "Phonological Features of Hindi Stops", *South Asian Languages Analysis*, 1: 79–88.

—— (1983). *Aspects of Hindi Phonology*. Delhi: Motilal Banarsidass.

—— (1991). "Phonological Areal Features of Some Indo-Aryan languages", *Language Sciences*, 13: 107–24.

—— (1994). "Hindi", *Journal of the International Phonetic Association*, 24 (1): 35–8. [Also published in *Handbook of the International Phonetic Association*. Cambridge: Cambridge University Press, 100–4.]

—— (1999a). "Hindi Syllabification", in J. J. Ohala, Y. Hasegawa, M. Ohala, D. Granville, and A. C. Bailey (eds.), *Proceedings of the XIVth International Congress of Phonetic Sciences*, i. Berkeley: Department of Linguistics, University of California, 727–30.

Ohala, M. (1999*b*). "The Seeds of Sound Change: Data from Connected Speech", in Linguistic Society of Korea (eds.), *Linguistics in the Morning Calm,* iv: *Selected papers from SICOL-'97.* Seoul: Hanshin Publishing Company, 263–74.

—— (2001). "Some Patterns of Unscripted Speech in Hindi", *Journal of the International Phonetic Association,* 31: 115–26.

—— (2003). "Integrity of Geminates and Homorganic Nasal Plus Stop: Evidence from a Word Game", in M. J. Sole, D. Recasens, and J. Romero (eds), *Proceedings of the 15th International Congress of Phonetic Sciences.* Barcelona, 1173–6.

—— (2006). "Experiments on Hindi Syllabification", in G. E. Wiebe, G. Libben, T. Priestly, R. Smythe, and H. S. Wang (eds.), *Phonology, Morphology, and the Empirical Imperative: Papers in Honour of Bruce L. Derwing.* Taipei: Crane, 115–56.

—— and Ohala, J. J. (1972). "The Problem of Aspiration in Hindi Phonetics", *Annual Bulletin N° 6, Research Reports for the Period June 1971–March 1972.* Research Institute of Logopedics and Phoniatrics, University of Tokyo, Faculty of Medicine, 39–46.

—— —— (1991). "Nasal Epenthesis in Hindi", *Phonetica,* 48: 207–20.

—— —— (1992). "Phonetic Universals and Hindi Segment Duration", in J. J. Ohala, T. Nearey, B. Derwing, M. Hodge, and G. Wiebe (eds.), *Proceedings of the International Conference on Spoken Language Processing.* Edmonton: University of Alberta, 831–4.

Öhman, S. E. G. (1967). "Word and Sentence Intonation: A Quantitative Model", *Speech Transmission Laboratory Quarterly Progress and Status Report,* 2–3. Stockholm: Speech Transmission Laboratory, Royal Institute of Technology, 20–54.

—— (1967). "Numerical Model of Coarticulation", *Journal of the Acoustical Society of America* 41: 310–20.

Onaka, A., Palethorpe, S., Watson, C., and Harrington, J. (2002). "Acoustic and Articulatory Difference of Speech Segments at Different Prosodic Positions", in *Proceedings of the 9th Australian International Conference on Speech Science and Technology,* 148–53.

Onsuwan, C. (2005). "Temporal Relations between Consonants and Vowels in Thai Syllables", Ph.D. dissertation (University of Michigan).

Orgun, C. O. (1995). "Correspondence and Identity Constraints in Two-level Optimality Theory", in J. Camacho. (ed.), *Proceedings of the 14th West Coast Conference on Formal Linguistics.* Stanford: Stanford Linguistics Association, 399–413.

Osborne, A. (1975). "A Transformational Analysis of Tone in the Verb System of Zahao (Laizo) Chin", Ph.D. dissertation (Cornell University).

Ostry, D. J., and Munhall, K. (1985). "Control of Rate and Duration of Speech Movements", *Journal of the Acoustical Society of America,* 77: 640–8.

Otake, T., Yoneyama, K., Cutler, A., and Lugt, A. V. D. (1996). "The Representation of Japanese Moraic Nasals", *Journal of the Acoustical Society of America* 100: 3831–42.

Ouni, S., and Laprie, Y. (2001). "Studying Articulatory Effects through Hypercube Sampling of the Articulatory Space", *International Congress on Acoustics,* iv, 6a.14. (Oral presentation). Rome. (Available at http://citeseer.ifi.unizh.ch/ouni01studeying.html).

Påhlsson, C. (1972). *The Northumbrian Burr: A Sociolinguistic Study.* Lund: Gleerup.

Palmeri, T. J., Goldinger, S. D., and Pisoni, D. B. (1993). "Episodic Encoding of Voice Attributes and Recognition Memory for Spoken Words", *Journal of Experimental Psychology: Learning, Memory, and Cognition,* 19: 309–28.

Pampel, F. C. (2000). *Logistic Regression: A Primer* (Quantitative applications in the social sciences, 132). Thousand Oaks, CA: Sage.

Panconcelli-Calzia, G. (1948). *Phonetik als Naturwissenschaft*. Berlin: Wissenschaftliche Editionsgesellschaft.

Pandey, P. K. (1989). "Word Accentuation in Hindi", *Lingua*, 77: 37–73.

Passy, P. (1890): *Étude sur les changements phonétiques et leurs caractères généraux*. Paris: Librairie Firmin-Didot.

Paul, H. (1880). *Prinzipien der Sprachgeschichte*. Halle: Niemeyer.

Pellegrino, F., Coupé, C., and Marsico, E. (2005). "Cross-Linguistic Comparison of Phonological Information Rate", MS, Laboratoire Dynamique du Langage, Université Lyon-2.

Penny, R. (2001). *Variation and Change in Spanish*. Cambridge: Cambridge University Press.

Penzl, H. (1961). "Old High German <r> and Its Phonetic Identification", *Language*, 37: 488–96.

Perkell, J. S., Matthies, M. L., Svirsky, M. A., and Jordan, M. I. (1993). "Trading Relations between Tongue-body Raising and Lip Rounding Production of the Vowel /u/: A Pilot "Motor Equivalence" Study", *Journal of the Acoustical Society of America*, 93 (5): 2948–61.

—— —— Lane, H., Wilhelms-Tricarico, R., Worniak J., and Guiod, P. (1997). "Speech Motor Control: Acoustic Goals, Saturation Effects, Auditory Feedback and Internal Models", *Speech Communication*, 22: 227–50.

Perkins, R. (1989). "Statistical Techniques for Determining Language Sample Size", *Studies in Language*, 13: 293–315.

—— (2001). "Sampling Procedures and Statistical Methods", in M. Haspelmath, E. König, W. Oesterreicher, and W. Raible (eds.), *Language Typology and Language Universals: An International Handbook* (Handbooks of Linguistics and Communication Science, 1–2). Berlin: Walter de Gruyter, 419–34.

Perlmutter, D. (1995). "Phonological Quantity and the Multiple Association", in J. A. Goldsmith (ed.), *The Handbook of Phonological Theory*. Oxford: Blackwell, 307–17.

Perrier, P. (2005). "Control and Representations in Speech Production", in S. Fuchs, P. Perrier and B. Pompino-Marschall (eds.), "Speech Production and Perception: Experimental Analyses and Models", *ZAS Papers in Linguistics*, 40: 109–32.

Peterson, G. E., and Barney, H. L. (1952). "Control Methods Used in a Study of Vowels", *Journal of the Acoustical Society of America*, 24: 175–84.

—— and Lehiste, I. (1960). "Duration of Syllable Nuclei in English", *Journal of the Acoustical Society of America*, 32(6): 693–703.

Pickett, J. M., and Pollack, I. (1963). "Intelligibility of Excerpts from Fluent Speech: Effects of Rate of Utterance and Duration of Excerpt", *Language and Speech*, 6: 151–64.

Pickett, E. R., Blumstein, S. E., and Burton, M. W. (1999). "Effects of Speaking Rate on the Singleton/Geminate Consonant Contrast in Italian", *Phonetica*, 56: 135–57.

Pierrehumbert, J. (1979). "The Perception of Fundamental Frequency Declination", *Journal of the Acoustical Society of America*, 66: 363–9.

—— (1980). "The Phonology and Phonetics of English Intonation", Ph.D. dissertation (MIT).

—— (1994). "Knowledge of Variation", in K. Beal et al. (eds.), *Proceedings of the 30th Meeting of the Chicago Linguistic Society*, ii: *Papers from the Parasession on Variation*. Chicago: Chicago Linguistic Society, 232–56.

Pierrehumbert, J. (2001*a*). "Exemplar Dynamics: Word Frequency, Lenition, and Contrast", in J. Bybee and P. Hopper (eds.), *Frequency Effects and the Emergence of Linguistic Structure.* Amsterdam: John Benjamins, 137–57.

—— (2001*b*). "Stochastic Phonology". *Glot International*, 5 (6): 195–207.

—— (2002). "Word-specific Phonetics", in C. Gussenhoven and N. Warner (eds.) *Laboratory Phonology*, 7. Berlin and New York: Mouton de Gruyter.

—— (2003*a*). "Phonetic Diversity, Statistical Learning, and Acquisition of Phonology", *Language and Speech*, 46: 115–54.

—— (2003*b*). "Probabilistic Phonology: Discrimination and Robustness", in R. Bod, J. Hay and S. Jannedy (eds.), *Probability Theory in Linguistics.* Cambridge, MA: MIT Press, 177–228.

—— and Beckman, M. E. (1988). *Japanese Tone Structure.* Cambridge, MA: MIT Press.

—— and Frisch, S. (1997). "Synthesizing Allophonic Glottalization", in J. P. H. van Santen, R. W. Sproat, J. P. Olive, and J. Hirschberg (eds), *Progress in Speech Synthesis.* New York: Springer, 9–26.

—— and Talkin, D. (1992). "Lenition of /h/ and Glottal Stop", in G. Docherty, and D. R. Ladd (eds.), *Papers in Laboratory Phonology*, ii: *Gesture, Segment, Prosody.* Cambridge: Cambridge University Press, 90–117.

—— Beckman, M. E., and Ladd, D. R. (2000). "Conceptual Foundations of Phonology as a Laboratory Science", in N. Burton-Roberts, P. Carr, and G. Docherty (eds.), *Phonological Knowledge: Conceptual and Empirical Issues.* Oxford: Oxford University Press, 273–303.

Pillot, C. (2004). "Sur l'efficacité vocale dans le chant lyrique : Aspects physiologique, cognitif, acoustique et perceptif", Ph.D. thesis (Université de la Sorbonne Nouvelle, Paris).

Pind, J. (1995). "Speaking Rate, Voice-Onset Time, and Quantity: The Search for Higher-order Invariants for Two Icelandic Speech Cues", *Perception and Psychophysics*, 57: 291–304.

—— (1999). "Speech Segment Durations and Quantity in Icelandic", *Journal of the Acoustical Society of America*, 106 (2): 1045–53.

Pisoni, D. B., and Luce, P. A. (1987). "Trading Relations, Acoustic Cue Integration, and Context Effects in Speech Perception", in M. E. H. Schouten (ed.), *The Psychophysics of Speech Perception.* Dordrecht: Martinus Nijhoff, 155–72.

Pitt, M. A., Johnson, K., Hume, E., Kiesling, S., and Raymond, W. (2005). "The Buckeye Corpus of Conversational Speech: Labeling Conventions and a Test of Transcriber Reliability", *Speech Communication*, 45 (1): 89–95.

Plag, I., Dalton-Puffer, C., and Baayen, H. (1999). "Morphological Productivity Across Speech and Writing.", *English Language and Linguistics*, 3: 209–28.

Plant R. L., and Younger R. (2000). "The Interrelationship of Subglottic Air Pressure, Fundamental Frequency, and Vocal Intensity During Speech", *Journal of Voice* 14 (2): 170–7.

Plauché, M. (2001). "Acoustic Cues in the Directionality of Stop Consonant Confusions", Ph.D. dissertation (University of California at Berkeley).

Polka, L., and Bohn, O.-S. (2003). "Asymmetries in Vowel Perception", *Speech Communication*, 41: 221–31.

Port, R. (1996). "The Discreteness of Phonetic Elements and Formal Linguistics: Response to A. Manaster Ramer", *Journal of Phonetics*, 24: 491–511.

—— and Crawford, P. (1989). "Incomplete Neutralization and Pragmatics in German", *Journal of Phonetics* 17: 257–82.

—— and Dalby, J. (1982). "C/V ratio as a Cue for Voicing in English", *Journal of the Acoustical Society of America* 69: 262–74.

Port, R., and O'Dell, M. (1985). "Neutralization of Syllable-final Voicing in German", *Journal of Phonetics*, 13: 455–71.

—— and Rotunno, R. (1979). "Relation between Voice-onset Time and Vowel Duration", *Journal of the Acoustical Society of America*, 66 (3): 654–66.

—— Al-Ani, S., and Maeda, S. (1980). "Temporal Compensation and Universal Phonetics", *Phonetica*, 37: 235–52.

—— Mitleb, F., and O'Dell, M. (1981). "Neutralization of Obstruent Voicing in German Is Incomplete", *Journal of the Acoustical Society of America* 70: S13, F10.

Prieto, P., d'Imperio, M., and Gili Fivela, B. (2005). "Pitch Accent Alignment in Romance: Primary and Secondary Associations with Metrical Structure", *Language and Speech*, 48 (4), 359–96.

Quené, H., and van den Bergh, H. (2004). "On Multi-level Modeling of Data from Repeated Measures Designs: A Tutorial", *Speech Communication*, 43: 103–21.

Raphael, L. J. (1972). "Preceding Vowel Duration as a Cue to the Perception of the Voicing Characteristic of Word-Final Consonants in American English", *Journal of the Acoustical Society of America*, 51: 1296–1303.

Recasens, D., Pallarès, M. D., and Fontdevila, J. (1997). "A Model of Lingual Coarticulation Based on Articulatory Constraints", *Journal of the Acoustical Society of America*, 102 (1): 544–61.

Renzi, L. (1985). *Nuova introduzione alla filologia romanza*. Bologna: Il Mulino.

Repp, B. H. (1978). "Perceptual Integration and Differentiation of Spectral Cues for Intervocalic Stop Consonants", *Perception and Psychophysics*, 24: 471–85.

Rhodes, R. (1992). "Flapping in American English", in W. Dressler, M. Prinzhorn, and J. R. Rennison, (eds.), *Proceedings of the 7th International Phonology Meeting*. Turin: Rosenberg and Sellier, 217–32.

Riber Petersen, P. (1973). "An Instrumental Investigation of the Danish Stød", *Annual Report of the Institute of Phonetics*, 7. Copenhagen: University of Copenhagen, 195–234.

Rickard, K. (2005). "An Acoustic–Phonetic Descriptive Analysis of Lanqi Citation Tones", Thesis (Australian National University, Canberra, Australia).

Rizzolatti, G., and Arbib, M. A. (1998). "Language within Our Grasp", *Trends in Neurociences*, 21: 188–94.

Robert-Ribes, J., Schwartz, J. L., Lallouache, T., and Escudier, P. (1998). "Complementarity and Synergy in BiModal Speech: Auditory, Visual and Audiovisual Identification of French Oral Vowels in Noise", *Journal of the Acoustical Society of America*, 103: 3677–89.

Rochet, A. P., and Rochet, B. L. (1991). "The Effect of Vowel Height on Patterns of Assimilation Nasality in French and English", *Actes du XIIème Congres International des Sciences Phonetiques*, 3. Aix-en-Provence: Université de Provence, 54–7.

Rochet-Capellan, A., and Schwartz, J. L. (2005a). "The Labial–Coronal Effect and CVCV Stability During Reiterant Speech Production: An Acoustic Analysis", *Proceedings of Interspeech 2005*, 1009–12.

—— —— (2005b). "The Labial–Coronal Effect and CVCV Stability During Reiterant Speech Production: An Articulatory Analysis", *Proceedings of Interspeech 2005*, 1013–16.

Roengpitya, R. (2001). *A Study of Vowels, Diphthongs, and Tones in Thai*. Ph.D. dissertation (University of California, Berkeley).

—— (2003). "(End) Truncation of the Thai Contour Tones on Different Durations of TBUs", in M. J. Solé, D. Recasens, and J. Romero (eds.), *Proceedings of the 15th International Congress of Phonetic Sciences*, 2. Barcelona, 1109–12.

Rogers, F. M. (1948). "Insular Portuguese Pronunciation: Porto Santo and Eastern Azores", *Hispanic Review* 16: 1–32.

Rosapelly, Ch.-L. (1876). "Inscription des mouvement phonetiques", in *Physiologie Experimentale. Travaux de Laboratoire de M. Marey*, 2. Paris: G. Masson, 109–31.

Rosch-Heider, E. (1972). "Universals in Color Naming and Memory", *Journal of Experimental Psychology*, 93: 10–20.

Rossato, S. (2004). "Quelques statistiques sur la nasalité vocalique et consonantique", in B. Bel, and I. Marlien (eds.), *Actes des 25èmes journées d'études sur le parole*. Fez, 433–6.

Rossi, M. (1971). "L'intensité spécifique des voyelles", *Phonetica*, 24: 129–61.

Rousselot, l'Abbé P. J. (1892). *Les modifications phonétiques du langage, étudiées dans le patois d'une famille de Cellefrouin (Charante)*. Paris: H. Welter.

—— (1897–1901). *Principes de phonétique expérimentale*. Paris: H. Welter.

—— (1936). "Bulletin of the International Society of Experimental Phonetics III", *Archives Néerlandaises de Phonétique Expérimentale*, 12: 133–47.

Rubach, J. (1977). "Nasalization in Polish," *Journal of Phonetics*, 5: 17–25.

Ryalls, J. H., and Lieberman, P. (1982). "Fundamental Frequency and Vowel Perception", *Journal of the Acoustical Society of America*, 72: 1631–4.

Sagart, L., Hallé, P., De Boysson-Bardies, B., and Arabia-Guidet, C. (1986). "Tone Production in Modern Standard Chinese: an Electromyographic Investigation", *Cahiers de Linguistique Asie Orientale*, 15: 205–11.

Sampson, R. (1999). *Nasal Vowel Evolution in Romance*. Oxford: Oxford University Press.

Sandow, W. (1958). "A Theory of Active State Mechanisms in Isometric Muscular Contraction", *Science*, 127: 760–2.

Saravari, C., and Imai, S. (1983). "Perception of Tone and Short–Long Judgement of Vowel Variants of a Thai Monosyllabic Sound", *Journal of Phonetics*, 11: 231–42.

Sato, M., Baciu, M., Lœvenbruck, H., Schwartz, J.-L., Cathiard, M.-A., Segebarth, C., and Abry, C. (2004). "Multistable Perception of Speech Forms in Working Memory: An fMRI Study of the Verbal Transformation Effect", *NeuroImage*, 23: 1143–51.

Savariaux, C., Perrier, P., Orliaguet, J.-P., and Schwartz, J.-L. (1999). "Compensation for the Perturbation of French [u] Using a Lip Tube, ii: Perceptual Analysis", *Journal of the Acoustical Society of America*, 106 (1): 381–93.

Sawashima M., Hirose, H., Ushijima, T., and Niimi, S. (1975). "Laryngeal Control in Japanese Consonants with Special Reference to Those in Utterance Initial Position", *Annual Bulletin Research Institute of Logopedics and Phoniatrics*. Tokyo: University of Tokyo, 9: 21–6.

Schacter, D. L., and Church, B. (1992). "Auditory Priming: Implicit and Explicit Memory for Words and Voices", *Journal of Experimental Psychology: Learning, Memory and Cognition*, 18: 915–30.

Schwartz, J. L., and Escudier, P. (1989). "A Strong Evidence for the Existence of a Large Scale Integrated Spectral Representation in Vowel Perception", *Speech Communication*, 8: 235–59.

—— Abry, C., Boë, L. J., and Cathiard, M.-A. (2002). "Phonology in a Theory of Perception-for-Action-Control", in J. Durand and B. Laks (eds.), *Phonetics, Phonology, and Cognition*. Oxford: Oxford University Press, 254–80.

—— Beautemps, D., Abry, C., and Escudier, P. (1993). "Inter-Individual and Cross-Linguistic Strategies for the Production of the [i] vs [y] Contrast", *Journal of Phonetics*, 21: 411–25.

—— Boë, L. J., Vallée, N., and Abry, C. (1997a). "Major Trends in Vowel System Inventories", *Journal of Phonetics*, 25: 233–53.

Schwartz, J. L., Boë, L. J., Vallée, N., and Abry, C. (1997*b*). "The Dispersion-Focalization Theory of Vowel Systems", *Journal of Phonetics*, 25: 255–86.

—— Abry, C., Boë, L. J., Ménard, L., and Vallée, N. (2005). "Asymmetries in Vowel Perception, in the Context of the Dispersion-Focalisation Theory", *Speech Communication*, 45: 425–34.

Scripture, E. W. (1902). *The Elements of Experimental Phonetics*. New York: Scribner's Sons/London: Arnold.

—— (1936). "Bulletin of the International Society of Experimental Phonetics, 3", *Archives Néerlandaises de Phonétique Expérimentale* 12: 133–47.

Searle, J. (1998). *Mind, Language and Society*. New York: Basic.

Semon, R. (1923). *Mnemic Psychology*, trans. B. Duffy. London: George Allen and Unwin. (Originally publ. as *Die mnemischen Empfindungen*, Leipzig: Wilhelm Engelmann, 1909).

Serkhane, J. E., Schwartz, J. L., Boë, L. J., and Bessière, P. (2005). "Building a Talking Baby Robot: A Contribution to the Study of Speech Acquisition and Evolution", *Interaction Studies*, 6: 253–86.

Sezer, E. (1981). "The k/Ø Alternation in Turkish", in G. N. Clements (ed.), *Harvard Studies in Phonology*. Bloomington: Indiana University Linguistics Club, 354–82.

Shadle, C. (1997). "The Aerodynamics of Speech", in W. J. Hardcastle and J. Laver (ed.), *Handbook of Phonetics*, Oxford: Blackwell, 33–64.

—— and Damper, R. (2002). "Prospects for Articulatory Synthesis: A Position Paper", *Fourth ISCA Workshop on Speech Synthesis*, Pitlochry, Scotland. 121–6 (http://www.isca-speech.org/archive/ssw4/ssw4_116.html).

Shannon, C. E. (1948). "A Mathematical Theory of Communication," *Bell System Technical Journal*, 27: 379–423, 623–56.

Shen, J.-X. (1993). "Slips of the Tongue and the Syllable Structure of Mandarin Chinese", in Sh-Ch. Yau (ed.), Essays on the Chinese Language by Contemporary Chinese Scholars. Paris: Editions Langages Croisées, 139–162.

Shosted, R. K. (2006*a*). "Vocalic Context as a Condition for Nasal Coda Emergence: Aerodynamic Evidence," *Journal of the International Phonetic Association* 36: 39–58.

—— (2006*b*). "Correlating Complexity: A Typological Approach", *Linguistic Typology* 10(1): 1–40.

Shotriya, N., Sarma, A. S. S., Verma, R., and Agrawal, S. S. (1995). "Acoustic and Perceptual Characteristics of Geminated Hindi Stop Consonants", in K. Elenius and P. Branderud (eds.), *Proceedings of the XIIIth International Congress of Phonetic Sciences*, iv. Stockholm, 132–5.

Sievers, E. (1876). *Grundzüge der Lautphysiologie zur Einführung in das Studium der Lautlehre der indogermanischen Sprachen*. Leipzig: Breitkopf and Härtel. (2nd edn. *Grundzüge der Phonetik zur Einführung in das Studium der Lautlehre der indogermanischen Sprachen*. 1881).

Silverman, D. (1997). "Tone Sandhi in Comaltepec Chinantec", *Language* 73: 473–92.

—— and Jun, J. (1994). "Aerodynamic Evidence for Articulatory Overlap in Korean", *Phonetica*, 51: 210–20.

Sjöstedt, G. (1936). *Studier över r-ljuden i sydskandinaviska mål*. [Studies of the r sounds in South Scandinavian dialects]. Dissertation, Lund University.

Skousen, R. (1989). *Analogical Modeling of Language*. Dordrecht: Kluwer.

—— (1992). *Analogy and structure*. Dordrecht: Kluwer.

Slater, J. C., and Frank, N. H. (1933). *Introduction to Theoretical Physics*, New York: McGraw-Hill.

Slis, I. H. (1986). "Assimilation of Voice in Dutch as a Function of Stress, Word Boundaries, and Sex of Speaker and Listener", *Journal of Phonetics* 14: 311–26.

Smith, D. R., and Patterson, R. D. (2005). "The Interaction of Glottal-Pulse Rate and Vocal-Tract Length in Judgements of Speaker Size, Sex, and Age", *Journal of the Acoustical Society of America* 118 (5): 3177–86.

—— —— Turner, R., Kawahara, H., and Irino, T. (2005). "The Processing and Perception of Size Information in Speech Sounds", *Journal of the Acoustical Society of America* 117 (1): 305–18.

Smith, J. (2004a). *Phonological Augmentation in Prominent Positions.* London: Routledge.

—— (2004b). "Functional Grounding in Phonology: Evidence from Positional Augmentation". paper presented at the Generative Linguistics of the Old World 2004 Workshop on Markedness in Phonology, Aristotle University, Thessaloniki.

Snijders, T., and Bosker, R. (1999). *Multi-level Analysis: An Introduction to Basic and Advanced Multi-level Modeling.* London: Sage.

Solé, M. J. (1992). "Phonetic and Phonological Processes: The Case of Nasalization", *Language and Speech* 35: 29–43.

—— (1995). "Spatio-Temporal Patterns of Velo-Pharyngeal Action in Phonetic and Phonological Nasalization", *Language and Speech* 38 (1): 1–23.

—— (1999). "The Phonetic Basis of Phonological Structure: The Role of Aerodynamic Factors", *Proceedings of the 1st Congress of Experimental Phonetics*, Tarragona, 77–94.

—— (2002). "Aerodynamic Characteristics of Trills and Phonological Patterning", *Journal of Phonetics* 30: 655–88.

—— and Estebas, E. (2000). "Phonetic and Phonological Phenomena: V.O.T.: A Cross-Language Comparison", *Proceedings of the 18th AEDEAN Conference.* Vigo, 437–44.

Standing, L., Conezio, J., and Haber, R. (1970). "Perception and Memory for Pictures: Single-trial Learning of 2560 Visual Stimuli", *Psychonomic Science* 19: 73–4.

Stark, J., Ericsdotter, C., Branderud, P., Sundberg, J., Lundberg, H. J., and Lander, J. (1999). "The APEX Model as a Tool in the Specification of Speaker-Specific Articulatory Behavior", *Proceedings from the XIVth ICPhS*, San Francisco, 2279–82.

Stelmachowicz, P. G., Small, A. M., and Abbas, P. J. (1982). "Suppression Effects for Complex Stimuli", *Journal of the Acoustical Society of America* 71: 410–20.

Stemberger, J. P. (1985). "An Interactive Activation Model of Language Production", in A. W. Ellis (ed.), *Progress in the Psychology of Language*, i. London: Erlbaum, 143–86.

Stephens, L. D., and Justeson, J. S. (1984). "On the Relationship between Numbers of Vowels and Consonants in Phonological Systems", *Linguistics* 22: 531–45.

Steriade, D. (1999). "Phonetics in Phonology: The Case of Laryngeal Neutralization", in M. Gordon (ed.), *Papers in Phonology, 3* (UCLA Working Papers in Linguistics, 2). Los Angeles: Department of Linguistics, University of California, 25–145.

—— (2001). "Directional Asymmetries in Place Assimilation: A Perceptual Account", in E. Hume and K. Johnson (eds.), *The Role of Speech Perception in Phonology.* San Diego: Academic Press, 219–50.

Stevens, K. N. (1972). "The Quantal Nature of Speech: Evidence from Articulatory-Acoustic Data", in E. E. Davis Jr. and P. B. Denes (eds.), *Human Communication: A Unified View.* New York: McGraw-Hill, 51–66.

—— (1989). "On the Quantal Nature of Speech", *Journal of Phonetics* 17: 3–45.

—— (1998). *Acoustic Phonetics.* Cambridge, MA: MIT Press.

Stevens, K. N. (2002) "Toward a Model for Lexical Access Based on Acoustic Landmarks and Distinctive Features", *Journal of the Acoustical Society of America* 111: 1872–91.

—— and Keyser, S. J. (1989). "Primary Features and Their Enhancement in Consonants", *Language* 65: 81–106.

Stollenwerk, D. A. (1986). "Word Frequency and Dialect Borrowing", in Brian D. Joseph (ed.), *Studies on Language Change* (The Ohio State University Working Papers in Linguistics, 34), 133–41.

Straka, G. (1963). "La division des sons du langage en voyelles et consonnes: peut-elle être justifié?", *Travaux de Linguistique et de Littérature*, i. Centre de Philologie et de Littératures Romanes de l''Université de Strasbourg, 17–99.

Strand, E. A. (2000). "Gender Stereotype Effects in Speech Processing", Ph.D. dissertation, (Ohio State University).

Strange, W. (1989). "Dynamic Specification of Coarticulated Vowels Spoken in Sentence Context", *Journal of the Acoustical Society of America* 85: 2135–53.

—— (1995). *Speech Perception and Linguistic Experience: Issues in Cross-Language Research*. Baltimore: York Press.

Strik, H., and Boves L. (1992). "Control of Fundamental Frequency, Intensity and Voice Quality in Speech", *Journal of phonetics* 20: 15–25.

—— —— (1994). "A Physiological Model of Intonation", *Proceedings of the Department of Language and Speech*, 16–17. Nijmegen: University of Nijmegen, 95–105.

Summerfield, A. Q. (1981). "On the Articulatory Rate and Perceptual Constancy in Phonetic Perception", *Journal of Experimental Psychology: Human Perception and Performance*, 7: 1074–95.

Summers, W. V. (1987). "Effects of Stress and Final-Consonant Voicing on Vowel Production: Articulatory and Acoustic Analyses", *Journal of the Acoustical Society of America*, 82: 847–63.

Susanne, C., and Polet, C. (eds.) (2005). "*Dictionnaire d'anthropobiologie*". Brussels: De Boeck.

Sussman, H. M., Duder, C., Dalston, E., and Cacciatore, A. (1999). "An Acoustic Analysis of the Development of CV Coarticulation", *Journal of Speech, Language, and Hearing Research* 42: 1080–96.

Svantesson, J.-O. (1983). *Kammu Phonology and Morphology*. Lund: Gleerup.

Svastikula, M. L. K. (1986). "A Perceptual and Acoustic Study of the Effects of Speech Rate on Distinctive Vowel Length in Thai", Ph.D. dissertation (University of Connecticut).

Syrdal, A. K., and Gopal, H. S. (1986). "A Perceptual Model of Vowel Recognition Based on the Auditory Representation of American English Vowels", *Journal of the Acoustical Society of America* 79 (4): 1086–1100.

Tanowitz, J., and Beddor, P. S. (1997). "Temporal Characteristics of Coarticulatory Vowel Nasalization in English", *Journal of the Acoustical Society of America* 101: 3194(A).

Teixeira, A., and Vaz, F. (2001). "European Portuguese Nasal Vowels: An EMMA study", *Seventh European Conference on Speech Communication and Technology, EuroSpeech—Scandinavia*, ii. Aalborg, 1843–6.

Tekavčić, P. (1963). "Un problema della fonematica italiana: la variazione s/ts", *Studia Romantica et Angelica Zagrabriensia* 15: 99–114.

Teleman, U. (2005). "Bakre r i svenskan. En alternativ hypotes" [Back r in Swedish. An Alternative Hypothesis], *Språk och Stil*, 15: 27–52.

Teston, B., and Galindo, B. (1990). "Design and Development of a Work Station for Speech Production Analysis", *Proceedings VERBA 90, International Conference on Speech Technologies*. Rome, 400–8.

Teston, B., and Galindo, B. (1995). "A Diagnostic and Rehabilitation Aid Workstation for Speech and Voice Pathologies", *Proceedings of the Fourth European Conference on Speech Communication and Technology (EUROSPEECH '95)*. Madrid: European Speech Communication Association, 1883–6.

Thorsen, N. (Grønnum) (1974). "Acoustical and Perceptual Properties of the Danish Stød", *Annual Report of the Institute of Phonetics*, 8. Copenhagen: University of Copenhagen, 207–13.

Thorsen, O. (1966). "Voice Assimilation of Stop Consonants and Fricatives in French and Its Relation to Sound Duration and Intra-Oral Air-pressure", *Annual Report Institute of Phonetics University of Copenhagen (ARIPUC)*, 1: 67–76.

Tingsabadh, K. M. R., and Deeprasert, D. (1997). "Tones in Standard Thai Connected Speech", in A. Abramson (ed.), *Southeast Asian Linguistic Studies in Honour of Vichin Panupong*. Bangkok: Chulalongkorn University Press, 297–307.

Titze, I. (1994). *Principles of Voice Production*. Englewood Cliffs, NJ: Prentice hall.

Tomiche, N. (1964). *Le Parler arabe du Caire*. The Hague: Mouton.

Traunmüller, H. (2005). "Auditory Scales of Frequency Representation", http://www.ling.su.se/staff/hartmut/bark.htm (last accessed 16 Nov. 2005).

Trautmann, M. (1880). "Besprechung einiger Schulbücher nebst Bemerkungen über die r-Laute", *Anglia* 3: 201–22.

Treiman, R. (1983). "The Structure of Spoken Syllables: Evidence from Novel Word Games", *Cognition* 15: 49–74.

—— Zukowski, A., and Richmond-Welty, E. D. (1995). "What Happened to the 'n' of *sink*? Children's Spellings of Final Consonant Clusters," *Cognition* 55: 1–38.

Trubetzkoy, N. S. (1935). *Anleitungen zu phonologischen Beschreibungen*, Brno: Edition du Cercle Linguistique de Prague. (Engl. transl. *Introduction to the Principles of Phonological Descriptions*. The Hague: Mouton, 1968.)

—— (1962). *Grundzüge der Phonologie*. Göttingen: Vandenhoeck and Ruprecht. (Orig. publ. 1939).

Tulving, E., and Craik, F. I. M. (2000). *Handbook of Memory*. New York: Oxford University Press.

Tumtavitikul, A. (1994). "Perhaps, the Tones Are in the Consonants?", *Mon-Khmer Studies* 23: 11–41.

Turchi, L., and Gili Fivela, B. (2004). "L'Affricazione di /s/ Postconsonantico nella Varietà Pisana di Italiano", *Atti del Convegno "Il Parlato Italiano"*, Naples: D'Auria, 1–25.

Tuttle, E. F. (1991). "Nasalization in Northern Italy: Syllabic Constraints and Strength Scales as Developmental Parameters", *Rivista di Linguistica* 3: 23–92.

Tyler, R. S., and Lindblom, B. (1982). "Preliminary Study of Simultaneous-masking and Pulsation-Threshold Patterns of Vowels", *Journal of the Acoustical Society of America*, 71: 220–4.

Umesh, S., Cohen, L., and Nelson, D. (1999). "Scale-transform Based Features for Application in Speech Recognition", *Proceedings of SPIE Conference on Wavelet Applications in Signal and Image Processing*, 3813: 727–31 (http://www.spie.org/web/meetings/programs/sd99/confs/3813.html).

Vaissière, J. (1988). "Prediction of Velum Movement from Phonological Specifications", *Phonetica* 45(2–4): 122–39.

—— (1995). "Teaching Acoustic-phonetics", *International Congress of Phonetics Sciences*, 4. Stockholm, 442–9.

Vaissière, J., and Michaud, A. (2006). "Prosodic Constituents in French: A Data-driven Approach", in I. Fónagy, Y. Kawaguchi and T. Moriguchi (eds.), *Prosody and syntax*. Amsterdam: John Benjamins, 47–64.

Vallée, N. (1994). "Systèmes vocaliques: de la typologie aux prédictions", Dissertation (Université Stendhal, Grenoble).

van Bergem, D. R. (1993). "On the Perception of Acoustic and Lexical Vowel Reduction", *Eurospeech '93*: 677–80.

—— (1994). "Reflections on Aspects of Vowel Reduction", *Proceedings from the Institute of Phonetic Sciences*, Amsterdam 18: 95–110.

van Santen, J. P. H., Shih, C., and Möbius, B. (1998). "Intonation", in R. Sproat (ed.), *Multilingual Text-to-Speech Synthesis: The Bell Labs Approach*. Dordrecht: Kluwer, 141–90.

Vennemann, T. (1988). *Preference Laws for Syllable Structure and the Explanation of Sound Change*. Berlin and New York: Mouton de Gruyter.

Vitevitch, M., and Sommers, M. (2003). "The Facilitative Influence of Phonological Similarity and Neighborhood Frequency in Speech Production in Younger and Older Adults", *Memory and Cognition* 31: 491–504.

Vitz, P. C., and Winkler, B. S. (1973). "Predicting the Judged Similarity of Sound of English Words", *Journal of Verbal Learning and Verbal Behavior*, 12: 373–88.

Viviani, P., and Stucchi, N. (1992). "Biological Movements Look Uniform: Evidence of Motor-Perceptual Interactions", *Journal of Experimental Psychology: Human Perception and Performance* 18: 603–23.

Volaitis, L. E., and Miller, J. L. (1992). "Phonetic Prototypes: Influence of Place of Articulation and Speaking Rate on the Internal Structure of Voicing Categories", *Journal of the Acoustical Society of America* 92: 723–35.

Wan, I.-P. (1999). "Mandarin Phonology: Evidence from Speech Errors". Ph.D. dissertation (SUNY).

Wang, H. S. (1995). "Nasality as an Autosegment in Taiwanese", in F. F. Tsao and M. H. Tsai (eds.), *Papers from the First International Symposium on Languages in Taiwan*. Taipei: Crane, 513–29.

—— (1996). "Are Taiwanese Syllables Segmented into Phoneme-sized Units?", in T.-F. Cheng, Y.-F. Li, and H.-M. Zhang (eds.), *Proceedings of the Joint Meeting of Seventh North American Conference on Chinese Linguistics and Fourth International Conference on Chinese Linguistics*. Los Angeles: Graduate Students in Linguistics, University of Southern California, 362–78.

Wang, W. S. Y. (1967). "Phonological Features of Tone", *International Journal of American Linguistics*, 33(2): 93–105.

—— (1969). "Competing Changes as a Cause of Residue", *Language* 45: 9–25.

—— and Fillmore, C. J. (1961). "Intrinsic Cues and Consonant Perception", *Journal of Speech and Hearing Research* 4: 130–6.

Warner, N., and Weber, A. (2001). "Perception of Epenthetic Stops", in *Journal of Phonetics*, 29: 53–87.

—— —— (2002). "Stop Epenthesis at Syllable Boundaries", in *Proceedings of the 7th International Conference on Spoken Language Processing*, Denver, 1121–4.

Warren, D. W., Dalston, R. M, and Mayo, R. (1994). "Hypernasality and Velopharyngeal Impairment", *Cleft Palate-Craniofacial Journal* 31: 257–62.

Watkins, K. E., Strafella, A. P., and Paus, T. (2003). "Seeing and Hearing Speech Excites the Motor System Involved in Speech Production", *Neuropsychologia* 41: 989–94.

Weber, A. (2001). "Help or Hindrance: How Violation of Different Assimilation Rule Affects Spoken-language Processing", *Language and Speech* 44: 95–118.

Wedel, A. (2002) "Phonological Alternation, Lexical Neighborhood Density and Markedness in Processing" paper presented at the Eighth Conference on Laboratory Phonology, New Haven, Yale University, 27–30 June 2002.

—— (2003). "Self-Organization and Categorical Behavior in Phonology", *Proceedings of the Berkeley Linguistics Society,* 29: 611–22.

—— (2004*a*). "Self-organization and the Origin of Higher-order Phonological Patterns", Ph.D. dissertation (University of California at Santa Cruz).

—— (2004*b*). "Lexical Category Competition Drives Contrast Maintenance within An Exemplar-based Production-perception Loop", paper presented at the Association for Computational Linguistics 42nd Meeting, Barcelona, July 2004.

Weenink, D. (2003). "Adaptive Vowel Normalization: Simulating Human Recognition in Mixed and Blocked Speaker Context", paper presented at the 15th International Congress of Phonetic Sciences, Barcelona.

Weismer, G. (1979). "Sensitivity of Voice-Onset Measures to Certain Segmental Features in Speech Production", *Journal of Phonetics* 7: 194–204.

Welling, L., Kanthak, S., and Ney, H. (1999). "Improved Methods for Vocal Tract Normalization", *Proceedings of the IEEE International Conference on Acoustics, Speech and Signal Processing*, ii, 761–4.

Werker, J. F., and Tees, R. C. (1984). "Cross-language Speech Perception: Evidence for Perceptual Reorganization During the First Year of Life", *Infant Behavior and Development* 7: 49–63.

Westbury, J. R. and Keating, P. A. (1986). "On the Naturalness of Stop Consonant Voicing", *Journal of Linguistics,* 22: 145–66.

—— Hashi, M., and Lindstrom, M. J. (1998). "Differences Among Speakers in Lingual Articulation of American English /ɹ/", *Speech Communication,* 26: 203–26.

Whalen, D. H. (1989). "Vowel and Consonant Judgments Are Not Independent When Cued by the Same Information," *Perception and Psychophysics* 46: 284–92.

—— and Beddor, P. S. (1989). "Connections Between Nasality and Vowel Duration and Height: Elucidation of the Eastern Algonquian Intrusive Nasal," *Language,* 65: 457–86.

—— and Levitt, A. G. (1995). "The Universality of Intrinsic f0 of Vowels", *Journal of Phonetics* 23: 349–66.

—— and Liberman, A. M. (1987). "Speech Perception Takes Precedence Over Nonspeech Perception", *Science,* 237: 169–71.

—— Benson, R. R., Richardson, M. L. Swainson, B., Clark, V. P., Lai, S., Mencl, W. E., Fulbright, R. K., Constable, R. T., and Liberman, A. M. (2006). "Differentiation of Speech and Nonspeech Processing within Primary Auditory Cortex", *Journal of the Acoustical Society of America,* 119: 575–81.

Wiebe, G. E., and Derwing, B. L. (1994). "A Forced-choice Word-blending Task for Testing Intrasyllabic Breakpoints in English, Korean, and Taiwanese", in M. J. Powell (ed.), *The Twenty-First LACUS Forum.* Chapel Hill, NC: Linguistic Association of Canada and the United States, 142–51.

Willerman, R., and Kuhl, P. (1996). "Cross-Language Speech Perception of Front Rounded Vowels: Swedish, English, and Spanish Speakers", in H. T. Bunnell and W. Idsardi (eds), *Proceedings of the International Conference on Spoken Language Processing ICSLP* 96.1, 442–5.

Wilson, C. (forthcoming). "Learning Phonology with Substantive Bias: An Experimental and Computational Study of Velar Palatalization", *Cognitive Science*.

Wingfield, A. (1968). "Effects of Frequency on Identification and Naming of Objects", *American Journal of Psychology*, 81: 226–34.

WonHo Yoo, I., and Blankenship, B. (2003). "Duration of Epenthetic [t] in Polysyllabic American English Words", *Journal of the International Phonetic Association*, 33 (2): 153–64.

Wood, S. (1986). "The Acoustical Significance of Tongue, Lip, and Larynx Maneuvers in Rounded Palatal Vowels", *Journal of the Acoustical Society of America* 80 (2): 391–401.

—— (1996). "Assimilation or Coarticulation? Evidence from the Temporal Co-ordination of Tongue Gestures for the Palatalization of Bulgarian Alveolar Stops", *Journal of Phonetics* 24: 139–64.

Xu, Y. (2004*a*). "Transmitting Tone and Intonation Simultaneously: The Parallel Encoding and Target Approximation (PENTA) Model", *Proceedings of International Symposium on Tonal Aspects of Languages—with Emphasis on Tone Languages*, Beijing, 215–20.

—— (2004*b*). "Understanding Tone from the Perspective of Production and Perception", in *Phonetics and Phonology* (Special Issue, *Language and Linguistics*, 5). Taipei: Academic Sinica, Institute of Linguistics, 757–96.

Yeou, M. (1996). "Une étude expérimentale des consonnes postérieures et pharyngalisées de l'arabe standard", Ph.D. thesis (Université Paris 3 Sorbonne Nouvelle, France).

—— and Maeda, S. (1995). "Uvular and Pharyngeal Consonants Are Approximants: An Acoustic Modelling and Study", in K. Elenius and P. Branderud (eds.), *Proceedings of the XIIIth International Congress of Phonetic Sciences*, iv. Stockholm, 586–9.

Yip, M. (1988). "Template Morphology and the Direction of Association", *Natural Language and Linguistic Theory* 6: 551–77.

—— (2002). *Tone*. Cambridge: Cambridge University Press.

Yoon, Y. B. (1995). "Experimental Studies of the Syllable and the Segment in Korean", Ph.D. dissertation (University of Alberta).

—— and Derwing, B. L. (2001). "A Language without a Rhyme: Syllable Structure Experiments in Korean", *The Canadian Journal of Linguistics*, 46 (3–4): 187–237.

Zawadski, P. A., and Kuehn, D. P. (1980). "A Cineradiographic Study of Static and Dynamic Aspects of American English /r/", *Phonetica*, 37: 253–66.

Zemlin, W. R. (1968). *Speech and Hearing Science: Anatomy and Physiology*. Englewood Cliffs, NJ: Prentice Hall.

Zerling, J-P. (1990). "Aspects articulatoires de la labialité vocalique en français. Contribution à la modélisation à partir de labio-photographies, labiofilms et films radiologiques. Étude statique, dynamique et contrastive", Ph.D. thesis (University of Strasbourg).

Zhan, P., and Westphal, M. (1997). "Speaker Normalization Based on Frequency Warping", in *Proceedings of the IEEE International Conference on Acoustics, Speech, and Signal Processing (ICASSP'97)*, ii, 1039–41.

Zhang, J. (2002). *The Effects of Duration and Sonority on Contour Tone Distribution: Typological Survey and Formal Analysis*. New York: Routledge.

—— (2004). "The Role of Language Specific Durational Patterns in Contour Tone Distribution", in B. Hayes, R. Kirchner, and D. Steriade (eds.), *Phonetically Based Phonology*. Cambridge: Cambridge University Press, 157–90.

Zhang, J. (2005) "Contour Tone Distribution is not an Artifact of Tonal Melody Mapping". Ms. Available at http://www.linguistics.ku.edu/faculty/Dr_Zhang.

Zimmer, K., and Abbott, B. (1978). "The k/Ø Alternation in Turkish; Some Experimental Evidence for its Productivity", *Journal of Psycholinguistic Research* 7: 35–46.

Websites:

LPP web site: http://ed268.univ-paris3.fr/lpp/ (to listen all the stimuli presented in the present paper, on Maeda's model and articulatory modeling, in preparation).

UCLA web site: http://phonetics.ucla.edu/course/chapter1/vowels.html (Jones's and Ladefoged's sounds) and http://phonetics.ucla.edu/course/chapter2/amerenglishvowels.html (British and American English vowels).

SUBJECT INDEX

A

accent 48–50, 52, 150, 194, 228, 230, 234, 243,
   271–2, 276, 289, 304–6
accidental gap 198
acoustic theory of speech production 54, 70
action theory 105, 113, 115–16, 122, 213
activation 27, 34–8, 40, 235, 339–42, 386
   level 37–8
   model of perception, see speech perception
   spreading 34
aerodynamics 62, 71, 76, 79–80, 85, 90, 92,
   131, 156, 158, 162, 169, 302, 312
affrication 156–7
airflow 59, 78–9, 82, 90, 116, 158, 312
   nasal flow 79, 159–3, 172
   oral flow 79, 159–1
allomorphy 16
allophonic variation 303, 307
alternations 23, 42, 90, 146–7, 202, 369–78,
   380, 382–4
   gradient alternations 370, 375
   morphophonemic alternations 42, 45, 373,
      375, 383
   semi-regular alternations 369–70
   tonal alternations 10, 24
American English 29–30, 33, 47, 130–1, 134,
   141, 156–7, 167, 170–3, 176, 186, 217,
   305, 307–9, 313, 317, 369, 374
analysis-by-synthesis 237, 245
APEX 179–82, 190
Arabic 57, 68–9, 107–8, 120, 319–20, 384
area functions 58, 65, 71
areal grouping 95–7
articulatory 17–19, 34, 46, 51, 54–8, 63, 66–7,
   71, 76, 90, 112–5, 117–18, 120, 123, 130–
   1, 141, 144, 146–7, 173, 176, 179, 182–4,
   189–90, 192, 209, 211–12, 215–16, 220–4,
   226–7, 229, 240, 302, 307 n., 312
   ambiguity 190

modeling 54, 70, 176, 179
movements 139, 209, 215–6, 221
reinterpretation 176, 183, 190
synthesis 58, 70, 176, 187–9
aspiration 56, 109, 308, 310–2, 314, 320
assimilation 5, 29, 45, 146, 148, 318, 365,
   387, 398
   complete 352, 365–7, 387–8
   gradient 387–8
   labial-to-velar 387–8, 394, 397
   place 145, 147–8, 366, 388, 390,
      392–3, 396
auditory 28, 34, 35, 42, 47, 53, 55, 70, 76,
   77, 112
   distance 35, 111; see also perceptual
      distance
   processing 114, 116
   representation 33–4, 107, 111, 144, 184
   theories 113

B

ballistic gesture, see gesture
binomial test 344
blend, see word-blending
boundary 183, 189, 203–4, 209–11, 213, 227,
   330, 353, 358; see also tone
   morpheme boundary 358, 366,
      389, 398,
   phrase boundary 50, 215, 221
   strength 220, 223, 226

C

canonical shape 270–2
Cantonese 234, 237–9, 241, 244–5
capitalization on chance 344, 349
Catalan 49, 51–2, 310–12, 315, 318
categorical perception 43, 53, 183, 187
categorization 27, 36, 48, 50–1, 141, 150, 153,
   183, 267, 248 n.

category 34–5, 43, 48, 53
　equivalence category 132–3, 138, 141
　linguistic category 28, 42
　membership 34, 95
　perceptual category 27
　prototype 27–8, 35, 40, 48, 60
citation form 45, 192, 243, 270, 272–3, 275–6,
　　285, 289, 366
closing-opening gesture, *see* gesture
cluster, *see* consonant cluster
coarticulation 5, 115, 120, 129–31, 141,
　　145–6, 156–8, 163, 172–4, 213, 220,
　　229, 274, 307
　coarticulatory nasalization 141, 155, 307, 309
　coarticulatory source 129–30, 142–3
coda, *see* syllable coda
cognitive psychology 27, 40
cognitive reality 193, 199
cohort size 370, 372, 382–3, 385
command-response model 230, 234, 243–4
　accent/tone command 234, 236–8, 243–5
compensation 62, 66, 76, 94, 98, 102–3, 129,
　　355, 394; *see also* perceptual
　　compensation
communicative function 44, 46, 52, 53, 229
compression (f0) 271, 272, 280, 281, 317; *see*
　　also end-truncation
concept formation technique 332, 363
conditioning environment 129, 133, 174, 308,
　　358
　morphological conditioning 200, 206
　phonological conditioning 200, 206
connected speech 30, 46, 127, 270, 273, 276,
　　285, 289
consonant 55, 57, 91, 96, 120, 161, 194–5,
　　198–9, 328, 332, 343, 346, 355–7, 364,
　　368, 373, 383, 388, 393, 395, 397
　cluster 146, 157, 362
　dorsal 47, 115, 175–6, 179, 182–4, 187, 190–1
　fricative 56, 58, 60, 62, 68–9, 77, 82–3, 85,
　　90, 108–9, 116–17, 123, 132, 142, 148,
　　155–8, 160, 163–4, 172–5, 180, 190, 315–6,
　　360–2
　gesture 150, 209–10, 212–3,218–20,
　　227

inventory 94, 97–8, 101–3
length 132, 358–9
nasal 128–34, 136, 139, 141–2, 155–7,
　　159–60, 162–4, 172–4, 307–9
palatal (noise) 56, 59–60, 62–4, 108–9, 146,
　　181–2
plosive 42 , 45–7, 108–10, 116–9, 121,
　　370–1, 374, 379
stop 19, 30, 46–8, 56, 58, 60, 76, 78, 91, 113,
　　132, 139, 146–8, 157–8, 161, 163–4, 172,
　　174, 197, 211–3, 239–41, 270, 272–6, 285,
　　287–9, 302–4, 307, 310–6, 318–9, 352–3,
　　358, 360, 362–3, 366–7, 390
system 105, 108–9, 113, 116, 123
constraints 14–7, 21–4, 75–7, 91–2, 124, 145,
　　149–53, 254, 302–4, 305 n., 306–7, 334,
　　338, 363, 365 n.
contextual variation, *see* variation
contour 11, 14, 18–21, 280–1, 288; *see also*
　　tone; fundamental frequency
　simplification 17–9, 21
contrast 42, 50, 52, 55–6, 63, 104, 110, 120,
　　183, 304, 310, 317
　consonant voicing 44, 142, 310, 314–5,
　　318–9
　phonological 28, 42, 45, 49, 67, 71
　tone 19, 49, 50, 52, 94, 96, 285
　vowel 29–30, 56, 64–5, 69–71, 120
　vowel duration 318–9
　vowel height 304
　vowel length 19
　consonant 56, 63
　singleton–geminate 353, 358
control 75–6, 78, 80, 89–92, 104–5, 113–7, 120,
　　200, 212–3, 215, 220, 229–30, 235, 237,
　　244, 302–4, 306–7, 313, 314 n., 320–1
controlled features, *see* features
Converter/Distributor model 210, 227
coronal 47, 108–10, 115, 119–20, 123, 146–7,
　　175–7, 179, 182–4, 187, 190, 374–5, 384,
　　387–97
　deletion 374–5
co-variation 130–2, 140–1
creaky voice, *see* voice type
cyclicity 371

D

Danish 175, 192–4, 197, 207

declination 75, 78, 83, 85–6, 229

definitions of language 325, 377

deletion 130, 142, 157, 201, 360, 363, 370–1,
374–7, 379, 380–3, 385

demisyllables 214, 217–26

derivational phonology, *see* phonology
(generative)

Devanagari script 352, 356, 364, 367

discrimination 51, 70, 134, 136–7, 139, 141,
183; *see also* identification
function 43, 51, 183, 189–90
task 129, 134–6, 186

dispersion 104–6, 108, 110, 113
dispersion-focalisation theory 62, 70, 104–5,
110, 120

distance, *see* perceptual distance

distinctive features, *see* features

distributor, *see* Converter/Distributor model

duration 18–21, 34, 45–8, 52, 59, 85, 89, 91–2,
130–1, 134–6, 139, 141–3, 145, 147–8, 151,
161–4, 170, 172, 174, 200, 209, 214–6,
220–4, 226–7, 240–2, 244, 259, 271, 273–9,
281–2, 285–7, 303–6, 310–5, 351–3,
355–62, 365, 368; *see also* vowel duration
durational factors 306, 320
temporal gap duration 210–11, 216,
223, 226–7

E

elicitation 7, 24

emphasis 200, 210, 214, 217–8, 221–3, 244

end-truncation 276, 283, 287, 289; *see also*
compression

English 31, 44, 46–8, 52, 57, 59–3, 78, 91, 94,
128, 131–2, 136–7, 141, 148–9, 155, 157,
159, 172–3, 230, 271, 310–13, 315, 318,
320, 326, 329–32, 361, 375; *see also*
American English

epenthesis 155–8, 163, 171–4, 304, 359, 364

excursion (of articulator movement) 209–10,
215, 218–20, 223, 225–7

exemplars 27–9, 33–8, 40
exemplar models 25, 37, 153 n., 266, 303

extrinsic and intrinsic vowel normalization,
see normalization

F

f0, *see* fundamental frequency

Falam Lai 7 n., 20, 23

falling tone, *see* tone

features 10, 22, 34, 44, 71, 105–7, 109–10, 113,
115, 145–6, 179, 199, 229, 240, 242–3,
245, 247, 302–6, 310, 313, 319–20, 353,
371, 373 n., 387–8, 398
controlled features 303–5, 306 n., 307, 310,
313, 317–8, 320
distinctive features 42, 104, 242–3, 319
feature-parsing 386–8, 392, 394, 398
language-specific features 303–4, 306, 310,
314, 321
mechanical features 302, 304, 306, 318–9, 321

feedback 76, 153, 213, 241, 341–2, 346–8, 350,
363
of activation 339, 341–2

field methodology 24, 29

final fall, *see* fundamental frequency

flapping 369, 374–6

focalization, *see* dispersion-focalisation theory

formal linguistics 326–7

formant 34, 54, 58, 60, 64–5, 110–12, 116–8,
120–1, 131, 146, 177–8, 184, 190, 254–6,
261, 353, 357, 365
amplitude 62–3
manipulation 70, 185, 266
patterns/frequencies, F-pattern 55–7, 62,
66–9, 179–82, 247–51, 253, 258, 264

frame/content theory 116, 119

French 44–5, 54–5, 57, 59, 60–8, 70–1, 79–80,
82, 85, 90–1, 96, 106, 115, 120–1, 175–6,
190, 305, 307, 309–10, 312, 314–15, 384

frequency code 53

frequency, *see* lexical frequency

fricative, *see* consonant

fundamental frequency 17, 34, 44, 48–9, 52,
75, 78, 80, 82, 84–6, 89, 91–2, 185, 228–30,
232–4, 236–8, 240, 243–5, 247–8, 251 n.,
252, 256, 260, 264, 266, 270, 271–2,
274, 276

fundamental frequency (*cont.*)
  alignment 44, 48–50, 305n.
  baseline value of 89, 91–2, 232, 237–8
  contour 52, 84, 185, 228–30, 234, 236–8,
    243–5, 270–1, 283
  final fall 78
  peak 49–52
  plateau 277, 281–3, 287–9
  rate of change 242, 272, 279, 281, 289,
    295–299
  range adjustment 276, 280, 282, 288–9
  slope 281, 283, 285, 312 n.,
  valley 51

G

geminate 157, 351–68, 372
  'apparent' geminate 351, 366, 368
  derived geminate 367–8
  duration 351–2, 358–60
  inalterability 372
  'integrity' of geminates 351, 364, 368
  underlying geminate 366–8
genetic grouping 95–7
generative phonology, *see* phonology
German 42–8, 51–2, 65, 106, 175–6, 190,
  200, 271, 315, 319, 320
gesture 48, 55, 66, 109, 142, 211, 218–9,
  227, 307 n., 394
  ballistic 199–200, 213
  closing–opening 46–7, 120
  consonantal 150, 209–10, 213
  jaw opening 179, 212, 215, 220
  lower lip 220, 221, 223
  reduction 46, 109
  tongue tip 179, 212, 214–15
  vocalic 212–3, 227
global timing, *see* timing
glottal closure 200
glottalization 19, 46–7
glottis 57–8, 63, 67–8, 77, 85, 89–92,
  113, 120, 179, 232 n.

H

Hakha Lai 15, 20, 23
heavy syllable, *see* syllable

Hindi 77–8, 91, 106, 109, 309, 351–3,
  355–8, 360–8

I

/i/-/y/ contrast 64, 66, 70
icebergs 211, 214, 217–21, 226–7
identification function 43, 183, 187,189
impedance 85, 89–90, 92
Impulse Response Function 212–3, 219, 237
informant work 20, 24
inner speech 339–42, 345–7, 350
intensity 75, 78–80, 82, 85–7, 89, 91–2,
  128, 185
intonation 17, 51, 53, 75, 78–9, 82, 92, 228,
  229, 243, 266; *see also* fundamental
  frequency
intraoral pressure, *see* pressure
intrasyllabic effects 358 n.
intrinsic vowel duration, *see* vowel
inventories 4, 53, 93–4, 104–110, 112–16, 121,
  123, 333; *see also* consonant inventory
  vowel inventory
Italian 49–51, 131, 142, 155–9, 164–5, 167,
  170–3, 175, 305, 307, 384

K

Kiel Corpus of Spontaneous Speech 52–3
  KIM - The Kiel Intonation Model 51
Korean 320, 325 n., 326, 330–7, 387–8, 390,
  394–5, 397–8
Kuki-Chin 9, 22–4
Kuki-Thaadow 22–3

L

labialization 63, 66, 177–8, 191
Laboratory Phonology 5, 41, 43–4, 49–50, 53,
  123, 270 n.
laboratory speech 45, 365, 367 n.
language games 329–30
language sample 95–6
Lanqi 228 n., 234, 238, 241, 243–4
laryngeal cartilages, 235–6; *see also* laryngeal
  muscles
  cricoid cartilage 79, 233
  thyroid cartilage 233–6

laryngeal cavity 64

laryngeal muscles, 78, 91, 213, 230, 234
  cricothyroid muscle (CT) 89, 232 n., 233–5
  sternohyoid muscle (SH) 234–5
  thyrohyoid muscle (TH) 235
  vocalis muscle (VOC) 200, 232, 235

larynx 55, 57, 64, 76, 80, 179
  lowering 55–6

lenition 46–8, 69, 71, 151

lexical:
  access 197, 199, 372
  bias 339–42, 345–50
  distinctions 96, 175, 243
  frequency 336, 343, 369–70, 372, 374–6,
    380–1, 385
  organization 8, 9, 24

lexicon 96, 121–2, 153–4, 197–8, 204, 327,
  369–70, 372–5, 380–5

light syllable, *see* syllable

linguistic phonetics 5

list recall task 325 n., 332–5, 337

loanwords 96, 363 n., 384

locus 33, 63, 118, 120

logistic regression:
  multi-level logistic regression 345
  multi-nomial logistic regression 348–9
  regression coefficients 225–6, 348–9

logit 348–9

M

Maeda's articulatory model 55, 57, 62, 66–8, 70

Mandarin 21, 96, 229–30, 234, 237–8, 241,
  243, 245, 334, 336, 337 n.

manner of articulation 46, 104, 108, 146, 175,
  316–17, 355 n., 362

mechanical features, *see* features

memory 31–2, 33 n., 34–6, 70, 76, 267, 279
  declarative memory 30, 32
  models 27, 34, 40
  recognition memory 30, 32, 267

mental processes 339

mental representation 32, 116, 363

methodology 3, 9, 24, 43, 53, 76, 123, 210,
  246, 283, 351–2, 362–3, 365, 370, 372; *see
  also* scientific method

Minnan 325 n., 326, 334–7

misperception 4, 144–5, 147–8, 151–3, 155

modal voice, *see* voice type

models, *see* speech production models, speech
  perception models

modeling, *see* articulatory modeling;
    perceptual modeling; phonological
    modeling; speech production modeling

mora 49–50, 192–4, 196, 198–9, 206, 362

morpheme boundary, *see* boundary

morphological conditioning, *see* conditioning

morphophonemics 8, 9, 369

morphophonemic alternations, *see* alternations

multisensory 105

muscular response 200

N

nasal consonant, *see* consonant

nasal place assimilation, *see* assimilation

nasalization, *see* vowel nasalization

nasal-fricative sequence 155–6, 158, 172, 174

naturalistic observation 326, 328, 330

naturalness 17, 134 n., 152

neighborhood density 369–70, 372–3, 376–8,
  380, 382, 385

neural command 200

neutralization 43, 46, 148, 238
  voicing neutralization 42, 44–5

nonderived environment 372

non-productive suffix 203; *see also* productive
  suffix

non-teleological (nature of sound change)
  4, 145, 150, 152, 154

normalization 28, 34, 246, 248–52, 256,
  259–60, 263, 266 n., 267, 274
  direct and indirect 263
  extrinsic and intrinsic vowel
    normalization 250, 267
  vowel normalization 246, 266 n.
  vocal tract length 251

O

obstruent voicing 43, 103, 315,
  318–9, 447

offline task 389, 397

onset, *see* syllable
opacity 9
optimality theory 7, 145–6
oral constriction 55, 59, 69, 77, 155, 161,
    163–4, 170, 310
orthography 45, 332, 352, 363, 367,
    373 n., 390
  orthographic influence 364
overlap-add synthesis 185
overt speech 341–2, 345–6

P
parameter tuning paradigm 264, 266
perception 4, 26–8, 37–8, 42–3, 46–7, 53–6,
    58, 70, 105, 110, 113–16, 123, 127–8, 130–
    2, 140–3, 145, 148, 150, 153–4, 174, 176,
    183–4, 187, 199, 241, 254, 260, 273,
    305 n., 306, 321, 358, 365, 367–8, 388,
    394 n.
  vowel perception 34, 112, 246–7
perceptual:
  compensation 128
  constancy 128
  distance 107, 110–11, 121–2, 184,
      186–90, 304–7, 309–10, 314, 321
  equivalence 130, 132–3, 136–9, 141
  modeling 253, 259, 263
  similarity 71, 146, 150
perceptibility 19
perceptuo-motor interactions 123
perturbations 64, 264, 274
phonetic:
  detail 26, 28–9, 34, 38, 40, 43, 128, 130,
      141–2, 302–3, 320
  knowledge 76, 124, 152–4
  transcription 60–1, 197
phonetics 3, 5, 7–10, 16–7, 23, 41–4, 46, 49,
    51, 53, 71, 104, 116, 123, 127 n., 145, 150,
    153, 244, 246, 259, 351, 353
  of speech communication 41, 44, 46, 53
phonological:
  category 128, 153 n., 246
  contrast 28, 45, 49, 54, 306, 367, 371
  generalization 28, 38, 40
  grammar 128, 130, 154

inference 386, 388–9, 391, 394, 397–8
  modeling 40, 154
  process 90, 94, 319
  rule 8–9, 28, 174, 365–6, 387, 391
  system 76, 94, 105, 153, 242
  theory 45, 123, 145, 192
  typology 95, 103, 149
  unit 40, 325–6, 328, 334, 338
  universals 75–6, 90, 92, 147
phonologization 8, 17, 23, 42, 141, 151
phonology 8, 17, 23, 28, 32, 36, 42–6, 48–52,
    104, 116, 123–4, 145–6, 150–4, 351, 362
  evolutionary phonology 145, 151–2
  exemplar-based phonology 26, 27–30, 32,
      34, 36, 38, 40
  generative phonology 8, 25, 44, 124, 146,
      326 n., 369
  laboratory phonology 5, 41, 43–4, 50,
      53, 123
  non-linear phonology 359, 366
  phrasal phonology 9
  probabilistic phonology 154
  synchronic phonology 26, 145–6, 148,
      150–4
phrase 9, 80, 91, 107, 226, 228–9, 310
  command 234, 237–8, 240, 245
  component 234, 238
  final elongation 214–15, 219–21
physiological mechanisms 75, 229–30,
    234, 245
pitch 21, 48–53, 80, 82, 89, 96, 151, 196, 229,
    241, 247, 259–60, 271, 274, 276, 289,
    303, 305
place of articulation 109, 118, 148, 157–8,
    176, 179, 181–3, 189–90, 312 n., 352
polar boundary tone, *see* tone
pressure 76, 90, 163, 213, 302, 310, 342–3
  intraoral 45, 79, 82–3, 88, 90, 163,
      302, 310
  subglottal 62, 75, 77, 92, 213
priming 32, 340–3, 345–50, 387
primitives 76, 78, 93, 229
productive 201–5, 271
  process 201
  semi-productive suffix 202–4

suffix 202; *see also* non-productive suffix
prosody 44, 75, 91, 209–15, 218–20, 224–7, 351, 356, 358–9, 368
   prosodic factors 210, 224, 304, 314
   prosodic prominence 150, 304, 315
prototype, *see* category prototype
psycholinguistic experiment 328, 336, 338, 368
psycholinguistics 5, 7, 116, 246, 326 n

Q
Quantal Theory 104, 112, 116

R
/r/:
   front r 183, 190–1, 175
   back r 175–6, 183, 186, 189–91
reading tests 333, 335–7
recognition 27–8, 36, 246–8, 250, 263–4, 267, 370, 372, 388–9, 394, 397
reduplication 331
regulation 46, 75–6, 78
resonance mechanism 36, 38
resonances (acoustic) 36, 38, 40, 55–6, 60, 62, 64–5, 67–8, 119
respiration 76
rhotic, *see* /r/
rhyme/rime, *see* syllable
rising tone, *see* tone

S
scientific method 5, 145
segment 4, 33–4, 44, 46–8, 52–3, 75, 79, 81, 90, 92–4, 98, 116, 130–1, 141, 164, 173, 193–4, 197, 199, 240, 271, 302, 304, 305 n., 314, 331
self-monitoring 339–42, 345–9
self-repair 347
sensory experience 27–8
Shanghainese 234, 237, 241, 243
similarity 36, 38, 71, 146, 150, 153, 176, 178, 332, 382
   similarity matching process 34–7
   sound-similarity judgments 331
singleton 157, 352–61, 363 n., 367–8; *see also* geminate

duration 352, 356–60
SLIP technique 339–42, 345
sound change 4, 30, 41–2, 46, 76, 127–30, 133, 140, 142–8, 151–2, 154–8, 163, 173–6, 190, 303–4, 320
Spanish 60, 106, 175, 307–10, 312, 315
spatio-temporal coordination 227
speaker size information 253, 267
speaking rate, *see* speech rate
speech comprehension system 341
speech error 329, 334 n., 339–47, 349–50
   spontaneous speech error 329, 340
   spoonerism 339–40, 342–3, 345–50
speech perception 26–8, 34, 42, 54, 70, 113–15, 127–8, 145, 154, 246, 305–6, 321
   activation models 27
   models 27–8, 34, 42
speech production 4, 26, 34, 47, 54, 70–1, 75–6, 78, 115–16, 127, 145, 176, 210, 213, 302–3, 305–6, 317, 320–1, 328, 339, 359, 365
   modeling 34, 47, 54–5, 58, 60–1, 63–7, 69–71, 176, 179, 210
speech rate 94, 157, 173, 200, 304–5, 307–9, 310–4, 318, 320, 375, 388
speech style variation, *see* variation
speech synthesis 228, 240, 246–7, 264, 266; *see also* articulatory synthesis; analysis-by-synthesis
speed of articulator movement 210, 211, 216, 218, 220
statistical pattern recognition 246–7, 260, 264
stød 192–205
stop consonant, *see* consonant
stop epenthesis 155–8, 163, 170, 172–4
strength (muscle activity) 200, 206
stress 49, 78, 85, 148, 151, 193, 201, 211–12, 229, 271, 275, 305–6, 314–20
subglottal pressure, *see* pressure
substance-based approach 104
Swedish 54, 57, 60, 64–5, 175–6, 180–1, 186–7, 191, 194–5, 230, 234, 272, 276, 305, 307, 309, 315
Swedish pitch accent 271, 289

syllabification 351, 362–5
syllable 120, 209–27, 326–37
  body 329–35, 337
  canon 94
  coda 96, 103, 132–6, 142, 209–10, 212, 215,
    240, 309, 318, 329–30, 333–4, 337, 362,
    369–70, 390–6
  duration 151, 209, 210, 212, 214–6, 220–3,
    225–7, 241, 313
  heavy 151, 193–4, 201, 202, 205
  light 212
  magnitude 212–4, 216, 218–21, 224, 226–7
  onset 95–6, 116, 131, 134, 158–60, 193,197,
    199, 200, 205, 209–10, 212–3, 273, 276,
    310, 329–31, 334, 336, 342
  rhyme 19–22, 116, 141–2, 193–4, 200, 205,
    215, 243, 273–9, 281, 287, 328–33, 336–7
  structure 19, 94–5, 98,101–3, 205, 270,
    272–3, 275, 287, 289, 304, 326, 329,
    360, 397
  weight 193, 365
synchronization, *see* fundamental frequency
  alignment
synchronic phonology, *see* phonology

T

talker-specific variation, *see* variation
temporal factors 306 n., 309, 310
Thai 132, 142, 234–5, 237–9, 241–5, 270–3,
  276, 280, 282–5, 287–90, 313–5, 320
Thlantlang Lai 7, 9, 17, 20–3
timing 46, 51–2, 120, 140–2, 150, 155, 158,
  173–4, 199–200, 220, 227, 230, 302–5,
  307, 313, 321, 359
  global timing 306 n., 314
  interarticulatory timing 158, 302, 313
  relative timing 140, 155, 307–9, 314–5
Tibeto-Burman 9, 93
ToBI 48, 51
tonal processes 282, 289
tonal word accent 194–5, 230, 234, 272
tone 9, 11–12, 14, 17–20, 23, 78, 80, 82, 270–89
  association 49
  boundary tone 14, 50
  falling tone 9–10, 14, 238–9

  five-level tone code 242–4
  polar boundary tone 14, 16
  rising tone 9–11, 14–15, 19, 21–22, 238–9
  spreading 14–17, 21–4
  system 94, 96–8, 100–2, 240, 242–3, 245
Tone Bearing Unit (TBU) 270, 272–82,
  287, 289
tone command 237–8, 243–5
  polarity 230, 236–8, 243
  timing 230, 244
tone language 9, 16, 18–24, 96, 100, 103, 228,
  230, 236–7, 240, 242–5
top-down processing 40
trading relation 62, 133
transitional probability 343
trills 79, 80, 82–3, 85, 90, 92, 175, 190
Turkish 369–78, 380, 384–5
typology (language) 20, 23, 105–6, 149; *see
  also* phonological typology

U

underlying form 8, 12, 386–395, 397–8
uniqueness point 382–3
unit 4, 40, 46, 48–9, 51–2, 105–9, 113, 210,
  325, 326, 327, 328, 330, 338, 364; *see also*
  tone bearing unit
universals, *see* phonological universals
'unscripted' speech 365–7
UPSID 95, 104 n., 105–6, 108–10, 112–4, 122,
  190–1

V

variables 76, 94, 102, 162, 213, 215, 224–6,
  256, 258–9, 344, 349, 369–70, 372, 374,
  376–77, 380, 382, 385
  categorical 96–7, 101
  numerical 94, 97
variation 170, 174, 270, 272, 275–6, 286
  contextual variation 26, 128–30, 174
  talker-specific variation 29, 30
  word-specific variation 30
velar palatalization 145–7
velum lowering 46, 67, 71, 131, 140–1, 156,
  307–10; *see also* nasalization
Vietnamese 234, 237, 241–4

visual perception 33, 110, 114, 116, 266

vocal fold 71, 78, 163, 185, 200, 213, 230, 232–4, 310, 312, 314
  length 231–5, 251–2
  tension 231, 232 n., 234–5

vocal tract 54–8, 60, 63–4, 66, 75–6, 85, 89, 90–2, 110, 113, 116, 118–120, 141 n., 179, 180–1, 251, 302–4
  constraints 76, 90, 302–4, 306–7

vocalic gesture, *see* gesture

vocoded speech 260

Voice Onset Time 47, 302, 306, 310–5, 320, 353

voice type
  breathy voice 91, 106, 109, 353 n., 406
  creaky voice 193, 196–200, 205
  modal voice 194, 200

voicing 42–5, 69, 76–7, 90, 103, 109–110, 133–136, 139, 141 n., 142, 157, 160, 163, 172–3, 213, 215, 240, 271, 302, 310–19, 353, 365–6, 370, 374–7, 379–85, 387

vowel 80–2, 89–90, 105–7, 110–8, 120–3
  duration 121–2, 134 n , 150, 157, 162, 171–2, 199, 273, 289, 307–10, 315–320, 353, 355, 357, 360, 362
  identification 59, 246, 254, 258–9, 264–5, 267
  intrinsic vowel duration 270, 273, 275, 289

inventory 97–8, 100–2
length (distinctive) 270, 273, 276, 320
nasalization 62–3, 67, 70–1, 97, 106, 109, 129–37, 139, 141–2, 155–159, 162, 164–7, 169, 171–4, 306–10
perception 34, 54, 112, 246–7
quality 97–101, 106, 111, 149–50, 158, 164, 169, 171, 247, 259, 267
reduction 67, 107, 115, 149–50
system 62, 67, 70, 105–7, 109, 111–14, 116, 121–3

W
word 9, 29, 30, 339–43, 345–50
  blending 328, 330–1
  form 33, 38, 44–5, 130, 153, 201, 341, 373
  frequency, *see* lexical frequency
  games 329–31, 363–4.
  length 271, 276, 375, 377, 381
  recognition 28, 370, 372, 386, 389
  structure 46, 201, 203, 205
  word-specific variation, *see* variation
World Atlas of Language Structures 95

X
x-ray microbeam data 211, 216, 220, 227

Y
yes/no questions 78, 84, 91

CPSIA information can be obtained at www.ICGtesting.com
Printed in the USA
BVOW03s1833080716

454533BV00026B/22/P